California Real Estate Law

Fourth Edition

Dawn Henry

Joseph Reiner

Jennifer Gotanda

Megan Dorsey

Rockwell Publishing Company

Table of Contents

Chapter 1

An Introduction to Law and the Legal System

Outline

Introduction

This chapter examines how our federal and state governments make and apply law. The better your understanding of how laws are created and interpreted, the less trouble you'll have with the real property cases and statutes discussed throughout this book.

Aside from some introductory material about the law, this chapter consists of two parts. The first part discusses differences between the criminal and civil law systems. The second part looks at the elements which comprise our legal system: constitutions, legislatures, courts, and administrative agencies. The interaction—and the occasional conflict—between these sources of law can be truly fascinating.

Let's begin with a few observations on the role of law, especially with regard to real estate.

The Role of Law

Law provides society with a number of benefits. Among other things, it:

- provides a minimum standard of acceptable behavior,
- punishes unacceptable behavior,
- settles disputes,
- preserves natural resources,
- protects various minorities from unfair treatment, and
- helps provide predictability in business.

In a book about real estate law, we are naturally concerned with the last item in our list: the law's role in helping to assure predictability in business dealings. In countries where the law is unsettled, commerce suffers. On the other hand, a stable and developed body of law, particularly business law, provides people with a common language; they can speak to each other and negotiate agreements with some certainty of the outcome.

What if judges deciding real estate contract disputes defined property terms like "fixtures" or "liquidated damages" differently in every case? Real estate contracts would have unpredictable consequences, and this uncertainty might discourage people from buying and selling property.

Any study of law involves learning a good deal of vocabulary, and this is certainly true of real estate. Admittedly, it can be a little overwhelming at first. As you read through this book, however, try to keep in mind how much a set of well-understood terms contributes to the completion of successful real estate transactions.

The Roots of U.S. Law

English settlers brought their legal system wherever they established colonies. The American colonies were no exception. By the time of the American Revolution, "common law"—as the English system is called—was entrenched in this country. Of course, since that time U.S. law on many subjects has departed from English law. Yet even today, a U.S. judge will occasionally settle an issue based on a rule established in eighteenth-century England (occasionally by some exotic-sounding court such as the "Exchequer").

The fact that a U.S. judge often relies on an earlier case to reach a decision reveals the main structural difference between the common law system and what is called the civil law system. In the **common law** system, judges follow rules or decisions made in earlier, similar cases. In doing so, they create a body of law distinct from the statutes passed by legislatures.

In the **civil law** system, the job of creating law falls more squarely on the legislature. Court cases are decided based on statutory law rather than the decisions in previous cases.

In civil law countries like France, Germany, Mexico, and Japan—indeed most places where England lacked a colonial presence—a judge's decisions have less effect on the behavior of later judges, and do not create a particularly significant body of law.

When we took our legal system from the English, we also took their legal terminology. Nowhere is that more apparent than in the real property arena. Many strange-sounding legal terms such as "seisin" (ownership), "metes" (measure), and "appurtenance" (a right attached to property) come from the medieval English or Latin used by our legal ancestors.

All 50 states, including California, share this English common law heritage. However, because of its history, California law was also influenced by Spanish legal traditions.

Spanish Influence in California

The Spanish first occupied the area that is now California in 1769. Mexico took over the territory in 1822 and continued to use Spanish-based law. In 1848, after losing the Mexican-American War, Mexico ceded California and considerable other territory to the United States.

Although U.S. law replaced Spanish-based law in California, traces of the older legal system still linger. The clearest example is community property law, a Spanish conception. We discuss community property in Chapter 5.

This concludes our look at legal history and the differences between the civil and common law systems. In the next section, we discuss the U.S. legal system's distinction between civil and criminal law, and use the word civil in a markedly different way.

Criminal and Civil Law

Probably the most basic legal distinction we can draw is the one between civil and criminal law. Simply put, civil law includes any legal matter that does not involve a criminal statute. Although we'll begin with a discussion of criminal law, the criminal code plays a relatively minor role in the real estate profession. We'll spend much more time discussing civil law.

Criminal Law

Legislatures generally decide which matters are criminal and which are not. For example, the California legislature has passed criminal statutes prohibiting, among other things, murder, embezzlement, insider trading, and certain kinds of drug use. All of California's criminal statutes are gathered in its Penal Code. Similarly, the U.S. Congress has passed laws against crimes of a federal nature, including mail and bank theft and the killing of federal officials. Federal criminal statutes are gathered in Title 18 of the U.S. Code.

Criminal law has its own set of legal procedures and penalties distinct from those of civil law. Penalties for violating criminal statutes include criminal fines, restitution, and incarceration. Civil law penalties, where they exist, are limited to fines and the revocation of licenses and benefits.

Another distinction between criminal and civil law is the restriction on who may bring a criminal case. Since only the government can prosecute crimes, all criminal cases are brought by the government, either at the federal, state, or local level. By contrast, any-one—either the government or a private person—may bring a civil case.

While criminal law looms large in news reports and legal dramas, in fact it makes up a relatively small part of the law. Most disputes involve civil law, our next topic.

Civil Law

In most civil cases, the government or a private person brings a claim for **damages**, seeking compensation for financial losses caused by the defendant's wrongful conduct. No jail time or other criminal penalty is involved. The term "guilty" isn't even used in a civil jury's verdict; a defendant is merely found financially liable for whatever injury, economic or physical, that he caused. Occasionally, the defendant may also be ordered to take a certain action—for example, to transfer title to a piece of real property or to stop a certain kind of trespass.

Let's review the criminal-civil distinction by considering the case of *Nollan v. California Coastal Commission* (1987) 483 U.S. 825. *Nollan* is a significant property rights case out of California and we will refer to it several times to illustrate points in this chapter. In *Nollan*, a married couple had an option to buy a small, decaying beachfront bungalow in Ventura County. The U.S. Supreme Court summarized some of the key facts as follows:

> The Nollans' option…was conditioned on their promise to demolish the bungalow and replace it…[This required that they] obtain a coastal development permit from the California Coastal Commission. On February 25, 1982, they submitted a permit application to the Commission in which they proposed to demolish the existing structure and replace it with a three-bedroom house in keeping with the rest of the neighborhood.

As you can see, the subject matter of the case involves contract law (the option to buy) and a development permit, both noncriminal matters. This is clearly a civil case, not a criminal case.

Types of Civil Law: Contract, Tort, and Property Law. Most civil law matters fall into one of three subject areas: contracts, torts, and property law. A civil case may involve all three of these subjects. Let's take a short look at each area.

Contract law. In a contract, each party makes a promise to the other. This exchange of promises forms a binding contract. Contract lawsuits result when one party fails to make good on his promise and the injured party sues over the resulting financial losses.

Legislatures have traditionally stayed out of the contract arena, leaving the courts to develop many general contract rules through common law. As a result, lawyers typically look to case law for rules regarding issues such as offer and acceptance in a real property transaction.

Tort law. In a contract, we voluntarily assume a duty in exchange for some benefit. By contrast, tort law imposes a duty on us: the duty to take reasonable care to avoid injuring people or damaging their property. Failure to exercise such reasonable care is called negligence. **Negligence** is simply the legal word for carelessness. If Sam's negligence causes injury, he has committed a tort.

Causing injury through negligence is an unintentional tort. An intentional tort, on the other hand, occurs when someone intends to cause injury to a person or property, and does so without legal justification. Intentional torts that arise in the real estate industry include trespass, fraud, and slander of title (falsely casting doubt on the validity of someone's title to property). Many intentional torts have their counterpart in the criminal code. For example, an employer may sue an embezzling employee for the tort of "conversion," while the state prosecutes that same person for theft.

Property law. Our third and last category of civil law is property law. This includes real property and also personal property. **Personal property** is any property that isn't real estate or permanently attached to real estate. The law provides many significantly different rules for real and personal property; thus, a court's classification of a certain piece of property as real or personal can have serious consequences, as the following case demonstrates.

Case Example:

More than a dozen San Francisco cable car operators suffered personal injuries while attempting to turn their cars around using the "turntables" (large rotating platforms) found at the end of the tracks. These operators sued Chin & Hensolt and others who had been involved in the design and manufacture of the turntables a number of years earlier.

If the turntables were real property (items permanently attached to land are called "fixtures" and are considered part of the real property), a certain four-year deadline applied, and that would mean the plaintiffs had filed their lawsuit too late. However, a ruling that the turntables were personal property would rescue the plaintiffs' case.

The plaintiffs pointed to an old California case that classified railroad tracks as personal property. The court found this case somewhat poorly reasoned and, at any rate, inapplicable. Turntables, the court declared, added value to the City's real estate "in the same way as affixed park benches." The turntables were unquestionably improvements to real property. Following cable car tradition, the court said it was ringing "the conductor's bell three times," signaling a stop to the plaintiffs' case. *Robinson v. Chin & Hensolt* (2002) 98 Cal.App.4th 702.

Standards of Proof in Criminal and Civil Cases

As we noted earlier, an act can constitute both an intentional tort and a violation of criminal law.

Example: Jake gives in to road rage and rams a fellow driver's car, causing the vehicle to slam into a highway guardrail. Jake will likely find himself the object of a civil lawsuit for damages brought by the injured driver. However, the state may also independently prosecute Jake for the crime of battery, or possibly vehicular assault.

A jury in Jake's civil lawsuit may find him financially liable for injuries caused during the intentional tort of battery. Yet another jury sitting in Jake's criminal case, and listening to the same set of facts, may declare him "not guilty." The same act will net different results.

The contrasting results might be due to different lawyers or differing personalities in the two juries. However, the explanation more likely turns on the differing standards

> **Lower Standard**

In 2002, the State of California charged Robert Blake, star of the 1967 movie *In Cold Blood*, with the murder of his wife, Bonny Lee Bakley. The recently married couple had just finished dining out and had gotten into their car, when Blake briefly returned to the restaurant (allegedly to retrieve a gun that had fallen out of his pocket). He told police that when he came back to the car, he found his wife shot in the head. Police arrested Blake, and he spent a year in jail awaiting trial.

The prosecution presented some alarming circumstantial evidence against Blake at trial, but nothing direct such as gunshot residue. The jury voted 11 to 1 for acquittal. The disgruntled prosecutor called the jurors "incredibly stupid," but several jurors said the state had simply failed to prove Blake guilty beyond a reasonable doubt.

Bonny Lee's children had already filed a civil suit against Blake for wrongful death. Half a year after Blake's "not guilty" verdict in the criminal trial, a civil jury applying the "more likely than not" standard had no trouble finding Blake responsible for his wife's death. The civil jury awarded $30 million in damages, and this caused the actor to declare bankruptcy.

of proof used in civil and criminal cases. Most people are familiar with the **standard of proof** required in a criminal case: the jury must find the defendant guilty "beyond a reasonable doubt." That is quite a hurdle to overcome. Suppose Jake claims that the injured driver started the whole thing. This claim might be enough to raise a reasonable doubt in the mind of some jurors.

However, Jake's claim might not work in a civil case. A civil jury merely needs to find that it is "more likely than not" that the defendant committed the wrongful act. This considerably lower standard represents society's belief that a defendant's money is less precious than his liberty, which is what is at stake in a criminal trial.

Before concluding our look at civil and criminal law, we will make one final general point. Civil law is almost entirely the province of state law. Federal law says little or nothing about such civil matters as breach of contract, negligence, or property deeds. To a somewhat lesser extent, the same is true of criminal law: crimes such as robbery and murder are defined and punished under state law, not federal law.

Are there some areas of law that can be addressed by both the U.S. Congress and the state legislature? The answer is yes. As you might expect, conflicts over whether federal or state law takes precedence can and do arise. How are these conflicts handled? The rest of this chapter, while exploring our various sources of law, attempts to answer this question.

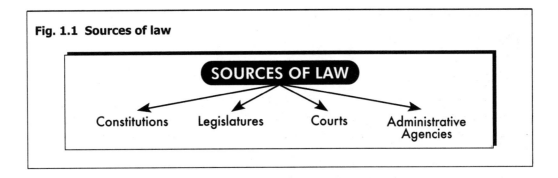

Fig. 1.1 Sources of law

Sources of Law

Federal, state, and local governments each have their own sets of laws. Federal and state governments have constitutions which provide the basic legal framework for government operation. In addition, new law is continually created by the judicial and legislative branches. Administrative agencies (e.g., the Federal Trade Commission or the California Coastal Commission) also contribute law in the form of regulations.

First we'll look at constitutional law, focusing on issues that figure significantly in real estate matters. We will then examine how the legislative and judicial branches engage in lawmaking, and conclude with a look at administrative agencies and their rulemaking activities.

The Constitution grants each branch of government a unique set of powers. For example, only the courts have the power to review legislative and executive acts for constitutionality. This "separation of powers" approach to government enables the different branches to act as "checks and balances" on each other. Both of these phrases were coined by the Enlightenment-era political philosopher Montesquieu, whose thinking was incorporated into the U.S. Constitution. The framers of the Constitution hoped that checks and balances would help keep the U.S. from ever becoming controlled by one king-like, central authority—something they wanted to avoid after their experiences with the English monarchy.

Constitutions

A constitution can be viewed as an engineering plan that specifies how the government is constructed and how it operates. It creates the branches of government, lists their powers—and the limits of those powers—and also provides a few detailed operating instructions. For example, the U.S. Constitution offers rules about who is eligible to run for federal office.

Since the U.S. Constitution is the source of our government and its laws, it is our highest legal authority. How do we know the Constitution is the highest authority? It tells us so. The U.S. Constitution makes clear its authority in Article VI, paragraph 2, which states in part, "This Constitution...shall be the supreme Law of the Land." This is known as the **Supremacy Clause**.

Thus, under the Supremacy Clause, if one of the governmental branches creates a law that conflicts with rules provided by the Constitution, that law is unconstitutional and void.

It is important that some source of law be the final authority—if this wasn't the case, some squabbles might never end.

The U.S. Constitution

The United States Constitution was adopted in 1789. It applies to both the federal government and to all 50 states. The original provisions are over 200 years old and yet they have served this country remarkably well.

The Constitution sets out areas of lawmaking authority for the different levels of government. The Constitution further provides that, except for certain specifically stated matters, each state has the right to legislate the conduct of persons within its borders.

Federal and State Lawmaking Responsibility. Article I, Section 8 of the Constitution grants the federal government sole lawmaking power over various matters, including:

- wars and the military,
- interstate commerce,
- copyrights and patents, and
- currency.

The logic behind these choices is fairly obvious. The success of a war, for example, may depend on unified action by the states. Similarly, allowing each state to mint its own currency would create a barrier to trade within our borders, hindering economic growth.

If a state enacts a law that encroaches on a subject area reserved to the federal government by the Constitution, the state law will have no effect. However, the Constitution's description of which lawmaking matters are exclusively the province of federal government is not very detailed. As a result, a court's assistance is sometimes needed to determine whether or not a certain state law is trampling on federal toes.

Case Example:

California's Compassionate Use Act permits medical use of marijuana. However, the federal Controlled Substances Act forbids consumption of the drug for any reason. In 2002, Oroville resident Diane Monson was growing six marijuana plants in her garden; the plants were legal under the Compassionate Use Act. That August, federal drug enforcement agents seized and destroyed her plants as part of a campaign against medical marijuana use.

Monson and others sued to stop the federal enforcement campaign. They argued that the states had the constitutional power to legislate medical matters. The U.S. argued that the federal government had the constitutional power to regulate interstate commerce and, since the marijuana trade involved interstate commerce, the states had no right to pass laws that conflicted with the federal Controlled Substances Act.

The Supreme Court ruled six to three in favor of the federal government: California could not permit medical marijuana use in violation of federal law. The dissent led by Justice Sandra Day O'Connor questioned whether Congress had encroached too far on states' rights by forbidding medical marijuana use. *Gonzales v. Raich* (2005) 545 U.S. 1.

Some areas of law, such as bankruptcy or patent law, are exclusively federal, while others, including contract and real property matters, are more or less left to the states. Finally, in some areas, such as illegal drug use, consumer protection, and pollution control, state and federal governments share an interest and provide overlapping legislation.

That raises an interesting question. What happens when overlapping state and federal statutes differ; for example, one law provides a more generous remedy than the other? The answer is fairly simple: plaintiffs can usually bring their claim under the more helpful law.

> **Example:** The federal Americans with Disabilities Act (ADA) states that a person is entitled to accommodation if their disability "substantially limits major life activities." In 2001, the California legislature dropped the word "substantially" from its definition of disability in the state's Fair Employment and Housing Act (FEHA). Thus, in employment and housing, California law now offers broader protection than federal law. Merely showing some difficulty caused by a disability will trigger statutory protection. As a result, some California plaintiffs with less severe disabilities may choose to sue under the FEHA rather than the ADA.

Aside from providing the different branches of government with specific areas of authority, constitutions also offer important protections of people's liberties. Before examining these constitutional protections, we should clear up a common point of confusion. The federal and state constitutions protect people's rights from violation by the government, not from violation by private individuals or entities. This is called the "state action requirement," as we explain below.

State Action. Only **state action**—an act by a government or government official—can violate someone's constitutional rights. A police officer who makes a warrantless search, a statute that discriminates against residents from a neighboring state, a public housing project manager who evicts someone because of race—all of these are examples of action by the government that might justify a constitutional claim.

In the following case, the Department of Real Estate (now the Bureau of Real Estate) provided the state action.

Case Example:

Anderson, a broker on inactive status with the California Department of Real Estate (DRE), compiled lists of local units for rent and sold them to apartment hunters for $25 or $30. At the time, this activity caused Anderson to meet the definition of "advance rental agent" under the Real Estate Law (an advance rental agent required an active license from the DRE).

After a few of Anderson's clients complained about lack of refunds, the DRE held a hearing and subsequently revoked Anderson's license. Anderson appealed, claiming that requiring a license simply to advertise lists of vacancies imposed an unnecessary burden on his constitutional right to free speech.

The appellate court began its analysis by reviewing the DRE licensing requirements. Real estate license applicants must be of good character and receive training in real estate law; this makes sense for people who will represent parties in real estate transactions. However, there was no legitimate reason to require all this of someone who merely drew up lists of available apartments. The statute lacked a rational basis and thus violated Anderson's

First Amendment right of free speech. The DRE was ordered to annul the revocation of his license. (Note: the statute was subsequently amended to eliminate this problem.) *Anderson v. Department of Real Estate* (1979) 93 Cal.App.3d 696.

Without state action, no constitutional violation can occur.

Example: Sam walks into a bar. After a number of whiskeys, he proclaims that drinking has ruined his life, Prohibition was a good thing, and America should once again ban alcohol. He offers to buy the bar a round of ginger ale. The bartender throws him out.

"You can't silence me," Sam bellows from the sidewalk. "I know my constitutional rights!"

No, actually, he doesn't. The bartender can't violate anyone's constitutional right to free speech. The bartender is a "private actor" and not part of the government; therefore, no state action has occurred.

Note, however, that federal and state legislatures have passed statutes protecting certain liberties from violation by private persons. For example, the federal Civil Rights Act of 1964 prohibits employers and private providers of public services (such as hotels and restaurants) from treating customers unequally because of race, color, religion, sex, or national origin. Civil rights statutes are discussed in Chapter 19.

Now that we've established the state action requirement, let's take a look at some specific rights protected by the federal and state constitutions.

Constitutional Rights. The United States clarified and strengthened its commitment to individual liberty in 1791 by adding the first ten amendments to the Constitution. These amendments are known collectively as the **Bill of Rights**, and they contain the bulk of our personal federal constitutional protections.

The Fourteenth Amendment, added soon after the Civil War, somewhat expanded the Bill of Rights as part of the effort to protect African-Americans. The amendment made clear that state governments, not just the federal government, had to honor constitutional protections.

The Bill of Rights, together with the Fourteenth Amendment, lists our personal freedoms in short simple phrases that allow fresh interpretation as society changes. Specific rights granted to persons in the U.S. include, for example, the right to due process, equal protection, and just compensation for property taken by the government. Because each of these particular rights has special relevance to the real estate practitioner, we will explore them in some detail.

Takings Clause. The Fifth Amendment reads in part, "No person shall…be deprived of life, liberty, or property; nor shall private property be taken for public use, without just compensation." The last provision requiring just compensation is known as the Takings Clause because it limits the government's power to take someone's property. Note that the clause doesn't forbid takings, it merely requires that landowners receive fair compensation in exchange for their property. If the city wants your land for a new park or airport runway, there's not much you can do about it except insist on receiving fair market value.

Let's consider an actual takings claim by returning to the *Nollan* case. Recall that the Nollans had applied to the California Coastal Commission for a permit to demolish their

Change is Hard

A country looks to its law, especially its constitution, to provide a sense of stability and permanence. The constitutional framers protected the Constitution from overly frequent change by requiring that any amendment first receive a two-thirds vote of approval by both houses of Congress, and then be ratified by at least 38 states. This isn't an easy thing to accomplish—the United States has only amended its Constitution a dozen times in the last hundred years.

Nonetheless, as many as 200 constitutional amendments are proposed each year in Congress. For example, the Supreme Court's decision in a somewhat infamous case, *Kelo v. New London* (2005) 545 U.S. 469, generated a wave of proposals for amending the federal and various state constitutions, including California's. In *Kelo*, the Supreme Court held that a city could force the sale (condemnation) of private homes to enable a large-scale private development (a mixed use shopping and condominium complex). Property rights advocates angered by *Kelo* proposed constitutional amendments banning condemnation for private development except to meet transportation or public utility needs. However, so far the proposals to amend the U.S. Constitution have met with the usual lack of success.

beachside shanty. The Commission granted this permit, but required the Nollans to provide the public with a beachfront easement that would make it easier for people to walk from one nearby beach park to another. The Nollans appealed; the basis of their appeal was, as you may have guessed, the Takings Clause.

The Nollans argued that the Coastal Commission had to pay for the easement; conditioning a building permit on the grant of an easement was merely a way of circumventing the Fifth Amendment's requirement of compensation. The Commission countered that the Nollans' larger house would burden public beach views and access, making the requirement of the easement a fair exchange. The issue eventually reached the U.S. Supreme Court.

Was the Coastal Commission taking the Nollans' property without just compensation? The Supreme Court had this to say:

> Had California simply required the Nollans to make an easement across their beachfront available to the public on a permanent basis in order to increase public access to the beach, rather than conditioning their permit to rebuild their house on their agreeing to do so, we have no doubt there would have been a taking. To say that the appropriation of a public easement across a landowner's premises does not constitute the taking of a property interest but rather (as Justice Brennan contends) "a mere restriction on its use,". . . is to use words in a manner that deprives them of all their ordinary meaning.

Permit or not, the Supreme Court ruled, the state could not claim an easement across the Nollans' beach without paying for it.

Case to Consider...

Plaintiffs offered to buy some agricultural land, but only on the condition that the seller obtain commercial zoning for the tract. Subsequently, the city rezoned the land as commercial and so the buyers completed their purchase. However, five years passed without the buyers making any improvements on the property. At this point, the city became concerned about protecting farm land and rezoned the land back to agricultural use only. The buyers' property became less valuable. Does a zoning change that reduces the value of property constitute a taking that requires paying the landowner compensation? *HFH, Ltd. v. Superior Court* (1975) 15 Cal.3d 508.

Due Process Clause. The Fifth and Fourteenth Amendments both provide that no one shall be "deprived of life, liberty, or property without due process of law." In both amendments, the word "process" refers to judicial process. In other words, the state cannot deprive a person of liberty or property without providing a fair hearing before some kind of impartial judge. Depending on the setting, the required due process may include anything from a full-blown trial involving attorneys, to a less formal hearing before the local land use board.

Equal Protection Clause. The Fourteenth Amendment does provide one important guaranty that the Bill of Rights does not: a provision entitling everyone to "equal protection of the laws." The equal protection requirement prohibits governments from: 1) adopting a law that unfairly discriminates between different groups of people; and 2) applying an otherwise acceptable law in a discriminatory fashion.

Almost every statute ends up discriminating against someone; the issue is whether the discrimination is justified. The government may treat groups of people differently if doing so achieves a reasonable state goal and does not single out individuals unfairly. In the *Nollan* case, for example, the Supreme Court noted that while protecting the public's access to beaches might be a legitimate state goal, the Equal Protection Clause would require that all beach front owners in the area share the burden—not just the Nollans.

This completes our examination of federal constitutional law. However, before we turn to the legislative branch, the subject of the next section, we will briefly consider California's constitution, focusing on how its provisions differ from those of the U.S. Constitution.

The California State Constitution

The California state constitution (adopted in 1879) begins with a Declaration of Rights. This Declaration provides, in part, that people have certain inalienable rights, including "acquiring, possessing, and protecting property." This wording suggests something of California's frontier character when compared to the phrasing of the U.S. Constitution (which makes no mention of "protecting" property). Nonetheless, this and other basic rights provided in the Declaration sound very similar to those provided at the federal level.

That said, California's Declaration of Rights is generally more detailed and covers more topics than the Bill of Rights. In fact, California's entire constitution covers more ground than the U.S. Constitution. Each document provides an organizational structure for its government, but the California constitution also creates law on a range of other issues that the U.S. Constitution ignores, such as labor (Article XIV) and private water rights (Article X).

We should also note that while the liberties protected by the Declaration of Rights resemble those found in the Bill of Rights, courts have occasionally interpreted certain California constitutional rights more broadly than their federal equivalents.

Case Example:

The U.S. Constitution protects speech on public property such as a street or park, but not on private property such as shopping centers. In the 1970s, several high school students were expelled from the Pruneyard Shopping Center in Campbell, California after they attempted to gather petition signatures inside the mall.

The California Supreme Court heard the students' case on appeal and declared that shopping centers, being "freely open" to the public, were a kind of public forum where free speech was protected by California's Declaration of Rights. The state constitution thus offered broader protection than the U.S. Constitution, at least for speech. The U.S. Supreme Court affirmed this interpretation of the state constitution. *Pruneyard Shopping Center v. Robins* (1980) 447 U.S. 74.

A follow-up to the above example: some two decades later, the California Supreme Court ruled that a tenants association had no right to distribute a newsletter in an apartment complex. The complex allowed only tenants and tenant guests on their property and this limitation meant the location wasn't a public forum.

Legislatures: Statutory Law

Both the federal and state constitutions place the primary duty to create new law on the legislature. Legislatures fulfill this responsibility by passing statutes.

The federal legislature consists of two "houses," the Senate and the House of Representatives. In California, the two houses of the legislature are known as the Senate and the Assembly. At the federal level, the two legislative houses together are referred to as **Congress**; at the state level, they are simply referred to as the **legislature**. Because the state and federal legislative processes resemble each other closely, we will discuss the two of them together.

The Legislative Process

A proposal to create a new statute or amend an existing one is called a **bill**. Bills are usually proposed to the legislature by legislators, although occasionally the president does so (or, at the state level, the governor). Legislators may introduce bills in response to voter request, but more commonly lobbyists provide the inspiration. In fact, lobbyists often provide the initial text of a bill.

After a bill is introduced, the appropriate legislative committee analyzes and redrafts the bill as necessary. For example, in the U.S. Congress, the House Committee on Energy and Commerce and the Senate Energy and Natural Resources Committee work on bills related to energy. If the house in which the bill was proposed passes the bill, that house sends it to the other house for consideration. The other house may:

- pass the bill as written,
- rewrite or amend the bill,
- vote the bill down, or
- let the bill die in committee.

If the second house passes the bill, it often does so only after amending or rewriting it. This means that each house has its own version of the bill; the two bills must be **reconciled**. Congress appoints members from both houses (usually important legislators from committees that worked on the bill) to serve on a **conference committee** to work out a compromise version. The compromise bill must receive a majority vote of approval from both houses or it dies.

Assuming the bill passes both houses, it still cannot become law until the executive branch has had a chance to act. The president (or governor) has three choices. She may: 1) approve the bill by signing it; 2) ignore the bill; or 3) **veto** the bill. Either of the first two choices allows the bill to become law. But if the executive vetoes the bill, it is unlikely to ever become law. Only if the legislature overrides the veto will the bill become law. Overriding a veto rarely happens, because it requires a two-thirds majority vote from both houses.

Local Laws. Just as federal and state legislatures pass statutes, local governing bodies pass ordinances. For example, city or county councils typically regulate a variety of issues, from construction standards to animal control.

 Veto Power

George W. Bush was the first president in 175 years not to veto a single bill during an entire term. In the middle of his second term, however, he ended this hiatus, and he went on to exercise the veto power a total of 12 times.

Yet it's inaccurate to say that President Bush failed to use the veto power even in his first term. A threatened executive veto can force a legislature to revise a bill or simply give up trying to pass it. Bush threatened to veto dozens of bills on issues ranging from stem cell research to modifying the Patriot Act. If both legislative houses are controlled by the chief executive's party, and that party is united, the mere threat of a veto works effectively.

These local laws often cover areas not addressed by federal or state law. For example, zoning laws are generally considered the realm of local governing bodies. But local laws may also address issues that are already covered by federal or state law, such as civil rights and discrimination. When this happens, the local laws may be stricter, but never weaker, than their federal or state counterparts.

Referenda and Initiatives. In California and many other states, voters are increasingly taking over some of the legislature's lawmaking responsibility by voting on referenda and initiatives. Technically, a referendum is a ballot measure that rejects or approves a statute passed by the legislature. It is a veto power for the voters. In contrast, an initiative is a proposal to amend the constitution or to modify or create a statute or ordinance. (Note that the U.S. Constitution does not provide for referenda or initiatives; our country has never included either type of measure in a national election, unlike most other democracies in the world.)

California's Codes

California's statutory law is grouped into 29 codes. The Civil Code contains many of the statutes governing the real estate profession. Other codes affecting real estate include the Business and Professions Code, the Financial Code, and the Corporations Code. You can search the state codes through the legislature's website. There, you can browse the table of contents for each code or search the text of the codes by keyword or phrase.

This completes our look at legislative lawmaking. We'll turn now to the courts and spend some time examining their unique method of creating law.

Case to Consider...

Three taxpayers challenged the passage of a 1982 proposition known as "The Victims' Bill of Rights," which contained several constitutional amendments concerning crime and public safety. The plaintiffs claimed, among other things, that the proposition violated the "single subject rule," a rule designed to prevent grab bag propositions (a practice that helps special interests pass measures that lack genuine public support). The plaintiffs cited as precedent *McFadden v. Jordan* (1948) 32 Cal.2d 330, a case in which the court rejected a proposition that addressed "gambling, civic centers, mining, fishing, city budgets, liquor control, senate reapportionment, and oleomargarine." Did the court distinguish McFadden or find it controlling precedent? *Brosnahan v. Brown* (1982) 32 Cal.3d 236.

The Courts: Case Law

While legislatures make new statutory law, the courts generate new case law. Judges are subject to more constraints than legislators, however, in their lawmaking activities. For one thing, judges can "make law" only regarding issues that arise in a particular lawsuit.

Judges can only interpret statutes, not create new ones. Further, judges must usually follow the judicial decisions that have come before them. Thus, lawmaking by the courts generally takes small steps rather than the legal leaps that occasionally characterize legislative action.

No matter how carefully and thoroughly the legislature drafts a certain statute, questions may arise when a court tries to apply that statute to a particular controversy. Judges in this situation must interpret the statute, attempting to follow what they believe the legislature intended to accomplish with the law. This process is called **statutory construction**.

A whole line of cases may develop interpreting a certain statutory word or phrase; in a sense, this interpretation becomes part of the statute. However, the legislature may decide that the courts have misinterpreted the statute and respond by rewriting the law to make it clear what was originally intended.

Court Opinions

Courts resolve disputes by applying the relevant law to the facts and reaching a decision. Trial courts typically limit themselves to a brief statement of their decision in a document called an order. In deciding an appeal, however, most reviewing courts do more: they explain how they reached their decision in a written **opinion**.

Opinions are generally quite detailed. In *Nollan* for example, the Supreme Court's decision was simple enough—the Coastal Commission could not require easements from people in exchange for a permit—yet the Court took eight full pages to explain this decision, carefully going over the facts and discussing how similar cases had been decided in the past. Furthermore, three judges disagreed with the *Nollan* majority and wrote a **dissent** (a contrary opinion that appears after the majority opinion) running another 13 pages.

As you read through the case examples in this book, keep in mind that they are merely summaries of opinions that typically run many pages.

Stare Decisis and Precedent

The rules found in judicial opinions are called **case law**. Once a case has been decided, it sets a precedent, and the rule developed in that case must be followed by judges in later cases. This is called the doctrine of ***stare decisis***. ("*Stare decisis*" means "to stand by settled decisions" in Latin.) However, the doctrine applies only in certain situations.

To begin with, *stare decisis* is not an absolutely rigid doctrine. Under common law tradition, courts that have established a certain precedent can later abandon it, either because social conditions have changed or because the precedent was flawed from the start. Yet overall, *stare decisis* gives litigants predictability and fair treatment—two primary goals of our legal system—so courts treat the doctrine seriously and rarely depart from it.

One famous and necessary break with *stare decisis* came in the case of *Brown v. Board of Education* (1954) 347 U.S. 483, in which the Supreme Court declared that segregating schools and other government facilities violated the Equal Protection Clause. With *Brown*, the Court overruled a terrible precedent that it had established over half a century earlier in *Plessy v. Ferguson* (1896) 163 U.S. 537.

Again, such outright breaks with the past are rare. Rather than reverse precedent, judges who are unhappy with the rule established in an earlier case more commonly find

> ▶ **Judicial Activism**
>
> Political commentators sometimes complain about "judicial activism." This term refers to judicial interpretations of statutes or constitutional provisions that go well beyond what the law actually says. Critics contend that judicial activism usurps the legislature's constitutionally mandated role of creating law. Cases as different as *Roe v. Wade* and *Bush v. Gore* have prompted allegations of judicial activism.
>
> In his confirmation hearing, Supreme Court Chief Justice John Roberts summarized what he called the principle of "judicial restraint" (the opposite of activism). "Judges are like umpires," he proclaimed. "Umpires don't make the rules." Yet in the common law system, many would say that judges are supposed to play a greater role than umpires do in sporting events.

a way to declare that particular case irrelevant. They do this by explaining in the written opinion how the facts of the earlier case are so different from those in the case at hand that applying the precedent makes no sense. This is called **distinguishing** a case. The effort to distinguish a case in order to avoid an unwanted ruling may occasionally lead judges to make factual distinctions that seem rather forced.

While a court that established a certain precedent may deviate from it for good cause, courts beneath that particular court cannot. For example, California Supreme Court decisions establish **binding precedent** for all the state's lower courts. In every state, trial and appellate courts must follow their state's supreme court rulings.

Creating a binding precedent requires the presence of three elements. A binding precedent is established only by an opinion that is: 1) from a higher court; 2) in the same jurisdiction; and 3) officially published.

Because precedent is the bedrock of the common law system, these three requirements deserve a more detailed look.

Higher Court. The U.S. Supreme Court is the highest court in the land and, as such, its decisions bind all federal appellate and trial courts (as well as all state courts on matters of federal law). So, for example, the Supreme Court's decision in the *Nollan* case has settled the law throughout the U.S.—a government agency cannot require an easement from a landowner in exchange for a permit, at least not without paying compensation.

Because the Court's ruling concerns federal law (the Takings Clause), it applies throughout the country, whether the easement condition is imposed by a state agency like the California Coastal Commission or by a federal agency like the U.S. Forest Service.

Jurisdiction. The term "jurisdiction" has several meanings. It can refer to the subject matter of the lawsuits handled by a certain court. For example, the U.S. Tax Court's subject matter jurisdiction is federal tax cases (we discuss this kind of jurisdiction in Chapter 2). However, when we use **jurisdiction** here, we mean the authority that higher courts have over the courts below them.

Citing a Case

Most appellate court opinions are published in hardbound volumes called **case reporters**. The citation tells you exactly where to find the case. Consider the citation, *Droeger v. Friedman, Sloan & Ross* (1991) 54 Cal.3d 26. The citation begins with the name of the case, followed by the year that the case was decided, 1991. Next comes the volume number—54—of the case reporter, Cal.3d, where the opinion can be found. Then the citation gives the page number, 26, where the opinion begins.

The following is a list of case reporter abbreviations relevant to California and federal law:

California courts

California Supreme Court decisions:

| California Reports | Cal., Cal.2d, etc. |

California Court of Appeals:

| California Appellate Reports | Cal.App., Cal.App.2d, etc. |

Federal courts

United States Supreme Court:

| United States Reports | U.S. |

United States Courts of Appeals:

| Federal Reporter | F., F.2d, F.3d |

United States District Courts (trial court):

| Federal Supplement | F.Supp., F.Supp.2d, etc. |

Federal appellate case citations and federal district citations include references to the specific district as well. For example, *Cantrell v. City of Long Beach* (9th Cir. 2001) 241 F.3d 674, was a federal case that was decided in the 9th Circuit.

Persuasive authority. Sometimes, a case involves a matter for which no binding precedent exists. This is known as a **case of first impression**. In such cases, judges are more or less free to rule as they think best. However, lawyers will often try to influence the judge's decision by mentioning a helpful case on the same issue from a nearby jurisdiction. Even though this case isn't binding authority, a judge may find it **persuasive**, showing respect for the approach of another court and possibly adopting that court's rule.

Publication. A court's opinion cannot become precedent without being published. To some extent, this is a practical requirement. If the opinion doesn't appear in a book (or online), how can other judges read and follow it?

A significant number of federal appellate court opinions are published. At the state level, all the opinions of the California Supreme Court are published. A limited number of state appellate opinions are also published. (Before they will be published, they must demonstrate some particular legal worth, such as establishing new law or providing a useful summary of existing law.) State trial courts never publish their opinions, largely because there are no courts below them so their opinions cannot create binding precedent.

This completes our discussion of lawmaking by the judicial branch. Although in the next chapter (Resolving Legal Disputes) we return to the courts, our focus there will be on issues that arise during the conduct of a lawsuit. Now, we will bring this chapter to a conclusion with a discussion of state and federal agencies and their role in the legal system.

Administrative Agencies

Administrative agencies are sometimes considered a fourth branch of government. They certainly deserve the title. Many agencies have hybrid powers: they can make law like a legislative body (through rulemaking) and they can also decide cases like a court (in hearings held by administrative law judges). In this section, we examine the different types of agencies and explore their special combination of powers.

Federal, State, and Local Agencies

Hundreds of federal agencies exist; some are so well-known that they have become household names. For example, we have the Internal Revenue Service, the Treasury Department, and the Environmental Protection Agency.

A number of federal agencies have an equivalent agency at the state level. For example, every state has some kind of environmental protection agency. The California Environmental Protection Agency is referred to as "CalEPA." California agencies also include the Bureau of Real Estate, the Department of Fair Employment and Housing, and, of course, the Coastal Commission.

Agencies exist at the local level, too. Every county and city has some kind of zoning authority, as well as agencies to administer matters such as parks and recreation, waste disposal, and certain social welfare programs.

What explains this huge array of agencies? Simply put, modern life requires more regulation of commerce and other activities than the legislative and executive branches can handle by themselves.

Rulemaking

Many agencies have the power to issue **regulations** (sometimes called rules) that have the force of law. State agency regulations are published in the California Code of Regulations; federal regulations are published in the **Code of Federal Regulations**.

Let's consider rulemaking by one California state agency, the Bureau of Real Estate (CalBRE). The Real Estate Commissioner has published over 150 pages of regulations covering many topics—including important issues such as discriminatory acts by licensees, but also more specialized topics such as the conditions under which resident aliens may receive real estate licenses (California Code of Regulations, Title 10, Chapter 6). The Commissioner can fine or revoke the license of those who violate these regulations.

Both state and federal agencies must publish a notice of any creation or proposed modification of a regulation. This gives interested "stakeholders"—for example, unions or environmental groups—the chance to study the proposal and possibly develop alternatives or modifications to the proposal. The agency will then hold a public hearing on the proposal. (For less controversial proposals, the agency may simply accept written comments.) The CalBRE's current regulatory proposals are available on their website.

Agency regulations must be constitutional and must also fall within the scope of authority granted to the agency. For example, if a regulation falls outside the subject matter area an agency is supposed to regulate, a court will declare the regulation void.

Adjudication and Enforcement

Agency law gives rise to disagreements over various matters: fines, suspended licenses, denied or revoked benefits—the list is endless. These disputes often involve specialized knowledge of agency regulations, so it makes sense for the agencies to try to settle these matters themselves rather than immediately handing them off to the court system for resolution.

Typically, anyone disputing an agency decision (such as a denial of benefits) must first appeal to the agency itself. The agency will usually hold an administrative hearing on the matter. At the hearing, the dispute will be heard by an **administrative law judge** (ALJ). The ALJ is part of the agency and is very familiar with agency policy and regulations. Nonetheless, she is supposed to decide disputes impartially, without favoring her employer.

If a claimant disagrees with the ALJ's decision, she can then appeal to superior court. The odds of success aren't great, however. Courts don't tamper with agency rulings unless the decision was arbitrary (without any substantial evidence), or the agency failed

 Filling Agency Vacancies

Currently, a California governor has the power to make some 2,000 appointments—this includes almost all state agency heads and key policy-making officials. Some appointments require legislative approval, such as appointment of University of California regents, but the legislature rarely denies confirmation. The governor also appoints all the state's judges, although appointments to the appellate and supreme court must be confirmed by the voters.

This vast number of appointments provides the governor with real power to shape state policy. To a degree, this compensates for the executive branch's general lack of direct lawmaking power. At the federal level, the president's agency appointments play a similar role.

Life and Death of an Agency

Legislative irritation with agency policy and rulemaking can lead to a statutory curbing of the agency's authority—or even the agency's outright extinction. Such was the case with the federal Office of Consumer Affairs (OCA), a consumer protection agency conceived of by John F. Kennedy and established by Lyndon Johnson. Within a few decades, Congress had decided that the OCA duplicated services provided by other agencies, and cut its funding until the OCA finally closed its doors in 1998.

to resolve all the necessary issues. Yet reversals of agency rulings do happen, as we saw in *Nollan*, where the Supreme Court declared a Coastal Commission's permit decision unconstitutional.

Agencies hold appeal hearings in order to satisfy a claimant's constitutional right to due process. Yet occasionally an agency can legally avoid holding a hearing. In the following case, a court had to decide if due process required the California Department of Real Estate to hold a hearing before suspending a broker's real estate license.

Case Example:

A broker negotiated a $20,000 loan for a client. The broker purposely didn't tell the lender that the borrower was insolvent, and the broker also failed to record a deed of trust on the borrower's property as requested by the lender. The borrower soon declared bankruptcy. The lender sued the broker for fraud, attempting to recover its losses on the loan, and won the case.

Responding to the court's finding of fraud, the Department of Real Estate sent the broker a notice stating that the agency intended to suspend the broker's license until he made financial restitution to the lender. The broker failed to object and the DRE went ahead and suspended the broker's license.

The broker then appealed to superior court, claiming that because he had never received an agency hearing, the DRE had violated his constitutional due process rights. The broker argued that a license could not be suspended without the right to examine witnesses at a live hearing. However, the court pointed out, the broker had enjoyed an opportunity to examine witnesses—in the earlier court case against him for fraud. Hearings cost an agency (and taxpayers) money and the court refused to require more due process when the wrongdoing had already been proved. The license suspension stood. *Rodriguez v. Department of Real Estate* (1996) 51 Cal.App.4th 1289.

Note that normally no professional license can be revoked or suspended without an agency hearing; the ruling in the above case is limited to instances where a trial has already occurred.

The due process requirement is very important. But, of course, agencies are also subject to scrutiny from the other branches of government. It is the job of the judicial branch, for example, to watch over agencies and to ensure that both agency decisions and regulations meet constitutional standards. This is just another example of our system of checks and balances at work. Courts, legislatures, executives, and agencies—all of these parts of government work together in the continuing effort to create a legal system that reflects society's needs and, of particular interest to us, the needs of a real estate market that is ever-changing.

Case Law in Depth

The following case involves some of the legal issues discussed in this chapter. Read through the facts and consider the questions in light of what you have learned. Then read what the court actually decided.

Lucas Valley Homeowners Assn. v. County of Marin (1991) 233 Cal.App.3d 130

Chabad (an orthodox Jewish congregation) sought Marin County's permission to convert a house into a synagogue that would hold small daily classes and host twice-monthly events involving up to 50 people. The County issued the permit but imposed several conditions. The Board of Supervisors upheld the County's decision and imposed further restrictions on Chabad. Local homeowners opposed the proposed conversion, citing concerns about the erosion of residential neighborhood qualities, impacts on parking and traffic, and excessive noise. They asked the court to overturn the Board's decision to approve the conversion.

Allegations of anti-Semitism were made and emotions ran high during what was a long and bitter struggle. In the end, the trial court invalidated Chabad's permit for the synagogue. The trial court stated the following: 1) it appeared that Chabad got preferential treatment by the Board when the permit was granted, based on the fact that it was a religious organization; 2) the findings by the Board that supported granting the permit were not backed up by evidence in the record; and 3) certain conditions imposed on Chabad as a requirement for the permit interfered with Chabad's religious freedom. Those conditions included the following: maintaining a weekly attendance log; permitting only six children outdoors at any one time; requiring that ceremonial or celebratory functions be conducted for the benefit of members only; restrictions on outdoor activities and outdoor music; and requiring that only events with "specific religious content" be permitted to occur on the site.

The questions:

Regarding Chabad's appeal: did Marin County's numerous conditions violate the Chabad members' constitutional right to religious freedom? Regarding the homeowners' claim: did enough evidence exist to support the Board's decision to grant the permit, or should the trial court's decision to invalidate the permit be allowed to stand?

The court's answers:

The court declared that the Board's decision to grant the permit was not improper, and the conditions did not violate Chabad's religious freedom. "The above conditions are concerned with mundane matters such as numbers, hours, location and noise restrictions. None entangle the County or the community in divining religious content or otherwise passing on the religious affairs of Chabad. Nor does the modest monitoring program inject the County in 'excessive and enduring' involvement with Chabad...

"[Evidence supported the Board's conclusion that impacts on the neighborhood would be minimal.] While unquestionably the proposed use would generate some traffic impact, the test is whether these impacts are potentially detrimental or significant. At the final level and intensity of use actually approved by the Board, there indeed was substantial evidence in the whole record demonstrating the absence of detrimental traffic impacts."

The result:

The trial court's decision invalidating Chabad's permit was overturned; Chabad proceeded with its synagogue plans subject to the conditions imposed by the County.

Chapter Summary

- Ideally, the law promotes order and stability, settles disputes, and protects the rights of minorities. Providing a set of rules makes business more predictable and therefore more likely to be profitable.

- A criminal action is brought by the government to punish a wrongdoer and protect society. In a civil action, an injured party sues for compensation. Some wrongful acts can give rise to both a criminal prosecution and a private suit for damages.

- Most civil law matters involve contracts, torts, or property. Contract law covers the voluntary exchange of promises and the breach thereof; tort law concerns the civil duty to act with reasonable care and to avoid causing injury to persons or property; finally, property law refers to the rights and responsibilities involved in owning real and personal property.

- Sources of law in the U.S. include the federal and state constitutions, legislative bodies, courts, and agencies. Constitutions provide a structure for government and protect personal rights. Each branch of government must meet constitutional requirements when making law or rendering decisions.

- The U.S. uses the common law system, in which courts follow law developed by courts in earlier decisions (precedents). Under the doctrine of *stare decisis*, higher courts create binding precedent for lower courts in the same jurisdiction. *Stare decisis* helps assure that the courts' interpretation of statutes and other laws remains reasonably consistent.

- Administrative agencies may be considered a fourth branch of government. Many agencies have a legislative-like power to issue regulations which have the force of law. Many agencies also have a judiciary-like power to adjudicate matters within their authority such as permitting decisions, licensing, etc.

Key Terms

- **Plaintiff** – The individual or entity who starts a lawsuit (or brings an action) by suing someone.

- **Defendant** – The individual or entity being sued.

- **Litigants** – The parties to a lawsuit; the plaintiff and defendant.

- **Criminal/civil law** – Criminal law involves the government's prosecution of persons charged with crimes. Civil law refers to all law of a non-criminal nature—chiefly, matters involving contracts, torts, and property.

- **Damages** – Money awarded to the winning party in a civil case.

- **Tort** – A type of civil wrong (as opposed to a criminal wrong); examples include negligence, defamation, battery, etc.

- **Due process** – A constitutional guarantee that the government will not deprive persons of liberty or property without a fair hearing.

- **Equal protection** – A constitutional guarantee that the government will not treat people unequally without legitimate reason.

- **State action** – An act of the government or a government official; only state action can violate a person's constitutional rights.

- **Just compensation** – The right to be fairly compensated if the government takes your land.

- **Bill** – A proposed law introduced in either house of the legislature.

- **Statute/ordinance** – Statutes are laws passed by state and federal legislatures; ordinances are laws passed by local legislative bodies such as city or county councils.

- **Code** – Statutes grouped together in logical order and published in official volumes, e.g., the U.S. Code, the California Codes.

- **Jurisdiction** – An area under the authority of a particular court.

- **Opinion** – The court's written explanation of its decision.

- **Case law** – Case law or "common law" is law established by the courts through their written opinions.

- *Stare decisis* – A doctrine that requires courts to follow common law established in earlier cases (precedents), though generally only precedents from higher courts in the jurisdiction are binding.

Chapter Quiz

1. The system in which judges create law through their published opinions is called:
   a) Spanish law
   b) feudal law
   c) civil law
   d) common law

2. Which one of the following parties can bring a criminal action against someone?
   a) The defendant
   b) The state
   c) A person injured by a drunk driver
   d) Any judge

3. Civil law includes:
   a) contract matters
   b) tort matters
   c) property matters
   d) All of the above

4. Tort law requires that people:
   a) honor valid contracts
   b) exercise reasonable care to avoid injuring others
   c) avoid violating any criminal law
   d) use the "beyond a reasonable doubt" standard of proof

5. The U.S. Constitution and the California state constitution:
   a) protect persons from having certain rights violated by the government
   b) protect persons from having certain rights violated by anyone
   c) are identical
   d) California has no state constitution

6. Due process includes:
   a) the right to equal protection of the laws
   b) the president's right to veto legislation
   c) the right to a fair hearing
   d) the distinction between civil and criminal law

7. A city council would most likely create law by:
   a) passing an ordinance
   b) making an agency decision
   c) passing a statute
   d) exercising the veto power

8. Legislatures:
   a) exist at both the state and federal level
   b) consist of two separate chambers
   c) can override an executive veto
   d) All of the above

9. A social welfare agency denies a claimant's application for benefits. Which of the following is true?
   a) The claimant may appeal the adverse decision directly to the appellate court
   b) There must be an agency hearing before the claimant can bring a court appeal
   c) The Takings Clause requires that the agency hold a hearing if a claimant contests a denial of benefits
   d) The Due Process Clause applies only to the judicial and executive branches; there is no right to appeal agency decisions so the claimant is out of luck

10. A lawyer appearing before the California Court of Appeal for the First District claims that the issue on appeal has been settled by a recent California Supreme Court decision. Which of the following answers best characterizes the situation?
    a) The appellate court must follow the rule announced in the supreme court case, under the doctrine of *stare decisis*
    b) The appellate court may avoid following the supreme court case by holding that the case concerned a different kind of situation and thus doesn't apply
    c) *Stare decisis* is federal court doctrine and doesn't apply to state courts, leaving the appellate court free to act without considering California Supreme Court decisions
    d) Both a) and b)

Chapter Answer Key

Chapter Quiz Answers:

1. d) In the common law system, decisions by higher courts are considered binding precedent that must be followed by lower courts in the same jurisdiction.

2. b) Only the state (the government) can prosecute a criminal action. Private parties may bring civil actions, however.

3. d) Civil law includes contract law, tort law, and property law.

4. b) Tort law imposes a duty on persons to exercise reasonable care to avoid injuring others.

5. a) Both the U.S. Constitution and the California state constitution protect individuals from having certain rights violated by the state (the government).

6. c) The right to due process means that a person cannot be deprived of life, liberty, or property without a fair hearing before an impartial judge.

7. a) An ordinance is a law passed by a local body, such as a city or county council.

8. d) Both the state and federal governments have legislatures that are each made up of two parts (the federal legislature is composed of the Senate and the House of Representatives; California's legislature is composed of the Senate and the Assembly). A two-thirds majority vote by both houses will override an executive veto.

9. b) Generally, a party disputing an administrative agency's decision must appeal to the agency itself, and a hearing is held. If the claimant is unhappy with the results of the hearing, she may then appeal to superior court.

10. d) Under the doctrine of *stare decisis*, the appellate court must follow the rule set in the supreme court case. However, if the facts of these cases are considerably different, the appellate court may decide that the rule doesn't apply.

Cases to Consider... Answers:

Constitutional Law

HFH, Ltd. v. Superior Court (1975) 15 Cal.3d 508. Merely changing the zoning of land does not constitute a taking by the government. So long as the new zoning allows some reasonable economic use of the property, compensation is not required—even when, as in this case, the property has become markedly less valuable. (Note: if the owner had actually started building on the property, that probably would have secured his rights under the old zoning laws, and the new zoning wouldn't have applied to his parcel.)

Statutory Law

Brosnahan v. Brown (1982) 32 Cal.3d 236. The court found it relatively easy to distinguish *McFadden's* random mix of issues from the Victims' Rights proposition, which focused on a single theme of concern to voters. The court noted that the voters' power to pass initiatives and referenda was one of the most precious rights in the democratic process. Courts have a duty to interpret this power liberally and protect it.

List of Cases

Anderson v. Department of Real Estate (1979) 93 Cal.App.3d 696

Brosnahan v. Brown (1982) 32 Cal.3d 236

Brown v. Board of Education (1954) 347 U.S. 483

Gonzales v. Raich (2005) 545 U.S. 1

HFH, Ltd. v. Superior Court (1975) 15 Cal.3d 508

Kelo v. City of New London (2005) 545 U.S. 469

Linmark Assoc., Inc., v. Willingboro (1977) 431 U.S. 469

Lucas Valley Homeowners Assn. v. County of Marin (1991) 233 Cal.App.3d 130

Nollan v. California Coastal Commission (1987) 483 U.S. 825

Plessy v. Ferguson (1896) 163 U.S. 537

Pruneyard Shopping Center v. Robins (1980) 447 U.S. 74

Robinson v. Chin & Hensolt (2002) 98 Cal.App.4th 702

Rodriguez v. Department of Real Estate (1996) 51 Cal.App.4th 1289

Chapter 2

Resolving Legal Disputes

Outline

Introduction

Most real estate agents will face at least one lawsuit during their careers. Hopefully, you will never have to sue anyone or be the subject of a lawsuit. However, a basic understanding of the legal system is useful for anyone engaged in any kind of business transaction. In this chapter, we'll discuss the dispute resolution process, from mediation to litigation. We'll begin with a look at alternative dispute resolution and then turn to dispute resolution by the courts. The judicial system in the United States is fairly complex, and discussing it will take up the lion's share of this chapter.

Throughout the chapter, you will find brief sections of commentary by a fictitious lawyer, Hank Howard, concerning the progress of a lawsuit brought against a real estate agent. This hypothetical piece of litigation closely tracks an actual California condominium sale dispute, although the names and other details have been changed. The case illustrates some litigation practicalities and will hopefully add some interest to the subject.

Let's turn to the details of this dispute right now.

A Real Estate Dispute: *Green v. Taslow*

Ten years ago, a San Francisco couple named Phil and Linda Green bought a two-bedroom condo in San Diego's Hook Canyon development. Shelly Taslow, the buyers' agent, had given the Greens a flyer describing the condo's "wonderful" prospects for appreciation. Taslow had visually inspected the property as required by law and saw nothing indicating trouble. The Greens made what they considered to be a slightly below-market offer and were pleased when it was accepted. Closing proceeded as scheduled.

The seller, Gary Crispin, provided a transfer disclosure statement that stated that there were no pending lawsuits affecting the property.

The Greens planned to live in the condo for two years, helping their daughter with her baby while her husband served in the military, and then sell the unit and use any profit to start a college fund for their granddaughter.

A few weeks after moving in, the Greens overheard a neighbor talking about "the lawsuit." Hook Canyon Homeowners Association, it turned out, had recently discovered water leaks that affected many of the units and some of the common areas. The homeowners association had filed a lawsuit against the builders and developers about one month before the Greens signed the offer for their unit.

Further investigation revealed that water damage had caused significant mold and structural damage to the common area hallway outside the Greens' unit. The condo was hardly the bargain they'd thought. Nor were its prospects for appreciation especially bright, at least not until the litigation was settled—something that might take years. The Greens wanted to undo the deal, get their money back plus expenses (for a total of about $350,000), and buy a different, less troubled property. A friend recommended a plaintiff's lawyer named Hank Howard.

Hank's Corner

I met with the Greens today and agreed to take their case. They bought a condo last month, and the seller's disclosure statement assured them that there was no litigation affecting the property. Turns out the homeowners association (HOA) had just filed suit against the builder for construction defects. The seller had to know: the HOA had sent letters to all the owners, and its newsletter mentioned the pending lawsuit several times. California law requires the seller to disclose any pending litigation, so this is a plain and simple case of fraud, if I ever saw one.

Negotiated Settlement

The first step in attempting to settle almost any dispute is **negotiation**. The parties talk to each other and try to hammer out a compromise. If they're too angry to talk, they can hire lawyers to handle the negotiation. Either way, if the parties reach a compromise they should have a lawyer draft a **settlement agreement** documenting the terms they've agreed to.

A negotiated settlement has several advantages over other methods of dispute resolution. It's fast. It's final—there's no question of an appeal, since the parties have both agreed to the terms of the settlement. Also, since negotiation doesn't take much attorney time, it's relatively inexpensive.

Negotiation starts with the parties presenting their initial positions to one another, either directly or through their lawyers. The party initiating the claim will usually want to be reimbursed for various losses or expenses. (With a personal injury claim, for example, the claimant is likely to ask for reimbursement for medical bills and lost pay.) If the claimant is represented by a lawyer, the lawyer will write a demand letter requesting payment of a specified amount. The letter indicates that unless the requested amount is paid, the claimant will take legal action against the other party.

Depending on the circumstances, the other party might accept the proposed settlement outright, agreeing to pay the requested amount. She might reject it outright, refusing to pay at all. Or she might make a counteroffer, offering to pay something less than the amount requested. The negotiations may continue with a series of offers and counteroffers, until finally one party accepts the other's latest offer.

In many cases, the parties cannot negotiate a compromise. If so, they may end up turning to the courts to resolve their disagreement. Using the court system presents some problems, however. The process is slow—the parties may have to wait more than a year for a trial date—and because of all the legal procedures involved, they'll face substantial attorneys' fees.

Beginning in the 1960s, parties and lawyers trying to avoid these drawbacks began relying more heavily on alternatives to courtroom litigation. Let's take a look at these alternative methods of dispute resolution.

Alternative Dispute Resolution

Alternative dispute resolution (ADR) includes two alternatives to the courtroom: mediation and arbitration. **Mediation** is basically negotiation with a referee and does not involve a hearing. **Arbitration** resembles a mini-trial, although the hearing is held outside the courtroom.

When a dispute arises, the parties may agree to try arbitration or mediation. Alternatively, they may be required to submit their dispute to arbitration or mediation as a result of:

- a contractual agreement (for example, employment contracts typically provide for ADR to settle any disputes between the parties);
- a statutory requirement (for example, California law requires mediation of marital dissolutions when children are involved); or
- a court order (in California, judges generally order arbitration in most types of cases involving claims of under $50,000).

Real estate purchase agreements and brokerage agreements commonly require mediation and/or arbitration of disputes, so real estate agents will want to be at least somewhat familiar with both processes.

Mediation

As noted, **mediation** is essentially negotiation conducted with the help of a neutral third party, usually someone with training in conflict resolution. Mediators use various techniques. For example, if the parties are hostile, the mediator typically avoids having the two sides meet face-to-face. Instead, the mediator will act as an intermediary, speaking first to one party and then to the other.

Mediators tend to encourage the parties to "split the difference." Often, a middle-of-the-road compromise makes sense. At other times, however, this result means that injured parties walk away with less money than they might have received in arbitration or the courtroom. Bringing a lawyer to the mediation may help avoid this. However, the presence of attorneys can create an adversarial atmosphere that reduces the odds of successful mediation.

> ### ▶ Six Signs You Have a Bad Mediator
>
> 1. He didn't read all the relevant documents beforehand.
> 2. She appears uncertain or otherwise fails to inspire confidence.
> 3. He can't manage the misbehavior of a party.
> 4. She doesn't offer settlement options.
> 5. He pushes too hard (for example, by keeping the mediation going late at night when everyone is tired: "serving the settlement, not the parties").
> 6. She drafts the settlement agreement, possibly practicing law without a license.

Mediation isn't binding, however. A party unhappy with the process can reject the result and take her claim to court—or to arbitration, if that form of dispute resolution is required.

The California Association of Realtors® (CAR) residential purchase agreement form requires buyers and sellers to mediate their disputes before proceeding to arbitration or the court system.

Cost of Mediation. Some California communities have organizations that provide free or low-cost mediation through the use of volunteer mediators. More complex disputes require mediators with a relevant professional background, such as construction industry experience, a social work degree, or a labor relations background. These specialized mediators generally charge a fee comparable to that of arbitrators, often from $200 to $300 an hour. The cost is shared by the parties.

Now let's discuss arbitration, a notably more complex process.

Arbitration

Arbitration is a formal hearing on a case, and both parties are usually represented by lawyers. The **arbitrator** is often a lawyer or a retired judge with experience in the subject matter of the dispute. There is no jury. The arbitrator often conducts the hearing in a rented conference room. In some cases, a court reporter is present. The atmosphere is fairly formal and many of the rules of evidence apply.

As with mediation, the parties typically split the costs. This would include room rental fees and other incidental charges, as well as the arbitrator's fee. A simple arbitration may take an afternoon, but a dispute of any complexity might require a day or two. Costs can add up. Still, arbitration is cheaper and faster than a full-blown trial.

Involuntary and Voluntary Arbitration. Arbitration is either involuntary or voluntary. It's considered involuntary when it is required by statute or court order. Involuntary arbitration is typically nonbinding. This means that any party can appeal an unsatisfactory result, which may help take the sting out of being forced to arbitrate. As we discuss below, there are reasons that parties sometimes prefer the courtroom.

Voluntary arbitration comes about through agreement-to-arbitrate provisions in contracts (although consumers buying insurance or entering into other contracts where they have almost no bargaining power may not find these provisions especially "voluntary").

> ### *Hank's Corner*
>
> I told the Greens today that we could sue the seller, Crispin, but it wouldn't do them any good. My investigator says that Crispin spent the proceeds of the condo sale paying off credit cards. In addition, he's run off to Show Low, Arizona, where his only assets are a little plot of land and a 28-year-old mobile home, both of which are mortgaged to the hilt. Any judgment we get would be useless.
>
> There's another option, though. We could go after the real estate agents. Over the years, there's been a trend towards expanding agent liability. There's not much case law to back up my theory, and it would be an uphill battle, but the Greens want to go ahead. Maybe we can get the real estate agents to settle.

This contractually required arbitration, also called **mandatory arbitration**, is generally binding—the parties cannot appeal the arbitrator's decision. The whole point of agreeing to arbitrate is to avoid the courtroom.

Even with binding arbitration, however, a court may occasionally get involved. It can overturn or vacate an award if the arbitrator's decision stemmed from fraud, corruption, or similar misconduct, or if the arbitrator exceeded her powers or refused to hear relevant evidence. While this may sound like a long list, in reality a court will rarely find any of these elements present. Further, the complaining party must show that the arbitrator's misconduct or other error actually affected the arbitration award.

Case Example:

Ramani agreed to arbitrate a dispute over property he owned jointly with several members of the Mahboubian-Fard family. A retired judge named Younger was appointed to arbitrate. Younger awarded the Mahboubian-Fards over $200,000.

Ramani asked the court to vacate the award, claiming that Younger was prejudiced against him. In the written arbitration award, Younger had labeled Ramani "slick" and an "operator" and, in this context, noted that he'd observed Ramani trying to hustle his former receptionist during breaks.

The reviewing court found that the amount of the award was supported by the expert witnesses' valuation testimony. Thus, even if Younger had formed a negative opinion about Ramani based on improper evidence, there was no evidence that Ramani had suffered harm because of it. The award was affirmed. *Mahboubian-Fard, et al. v. Superior Court* (Super.Ct. Los Angeles, Mar. 6, No. LS007911) 2003 WL 768905.

Let's return to the Greens' case for a moment. Will they arbitrate their dispute? Well, we know that court-ordered arbitration isn't a possibility, because the Greens are seeking return of their purchase money and this amount greatly exceeds $50,000—the maximum for court-ordered arbitration in California. As for contract-specified arbitration, the dispute

Arbitration Provisions: Buyers vs. Sellers

Arbitration provisions tend to favor either buyers or sellers, depending on the state of the housing market.

In a flat or falling market, a better-priced house is always lurking right around the corner. Buyers might be tempted to back out of a sale, knowing they risk losing only their deposit. In this economic environment, arbitration looks attractive to a seller: it will allow her to enforce her right to the buyer's deposit with relative speed and economy, avoiding a costly, time-consuming lawsuit. Thus, sellers in a sluggish or sinking market will probably want to require arbitration.

A rising market reverses the equation, however. As a purchase transaction winds towards closing, other buyers may appear and make attractive backup offers that seem to invite the seller to reevaluate his position. In a hot market, it's the buyers who typically end up wanting to enforce purchase agreements.

resolution section in the California Association of Realtors® purchase agreement form does require arbitration, but only if both parties initial the provision.

The relevant language in the form states:

> **NOTICE: BY INITIALING IN THE SPACE BELOW, YOU ARE AGREEING TO HAVE ANY DISPUTE...DECIDED BY NEUTRAL ARBITRATION AS PROVIDED BY CALIFORNIA LAW AND YOU ARE GIVING UP ANY RIGHTS YOU MIGHT POSSESS TO HAVE THE DISPUTE LITIGATED IN A COURT OR JURY TRIAL...YOU ARE [ALSO] GIVING UP YOUR JUDICIAL RIGHTS TO DISCOVERY AND APPEAL...**

The law requires this provision to be in attention-getting type (Code of Civil Procedure § 1298(c)). Some attorneys recommend against the parties initialing the provision. The worry is that arbitrators can be, well, arbitrary. Arbitrators' decisions can't easily be reversed on appeal, and this sometimes encourages eccentric decision-making on their part.

Further, arbitrators tend to be more conservative than juries, which makes it harder to win a large damage award. This consideration helps explain why businesses tend to like arbitration. Yet arbitration isn't necessarily a net win for business. Evidence suggests that arbitrators often compromise by offering plaintiffs a little something in the way of damages, while a court might very well have decided that the claim had absolutely no legal merit and awarded nothing.

In the Greens' case, both the buyers and the seller initialed the arbitration provision on the purchase agreement form. Thus, the Greens' claim against Gary Crispin will have to be arbitrated. It doesn't seem likely that Crispin will come to California for an arbitration hearing, however.

The dispute resolution provision in the CAR buyer-broker agreement form is very similar to the one found in the purchase agreement form. However, both the Greens and their broker, Shelly Taslow, failed to initial the arbitration provision.

Hank's Corner

The lawyer representing both real estate agents called today after getting my settlement offer. He claimed my theory of liability is outrageous and refused to talk settlement.

The buyer-broker agreement requires us to mediate before proceeding to arbitration, but I don't expect much from the process. The lawyer doesn't want to arbitrate, anyway. "We're going to court," he said. "I don't think a judge will give you one penny for this claim."

"Maybe not a judge," I said. "But I'm willing to bet a jury of homeowners might."

He and I both know that most cases settle long before they get to trial, but if he's not willing to talk settlement, I've got to go ahead and file the complaint.

Case to Consider...

The plaintiffs were various buyers of "entry-level" houses from Pardee Construction, a large-scale developer. These houses had construction defects. The dispute resolution provision in the purchase agreement required arbitration, but this provision was confusingly labeled and somewhat difficult to understand. It also barred the buyers from seeking punitive damages. A court will not uphold unconscionable provisions in a contract—that is, provisions that take advantage of naïve buyers and that unfairly favor the seller. Did this arbitration provision sink to the level of unconscionability? *Pardee Construction Co. v. Superior Court* (Rodriguez) (2002) 100 Cal.App.4th 1081.

Litigating in Court

The rest of this chapter focuses on how courts resolve disputes. Let's start with a basic question: how does Hank Howard—or any other lawyer—know where to file a lawsuit?

Most state court systems are set up in a similar manner. There is a local trial court for the initial hearing of disputes, an intermediate appellate court for appeals of trial court decisions, and a supreme or high court that hears certain appeals from the appellate court. (A number of states don't bother with a mid-level appellate court, so their high court hears all trial court appeals.)

We know that Hank must start with a trial court. But state or federal trial court? And in what state? Choosing the correct court turns on the concept of jurisdiction.

Determining the Proper Court for Trial: Jurisdiction

Lawyers can't file their case in whatever trial court they please. The chosen court must have jurisdiction over both the parties and the subject matter. **Jurisdiction** is the authority a court has to make legally valid judgments on the matters before it. A court decides whether it has jurisdiction by analyzing the following elements:

- the state(s) where the parties reside and where the alleged wrong took place,
- the type of claim at issue (for example, a breach of contract or a crime), and
- in a civil case, the amount of money at stake.

There are two types of jurisdiction, personal jurisdiction and subject matter jurisdiction, both of which must be present in order for a court to hear the case. Let's begin by analyzing personal jurisdiction, which involves aspects of the first element in the above list.

Personal Jurisdiction. A court cannot hear a case unless it has personal jurisdiction over the defendant. **Personal jurisdiction** refers to a court's legal right to force the defendant into court. The constitutional right to due process (see Chapter 1) places limits on personal jurisdiction, however. A court can't just arbitrarily order residents of other states or countries into the courtroom. The defendant must have committed some act in the state, or have some connection with the state to justify requiring his presence.

> **Example:** A Sacramento resident named Banhart drives to Eugene, Oregon for the Bach Festival. While there, an elderly music fan named Rudy accidentally rear ends Banhart's car. The Californian returns home and promptly files a lawsuit against Rudy in Sacramento County Superior Court. This court dismisses Banhart's case for lack of personal jurisdiction over Rudy. Rudy had no contact with California that would give the court personal jurisdiction over him.

In the last few decades, an interesting line of cases has developed over whether Internet contacts with a state can create personal jurisdiction. The following case illustrates how a court may look at a defendant's level of Internet activity (or interactivity) in a given location when considering the issue of personal jurisdiction over the defendant.

Case Example:

A Silicon Valley company called Dot Com provided Internet news services to subscribers. Dot Com's web pages could be viewed worldwide, but it had no physical presence anywhere except in California. The company owned and used the domain names zippo.com, zippo.net, and zipponews.com.

Zippo Manufacturing, maker of the famous Zippo lighter, has its home in Pennsylvania. Zippo filed a trademark infringement claim against Dot Com in a Pennsylvania federal district court. Dot Com moved to dismiss the case, arguing that the court lacked personal jurisdiction.

About 3,000 of Dot Com's customers lived in Pennsylvania at the time. They paid for Dot Com's services online by using a credit card. Additionally, Dot Com had contracts with several Pennsylvania Internet service providers.

Earlier court decisions had already determined that business websites that simply provided information, but did not allow products to be ordered over the web, couldn't confer personal jurisdiction. These so-called "passive websites" do not create sufficient contact with the state where the customer resides. But in this case, Dot Com had entered into transactions with Pennsylvania customers via its webpage, and this gave the Pennsylvania court personal jurisdiction over the defendant. *Zippo Mfg. Co. v. Zippo Dot Com, Inc.* (W.D. Pa. 1997) 952 F.Supp. 1119.

Subject Matter Jurisdiction. Along with jurisdiction over the defendant, a court must have jurisdiction over the **subject matter** of the case—that is, the particular type of case being brought. For example, a state's trial courts can decide cases involving that state's civil or criminal law. Because state trial courts have such broad scope, they are called courts of **general jurisdiction**.

Yet even courts of general jurisdiction have some limits on the subject matter they can hear. For example, California superior courts cannot hear federal tax or bankruptcy cases. Those cases must be filed in a U.S. Tax Court or U.S. Bankruptcy Court. (Because of their specialized nature, tax courts and bankruptcy courts are called courts of **limited jurisdiction**.)

Now that we've introduced subject matter jurisdiction, let's look at some specific applications of this concept in the state and federal court systems.

Federal Trial Court Jurisdiction. Most federal trial courts are called U.S. district courts. Each state has at least one U.S. district court, and larger states have two or more. California has four, one each for the northern, eastern, central, and southern portions of the state.

The U.S. Constitution grants federal courts subject matter jurisdiction over cases where:

- the United States government is a party,
- a question of federal law is at issue, or
- there is diversity of citizenship (defendants and plaintiffs reside in different states).

Jurisdiction also exists over slightly more obscure matters, such as maritime cases and disputes with foreign citizens and governments. We'll briefly discuss the first two types of federal subject matter jurisdiction, U.S. government and federal law cases, and then spend slightly more time on diversity jurisdiction—if only because it may apply to our *Taslow* case.

U.S. government cases. The United States goes to federal district court to prosecute federal crimes such as racketeering or mail fraud. The federal government also brings suit in U.S. district court over civil matters such as breach of contract. The U.S. government may be sued there, as well. For example, a flood levee builder might sue the U.S. Army Corps of Engineers over a dispute concerning payment for construction work.

Fig. 2.1 California's federal court districts

Federal law cases. Federal district courts have subject matter jurisdiction over cases where private parties raise federal law issues. These include claims made under the U.S. Constitution, a federal statute, or a U.S. treaty.

A case can involve both federal and state law. For example, a tenant may allege that her eviction violated federal antidiscrimination law and also her state's landlord-tenant law. Cases that contain mixed federal and state legal issues may be brought in either federal or state court.

Diversity cases. When plaintiffs and defendants live in different states, there is **diversity of citizenship**. The framers of the Constitution created this brand of jurisdiction to protect an out-of-state party from the favoritism a state court might show towards its residents. However, in order to prevent minor cases from clogging the federal court system, Congress added a requirement that diversity cases must involve claims of at least $75,000.

Diversity jurisdiction is optional. That is, a case with diversity of citizenship will nonetheless be tried in state court unless one of the parties opts for federal court. A party unhappy about being in federal court may try and attack the basis for diversity jurisdiction.

 Federal Court Pros and Cons

If you have a choice, should you go to federal court? That depends; your lawyer will offer clear direction. Federal judges on average possess greater legal sophistication than their state counterparts—although this becomes a disadvantage if the legal basis for one's position is shaky.

Federal trials tend to proceed more quickly. However, this may be an advantage only if you anticipate winning. Also, the rules of procedure and evidence vary somewhat, and that may be a factor in some cases.

Finally—a less honorable consideration—if the federal courthouse is significantly farther from the opposing party's residence than the state court, sometimes a party will burden their opponent by removing the case to the more distant federal court.

Case Example:

Various trucking companies sued the makers of their trucks in California state court. The truck manufacturers petitioned to remove the case to federal trial court, apparently believing they would receive better treatment at the federal level.

Plaintiffs had added or "joined" a trucking company called RCI as a fellow plaintiff. The company was located in the same state as one of the defendant manufacturers and this joinder created a lack of diversity between the parties (putting federal court out of reach). The manufacturers appealed in federal court, arguing that the plaintiffs had added RCI for only one reason: to defeat federal jurisdiction. Adding a party who has no real role in the litigation, with the intent to defeat jurisdiction, is called fraudulent or egregious joinder.

The complaint failed to explain the basis for RCI's claim. However, there were dozens of plaintiffs and this omission may have been an oversight. At any rate, merely noting the failure to state a claim didn't satisfy the defendants' burden of proving that no claim existed;

the plaintiffs could amend their complaint and flesh out RCI's cause of action. Without positive proof of fraud, the case was headed back to California state court. *California Dump Truck Owners Association. v. Cummins Engine Co., Inc.* (9th Cir. 2001) 24 Fed. Appx. 727.

We mentioned that diversity jurisdiction might apply to the *Taslow* case. Remember that the seller, Gary Crispin, moved to Arizona and that the Greens reside in California. What's more, the Greens are seeking over $75,000 in damages. However, for diversity jurisdiction to exist, every defendant must live in a different state from every plaintiff. In our case, defendant Shelly Taslow lives in California along with the Greens. That destroys diversity jurisdiction and eliminates the possibility of federal court.

The Greens must bring their suit in state court. Since litigation concerning real property is brought in the county where the property is located, they must file suit in the California Superior Court, County of San Diego.

State Trial Court Jurisdiction. The trial courts in California and most other states are called **superior courts**. State trial courts are found in each county and for that reason are often informally referred to as "county courts." As mentioned, these courts have jurisdiction over state civil and criminal cases.

Note that California plaintiffs with claims of $10,000 or less ($5,000 or less if the plaintiff is a business) may choose to save time and money by bringing their cases in

 A Crowded Bench

California has over 2,000 judges. Most of these judges serve in superior court, elected by the voters to six-year terms. It is the governor who appoints judges to the court of appeals and supreme court, and they serve 12-year terms. However, voters can reject the governor's higher court appointments at the next general election.

California voters can recall any judge for misconduct, in theory. Recall efforts rarely succeed. In 1997, some furious citizens sought the recall of Judge Stock of Orange County Superior Court after the judge granted O.J. Simpson custody of his children (following their mother's murder). However, the organizers couldn't get enough signatures to put the recall measure on the ballot.

In 2004, a group of conservative Sacramento residents attempted to oust California superior court Judge Loren E. McMaster after he upheld California's Domestic Partnership Act. State voters had recently passed Proposition 22, which limited marriage to male-female couples, and the group believed that Proposition 22 had repealed the Partnership Act. Again, the necessary petition signatures failed to materialize and the recall effort stalled.

Court Costs

California superior courts hear about eight million cases a year. More than two-thirds of these cases concern criminal matters (mostly relating to traffic).

The state imposes various filing fees on civil parties, forcing them to share part of the court system's expenses. For instance, the plaintiff pays between $225 and $435 to file her case, depending on the amount in controversy. The defendant must pay a matching fee when responding to the complaint. The filing fee to initiate a small claims court case is much smaller, ranging from $30 to $75 depending on the claim amount. Low-income parties can apply for a waiver of any filing fee.

Convicted criminals may also have to pay some fees and/or court costs as a condition of their sentence.

small claims court rather than superior court. There is no jury in small claims court, and the procedural rules are simplified. Lawyers cannot appear in the courtroom, but they can give clients advice before and after the proceedings.

Some states also have a layer of city courts called municipal, police, or district courts—with jurisdiction over traffic infractions and other city ordinance violations. Until relatively recently, California also had municipal courts, but beginning in 1998 the state merged its municipal courts into the superior court system.

How a Lawsuit Begins

Our plaintiffs, the Greens, want to sue. Exactly how do they begin? Actually, starting a lawsuit is relatively simple: draft the complaint, file, and serve. Then, the plaintiff sits back and awaits the defendant's answer.

We will discuss each of these initial steps before turning to the more central elements of a trial.

Complaint. The **complaint** is a document from the plaintiff that outlines the case against the defendant. Complaints may be quite brief or, in complex litigation, run dozens of pages.

Generally, the first few paragraphs of the complaint contain facts assuring the court that it has personal jurisdiction over the defendants. In most complaints, the paragraphs following the jurisdictional facts describe the defendant's misconduct. Then, with these wrongful acts described, the plaintiff makes legal claims against the defendant.

The complaint typically concludes by stating what **relief** or **remedy** the plaintiff seeks. There's no point in paying a filing fee and complaining about your suffering if you don't ask the court to do something about it. We'll discuss remedies shortly.

Filing. The complaint is filed with the clerk of the court. The clerk date-stamps the complaint; the person filing the document makes copies and then returns the original to the clerk for inclusion in the court file.

Service. A copy of the complaint must be served on the defendant. Generally, service requires hand delivery. The plaintiff cannot serve the defendant; that task must be handled by someone who isn't a party. Usually, this means hiring a professional process server.

Along with the complaint, the service also includes a summons—a simple document from the court telling the defendant that he must answer the complaint and appear in court.

Hank's Corner

I filed and served the Greens' complaint today. San Diego Superior Court case number: 668406. We claimed breach of contract, fraud, and negligence. We're seeking compensatory damages for closing costs, interest, legal fees, and emotional distress. Total: $480,000. Hopefully, the number will encourage the other side to rethink a settlement.

The other side has 30 days to answer our complaint. I imagine they'll deny most of it. Still, all we can do now is wait.

Answer. After the process server's unwelcome visit, the defendant must file and serve an answer to the complaint. The **answer** responds to the various allegations made in the complaint. The complaint, the answer, and similar documents filed in a lawsuit are often referred to as the **pleadings** in the case.

Often a defendant's answer denies almost every assertion made in the complaint except for the spelling of his name and address—and occasionally even that. In our *Taslow* case, the defendant real estate agents will certainly deny that they committed fraud, probably pointing out that they lacked the intent to mislead that fraud requires. They will also deny the Greens' claim of negligence, stating that they had no legal duty to investigate whether the condo complex was involved in litigation.

A defendant in California superior court generally has 30 days to answer (less time in certain simple court procedures like eviction). If the defendant fails to answer within this period, the court may find him in default and grant the plaintiff's request for damages or other relief. However, a defendant with a good reason for delay may seek an extension of time to answer.

Defenses. Along with denying the plaintiff's allegations of wrongdoing, the answer can also raise what are called **affirmative defenses**. This type of defense doesn't involve denying the wrongdoing. With an affirmative defense, even if the facts claimed by the plaintiff are proven true, the defendant will not be found liable. This occurs, for example, when a defendant alleges that the court lacks personal jurisdiction. If the court agrees with this lack of jurisdiction defense, it will dismiss the plaintiff's claims.

Arguing that a party has waited too long to file her claim is another affirmative defense. State and federal **statutes of limitations** limit how much time a plaintiff has to bring a lawsuit. For example, in California a plaintiff must file a claim concerning a written contract within four years of when the breach occurred (and within only two years if the contract was oral). If a plaintiff files after this time period, the statute of limitations bars her claim.

Statutes of limitations help prevent trials from taking place after so much time has passed that witnesses have either moved or no longer remember what exactly was said or intended. However, the clock on many statutes of limitations does not begin to run until the plaintiff has had a reasonable chance to discover the breach or other injury. This is called the **delayed discovery rule**.

> **Example:** During brain surgery, the surgeon absentmindedly leaves a tiny clamp inside Mike's head. Over time, this clamp causes a blood clot to form. One day, four years later, Mike has a stroke.
>
> The statute of limitations for California tort actions is generally two years; three years are allowed for medical malpractice (unless the injury should have been discovered sooner than it was). However, the delayed discovery rule applies to cases of foreign objects left inside a patient's body. As long as Mike files his lawsuit within three years after discovering his injury, his doctor won't be able to raise the statute of limitations as an affirmative defense.

Occasionally, parties enter into contracts containing a **limitation on actions clause**. This clause gives the parties less time to bring a lawsuit for breach than the statute of limitations allows. Sometimes courts uphold these provisions, sometimes not. In the following case, a homeowner argued against a contractual time limit on public policy grounds.

Case Example:

Moreno and Contreras contracted to buy a house in Whittier. They had the building inspected. The inspector's contract required that any claim against the inspector had to be brought within one year.

After moving in Contreras fell ill, suffering various unpleasant chronic symptoms such as nosebleeds. She was eventually diagnosed with a bacterial infection. A new building

---

The Process Server's Life

Most people stonily accept their "papers" from a process server. Some defendants get angry, however. Process servers report defendants turning dogs loose and even firing guns. For all this, the server earns an average of about $50 per service.

A more common professional problem than outright hostilities is a defendant who evades service. Pretending to be someone else, refusing to answer the door, sneaking out the back—such are the tricks of the "difficult serve." But process servers can be equally tricky: showing up with a floral bouquet or holding a pizza box, for example. One New York process server who faced a reluctant dermatologist claimed to be suffering a rash in order to gain admittance to the doctor's examining room.

inspector discovered problems the first inspector had missed, including a ventilation system that was contaminated by dirt, dust, and dust mites due to an unsealed component. The buyers sued the first inspector several months after their contract's one-year limit expired.

Noting that the public relies on professionals and skilled tradespeople like building inspectors, the court ruled that any attempt by these service providers to shorten the four-year statutory time limit on contract actions violated public policy. *Moreno v. Sanchez* (2003)106 Cal.App.4th 1415.

Counterclaims. The defendant may also make counterclaims against the plaintiff in the answer. For example, the defendant may counterclaim that it was the plaintiff who first breached the contract and thus owes the defendant damages. In a sense, **counterclaims** turn the defendant into a quasi-plaintiff and require the plaintiff to file a pleading that answers the defendant's allegations.

Lis Pendens. In a lawsuit affecting title to real property, the plaintiff's lawyer will file a lis pendens against the property in the county recorder's office. A **lis pendens** (Latin for "suit pending") is a notice that essentially tells the public, "Warning—a lawsuit has been filed that potentially affects title to this property." By the way, "lis pendens" remains a commonly used term among practitioners, but the California Code of Civil Procedure uses the term "notice of pendency."

The lis pendens or notice of pendency warns prospective purchasers or mortgagees that if they take an interest in the property, it will be subject to any judgment in the plaintiff's favor. The presence of a lis pendens may scare off potential buyers and lenders, forcing the defendant-owner to the settlement table.

Case Example:

Brent sued Vicki for breach of a contract to share the proceeds from selling certain pieces of property. Unfortunately, Brent had lost the contract itself. However, his attorneys took his word that it existed and placed a lis pendens on Vicki's property.

Vicki argued that Brent's breach claim was meritless, and that the lis pendens was intended solely to extort settlement from her by preventing her from closing a sale on one of the properties. Perhaps there wasn't much to Brent's suit, because he subsequently withdrew the action and the court expunged (removed) his lis pendens from Vicki's property.

Vicki then sued Brent's attorneys, alleging, among other things, "slander of title" (for placing a lis pendens on property in bad faith). While support for Brent's lawsuit had been thin, Vicki produced no evidence that Brent's attorneys knew he was lying about the contract's existence; thus, the court couldn't find bad faith. And even if Vicki had proved bad faith, she'd failed to show that the lis pendens had caused her direct financial loss. She had no case. *Vallis v. Collinson, et al.* (3rd Cir., Sept. 8, 2004, No. C045374) 2004 WL 1987103.

In our condominium case, had Shelly Taslow (the Greens' agent) searched the county records for a lis pendens against the property, it's unlikely that she would have found one. Construction defect litigation doesn't affect title to the property, since the property in question is not owned by the construction company. So a lis pendens isn't filed when this type of lawsuit begins. On the other hand, a check of the San Diego Superior Court records would have immediately revealed the lawsuit.

Remedies. As mentioned, the complaint must request some form of remedy from the court. And if a defendant makes any counterclaims against the plaintiff in her answer, she too must include a request for relief.

We're going to focus on three relatively common forms of legal remedies in this section. Keep in mind, however, that there are other, more specialized remedies that we'll address in later chapters. For example, in certain real property actions including eviction and partition, the relief takes the form of a court order modifying or clarifying property rights.

The three remedies we'll discuss here are:

- compensatory damages,
- punitive damages, and
- specific performance.

Compensatory damages. The most commonly requested legal remedy is compensatory damages. Compensatory damages reimburse a party for actual financial losses suffered due to the other party's actions. For example, suppose a computer wholesaler failed to provide some below-market-priced laptops it had promised an electronics store. The store's request for compensatory damages would include the extra cost it incurred when it substituted laptops from another wholesaler at the full market price. In the context of a personal injury case, compensatory damages would include items like medical bills or lost wages.

Punitive damages. If the defendant's wrongdoing had a severe, flagrant quality, the plaintiff may sometimes successfully claim punitive damages in addition to compensatory damages. The point of punitive damages is to deter the defendant and others like her from similar misbehavior in the future. This award may be up to ten times the plaintiff's compensatory damages and is something of a windfall. However, courts only occasionally find a defendant's behavior appalling enough to justify punitive damages.

Specific performance. The third form of relief we're going to discuss, specific performance, actually isn't requested very often—although parties seek it more frequently in disputes over real property sales than in other types of contract litigation. A court order granting specific performance forces a party to perform as the contract provided. For example, in a lawsuit over a real estate transaction that failed to close, the court might order the seller to sign a deed and deliver it to the buyer as required by the purchase agreement.

Courts order specific performance only when monetary damages alone won't satisfy the plaintiff. This situation generally arises only in connection with a contract to purchase something that's one-of-a-kind—art works and real estate are obvious examples. In short, it has to be something that no one but the opposing party can provide. Specific performance would never be ordered in litigation over a breach of contract to sell laptops. There's nothing unique about laptops; money damages would enable the plaintiff to purchase them from someone else.

This completes our discussion of legal remedies, at least for now. Let's return to our study of the steps leading directly to trial.

Jury Demand. Both plaintiffs and defendants have the right to request a jury, although they must do so fairly quickly after the answer is filed. If neither party files a **jury demand**, the judge will decide the case. This is called a **bench trial**.

Deciding whether to request a jury requires experience. A likeable or sympathetic client makes a jury seem desirable, since judges are less likely to be swayed by emotional considerations. Conversely, a lawyer whose case depends on sophisticated legal arguments may prefer to have the judge decide the case.

Discovery

The complaint and answer have been filed and served, and any hope of a quick settlement has dissolved. Now things can turn ugly—and costly. The lawsuit enters what is called the discovery phase. **Discovery** is the process of learning about the opposing party's case by using any combination of these methods:

- written questions (interrogatories),
- oral questions (depositions), and
- document requests (requests for production).

Each side is required by law to respond to the other's discovery requests. Requiring parties to reveal their case to the other side might seem a little odd, especially if you were raised on traditional courtroom dramas, stories where lawyers introduce surprise witnesses or experts take the stand and drop bombshells. In modern legal practice, each side uses discovery to learn which witnesses will appear at trial and also what they will have to say.

While this approach doesn't make for strong television, it does give the parties a realistic view of their chances of success at trial. Why does this matter? Because having a sense of the trial's likely outcome encourages the parties to make realistic settlement offers. And settlement saves everyone money—including taxpayers, who cover most of the court system's costs.

Interrogatories. Early in the lawsuit, the parties typically send each other sets of questions about the case called **interrogatories**. Note that when we say "parties" here, we follow the legal convention that tends to blur the distinction between the acts of the parties themselves and the acts of their attorneys. In reality, the lawyers usually draft the interrogatories and their clients often never see them. They do see the opposing side's interrogatories, however, because they have to answer them (with the aid of their lawyer).

Generally, interrogatories are used to get addresses, histories, and other detailed information by written answer. In the *Taslow* case, for example, Hank Howard is likely to send Shelly Taslow interrogatories asking for the date and time of every conversation she held with the seller and a summary of what was discussed.

Parties tend to answer discovery questions as narrowly as possible—especially with interrogatories. A lawyer typically goes over her client's responses with a fine-tooth comb before sending them back to the other side.

> ### *Hank's Corner*
>
> Taslow, the listing agent, served her answer last week. As expected, she denied everything.
>
> Still no talk of settlement, which means it's time to go ahead with discovery. Hopefully we can get something on paper that we can use in court to prove that Taslow knew about the construction defects or, at the very least, the pending litigation. If discovery makes her look bad, we may convince them to settle, after all.

Depositions. After sending and receiving interrogatories, both sides schedule meetings with each other to ask questions in person. These **deposition** sessions are usually held in a law firm's conference room, under oath, with a court reporter present to create a transcript. Depositions are useful both for gauging the personalities of the opposing parties and witnesses (how credible are they? how likeable?) and for gathering factual information about the case. Sometimes, in the give and take of oral interrogation, people reveal information that they managed to mask when answering the written questions.

Requests for Production. The last method of discovery that we'll discuss is the **production request**: a written request to the opposing side to send copies of documents relevant to the case. In a personal injury case, for example, the defendant would request copies of the plaintiff's medical records and pay stubs (to verify claims of lost income). In the *Taslow* case, the Greens might request a copy of Shelly Taslow's real estate license and copies of any correspondence from clients that contain complaints of any kind.

> ### *Hank's Corner*
>
> I deposed Taslow yesterday. Unfortunately, she's likable and comes across as very honest— not good for our case; very good for theirs. I might be able to use this against her at trial, though. If I admit that Taslow is competent, the jury may agree with me that a competent agent should have had no trouble finding out about some pending litigation. All Taslow had to do was pick up the phone and call the homeowners association.
>
> I need to convince the jury that Taslow was negligent in not making that phone call. "We know she had a duty to inspect the premises," I'll say. "And to report any material facts that she found. How hard was it to pick up the phone?"

Taslow's lawyer might object to the latter request on the grounds of relevance. For example, how does his client's failure to forward a counteroffer last year relate to whether she should have examined the public records for litigation for the Greens? Hank Howard may or may not find an effective counterargument to this—but he would try. At any rate, lawyers sometimes end up taking their discovery disputes to court for a judge to settle. You can see how the legal bills and the emotional toll start to add up well before trial.

If a judge repeatedly has to order a party to comply with legitimate discovery requests, the court may eventually fine or sanction the party and/or his attorneys for **abuse of discovery**. Endless stonewalling can actually lead a court to punish a party by terminating his entire case. This drastic step is sometimes referred to as the "doomsday sanction."

Case Example:

Plaintiffs signed an agreement with the Moiselle, Dorsey & Hochman Advertising Agency (MDH) to market an instructional golf aid called "The Secret." Later, plaintiffs sued MDH, alleging the agency had stolen money from them. Plaintiffs filed requests for production of financial records. MDH eventually produced some records, but not all of them, despite repeated requests.

The trial court initially denied the plaintiff's motion for a terminating sanction (which would mean rendering a verdict for the plaintiff without a trial). The court did require MDH to pay the plaintiffs $10,000 in attorneys' fees, however. After dragging its feet, MDH paid this money, but still failed to provide the missing documents.

Over half a year passed with continued motions and delays. The court characterized MDH's discovery abuse as the most egregious it had ever witnessed. The court finally dropped the bombshell: it struck MDH's answer and entered a default judgment against them—and added financial sanctions. The terminating sanction was upheld on appeal. *Lang v. Hochman* (2000) 77 Cal.App.4th 1225.

Motions

Judges usually impose discovery sanctions in response to a motion—that is, a formal request by a party for a particular order. Generally, both sides will present written arguments regarding the request, citing legal authority for their positions.

There are many kinds of motions. Probably the most important is the summary judgment motion. In a **summary judgment motion**, a party asks the court to rule on the validity of a legal issue or even an entire claim before the trial begins. It's an extremely important litigation tool (although it's difficult to convince the judge to rule in your favor).

Hank's Corner

The defendant real estate agents filed a summary judgment motion today seeking to dismiss all our claims. I'm willing to agree to dismiss the fraud claim, because I never found any evidence of fraud during discovery. I'm drafting a second set of interrogatories and I can always reinstate the claim if something turns up. But negligent failure to investigate is the basis of our lawsuit, and I'm going to fight that.

I'll admit the only real legal authority I have is *Montoya v. McLeod*, a 1985 case. In *Montoya*, a real estate agent named McLeod arranged a loan of her client's money to a real estate investment company without investigating whether the company was creditworthy. The court found her negligent. Now I just need to convince the judge that *Montoya* should apply in our case, too.

Hank did the right thing in accepting a dismissal of his fraud claim. If he hadn't, he would have lost the summary judgment motion and driven up his clients' legal fees.

Let's imagine that discovery had gone differently, however, and Hank had found incriminating evidence—for example, a neighbor who said in deposition that she'd told Shelly Taslow "all about the lawsuit." This evidence would raise a **factual issue** concerning the fraud claim. What exactly did Shelly know? Courts can't grant summary judgment if the claim involves unanswered questions about the facts. Summary judgment is only appropriate when the issues are purely legal. Factual issues require a trial, so that witnesses can testify about what took place.

Hank's Corner

We lost the summary judgment hearing on all claims—even negligence. So much for my theory. The judge wasn't impressed with *Montoya* and ruled as a matter of law that the real estate agent's duty to inspect doesn't extend beyond the unit in question. In other words, Taslow had no duty to question the homeowners association about pending litigation.

On the other hand, the seller, Gary Crispin, didn't even bother responding to our arbitration request, so the judge entered a default judgment against him for the full amount of our claim. Not much of a victory, though, since my clients will probably never get a penny out of Crispin.

The Trial

We've finally arrived at the trial stage of litigation. Again, most cases never make it this far, often because the discovery phase provided enough information to bring about a reasonable settlement.

In this section, we'll explore the state and federal trial court system and get into the nitty-gritty of trying a case.

Jury Selection. A trial that will be heard by a jury begins with jury selection. The judge or the parties' lawyers ask potential jurors questions to ferret out biases that could affect their deliberations. This process is called *voir dire* ("speak the truth").

During *voir dire*, the judge can dismiss certain potential jurors for cause. A dismissal **for cause** means the juror said something indicating an inability to consider the facts impartially.

> **Example:** A potential juror in the Taslow case reveals during voir dire that his sister is a real estate agent. He then comments angrily, "Buyers think that agents are easy pickings and it's just not fair." The judge dismisses the juror for cause. He probably wouldn't weigh the Greens' claims against the real estate agents fairly.

A lawyer can request the dismissal of a particular juror without cause—in other words, even if she didn't reveal a bias. This is called a **peremptory challenge**. If Hank had succeeded in getting the Greens' case to trial, he might have used peremptory challenges to eliminate anyone who works in the real estate industry. The lawyers get to play a few hunches about which jurors are likely to favor the other side. But peremptory challenges are limited (in California, each side generally gets six), so lawyers treat them like gold.

Opening Statements. The trial itself begins with the plaintiff's **opening statement**, in which the plaintiff's lawyer describes the case he intends to make. Then the defendant's lawyer delivers another opening statement, countering the plaintiff's statement with the defendant's view of the facts and the law.

Lawyers making opening statements must limit themselves to assertions for which they have at least some evidence or legal authority. Even so, there's room to paint a vivid picture. The goal is to tell the jury a clear, sympathetic story. Thus, lawyers often begin with strong narrative lines like, "This is a case about breach of trust." Or greed, or carelessness, or whatever theme pulls the lawyer's case together.

Testimony. After the opening statements, the plaintiff presents witnesses who support the plaintiff's case. Had Hank been more successful on summary judgment, his first witness would no doubt be one of the Greens. Then, perhaps, someone from the homeowners association to explain about the construction defect lawsuit.

After Hank had presented everyone on his witness list, the defendants would put their witnesses on the stand. Note that whenever one side has a witness testify, the other side has a right to **cross-examine** that person. A lawyer will try to raise doubts about the witness's accuracy or expertise during cross-examination. However—again somewhat contrary to television—the lawyer will generally use a mild tone of voice, to avoid striking the jury as bullying or self-righteous.

Fact witnesses vs. expert witnesses. There are two types of witnesses: fact witnesses and expert witnesses. **Fact witnesses** testify to events they actually witnessed. For example, "I saw the defendant run out of the bank," or "The seller told me there was no litigation pending that involved the condominium."

Not everything a witness says is admissible in court. There are many **evidentiary rules** designed to exclude poor-quality or irrelevant evidence. The following example should sound somewhat familiar: witnesses generally can't testify about what someone told them a third party said. This testimony would be "hearsay," which is usually inadmissible. Why? Well, secondhand reports about what someone said are inherently unreliable; furthermore, since the third party isn't present on the stand, the opposing party can't exercise its right to cross-examine him concerning the statements he allegedly made.

Let's imagine that the real estate agents' summary judgment motion was not successful and so the Taslow case proceeded to trial. Consider the following hypothetical court transcript:

Hank:	You were Gary Crispin's neighbor before he sold his condo to the Greens?
Witness:	Yes.
Hank:	Did Mr. Crispin ever say anything about Shelly Taslow?
Witness:	That girl who was the Greens' agent?
Hank:	The woman, yes.

Witness:	Yeah, well, she gave me her card once. Anyway, Gary said he'd told Shelly Taslow all about the defect lawsuit—on the first day she came to see the property.
Defense:	Objection, your honor. Hearsay.
Judge:	The jury will ignore the witness's statement about what Gary Crispin allegedly told Shelly Taslow. That testimony will be stricken from the record.

Fact witnesses are supposed to stick to the facts, not offer their opinions. In contrast, the role of expert witnesses is to give opinions. An **expert witness** is qualified by education or experience to analyze some aspect of the case. Common types of expert witnesses include doctors, engineers, and appraisers.

Had any of Hank's claims in *Taslow* survived summary judgment, the expert witnesses would have included experienced brokers or real property law experts offering opinions about whether or not Shelly Taslow should have checked court records for pending lawsuits. And each side would have presented its own appraiser, each one with a very different view about how much of a financial loss the Greens suffered.

Closing Arguments. When all the witnesses have finished their testimony, the lawyers for each side conclude their portion of the trial by making closing arguments. A lawyer's **closing argument** is supposed to sum up the meaning of the evidence and emphasize key points for the judge or jury to consider during deliberations. It usually echoes the tone of the opening statement.

The defendant's closing argument follows the plaintiff's, as with the opening statements. However, sometimes the plaintiff gets a second chance, an opportunity to briefly rebut the defendant's closing argument.

Jury Instructions. After the closing arguments, the judge instructs the jury (if there is one) about the law relevant to the case. These **jury instructions** will include direction about procedural law, such as the degree of proof needed to reach the civil or criminal verdict (something we discussed in Chapter 1).

Often the jury instructions will also include directives on matters more specific to the particular case. For example, the judge might instruct the jury that even though the defendant real estate agent might be liable for negligence, as a matter of law her behavior was not egregious enough to merit punitive damages.

Verdict. In California civil cases, at least three-quarters of the jurors must agree on a decision (for example, five out of six or, for a larger jury, nine out of twelve). Unanimous verdicts are required only in criminal trials. A **hung jury**—a jury that cannot agree on any verdict—forces a new trial with a fresh jury. Unless, of course, the financially and emotionally exhausted parties decide to settle, or the plaintiff drops the case.

In cases where there is no jury, the judge decides on the verdict.

Enforcing Judgments

Winning isn't everything. You also have to collect what the judge awarded you. The process of collecting money from a defendant after winning a damages award against him is called **enforcing a judgment**. Sometimes it's the hardest part of the whole case. The Greens have an award against the defendant Crispin. But a defendant who saw so little at risk that he didn't bother showing up for arbitration probably doesn't care what amount was awarded: $38,400 or $384,000, it doesn't matter. He can't pay it. He's considered judgment proof.

Still, the **judgment creditor**—the party who wins an award—has ten years to collect. Crispin's fortunes might change. It's something Hank and the Greens could keep an eye on.

With wealthier defendants, when the judge announces the award in court, the defendant takes out her checkbook and writes a check for the full amount. Right? Not usually. In reality, collecting a judgment often requires significant legal exertion, beginning with the filing of a lien, our next topic.

Judgment Liens. A judgment creditor can secure his award with a **lien** against real property owned by the judgment debtor.

Don't confuse a judgment lien with a lis pendens. During an ongoing case, a lis pendens warns others of a possible judgment against the defendant property owner. A judgment lien, on the other hand, attaches after the case has been decided in favor of the plaintiff. Note that you can claim a judgment lien even if the underlying case didn't involve the defendant's property (for example, when damages are awarded for a personal injury). When the proper procedures are followed, judgment liens can attach to all the real property the judgment debtor owns anywhere in the country.

When property has a judgment lien against it, the judgment creditor can foreclose, force the sale of the property, and collect her judgment from the proceeds. (For more about the foreclosure process, see Chapters 13 and 14.)

Hank's investigator ran a county property records search in Show Low and discovered that Crispin's lot is mortgaged to the hilt. After a foreclosure sale, once the earlier creditors had been paid off out of the sale proceeds, nothing would be left for the Greens.

Crispin, the investigator also reports, owns an older model car and some other personal possessions. While some jurisdictions allow judgment liens against personal property, basic possessions like a debtor's household furnishings and an inexpensive vehicle are exempted. Judgment creditors can also file liens against business equipment and inventory. But Crispin doesn't own a business, so that doesn't help the Greens.

Garnishment. Judgment creditors can use **wage garnishment** to collect their judgments from a debtor's pay. The creditor serves an "earnings withholding order" on the debtor's employer, who then holds back some of the debtor's earnings—typically, up to 25%—for the creditor each pay period. However, the amount of money needed to support the debtor (and his family, if any) can't be garnished. The Greens have to be practical: Crispin simply doesn't earn enough to make garnishment worthwhile.

Finally, a judgment creditor can garnish the debtor's bank account. When asked about garnishing Crispin's bank account, the investigator just laughed. The win against Crispin seems hollow indeed.

Case to Consider...

Patterson received rental income of $800 a month from a property. His ex-wife got a trial court order of garnishment, directing the renter to pay the rent to her (to satisfy Patterson's child support obligations). No prior California case had addressed whether installments of rent due in the future could be garnished. Garnishment is allowed only on amounts certain to become due. Was the stream of rental income certain enough to support a garnishment order? *Hustead v. Superior Court* (1969) 2 Cal.App.3d 780.

The Appeal

In this section, we'll examine the appeals process in the state and federal court systems.

Right to Appeal. Any litigant unhappy with a trial court decision has the right to a review by a court of appeals (or by the state supreme court in those states that lack appellate courts). California has an exception for death penalty cases, which are appealed directly from superior court to the state supreme court.

Even losing at the appellate court level isn't necessarily the end of the road. Dissatisfied parties may try to secure a higher-level review from the supreme court. For a California case, this means going to the courthouse in San Francisco, or to one of the state supreme court branches in Sacramento or Los Angeles. If review of a federal appellate case is granted by the U.S. Supreme Court, the lawyers head to Washington, D.C.

As we suggested earlier, appeals to the high court are discretionary (again, with the exception for state death penalty appeals). A **discretionary appeal** means the high court can refuse to review the appellate court opinion. And in fact the court usually does refuse; most requests for discretionary appeals are denied. The high courts simply can't handle much volume. The state and federal supreme courts limit themselves to appeals involving important legal questions, especially ones where the appellate courts have come up with conflicting answers.

Generally, the federal and state appellate systems are separate worlds. Yet occasionally a case crosses from one system to the other. For example, a state supreme court decision can be appealed directly to the U.S. Supreme Court. As with any other high court appeal, however, the request for a hearing is likely to be denied. Petitioners file over seven thousand cases each year with the U.S. Supreme Court, but the Court grants review for less than 2% of them.

Filing an Appeal. Now that we've described the system of courts of review, let's look at some of the nuts and bolts involved in filing an appeal.

The first step in appealing a ruling is to file a **notice of appeal** both with the court and the parties. After the lower court's judgment has been entered, the disgruntled plaintiff or defendant only has a short period (usually 30 days) to file the appeal notice. After that, appeal is barred. Shelly Taslow will hold her breath during this time, hoping the Greens give up on their case against her.

The party who files the appeal is called the **appellant**. The party arguing against the appeal is called the **respondent**, or sometimes the **appellee**.

The reviewing court reads written arguments from the parties and reviews the trial record (a transcript of the trial prepared by a court reporter). Most appellate cases are heard by a panel of three judges, whereas nine judges (referred to as justices) hear appeals at the supreme court level. After reading the written materials, the judges typically hold a hearing. While appellate courtrooms superficially resemble a trial court, the appellate lawyer has no jury or witnesses to deal with. Instead, she stands at a podium, delivers an oral argument, and hopes the judges don't ask too many tough questions.

State and Federal Courts of Review. Which state appellate court would handle the Greens' appeal? The location of the trial court determines the answer. California is divided into six appellate court districts based on geography, and these courts handle appeals from every superior court in their district.

The California Superior Court, County of San Diego falls under the jurisdiction of the California Court of Appeal for the Fourth District. The Greens would file in the Fourth District court.

The U.S. appellate courts are organized in a similar fashion. The country is divided into 11 geographical territories that are called "circuits." Each circuit handles appeals from all the federal trial courts within its territory. For example, the decisions of the U.S. district courts in California are appealed to the 9th Circuit U.S. Court of Appeals. The 9th Circuit also includes Alaska, Washington, Oregon, Idaho, Montana, Nevada, Arizona, and, farther afield, Hawaii and Guam. The 9th Circuit may seem disproportionately large. However, when the circuits were created after the Civil War, the population covered by the 9th Circuit more or less matched that of the others.

There are two additional federal appellate courts as well: an appellate court for the District of Columbia, and an appellate court that has jurisdiction over federal subject matter, such as international trade, patents, and trademarks.

Hank's Corner

The Greens thought it over and want to appeal. I reminded them that in recent years the California Court of Appeals has only overturned about 20% of the civil cases submitted to them for review. Not to mention that it can take more than a year for a case to be heard on appeal.

But they seem determined, so I agreed. We've got 30 days to file the notice of appeal. After that, we wait.

Issues on Appeal. Most appeals are limited to the trial court record, meaning that the parties can't ask the reviewing court to consider any new facts or legal issues. Even if the Greens' appellate lawyer could come up with a brilliant new theory of liability, it's too

Breaking Up Is Hard to Do

For years, some members of Congress have tried to break up the 9th Circuit; as it stands now, it's a huge and extremely influential circuit. By creating a new 12th Circuit containing Alaska, Washington, Oregon, Idaho, Montana, Nevada, and Arizona, the 9th Circuit would be reduced to California, Guam, and Hawaii—considerably humbled and less important.

The House of Representatives passed a 9th Circuit breakup proposal in 2004, but the Senate voted it down, reluctant to cripple a court that has such a venerable history. Yet vigorous efforts continue, and someday the new 12th Circuit may come to pass.

late: the time for making new claims ended with the trial. The appellate lawyer simply searches for better case law and statutory law to support his client's position, and tries to offer a more convincing analysis than was provided at trial.

Other limitations also affect appeals. Let's examine two fairly significant ones.

Questions of law vs. questions of fact. Generally, issues at trial concern either questions of law or questions of fact. A **question of law** involves interpreting a statute or case law. Here's an example: What are the elements of the tort of fraud?

A **question of fact**, in contrast, does not involve legal analysis. Did Crispin (the seller) tell either real estate agent about the defect litigation? That's purely a question of fact.

An appellate court generally won't overturn a trial court's decision on a question of fact unless the ruling lacked substantial supporting evidence. And that doesn't happen very often. Trial judges and juries hear testimony firsthand and can evaluate witness credibility, something that appellate judges who merely read the trial transcript can't do very well. That's why trial court findings of fact are given deference.

On the other hand, judges at the reviewing court level generally have fancier legal credentials than trial court judges. There's no reason why they shouldn't review decisions on questions of law. In fact, evaluating questionable legal decisions from the lower court could serve as a one-line job description for appellate judges.

Prejudicial error vs. harmless error. Even if a reviewing court rules that a lower court has decided a legal issue incorrectly, it won't do anything about it unless the error was prejudicial. A **prejudicial error** is one that probably affected the trial's outcome in a way that harmed the appellant. Prejudicial errors require corrective action, as we discuss below. In its opinion, the reviewing court will also note any **harmless errors**—errors that didn't materially affect the outcome of the case. Harmless errors don't need correction.

The following case illustrates the distinction between prejudicial and harmless errors.

Case Example:

During an argument, LaShawn Harris shot and wounded a man. The state charged him with first-degree assault. Harris claimed self-defense. The trial began on January 17, 1991. Three days later, the first President Bush announced that military action against Iraq had begun in response to Saddam Hussein's attack on Kuwait. Later that same day, Harris's prosecutor made his closing argument.

The prosecutor described Harris as a bully and a thug anxious to use a deadly weapon. The prosecutor then went on to describe another man, "filled with a sense of the power of his killing weapons that he wanted to use, [who] acted like a thug and bully. . . I speak of course of Saddam Hussein."

Naturally, the defense lawyer objected to the comparison of his client to the Iraqi dictator. The trial court did not stop the prosecutor, however. In fact, the prosecutor continued on like this; if anything, his statements grew even more outrageous. Harris was convicted.

On review, the appellate court labeled the prosecutor's comments "improper," but concluded that so much evidence pointed to Harris's guilt that the jury would have convicted him anyway, making the error harmless.

The state supreme court disagreed. The prosecutor's attempt to inflame the jury with patriotic passion was misconduct and unacceptable—and it might very well have harmed the defendant. Specifically, if not for the prejudicial comments, the jury might have found that Harris had acted in self-defense. The high court ordered a new trial. *LaShawn Harris v. The People of the State of Colorado* (1995) 888 P.2d 259.

Disposition of the Appeal. When a reviewing court agrees with the court below, it simply affirms the lower court's decision. When the reviewing court finds reversible error, however, things become more complex. A reversible error is an error made during the trial that is harmful enough to justify reversing the decision of the lower court. When the court finds reversible error, it may:

- issue a substantive ruling or verdict (for example, freeing the defendant or ordering the plaintiff to pay damages for breach of contract);
- remand (return) the case to the trial court for further proceedings; or
- order a new trial.

Why did the high court in LaShawn Harris's case choose the last option? Well, the first option wasn't appropriate; a prosecutor's prejudicial comments during closing don't really merit letting a defendant evade trial completely. Option number two wouldn't work, either; since the jury had already voted to convict, the trial was over. The only reasonable solution in this case was the third one: ordering a new trial. The defendant might very well be convicted again, and at taxpayer expense, but there will always be certain costs to maintaining the integrity of our judicial system.

> ### *Hank's Corner*
>
> Well, it's been almost two years, but the California Court of Appeal for the Fourth District affirmed the lower court's decision, refusing to broaden an agent's duty of inspection to include more than making a visual inspection of the property.
>
> I mentioned appealing the case to the California Supreme Court, but the Greens declined. They don't feel there's much of a chance, and I agree. In his opinion, the appellate judge suggested that this was a matter for the state legislature. In time, statutes may change to protect clients like mine but, for now, they are out of luck.

The outcomes of both the *LaShawn Harris* case and our own hypothetical *Green v. Taslow* case illustrate the long, frequently costly process involved in resolving legal disputes. Understanding how our legal system works will help you decide when it's best to pursue the unpaid commission, cut your losses, settle out of court, or pursue an appeal. Obviously, most people don't seek out legal disputes, but it is the rare real estate agent who can avoid them completely.

Case Law in Depth

The following case involves some of the legal issues discussed in this chapter. Read through the facts and consider the questions in light of what you have learned. Then read what the court actually decided.

Woodside Homes of Cal., Inc. v. Superior Court (2003) 107 Cal.App.4th 723

A group of home buyers (Buyers) sued their builder/developer, Woodside Homes of California, Inc. (Woodside). A clause in the purchase agreements provided that disputes would be settled by judicial reference (which is similar to arbitration) rather than by a jury trial. However, Buyers wanted to have the case decided in court instead.

Buyers claimed that the judicial reference clause was not enforceable because it was unconscionable. The clause provided that Buyers were to pay half the referee's fee, and they claimed this was an undue expense. They argued that the clause, in effect, waived their right to a jury trial, but the print was too small for it to constitute a voluntary waiver. Buyers also argued that waiving the right to a jury trial unfairly limited their right to compensation, because juries tend to reward plaintiffs with more generous verdicts than referees and arbitrators do. Therefore, this waiver compromised their right to adequate damages.

The question:

Did these factors—the small type, the requirement to pay half of the costs, and the possible limitation on compensatory damages—make the provision unconscionable?

The court's answer:

"We do not think the [purchase] contracts here can be described as misleading or hard to penetrate. Although the contracts are several pages long, the Buyers were made aware of the existence of [the judicial reference] provision because they had to initial the paragraph separately. Not only that, but immediately above the spaces for the buyers' initials is the large, bolded statement: 'By initialing below, the parties acknowledge that they have read and understand the foregoing and accept that they are waiving their right to a jury trial.' The fact that there would not be a jury trial was clearly and conspicuously set forth."

The court went on to address the issue of the fees. Here the trial court speculated that costs could run up to $600 per hour, a substantial expense. However, the expenses of arbitration (and presumably judicial reference as well) are typically less than courtroom expenses. For their argument to be persuasive, the buyers "must demonstrate at the least that the fees they are likely to pay are in fact greater than those which would accrue in litigation before the court." No such showing was made.

Finally, the court turned to the issue of Buyers' waiver of the right to a jury trial. "As we have discussed above, this waiver was not obtained by 'stealthy device' such as the burial near the end of 70 pages of text...but was clearly set forth." There are many reasons why alternative dispute resolution provisions have become popular. But even if the court were to assume that the reason Woodside included the provision was to avoid large damage awards by juries, this does not in and of itself make the provision unconscionable.

"Nothing in the record before us suggests that a truly neutral decision maker chosen under the sales contracts will not return a fair decision, or that, if the decision is in favor of Buyers, the award will not represent complete and reasonable compensation for their damages. There is nothing 'unconscionable' in requiring a party to a contract to give up the possibility of obtaining a windfall from a jury irresponsibly generous with someone else's money."

The result:

The ADR clause was not unconscionable and therefore was enforceable. As agreed to by the parties, the dispute had to be resolved by judicial reference, not in court.

Chapter Summary

- The federal and state court systems usually have a three-level hierarchy, consisting of trial courts, appellate courts, and a supreme court. The appellate courts and the supreme court review the trial record for errors of law and generally defer to the trial court decisions on issues of fact.

- The federal and state court systems are generally independent. However, some cases can be brought in either state or federal court. Federal subject matter jurisdiction exists for cases involving questions of federal law, diversity of citizenship, or the U.S. government.

- A court cannot hear a case unless it has personal jurisdiction over the defendant. The defendant must have some connection with the state where the lawsuit was filed to justify forcing him into court.

- To start a civil suit, the plaintiff files a complaint with the court and serves the defendant with a summons and complaint. Generally, the defendant must answer within 30 days. Discovery usually follows; the parties use depositions and interrogatories to learn about the other side's case. Settlement negotiations typically take place based on the information developed during discovery.

- In a trial, the case is heard and decided either by a judge alone, or (at the request of one of the parties) by a jury under the supervision of a judge. The plaintiff presents her case, and then the defendant presents his. Witnesses are either experts offering opinions, or fact witnesses testifying about their first-hand knowledge of the events. Numerous rules limit the admissibility of evidence, to ensure that the court's decision is based on fair and reliable information.

- A trial court's judgment for or against the plaintiff does not necessarily end a legal dispute; the other side may appeal the trial court's decision. And once the legal proceedings have ended, the winning party may have to use wage garnishment or judgment liens in order to collect the judgment.

Key Terms

- **Settlement agreement** – A contract between the parties to a legal dispute, in which the claimant agrees to settle the dispute.

- **Alternative dispute resolution (ADR)** – Using mediation or arbitration to resolve a legal dispute as an alternative to a courtroom trial.

- **Complaint** – The document a plaintiff files with the court to formally initiate a lawsuit.

- **Answer** – The defendant's response to the plaintiff's complaint.

- **Service of process** – Hand delivery to the defendant of the plaintiff's complaint, along with a summons from the court.

- **Personal jurisdiction** – A trial court's authority to order a particular defendant into the court and pass judgment on him.

- **Subject matter jurisdiction** – A trial court's authority to hear the kind of case being brought.

- **Discovery** – The stage of a lawsuit in which each party is required to provide information about the case to the other party, in response to interrogatories (written questions), depositions (formal interviews of witnesses), and requests for the production of documents.

- **Trial record** – An official transcript of trial proceedings prepared by a court reporter.

- **Damages** – A trial court's award of money to one of the parties to a lawsuit, either as compensation for losses or injuries (compensatory damages) or as punishment for willful wrongdoing (punitive damages).

- **Superior court** – The basic state trial court, having at least one courthouse in each county.

- **Appeal** – A losing party's petition to a higher court to have a lower court's decision reviewed and possibly overturned.

- **Appellant** – The party that appeals a decision.

- **Appellee** – The party that responds to an appeal, arguing that the lower court's decision should be affirmed instead of overturned. Also called the respondent.

Chapter Quiz

1. Which of the following is true of an appeal?
   a) It is essentially a second trial, only without a jury
   b) The trial transcript is reviewed
   c) Expert witnesses may testify
   d) A fresh jury must be chosen

2. Which of the following is a question of law?
   a) Did the agent sign the arbitration provision?
   b) Was the agent negligent?
   c) Did the seller tell the agent about the lawsuit?
   d) How much money did it cost to repair the water damage?

3. Prejudicial error:
   a) means that the defendant made a religious slur during trial
   b) never involves a question of law
   c) requires some kind of modification of the lower court's decision
   d) didn't necessarily affect the outcome of the trial

4. Arbitration differs from mediation in that:
   a) arbitration is more like a mini-trial
   b) mediation is more like a mini-trial
   c) arbitration is never required, mediation always is
   d) mediation is generally binding and the parties cannot appeal

5. Whether a court has jurisdiction over a matter may depend on:
   a) where the parties live
   b) the amount of damages claimed by the plaintiff
   c) the type of case
   d) All of the above

6. Which of the following is true of California's court system?
   a) The superior court is the state's highest court
   b) Appellate courts can review superior court decisions
   c) There are no appellate courts
   d) The larger cities typically have municipal courts

7. Lawrence sues Carlos for negligence, claiming $85,000 in damages. Carlos lives in San Francisco and Lawrence lives in Los Angeles. Which of the following is true?
   a) Federal diversity jurisdiction exists because the parties live in different counties and the amount in controversy exceeds $75,000
   b) Negligence is a federal law issue and must be heard in a federal court
   c) There is no federal diversity jurisdiction here: the parties must live in different states
   d) U.S. citizens can always choose to bring their case in federal court

8. During discovery, the plaintiff in a contract dispute sends the defendant interrogatories that ask if he has ever received treatment for substance abuse and, if so, to list the dates of treatment and the names of providers. Which of the following is true?
   a) This question is clearly more suited to a deposition than to interrogatories
   b) The defendant may try to object to the question on the grounds of relevance
   c) Discovery does not apply to civil suits; it is reserved for criminal cases
   d) Interrogatories and depositions are tools that enable the defendant to learn about the plaintiff's case; plaintiffs can never use these forms of discovery

9. During trial, a doctor testifies that a certain medical condition is best treated with a particular prescription drug. Which of the following is true?
    a) This testimony may be proper if the witness is an expert
    b) This is opinion testimony and the rules of evidence forbid opinion testimony
    c) Any witness can offer opinion testimony, provided there is substantial factual support for the opinion
    d) All of the above

10. A listing agreement provides that any dispute arising out of the agreement will be settled through binding arbitration. A dispute over the commission arises, and the listing agent begins an arbitration action. The arbitrator rules in favor of the listing agent. Can the seller appeal this decision?
    a) Yes, because any arbitration award may be appealed
    b) Yes, because this was court-ordered arbitration
    c) No, because this was contract-required binding arbitration
    d) Yes, because this was contract-required binding arbitration

Chapter Answer Key

Chapter Quiz Answers:

1. b) The appellate court reviews the transcript of the trial to determine whether there were any prejudicial errors on questions of law. Lawyers present oral arguments to the appellate court, but no witnesses testify, and there is no jury.

2. b) "Was the agent negligent?" is a question of law, because the answer depends on the legal definition of negligence. The other options are questions of fact, because they concern factual matters such as whether or not certain events occurred and how much something cost.

3. c) If there was prejudicial error in a trial (an error that affected the outcome), the appellate court will modify the trial court's decision.

4. a) Arbitration involves a more formal proceeding than mediation. Arbitration may be required, and the decision may be binding.

5. d) A court's jurisdiction may be limited by where the parties reside, the amount of money at issue, and by the type of case (for example, only bankruptcy courts can hear bankruptcy cases).

6. b) California has appellate courts (courts of appeal) that review decisions by its trial courts, which are called superior courts. Decisions of the courts of appeal can be reviewed by the California Supreme Court.

7. c) For federal diversity jurisdiction, the parties must live in different states. This case can't be heard in federal court, because there isn't diversity jurisdiction, a question of federal law, or the United States as a party.

8. b) The defendant might refuse to answer the question on the grounds that it isn't relevant to the issues in the contract dispute. Discovery is used in civil suits, and both the plaintiff and the defendant are entitled to use interrogatories and depositions to obtain information about the other party's case.

9. a) Expert witnesses are allowed to give opinion testimony. (Fact witnesses are not allowed to do so.)

10. c) Contract-required arbitration generally cannot be appealed.

Cases to Consider... Answers:

Arbitration

Pardee Construction Co. v. Superior Court (Rodriguez) (2002) 100 Cal.App.4th 1081. The court struck the one-sided arbitration provision as unconscionable. If consumers are going to forego punitive damages or other substantial rights, they can do so only through provisions that are reasonably clear. Arbitration is a tool to promote more efficient administration of justice, not to take advantage of weaker parties.

Garnishment

Hustead v. Superior Court (1969) 2 Cal.App.3d 780. The appellate court ruled that because a tenant could abandon the premises or the landlord could interfere with the tenant's enjoyment of the premises, causing the lease to terminate, the rental income stream was uncertain. The appellate court reversed the trial court's decision and vacated the garnishment order.

List of Cases

Cal. Dump Truck Association v. Cummins Engine Co., Inc. (9th Cir. 2001) 24 Fed. Appx. 727

Hustead v. Superior Court (1969) 2 Cal.App.3d 780

Lang v. Hochman (2000) 77 Cal.App.4th 1225

LaShawn Harris v. The People of the State of Colorado (1995) 888 P.2d 259

Mahboubian-Fard, et al. v. Superior Court (Super.Ct. Los Angeles, Mar. 6, No. LS007911) 2003 WL 768905

Montoya v. McLeod (1985) 176 Cal.App.3d 57

Moreno v. Sanchez (2003)106 Cal.App.4th 1415

Pardee Construction Co. v. Superior Court (Rodriguez) (2002) 100 Cal.App.4th 1081

Vallis v. Collinson, et al. (3rd Cir., Sept 8, 2004, No. C045374) 2004 WL 1987103

Woodside Homes of Cal., Inc. v. Superior Court (2003) 107 Cal.App.4th 723

Zippo Mfg. Co. v. Zippo Dot Com, Inc. (W.D. Pa. 1997) 952 F.Supp 1119

Chapter 3

Real Property

Outline

Introduction

Now that we've discussed general legal concepts, let's turn our attention to the specific legal aspects of real property ownership. In this chapter, we'll discuss how real property is defined and how it differs from personal property. Then we'll examine attachments and fixtures, and why they're classified as real property. Finally, we'll look at the rights that are transferred with real property when it changes ownership, as well as the rights that may be sold or transferred separately from the land and its improvements.

The Nature of Property

Typically, when we think of property, we think of physical objects, such as an acre of land or a boat. But in a broader, more generic sense, property is any interest capable of being transferred and enjoyed. In fact, California Civil Code § 655 defines property in this manner:

> There may be ownership of all inanimate things which are capable of appropriation or of manual delivery; of all domestic animals; of all obligations; of such products of labor or skill as the composition of an author, the good will of a business, trademarks and signs, and of rights created or granted by statute.

Property can be divided into two major types. According to Civil Code § 657, property is either:

- real (immovable), or
- personal (movable).

Although we are mostly concerned with real property, we also need to understand the concept of personal property.

Real Property vs. Personal Property

Let's say that you represent the seller in a transaction involving a home with a patio and a small apple orchard. The buyer is interested in purchasing some of the seller's patio furniture. The seller wants to know if he can come back for the apples that will be ready to pick about a month after closing. Do you know which of these items are considered personal property and which are considered part of the realty? Does your client need a written contract to sell the patio furniture to the buyer, or will a mere verbal agreement be sufficient?

Because real property is treated differently from personal property (see Figure 3.1), it is important to know how a particular item will be categorized. Civil Code § 663 simply defines personal property as whatever is not real property: "Every kind of property that is not real is personal."

California statutes are a little more specific when it comes to defining real property. By law, real property consists of:

- land,
- that which is affixed to land,
- that which is incidental or appurtenant to land, and
- that which is immovable by law.

The third component ("that which is incidental or appurtenant to land") includes the rights inherent in ownership of real estate, such as the right to transfer, sell, or encumber the property, and the right to occupy or use the real estate in a variety of ways. These rights are distinct from the land itself, and may be transferred, sold, or encumbered separately. It's possible that a listed property may not be "complete"; that is, some of these rights and benefits already may have been transferred in an earlier transaction. This is something real estate agents should be on the lookout for when listing or selling property.

The last component ("that which is immovable by law") consists of things that, while technically easy to move, are considered by law to be so attached as to be immovable.

We'll take a closer look at all of these elements.

Bundle of Rights Theory

To explain how property rights may be sold or transferred separately from the physical property itself, we use the **bundle of rights** theory. The bundle of rights refers to all the rights, tangible and intangible, that a person has in real property. It may be helpful to think of this combination of rights as a bundle of sticks, in which each stick represents a separate, distinct right. One stick may represent the right to sell the property, for example;

Fig. 3.1 Real property vs. personal property

Real Property	Personal Property
• The sales agreement must be in writing to be enforceable	• The sales agreement must be in writing if value is over $500
• Real property is governed by the law of the state in which it is located	• Commercial sales of personal property are subject to federal and state laws
• A recording system traces title transfers	• There is no recording system
• Different tax laws govern real property and personal property	• Different tax laws govern personal property and real property

another stick might represent the right to mine for minerals. Still another might represent the right to use the water that crosses one's land.

A property owner may remove one or more of these sticks, give them to someone else, and keep the rest of the bundle for himself. For example, an owner might remove and sell the stick labeled "subsurface rights" to a mining company but retain the remaining sticks for himself.

Balancing Individual Interests

An individual's property rights are not absolute; they must be balanced against the rights of other property owners as well as the health and safety of the general public. For example, your right to use, possess, and dispose of your property is not unlimited. Rather, your property rights are relative to the rights of neighboring property owners. This means that you can't interfere with someone else's use or possession of his property. If you own a property along a road, you can't fence it in so as to prevent the landlocked property owner behind you from having access to the road.

Other things may also affect an individual's property interests and rights. Government restrictions, such as zoning laws and building codes, limit what a person can do with her property. So do private restrictions, such as a rule against parking a recreational vehicle in the sideyard of a subdivision home. As you can see, no property is completely free from the interests of others.

Natural Attachments

California's Civil Code treats the distinction between real and personal property as a simple one, but figuring out which items belong in which category can sometimes be confusing. The house itself is easy to categorize as real property. But what about the appliances or an above-ground pool? What about the flowering shrubs in the backyard?

It's important to remember that real property includes more than just the land; it also includes attachments. **Attachments** are things that are either growing on the land, like grass or trees; or things that are attached to the land, like a greenhouse or a fountain set in cement.

Attachments can be divided into two groups:

- natural attachments, such as the grass and trees; or
- man-made attachments, such as the greenhouse and the fountain.

Man-made attachments are also called fixtures, and will be discussed later in the chapter. First, let's take a look at natural attachments.

Naturally Occurring vs. Cultivated

Natural attachments are either naturally occurring plants (*fructus naturales*, or fruits of nature) or plants cultivated by people (*fructus industriales*, or fruits of industry).

Naturally occurring plants are considered part of the real property, and they're transferred with the property unless specifically reserved by the seller. For instance, a small grove of oak trees growing wild in the back of a lot are naturally occurring plants that would be considered part of the real property.

Cultivated plants are also generally considered part of the real property and transferred along with it, unless specifically reserved. In some states, however, the crops produced by cultivated plants are treated as personal property, even before they've been harvested. For example, the cultivated apple trees in an orchard would be real property, but the apples themselves would be personal property even while they were still on the trees. As personal property, the apples would not automatically be transferred with the real property. Without a provision in the purchase agreement specifying that the apples were part of the sale, they would remain the seller's property.

However, California does not recognize this distinction. Instead, unharvested crops are ordinarily considered real property. Unless they are expressly reserved by the seller (in writing), they transfer automatically with the land when it is sold or otherwise conveyed. Crops harvested before the buyer takes title or possession belong to the seller as personal property.

In California, crops become personal property only when they have been harvested or upon constructive severance. **Constructive severance** occurs when an interest has been sold or transferred separately from the real property, but the interest remains on or attached to the land itself.

> **Example:** The Clines own five acres of land that they've cultivated as an apple orchard. In July, they sell their entire crop of apples to a juice company, even though the apples won't be harvested until October. This sale results in a constructive severance of the apples from the real property. The apples are now the personal property of the purchaser (the juice company), even though they're still on the trees that belong to the Clines.
>
> If the Clines sell the orchard itself in September, before the apple harvest, ownership of the apple trees would pass to the buyer along with the land, but the apples would not. Since the apples are the personal property of the juice company, they aren't included in the sale of the real property.

Because of constructive severance, any contract for the sale of unharvested crops is a contract for the sale of personal property, not realty. The sale of personal property is governed by a different set of rules than the ones that govern the sale of real property. California has adopted a statute called the **Uniform Commercial Code** (UCC) to deal with the sale of personal property, or **goods**. The UCC defines the sale of crops and timber as a sale of goods and governs their sale, even when they are still attached to the land.

Other property interests that can be constructively severed from real property include mineral rights, air rights, and oil and gas rights. We will discuss those interests later in this chapter.

Leased Land. When a farmer leases land upon which to grow her crops, some different rules apply. California Civil Code § 1926 generally provides that "products of a thing hired, during the hiring, belong to the hirer." In other words, the tenant farmer is entitled to the crops she produces during the term of her lease. However, she is only entitled to the crops that can be harvested before the end of the lease term. To require the landlord to provide use of his land after the lease term, without compensation, would be unfair since the tenant knew her lease was ending.

> **Example:** In August, Theresa leased ten acres of land from Bill for five years to grow organic lettuce. In the spring of the fifth year, Theresa began planting seeds every few weeks in anticipation of a full harvest throughout the summer and into the fall on a staggered basis. She carefully cultivated the plants and tended to them daily. When Theresa's lease expired in August, there were still lettuce plants that wouldn't reach maturity for another three or four weeks. However, Theresa had no right to the lettuce that matured after the termination of her lease. Her right to harvest the plants ended when her lease did.

However, tenant farmers who lease land for indefinite periods of time are protected by the **doctrine of emblements**. This rule states that if a month-to-month tenancy is terminated, through no fault of the tenant, he will be able to re-enter the property to harvest any crops that mature after the lease has been terminated. This is because it would be unfair to deny a tenant farmer the result of all his hard work, unjustly enriching the landlord in the process. Note, however, that this rule applies only to tenants who lease property for an indefinite period of time; tenants who know their lease is ending are responsible for planting their crops so they can harvest them before the termination date.

> **Example:** Returning to our previous example, instead of a five-year lease, Theresa and Bill sign a month-to-month lease, in which Theresa pays Bill $250 a month to rent ten acres on which to grow her lettuce. They continue this arrangement for many years. On August 1, Bill suddenly announces that he is terminating the lease, and that Theresa will have until September 1 to vacate the premises. Her last crop of lettuce won't be ready to harvest until the third or fourth week of September. Under the doctrine of emblements, because Theresa's lease was for an indefinite period of time and the lease was terminated through no fault of her own, she is entitled to re-enter the land after September 1 to harvest the lettuce she has already planted.

But what if the tenant wants to come back to harvest the wild blackberries growing in the woods at the back of the property? In this situation, the doctrine of emblements doesn't apply. The crops subject to the rule must be planted or cultivated by the tenant farmer. In addition, if the crop is one that produces multiple crops for harvest throughout the year, then the rule applies only to the first crop that matures after the lease has ended.

Profit à Prendre vs. Separate Title

Let's take a moment to discuss the interests that are transferred in constructive severance. Constructive severance may simply involve the transfer of a nonpossessory interest in the property known as a ***profit à prendre***: the right to enter another's land to remove the soil or a product of the soil, such as oil, gas, crops, or timber. A *profit à prendre* is a property interest, but it is not a form of real property ownership.

On the other hand, constructive severance may involve a transfer of title. The party receiving **separate title** actually owns the land or interest in land that is the subject of that title, rather than merely leasing it. In other words, a person with separate title takes possession of one of the sticks in the bundle of rights, and the landowner's bundle is reduced.

> **Example:** Big Mining Company purchases the right to enter Brown's 400-acre property in San Bernardino County to mine for iron. Big Mining Company's right is limited to entry and mining; it doesn't have the right to possess the land being mined. Big Mining Company holds a *profit à prendre*.

After a year of mining in this manner, Big Mining Company asks to purchase the subsurface rights to Brown's property for a substantial amount of money. Brown agrees. Although Brown maintains ownership of and continues to live on the property, Big Mining Company now holds separate title to the subsurface of Brown's 400 acres.

As owner of a separate interest, Big Mining Company has the right to sell, encumber, give away, or otherwise dispose of its property in any way it sees fit.

Fixtures

Now let's take a look at man-made attachments, which are usually referred to as fixtures. **Fixtures** are items that were once personal property, but have since become attached to the land and are now presumed to be real property. For example, cement and bricks are personal property when purchased at the home improvement store. But once they are used to build a patio, the patio becomes part of the real property. As part of the real property, these items will transfer with the land when it's conveyed, even if not specifically mentioned in the purchase agreement or deed.

The patio may be an obvious fixture, one that the buyer has every reason to believe will be there on moving day, and one that the seller would never think to dig up and take with him when he goes. But what about the birdbath and the patio furniture? What about the gardening shed nearby? These kinds of items can often lead to disputes between buyers and sellers. To guard against disputes, it should be clearly stated in the purchase agreement which items will be transferred in the sale and which will not.

The California Civil Code gives us one test for determining whether an item of personal property has become a fixture. However, the courts also use additional fixture tests that take into consideration other factors not mentioned in the statute. We'll look at the statutory fixture test first, and then move on to the common law tests.

Statutory Fixture Test

According to California Civil Code § 660, whether an item has been permanently attached to land depends on the manner in which it is attached. This is referred to as the **method of attachment** test.

Under this test, when personal property is permanently attached to the land, it becomes part of the real estate. In this context, permanently attached means:

- attached to the land by roots (as with trees, shrubs, and vines);
- embedded in the earth (like foundations, septic tanks, and sprinkler systems);
- permanently resting on the land (as with houses, gazebos, and barns); or
- attached by any enduring method (such as with cement, plaster, nails, bolts, or screws).

Note that physical attachment—called **actual annexation**—is not a necessary requirement for permanent attachment. The force of gravity, for example, may be sufficient to render a theoretically moveable item immovable.

Example: The Alvarez family has a large prefabricated cedar tool shed on their property. The building was trucked in on a flatbed and now rests on cinderblocks. Even though it is not physically attached to the property, the tool shed would probably be considered a fixture and thus part of the real property.

If removing an item of personal property would result in damage to the item or the property, it may be considered a fixture. This sometimes happens when the personal property item has been permanently enclosed within a room or building.

> **Example:** When the Yungs built their large contemporary home in the hills above Los Angeles, they had a custom-made billiards table placed by crane into their family room before the walls and roof were completed. This is the only way it would fit into the house. When the Yungs move, the table will be considered a fixture.

Constructive Annexation. The doctrine of constructive annexation can turn a completely moveable item into real property. This doctrine applies to small, unattached items that are easily moveable, but that are so important to the real estate that they are considered fixtures.

> **Example:** The Yungs have also installed several ceiling fans and specialized lighting sources in their home that are operated from a single remote control. Although completely moveable, the remote control is integral to the performance and function of the ceiling fans and lighting fixtures. It is therefore considered constructively annexed to the property and is a fixture itself.

When items that would normally be considered fixtures have been temporarily removed for repair, the doctrine of constructive annexation also applies. Though not physically present on the real property, they are considered so attached as to be fixtures even when temporarily absent.

> **Example:** At the time the Yungs sell their home, the custom cabinet-faced built-in oven has been taken to a repair shop. The oven is constructively annexed to the property and is therefore still a fixture.

Common Law Fixture Tests

The statutory test for fixtures (the method of attachment test) is just part of the analysis of what is or is not a fixture. In determining whether an item is a fixture, the courts will also apply other, common law tests as well.

Intention of Annexor. The most important test is the intention of the **annexor**, the person who placed the item on the property. This test asks: "Did the annexor intend the item to remain personal property or to make it part of the real property?" If the annexor intended the item to become part of the realty, then the item will generally be considered real property. But if the annexor intended the item to remain personal property, then it won't be considered part of the realty.

However, the evidence of the owner's intent must be objective—that is, easily apparent; the secret intent of the owner doesn't count. Each of the other tests (including the method of attachment) is viewed as objective evidence of the owner's intent.

> **Example:** A property owner installed a fountain that was embedded in concrete. This method of attachment (embedding in concrete) is objective evidence that the owner in-

tended the fountain to become part of the property. He cannot later claim that he secretly intended to take the fountain with him when he moved.

Adaptation to the Realty. The next test is the item's adaptation to the realty. An item will probably be considered a fixture if it was specifically designed for the property or is integral to its use.

> **Example:** A commercial property's custom-made blinds would probably be considered a fixture, as would the computer system used to control the building's heating and cooling system.

Relationship of the Parties. When a court is determining intent, it will look at the relationship between the parties in question: are the parties landlord and tenant, creditor and debtor, or seller and buyer? The courts know that the intent of a tenant is often entirely different from the intent of an owner.

> **Example:** Items installed by a tenant are usually considered personal property. It's generally assumed that these items will be removed when the tenant leaves. So if a tenant installs a medicine cabinet over the bathroom sink, both the landlord and the tenant expect her to remove the medicine cabinet when she moves out.
>
> However, it's usually assumed that an owner making the same installation is attempting to improve the property and doesn't intend to remove the item later on. An owner-installed medicine cabinet would be considered a fixture, and a prospective buyer could assume it would stay with the property.

Trade Fixtures. Tenants who lease commercial space to carry on a trade or business frequently install fixtures that are integral to the use of the space, such as countertops, refrigeration units, or built-in displays. These items are referred to as **trade fixtures**. The tenant may intend to remove the trade fixtures at the end of the lease, either to sell or to use in the next place of business. Unless the lease states otherwise, trade fixtures generally may be removed by the tenant at the end of the lease term, regardless of how they are attached.

Why are trade fixtures an exception to the general rule that fixtures remain with the property when it's sold? The reason is one of public policy: allowing tenants to take equipment with them when they leave means that tenants are more likely to install newer and safer equipment. A tenant would have little incentive to modernize if he had to leave everything behind when his lease expired. However, note that if the tenant does leave any trade fixtures behind after the expiration of his lease, those items automatically become the property of the owner.

If the trade fixture has become an intrinsic part of the leased property, the tenant may remove it even if it will cause damage to the existing property. However, the tenant has a legal duty to restore the leased property to its original condition or to compensate the owner for any damage caused by removing the fixture.

It's important to note that if the property owner cannot be compensated adequately for the damage caused by an item's removal (for instance, the removal would cause irreparable structural damage to the building), the item may not be considered a trade fixture after all.

A rule similar to the trade fixtures rule applies to items installed by agricultural tenants to farm the land. Farming equipment and items such as small tool sheds or prefabricated henhouses may be considered **agricultural fixtures** and, if so, may be removed by the tenant farmers when they leave the property.

Case to Consider...

Beebe operated a beauty salon on a seasonal basis out of a room she leased at the Del Tahquitz Hotel. Under the terms of the lease, half of the rent was due at the beginning of the season, and half was due at the end of the season. Beebe brought in salon equipment consisting of four dryers, four dryer bowls, two manicure tables, a shampoo bowl, three small dressers, and five mirrors. She attached the shampoo bowl, dressers, and mirrors to the walls with lag bolts. She also installed a neon "Salon" sign.

When the manager of the hotel told Beebe he had orders to raise her rent or require her to move immediately, Beebe hired a truck to move her belongings. However, the manager prevented her from removing the salon equipment from the room. He later argued in court that the items were so attached as to become part of the realty. Who had a right to the fixtures and why? *Beebe v. Richards* (1953) 115 Cal.App.2d 589.

Contractual Agreements. Written agreements always trump all these fixtures tests. If the parties entered into a written agreement that states how a particular item is to be treated, that agreement will be enforced by the courts. As you might guess, a written agreement provides irrefutable evidence of the intent of the parties.

> **Example:** A seller wants to remove a custom designed stained-glass window and take it with her when she leaves the home. She tells the buyer this and includes the information in the purchase agreement. The buyer agrees and signs the contract. The parties' contractual agreement overrides any consideration of intent or adaptation to the realty.

Case Example:

A lease clause stated that all fixtures and improvements to a restaurant became part of the real property and belonged to the landlord at the end of the lease. Cal-Pacific held an unrecorded security interest in the tenant's restaurant equipment and argued that the items were trade fixtures belonging to the tenant. However, the court found that a special agreement between the parties supersedes general landlord-tenant rules. Therefore, the usual rights of the lessor and lessee regarding trade fixtures were changed by written agreement. *Bridges v. Cal-Pacific Leasing* Co. (1971) 16 Cal.App.3d 118.

Secured Financing and Fixtures

In the previous case example, Cal-Pacific held a security interest in the restaurant equipment, which means that the equipment was purchased using secured financing. **Secured financing** refers to an arrangement in which personal property or fixtures are used to secure a loan or line of credit.

Example: Pam wants to start a restaurant and needs money to buy a commercial refrigerator for the kitchen. The bank agrees to loan her $10,000 in return for the right to repossess the refrigerator if Pam defaults on her loan payments. To accomplish this, Pam and the bank enter into a secured financing agreement.

As long as it is properly recorded, a secured financing agreement will trump the usual rules regarding fixtures and personal property, much as a contractual agreement will. Secured transactions are governed by Article 9 of the Uniform Commercial Code. (Note that in the case example, Cal-Pacific's security interest was not recorded; this is why the agreement between the landlord and tenant took precedence.)

When secured financing is used, the terms of the loan are specified in the security agreement. The lender files a **financing statement**, which gives constructive notice that a security interest exists in the fixture. In other words, current and future lienholders, as well as anyone who buys the property after the statement is filed, are put on notice of the security interest. If the property is transferred, the items subject to the security agreement that normally would be considered fixtures can be repossessed by the holder of the security interest.

Example: Sarah Williams owns an office building that is mortgaged to State Bank. She purchases an elaborate heating and cooling (HVAC) system that is installed on a large concrete pad in the building's basement. She buys the HVAC system on credit, and the HVAC company files a financing statement containing a description of the system.

Sara eventually defaults on both her mortgage payments and her payments to the HVAC company. Normally, such a heating and cooling system would be considered a fixture and, upon default, ownership of the system would transfer to the bank as part of the real property along with the office building. But because a financing statement has been filed, the HVAC company has the right to repossess the heating and cooling system.

Buyers and lenders should check with both the county recorder's office and the office of the Secretary of State to be sure no financing statements have been filed that give notice of an interest in any of the fixtures on the property.

Mobile Homes

Special rules apply to mobile homes. A mobile home on a foundation may be either a fixture or personal property, depending on whether or not it has been **affixed** to the real property. If a mobile home is considered personal property, it must be licensed and registered as a motor vehicle and sold by a licensed mobile home dealer (not a real estate agent). In addition, its sale will be subject to sales tax laws. On the other hand, if a mobile home is considered a fixture, it will be taxed as part of the real property and its sale is subject to the requirements of the real estate license law.

California Health and Safety Code § 18551 states that for a mobile home to be considered affixed to the real property, more than mere attachment to a foundation is required. Instead, to make a mobile home part of the real property, the owner must do the following:

1. obtain a building permit by showing:
   - written evidence of ownership of the underlying land, or proof of a lease for more than 35 years (certain other leases may qualify);

- proof that there are no liens against the mobile home, or that if there are, that the lienholders consent to the attachment to real property;
- plans and specifications by the mobile home manufacturer or signed by a licensed California architect, that detail the installation of the individual mobile home; and

2. obtain a certificate of occupancy.

Once again, California law looks to the intent of the annexor; obtaining the required documents demonstrates the owner's intent to annex the mobile home to the property.

Affixation status is permanent as of the day the certificate of occupancy permit is issued. The affixation must be recorded in the county where the real property is located, to provide constructive notice to anyone who might acquire an interest in the real property in the future.

Once installed as a fixture, the mobile home cannot be removed without the consent of all parties who have an interest in the real property. The mobile home owner must give the Department of Housing and Community Development and the county assessor 30 days' notice of intent to remove, and proof of consent of all concerned parties.

Appurtenances

Clearly, a real property purchaser wants to know what items are included in the sale. But she should also understand what property rights transfer with the property when it is conveyed.

An **appurtenance** is a right, privilege, or improvement that is associated with a piece of real property. For example, the rights to use air, water, and minerals in or on the land are all appurtenances. When real property is sold or transferred, these rights "run with"—automatically transfer with—the property. However, individual rights (those individual "sticks" we talked about previously) may be sold separately, and may have been affected by previous transactions. When you are involved in a real estate transaction, it is important to be aware of these rights and how they can be limited.

Air Rights

A property owner's rights theoretically extend to the upper limits of the sky. However, as we noted above, the rights of the individual are often balanced against the rights of the public. In the Air Commerce Act of 1926 and the Civil Aeronautics Act of 1938, Congress made it clear that the United States government has control over U.S. airspace.

Use of Airspace. Individual owners still have the right to use and enjoy the airspace above their own properties, despite the government's control over the airways. That use is limited, however. For example, a landowner cannot obstruct or interfere with air traffic. Also, a landowner cannot use her airspace in such a way that it interferes with a neighbor's use of his own land or airspace.

> **Buying Air Rights**

In downtown areas of cities like San Francisco and Los Angeles, where land is precious and building towards the sky tantalizes developers, those who want to exceed zoning height restrictions can buy unused air space from the owners of low-rise, typically older buildings.

Sales of these "transferable development rights" (or TDRs), as they are called, can help keep older buildings commercially viable by providing cash for renovation. For example, in the early 1980s owners of the architecturally classic Bradbury Building in Los Angeles sold their unused air rights to Mitsui Fudosan, Japan's largest real estate investment firm. Fudosan also bought the air rights of two other properties, spending a total of over $8 million on TDRs. Fudosan gained the right to add nearly half a million square feet to their planned high-rise.

Not long after Fudosan acquired these air rights, the tax man came calling. The county assessor's revaluation of the Fudosan site resulted in a hefty property tax increase—over a quarter of a million dollars. Fudosan sued to overturn the assessment. While the trial court ruled in the company's favor, the appellate court disagreed and declared that TDRs were part of the bundle of rights that gave a property its value, and thus were fair game for taxation.

Case Example:

Sneed owned over 200 acres of land that he used as a thoroughbred farm and breeding facility. The property was located next to an airport owned by Riverside County. When the county enacted a zoning ordinance limiting the height of buildings near the airport, Sneed sued. The court found that the ordinance was a reasonable exercise of the police power. However, the court did find that the frequent and low flights over Sneed's property resulted in an easement and inverse condemnation for which Sneed was entitled to compensation. *Sneed v. County of Riverside* (1963) 218 Cal.App.2d 205.

Sale of Airspace. Airspace rights can be sold separately from the land below. In metropolitan areas where land is scarce, the sale of airspace has become increasingly popular. This sale of airspace is what makes condominiums possible.

> **Example:** The state owns a strip of land under which it recently built a tunnel to ease traffic congestion. The state may retain ownership of that land, yet enter into a contract with ABC Builders to sell ownership of the airspace above the tunnel for a condominium development.

Water Rights

Water is a scarce resource in California, and has been the cause of many lawsuits as well as the motivation for many laws. Questions constantly arise as to ownership of the water, the right to use the water, and ownership of a lake or stream bed.

In the United States, the two main types of water rights are riparian rights and appropriative rights. California uses a combination of the two systems.

Riparian Rights System. The riparian rights system is based in English common law and is still used in some states. Under this system, every landowner who has land that touches water (such as a river) has an equal right to use that water. **Riparian rights** arise on lands that are adjacent to or crossed by water. **Overlying rights** are similar to riparian rights but apply to subsurface or percolating water (such as a spring). Riparian and overlying rights are appurtenant to and run with the land. When the property is sold, the right to use the water automatically transfers to the new owner.

Under this traditional system, all riparian owners have the right to take water for reasonable and beneficial use. This includes domestic uses such as drinking and bathing, as well as recreational uses such as swimming and boating. At one time, upstream riparian users could use all the water touching their land, without regard for downstream users. But an amendment to the California Constitution (Article X, Section 2) now limits riparian use to water that is taken for a "reasonable and beneficial use." Wasteful or unreasonable uses, as well as unreasonable methods of diversion, are prohibited. Furthermore, landowners cannot use riparian water on non-riparian land (land that does not adjoin the water).

> **Example:** Wilson and Alvarez both own property along Mountain Creek. Wilson, the upstream owner, decided to turn a field across the road into an orchard. To irrigate the orchard, he diverted so much water from Mountain Creek that there wasn't enough for Alvarez to water his flower garden. A court could prohibit Wilson from using the water in this way because it was used on non-riparian land, was not a domestic use, and interfered with Alvarez's riparian right to use the water.

Appropriative Rights System. When California gained statehood in 1850, it adopted an English common law system of riparian rights similar to those used in the eastern states. But just one year later, the appropriative system was adopted in response to a growing population and agricultural and mining demands.

The appropriative rights system (also known as the **prior appropriation system**) has its roots in the 1849 California gold rush. The miners developed elaborate systems of flumes and conduits to divert large quantities of water across arid stretches of land to their mining operations. These miners even posted notice of their water claim to alert other miners to their rights—a sort of "finders-keepers" system. From this modest beginning, the "first in time, first in right" concept of water rights was born, and in 1851 the California legislature formally recognized the appropriative water rights system. (The Water Commission Act of 1914 establishes the water permit process currently used in California.)

Under the appropriative rights system, the right to use water in a way that diminishes the normal quantity is established by obtaining a water permit from the state government.

> **▶ The Law of the River**
>
> The use and allocation of the Colorado River is controlled by numerous federal laws, compacts, court decisions and decrees, and regulatory guidelines—collectively known as "The Law of the River." In 1922, the seven states that comprise the Colorado River basin negotiated the Colorado River Compact, which divided the states into two basins, upper and lower, and apportioned the river's flow between them. Each basin received approximately 7.5 million acre feet per year (an acre foot is the amount of water needed to cover an acre one foot deep). The Boulder Canyon Project Act of 1928 established California's share at 4.4 million acre feet per year. In addition, in 1944, the U.S. signed a water treaty with Mexico, in which the U.S. agreed to deliver 1.5 million acre feet per year to Mexico. However, while original negotiations estimated the flow of the Colorado River to be at least 17.5 million acre feet per year, since 2000 the flow has averaged only about 12 million. As a result, the seven states have undertaken joint conservation efforts.

Once a permit is obtained, water may be used on any land for the purpose specified in the permit application. Unlike riparian rights, appropriative water rights do not run with the land. Furthermore, if the use is abandoned for five years, the water reverts to the general public as unappropriated water.

If multiple parties have appropriation permits for the same body of water, the party who obtained a permit first can use the full amount of water specified in the permit, even if this leaves too little water for those who obtain permits later.

> **Example:** Consider the previous example. Now suppose that instead of relying on riparian rights, Wilson obtained a permit to use the amount of water necessary to sufficiently irrigate his orchard. Since fruit production is a beneficial use, Wilson will be allowed to divert the amount of water specified in his permit, even if it diminishes the normal flow of the creek.

Combination of Riparian and Appropriative Rights. Even though California uses appropriative rights, riparian rights still apply as well. Riparian owners are entitled to take water from natural water sources that cross or abut their property. There is no loss of rights due to non-use.

Non-riparian users may apply for a permit to use unappropriated or excess riparian water, but riparian users always have higher priority than appropriative users. During times of shortage, riparian users share equally in the available water; appropriative users receive any excess, which is distributed based on the first in time, first in right theory. Junior appropriative users might not receive anything at all. All users are subject to the state's limitations on reasonable and beneficial use.

Water Wars

In 1913, workers completed a 233-mile-long aqueduct from the Owens River to the San Fernando Valley and into LA. (The movie *Chinatown* describes the scheming and bribery that surrounded this project.) The insatiable water demand from the San Fernando and LA areas soon began to suck the Owens aquifer dry. Owens Valley, once delightfully lush and green, grew desert-like. By 1924, Owens Lake had ceased to exist. Furious Owens Valley ranchers and farmers armed themselves, seized an aqueduct gateway, and blew it up with dynamite.

This rebellion had little effect. The water flow only increased over the decades. Indeed, in the early 1970s, Los Angeles added a second aqueduct. Groundwater pumping soon reached the rate of several hundred thousand acre feet per year.

Before building the second aqueduct, the City of Los Angeles had failed to complete an environmental impact report (EIR) as required by law. Environmental groups fighting to restore this ecologically devastated area brought lawsuits and forced the City to publish an EIR, and then a second one. However, the courts threw out both reports as inadequate. Meanwhile, the water pumping continued unabated.

In 1991 and again in 1997, the City signed river restoration agreements with various parties including Inyo County (where the Owens River runs—or ran). The City agreed to reduce its pumping and rewater the Owens River by 2003. However, the City failed to restore the lower part of the river by the promised date. The City then signed another agreement to meet the obligation by 2005. Missing this deadline too, the City finally started some of the reflow at the end of 2006. The river appears to be recovering.

Because water is such a valuable resource, water uses have been prioritized under California's water law. The use of water with the highest priority is domestic purposes; the next highest use is irrigation.

Case to Consider...

Deetz and Carter owned adjoining parcels of agricultural property. Various streams crossed the Carter property to the Deetz property, and were used by both parties for irrigation. Deetz used the entire flow of one stream, Cold Creek, for domestic and agricultural purposes. Cold Creek was the only stream providing a domestic water supply for the Deetz family, and its entire flow was diverted to a ditch and led by pipe to serve the Deetz house. Excess water was used for agricultural purposes.

Between 1956 and 1962, the Carters began to divert Cold Creek for irrigation and livestock watering. The water was diverted to a ditch through Carter's pens and corrals and then back to its natural channel before entering the Deetz property. As a result, the water was often muddy and polluted by the time it reached the Deetz ranch. Both parties claimed conflicting riparian rights in the waters of Cold Creek. Who had first right to the water from Cold Creek? Deetz or Carter? *Deetz v. Carter* (1965) 232 Cal.App.2d 851.

Mineral Rights

Mineral resources are vital to the prosperity of governments, industries, and individuals. Gold changed California's fortunes in the 1800s, and we have seen how the discovery of oil affected states like Texas, Louisiana, and Alaska. Other, less dramatic minerals are also important economic resources, such as coal, copper, iron, limestone, and gypsum. You can guess that the question of who owns the rights to these minerals is an important one.

A landowner owns all the minerals located in or under her property. Minerals are real property while they are in the earth; once they are removed from the earth, they become personal property. Like other appurtenant rights, a landowner may sell his mineral rights, keeping the surface estate for himself. His right to use the surface property will be separate and distinct from the right to the subsurface property (the minerals). This type of sale is known as a **horizontal division**. Selling mineral rights is fairly common, as many landowners don't have the expertise or financial resources to extract the minerals on their own.

The surface land rights and subsurface mineral rights may be divided in the following ways:

- mineral rights option,
- mineral lease,
- mineral deed, and
- mineral reservation.

A **mineral rights option** gives someone the right to explore for minerals on another's land. Based on the results of this exploration, the holder of the option may decide to proceed with a lease or purchase of the mineral rights.

With a **mineral lease**, the leaseholder (the lessee) has a right to mine the land for a certain number of years, and will own all the minerals extracted. However, the owner of the surface land (the lessor) keeps the right to mine for minerals when the lease ends. Under most mineral leases, the "rent" is a percentage of the value of the minerals that are mined.

In some situations, a mining company may wish to purchase (rather than lease) the mineral rights to a piece of land. This is accomplished with a **mineral deed**, which transfers all rights to the minerals, along with an implied right to access the surface property to mine, develop, and transport the minerals. The seller keeps title and possession of the surface property.

The final type of horizontal division is by **mineral reservation**. A mineral reservation

 Forgotten, but not Gone

Federal lands contain approximately 67% of the abandoned mines in the State of California (primarily on Bureau of Land Management, National Park Service, and U.S. Forest Service property). Approximately 31% are on private lands, and about 2% are on lands owned by the state or local government.

is very similar to a mineral deed, but the seller transfers title to the surface estate while keeping title to the mineral rights instead.

Case to Consider...

Trklja and Keys both received their deeds from a common grantor. Trklja held fee title to the creek bottom; Keys owned a mineral deed to the same land. Trklja believed that Keys should not have the right to extract minerals if the process would injure or destroy his surface property. Did Trklja have the right to prevent Keys from mining the creek bottom? *Trklja v. Keys* (1942) 49 Cal.App.2d 211.

Support Rights

A landowner has support rights, which refers to the right to the natural support that is provided by the land surrounding his property. **Lateral support** is support provided by adjacent land. The right to lateral support applies not only to land, but also to improvements such as buildings. If the support is removed and causes damage to the property or improvements, liability may result. However, the added weight of the improvements cannot be the cause of the problem. The soil's slipping and sliding must occur because of the soil's own weight, not because of the superimposed weight of improvements.

Case to Consider...

In 1947, Sullivan purchased a large tract of land and subdivided it. The Pucketts bought one of the lots and built a house, carport, and other improvements. In 1950, Sullivan began excavating the land downhill from the Pucketts' property in order to build a shopping center. In 1954, water lines on the Pucketts' property began breaking and power poles began shifting position. The Pucketts sued for damages to their property resulting from the landslides caused by the removal of lateral support. Did the Pucketts have a right to recovery? *Puckett v. Sullivan* (1961) 190 Cal.App.2d 489.

While lateral support is support from neighboring land, **subjacent support** is support from the subsurface. The right to subjacent support is especially important when the surface and subsurface estates are owned by two different people. If a mining company owns the mineral rights beneath a surface owner's property, the mining company will be liable for any damage caused to the surface owner's land as a result of excavations.

Oil and Gas Rights

The prevalence of oil and natural gas deposits in California has resulted in many statutory provisions regulating oil and gas production, as well as case law regarding the nature of oil and gas rights. While oil and gas are technically minerals, their unique nature has given rise to special legal treatment.

Rule of Capture. Unlike other kinds of minerals found on real property, gas and oil are ever-changing (sometimes called fugacious) and transitory. A single deposit may extend below several pieces of property and migrate over large areas. Because of this, California follows the **rule of capture**: oil or gas is not owned until it is pumped to the surface and reduced to possession. However, a real property owner does have the exclusive right to drill for oil or gas on her property. This right is part of the property's title; it is appurtenant and runs with the land. This right to drill may be conveyed, leased, or reserved, as long as it is in writing and recorded.

Slant Drilling. Oil and gas in their natural states lie trapped under great pressure beneath the surface of the earth. However, once an oil or gas reservoir has been tapped, the oil and gas begin to flow toward the point where the reservoir was pierced by the well, since this is the area of lowest pressure. By drilling a well on her own property, it is possible for a property owner to tap and drain a pool of oil or gas beneath her neighbor's property.

In California, **slant drilling**—using owned or leased property to purposefully tap a reservoir under a neighboring piece of property—is allowed, provided the well doesn't terminate under the neighboring property. Slant drilling is also subject to set-back requirements (usually 100 feet from adjacent property).

Lease Agreements. As previously mentioned, a real property owner may convey, reserve, or lease her right to drill for oil or gas. As with mineral rights, most landowners lack the necessary equipment, skills, and resources to drill for oil or gas. As a result, lease agreements allowing oil or gas companies to drill and extract the oil or gas are fairly common. This type of lease agreement usually includes an implied right to enter the surface property to conduct the mining operations.

Obviously, the right of an oil or gas leaseholder to enter the surface estate is a factor your buyer may want to consider when purchasing property. As an agent, you need a basic understanding of the rights to oil and gas, minerals, water, natural attachments, and fixtures.

Case Law in Depth

The following case involves some of the legal issues discussed in this chapter. Read through the facts and consider the questions in light of what you have learned. Then read what the court actually decided.

Wall v. Shell Oil Co. (1962) 209 Cal.App.2d 504

In 1894, George Briggs was the owner in fee simple absolute of a large tract of land in California. He deeded the subsurface estate to Edward Haskell, including all "beds, deposits, lodes, veins and ledges of minerals of every description, and all the petroleum" located under the property. Along with the subsurface estate, Haskell also received the right to enter the surface estate for drilling purposes, and even the right to build any structures required to extract the minerals. Over time, 590 acres of Haskell's subsurface estate ended up in the hands of Shell Oil.

The surface estate was eventually subdivided into many smaller parcels and conveyed to many different owners. One of these parcels was a 17-acre estate owned by the Walls.

Shell Oil had 17 oil wells situated within its 590 acres; four of them were located on the Walls' parcel. Shell Oil had also constructed a road, pipeline, and other facilities on the Walls' parcel that served not just those four wells, but the entire 590 acres. The four wells on Parcel A bottomed out (or terminated) outside the boundaries of the Walls' property.

The question:
Was Shell Oil's use of the Walls' property a trespass?

The court's answers:
The court stated that it was settled law that a property owner may transfer his oil and mineral rights to another. Furthermore, whoever acquires this subsurface estate also acquires a right to "such possession of the surface as is necessary and convenient" to exercise his right to remove the oil or minerals.

The rule regarding subsurface estates is twofold. 1) The owner of the subsurface estate can only subject the surface estate to "such burdens as are reasonably necessary to the full enjoyment of the mineral estate," and the surface estate cannot be burdened by structures that serve the subsurface estates located under other parcels. 2) On the other hand, the owner of the surface estate cannot, after the sale of the mineral rights, divide or sell the property in a way that hinders the subsurface owner from using his entire estate.

According to the court, each subsequent purchaser of these parcels of property purchased it with notice of the prior sale of the subsurface estate, "knowing that his surface ownership may be burdened in part, and, in very rare cases perhaps, in its totality, by the reasonable exercise of the rights of the owner of the oil and mineral estate; and this without regard to whether or not the oil or mineral underlies the particular subdivision, or whether the facilities located thereon serve facilities located without the subdivision..."

"If a particular facility is necessary and convenient to the operations of the oil and mineral owner, it may be placed anywhere upon the surface area...so long as such placement is reasonable under prevailing conditions and even though such placement in particular instances may work a hardship on the surface owner. Certainly, the owner of the oil and mineral estate cannot be required to spread his facilities over a multiple division tract solely in order that a pro rata burden must fall on each subdivision."

The result:
Shell Oil's right to use its subsurface property was equal to the Walls' right to use their surface estate. Therefore, no trespass had occurred.

Chapter Summary

- Real estate refers to the physical land, appurtenances, structures, and other tangible items attached to land, such as trees, crops, and rocks. Real property, on the other hand, includes not only this physical manifestation of property, but also the benefits and rights inherent in ownership of real estate, such as the right to sell, transfer, encumber, occupy the property, or exclude others from it.

- The most important test to determine whether an item has been affixed to the real property is the intention of the annexor. The main purpose of the other tests (method of attachment, relationship between the parties, and adaptation to the realty) is to help the court determine the annexor's intent based on objective evidence.

- California uses a mixture of appropriative and riparian water rights systems. Riparian users have higher priority, but are limited to using the water for reasonable and beneficial use. The highest use of water in California is for domestic purposes; the next highest use is irrigation.

- A property owner theoretically owns not only the surface of the land, but also everything underneath it and everything above it to the far reaches of the sky. Items such as crops and timber may be constructively severed from the land and sold to another party. It is also possible for a landowner to keep the surface property to himself, but sell the rights to everything below the surface to a third party. When this happens, all future owners of the surface property are bound by the rights of the subsurface owner.

Key Terms

- **Real property** – The physical manifestation of property, but also the benefits and rights inherent in ownership of real estate, such as the right to transfer, sell, or encumber the property; and to occupy or use the real estate in a variety of ways.

- **Bundle of rights** – The combined rights, tangible and intangible, that are associated with ownership of real property.

- **Constructive severance** – When an interest in the land has been sold or transferred separately from the real property, but the interest in question still remains in, on, or attached to the land itself.

- **Doctrine of emblements** – The right of a tenant farmer, under a lease of unspecified length, to re-enter a property to harvest the first crop that matures after termination of his lease.

- **Profit à prendre** – The right to enter another's land to remove the soil or a product of the soil, such as oil, gas, crops, or timber. A *profit à prendre* is a property interest, but it is not a form of ownership of real property.

- **Fixtures** – Man-made attachments that were once personal property, but are now attached to the real estate in such a way that they are considered part of the real property and transfer automatically upon conveyance of the land.

- **Appurtenance** – A right, privilege, or improvement that is associated with a piece of real property. Examples of appurtenances are the rights to use air, water, and minerals in or on the land.

- **Rule of capture** – The rule that states that there is no ownership of oil or gas beneath one's property until it is brought to the surface and reduced to possession.

Chapter Quiz

1. Man-made attachments are also known as:
   a) crops
   b) fixtures
   c) emblements
   d) None of the above

2. In California, growing crops:
   a) are fixtures and transfer automatically with the land
   b) belong to the seller
   c) are natural attachments and transfer automatically with the land, unless expressly reserved by the seller
   d) None of the above

3. The doctrine of emblements refers to a tenant's right to:
   a) live on the land after her lease is terminated until she harvests her crops
   b) re-enter the land after termination of a five-year lease to harvest her crops
   c) re-enter the land after termination of an indefinite lease to harvest her crops
   d) None of the above

4. Timber is attached to real property and transfers with the land, but may be considered personal property:
   a) upon actual severance
   b) upon constructive severance
   c) only once it's been cut down
   d) Both a) and b)

5. The rule of capture states that:
   a) the owner of surface property also owns all the oil and gas under it
   b) oil or gas is not owned until it is pumped to the surface and reduced to possession
   c) there is no ownership of solid minerals until they have been mined
   d) Both b) and c)

6. Property is either real (immovable) or:
   a) appurtenant
   b) naturally attached
   c) personal (movable)
   d) tangible

7. The water rights of someone who owns property beside a river are called:
   a) appropriative rights
   b) overlying rights
   c) riparian rights
   d) All of the above

8. A commercial tenant signs a lease that states, "All fixtures installed by tenant, including counters and shelving, become part of the premises and belong to the landlord on termination of the lease." At the end of the lease, the tenant wants to remove some built-in shelves he installed, claiming they are trade fixtures. In this case, the tenant:
   a) has the right to remove the shelves because they are trade fixtures
   b) can remove the shelves if he doesn't damage the landlord's property
   c) can't remove the shelves; they would normally be considered trade fixtures, but the parties agreed that they would become part of the real property
   d) Both a) and b)

9. Custom-made curtains for unusually shaped windows in a home will likely be considered fixtures based upon which test?
   a) Adaptation to the realty
   b) Constructive annexation
   c) Method of attachment
   d) None of the above

10. Constructive severance occurs when:
    a) an interest in the land has been sold or transferred separately from the real property, but the interest in question still remains in, on, or attached to the land itself
    b) an item has been cut down or harvested, such as timber or crops
    c) a landowner terminates a tenant farmer's lease
    d) None of the above

Chapter Answer Key

Chapter Quiz Answers:

1. b)   There are two main categories of attachments: natural attachments, such as trees and crops; and man-made attachments, also known as fixtures.

2. c)   In California, growing crops are natural attachments that are part of the realty and transfer automatically with the land unless expressly reserved by the seller in the deed of sale.

3. c)   The doctrine of emblements applies to crops planted by tenant farmers who lease land for indefinite periods of time, rather than for a specific number of years. If the tenancy is terminated, through no fault of the tenant, and the lease is for an indefinite period of time, the tenant has the right to re-enter the land and harvest the first crop that matures after the end of the lease.

4. d)   Trees and timber are attached to real property and transfer automatically with the land upon conveyance. However, naturally occurring trees and plants, once actually or constructively severed from the land, may also be considered personal property. The sale of standing timber constructively severed from the land is governed by the UCC.

5. b)   The rule of capture states that there is no ownership of oil or gas until it has been pumped to the surface and reduced to possession. Note that this is because oil and gas are transitory. For that reason, the rule of capture does not apply to solid minerals.

6. c)   Section 657 of the Civil Code defines property in California as either real (immovable), or personal (movable).

7. c)   Someone who owns land beside a river is called a riparian landowner, and her water rights are called riparian rights.

8. c)   While the shelves installed by a commercial tenant would normally be considered trade fixtures and removable at the end of the lease, if there is written agreement between the parties stipulating how a particular item is to be treated, a court will respect and enforce the written document.

9. a)   Custom-made curtains for unusually shaped windows will likely be considered fixtures based upon the adaptation to the realty test. Items will usually be considered fixtures if they were specifically designed for the property or are integral to its use, even if they are not permanently attached.

10. a)   Constructive severance occurs when an interest in the land has been sold or transferred separately from the real property, but the interest in question still remains in, on, or attached to the land itself. Once constructively severed, the item in question becomes personal property.

Cases to Consider... Answers:

Trade Fixtures

Beebe v. Richards (1953) 115 Cal.App.2d 589. The court ruled in favor of Beebe. The salon items were trade fixtures that belonged to the tenant upon termination of the lease.

Riparian Rights

Deetz v. Carter (1965) 232 Cal.App.2d 851. The court found for Deetz. Regarding apportionment of water between riparian claimants, the need for domestic purposes receives first preference over irrigation and livestock. Quality and quantity are both factors, and domestic use must be effective. Domestic water that has been polluted by upstream irrigation and livestock is not effective.

Mineral Rights

Trklja v. Keys (1942) 49 Cal.App.2d 211. Keys was entitled to mine the creek bottom. A mineral deed carries with it, by necessary implication, the right to remove minerals by "the usual or customary methods of mining," even if the surface may be injured or destroyed as a result (though in some cases, the miner may be liable for damages). Because Keys intended to use normal methods to extract his mineral estate, Trklja could not deny him access.

Support Rights

Puckett v. Sullivan (1961) 190 Cal.App.2d 489. The Pucketts were entitled to recovery. Sullivan's excavations had changed the drainage, removed protective surface cover, changed the balance of weights, and allowed saturation of the lower area. As a result, these excavations withdrew the "natural, necessary support of Puckett's property in its natural state." Section 832 of the Civil Code states that adjacent landowners are entitled to lateral support. The owner of adjoining land may excavate, but he must provide notice and use ordinary care and skill.

List of Cases

Beebe v. Richards (1953) 115 Cal.App.2d 589
Bridges v. Cal-Pacific Leasing Co. (1971) 16 Cal.App.3d 118
Deetz v. Carter (1965) 232 Cal.App.2d 851
Puckett v. Sullivan (1961) 190 Cal.App.2d 489
Sneed v. County of Riverside (1963) 218 Cal.App.2d 205
Trklja v. Keys (1942) 49 Cal.App.2d 211
Wall v. Shell Oil Co. (1962) 209 Cal.App.2d 504

Chapter 4

Estates in Land

Outline

Introduction

A person's claim to real property is called an interest in real property. An interest in real property may be either possessory or nonpossessory. In this chapter, we'll look at possessory interests in real property, which are also known as estates. We'll cover nonpossessory interests, such as mortgages and easements, in later chapters.

Our discussion will begin with the nature of possessory interests and how estates are classified. Then we'll examine some of the legal issues surrounding the various types of estates. Our main focus will be on freehold (ownership) estates, but we'll also describe the different non-freehold (leasehold) estates.

Possessory Interests

In this book, you'll hear the word "estate" used in two different ways. In some contexts, estate is used to refer to all of the property (both personal and real property) that someone owns. For example, in connection with wills and inheritance, all of the property a person owns when she dies is referred to as her estate. The second, narrower, definition is the one we'll be using in this chapter. Here, when we discuss "estates in land," the term refers to the duration, quality, and extent of the interest a person has in real property.

In this sense of the word, all estates are interests in real property. Not all interests in real property are estates, however. An **estate** is an interest in real property that is or may become **possessory**. That means the owner of an estate in real property has the right to possess and enjoy the property, either now or in the future. It is this right of possession that differentiates estates from other types of interests in real property such as liens, easements, and restrictive covenants. Someone who holds one of those other nonpossessory interests still has rights in regard to the property, and may even have some control over how the property is used, but she has no right of possession.

Classification of Estates

California's Civil Code classifies estates based on duration, quality, and time of possession and ownership. We will briefly describe these characteristics to establish the framework for our discussion of the types of estates.

The first characteristic that distinguishes different types of estates is the **duration of possession**: how long is the holder of the estate legally entitled to possess and enjoy the property? Civil Code § 688 states that an interest in property is either perpetual or limited. A **perpetual interest** has a duration (or potential duration) equal to the duration of the property, which means that the interest could potentially last for as long as the property exists. The duration of a **limited interest** is less than the duration of the property.

Civil Code § 761 sets forth four types of estates, each with a different duration:

- estates of inheritance or perpetual estates,
- estates for life,
- estates for years (also known as term tenancies), or
- estates at will (also known as tenancies at will).

Estates of inheritance and life estates are **freehold estates**. Estates for years and estates at will are non-freehold estates, also called **leasehold estates**. Briefly, someone who has a freehold estate is the owner of the property, while someone who has a leasehold estate is a tenant. Freeholds and leaseholds, the two main categories of estates, will be examined in more detail later in the chapter.

The next consideration in the classification of estates is **quality of possession**: are there any limitations on how the estate holder can possess and enjoy the property? Does someone else have a right to control or terminate the estate holder's possession? With respect to quality of possession, an estate is either absolute or qualified.

Ownership of property is **absolute** when only one person has complete authority over the property and may use it or transfer it in any way he chooses—or, as Civil Code § 679 puts it, "when a single person has absolute dominion over [the property], and may use or dispose of it according to his pleasure, subject only to general laws."

Ownership of property is considered **qualified** when it is shared with more than one person (see Chapter 5), when the time of possession is deferred or limited in some way, or when the use of the property is restricted in some fashion.

 Property Ownership Rights

Historically, owning a freehold estate entitled you to more than just use and possession of the land. From the earliest times, property ownership was tied to other important rights, such as the right to vote. When the U.S. Constitution was written, only white male property owners were granted the right to vote. It wasn't until the 1850s that property ownership was eliminated as a prerequisite to voting in the United States.

The last consideration in classifying estates is **time of possession**: when is the estate holder entitled to possession of the property? Civil Code § 688 states that, in respect to the time of enjoyment, an interest in property is either a present interest or a future interest.

A **present interest** in real property gives the estate holder a right to immediate possession of the property. A **future interest** gives the estate holder the right to take possession only at some future time.

Keep these characteristics and classifications in mind as we go on to consider the different types of estates—first freeholds, then leaseholds.

Freehold Estates

The term "freehold"—like a lot of real estate terminology—comes from the English feudal system, when all land was owned by the king. The king would grant large parcels of land to his loyal followers in return for their service and their pledge of fealty (faithfulness). These landholders, called lords, could then grant portions of their holdings to others in a similar fashion. A person who was granted a freehold, known as a freeman, had the right to sell or transfer his property interest, as long as the new freeholder agreed to give a pledge of fealty to the lord.

In our modern system, a **freehold estate** is a possessory interest in real property that is of undetermined duration. That is, the holder of a freehold estate has the right to possess and enjoy the property for an unspecified and indefinite period of time. In everyday language, she is the property owner, as opposed to a renter or tenant. There are two main categories of freehold estates: estates of inheritance (fee simple estates) and life estates.

Estates of Inheritance

An estate of inheritance, or **fee simple estate**, is freely transferable and inheritable. In theory, a fee simple estate can last forever; it has no termination point, and can be passed on to the owner's heirs. The two types of fee simple estates are the fee simple absolute and the fee simple defeasible.

Fee Simple Absolute. A fee simple absolute is the greatest estate that can exist in land, the highest and most complete form of ownership. It is of potentially infinite duration. In California, no special words are required in a deed to create a fee simple absolute estate; a grantor who has a fee simple absolute estate is presumed to be conveying a fee simple absolute estate. If the grantor intends to convey a lesser estate, the deed must include language expressing that intent.

Fig. 4.1 Characteristics of a fee simple absolute

Fee Simple Absolute	
Duration	perpetual, inheritable
Quality	absolute
Time	present

Fee Simple Defeasible. A fee simple estate may be made conditional, or restricted in some way, when it is transferred from one owner to another. This is called a **fee simple defeasible** or a **defeasible fee**. In the deed, it is clearly stated that ownership is subject to termination if a specified event occurs or a specified condition is not met. Upon termination, title will return to the grantor.

> **Example:** Warren is selling some commercial property he owns. Because he is opposed to drinking, Warren includes a provision in the deed prohibiting the operation of a bar, tavern, or other establishment serving alcoholic beverages on the property. If the grantees or any subsequent owners violate this provision, their title will terminate and ownership will return to Warren or, if Warren is no longer alive, pass to Warren's heirs.

Defeasible fees are comparatively rare. The vast majority of real property is owned in fee simple absolute, unconditionally and without qualification. But you may occasionally encounter a fee simple defeasible in the course of your real estate career.

Historically, there were two types of defeasible fees:

- the fee simple determinable, and
- the fee simple subject to a condition subsequent.

The type of defeasible estate a grantee had was determined by very technical rules concerning the language in the deed. (For example, it made a difference whether the deed said "unless," "so long as," "if," or "on condition that.") Under California law, only the fee simple subject to a condition subsequent remains, so we won't go into those technical rules, but we'll explain the basic distinction between the two types of defeasible fees.

Fee simple determinable. Under common law, a fee simple determinable was an estate that would terminate automatically if the triggering event specified in the deed occurred. After transferring title to a grantee in fee simple determinable, the grantor retained an interest in the property known as a **possibility of reverter**.

With a fee simple determinable, the grantor didn't have to take any action to terminate the grantee's estate or regain title to the property. Both of those things happened automatically if the triggering event occurred.

An automatic forfeiture of property is regarded as a harsh result in the law. Therefore, courts generally treated an estate as a fee simple determinable only if the language in the deed left no doubt that was what the grantor intended to create. When it was possible, a court would interpret a defeasible estate as a fee simple subject to a condition subsequent rather than a fee simple determinable.

Fee simple subject to a condition subsequent. Like a fee simple determinable, a fee simple subject to a condition subsequent carries a condition or qualification imposed by the grantor. This condition or qualification can defeat the grantee's estate. But there's one important difference: instead of a possibility of reverter, the grantor of a fee simple subject to a condition subsequent holds a future interest known as a **power of termination** (also called a **right of re-entry**). The key feature of this future interest is that termination of the grantee's estate is not automatic; the grantor must exercise the power of termination to regain ownership of the property. We'll explain more about this process shortly.

Defeasible fees in California. As noted above, courts have long favored the fee simple subject to a condition subsequent over the fee simple determinable, because the former requires action on the part of the grantor instead of allowing an automatic forfeiture. California has codified this preference in the Civil Code.

California Civil Code § 885.020 abolishes the fee simple determinable. Every estate that would be a fee simple determinable at common law is now deemed to be a fee simple subject to a condition subsequent. Similarly, every interest that would be a possibility of reverter at common law is now a power of termination (a right of re-entry).

The grantee of a fee simple subject to a condition subsequent has all the same rights and is in the same position as the owner of a fee simple absolute, provided that:

- the condition is not broken; or
- if the condition is broken, the grantor chooses not to exercise her power of termination.

Like a fee simple absolute, a fee simple subject to a condition subsequent is freely transferable and inheritable, but the grantee and later owners take the property subject to the condition. (These later owners are often referred to as the grantee's "heirs and assigns." An assign is anyone who takes title from the grantor by any means, including deed or will.) The recording of the original deed provides constructive notice to all subsequent purchasers, so that the condition remains in force even if later deeds fail to mention it. The grantor's future interest (which is based on her power to terminate the estate if the condition is broken) is also freely transferable and inheritable.

Power of termination. The power of termination gives the original grantor, or her heirs or assigns, the right to petition a court for return of the real property if the condition attached to the grantee's estate has been broken. Note that the power of termination can be exercised only by the original grantor or her heirs or assigns.

Example: Mary grants two acres "to the town of Smithville, on condition that the land is used as a playground." This gives the town a fee simple subject to a condition subsequent. Several years pass and Mary dies, leaving everything she owns to her son George. Sometime later, the town of Smithville decides to take down the playground equipment and put up a storage facility. Neighbors on either side of the property, who know about the condition Mary included in her deed to Smithville, are annoyed at the change and want to force the town to maintain the property as a playground. But only George, Mary's heir, has the right to exercise the power of termination and ask a court to end the town's ownership. The neighbors cannot enforce the condition in the deed.

Even with a fee simple subject to a condition subsequent, courts will try to avoid forfeiture. The condition will generally be interpreted to favor the grantee, as in the following case.

Case to Consider...

In 1967, Marjorie Springmeyer and her two siblings granted almost six acres to the city of South Lake Tahoe, "to be used for government office purposes." The deed provided that, should the land ever stop being used for government office purposes, it would revert back to the grantors. The city did erect office buildings on the property, but then allowed the county to build some offices of their own. Springmeyer claims that this violated the condition in the deed, so the land should now revert back to the grantors. Should the property revert back to Springmeyer and the other grantors? *Springmeyer v. City of South Lake Tahoe* (1982) 132 Cal.App.3d 375.

Limits on defeasibility. In California, there are limits on the defeasibility of a fee simple subject to a condition subsequent. Civil Code § 885.030 provides that a power of termination will expire 30 years after the document that created the interest was recorded. Before the power expires, the grantor (or her heirs or assigns) may record a notice of intent to preserve and extend the power of termination for another 30 years. And if another notice is recorded before the extension period ends, the power will be extended for an additional 30 years. But if the power of termination is allowed to lapse, the grantor's interest dissolves, and the defeasible fee becomes a fee simple absolute.

The exercise of the power of termination is also limited by California law. According to the statute of limitations, from the time the condition is breached, the grantor or his heirs or assigns have five years in which to use the power of termination. After that, the power of termination is lost. However, the period created by the statute of limitations may be waived or extended by a document signed by both parties.

Defenses to termination. Grantees are not entirely at the mercy of a grantor's power of termination. In addition to the limitations discussed above (the 30-year expiration rule and the five-year statute of limitations for exercise of the power of termination), a grantee may raise other defenses, including the following.

Fig. 4.2 Characteristics of a fee simple defeasible

Fee Simple Defeasible	
Duration	perpetual, inheritable (as long as the condition is met)
Quality	qualified
Time	present

- **Expiration by obsolescence.** The grantee may argue that the condition in the original deed is no longer of substantial benefit to the grantor. The grantee may also claim that enforcing the power of termination would not fulfill the purpose of the condition, or that changed circumstances would make it unfair to enforce the power against the grantee at this point.
- **Compensation.** Instead of ordering forfeiture of the grantee's estate, a court may allow the grantee to pay compensation to the grantor, especially in circumstances where an appropriate amount of compensation can be easily determined. This is especially likely to occur in cases where the breach of the condition has not been substantial. A court may also order forfeiture of only the minimum amount of property necessary to compensate the grantor.
- **Laches.** The power of termination must be used within a reasonable amount of time. Even if the five-year period allowed by the statute of limitations has not expired, a delay that causes unreasonable difficulties for the grantee may prevent the grantor from recovering the property. (This is an application of the **doctrine of laches**, which holds that legal rights may be lost if they aren't asserted in a timely manner.)
- **Waiver and estoppel.** The grantor may be denied possession if her actions have been inconsistent with a claim of forfeiture. For example, if the grantor's own acts have violated the condition in the deed, she will be deemed to have waived her power of termination.
- **Public policy.** A grantor's claim of forfeiture may be denied if a court deems the restriction in the original deed to be a "restraint on alienation" (a provision that unreasonably limits the free transferability of property).

Life Estates

Fee simple estates (absolute and defeasible), covered in the previous section, make up one of the two main categories of freehold estates. The other main category of freeholds is **life estates**, also called estates for life. The duration of a life estate is determined by the length of a person's lifetime; the estate lasts as long as a specified person is alive. This person, referred to as the **measuring life**, may be the **life tenant**—the person who has the life estate, and is entitled to possession of the property—or it may be someone else.

> **Example:** Suppose Ahmed executes a deed granting his property "to my sister Eva, for life." Eva is the life tenant, and she is also the measuring life. She will have a possessory interest in the property—a life estate—for the rest of her life.
>
> On the other hand, suppose Ahmed grants his property "to my sister Eva, for so long as our mother is alive." In this case, Eva is still the life tenant, but the mother is the measuring life. Eva's possessory interest in the property—her life estate—will end when their mother dies.

A life estate based on the life of a third party is known as a life estate *pur autre vie* ("for the life of another" in Old French). In the second example above, where the measuring life is the mother, Eva has a life estate *pur autre vie*.

To create a life estate, a deed or will must include language limiting the duration of the estate to someone's lifetime. The specific words "life estate" are not necessary, as long as it's clear that's what the grantor or testator intended to create.

Life Estates for a Good Cause

Although life estates have fallen out of favor for estate planning purposes, many charities still encourage donors to use them. A charitable organization may receive a donation of real property where a life estate is reserved by the donor. By making this kind of gift, homeowners can take a charitable deduction on their current income tax return, while keeping the use of their homes for their lifetimes.

Here's how the arrangement (referred to as a retained life estate) works: the donor gives the remainder estate to the charity and keeps a life estate for herself. She's entitled to a charitable tax deduction based on the fair market value of the donated property, minus the expected value of the retained life estate. The younger the life tenant is (or the more of them there are), the lower the value of the remainder interest and the lower the tax deduction.

During the life estate, the donor continues to be liable for any mortgage or other encumbrances on the property, pays the property taxes, and maintains the property. Once the life estate terminates, the charity receives the remainder interest in the property (which becomes a fee simple estate).

Conditional Life Estate. A life estate may be conditioned on some action of the life tenant. For example, a deed may grant real property "to my son Jacob, for life, so long as he lives on the property; otherwise, to my brother John, for life; remainder to my daughter Sarah."

Reversion or Remainder. What happens to the property when the measuring life dies? Whenever a life estate is created, a future interest is also created. This future interest is held by the person who is entitled to the property when the life estate ends (when the measuring life dies). The future interest is either an estate in reversion or an estate in remainder. It's an **estate in reversion** if ownership of the property will revert to the grantor at the end of the life estate. It's an **estate in remainder** if ownership will pass to a third party, known as the **remainderman**, at the end of the life estate.

> **Example:** In Ahmed's will, he leaves his real property to "my sister Eva, for life; then to our brother Ali." Ali has an estate in remainder. He is the remainderman.

If the document creating a life estate does not name a remainderman, the future interest will be an estate in reversion, and the property will return to the grantor (or her heirs or assigns) when the life estate ends.

> **Example:** Ahmed deeds his property "to my sister Eva, for life," without specifying who will own the property after the measuring life ends. In this case, it's assumed that he intends for ownership of the property to revert to himself.

We'll return to the subject of future interests later in the chapter.

Rights and Powers. During the term of a life estate, if there's no provision in the deed or will to the contrary, the life tenant has all the same rights in regard to the property that a fee simple owner would have. This means that a life tenant has full rights of possession and enjoyment, including:

- the right to any rents and profits generated by the property;
- the right to declare a homestead (see Chapter 14); and
- the power to lease, mortgage, or transfer the property.

It's important to realize, however, that the life tenant's power to lease, mortgage, or transfer the property lasts only as long as her life estate.

> **Example:** Linda's will gave her beachfront property, "to my daughter Susan, for life; remainder to my granddaughter Chloe." Susan would like to sell the beachfront property, since it's worth a lot of money and she has a lot of bills to pay. However, all she can sell is her life estate in the property. If Susan finds buyers willing to purchase the life estate, the buyers will have only what Susan had. In other words, when Susan dies, the buyers' interest will end, and the beachfront property will pass to Linda's granddaughter, Chloe, as specified in Linda's will.

Duties and Liabilities. A life tenant has a legal duty to treat the property as his own, meaning that he must do what an ordinary owner in fee simple would do to preserve and maintain it. This usually includes the payment of property taxes, special assessments, and maintenance or homeowners association fees. However, the granting instrument may provide for some other division of responsibility. For instance, it could provide that the life tenant will pay for maintenance, but the remainderman will pay for special assessments.

A life tenant is also forbidden from committing waste. **Waste** is any act or failure to act that materially reduces the market value of the property. Waste is prohibited because it lessens the value of an interest (the future interest) owned by another. So while a life tenant has the right to exclusive possession of the property during the measuring life, the holder of the future estate has a right to enter and inspect the property periodically, on reasonable terms, to ensure that no waste is being committed.

Ordinary wear and tear will not be considered waste. In fact, the reversioner or remainderman won't be able to claim waste unless she can show the court that there's been a material reduction in value, such as would result from the cutting of timber or the removal of minerals from the property. If she can prove waste, she'll be awarded three times the amount of actual damages.

Note, however, that the life tenant is under no obligation to make improvements to the property. For example, a life tenant would not have to pave a dirt road or install fencing unless he chose to do so. If building improvements are required by law to meet minimum building code standards, the reversioner or remainderman may be required to

Fig. 4.3 Characteristics of a life estate

Life Estate	
Duration	life of a specified person
Quality	qualified
Time	present

reimburse the life tenant for an appropriate share of the cost. This is because physical improvements to the property may last beyond the term of the life estate, so that not only the life tenant but the person who holds the future interest will benefit from the added value.

Termination, Merger, and Partition. A life estate terminates automatically at the end of the measuring life. The life tenant's rights of possession and enjoyment, and her ability to transfer or encumber the property, end at the moment that the person who is the measuring life dies.

Case to Consider...

In 1943, Mattie Stanley died, leaving a life estate in the house she owned to her husband, Milledge Stanley, with the remainder going to her daughter, Juanita Clarke. Milledge's niece, Marnie, moved in with him. When Milledge died five years later, he left all of his property by will to Marnie. Juanita sued for possession of the house. Who was entitled to the house, Marnie or Juanita? *Clarke v. Bates* (1951) 104 Cal.App.2d 597.

A life estate will also terminate if the life estate and the future estate become vested in a single individual. For example, a life tenant and a remainderman might agree to sell their interests to a third party. When that happens, the two estates merge into a fee simple absolute owned by the buyer. Merger also occurs if the life tenant purchases the future estate, or if the owner of the future estate purchases the life tenant's interest.

Finally, a life estate will terminate automatically upon partition of the real property. When either the life tenant or the holder of the future interest sues for partition, the property will be sold and the proceeds divided between them. The following case example involves this type of partition action.

Case Example:

In her will, Alice gave her son Fern a life estate, "for so long as he lives upon the property, and upon his removal from the property, or upon his death, then the property is to be distributed to those children living at that time, share and share alike." Fifteen years after Alice's death, Fern filed a partition action against his three siblings. He wanted the property to be sold, the value of his life estate deducted from the proceeds and given to him, and then the balance of the proceeds divided between the four siblings (Fern included). Fern's siblings were willing to sell the estate and split the proceeds four ways, but were unwilling to grant Fern the value of his life estate first.

The trial court found (and the appeals court affirmed) that Fern had abandoned the life estate by maintaining the partition action and agreeing to the sale of the property. While the owner of a life estate is entitled to bring a partition action, Fern's life estate was conditional: his "removal" ended the life estate. In this case, Fern's motion for partition was a removal and the life estate ceased to exist. Fern was entitled to share equally in the proceeds of the sale with his siblings, but he was not entitled to the value of a life estate that had been abandoned. *Forrest v. Elam* (1979) 88 Cal.App.3d 164.

A Trust for Fido

California and most other states now allow pet trusts—money and/or property set aside for the care of an animal. Section 15212 of the Probate Code limits the duration of the trust to the lifetime of an animal that was alive when the trust's creator died.

As you can also see from this case example, a conditional life estate will terminate automatically if the condition is no longer met.

> **Example:** Bart grants his estate, "to my brother Charlie, for life, so long as he lives on the property; otherwise to Joan for life." Charlie lives on the property for ten years and then moves to another state and leases the property to Alan. However, the moment Charlie ceased to occupy the property, his life estate terminated automatically and Joan's life estate began. Charlie had no right to lease what he no longer owned, so Alan's lease is invalid.

Trusts. In modern legal practice, life estates are seldom used, because trusts provide the same benefits, with the additional safety factor of a trustee who looks out for the interests of the specified beneficiary. When a trust is created to serve the same function as a life estate, a trustee is given legal title to property that she holds for the life of the beneficiary. When the beneficiary dies, the property is disposed of according to the wishes of the trustor.

Leasehold Estates

The types of estates we've discussed so far, fee simple estates and life estates, make up the category of freehold estates. The other major category of estates is less-than-freehold, or **leasehold**, estates. As the term "less-than-freehold" indicates, a leasehold is a more limited interest in property than a freehold. A leaseholder (a **tenant**, also called a **lessee**) rents or leases property from a **landlord** (or **lessor**). The landlord, who almost always owns the property in fee simple, retains title to the property but grants the tenant a temporary right of possession.

A leasehold estate is created with a **lease**, a contractual agreement that establishes and governs the relationship of landlord and tenant. It grants the tenant the right of exclusive use and possession of the property, in return for the payment of rent (or sometimes services provided). The lease may last for a definite or indefinite period of time. In either case, possession of the property ordinarily reverts to the landlord when the lease ends. Thus, during the term of the lease, the landlord has an estate in reversion, like the grantor of a life estate.

Any interest in real property may be the subject of a lease; for example, it's possible to lease mineral rights, water rights, or air rights. A lease differs from a *profit à prendre* or a license (see Chapter 15) in that a lease grants the right of possession. It is this right of possession that gives the lease its estate status and makes it more than a mere right of entry (to mine for minerals, for example) or right of use.

We will discuss leases and the landlord-tenant relationship in more detail in Chapter 20. For now we'll just describe the different types of leasehold estates.

California Civil Code § 761 specifically lists two types of leaseholds: the estate for years (term tenancy) and the estate at will (tenancy at will). Generally, however, four types of leaseholds are recognized:

- the term tenancy,
- the periodic tenancy,
- the tenancy at will, and
- the tenancy at sufferance.

Technically, the tenancy at sufferance is not really an estate at all (because there is no right of possession), but it is commonly discussed along with the leasehold estates.

Term Tenancy

A **term tenancy**, also known as an **estate for years**, is a tenancy for a fixed period of time. Any lease with a fixed term—one that has definite beginning and ending dates—is a term tenancy, even if the term of the lease is just a few days, weeks, or months.

> **Example:** Mary and Julio lease an apartment in Los Angeles, "For a term beginning August 1 and ending November 30." Mary and Julio have a term tenancy.

A term tenancy ends automatically when the term expires. It's not necessary for either the tenant or the landlord to give the other party notice of termination. This is true no matter how long or how short the term is.

During the term of a lease, the landlord may still sell, give, or will the property to a third party. The new owner will take title subject to the existing lease, however, and must honor its terms. The tenant's interest (the term tenancy) is not affected by the transfer of title.

Fig. 4.4 Characteristics of a term tenancy

Term Tenancy	
Duration	a specific term
Quality	qualified
Time	present

Periodic Tenancy

With a periodic tenancy, property is leased on a weekly, monthly, or yearly basis. The lease doesn't terminate automatically at the end of the specified period, however. Instead, it will renew itself for the same period until one party gives the other notice to terminate. This kind of tenancy is often called a week-to-week, month-to-month, or year-to-year tenancy, depending on the length of the rental period.

> **Example:** Samantha and Eric lease 25 acres of farm land on a year-to-year lease. Until they either give or are given notice of termination, their lease will continue for successive years, indefinitely.

When a lease lacks either a termination date or an express provision that states the duration of the rental period, the rental period is determined by the frequency of the rental payments. So a tenant who pays rent on a monthly basis will have a month-to-month tenancy, unless otherwise agreed. If rent is paid once a year, it will be a year-to-year tenancy. The exception to this rule is agricultural land, which is presumed to renew on a year-to-year basis, even if the rent is paid monthly.

Fig. 4.5 Characteristics of a periodic tenancy

Periodic Tenancy	
Duration	indefinite
Quality	qualified
Time	present

We'll discuss the rules for notice of termination of a periodic tenancy in Chapter 20. In general, either party may terminate a month-to-month tenancy by giving the other notice of termination 30 days in advance, but under certain circumstances a residential tenant may be entitled to 60 days' notice.

Tenancy at Will

A **tenancy at will**, also called an estate at will, is created when a tenant enters into possession of real property with the landlord's permission, with no termination date set and without the payment of rent. (Payment of rent would transform a tenancy at will into a periodic tenancy. For example, monthly rental payments would create a month-to-month tenancy, as explained above.) A tenancy at will may be created by either express or implied agreement.

Under common law, no notice was required to end a tenancy at will, but Civil Code § 789 requires a landlord to give the tenant 30 days' notice. A tenancy at will terminates if either the tenant or the landlord dies.

Case Example:

Raymond Marquez lived with his father. When the father died, Raymond refused to move out, and the rest of the family sued to evict him. The court found that Raymond had a tenancy at will before his father's death: his occupancy was consensual, for an indefinite period of time, and did not involve the payment of rent. However, when his father died, Raymond's tenancy at will terminated. *Marquez-Luque v. Marquez* (1987) 192 Cal.App.3d 1513.

Note that a tenancy at will is not the same as a trespass, which is entry without permission. Nor is it the same as a tenancy at sufferance, which is created without express or implied agreement between the parties.

Tenancy at Sufferance

The **tenancy at sufferance** is not mentioned specifically in the Civil Code, but courts have long used this term to describe possession by a tenant who holds over after the expiration of a prior leasehold estate, without the property owner's consent. A tenant at sufferance takes possession of the property legally, but continues to occupy it after the

Fig. 4.6 Comparison of tenancy at will, tenancy at sufferance, and trespass

Tenancy at Will	Tenancy at Sufferance	Trespass
• Entry with permission • Possession with permission • Express or implied agreement between the parties • Terminates when period of permission ends	• Entry with permission • Possession no longer with permission • No express or implied agreement between the parties	• Entry without permission • Possession without permission

right to possession has ended. (In the case example given above, Raymond became a tenant at sufferance when his father died and his tenancy at will terminated.) In contrast to a tenancy at will, there was no express or implied agreement between the parties to create this "tenancy." Therefore, California law does not give a tenant at sufferance the same protection as a legitimate tenant; no 30-day notice of termination is necessary. (If a tenant at sufferance refuses to leave, however, the landlord must follow the eviction procedures prescribed by law to regain possession of the property. See Chapter 20.)

There's an exception to the rule that a tenant at sufferance is not entitled to notice of termination. When the property in question is agricultural land, if a tenant at sufferance does not receive a notice to leave within 60 days, continued possession will be presumed to be with permission of the landlord, and the tenant will have the right to hold the property for another year.

Note that with either a tenancy at will or a tenancy at sufferance, if the landlord accepts rent at any point, the tenant's occupancy will be converted to a periodic tenancy.

Case Law in Depth

The following case involves some of the legal issues discussed in this chapter. Read through the facts and consider the questions in light of what you have learned. Then read what the court actually decided.

Miller & Desatnik Management Co. v. Bullock (1990) 221 Cal.App.3d Supp. 13

In 1983, Marianne Jones executed a written rental agreement for a rent-controlled apartment in Santa Monica. The tenancy began on January 15. There was no specific termination date, rent was to be paid on a monthly basis, and the tenancy could be terminated by either party with 30 days' advance notice. Marianne lived in the apartment until her death on September 21, 1984.

Marguerite Bullock (Respondent) was Marianne's mother. After Marianne's death, Respondent assumed the rental payments with money orders purchased in Marianne's name as payor. Respondent never lived in the apartment, but did visit it three or four times a week to take care of Marianne's plants and to be "close to her daughter."

Respondent never informed the apartment managers (Appellants) of Marianne's death. Nearly four years later, Appellants discovered that Marianne had died in 1984. When confronted, Respondent denied that Marianne was dead. On July 29, Appellants served Respondent with a 30-day written notice to vacate the premises. Appellants never accepted rent from Respondent after serving the notice to vacate. Respondent refused to move, and Appellants sued to regain the premises.

A trial court found that Marianne's tenancy survived her death and that Respondent was a tenant entitled to remain in possession. Furthermore, as a tenant, Respondent was entitled to proper eviction notice and procedures that complied with the good cause termination provisions of the Santa Monica Rent Control Charter Amendment. The property management company appealed.

The question:

What kind of leasehold interest did Marianne have, and did that interest survive her death?

The court's answer:

The court stated that the lease in this case clearly created a month-to-month tenancy. "The death of a tenant who holds from month to month prevents the tenant from exercising her right to continue in possession. If she has assigned her rights under the tenancy before her death, her assignee only obtains the right which the assignor herself had: the right to possess and use the premises for one month. After her death, the assignor is not able to exercise her renewal for a successive monthly period or periods. Consequently, the assignee does not receive such right to possess for successive periods."

The court held that the month-to-month tenancy was terminated by notice of the tenant's death. Marianne's mother was not an assignee, but rather a trespasser.

The result:

As the respondent was a trespasser and not a tenant, she had no protection under the Santa Monica Rent Control Charter Amendment, and the lease could be terminated.

Chapter Summary

- The term "estate" refers to the duration, quality, and extent of the interest a person has in real property. While all estates are interests in real property, not all interests in real property are estates. An estate is an interest in land that is, or may become, possessory.

- Every estate is either absolute or qualified; present or future; and perpetual or limited.

- There are two main categories of estates: freehold and leasehold. The freehold estates, which are considered ownership interests, are the fee simple (estate of inheritance) and the life estate (estate for life).

- A fee simple estate may be further classified as either a fee simple absolute or a fee simple defeasible. Under common law, a fee simple defeasible could be either a fee simple determinable (with a possibility of reverter) or a fee simple subject to a condition subsequent (with a power of termination). Under California law, the fee simple determinable has been abolished and only the fee simple subject to a condition subsequent remains.

- A life estate lasts as long as a specified person (the measuring life) is alive. The measuring life may be the life tenant herself, or it may be a third person. A life tenant has most of the same rights in regard to the property as a fee simple owner, but the life tenant can only convey or encumber the life estate and must not commit waste.

- Creation of a life estate also creates a future interest: either an estate in reversion or an estate in remainder. It's an estate in reversion if ownership will revert to the grantor when the life estate ends. It's an estate in remainder if ownership will pass to a third party when the life estate ends.

- The holder of a leasehold estate (the tenant) has only a temporary right to possession and enjoyment of the property, and does not have title to it. The leasehold estates are the term tenancy, the periodic tenancy, the tenancy at will, and the tenancy at sufferance.

Key Terms

- **Estate** – An interest in land that is, or may become, possessory.

- **Freehold estate** – An indefinite possessory interest in real property. The two types of freehold estates are the fee simple and the life estate.

- **Fee simple absolute** – The greatest estate that can exist in land. It is complete ownership, without qualifications.

- **Fee simple defeasible** – A qualified estate in land that may terminate if certain conditions are not met. Also called a defeasible fee.

- **Power of termination** – In connection with a fee simple defeasible, the right to sue for return of the real property if the condition attached to the grantee's estate has been broken.

- **Life estate** – A freehold estate that lasts for the life of a specified person (the measuring life); the measuring life may be the grantee (the life tenant) or a third party. If the measuring life is a third party, the life tenant has a life estate *pur autre vie*.

- **Reversion** – A future interest held by the original grantor that becomes possessory after a life estate ends.

- **Remainder** – A future interest held by a third party that becomes possessory after a life estate ends.

- **Waste** – Any act or failure to act that materially reduces the market value of property.

- **Leasehold** – The holder of a leasehold estate (the tenant) has a temporary right to exclusive possession and use of the leased property.

- **Term tenancy** – A leasehold estate for a fixed period.

- **Periodic tenancy** – A leasehold estate that continues for successive rental periods of equal length until terminated by one of the parties.

- **Tenancy at will** – A tenancy with no fixed term and no payment of rent, based on an express or implied agreement between the tenant and the landlord.

- **Tenancy at sufferance** – Occupancy of property by a tenant who remains in possession after his right to possession has ended, without the landlord's express or implied consent.

Chapter Quiz

1. An interest in land that is, or may become, possessory is a/an:
   a) estate
   b) *profit à prendre*
   c) license
   d) None of the above

2. Mary grants her property "to Billy for life, then to Susan." Susan's interest is a:
   a) reversion
   b) remainder
   c) contingent estate
   d) life estate

3. Mary grants her property "to Billy for life." When Billy dies, the property will:
   a) pass to the remainderman
   b) pass to the life tenant
   c) revert to Mary or her heirs or assigns
   d) pass to the state

4. Mark grants his property, "To the City of Malibu for so long as the property is used as a youth center." Several years later, the city tears down the youth center to build an office building. Mark's right to sue for return of the property is known as a:
   a) right of re-entry
   b) possibility of reverter
   c) power of termination
   d) Both a) and c)

5. A will states, "To Laura for the life of Sally, remainder to Janet." Sally is the:
   a) life estate
   b) measuring life
   c) remainderman
   d) None of the above

6. Peter holds a life estate in Mariko's property. Without Mariko's permission, Peter lets a lumber company clear the property of all standing timber. A court would probably find that Peter has:
   a) the right to sell the timber, since he has possessory interest in the property
   b) the right to sell the timber, since Mariko gave Peter a life estate
   c) committed waste and is liable for the diminished value of the property
   d) None of the above

7. Alice leases an apartment to Steven for a period "beginning August 1 and ending October 31." Steven's leasehold estate is a:
   a) term tenancy
   b) periodic tenancy
   c) tenancy at will
   d) tenancy at sufferance

8. Ed rents an apartment for an unspecified period of time. The rental agreement requires him to pay the landlord $600 per month. Ed's leasehold estate is a:
   a) term tenancy
   b) periodic tenancy
   c) tenancy at will
   d) tenancy at sufferance

9. Catherine lives with her aunt, free of charge, in exchange for caring for her aunt in her old age. When the aunt dies:
   a) Catherine's tenancy at will terminates automatically
   b) Catherine can continue to live on the property, since the aunt gave her permission
   c) Catherine will become a tenant at sufferance if she refuses to move
   d) Both a) and c)

10. Curt is living in one of Bob's apartment units without permission. Curt offers to pay rent if Bob will let him stay, but Bob refuses. Under California law, Curt is a:
    a) periodic tenant
    b) tenant at will
    c) tenant at sufferance
    d) trespasser

Chapter Answer Key

Chapter Quiz Answers:

1. a) An estate is an interest in land that is, or may become, possessory. The other two options are not possessory interests.

2. b) Susan is a third party, so her future interest is a remainder.

3. c) Since Mary didn't name a remainderman, the future interest is an estate in reversion, and the property will revert to the grantor or her heirs or assigns when the life estate ends.

4. d) Under common law, Mark's right to sue for return of the property would be a power of termination, also known as a right of re-entry. A possibility of reverter refers to automatic termination under the common law fee simple determinable, which has been abolished in California.

5. b) Sally is the measuring life. When Sally dies, Laura's life estate ends.

6. c) A court would probably find that Peter has committed waste and is liable to Mariko for the diminished value of her reversionary interest.

7. a) A term tenancy is any tenancy for a fixed period of time, even if the term of the lease is less than one year.

8. b) Ed has a periodic tenancy (specifically, a month-to-month tenancy). When property is leased for an unspecified period of time and the tenant pays rent, it's a periodic tenancy, with the length of the rental period determined by the frequency of the rent payments.

9. d) When Catherine's aunt dies, her tenancy at will terminates automatically. If she refuses to move, she will become a tenant at sufferance.

10. d) Curt is a trespasser because he never had permission to enter or possess the apartment unit. He would only be a tenant at will or at sufferance if he'd originally had Bob's permission to enter and possess the property, but then overstayed the period of permission.

Cases to Consider... Answers:

Defeasible Fees

Springmeyer v. City of South Lake Tahoe (1982) 132 Cal.App.3d 375. The court disagreed with Springmeyer. Since forfeiture is a drastic remedy, it won't be applied unless the grantor showed a "clear and unmistakable" intention to cause a reversion. Here, the term "government offices" could apply to county municipal offices, as well as city offices. Therefore, the language in Springmeyer's grant wasn't a clear enough expression of intent to require a reversion under the circumstances. [NOTE: This case was decided before Civil Code § 885.020 became effective; under current law, Springmeyer's possibility of reverter would be a power of termination.]

Termination of Life Estates

Clarke v. Bates (1951) 104 Cal.App.2d 597. The court found for Juanita, stating that her remainder interest became a fee simple absolute when Milledge died. Milledge's life estate ended at the moment of his death, and his will could not transfer title to property he no longer owned.

List of Cases

Clarke v. Bates (1951) 104 Cal.App.2d 597
Forrest v. Elam (1979) 88 Cal.App.3d 164
Lucas v. Hamm (1961) 56 Cal.2d 583
Marquez-Luque v. Marquez (1987) 192 Cal.App.3d 1513
Miller v. Desatnik Management Co. v. Bullock (1990) 221 Cal.App.3d Supp. 13
Springmeyer v. City of South Lake Tahoe (1982) 132 Cal.App.3d 375

Chapter 5

Co-ownership of Real Property

Outline

Introduction

Let's now turn our attention to co-ownership of real property. How co-owners take title to real property affects control over and use of the property, as well as how the property is divided when the co-ownership ends. It's important for real estate agents to be familiar with the different forms of co-ownership and to understand which signatures are required when co-owned property is transferred.

In this chapter, we'll look at the three main types of co-ownership recognized in California: tenancy in common, joint tenancy, and community property. We'll also discuss the basic types of business entities and explain how they take title to real property. Finally, we'll take a quick look at some of the issues business owners consider when they're deciding how to organize their business.

Forms of Co-ownership

Ownership of property by one person is fairly straightforward. When a piece of property is owned by only one person, ownership is said to be **several** or held **in severalty**. Although this term may sound like the opposite of what it means, it's helpful to remember that the usage stems from the word "sever." Ownership in severalty is ownership severed from all other people—title isn't shared in any way.

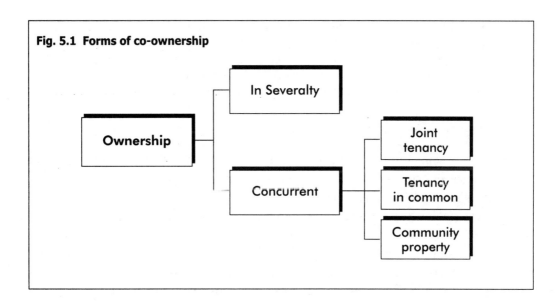

Fig. 5.1 Forms of co-ownership

Not surprisingly, ownership of property by two or more people is more complex than ownership in severalty. In California, two or more people may hold title to property in one of the following ways:

- tenancy in common,
- joint tenancy, or
- community property.

Tenancy in Common

Tenancy in common (TIC) is the default form of co-ownership. If a grantor conveys property to two or more unmarried people and the deed doesn't specify the form of co-ownership, the grantees take title as **tenants in common**. Nonetheless, to avoid any possible confusion, co-owners who specifically want tenancy in common should say so in the deed, adding "as tenants in common" after their names.

Why would property owners choose tenancy in common? The chief difference between TIC and the alternative—joint tenancy—is that a TIC is an interest that passes to the owner's heirs upon his death. In contrast, any joint tenancy property passes automatically to the other surviving owner(s). We will discuss joint tenancy more thoroughly in the next section.

To show you how tenancy in common works, let's start with an example, which we'll be returning to throughout the discussion.

> **Example:** Angela and Kyle are engaged to be married. They've been living together for a few years in a condo south of Oakland. When they purchased the condo, the deed contained the following conveyance language:
>
> *The undersigned grantor, for valuable consideration, hereby grants to Angela Mondavi, a single person, an undivided 70 percent interest, and to Kyle Pinsky, a single person, an undivided 30 percent interest, as tenants in common, in the following described real property...*

Kyle, who is a freelance carpenter, had almost no money to contribute to the purchase of the condo. Even so, Angela agreed that Kyle would have a 30% interest in the property. This arrangement was based on their love for one another, but also on the understanding that Kyle would undertake a major remodel of the bathroom and kitchen. He has put a great deal of time into the remodeling project, but progress has been slow.

Undivided Interests

Tenancy in common is a very flexible form of co-ownership. The co-tenants may have equal interests, or one co-tenant may own almost 100% of the property while a dozen or more others share slivers of the remainder.

However, no matter how small a tenant in common's percentage of ownership, her interest is always undivided. As a result, tenants in common are said to have unity of possession. Co-tenants have **unity of possession** when each one has a right to use the entire property and no co-tenant can keep the other owners out. Note, however, that the co-tenants can provide in their TIC agreement that a particular co-tenant has an exclusive right to possession of the premises.

Usually, differing interests in co-owned property, like the 70/30 split in our example about Angela and Kyle, mean that one party contributed proportionally more money to the purchase. If a deed creating a tenancy in common says nothing about the co-owners' fractional interests, a court will presume that the interests are equal. However, a tenant in common can rebut that presumption, usually by showing a canceled check or other evidence of having contributed more than an equal share of the purchase price.

Rights and Duties of Tenants in Common

For tenants in common, there are legal rules concerning contributions for expenses and improvements, contribution of labor, profits from the property, and waste. Note that some of these rules also apply to other forms of co-ownership.

Contributions for Expenses and Improvements. Absent an agreement to the contrary, tenants in common share the property's expenses in proportion to their percentage of ownership.

> **Example:** In the years since they bought their condo, Angela has been shouldering 70% of the mortgage, taxes, and other expenses, while Kyle has been handling his proportionate share of 30%. However, the last two months he's come up short (he's had trouble finding work), so Angela has had to make up the difference.

If a co-tenant ends up paying more than her pro rata share of expenses, she has a right to reimbursement from her fellow co-tenants. This is the **right to contribution**. (Angela hasn't seen much point in invoking this right against her fiancé.)

The right to contribution applies automatically to all necessary expenses. It applies to optional improvements only if the other co-tenants authorized the improvement.

> **Example:** Cassie, Jean, and Marcie live together in a house that they own as tenants in common. The house consists of four levels built into a steep bank that continues down to the lake shore. Each level has a deck. There is a simple tram that stops at each deck, and then descends to the shore of the lake.

▶ Equity Sharing

In response to the huge increases in housing prices in California, a co-ownership arrangement called **equity sharing** was developed to help home buyers share the cost of purchasing a home. In an equity sharing arrangement, the co-owners usually take title as tenants in common, though joint tenancy is also used. The co-owners agree that one of them (usually the poorer one) will live in the house as the occupant. The occupant is both an owner and a tenant at the same time. The owner-occupant pays the mortgage and maintenance expenses, and perhaps some rent. The occupant typically lacks funds for the downpayment, so the non-resident investor pays most or all of that expense.

In return, the non-resident investor takes a tax deduction for depreciation based on his percentage of ownership in what is, to him, rental property. (Note that a lawyer should prepare the equity sharing agreement, if only to ensure that IRS requirements for these deductions are met.)

The equity sharing agreement specifies a certain period, commonly five to seven years, after which the residence will be sold. If it's sold to a third party, the occupant and the investor split the net proceeds in proportion to their contributions. If the occupant wants to buy the investor out—often the whole point of the arrangement, from the occupant's perspective—a professional appraiser provides a purchase price for the investor's share.

Equity sharing is relatively new. The courts have only recently begun to grapple with some of the issues raised by these arrangements, as in the following case.

Case Example: Four people bought an investment residence as tenants in common. They had an agreement which allowed a co-owner to live in the residence in exchange for paying all of the association dues, property taxes, and mortgage payments. Pursuant to this agreement, Regina Ann Barross moved into the residence, but she failed to make the required payments.

When the other co-owners told Barross she had to move out, she claimed that as a co-owner she could not be evicted. She argued that the parties were not in a landlord-tenant relationship, and so the other co-owners' only remedy was to sue her for breach of contract.

The court noted the lack of clear precedent on how to interpret their arrangement. Barross's "rent" varied depending on the property taxes and other expenses, and there was no term to her "lease." However, Barross's right to exclusive possession against the other owners, in addition to the court's interpretation of numerous other provisions in the equity sharing agreement, strongly indicated lessee status. The court concluded that she was indeed a tenant and could be evicted for non-payment. *Rossetto v. Barross* (2001) 90 Cal.App.4th Supp. 1.

One day the tram motor burns out. Cassie does the research and reports that it will cost about $12,000 to fix it, as the building code now requires a more powerful motor as well as safety rails. Jean objects to the expenditure, pointing out that she never uses the tram and prefers the exercise she gets from walking.

Is rebuilding and upgrading the tram necessary maintenance or a voluntary improvement? The women's TIC agreement doesn't address this issue. It may take a court to settle the matter.

If the tram is a voluntary improvement, Cassie and Marcie would have to split the $12,000 between themselves—they can't force Jean to contribute. If Jean refuses to contribute, she can't share in the increased market value that a refurbished tram would bring to the property. It's not fair for a non-contributing tenant to reap the rewards of an improvement.

At any rate, you can see how the distinction between necessary maintenance and voluntary improvements may lead to disputes. Carefully drafted TIC agreements can help avoid disputes and make lawsuits less likely. For example, a TIC agreement could provide that if the majority of tenants in common vote in favor of a voluntary improvement, everyone must contribute.

Contribution of labor. Tenants in common may allow a co-owner to meet financial obligations of the TIC by contributing labor instead of money.

Example: When they bought their condo, Angela and Kyle drafted a very simple TIC agreement. It stated that Kyle's 30% ownership was based on his agreement to provide the labor and materials necessary to remodel the bathroom and kitchen, with the design to be "as agreed." The couple had estimated that this remodeling was worth about $54,000—a little less than one-third of the condo's $180,000 purchase price.

Angela has learned the hard way that Kyle is a fussy craftsman. He's spent about $17,000 on expensive materials, including an extravagant sunken tub of forest green Italian marble (which was definitely not part of the "as agreed" design). He says he has contributed almost $19,000 in labor, although he's more interested in doing the work than

> ▶ **Contribution of Labor: Making it Work**
>
> When a co-owner is planning to contribute labor as part of her share of expenses, the other co-owner(s) should insist on a written contract concerning the contribution, to lessen the likelihood of trouble. The following are worthwhile guidelines:
>
> 1. Approval: Significant work or changes should require the agreement of all parties.
>
> 2. Bids: Professional bids should be obtained to help set a reasonable price on the work.
>
> 3. Flat fee for work: Setting fixed fees for the work (instead of an hourly rate) will encourage efficiency.
>
> 4. Materials costs: The contract should address materials costs. Non-professional workers tend to underestimate materials costs and make wasteful mistakes.
>
> 5. Schedule: Prevent projects from dragging out indefinitely by providing a completion schedule, with payment or ownership credit linked to specified dates.

keeping records of his time. The bathroom is certainly lovely, but much more than Angela wanted or that makes sense in their relatively modest condo.

Again, a carefully drafted TIC agreement can help prevent this type of situation.

Profit. Every co-tenant has a right to profit from his share in the property. In the case of rental property, this means a fairly straightforward sharing of rental income. However, with unimproved land that contains valuable natural resources—such as oil, minerals, or timber—disagreements can sometimes arise over whether a co-tenant may profit from a portion of these assets and, if so, exactly how much.

Case Example:

Henry, Clarence, and their sister Elvira each owned an undivided one-third interest in 1,500 acres of mountain timberland. Clarence wanted to make money from his share, so he sold logging rights to 500,000 board feet of fir and ponderosa pine. His siblings objected, but the logging went ahead.

Henry and Elvira sued for a share of the logging proceeds. The appellate court ruled that any of the co-tenants had a right to log one-third of the property's total timber, and remanded the case to determine if more than that amount had been logged. If it was more than one-third, Clarence would owe his siblings the excess amount. *Garibaldi v. Garibaldi* (1968) 264 Cal.App.2d 9.

Waste. In Chapter 4, we explained that a life tenant can't commit **waste**; that is, he may not physically damage the property and reduce its value. The same rule applies to co-owners.

In a co-ownership situation, as the *Garibaldi* case (above) illustrates, harvesting an appropriate share of the timber or other resources, or otherwise taking a reasonable profit from the property, does not count as waste. However, in *Garibaldi*, the brother's logging damaged the timberland roads and waterways to the tune of $25,000. The court ruled that this was waste and ordered Clarence to reimburse his siblings for the cost of repairs.

Transfer and Encumbrance. A tenant in common doesn't need the consent of the other owners to mortgage his share of the property. He may freely mortgage, sell, gift, or otherwise transfer his interest. This transfer may take place voluntarily or involuntarily.

Example: Let's return to Angela and Kyle. Yesterday, they became husband and wife. Just before the ceremony, Kyle—who had promised Angela a surprise honeymoon—presented her with tickets for ten days in Bali. Naturally, she was thrilled, although a little puzzled as to how Kyle had paid for the trip. He assured her that he hadn't used their credit card. What Kyle had done, however, was borrow $18,000 from his uncle, quietly exercising the right to unilaterally encumber a TIC interest, specifically by mortgaging his condo share to secure the loan.

If Kyle ever defaults on this loan, the uncle could foreclose on the security. Angela might have to buy him out to avoid a forced sale of her condo. At least Angela's 70% interest is safe: the share of a tenant in common can't be encumbered without her consent.

Bankruptcy is another situation that could lead to an involuntary transfer of a TIC interest. A bankruptcy trustee may sell a bankrupt co-tenant's interest to pay a creditor.

Since there isn't much of a market for most TIC shares, the creditor is likely to end up purchasing the interest and becoming a co-owner with the remaining tenant(s) in common.

Right of first refusal. Co-tenants can lessen the risk of unwanted new co-owners (such as Kyle's uncle, or a creditor in a bankruptcy) with a TIC agreement containing a **right of first refusal**. A right of first refusal provision requires that any owner who wants to sell his share must first offer that share to the existing owners, generally for purchase on the same terms. This provision can also apply to involuntary transfers such as a foreclosure or a bankruptcy sale.

Case to Consider...

A group of tenants in common signed a TIC agreement that contained a right of first refusal. Later, a co-tenant named Cathryn borrowed money from another co-tenant using her TIC interest as collateral. Cathryn then defaulted and, as a result, deeded her interest in the property to the co-tenant to avoid foreclosure. Was this deeding of Cathryn's interest in lieu of foreclosure a "sale" that triggered the right of first refusal? *Pellandini v. Valadao* (2003) 113 Cal.App.4th 1315.

Terminating a Tenancy in Common

What if the needs of the tenants in common change? Can they escape their co-tenancy? The answer is yes. They can either agree to terminate their co-ownership; or if that fails, they can seek termination in a courtroom.

 Refusing the Right of First Refusal

Examine any right of first refusal provision carefully. The requirements can handcuff an owner who needs to sell quickly—and that owner could be you.

For example, sometimes the buyout portion of the provision gives existing owners extra time to raise cash for purchasing the share. Or the provision may even grant the existing owners a right to purchase the share for less than its fair market value (see the case example *Schwartz v. Shapiro*).

Another consideration: perhaps you simply don't want to sell to your co-tenants. Imagine you own a TIC interest in a lakeside cabin where you used to take the kids on family vacations. Now your kids have kids. They'd like to be able to continue the family tradition by vacationing at the cabin. For financial reasons, you need to sell your interest, but you'd like to sell it to your children. Yet your co-owners can exercise their right of first refusal and buy out your interest, preventing your kids from buying it.

Voluntary Termination. If the co-tenants want to terminate the tenancy, they can agree to a physical division of their property, then sign and record the necessary deeds. Each co-tenant receives a piece of property owned in severalty. This is **voluntary partition**.

> **Example:** The Chens, a large close-knit family, decide they want to spend all their vacations together, so they buy a vacation property in Big Sur. They choose a ten-acre parcel of undeveloped land with lovely views. Before they can build their dream house, however, the family erupts into a prolonged argument over a family member's behavior at a wedding. Instead of resolving the argument, the two factions decide they no longer want to vacation together. They have the land surveyed and split into north and south parcels. One family group deeds its undivided ½ interest in the southern half to the other family group, and vice versa. Now each family group owns a five-acre tract in severalty. No further communication between them is needed.

Sometimes tenants in common decide that another form of co-ownership—joint tenancy or, for married co-tenants, perhaps community property—offers advantages over TIC. They agree to terminate their TIC, but no partition is needed: the parties just sign and record deeds granting themselves title in the new form.

Judicial Termination. The court can terminate a tenancy in common if a co-tenant refuses to agree to voluntary termination. Suppose the Chens couldn't decide if or how to divide their vacation property. One of the owners could have filed a **partition action** in superior court.

The plaintiff—the co-tenant seeking partition—must name everyone else with an interest in the property as a defendant in the action. The court settles on a plan for satisfying any lien holders with claims on the property and then, if possible, divides up the property into pieces proportionate to each co-tenant's interest. However, if there is an agreement between the parties that contradicts a partition, such as a right of first refusal, the partition action may not necessarily happen. This is illustrated in the next case.

Case Example:

Esther Schwartz and David Shapiro bought an apartment building as tenants in common. A week later, they signed an agreement creating a right of first refusal. Under the agreement, neither could sell his or her interest in the property without first offering to sell it to the other co-tenant for the original price.

Disputes later arose over management of the apartment house, and Schwartz sued for partition. Shapiro objected, and the court ruled in his favor. Partition constitutes a sort of forced sale, the court concluded, and therefore Schwartz had to offer Shapiro a chance to buy her interest for the original (now below-market) price before seeking partition. *Schwartz v. Shapiro* (1964) 229 Cal.App.2d 238.

Fairly often, physical partition won't work. For example, there's no practical way to divide the condo unit that Angela and Kyle own as tenants in common. In this situation, the court will order the sale of the property and divide the proceeds, with each co-tenant receiving his or her proportionate share of the money.

Extortion by Partition

It sometimes happens that a tenant in common threatens a partition action purely to extort concessions from his co-tenants. The co-tenants may reluctantly agree to give him special privileges in regard to the property, hoping to avoid a court battle and any decrease in property value from the partition.

To prevent blackmail by a cranky co-tenant, a TIC agreement should give the owners the right to buy out any co-tenant seeking a partition. Of course, if the co-tenants can't easily raise the purchase money, this provision won't protect them against a threatened partition.

Even if physical division is possible, dividing the property often renders it less valuable than it would be if sold as a whole. That would be true, for example, if commercial development would only be practical for the property as a whole. In that case, a court would probably order the property sold instead of partitioning the land.

Let's return to Angela again. Not long before she and Kyle married, Angela's father died. He left his artichoke farm in Castroville to Angela and her brother, Cesar. The farm isn't large, but the land is fully paid off.

Angela and Cesar have been arguing over management of the farm (Angela wants to take the farm organic and her brother doesn't). For them, however, partition is not a solution. Farming would hardly be profitable on half-sized lots. On the other hand, neither sibling wants to dishonor their father's memory by selling the property to a housing developer. Neither can afford to buy out the other's interest, so for now, at least, they'll continue as co-owners and try to get along.

Joint Tenancy

Let's turn now to the second type of co-ownership on our list: joint tenancy. Like tenants in common, joint tenants share undivided interests in the entire property. And the rights and duties of joint tenants are similar to those of tenants in common—the right to demand contribution, the right to profit from the property, and the duty not to commit waste. A joint tenant can also encumber her interest without consent from her fellow owners.

The most important difference between a TIC and a joint tenancy is the **right of survivorship**. On the death of a joint tenant, her share automatically passes in equal shares to the surviving joint tenants. People choose joint tenancy to avoid probate (the process of distributing a deceased person's property), but they must keep in mind that their heirs will not get the property when they die.

Example: Brothers Irving and David buy a vacation home near Lake Tahoe together, splitting the cost between them. Sometime later Irving dies while waterskiing on the lake.

If the brothers were tenants in common, Irving's undivided ½ interest would pass to the beneficiaries named in his will (his two daughters). David and his nieces would then own the property as tenants in common. David would still have a ½ interest, and each niece would have a ¼ interest.

But if the brothers were joint tenants, from the moment of Irving's death, David would have owned the entire property in severalty. Because of the right of survivorship, the provision in Irving's will leaving his interest to his daughters would have had no effect.

Case Example:

William and Loretta Petersen were married for 32 years. William had a daughter from a previous marriage. He recorded an assignment of his residence to himself and Loretta as "Husband and Wife, as joint tenants," and later a grant deed was recorded using the same language.

William died in 1992. His will mentioned his wife Loretta, but left nothing to her, instead giving his entire estate to his daughter and her family. Loretta sued, claiming that because of the joint tenancy, William had no interest in the residence that he could will to his daughter. The court recited the presumption that when determining the character of property after the death of a spouse, deeds are taken at face value. The daughter failed to overcome this presumption, and Loretta got the house. *Estate of Petersen* (1994) 28 Cal.App.4th 1742.

Creating a Joint Tenancy

The law makes tenancy in common the default form of co-ownership to help protect people from unwittingly making their will meaningless. Forming a joint tenancy requires clear evidence of intent.

The deed creating a joint tenancy should state that the co-owners take title "as joint tenants" or "in joint tenancy." Less specific wording may fail to show intent. Years ago, a California court stated that the phrase "to A and B, with the right of survivorship" would not create a joint tenancy, at least by itself. Even with unambiguous wording, a co-owner may argue that the grantor or the testator mistakenly confused joint tenancy with tenancy in common.

At any rate, using the correct language is only part of the formula for joint tenancy. Unless four particular conditions—known as the **four unities**—are fulfilled when creating and maintaining a joint tenancy, the joint tenancy fails and with that, the right of survivorship disappears. Instead, the property becomes either a tenancy in common or, for married couples, possibly community property.

Four Unities. The four unities required for a joint tenancy are unity of possession, interest, time, and title.

Unity of possession requires that all the joint tenants have the right to occupy the entire property—as with a tenancy in common. **Unity of interest** means that all the joint tenants must have the same size interest in the property (that is, two tenants would have to each own half the property, three tenants each own a third, and so on). **Unity of time** requires that all the joint tenants must take title to the property at the same time. And finally, for **unity of title** to exist, the joint tenants must all receive their ownership from the same deed.

This last unity—title created through a single deed or other instrument—doesn't pose much of an obstacle for property owners who want to establish a joint tenancy with someone new. A grantor owning property from an earlier conveyance can create a joint tenancy simply by deeding the property to herself and the new party as joint tenants. Before the legalization of same-sex marriage, same-sex couples often used joint tenancy to ensure that property passed to the surviving partner. If one partner owned property from before the relationship began, she would deed it to herself and her partner as joint tenants.

Note that as with TIC property, the joint tenants can grant a particular joint tenant exclusive use of the property in return for rent. California courts have held that this occupancy does not break the unity of possession—a sensible approach, since it allows the full range of use for joint tenancy property.

Liens and Joint Tenancy

Along with the right of survivorship, joint tenancy possesses one other unusual characteristic: surviving joint tenants take their interests free of any liens incurred by the deceased co-owner. The creditor's right to payment continues as an unsecured claim, but the deed of trust, judgment, or other lien on the property evaporates—along with the surviving tenant's obligation to pay it. This doesn't occur with any other form of property transfer. For example, when a tenant in common dies, her heirs take the property with any liens against it remaining intact.

Of course, this doesn't mean that converting ownership of a house into a joint tenancy will somehow erase a lifetime's worth of debt stacked up against the property. Consider the following case.

Case Example:

The Diedens sued Schmidt over a matter and lost. The court awarded Schmidt attorney's fees and costs. He recorded a judgment lien against some property in Berkeley that the Diedens owned as tenants in common. Schmidt later renewed his judgment lien against Mr. Dieden, but failed to do so against Mrs. Dieden.

A number of years later, the Diedens conveyed the Berkeley property to themselves as joint tenants. Only a year later, Mr. Dieden died. Liens attached to the interest of a joint tenant's property die with the tenant; Mrs. Dieden claimed that Schmidt's judgment lien on the property was thus extinguished on her husband's death. The court disagreed. Trying to evade an already-existing lien by converting the property to joint tenancy doesn't work. The lien remained in effect. *Dieden v. Schmidt* (2002) 104 Cal.App.4th 645.

Sophisticated creditors rarely accept a joint tenant's interest as security for a loan, knowing that their lien could disappear so easily. This would seem to make financing improvements on undeveloped joint tenancy property difficult. However, joint tenants acting together can raise money for development or other purposes by agreeing to a lien against the entire property. The document creating the lien must be signed by all the owners, which will allow the lien to survive the death of any particular joint tenant.

Right of Survivorship

Let's take a closer look at the right of survivorship. In a joint tenancy, the right of survivorship is automatic, with the surviving tenant(s) taking title at the moment of death. However, certain aspects of survivorship involving marketable title and simultaneous death merit a few comments.

Creating Marketable Title. Although a transfer of title by right of survivorship occurs at the moment a joint tenant dies, buyers and title companies will require a paper record of the transfer. Surviving joint tenants must record certain documents to clear their title and make it marketable. A title company will not insure a title that is not marketable.

Clearing title is accomplished by recording either:

- a certified copy of a court order stating the fact of death, describing the property, and identifying the surviving joint tenant(s); or
- a notarized affidavit of death that identifies the deceased as a joint tenant in the described real property, along with a certified copy of the death certificate.

When a notarized affidavit of death is used, the survivor also normally records an affidavit that identifies herself as the surviving joint tenant. However, title company permitting, there's no reason why these two affidavits can't be combined into one document.

 Nothing is Certain but Death and Taxes…but Costs Can Be Cut

In many states, probate lawyers charge by the hour and, with a relatively simple probate, the cost isn't all that great. California, however, allows probate lawyers to charge a percentage of the estate as a probate fee. A large but not particularly complex estate can provide a lawyer with a windfall.

Probate Code § 10810 allows an attorney to charge the following probate fees:
- 4% of the first $100,000 of the estate,
- 3% of the next $100,000,
- 2% of the next $800,000,
- 1% of the next $9,000,000,
- 0.5% of the next $15,000,000, and
- a reasonable amount (to be determined by the court) for all amounts above $25,000,000.

For an estate that consists of only a house worth $700,000, the probate fee works out to about $17,000—certainly enough to make joint tenancy look appealing to some property owners.

Note, however, that the lack of probate for joint tenancy does not mean that the property escapes estate taxes.

Simultaneous Death. What happens if all the joint tenants die at once? For example, suppose two cohabiting joint tenants perish together in a house fire. In that case, each co-owner's interest in the joint tenancy property would pass to his or her heirs; all the heirs of the deceased joint tenants would share title as tenants in common, at least until they arranged a sale.

Terminating a Joint Tenancy

Let's wind up our discussion of joint tenancies by exploring how people terminate them, voluntarily or involuntarily.

Partition. Joint tenants, like tenants in common, can voluntarily agree to partition their property. Alternatively, one joint tenant can force a partition with a lawsuit. In either situation, the partition ends the unity of possession and thus the joint tenancy, and results in

---

 Slayer Statute

Let's take a moment to discuss the scenario of one joint tenant killing the other, with an eye toward taking the property by survivorship. Although co-tenant killings certainly occur, the killer isn't likely to profit from the right of survivorship. For one thing, California's "slayer statute" prohibits people from taking property from anyone they've murdered.

Section 251 of the California Probate Code reads in part:

> A joint tenant who feloniously and intentionally kills another joint tenant thereby effects a severance of the interest of the decedent so that the share of the decedent passes as the decedent's property and the killer has no rights by survivorship.

But what happens to the killer's interest in the joint tenancy property? Before enactment of the slayer statute, the court addressed this issue in *Johansen v. Pelton* (1970) 8 Cal. App.3d 625. In *Johansen*, a man killed his joint tenant wife and then himself. While the husband certainly couldn't take his wife's half of the property as survivor, the court did allow the killer's heirs to take the man's original undivided one-half interest in the property. This rule does not allow the killer to benefit from wrongdoing; it merely prohibits civil confiscation of his property and leaves punishment to the Criminal Code.

A more recent case, *Estate of Castiglioni* (1995) 40 Cal.App.4th 367, concerned a 51-year-old woman who killed her 85-year-old joint tenant husband. The slayer statute had been enacted by then, and the court extended the approach taken in *Johansen*, ruling that a homicidal spouse keeps her half interest in joint property when she survives.

the former co-tenants each owning a piece of property in severalty. Note that a partition lawsuit doesn't actually terminate, or sever, the joint tenancy until the court enters its partition order.

As in a TIC, the threat of partition and sale can sometimes be used by one joint tenant to force concessions from the other(s). Here again, the parties may find some protection by including a right of first refusal in their joint tenancy agreement.

Other Methods of Severance. Joint tenancy can terminate without ending the parties' co-ownership. The owners may simply change their joint tenancy into a tenancy in common—or possibly, in the case of a married couple, to community property. A change in the form of co-ownership can result from transfer, declaration, or mutual agreement.

Transfer. A transfer of a joint tenant's interest can be voluntary or involuntary. Again, the obvious example of involuntary transfer is a trustee's sale to satisfy the creditors of a joint tenant in bankruptcy. Whether voluntary or involuntary, the transfer severs the joint tenancy. Bringing a new co-owner to the table breaks the unities of time and title.

Yet while a sale or other transfer ends the joint tenancy between the transferring co-tenant and the other co-tenant(s), if there are two or more remaining co-tenants these parties are still joint tenants in relation to one another. The severance of one joint tenant's interest does not disturb the joint tenancy of the others.

> **Example:** The Bad Hombres own their motorcycle clubhouse in joint tenancy. One night during a biker meet in Reno, an Hombre named Leech falls in love and marries a woman named Daisy. To prove his love, he secretly deeds his share in the clubhouse property to Daisy as separate property. This act severs the joint tenancy as far as Leech's undivided 1/19th interest is concerned, and Daisy is a tenant in common. However, the rest of the Hombres remain joint tenants in relation to one another.
>
> If Leech's wife dies, her interest will pass to her heirs. The right of survivorship does not apply to Daisy. But if one of the other bikers dies, the surviving Hombres will acquire his interest, because the right of survivorship still operates among them.

In California (and most other states), a joint tenant may sever the joint tenancy simply by deeding his interest in the property to himself in severalty. Prior to 1980, however, this wasn't allowed: California required a person who wanted to end a joint tenancy to first deed the interest to a "straw man," an intermediary. The intermediary would then immediately deed the property back to the party in severalty, terminating the joint tenancy. In 1980, a California court ended this rather pointless requirement, and a few years later, legislation was enacted specifically to allow joint tenants to unilaterally sever a joint tenancy. California Civil Code § 683.2 provides for severance of a joint tenancy by "execution of a written instrument that evidences the intent to sever the joint tenancy," such as a deed, a written declaration, or another written instrument.

Declaration. A co-owner can sever a joint tenancy simply by declaring, in writing, that the joint tenancy is severed. This declaration must be recorded to give the other co-owners constructive notice that one of them is now a tenant in common instead of a joint tenant (or, if there were only two joint tenants to start with, constructive notice that they now have a tenancy in common instead of a joint tenancy).

Written agreement. A joint tenancy may also be severed by written agreement between the joint tenants, even if the agreement doesn't expressly refer to termination. Suppose that two college friends buy property together as joint tenants. One friend later has children. If they sign an agreement stating that this friend can leave his half interest in the property to his kids, this permission cancels the right of survivorship and severs the joint tenancy.

Agreement not to sever. With all these methods of severance available, the right of survivorship is easily lost. Although a joint tenant's declaration of severance requires recording to take effect, most co-owners do not routinely check the public records and may have no idea that their joint tenancy has been severed. A dying old man, for example, might re-title his house in joint tenancy with his caregiver, as payment for her faithful nursing. If, sometime later, he quietly recorded a declaration of severance and made a will leaving his ½ interest in the house to his nephew, the caregiver would not know that this had happened. After her patient's death, she'd discover that she co-owned the house with the nephew instead of owning it in severalty.

Earlier, we mentioned that joint tenants can protect themselves against the threat of a partition action with a joint tenancy agreement; similarly, the agreement could prohibit co-owners from severing the joint tenancy without mutual consent. If this agreement is recorded, it puts potential buyers on notice that the sale of an interest in the property could be rescinded.

However, a mutual consent requirement should be approached with caution. As with a right of first refusal provision, you could end up trapped by the restriction.

Case to Consider...

A court order of dissolution severs any joint tenancy between married people. However, if one of the spouses dies during the dissolution proceedings, the surviving spouse takes title to the property.

Robert and Shirley owned real property as joint tenants. Their marriage soured and they started dissolution proceedings. A standard court order prohibited either spouse from disposing of any property during the proceedings. To prevent Shirley from taking the joint tenancy property if he died, Robert recorded a declaration of severance. Sure enough, Robert died while the dissolution was still pending. His wife claimed that his severance declaration was a disposition and hence invalid because it violated the court order. Was she right? *Estate of Mitchell* (1999) 76 Cal.App.4th 1378.

Community Property

Third on our list of co-ownership forms is community property. In a state that has a **community property** system, most property acquired by a couple during the marriage—including their wages—belongs to both parties equally, as the two halves of a marital community. However, only California, Arizona, Idaho, Louisiana, Nevada, New Mexico, Texas, Washington, and Wisconsin have community property systems.

In the majority of other states, married couples co-own real property as **tenants by the entirety.** Tenancy by the entirety resembles joint tenancy, but is limited to married couples. California does not use tenancy by the entirety. However, not long ago the state added an optional survivorship feature to the community property form of title; we'll discuss this at the end of the section.

The community property concept is a legacy of Spanish law. Shortly after the United States' treaty with Mexico in 1848, California adopted its first state constitution and honoring Spanish legal principles—included a provision that recognized community property rights. Since then, statutes and case law have further developed California's community property system.

Community property law gives each spouse an undivided ½ interest in most assets acquired during marriage. Requiring the sharing of marital assets is intended to strengthen families and to protect a non-wage-earning spouse from financial destitution if the marriage ends.

The Internal Revenue Code provides a significant tax advantage for this form of co-ownership. Upon the death of the first spouse to die, the adjusted basis of all the community property steps up (increases) or steps down (decreases) to the current fair market value. This allows the surviving spouse to sell the couple's residence or other property without having to pay tax on any profit.

Who Can Own Community Property?

In the context of community property law, California recognizes three types of couples: married people, registered domestic partners, and unmarried cohabitants. The first two groups can own community property; the last cannot.

Domestic Partners. Under California's Domestic Partner Rights and Responsibilities Act, couples may register as domestic partners by filing a **Declaration of Domestic Partnership** with the secretary of state. Domestic partners must share a common residence and agree to joint responsibility for each other's basic living expenses.

Section 297.5 of the Family Code gives registered domestic partners essentially all the rights and obligations of spouses, including the ability to hold property as community property. As you read along, keep in mind that our discussion of the property rules governing married couples also applies to registered domestic partners.

Unmarried Cohabitants. In about ten states, a man and woman who live together and publicly hold themselves out as married (for instance, living together and calling themselves husband and wife) for a certain number of years are considered legally married despite the lack of a ceremony or marriage license. This is known as a **common law marriage.** California law doesn't provide for common law marriage. However, if a couple is considered married under the common law of another state and then moves to California, California will recognize their marriage.

Classifying Property as Separate or Community

In California, all of the property owned by a married couple is classified as either the **separate property** of one spouse or the **community property** of both spouses. This classification determines who will get what when death or dissolution ends a marriage. Separate property is like any other property owned in severalty. The other spouse has no ownership rights to it.

Case Example:

Lulu Belle Washington sued her husband Alious for divorce. The court had to decide if their Los Angeles residence was community or separate property. At trial, Lulu Belle testified that she had paid $1,200 down for the property and had made all of the subsequent payments. Alious had contributed only $125 toward those payments.

The trial court ruled that Lulu Belle owned the house as separate property and the appellate court found insufficient evidence to overturn this decision. Alious did receive an award of $500 to compensate him for any community interest acquired in the separate property. *Washington v. Washington* (1949) 91 Cal.App.2d 182.

In a marital dissolution or upon the death of a spouse, courts often have to classify five different types of assets as either community or separate property. Specifically, they have to classify assets acquired:

- before marriage,
- by spousal effort (usually wages),
- by gift and inheritance,
- during separation, or
- in non-community property states.

Let's look at classification issues that arise with each of these types of assets.

Property Acquired Before Marriage. Property owned by either party before marriage is his or her separate property. For example, if Kyle owned a car before he and Angela got married, the car would remain Kyle's separate property after the marriage.

Case Example:

Steven Joaquin leased a 97-acre almond orchard from his father in 1972. The lease was for five years and contained an option to renew. Steven married Janiece in 1974. Steven's almond orchard income helped support the marital community. During the marriage, Steven exercised the option to renew the lease. Then in 1980, he filed for dissolution.

At trial, the parties agreed that the original five-year lease term rights were Steven's separate property. However, Janiece contended that his renewal transformed the lease into community property for the second five-year term.

By statute, property acquired during a marriage is presumed to be community property. The court's analysis turned on the word "acquired." An option to renew is acquired at the time the lease is originally signed, the court decided, not when it is later exercised. Thus, both lease terms were separate property. *In re Marriage of Joaquin* (1987) 193 Cal. App.3d 1529.

Note that a property doesn't lose its separate property status merely because a spouse sells it and then uses the proceeds to buy something else. The new asset will remain separate property, unless something else occurs to change it into community property. (We'll discuss how separate property can be converted into community property later in the chapter.)

Spousal Earnings from Efforts. Any money or property gained through the efforts of a spouse during the marriage belongs to the marital community. Even if only one spouse works, the income earned is considered community property.

If a spouse puts time and labor into his separate property during the marriage, any profits (or appreciation) resulting from these efforts are essentially earnings, and thus are also considered to be community property.

Gifts and Inheritance. Assets acquired during marriage by gift, inheritance, or descent (property from a relative who died without a will) are separate property. The reasoning behind this rule is that gifts and inheritances have nothing to do with the efforts of the community.

This rule extends even to gifts purchased with community funds by one spouse for the other. For example, birthday gifts received over the years would not be included in the marital asset pool during a division of community property.

People sometimes try to disguise a payment for services as a "gift" to avoid having the payment classified as community property.

> **Example:** Phil's elderly mother "gifts" him her vintage Cadillac. It's understood between the two of them that she's actually paying Phil for helping her with rent collection, yard work, and even a little nursing.
> The car is not a gift; Phil has earned it. That makes the vehicle the community property of Phil and his wife Anne, not Phil's separate property.

Property Acquired During Separation. For married couples who have obtained a judgment of legal separation, all income earned and property acquired after the date of the judgment is separate property. Earnings and acquisitions of a couple who are living "separate and apart" are also separate. Living separate and apart means the marriage has essentially ended; it doesn't include a merely temporary separation.

Case Example:

A Stanford University professor contended that he and his wife had lived "separate and apart" for two periods of approximately one year each. How much money his wife got in compensation for the increased value of certain real property and stock would turn on whether he could prove his claim.

The couple had been married for four years when the wife first moved out of their house and got an apartment nearby. She filed a petition for dissolution, but didn't pursue it. After about a year, they lived together again for nine months or so, and then the wife moved out again. A year later, she filed a fresh dissolution action; this time, she did not abandon her suit.

During the alleged separations, the parties' sexual relationship continued and they met each other several times in Puerto Vallarta. The husband traveled and the wife wrote him loving letters (although at the same time she wrote to her mother that she was thinking about ending the marriage).

The court found all this painted too muddy a picture of the parties' intentions for the husband to claim that they had truly lived "separate and apart" during the two periods. The wife was entitled to her share of the property value increase during the periods of semi-separation. *In re Marriage of Marsden* (1982) 130 Cal.App.3d 426.

Property Owned in Non-Community Property States. If a married couple moves to California from a non-community property state, California will treat any property they previously acquired in the other state as community property (provided it was acquired with community-type assets such as spousal effort or wages). Technically, this kind of property is called **quasi-community property**.

Converting Separate Property into Community Property

The characterization of an asset as separate or community property does not always remain fixed. Sometimes the marital community acquires an interest in one spouse's separate property almost by accident; at other times the spouses act intentionally to turn separate property into community property. We'll discuss the four ways separate property gets converted into community property: spousal labor, expenditure of community funds, deed or community property agreement, and commingling.

Spousal Labor. We mentioned that a spouse's labor or effort is community property. If the spouse expends labor on her separate property, a portion of that separate property equal to the value of her effort gets converted into community property. To see how this works, let's return to Angela and Kyle.

As you'll recall, Angela and her brother Cesar inherited their father's artichoke farm and are trying to make a go of the business.

To begin with, Angela's ½ interest in her father's farm was her separate property. (It was separate property because she acquired it before their marriage; but it would have been separate property even if she'd acquired it after the wedding, because she acquired it by inheritance.) However, Angela has been spending community effort on this separate property. She's met with Cesar many times to argue about farm business, and she spends several hours each month on conference calls with the farm manager. In addition, she drives out to the farm every few weeks.

Because Angela is investing effort in the business, a small but increasing portion of Angela's share of the farm is taking on a community character. If Angela and Kyle were to divorce, Kyle could claim an interest in Angela's share of the farm.

Community Funds. Instead of expending effort, a spouse may spend community funds on separate property and convert it to community property (intentionally or otherwise).

Angela and Kyle purchased their condo before marriage. That means each of them owns it as separate property, at least initially: Angela's 70% interest is her separate property, and Kyle's 30% interest is his separate property. Yet each month, Angela and Kyle pay the condo mortgage and other expenses from their earnings. In other words, they are using 100% community funds on separate property. Use of these community resources means that each spouse is slowly but steadily acquiring a community interest in the other's separate interest in the condo.

Note that it doesn't work the other way. Use of separate funds doesn't convert any portion of community property into separate property. However, a spouse who spends her separate funds on community property (for instance, making mortgage payments on the marital residence from a separate bank account) can seek reimbursement for these expenditures under Family Code § 2640. Obviously, she should keep a careful record of these payments.

Deed or Community Property Agreement. The quickest and most direct way to convert an asset into community property is with a deed: the parties simply deed their tenancy in common, joint tenancy, or separate property interests to themselves as a married couple.

A common method for accomplishing a blanket conversion of property to community status is through a written **community property agreement** (CPA). A CPA is three-pronged. First, the agreement converts all property currently owned by either spouse into community property. Second, it converts all property they will acquire in the future into community property. The third and final prong provides that on the death of one spouse, all community property immediately vests in the survivor, which keeps the property out of probate. After that, because death dissolved the community, the CPA has no further effect. The CPA is typically recorded along with the proof of death to evidence the transfer of title.

 Separate is as Separate Does

A spouse who wants to keep separate property separate can't spend community funds on the property's expenses. The spouse must maintain a checking account funded only with separate funds and use this account to pay separate property expenses. This practice provides the court with a solid paper trail if litigation occurs.

But consider the following scenario: A married man inherits a six-unit apartment building. It is tempting and economical for him to handle some of the maintenance or leasing tasks by himself. Yet when it comes to spousal effort, there's no way to set up a separate account. If he wants to make sure the apartment building remains entirely his separate property, his safest course would be to a hire a property management firm to run the building and pay the management fees from a separate property bank account funded by the rental income.

Commingling. The last way that separate property is converted to community property is through **commingling**. This applies mostly to money. If a spouse mixes or commingles his separate property with community assets in such a way that a court can't distinguish or trace which is which, the separate property is presumed to be a gift to the community—unless the amount of community property mixed in is negligible.

Commingling may occur intentionally or unintentionally.

> **Example:** When Consuelo got married, she started a joint checking account with her husband, Ricardo, by depositing $12,000 that she'd saved during her single days. Ricardo had no money to contribute, but afterwards both spouses proceeded to deposit their paychecks in the account and pay bills from it. A court would have no way to tell if any money remaining in the account was Consuelo's original $12,000 or community funds.

Rebutting the presumption that commingled separate property is a gift to the community isn't easy. The following case suggests that sometimes the character of the litigants can play a role in the court's decision.

Case Example:

Richard and Esther Mix were married in 1958. Esther was an associate attorney earning $400 a month. By the end their marriage ten years later, she was a law firm partner earning some $2,000 a month. Richard's work as a musician with the Sacramento Symphony Orchestra had proved "a good deal less remunerative," the court noted. His annual income averaged between $1,000 and $3,000.

Esther had entered the marriage with significant separate property—income-producing real property, life insurance, and bank accounts. The couple changed Richard's checking account into their joint account and used it to hold all their earnings, including Esther's income from her separate property. However, after five years, Esther began depositing most of the income from her law practice and various investments into a separate account.

In the dissolution trial, the court awarded Esther as her share of the community property the equity in the residence, an Oldsmobile, her law partnership, and a small amount of investment property. Richard got $6,137, two sailboats, and a Volkswagen. The court also ruled that the property Esther owned before the marriage had not lost its character through commingling and was still separate. Unsurprisingly, Richard appealed.

Esther had entered into evidence a schedule showing that each expenditure for separate property was closely paralleled in time and amount by income from separate property. Bank records showing specific deposits and withdrawals were unavailable, however, and Esther had failed to keep such records herself. Richard argued that the schedule alone wasn't enough to overcome the presumption that property acquired during a marriage is communal. The court agreed that the schedule by itself was insufficient. However, the schedule was backed up by Esther's personal testimony, which the trial court found credible, and that was good enough to affirm the ruling. *In re Marriage of Mix* (1975) 14 Cal.3d 604.

Spousal Control over Community Property

Generally, the spouses have equal say in managing community property. There is one notable exception: when one spouse runs a business, even if the business is community property, the other spouse has no right to participate in its management.

Let's look at the other rules governing control of a community's personal and real property.

Control of Personal Property. Generally, a spouse can sell or encumber the community's personal property without the other's consent.

> **Example:** Lowell and Gina own a 1960s Airstream trailer as community property. One day, a passerby knocks on the door of their house and offers Lowell $3,500 for the trailer. That strikes Lowell as a great deal, so he accepts the offer without consulting Gina.
>
> When Lowell tells Gina that he sold their trailer, she's furious. But it doesn't matter: Lowell's unilateral action was legally binding.

However, if Lowell had given the trailer away instead of selling it, Gina could have demanded it back. One spouse can't give away community personal property without the other's written consent. Further, a spouse can't sell or encumber the family's household furnishings, clothing, or personal property residence (such as a live-aboard boat) without the other's consent.

Control of Real Property. Documents for the purchase, transfer, or encumbrance of community real property (including leases for a period over one year) must be signed by both spouses. This is the **joinder requirement**, codified in Family Code § 1102.

Failure to get the signatures of both spouses makes the transfer or encumbrance of community real property voidable by the non-signing spouse. However, the legislature carved out an exception for a particular kind of encumbrance in response to the following case.

Case Example:

Joanna Droeger started a marital dissolution proceeding against her husband in 1982. She retained an attorney. Four years later, the dissolution action was still ongoing.

By this time, Joanna owed her attorney over $31,000 in fees and costs. She signed a deed of trust on some community real property to secure the debt. Joanna's husband objected, arguing that she needed his consent to encumber the community real property.

The court noted that although "economically weak" spouses were at a disadvantage in dissolution proceedings, the statute concerning the joinder requirement did not make any exception for spouses in dissolution actions. Thus, the husband could void the lien. *Droeger v. Friedman, Sloan & Ross* (1991) 54 Cal.3d 26.

The legislature responded to the *Droeger* case by passing a law permitting a spouse involved in a dissolution to encumber community property with a lien to pay attorneys' fees without obtaining the other spouse's consent. The lien attaches only to the interest of the spouse creating the lien. This exception to the joinder requirement is set forth in Family Code § 2033.

Obviously, a real estate agent should try to determine if the parties to a transaction are married (or in a registered domestic partnership) and, if they are, help secure all the necessary signatures. Even when a married person is selling only her own separate property, the safest course is to have her spouse sign a quitclaim deed releasing any interest in it. This will prevent the spouse from later claiming that the property was actually wholly or partly community property.

A spouse can lose his right to object to a transaction. If he doesn't consent to a transfer or encumbrance, but nonetheless accepts benefits from the transaction (for example, by using the proceeds of a mortgage), or if he fails to bring a timely lawsuit to void the transaction, he may be barred from contesting the transaction.

Distribution of Community Property on Dissolution or Death

Characterization of the property owned by a married couple as community or separate property is largely theoretical until the marriage ends, either in divorce or because one of them dies. When one of those events occurs, the extent of the community property must be determined and the property must be distributed.

Distribution on Dissolution. A court deciding a marital dissolution case must divide the community property equally between the spouses. In some community property states, the court can also distribute some or all of a spouse's separate property to arrive at what it considers to be a fair property settlement. California does not allow this, however.

During dissolution proceedings, both spouses must disclose all assets they hold that are (or that may be) community property. The penalty for failing to disclose an asset is fairly stiff: a spouse loses her right to her ½ interest in the undisclosed property (Family Code § 1101(h)).

Distribution at Death. When a married person dies, his separate property (if any) and his half of the community property are distributed according to his will. If no will exists, his property is distributed according to the rules of intestate succession.

By will. A spouse is entitled to will his undivided ½ interest in community property to anyone—for example, to a child from a previous marriage, to a friend, to a charity, or to anyone else.

> **Example:** Jules and Frank are married. The couple owns a home as community property. Jules wills his ½ interest in the property to his business partner, Conrad. When Jules dies, Frank and Conrad each own an undivided ½ interest in the property as tenants in common. Frank and Conrad don't get along, so Frank decides to seek a judicial partition of the property.

By intestate succession. If a married person dies **intestate**—without having made a valid will—all the community property vests in the surviving spouse. This default rule reflects what most married people would actually like done with their community property.

Nice Try

In December 1996, Denise Rossi had some good luck. She won $1,336,000 in a state lottery, her share of a ticket purchased in a pool at her workplace. The winnings were to be paid over 20 years. She immediately filed for divorce, but failed to tell her soon-to-be ex-husband about her lottery win. To carry out the deception, she gave the lottery commission her mother's address for the payments.

All went well for a year and a half. Then a company sent Denise an offer to buy out her payment stream in return for a lump sum—mailing this offer to her old address. The husband opened the letter and then sued for his share of the lottery winnings. The trial court awarded him all of the lottery winnings—Denise's ½ interest as well as his own ½ interest—as permitted by statute. The state appeals court affirmed the decision, though rather than add insult to injury, it did not award the husband his attorney fees. *In re Marriage of Rossi* (2001) 90 Cal.App.4th 34.

The law treats the separate property of an intestate spouse differently. If the decedent left a child, parent(s), sibling(s), or a sibling's children, the surviving spouse shares half of the deceased spouse's separate property with that relative or group of relatives. With two or more children, or with one child and one or more grandchildren from a deceased child, or with some other combination of children and grandchildren, the spouse gets a third and those other family members share the remainder. The spouse gets all the separate property if the decedent left no other immediate family. Probate Code § 6401 provides further details.

Community Property with Right of Survivorship

In 2001, California began allowing married couples to take title to property as **community property with right of survivorship** (CPRS) (Civil Code § 682.1). This hybrid of community property and joint tenancy provides the tax advantage of community property (the step-up in basis to fair market value on death) and the probate avoidance of joint tenancy. Because of this, community property with right of survivorship has rapidly become the common choice for California married couples.

The surviving spouse takes title to this type of community property automatically and regardless of what the decedent's will states. Most people view this as an advantage.

> **Example:** May and Graham are married. Their assets consist of a residence owned as community property with right of survivorship, two vehicles, a bank account, and shares of stock. When Graham dies, May learns that he has left his half of the community property to his cousin. The right of survivorship means that the house remains safely in May's hands. The cousin will take Graham's ½ interest in the rest of the community property, however.

May will still need to make her title marketable by taking the steps described earlier for surviving joint tenants: recording a proof of death (a court order or death certificate), and recording an affidavit that identifies Graham as one of the two co-tenants named in the deed and states that May is now the sole owner of the property.

We'll end this discussion of community property with right of survivorship—and community property generally—with an update on Angela and Kyle. They're doing pretty well. Last week, to celebrate their two-year wedding anniversary, the couple deeded their TIC interests in the condo to themselves as community property with right of survivorship. Now they each have an undivided 50% interest in the property, and Kyle can't obtain an additional mortgage on the condo without Angela's consent.

Ownership by Business Entities

So far, we've been discussing ownership of property by individuals; now we'll take a look at ownership by business entities. In most cases, an entity holds title in severalty, but it may also co-own property with other entities or individuals as tenants in common. Note that joint tenancy is ruled out; since business entities potentially never "die" (terminate), the survivorship aspect of joint tenancy would be meaningless.

In this section we'll take a look at the different types of business entities and how real property transactions are handled for each type. We'll conclude by examining the main considerations that influence an owner to choose one type of business organization over another.

Business Entities: the Basics

Co-owners of a business can form their enterprise in one of four common ways:

1. a general partnership,
2. a limited partnership,
3. a corporation, or
4. a limited liability company (LLC).

In addition, a business will occasionally be organized as a trust or joint venture. Let's take a short look at the governance structure for each of these forms.

General Partnerships. A **general partnership** springs into existence as soon as two or more people start a business together. No legal document is required. Each partner is an agent of the partnership and can bind the partnership to contracts. (See Chapter 6.) For this reason, no one should form a partnership with someone they don't fully trust.

Partnerships are governed by California's Uniform Partnership Act of 1994 (Corporations Code §§ 16100 – 16962.) The act provides that partners have an equal share in decision-making and profit-taking. This means that a partner who contributes 60% of the business capital will have no more voting power and no greater share of the profits than one who merely contributes 15%.

However, this and most other partnership rules can be altered through a **partnership agreement**. Partners in a small business who decide to forego the "unfriendliness" of a written agreement often later regret it. Drafting an agreement forces the parties to settle on a plan in case the relationship goes awry.

A partnership may acquire real property in its name or in the names of one or more partners. Partnership property may be bought or sold by any partner with the authority to do so. A partner's authority normally extends only to transactions that are in the course of ordinary business. So if the partnership routinely deals in land, any partner's signature on a deed or contract is likely to make the document enforceable. But an extraordinary transaction, such as the sale of the partnership's building, would require a partnership vote and the authorization of a particular partner to sign the deed and other necessary documents.

When one partner dies, his interest in the partnership property goes to the surviving partners. Although this may sound like joint tenancy, in this case the deceased partner's heirs actually do inherit something: the deceased partner's right to partnership profits. This means that the value of the partnership property stays in the deceased partner's estate.

Case to Consider...

The Patels owned the City Center Motel in Eureka. Their son Rajeshkumar became a 35% partner in the motel operation, and the partnership agreement provided that the son's approval must be obtained before the motel could be sold. But the Patels never recorded a deed or other document indicating the son's interest in the motel. A few weeks after forming the partnership, the elder Patels put City Center on the market. Another motel operator (also named Patel) made an offer on the property, and Rajeshkumar's parents accepted it. To the parents' dismay, however, when Rajeshkumar learned of the sale, he refused to consent.

Generally, an undisclosed partner like Rajeshkumar (someone not named on the deed or otherwise made known) cannot overturn a sale to a good faith purchaser. Yet the law also provides that partners must give unanimous consent to a contract or other act that puts an end to ordinary partnership business. The two rules conflict. How did the court decide which Patel got the motel? *Patel v. Patel* (1989) 212 Cal.App.3d 6.

Limited Partnerships. A **limited partnership** has one or more general partners and one or more limited partners. We've already described general partners in our discussion of general partnerships, so here we'll focus on limited partners. Limited partners have limited liability for the debts, obligations, and actions of the business. (We'll discuss the issue of liability later in the chapter.) In the real estate arena, limited partners are often real estate investors; they rely on their general partner(s) to find and manage commercial or residential properties for them.

A limited partnership requires formal creation. The partnership must file a **certificate of limited partnership** with the California secretary of state's office, identifying the general partners and providing an office address. The limited partnership must also identify an agent for receiving service of legal process; this is necessary in case someone wants to sue the partnership.

Corporations. In a corporation, ownership interests are divided into shares of stock; the **shareholders** are the owners of the business. The corporation sells shares of stock to raise money for operations.

Like limited partnerships, corporations require formal creation. **Articles of incorporation** must be filed with the secretary of state. The articles name the corporation, provide some general information, and—as with a limited partnership—state the name and address of an agent for receiving service of legal process.

Practically speaking, corporations may be divided into two types: those with numerous shareholders and those with few. When ownership is spread out among many, most shareholders lack real voting power and are relegated to a minor role, usually doing little more than approving the election of a board of directors at the required annual shareholders' meeting.

The corporation's **board of directors** makes policy decisions and appoints corporate officers—the president or CEO, vice president, and so on—who run the business day-to-day. In smaller corporations, the shareholders either serve on the board directly or control those who do.

How does a corporation handle buying and selling real property? Generally, the board must pass a resolution authorizing the transaction, unless the corporation routinely deals in real estate. Note, though, that corporate shareholders must approve any transaction involving the sale of property that constitutes the bulk of the corporate assets. So if real estate is being sold as part of a corporation's sale of itself, the buyer will want evidence of approval by the shareholders as well as by the board of directors.

Limited Liability Companies. Last, but certainly not least in our discussion of major business forms is the **limited liability company** (LLC). The LLC has become the most popular choice for small and medium-sized businesses since its introduction in the U.S. in the 1970s (the California legislature didn't authorize this form until 1994). We mention the LLC last because describing its structure is much easier now that we've covered partnerships and corporations. The LLC is a flexible form of entity: owners can fashion their LLC into something very much like a corporation, or into something more like a partnership.

LLC owners are called **members**. They own percentage interests in the entity, not shares of stock. In a member-managed LLC, the members act like partners and have agency authority and participate and vote on the issues confronting the business. In a manager-managed LLC, by contrast, governance is handled as in a corporation, with a manager or managers taking charge of day-to-day operations like a president and other corporate officers. The management structure chosen by the LLC will determine whether it authorizes real estate transactions like a partnership or like a corporation.

To create an LLC, **articles of organization** must be filed with the secretary of state. The articles of organization spell out which management structure the LLC has adopted and provide other basic information about the business, very much like a corporation's articles of incorporation.

Other Business Forms. While partnerships, corporations, and LLCs make up the bulk of business entities, a few other types are worth mentioning: joint ventures, trusts, and syndicates.

Joint ventures. A joint venture is like a partnership, but one whose life is limited to a single transaction or set of transactions. It isn't meant to be an ongoing business of infinite duration. An example of a joint venture would be a property owner, an architect, and a building contractor joining together to design and construct a particular building. Joint ventures are generally governed by partnership law.

Trusts. When a trust is created, the trustee is given the power to manage the trust property for the benefit of the beneficiaries. The trustor (also called the grantor) signs the trust documents, which appoint the trustee and establish the rules the trustee must follow. Certain types of trusts can hold title to real estate.

A **real estate investment trust** (REIT) is an entity created by investors to finance large real estate projects. The Internal Revenue Code offers tax benefits to real estate investors who organize their business as a REIT. A REIT must have at least 100 investors and at least 75% of its investment assets must be in real estate. Shares in a REIT are securities and subject to federal regulation.

A REIT avoids double taxation (discussed later in the chapter). As long as at least 90% of its income is distributed to the shareholders, the trust pays taxes only on the earnings it retains. Yet the investors, like corporate shareholders, are shielded from liability for the REIT's debts.

Syndicates. A syndicate is any business association in which investors pool their money together to establish and carry on an enterprise. A real estate syndicate is one in which the investors' money is used to purchase, manage, and/or develop a piece of real estate.

Note that a syndicate is not a specific type of legal entity. It may be organized as a partnership, corporation, limited liability company, or trust. Real estate investment trusts and real estate limited partnerships are both examples of real estate syndicates.

Considerations When Choosing a Form of Organization

Now that we've introduced the common types of business entities, let's examine the issues of liability and taxation. These two considerations largely determine whether business owners decide to organize their business as a general partnership, limited partnership, corporation, or limited liability company.

Liability. Like an individual, a business entity has contract and tort liability—that is, financial liability for contractual obligations it takes on and injuries it causes. For example, growers and sellers of contaminated vegetables may be forced to compensate consumers made ill by the produce. Business owners should consider the risk of personal liability when choosing a business form.

Personal liability: general partnerships. As a rule, the only business owners who have personal financial liability for business debts are general partners. If a partnership's assets can't satisfy a creditor's claim, the remaining financial liability passes straight through to the individual partners.

> **Example:** Linda, Yolanda, and Dominique are partners in LYDia, an haute couture fashion import business. They have contracts with boutiques all over the country to provide Karl Uber's fall line. However, Karl refuses to ship after Yolanda enrages him by suggesting he should've used fewer feathers in his current collection. The boutiques counting on Karl's clothing successfully sue LYDia for $380,000. However, LYDia's bank account,

inventory, and other assets amount to only $80,000. The three women must write personal checks totaling $300,000 to the judgment creditors.

By law, creditors can go after any one partner for the complete unpaid amount of a partnership debt. Thus, in the example above, if Linda and Yolanda are broke, Dominique would have to pay the entire $300,000.

So why does anyone organize their business as a partnership, a comparatively risky form? Well, for one thing, most partnerships have insurance that limits the partners' financial exposure, at least for tort liability. And there are practical advantages: the partnership offers an appealingly simple structure and an income tax advantage, as we'll discuss shortly. It's true, though, that many business owners who would have considered a partnership in the past now choose the LLC instead.

Limited liability: limited partnerships, corporations, LLCs. The limited partnership, the corporation, and the LLC all protect owners from personal liability. The most owners with limited liability can lose is whatever they have invested in the business.

However, banks and other significant creditors of small corporations or LLCs often require that owners personally sign for loans, leases, and other important transactions. This makes the limited liability issue somewhat moot.

Also, liability protection does not extend to one's own acts of negligence, intentional misconduct, or knowing violation of law, even when committed in a business capacity.

Case Example:

Pacific Landmark, an LLC, owned a business called Victoria's Health Care in a Los Angeles strip mall. Victoria's was an illegal massage parlor and house of prostitution. Ron Mavaddat managed the business. The city brought a "red light abatement" action to shut down the operation. The criminal code provided for collection of damages and, in some cases, fines.

Ron claimed personal immunity from the prosecution. He pointed to Corporations Code § 17158 (now § 17703), which protects individuals from liability solely because of their status as a manager of an LLC. (A similar law protects corporate officers.) However, the court declared, that statute wasn't intended to insulate individuals from their own wrongdoing. Ron knowingly abetted criminal activities and could not seek shelter under the Corporations Code. *People v. Pacific Landmark* (2005) 129 Cal.App.4th 1203.

Taxation. The other important factor that owners weigh when deciding on a business form is how the business will be taxed. Specifically, choosing the corporate form can have the undesirable result of "double taxation."

Taxation of corporations. Different types of corporations receive different tax treatment. The IRS classifies a corporation that has more than 100 shareholders or any foreign shareholders as a "C corporation." Certain small corporations may be eligible for S corporation status, which entitles them to a more advantageous tax treatment. A C corporation files a corporate tax return and pays income tax on its net profits. These profits are taxed again when the owners report their stock dividends on their personal income tax returns. This double taxation can have a fairly drastic effect on an owner's bottom line.

Formation Facts

No owner has protection from personal liability until the moment the articles of incorporation, organization, or limited partnership are time-stamped by the secretary of state's office. Until then, if the owners are conducting business, they do so essentially as a partnership and have personal liability.

The state doesn't charge much for filing articles: incorporation costs $100 and organization as an LLC costs $70. However, California also charges corporations and LLCs an annual minimum franchise tax of $800.

Example: A C corporation enjoys a million dollar profit for the year. It pays 34% in federal income taxes, resulting in a tax bill of $340,000 and leaving an after tax profit of $660,000. This profit is distributed in the form of dividends to the corporation's 200 shareholders.

Each shareholder reports their $3,300 of dividend income on their personal income tax return. The government takes another cut at this level, reducing each owner's share to $2,200 (assuming the owner's personal tax rate is 33%).

S corporations, however, do not pay corporate income tax. If this corporation had qualified as an S corporation, each shareholder would have received her dividend share of corporate earnings untaxed; that is, each would have received $5,000. The owner's personal income tax would reduce this amount to $3,350—much better than the $2,200 netted from a C corporation on the same profit.

Taxation of other entities. The earnings of S corporations, partnerships (both limited and general), and LLCs pass through to the owner intact; no income tax is paid at the entity level. The investor simply reports her share of the profits on her personal tax return.

Looking at the business entity issues we've discussed, you can see why the LLC has emerged as the favored form. An LLC offers liability protection and avoids double taxation, and there are no size restrictions the way there are for S corporations. Finally, an LLC may be managed in any way the owners want. It's a win-win form of organization for the owners.

As you can see, an owner must consider many different issues when deciding how to organize her business; how the business will take title to property is just one of these considerations. Similarly, individuals must make co-ownership decisions, too; for example, when two friends purchase property together, they must decide whether to take title as joint tenants or tenants in common. Whether your clients are buyers or sellers, individuals or a business, an understanding of co-ownership issues will help you recognize legal problems before they occur.

Case Law in Depth

The following case involves some of the legal issues discussed in this chapter. Read through the facts and consider the questions in light of what you have learned. Then read what the court actually decided.

In re Marriage of Delaney (2003) 111 Cal.App.4th 991

Steven bought a house in San Anselmo in 1982. Eight years later, Linda Sue began living with him on the property. They married five years after that. Steven had a learning disability that severely limited his reading comprehension; he relied on Linda Sue to handle all the legal and financial matters. Linda Sue had worked as a legal assistant doing probate work. She was familiar with joint tenancy, having gained an interest in real property through a survivorship deed created during a previous marriage.

In 1996, the couple sought a loan to enlarge their house to accommodate the birth of a second child. During this process, Steven signed a grant deed conveying the residence to himself and his wife as joint tenants. He testified that he did not realize he had given up any property rights until he noticed his wife's name on the property tax bill.

Some three years later, Steven filed a petition to dissolve the marriage. He sought to set aside the grant deed, claiming undue influence by his wife. The trial court found for Steven, ordering Linda Sue to sign a quitclaim deed and move out of the house. She appealed (and she also refused to leave the premises—a sheriff had to dislodge her).

On review, the appellate court noted that spouses owe each other a duty of utmost fair dealing. When one spouse comes out ahead in a transaction, courts will presume undue influence. However, the wife pointed out that courts also presume that the holder(s) of record title are the property's owners (and she and Steven were the record owners, as joint tenants).

The questions:

Did the presumption of undue influence apply? If so, did Linda Sue rebut this presumption? What about the presumption that a recorded title should be taken at face value—does that outweigh a presumption of undue influence?

The court's answers:

The appellate court addressed these issues by quoting from the case *In re Marriage of Haines* (1995) 33 Cal.App.4th 277: "'We conclude that application of [the presumption of record ownership]...is improper when it is in conflict with the presumption of undue influence...Any other result would abrogate the protections afforded to married persons and denigrate the public policy of the state that seeks to promote and protect the vital institution of marriage.'"

The court went on to say, "[T]he trial court properly determined that the presumption of undue influence applies to the facts of this case. Consequently, it was Wife's burden to establish that Husband's transmutation of the Property to joint tenancy was freely and voluntarily made, with full knowledge of all the facts, and with a complete understanding of the effect of a transfer from his unencumbered separate property interest to a joint interest as Husband and Wife."

The court found there was "substantial evidence" to support the trial court's conclusion that the wife failed to meet this burden. "This evidence showed that Husband suffered cognitive impairments and as a consequence had entrusted all marital financial and legal matters to Wife, trusting and relying upon her judgment and management in this regard. Wife, on the other hand, had extensive experience in legal and financial matters, and had personal experience in her previous marriage with the transmutation of separate property to joint tenancy. Husband signed the documents conveying his unencumbered separate interest in the Property to himself and Wife jointly without questioning her instruction that it was necessary to do so. On this record, we have no basis for overturning the trial court's determination that Wife had failed to rebut the presumption of undue influence."

The result:

The presumption of undue influence outweighed the presumption that a recorded title is valid. The court overturned the joint tenancy deed and the husband regained ownership of the residence as his separate property.

Chapter Summary

- Tenants in common may have unequal percentages of ownership, but they each have the right to possess the whole property (unity of possession). They must contribute to the payment of necessary property expenses, and they may sell or encumber their interests without the consent of their co-tenant(s). Voluntary or involuntary partition divides the property into parcels owned in severalty and ends the tenancy in common.

- A joint tenancy requires unity of time, title, interest, and possession. Joint tenants have the right of survivorship: when a joint tenant dies, the surviving co-tenant(s) take equal shares of the deceased's interest. A joint tenant cannot transfer her joint tenancy interest by will. However, joint tenancies can easily be severed.

- All property acquired by the effort of a California resident who is married or in a domestic partnership is community property. Property acquired before marriage or by gift or inheritance is separate property. Transfer or encumbrance of community real property requires the signatures of both spouses; otherwise, the non-consenting spouse has a reasonable period in which to void the transfer. California allows community property to be held with right of survivorship.

- A general partnership begins as soon as two or more people start a business together. Each partner is an agent of the partnership and can bind the partnership to contracts. California's Uniform Partnership Act gives partners an equal share in decision-making and profit-taking regardless of their percentage of interest. However, a partnership agreement may provide for a different allocation of voting rights and profit-taking.

- A limited partnership consists of one or more general partners and one or more limited partners. The limited partners have limited liability, and usually play only a limited role in managing the partnership. To create a limited partnership, a certificate of limited partnership must be filed with the secretary of state's office.

- A corporation is owned by shareholders. The corporation sells shares of stock to raise money for operations. To create a corporation, articles of incorporation must be filed with the secretary of state. The corporation's board of directors makes policy decisions and the officers run day-to-day operations.

- The owners ("members") of a limited liability company (LLC) own percentage interests in the entity, not shares of stock. In a member-managed LLC, the members act like partners; they have agency authority and participate and vote on the issues confronting the company. In a manager-managed LLC, governance is handled as in a corporation; a manager or managers take charge of day-to-day operations like a president and other corporate officers.

Key Terms

- **Severalty** – Sole ownership; an individual or entity that does not share title with anyone holds title in severalty.

- **Tenancy in common (TIC)** – The default form of co-ownership between unmarried individuals; each co-tenant has an undivided interest in the whole and may freely encumber or sell that interest.

- **Joint tenancy** – In a joint tenancy, the co-tenants have the right of survivorship, so that a deceased co-tenant's interest in the property automatically passes to the other co-tenant(s) on his death, without probate.

- **Partition** – A voluntary or court-ordered physical division of real property held in co-ownership into parcels owned in severalty.

- **Community property** – In California and a number of other states, most property acquired by a couple during marriage belongs equally to the two spouses as a marital community; also applies to registered domestic partnerships in California.

- **Community property with right of survivorship** – Community property that automatically passes to the surviving spouse when a spouse dies.

- **Separate property** – Any property owned by a married person that is not community property, such as property acquired before marriage or after marriage by gift or inheritance.

- **Commingling** – When separate and community property interests have been mixed so thoroughly that a court cannot trace the asset's origins; the separate property interest is usually treated as community property.

- **General partnership** – A form of business entity that springs into existence as soon as two or more persons enter into a business together; doesn't offer protection from personal liability.

- **Limited partnership** – A form of business entity that includes one or more general partners (who have unlimited liability) and one or more limited partners (who have limited liability).

- **Corporation** – A form of business entity owned by shareholders and run by a board of directors and officers; offers limited liability but may be subject to double taxation.

- **Limited liability company (LLC)** – A business entity owned by "members" and either "member-managed" like a partnership or "manager-managed" like a corporation; all members have limited liability.

Chapter Quiz

1. Two brothers inherit a piece of property. They own it as:
   a) community property
   b) joint tenants
   c) tenants in common
   d) Either b) or c)

2. Marcia works in San Francisco as a lawyer. Her husband is an unemployed writer. After five years, Marcia divorces her husband. She saved $120,000 during the marriage. The court awards her husband half of this money, in accordance with the rules of:
   a) joint tenancy
   b) equity
   c) community property
   d) tenancy by the entirety

3. Phil, Bill, and Jill own property as tenants in common. Phil wants to sell his interest to a third party for $145,000. A provision in the TIC agreement requires that he first offer his interest to Bill and Jill for an amount equal to any third party offer (here, $145,000). This provision is called a/an:
   a) option
   b) agreement not to sever
   c) right of first refusal
   d) covenant not to compete

4. A tenancy in common requires unity of:
   a) title, interest, and possession
   b) time, title, interest, and contribution
   c) time, title, interest, and entirety
   d) possession

5. Richworth and Poormouth took title to a house as joint tenants and agreed that Poormouth would live there. Poormouth paid rent for the privilege of exclusive occupancy. Did this arrangement sever their joint tenancy?
   a) Yes, because unity of possession is one of the four unities
   b) No, because unity of possession is not one of the four unities
   c) No, because joint tenants can give up the right to possession in return for rent from a joint tenant
   d) No, because a joint tenancy can only be severed by recording a declaration of severance

6. Jack and Jill have been married 25 years. Eight years ago, Jack secretly bought a Mt. Shasta area cabin using salary he had hidden away. Recently, he mortgaged the cabin property with plans to buy a boat. Jill saw the check for the loan proceeds and learned of the cabin's existence. Which of the following is true?
   a) Jill cannot challenge the mortgage because each spouse has the right to manage all real or personal community property
   b) Because Jill did not consent, the mortgage is voidable by Jill
   c) The cabin is not community property because Jack saved his earnings separately
   d) California does not recognize community property, so Jill cannot challenge the mortgage

7. Sally and Sam are married. When Sam inherits his mother's house and its modest mortgage, both Sally and Sam use their salaries to make the monthly mortgage payments. A court would probably classify the house as:
   a) separate property because inheritances are separate property
   b) a mix of separate property and community property
   c) entirely community property
   d) quasi-community property

8. A, B, and C own land as tenants in common. A and B each own an undivided ¼ interest, and C has an undivided ½ interest. C wills all his property to his son, C Jr. When C dies, how is the land ownership shared?
   a) A and B each own an undivided ¼ interest, and C Jr. has an undivided ½ interest
   b) A and B each own an undivided ¾ interest
   c) A and B each own an undivided ½ interest
   d) A and B and C Jr. each own an undivided ⅓ interest

9. A real estate broker organizes her business as an LLC. One day, she tells a lie about a property to move a sale along. The buyer finds out about the deception and backs out of the deal. The seller wants to sue the broker and her LLC for fraud. The LLC only has $10,000 in assets, but the broker has a great deal of equity in her home. Which of the following is true?
   a) LLCs offer limited liability, so all the seller could do is sue the LLC
   b) The seller could sue the broker personally, as LLCs do not offer limited liability
   c) LLCs offer limited liability, but this protection doesn't extend to a member's wrongful acts, so the seller can sue the broker personally
   d) None of the above

10. Jack and Francine own a ski shop. One day, a clerk fails to properly adjust a customer's bindings; as a result, the customer falls and suffers a paralyzing injury. Jack and Francine are forced to sell their home to pay the judgment. Their business is probably organized as a/an:
    a) LLC
    b) S corporation
    c) C corporation
    d) partnership

Chapter Answer Key

Chapter Quiz Answers:

1. d) People can inherit property as either joint tenants or tenants in common. A will might also specify that a married couple or domestic partnership will take property as community property, but because blood relations can't become domestic partners, that answer wouldn't apply here.

2. c) California is a community property state; the general rule is that community property is divided equally between the spouses on dissolution.

3. c) People include a right of first refusal to avoid becoming tenants in common with strangers. In contrast, an option is a contractual right to purchase something and is rarely, if ever, linked to an offer by a third party.

4. d) While joint tenancy requires a number of "unities," tenancy in common only requires that the owners share possession of the property.

5. c) Joint tenants must share an equal right to possession. But for practical reasons, the courts allow joint tenants to grant exclusive possession to one of their number in return for rent.

6. b) If community real property is mortgaged without the consent of the spouse, that spouse may consent to the encumbrance after the fact or, alternatively, void the mortgage.

7. b) Sam inherits the equity in the house as separate property. The marital community acquires an interest in the house proportionate to the amount the community expends on mortgage payments.

8. a) Tenants in common pass their interest to their heirs. Thus, C Jr. takes his father's ½ interest. If it had been a joint tenancy, C Jr. wouldn't inherit any interest in the property.

9. c) LLCs only protect an owner from liability for the wrongful acts of others (for example, employees or contractors). Insurance can protect personal assets from liability for one's own negligence.

10. d) Investors in LLCs and corporations have limited liability; general partners do not.

Cases to Consider... Answers:

Tenancy in Common

Pellandini v. Valadao (2003) 113 Cal.App.4th 1315. Deeding a property to a lender to avoid foreclosure can sometimes trigger a right of first refusal, since it's a transfer of ownership. However, like most right of first refusal provisions, the provision in this agreement was designed to prevent unwanted third parties from becoming co-tenants. Thus, the court ruled, the transfer of Cathryn's interest to an existing co-tenant did not trigger the right to buy.

Joint Tenancy

Estate of Mitchell (1999) 76 Cal.App.4th 1378. The right of survivorship doesn't vest until someone actually dies. All Robert disposed of was a potential right. Survivorship isn't a true real property interest, and therefore his severance wasn't a disposition of real property and did not violate the court order. Robert's heirs took his half of the joint tenancy property, not Shirley.

Ownership by Partnerships and Other Associations

Patel v. Patel (1989) 212 Cal.App.3d 6. All partners must approve any act that makes it impossible for the partnership to continue ordinary business. The court decided that this rule was fundamental and trumped the undisclosed partner rule. The motel could not be sold without the son's approval.

List of Cases

Dieden v. Schmidt (2002) 104 Cal.App.4th 645
Droeger v. Friedman, Sloan & Ross (1991) 54 Cal.3d 26
Estate of Castiglioni (1995) 40 Cal.App.4th 367
Estate of Mitchell (1999) 76 Cal.App.4th 1378
Estate of Petersen (1994) 28 Cal.App.4th 1742
Garibaldi v. Garibaldi (1968) 264 Cal.App.2d 9
In re Marriage of Delaney (2003) 111 Cal.App.4th 991
In re Marriage of Joaquin (1987) 193 Cal.App.3d 1529
In re Marriage of Marsden (1982) 130 Cal.App.3d 426
In re Marriage of Mix (1975) 14 Cal.3d 604
In re Marriage of Rossi (2001) 90 Cal.App.4th 34
Johansen v. Pelton (1970) 8 Cal.App.3d 625
Patel v. Patel (1989) 212 Cal.App.3d 6
Pellandini v. Valadao (2003) 113 Cal.App.4th 1315
People v. Pacific Landmark (2005) 129 Cal.App.4th 1203
Rossetto v. Barross (2001) 90 Cal.App.4th Supp. 1
Schwartz v. Shapiro (1964) 229 Cal.App.2d 238
Washington v. Washington (1949) 91 Cal.App.2d 182

Chapter 6

Agency Law

Outline

Introduction

Agency relationships are fundamental to the real estate profession, and agency law shapes a real estate agent's work with clients and customers. This chapter examines the nature of agency and gives an overview of agency relationships in real estate transactions. It discusses the agent's authority and the principal's liability for the agent's actions, and it also explains how agency relationships are created and terminated. California's laws concerning the specific duties real estate agents owe clients and customers will be covered in Chapter 7.

Agency Law and the Real Estate Profession

An **agency relationship** exists when one person (known as the **agent**) acts as the legal representative of another person (known as the **principal** or **client**). A **third party** is someone outside the agency relationship whom the agent interacts with on behalf of the principal. (Third parties are also sometimes referred to as customers.)

For example, when a seller lists her home with a real estate broker, it creates an agency relationship between them. The broker is the agent, and the seller is the principal or client. If the broker negotiates with a prospective buyer, the prospect is a third party.

A principal can empower an agent to do almost anything the principal could legally do herself. In the eyes of the law, when an agent performs an authorized action as the principal's representative, it's as if the principal had performed that action herself. The act of the agent is treated as an act of the principal.

An agency relationship is a **fiduciary relationship**, which means that the agent occupies a special position of trust in regard to the principal. The agent owes special legal duties (fiduciary duties) to the principal that she does not owe to third parties. (See Chapter 7.)

Agency relationships arise in many different arenas, not just in real estate transactions. For example, an agency relationship exists between an attorney and her client, between a trustee and his beneficiary, and between an author and her publishing agent.

The body of law that applies to agency relationships regardless of the context, including real estate, is called **general agency law**. The rules of general agency law originally developed as common law rules (in other words, they were established in court decisions), but in California they have been codified in Civil Code §§ 2295 – 2357.

California has some additional statutory provisions that specifically concern agency relationships in real estate transactions. These appear in Civil Code §§ 2079.13 – 2079.24. Some of the rules we'll be discussing in this chapter are from those statutory provisions concerning real estate agency, and others are from the general agency law provisions.

Although our discussion will focus on agency relationships in real estate sales transactions, keep in mind that these rules also apply to lease transactions, where a real estate broker serves as the agent of a landlord or tenant instead of a seller or buyer.

Agency Relationships in Real Estate Transactions

Let's start with an overview of the various types of agency relationships that may exist in a real estate transaction. We've already mentioned the agency relationship between a seller and the broker who lists her property, but that's not necessarily the only agency relationship in the transaction.

The seller and the buyer may each be represented by their own agent, or one party may have an agent while the other party does not. In some cases, an agent represents both the seller and the buyer at the same time. Agency relationships can seem complicated and confusing even in the most ordinary real estate transactions.

Terminology adds to the confusion. "Real estate agent" is the common term for a real estate licensee (either a broker or a salesperson). As a result, a buyer might regard a licensee he's been working with as "my real estate agent" when no agency relationship has actually been established.

We'll use an example to review how a typical home sale works and lay the groundwork for our discussion. Then we'll examine the possible agency relationships in this example and other transactions. The basic question is, "Who's representing whom?"

> **Example:** A property owner named Sally wants to list her home for sale, so she calls ABC Realty, a local brokerage. Steve, a real estate salesperson who works for ABC, comes to Sally's house and takes the listing. Steve is the listing agent. ABC Realty may also be referred to as the listing agent, or may be called the listing broker.
>
> Steve submits information about Sally's property to the multiple listing service (MLS) that ABC Realty belongs to, so that the information can be shared with other real estate agents. Other real estate agents who belong to the MLS start bringing buyers to see Sally's property.
>
> Meanwhile, a potential buyer named Burt contacts a different brokerage, XYZ Realty, for help in finding a home to buy. Barbara, a real estate salesperson who works for XYZ, reviews the MLS listings and takes Burt to look at several suitable properties, including Sally's. Burt decides he'd like to buy Sally's house.
>
> The next step is for Burt to make an offer to Sally. Barbara, Burt's real estate agent, prepares the offer for him, filling out a purchase agreement form. In this situation, because she's helping a buyer to make an offer, Barbara is referred to as the selling agent. Her employing broker, XYZ Realty, may also be called the selling agent, or else the selling broker.
>
> Barbara submits Burt's offer to Steve, the listing agent, and Steve presents the offer to Sally for her consideration. Then there are negotiations, until the parties reach a final

agreement. These negotiations don't take place directly between Sally and Burt, however; instead, they're mainly carried out by Steve, the listing agent, and Barbara, the selling agent, on behalf of the parties.

In a transaction like this, it's easy to assume that the listing agent is representing the seller and the selling agent is representing the buyer, but that may or may not be the case. Before going into the issue of the agency relationships between the agents and the buyer and seller, however, we need to explain the agency status of real estate salespersons in relation to their brokers and the principals.

The Salesperson as the Broker's Agent

A real estate salesperson's license does not authorize the salesperson to represent members of the public (buyers and sellers) directly. Instead, a salesperson must be employed by a real estate broker. He can work with members of the public only as an agent of his employing broker.

In the example given above, Sally (the seller) probably thinks of Steve (the listing agent) as "my agent." But technically, ABC Realty, Steve's employing broker, is Sally's agent. In his work with Sally, Steve is acting as an agent of ABC Realty.

Similarly, Barbara (the selling agent) is an agent of XYZ Realty, her employing broker. (As we'll discuss below, XYZ Realty may or may not have an agency relationship with the buyer or the seller.)

This technical point—that a real estate salesperson is the agent of her employing broker, not the agent of the seller or the buyer—doesn't make a lot of practical difference. The Real Estate Law specifically provides that as an agent of her broker, a salesperson has the same duties and obligations to clients and customers that her broker does. Even so, it's an important point to keep in mind. It affects the broker's liability for the salesperson's actions, as we'll discuss later in the chapter.

In this book, we generally follow standard usage and refer to real estate licensees as real estate agents, distinguishing between brokers and salespersons only when necessary. And we usually call a salesperson a seller's or buyer's agent, even though it's actually the employing broker who's the seller's or buyer's agent. So, for instance, we'll refer to Steve, the listing salesperson, as Sally's agent.

Here's one other point concerning the relationship between brokers and salespersons. In California, either an individual (Jan Jones) or a corporation (ABC Realty, Inc.) can be licensed as a broker. An individual licensed as a broker is directly responsible for supervising the real estate salespersons who work for her. When a corporation holds a broker's license, a person called the **designated broker** is responsible for supervising the salespersons who work for the company. The salespersons are the corporation's agents, under the supervision and control of the designated broker. (See Chapter 8 for more about brokers and salespersons.)

Agent-Client Relationships

Now let's turn to the central issue: the different types of agency relationships that a real estate broker (and, through the broker, a real estate salesperson) can have with clients.

California law recognizes three types of real estate agency relationships: seller agency, buyer agency, and dual agency. The main differences between them can be summarized as follows:

- **Seller agency.** A seller's agent represents only the seller. He must obey the seller's instructions and promote the seller's interests.
- **Buyer agency.** A buyer's agent represents only the buyer. She must obey the buyer's instructions and promote the buyer's interests.
- **Dual agency.** A dual agent represents both the seller and the buyer, and must not favor either party over the other.

Some real estate agents specialize in seller agency or buyer agency, but many vary their role from one transaction to the next. In other words, an agent might serve as a seller's agent in the sale of Property A, a buyer's agent in the sale of Property B, and a dual agent in the sale of Property C.

Confusion About Agency. Although the differences between the three types of real estate agency relationships sound simple enough, it isn't always obvious which party an agent is representing in a particular transaction. For example, a buyer might think that a real estate agent is representing him, when the agent is actually representing the seller. Or a seller might think that an agent is representing only her, when in fact he's acting as a dual agent. This type of confusion is a serious problem, because it may lead a buyer or seller to confide in or rely on the advice of a real estate agent who actually has a duty to promote the other party's interests.

> **Example:** In our earlier example, Barbara from XYZ Realty showed Burt, the buyer, several properties, and when he decided he wanted to buy Sally's property, Barbara prepared his offer for him. Even though Barbara has been providing services to the buyer, she isn't necessarily the buyer's agent. Under certain circumstances, she could be representing Sally, the seller, instead. In other words, both the listing agent, Steve, and the selling agent, Barbara, may be seller's agents in this transaction. If so, it's Barbara's duty, as well as Steve's, to promote the seller's interests.
>
> Suppose Burt doesn't understand that Barbara is the seller's agent. He asks her how much he should offer for Sally's property. He says he really wants the house and is willing to pay the full asking price, but he's thinking about starting out with an offer of $17,000 less. As the seller's agent, Barbara has a legal duty to pass this information along to Sally. If Burt had understood Barbara's role, he probably wouldn't have confided in Barbara.

A buyer's confusion about the role of the agent he's working with may result in an **inadvertent dual agency**. If a seller's agent gives the buyer the mistaken impression that she's representing him, it could create an agency relationship between them by implication. If that happens, then the agent is inadvertently (accidentally) representing both the seller and the buyer in the same transaction; she's become an inadvertent dual agent. Either the buyer or the seller, or both, could end up suing the agent for breach of her agency duties.

Some of California's current laws concerning real estate agency are intended to prevent this type of situation. But to fully understand the current laws, it's necessary to know a little about how real estate agency relationships used to work.

The Growth of Buyer Agency

In 1983—long before buyer representation became a household word—the Federal Trade Commission (FTC) completed a study on the real estate industry. According to this study, 72% of all property buyers thought that the real estate agent they worked with represented them, even though virtually all agents at that time represented the seller. The report sent shock waves through the industry. Why was this statistic a problem? It meant that almost 75% of all buyers were "spilling their guts to agents who weren't representing them," according to one buyer's agent.

The results of the 1983 FTC study led to a flurry of state legislation that mandated real estate agency disclosure. California was one of the first states to pass an agency disclosure statute; its law went into effect in January of 1988. By the end of 1988 most states had passed some kind of disclosure law.

A perhaps unforeseen by-product of this study and the subsequent disclosure laws was the growth of buyer agency. Once buyers became more aware that agents were representing the seller, many decided that they wanted their own agents. In 2015, over 85% of all home buyers in the United States used a buyer's agent.

MLS listings and subagency. A multiple listing service usually requires its member brokers to use standard listing agreement forms. For many years, MLS listing forms included a provision called the **unilateral offer of subagency**. Under this provision, the broker of any agent who brought buyers to see a property listed through the MLS automatically became an agent of the listing broker and a subagent of the seller. A **subagent** is an agent of an agent. An authorized subagent represents the principal just as the agent does.

> **Example:** Let's go back to our earlier example again. As you'll recall, Sally's house is listed with ABC Realty. Barbara, from XYZ Realty, found a buyer for the house. Under the unilateral offer of subagency provision in the old MLS form, XYZ Realty would automatically have been an agent of the listing broker, ABC Realty, and a subagent of the seller. As a result, Barbara would automatically have been representing the seller, even though she had been working closely with the buyer.

Because of this unilateral offer of subagency provision, in most transactions all of the real estate agents involved were representing the seller. That was true even if they worked exclusively with the buyer and never met the seller. To create a buyer agency, a real estate agent working with a buyer would have to formally reject the unilateral offer of subagency, then enter into an agreement with the buyer. This was done very rarely.

Cooperation provision. In the 1990s, as new legal requirements and other considerations made real estate transactions more complex, buyers became interested in having their own agents represent them. In response to the growing popularity of buyer agency, multiple listing services replaced the unilateral offer of subagency in their listing agreements with a "cooperation and compensation" provision. Under this provision, other members of the MLS are only cooperating agents, not subagents. A **cooperating agent** is simply any member of the MLS who tries to find a buyer for another broker's listing.

With the cooperation and compensation provision, MLS listing agreements don't automatically assign an agency role to cooperating agents. Instead, individual cooperating agents decide whether to represent the buyer or the seller in a given transaction. So with a current MLS listing form, XYZ Realty and Barbara don't automatically represent the seller. Barbara is free to act as Burt's agent if she chooses to do so.

Agency disclosures. The change in the listing agreement made it so that a cooperating agent isn't automatically the seller's agent. But that doesn't mean she's automatically the buyer's agent, either. So it's still possible for a buyer to assume that the real estate agent he's been working with is his agent when she hasn't taken on that role. To prevent this problem, California real estate agents must comply with the **agency disclosure law** in most real estate transactions. This law requires agents to inform buyers and sellers, in writing, whether they're representing the seller, the buyer, or both parties in a particular transaction. We'll discuss the details of the disclosure requirements in the next chapter; for now, let's take a closer look at seller agency, buyer agency, and dual agency.

Seller Agency. As we said, listing a property with a real estate broker establishes an agency relationship between the seller (the principal) and the broker (the listing agent). In the listing agreement, the seller authorizes the listing agent to act as her representative in interactions with prospective buyers. (Listing agreements are covered in Chapter 9.)

Listing agent's role. As the seller's agent, the listing agent helps the seller set a listing price based on current market conditions; advises his client on preparing the property for showings; markets the property, keeping his client's goals in mind; and negotiates on his client's behalf with buyers and selling agents. The listing agent must treat buyers fairly and honestly, but his primary duty is to promote the seller's interests, putting them above everyone else's, including his own. (We'll discuss the specific duties that real estate agents owe clients and third parties in the next chapter.)

Under California law, a listing agent always represents the seller. There are situations in which a listing agent may also be representing the buyer in the same transaction; in other words, the listing agent may be a dual agent (see below). But a listing agent can never be the buyer's agent and not the seller's. (Civil Code § 2079.18.)

Other seller's agents. While the listing agent is always the seller's agent, other agents involved in the transaction may also be representing the seller. In our example, Barbara, the selling agent, may represent Sally, the seller, through a traditional subagency arrangement. In that case, Barbara can provide various services to Burt, the buyer, but she must not put Burt's interests ahead of Sally's.

Don't confuse the terms "seller's agent" and "selling agent." A seller's agent is an agent who is acting as a representative of the seller. A selling agent is the agent who finds a buyer for the property. The selling agent may or may not be the seller's agent.

> ### ▶ Agency Alternatives?
>
> There are two other types of representation that are missing from our list of the types of real estate agency relationships: designated agency and transactional agency. They're not on the list because neither of them is recognized by California law. While other states have permitted these alternatives as a way to avoid some of the agency problems we've discussed—particularly problems with dual agency—California has not adopted them. (Under California law, a real estate agent must be representing either the seller or the buyer, or both parties, in every transaction.) Even so, it's helpful to know what they are and perhaps consider why California doesn't allow them.
>
> **Designated Agency:** This type of agency relationship was designed to help avoid the conflict of interest involved in dual agency. If the salesperson who's representing the buyer and the salesperson who's representing the seller both work for the same broker, in California that creates a dual agency situation; both of the salespeople and their broker are dual agents. In some other states, however, if the broker practices designated agency, the broker would designate the first salesperson as the agent of the buyer (and only the buyer), and designate the second salesperson as the agent of the seller (and only the seller). Each client is represented only by the individual salesperson who has been designated as that client's agent; the rest of the broker's salespeople do not represent that client. The designated agent can fully represent her client, instead of walking the tightrope of dual agency. In some states that allow designated agency, even the broker avoids a dual agency relationship in this situation.
>
> **Transactional Agency (Non-Agency):** Some states allow brokers to have what is essentially a "non-agency" relationship with their clients. Brokers acting in this capacity may be referred to as "transaction brokers" or "facilitators." Instead of acting as an agent and owing fiduciary duties to the client(s), the broker is merely a middleman, shepherding the parties through the transaction to closing without serving as an advisor to either one of them.

Listing agent may be selling agent. Sometimes the listing agent is the only agent involved in a transaction. If no other agent has been assisting the buyer, then the listing agent is also considered to be the selling agent.

> **Example:** Suppose that Burt, the buyer, wasn't working with another real estate agent when he came to see Sally's property. As a result, it was Steve, the listing agent, who showed Burt the house. When Burt decided to make an offer, Steve filled out the purchase agreement form for him. This makes Steve the selling agent as well as the listing agent in the transaction between Sally and Burt.

As with any other selling agent, when the listing agent is also the selling agent, there isn't necessarily any agency relationship between him and the buyer (Civil Code § 2079.22). In the example, Steve may still be representing only Sally, instead of both Sally and Burt.

Buyer Agency. Nowadays, a buyer often has an agent of his own to represent him. In addition to taking care of the tasks that can be performed by seller's agents (such as preparing the buyer's offer), a buyer's agent can give the buyer objective advice, helping him to evaluate properties and decide how much to offer when the right one is found. A buyer's agent promotes the buyer's interests in the same way that a seller's agent promotes the seller's.

A buyer agency relationship is ordinarily established with a written contract called a buyer representation agreement (see Chapter 9).

> **Example:** When Burt goes to XYZ Realty and talks to Barbara about buying a home, he decides he doesn't just want her to show him houses, he wants her to represent him as a buyer's agent. She and Burt sign a buyer representation agreement making XYZ Realty Burt's agent.

Although that's the usual way of establishing a buyer agency, there are circumstances in which a real estate agent can become a buyer's agent without a written agreement. We'll discuss this later in the chapter.

Compensation and agency. A buyer representation agreement may provide that the buyer will pay his agent a flat fee, an hourly rate, or a percentage commission. But most buyer's agents receive their compensation from the seller, not the buyer. This is the result of the **commission split** arrangement used by multiple listing services.

Under MLS membership rules, when a property is sold, the listing broker is required to split (share) the brokerage commission with the selling broker. That's true whether or not the selling broker was representing the buyer. Civil Code § 2079.19 provides that the selling broker's acceptance of compensation that was originally paid by the seller doesn't affect the agent-client relationships. It doesn't create an agency relationship with the seller, and it doesn't compromise an existing agency relationship with the buyer.

Dual Agency. A dual agency exists when a real estate agent represents both the seller and the buyer in a real estate transaction. Before acting as a dual agent, a broker must have the informed written consent of both parties to the transaction. Dual agency without full disclosure is a violation of the Real Estate Law (Business and Professions Code § 10176(d)) and may lead to suspension or revocation of the broker's license. (See Chapter 8.) In addition, both the buyer and the seller may be released from any obligation to pay a commission, and either party may be allowed to terminate the purchase agreement.

A dual agent owes fiduciary duties to both principals and must do his best to treat them equally. Because the interests of the buyer and seller usually conflict, it can be difficult for a dual agent to promote both parties' interests at the same time. It would be easy for a dual agent to use one party's confidential information to the advantage of the other party, but this clearly would violate his agency duties. In fact, Civil Code § 2079.21 specifically states that a dual agent must have express written consent to disclose to the buyer that the seller is willing to sell the property for less than the listing price, or to disclose to the seller that the buyer is willing to pay more than the price offered.

Dual agency isn't always a deliberate choice; it may arise out of circumstances. For example, a real estate agent who's both the listing agent and the selling agent in a transaction may be a dual agent. This might happen when a buyer the agent has been representing decides to buy one of the agent's own listings. More commonly, a dual agency arises when the selling agent works for the same broker as the listing agent. In that situation, the broker becomes a dual agent.

> **Example:** Suppose that Steve and Barbara both work for ABC Realty, instead of for two different brokerages. Steve has the listing for Sally's property, and Barbara has a buyer agency agreement with Burt. When Burt makes an offer to purchase Sally's property, ABC Realty becomes a dual agent.

Now that you're familiar with the different types of real estate agency, we'll take a closer look at the legal consequences of an agency relationship.

Agency Authority and Liability

Once an agency relationship has been established, the acts of the agent are treated as the acts of the principal. This means the agent's acts can be legally binding on the principal, and the principal can be held liable for harm caused by the agent's acts. However, there's an important limitation on that rule: the principal is bound by or liable for the agent's acts only if they're within the scope of the agent's authority. If the agent exceeds his authority, the principal usually won't be obligated or liable to a third party. As a result, it's important to know how far a particular agent's authority extends.

Scope of Authority

The scope or extent of an agent's authority is generally determined by agreement between the parties and by customary business practices.

For example, a listing broker's authority depends on the terms of the listing agreement, interpreted in the light of customary practices in the real estate industry. A standard listing agreement is understood to authorize the broker to find potential buyers for the seller's property and negotiate with them on the seller's behalf. The broker isn't authorized to enter into a contract with a buyer or to convey the seller's property. A seller could authorize a broker to do those things, but a standard listing agreement doesn't give the broker that authority.

Depending on the nature of the agency and the principal's goals, an agent's authority may be either ongoing or limited to a single transaction. Civil Code § 2297 states that an agent for a particular act or transaction is called a **special agent**. In an ordinary sales transaction, a real estate agent is a special agent.

> **Example:** Alvarez lists his commercial property in San Diego with Broker Jones. Jones has the authority to negotiate with third parties concerning the sale of Alvarez's property. Once a buyer for the property is found, Jones's agency will end. Thus, Jones is a special agent.

A **general agent**, by contrast, is authorized to handle matters for his principal in a specified area on an ongoing basis. For example, a property manager is usually a general agent.

> **Example:** Suppose that Alvarez has hired Broker Jones to manage the San Diego property rather than sell it. Jones has the authority to act as Alvarez's representative in the

management of the property on an ongoing basis, not just in a single transaction. Jones is a general agent.

Whether the agency is special or general, the principal may give the agent broad powers or very limited ones. For example, a property management agreement might authorize the property manager to handle virtually all of the day-to-day tasks involved in managing the property: to set the rental rates, sign leases, hire and fire a resident manager and maintenance staff, contract for repairs, collect rents, and so on. Or, if the property owner wants to be closely involved in the day-to-day management and make most of the decisions, the agreement could give the property manager much more limited authority.

Actual and Ostensible Authority

While an agent's authority is largely determined by agreement between the parties, an action doesn't have to be specifically authorized by the principal in order to fall within the scope of the agent's authority. There are essentially three types of agency authority:

- express actual authority,
- implied actual authority, and
- ostensible authority.

Actual Authority. The authority that a principal grants to his agent is known as **actual authority**. Actual authority is either express or implied.

Express. Authority communicated to the agent, whether orally or in writing, is called **express actual authority**. For example, a listing agreement signed by the seller expressly authorizes the broker to find a buyer for the seller's property. The broker has express actual authority to find a buyer.

Implied. In addition to expressly granted authority, an agent also has the **implied actual authority** to do "everything necessary or proper and usual in the ordinary course of business" to achieve the purpose of the agency. (Civil Code § 2319(1).) Express and implied authority work hand in hand, but implied authority isn't written or spoken; it's simply understood to have been granted, because the goals of the agency couldn't be achieved without it.

> **Example:** Let's consider Broker Jones and her client, Alvarez, again. As the listing agent for Alvarez's property, Jones has been given the express authority to find a buyer. Jones has also been given the implied authority to do whatever is considered necessary, in the ordinary course of business, to achieve that goal. This would include advertising the property on her website, putting a "For Sale" sign on the property, receiving offers from prospective buyers, and so on. The broker has implied actual authority to do those things, even though they're not specified in the listing agreement.

Implied authority is necessary because it isn't practical for the principal to anticipate and authorize every possible action needed to fulfill the purpose of the agency. But implied authority can't conflict with the agent's express authority; implied authority merely allows the agent to take actions reasonably necessary to make sure that the principal's express instructions are carried out. A court evaluating the reasonableness of a particular action may look at customary business practices in the community.

Ostensible Authority. While actual authority is authority that a principal has actually granted to an agent, **ostensible authority** is authority that the principal, intentionally or negligently, allows a third person to believe the agent has been granted. Ostensible authority is also called **apparent authority**. The ostensible agent (or apparent agent) appears to have been authorized to do something, but in fact has not. In some cases, the ostensible agent had no actual authority whatsoever; in other cases, he simply exceeded his actual authority.

If a third party relies in good faith on an ostensible agent's authority, the principal will be bound by actions within the scope of the ostensible authority.

> **Example:** Seller Michael watches his listing agent, Broker Camilla, sign a purchase agreement in his name, and then tell the buyer that it is a binding contract. Michael says nothing to contradict Camilla's statement to the buyer. In fact, Camilla was not authorized to sign a contract that would bind Michael, but Michael allowed the buyer to believe that Camilla's signature was an authorized action. In this situation, Camilla might be considered to have ostensible authority to sign the contract on Michael's behalf.

Ostensible agency is based on the doctrine of **estoppel**. Under this legal doctrine, someone who causes another person to rely on her actions or words is prohibited, or "estopped," from later taking a different position that would be to the other person's disadvantage. A principal is estopped from denying an obligation that was based on an ostensible agent's acts. In the example above, if Michael later refuses to fulfill the terms of the purchase agreement, a court could hold that he is estopped from denying the contract, because Broker Camilla had ostensible authority to sign it for him.

Whether an ostensible agency exists is a question of fact based on the circumstances of a particular case. In general, for an ostensible agency to exist, the following requirements must be met:

- the third party's belief in the agent's authority was reasonable;
- the belief was based on a deliberate or negligent statement, act, or failure to act by the principal (not just on the agent's acts or statements);
- the third party had reason to rely on the agency;
- the third party's reliance was not negligent; and
- the third party will be harmed if the agent's ostensible authority is denied.

There are limits on the types of actions that can be binding on the principal based on ostensible authority. Civil Code § 2306 states that an agent never has the authority, either actual or ostensible, to perform an act that the third party she's dealing with knows or suspects would be a fraud against the principal.

Also, a third party dealing with an agent must make a reasonable effort to determine the scope of the agent's actual authority. As we said above, an agent won't be considered to have ostensible authority to do something if the third party's reliance on the agent's supposed authority was not reasonable. Depending on the circumstances, failure to inquire into the scope of the agent's authority could be considered negligent. If so, there was no ostensible authority, and the principal would not be bound by or liable for the agent's acts.

Case to Consider...

Kaplan purchased three parcels of agricultural property for $1,000,000. Broker Marsh, who operated a Coldwell Banker franchise called Coldwell Banker Citrus Valley Realtors (CVR), negotiated on behalf of the sellers. Kaplan later discovered that the property was not as the sellers and Marsh had represented. Kaplan sued the sellers and Marsh, and also named Coldwell Banker as a defendant under an ostensible agency theory. Kaplan claimed that Coldwell Banker should be liable, because the misrepresentations had been within the scope of CVR's ostensible authority as Coldwell Banker's agent.

Kaplan later settled with the sellers, and Marsh went bankrupt, leaving only Coldwell Banker as a defendant. The trial court granted Coldwell Banker's summary judgment motion (a motion to decide the issue in Coldwell Banker's favor without a jury trial). Kaplan appealed.

Kaplan's argument was that he "went for the sign" and trusted the Coldwell Banker name because it was a large, reputable company. Kaplan believed that CVR was an agent of Coldwell Banker, and had purchased the property in reliance on that belief. Coldwell Banker argued that CVR was merely a franchise operation and pointed to disclaimer language in the franchise agreement that required CVR to hold itself out to the public as "an independently owned and operated member of Coldwell Banker," language that was found in small print on CVR's advertising. Should the court find for Kaplan or Coldwell Banker? Why? *Kaplan v. Coldwell Banker Residential Affiliates, Inc.* (1997) 59 Cal.App.4th 741.

Warranty of Authority

Someone who acts as an agent without authority, or who acts outside the scope of his authority, is liable to third parties for a breach of an implied **warranty of authority**. Civil Code § 2342 states that a person who acts as an agent warrants that he has the authority to do so. The implied warranty of authority is like an unspoken promise, made by the agent to third parties, that the principal has granted him the authority to act as the principal's agent.

This warranty protects third parties in situations when the principal isn't liable, because the supposed agent had neither actual nor ostensible authority. (In other words, the principal didn't grant authority, and the principal also didn't intentionally or negligently allow a third party to believe that she had granted authority.) Without the implied warranty of authority, a third party would have no way to recover damages for the harm caused by the agent's unauthorized actions.

Civil Code § 3318 provides the remedy for breach of the implied warranty of authority: the agent will be required to compensate the injured party by paying the same amount that would have been collected from the principal had the agent been authorized to act on the principal's behalf.

Case Example:

From 1934 to 1942, Cheda rented a garage from Henry Grandi on a month-to-month basis. In 1941, Henry suffered a mental breakdown due to a stroke. Henry's brother, Lloyd Grandi, a real estate broker, began acting for Henry in connection with the garage and other matters. Henry had not authorized Lloyd to be his agent, however. (Henry was eventually declared incompetent by a court, although that didn't occur until 1943.)

In 1942, Cheda decided to expand his business, but only if he could get a long-term lease and make some physical changes to the property. Lloyd wrote Cheda a letter offering him a five-year lease with an option to renew. The letter contained language such as, "I have analyzed the matter of your leasing Henry's garage...and I have attempted to arrive at a solution which would be fair to you and also to him. I have decided as follows...." Cheda replied that the terms were acceptable and Lloyd prepared three copies of the lease, instructing Cheda to sign and return them. The lease provided for Henry's signature, but Lloyd never discussed the lease with his brother, and Henry never signed it. Cheda was unaware of these facts; however, Cheda had known the Grandi family for many years and knew that Lloyd often acted as the family representative.

In 1946, the McFaddens started negotiations with Lloyd to purchase the garage property. Lloyd told them that Cheda had only a month-to-month tenancy, but Cheda told them he had a lease. Lloyd finally produced the lease copies, unsigned by either himself or Henry, and the McFaddens concluded that the unsigned lease was invalid. They subsequently bought the property and doubled Cheda's rent. Cheda sued.

The court found that Lloyd had breached his warranty of authority to Cheda. Lloyd's actions implied that he had the authority to act on Henry's behalf. Cheda relied on these representations; therefore, Cheda was entitled to damages against Lloyd for the breach of the warranty of authority. *Cheda v. Grandi* (1950) 97 Cal.App.2d 513.

Liability Issues

So far we've mainly discussed how an agent's actions can be legally binding on the principal. For example, a contract signed by an agent can be enforced against the principal if signing the contract was within the scope of the agent's authority. Now let's consider agency and tort liability: liability for negligent or wrongful acts committed by an agent.

Vicarious Liability. As we discussed in Chapter 1, when a person does something negligent or intentional that causes harm to another person, it's called a tort. Someone who commits a tort may be held liable and required to compensate the person who was harmed. This rule applies to someone acting as an agent, just like it does to anyone else. An agent is liable for harm caused by his own negligent or wrongful acts.

> **Example:** Victor's property is listed with Broker Jones. Broker Jones makes misrepresentations about the property to a prospective buyer, resulting in a financial loss for the buyer. The broker can be held liable and required to pay damages to the buyer.

But the agent isn't the only one who can be held liable. Under a very old common law doctrine called **respondeat superior**, a master (an employer or principal) is legally responsible for the actions of a servant (an employee or agent). This rule prevents a person from avoiding responsibility for an action by having someone else carry it out.

Thus, when a third party is harmed by something an agent did or failed to do, the principal as well as the agent may be required to compensate the third party. This is called

vicarious liability. (An event or condition is experienced "vicariously" when a person indirectly suffers or enjoys something that's actually happening to another person, not to him.)

> **Example:** In the previous example, not only can Broker Jones be held liable for harm caused by her own misrepresentations, her principal (the seller) can be held vicariously liable for harm caused by Broker Jones's misrepresentations. That's true even if the seller was unaware of the misrepresentations and would not have authorized them if he had been aware of them.

In this type of situation, a court is likely to impose **joint and several liability**, which means that both the seller and the broker would be fully liable for the buyer's loss. If the broker failed to pay, the seller could be required to pay the full amount of the judgment awarded to the buyer. (The seller would then have the right to sue the broker.)

Vicarious liability applies only to torts that the agent commits "in the transaction of the business of the agency." (Civil Code § 2338.) In other words, the principal isn't liable for absolutely everything the agent does wrong while he's representing the principal. The negligence or wrongdoing must occur in connection with tasks the agent performs to carry out the purpose of the agency.

Vicarious liability for salesperson's torts. Just as a principal is vicariously liable for his real estate broker's torts, a broker is vicariously liable for torts committed by a real estate salesperson who works for her, since the salesperson is the broker's agent. In addition, since the salesperson's principal (the broker) is responsible for the salesperson's actions, and the broker's principal (the client) is responsible for the broker's actions, the client may also be liable for the salesperson's actions.

> **Example:** Marie is a salesperson who works for Broker Jones. She's the listing agent for Victor's property. She misrepresents the property to a prospective buyer. Marie herself, Marie's principal (Broker Jones), and Broker Jones's principal (Victor, the seller) can all be held liable to the buyer.

Imputed Knowledge. Another rule that may affect the liability of a principal and an agent is the **imputed knowledge** rule. This concerns information that the principal should communicate to the agent, and information the agent should communicate to the principal. Under California Civil Code § 2332, if either the agent or the principal has information that ought to be communicated to the other "in good faith and the exercise of ordinary care and diligence," then the other is also considered to know that information—even if the information was never actually conveyed. In other words, the principal's knowledge is automatically imputed to the agent, and the agent's knowledge is automatically imputed to the principal.

> **Example:** A home inspector tells the seller's agent that there's dry rot in a crawl space in the house. In the inspection report, the inspector fails to include any information about the dry rot. The agent also forgets to tell the seller about the problem and, as a result, the seller never learns about it. Even so, if the problem later becomes an issue in a lawsuit, the seller could be held to have known about it when she conveyed the property to the buyer. The agent's knowledge of the problem is imputed to the seller.

Because of the imputed knowledge rule, a principal can be held liable for her agent's failure to disclose information to a third party, even if the principal had no knowledge of that information. (We'll discuss the duty to disclose information to third parties in Chapter 7.)

Delegation of Agency Authority: Subagency

The last aspect of agency authority and liability we'll examine is what happens when an agent delegates some of his authority to a subagent. As explained earlier, a subagent is the agent of an agent. Let's take a look at the rules of subagency.

We'll start with the rules from general agency law, which appear in Civil Code §§ 2349 – 2351, and then explain how they're applied in the context of real estate agency.

Appointing Subagents. There are two main issues in connection with subagency:

1. whether the principal is responsible for a subagent's actions, and
2. whether the original agent is responsible for a subagent's actions.

The answers to these questions depend on whether the subagent was lawfully appointed or not. Civil Code § 2349 states the circumstances under which an agent is allowed to appoint subagents. Unless specifically forbidden by the principal, an agent may delegate his powers to another person in the following situations (and in no others):

- the required act is purely mechanical (for example, putting up "For Sale" signs);
- the required act is one that the subagent can lawfully perform and the agent cannot (for example, performing an inspection that requires special licensing, or providing legal advice);
- it's the custom in the local community to delegate the type of powers in question; or
- the principal has specifically authorized the delegation.

Principal responsible for actions of authorized subagent. According to Civil Code § 2351, a lawfully appointed subagent represents the principal in "like manner with" (in the same way as) the original agent. As a result, the principal may be bound by or liable for the subagent's actions.

On the other hand, Civil Code § 2350 states that if an agent employs a subagent without the authority to do so, then there is no agency relationship between the principal and the subagent. In that case, only the agent, not the principal, is bound by and liable for the subagent's actions.

Agent not responsible for actions of authorized subagent. After establishing that a lawfully appointed subagent represents the principal, Civil Code § 2351 goes on to say that the original agent is not responsible to third parties for a lawfully appointed subagent's actions. In other words, once there's an agency relationship between a principal and a subagent, there's no longer an agency relationship between the original agent and the subagent. The original agent is off the hook, in effect, even though he was the one who appointed the subagent. The principal has agency relationships with both the original agent and the subagent, but there's no agency relationship between the agent and subagent.

Again, however, if the subagent wasn't lawfully appointed, there's no agency relationship between the principal and the subagent, and the agent who appointed the subagent remains liable for the subagent's actions.

Cooperating Brokers May Be Authorized Subagents. In the real estate context, a court may apply these rules from Civil Code §§ 2349 – 2351 to decide whether a seller can be bound by or liable for the actions of a cooperating broker. A listing agreement may expressly authorize the listing broker to delegate agency authority to cooperating brokers who belong to the multiple listing service. Even in the absence of such a provision in the listing agreement, the delegation might be considered authorized because it's customary in the real estate industry. So a cooperating broker's actions can be binding on the seller, and the seller can be held liable for things a cooperating broker has done. Whether a cooperating broker will be considered an authorized subagent of the seller in a particular case will depend on the circumstances.

Even when a cooperating broker is held to be the seller's subagent, the listing broker as well as the seller may be held liable for the cooperating broker's actions. The listing broker isn't necessarily off the hook, in spite of Civil Code § 2351, discussed above. This area of the law is complicated and somewhat unresolved.

Salespersons Aren't Subagents. A listing broker can delegate agency authority to a cooperating broker, so that the cooperating broker is an authorized subagent of the seller. However, a salesperson from the listing broker's firm can't be a subagent of the seller. Civil Code § 2079.13(p), which gives a definition of "subagent," specifically says, "[The term] "subagent" does not include an associate licensee who is acting under the supervision of an agent in a real property transaction."

> **Example:** Carlos hires ABC Realty, owned by Broker Finch, to sell his home. Ann is a salesperson who works for Broker Finch. Ann is an agent and employee of Broker Finch, but she is not Carlos's subagent.

What's the point of this statutory provision? Essentially, to make it perfectly clear that a salesperson's employing broker is always responsible for the salesperson. A broker will be held vicariously liable for the actions a salesperson takes while carrying out her duties as a real estate licensee. The broker is never off the hook where his salespersons are concerned. (See Chapter 8 for more information about a broker's supervisory responsibilities.)

Creation of an Agency Relationship

The principal and the agent take on the duties and liabilities imposed by agency law automatically when an agency relationship is created. So it's important to understand the various ways in which an agency relationship can arise.

In this section, we'll begin with a brief look at how agency relationships and contractual relationships overlap. Then we'll examine the issue of intent to enter into an agency relationship, and how courts evaluate whether the parties had that intent. Finally, we'll look at the four main ways that agency relationships can be created.

Agency: an Ongoing Source of Legal Problems

Just in case real estate agents think agency issues aren't important anymore, here are some sobering statistics.

According to the National Association of Realtors® 2015 legal survey, agency issues are still among the most common causes of real estate-related legal disputes. Out of a total of 195 recent real estate cases that were reviewed, there were 74 cases that involved agency issues. Breach of fiduciary duties was addressed in 45% of the agency cases, buyer representation in 16%, and dual agency in 11%.

Agency issues were also subjects of legislative and regulatory attention: agency disclosure and designated agency were both common targets of recent laws and regulations.

Agency Formation and Contract Law

Many agency relationships are established when the principal and the agent enter into a contract with one another. For example, the agency relationship between a seller and her listing broker is created when they enter into a listing agreement. That means the principal and agent are taking on contractual obligations at the same time that they're taking on agency duties. The contractual obligations—such as the seller's obligation to pay the broker a commission—are determined by the terms of the agreement and by the rules of contract law. The agent's powers and both parties' agency responsibilities are determined by the terms of the agreement and by the rules of agency law. Agency law and contract law overlap in governing the relationship between the broker and seller under the terms of their listing agreement.

Although an agency relationship is often created by a contract, it isn't necessary for the parties to have a legally enforceable contract in order to have an agency relationship. For example, as we'll discuss in Chapter 9, a listing agreement must be in writing to be enforceable. A broker isn't entitled to sue for a commission unless she has a written agreement with the seller. Yet if a broker and a seller have an oral listing agreement, that's sufficient to establish the broker's agency. As the seller's agent, the broker owes fiduciary duties to the seller and can represent the seller in dealings with third parties, even though she can't sue for compensation if the seller decides not to pay her.

Intent to Create an Agency

Not only is it unnecessary to have a written contract in order to create an agency relationship, no other legal formalities are required. Instead, the intent to create an agency relationship is essentially all that's needed to create one. In other words, the principal must intend to employ the agent to act on his behalf, and the agent must intend to accept that employment. Agency is a consensual relationship, requiring the mutual consent of both parties.

The most straightforward indication of intent to create an agency is a written agency agreement, such as a signed listing agreement or buyer representation agreement. But intent may also be established through the parties' spoken words or actions. For example, if a real estate broker acts as if she's representing a buyer, that can be interpreted as intent to accept the role of the buyer's agent. (Remember the problem of inadvertent dual agency, discussed earlier in this chapter.)

However, when a broker merely responds to a buyer's inquiries about a property, that isn't enough to show intent to create an agency.

> **Example:** The Smiths are vacationing in Napa Valley. One afternoon, while strolling through a town, they pass a real estate office and notice a listing flyer in the window advertising a house for sale nearby. There's no price stated on the flyer and the Smiths are curious, so they go in; they've fallen in love with the area and might consider a move. Inside, the Smiths meet Broker Crenshaw. They ask the price of the property on the flyer, and Crenshaw looks it up for them. This act alone does not create an agency relationship between the Smiths and Broker Crenshaw.

On the other hand, if a buyer asks a real estate broker's advice or, by words or actions, engages the broker's negotiating skills, and the broker seems to accept the role of the buyer's agent, then an agency may be created.

> **Example:** After learning the price of the house, the Smiths decide to go look it over. Later Mrs. Smith says to Broker Crenshaw, "They're asking a lot for it, considering the shape it's in. How much less do you think they'd sell it for?" Crenshaw says, "Oh, I bet we can talk them down quite a bit—I know they're eager to sell." A court could rule that this interaction created an agency relationship: the Smiths intended to engage Crenshaw's expertise, and by implication Crenshaw accepted an agency role when he indicated he would negotiate on their behalf.
>
> Now suppose instead that Crenshaw replies, "I usually only handle commercial real estate, but I'll give you the number of another agent who will be able to help you." In this case, the Smiths may have intended to create an agency relationship, hoping that Crenshaw would advise and represent them. But Crenshaw clearly did not accept that role. Therefore, no agency relationship has been formed.

Here's a side note regarding the first scenario in the example: If Crenshaw is the listing broker for the house the Smiths are interested in, then he's already the sellers' agent. By creating an agency relationship with the Smiths, he has become a dual agent; and by saying that the sellers will accept less than the listing price, he has violated his duties to the sellers.

Factors Indicating Intent. When deciding whether there was intent to create an agency relationship, courts consider the nature of the relationship between the parties. An agency relationship is characterized by the principal's right to control the agent's actions, and by the agent's right to exercise discretion (use her own judgment) in carrying out the principal's instructions.

Another factor that courts will take into account when deciding whether an agency relationship has been established is whether and how the alleged agent was compensated. Payment of a fee is considered an indication of intent to create an agency. However, a fee (or lack of a fee) won't by itself prove (or disprove) that intention. It's possible to be someone's agent and owe duties to the principal even with no promise of compensation, and it's possible to receive compensation without becoming the agent of the person who pays it.

This is an important issue in real estate transactions, since buyer's agents often receive a share of the commission paid by the seller. As mentioned earlier, Civil Code § 2079.19 specifically provides that compensation doesn't determine real estate agency relationships: "The payment of compensation or the obligation to pay compensation to an agent by the seller or buyer is not necessarily determinative of a particular agency relationship between an agent and the seller or buyer."

Methods of Creating an Agency Relationship

Under general agency law, an agency relationship may be created in four different ways:

- by express appointment,
- by ratification,
- by estoppel, and
- by implication.

Agency by Express Appointment. When a principal asks someone to act as his agent, and the agent accepts, an agency has been created by express appointment. An agency agreement, such as a listing agreement or a buyer representation agreement, creates an agency by express appointment.

Most agency agreements are in writing, but as we said earlier, a written agreement is not required. As far as agency law is concerned, an oral agreement creates the same duties and responsibilities as a written agreement. Remember, however, that if the principal breaches the agency agreement, the real estate broker will be able to claim a commission only if the agreement was in writing.

Another way of creating an agency by express appointment is with a **power of attorney**. This is simply a document in which a principal appoints another person to act as his agent and specifies the agent's powers. A power of attorney is required in order to empower an agent to do certain things, such as convey real property (see Chapter 10).

Agency by Ratification. An agency relationship can also be created without an express appointment. When the principal gives her approval to unauthorized actions after the fact, this creates an agency by **ratification**. Before the ratification, the agent may have had no authority at all to act for the principal, or may have exceeded his authority.

When the principal ratifies unauthorized actions, it's just as if the actions had been authorized in advance. They have the same power to bind the principal, and the same liability rules apply.

Even without an express ratification, unauthorized acts can be considered ratified if the principal is aware of the actions and accepts the benefits of them. However, if authority to perform the action could only have been given to an agent in writing beforehand, it can only be ratified afterward in writing. (Civil Code § 2310.)

Civil Code § 2311 states that ratification of part of an indivisible transaction is a ratification of the whole transaction. In other words, the principal must accept all or none of the consequences of the unauthorized actions related to a transaction. It wouldn't be fair if the principal could ratify only the actions that benefit her, and deny the actions that would cause her harm or financial loss. The principal must take the bad with the good.

Case to Consider...

Friddle represented a buyer named Epstein in negotiating the purchase of 142 acres in Livermore, California. A preliminary purchase agreement included the following line: "Robert Epstein hereby agrees to pay a commission of 10% to Friddle Real Estate." About a week later, a second and final purchase agreement was prepared; it stated, "The payment of Buyer's Broker's commission is the subject of a separate agreement between [Epstein] and Buyer's Broker." Although Epstein never signed this second purchase agreement, his offer was accepted by the sellers, and the property was sold to Epstein for $5.2 million. Less than a week after that transaction closed, Epstein resold part of the property for $7 million.

Friddle claimed that he was entitled to a $520,000 commission on the purchase transaction. Epstein refused to pay it, claiming that he didn't have to because he hadn't signed the purchase agreement. Epstein had, however, paid the $5.2 million to the sellers and accepted title to the property. Friddle sued for his commission.

The trial court found that Epstein had ratified the purchase agreement when he went ahead with the transaction, but that he had only ratified those portions of the agreement that dealt with the purchase itself, not the part of the agreement referring to the "separate [commission] agreement." Friddle appealed. Was Friddle entitled to his commission? *Friddle v. Epstein* (1993) 16 Cal.App.4th 1649.

Agency by Estoppel. As we explained earlier, in the section on ostensible authority, estoppel is a legal doctrine that prevents a person from changing her position to another person's disadvantage if her past words or deeds caused the other person to act in reasonable reliance on them. An agency is created by estoppel when an unauthorized person (an ostensible agent) is performing actions as if he were the principal's actual agent, the principal is aware of this, and the principal's conduct or statements cause a third party to think that the actions are in fact authorized.

However, the estoppel doctrine will not be used against an innocent principal who has no knowledge that someone is claiming to represent him, as in the following case.

Case Example:

Jones owned real property that Bernstine wanted to purchase. Miller pretended to be Jones's agent, signed a contract agreeing to sell Jones's property to Bernstine, accepted $500 from Bernstine as payment under the contract, and ran away with the money. Bernstine then sued Jones for a return of the money, claiming that Miller had been Jones's agent by estoppel.

The court sided with Jones. Jones had never authorized Miller to act as his agent or to sell his property, and an agency had not been created by estoppel. Bernstine's belief that Miller was Jones's agent was based only on Miller's conduct, not on Jones's conduct. Jones never led Bernstine to believe that Miller was his agent, nor did Jones benefit from Miller's actions. Miller was acting on his own. *Bernstine v. Jones* (1951) 108 Cal.App.2d 135.

Agency by Implication. Like agency by estoppel, an agency by implication is created when a person is allowed to believe that an agency relationship exists, even though there isn't an actual relationship. However, unlike agency by estoppel (which is based on the conduct or statements of the supposed principal), an agency by implication is based on the conduct or statements of the supposed agent. If a person reasonably believes that someone else is acting as his agent, and the supposed agent fails to do anything about this misunderstanding, she may find herself owing agency duties to the other person. This is how an agency relationship can arise between a buyer and a real estate agent when the agent doesn't make it clear to the buyer that she isn't his agent.

Agency by estoppel protects a third party who is misled by the supposed principal's conduct. Agency by implication protects a principal who is misled by the supposed agent's conduct.

Termination of an Agency Relationship

Understanding how agency relationships may terminate is as important as understanding how they may be created. When an agency relationship is terminated, the agent is no longer authorized to represent the principal.

The ways that agency relationships may terminate can be divided into two groups:

- termination by actions of the parties, and
- termination by operation of law.

Termination by Actions of the Parties

The parties to an agency may mutually agree to terminate it; or it may be terminated unilaterally, either by the principal's revocation or by the agent's renunciation.

Mutual Agreement. The principal and agent may agree to terminate their relationship at any time. If their original agency agreement was in writing, their termination agreement should also be put into writing. If the agency was created with a recorded power of attorney, a document canceling the power of attorney should be recorded. (Under Civil Code § 1216, when a recorded power of attorney grants authority to convey real property or execute documents that affect real property, that authority can only be withdrawn with another recorded document.)

Unilateral Termination. Agency requires the consent of both parties, and either of them can withdraw consent and terminate the agency at any time. The relationship between principal and agent is based on trust and confidence; it would be contrary to the nature and purpose of agency to make them continue the relationship in the absence of trust and confidence. So the principal can **revoke** the agent's authority, or the agent can **renounce** his agency authority.

However, sometimes the unilateral termination of an agency relationship is a breach of contract, and the terminating party may be liable to the other party for the breach.

Case to Consider...

The Vasquezes listed their restaurant for sale with a broker in October 1992; the listing was to expire in March 1993. In the listing agreement, the Vasquezes agreed to pay the broker a commission if the property was sold during the listing period, no matter who found the buyer. In November 1992, unhappy with the broker's services, the Vasquezes terminated the agency relationship by letter. They then hired another broker, who arranged the sale of the property in February 1993, before the ending date of the original broker's listing. Was the original broker entitled to a commission? *Century 21 Butler Realty, Inc. v. Vasquez* (1995) 41 Cal.App.4th 888.

Note that there's one exception to the rule that a principal can revoke the agency at any time: a principal can't revoke an agency coupled with an interest. We'll discuss that shortly.

Termination by Operation of Law

An agency is terminated by operation of law when an event occurs that causes the agency to end automatically. Any of the following events will terminate an agency:

- fulfillment of the purpose of the agency;
- expiration of the agency agreement;
- extinction of the subject matter of the agency; or
- the death, incapacity, or bankruptcy of either party.

Fulfillment of Purpose. When a seller lists a home with a broker, the agent's job is to find a ready, willing, and able buyer, and to oversee the completion of the transaction. Once a buyer is found and the sale has closed, the agency relationship between seller and broker ends. The same is true for a buyer's agent: once the agent finds the buyer a home she wants and the purchase is completed, the purpose of the agency has been fulfilled, so the agency ends. This may be the most common reason for agency termination.

Expiration. If an agency agreement has a specific expiration date, the agency will automatically end on that date (unless the parties choose to extend the agreement before it expires).

An agency agreement without an expiration date is considered to expire after a reasonable time. A court will decide how much time is reasonable based on the type of agency and the circumstances of the case.

Note that in California, it's illegal for a real estate broker to demand or collect compensation under an exclusive agency agreement that doesn't have a specific expiration date (Business and Professions Code § 10176(f)).

Extinction of the Subject Matter. The subject matter of the agency relationship between a seller and a real estate broker is the seller's property. If the property is destroyed (by fire or an earthquake, for example), the agency relationship automatically terminates.

When sale of the property isn't the purpose of the agency—in a property management context, for example—a sale would be considered extinction of the subject matter.

It would automatically terminate the agency relationship between a property owner and a property manager.

Death, Incapacity, or Bankruptcy. Because agency is a personal relationship based on trust and confidence, an agency terminates if either party can no longer participate personally in carrying out its purpose. So the death or incapacity of either the principal or the agent terminates their agency relationship. Incapacity includes not only mental incompetence, but any other events that make it legally impossible for the principal or agent to continue with the agency. For example, if a broker loses her real estate license, her agency relationships with clients terminate due to incapacity. Bankruptcy may also prevent the principal or the agent from continuing with the agency and cause it to terminate.

Case to Consider...

In May 1967, Dr. Moore entered into a listing agreement with a broker to sell a 156-acre vineyard. In the contract, Dr. Moore agreed to pay the broker a commission if the property was sold during the listing period. The agreement was to expire December 31, 1968. Dr. Moore died in June 1968, and Rickard was appointed executor of the estate. In November 1968, Rickard sold the vineyard for $152,000, without any help from the listing broker. The broker subsequently sued for the commission, citing the terms of the agreement with Dr. Moore. Did the court enforce the listing agreement and require the estate to pay the broker a commission? *Charles B. Webster Real Estate v. Rickard* (1971) 21 Cal.App.3d 612.

Effect of Termination on Third Parties

When an agency relationship terminates, how does that affect third parties who were dealing with the agent? That depends on the way in which the agency terminates, and on whether the third party had notice of the termination (whether he knew or should have known about it).

Under Civil Code § 2355, if an agency is terminated by expiration of the term, extinction of the subject matter, the death or incapacity of the agent, or the agent's renunciation, the termination is effective as to a third party who has notice of the termination. But if the third party doesn't have notice, it's reasonable for him to assume that the agent is still authorized to represent the principal.

> **Example:** Martha's house has been listed with Broker Nicholson. Martha hasn't been very pleased with Nicholson's work, so when the listing is about to expire, Martha doesn't extend it.
>
> Right before the listing expired, Nicholson was negotiating with a potential buyer named David. Martha is aware of these negotiations. Unless Martha informs David of the agency termination or he learns of it in some other way, it's reasonable for him to assume that Nicholson is still acting as Martha's representative.

If the third party doesn't have notice that the agency has been terminated, the principal may still be liable to the third party for the former agent's actions. The former agent's actual agency authority has ended, but she may still have ostensible authority if the principal negligently allows the third party to think that the agency is still in effect.

Example: Suppose Martha doesn't inform David that Nicholson is no longer her agent. David gives Nicholson a written offer to purchase Martha's property, along with a check for the good faith deposit. Nicholson then runs off with the funds. Depending on all of the circumstances, it's possible that Martha would be held liable and required to reimburse David. If Martha allowed David to think Nicholson was still authorized to represent her, then Nicholson was acting within the scope of her ostensible authority.

When an agency is revoked by the principal or terminated by the death or incapacity of the principal, a different rule applies. In those cases, the termination may be effective as to a third party even if the third party has no notice of the termination. (Civil Code § 2356.)

Agency Coupled with an Interest

Civil Code § 2356(a) provides that an **agency coupled with an interest** cannot be revoked and is not terminated by the death or incapacity of the principal. An agency is coupled with an interest if the agent has a financial interest in the subject matter of the agency.

For instance, if a real estate broker co-owns a property with other people, and they've authorized him to represent them in selling the property, the agency is coupled with an interest. The co-owners can't revoke it.

However, the mere promise of compensation does not create an agency coupled with an interest. In most real estate transactions, the broker is promised a commission if the sale closes. But the possibility of earning this commission doesn't create an agency coupled with an interest. A financial interest in the subject matter of the transaction is necessary.

Whether an agency is coupled with an interest or not, the creation and termination of agency relationships are very important aspects of the real estate business. The nature of the agency relationship will determine both the extent of the agent's authority and the principal's liability in transactions. It also creates a framework for the duties and responsibilities that a real estate agent owes to clients and customers (the subject of our next chapter). By understanding this framework, and the importance of agency law, a real estate agent can better avoid the kinds of situations that invite legal problems.

Case Law in Depth

The following case involves some of the legal issues discussed in this chapter. Read through the facts and consider the questions in light of what you have learned. Then read what the court actually decided.

Boquilon v. Beckwith (1996) 49 Cal.App.4th 1697

A friend introduced the Boquilons to Mary Beckwith, a licensed real estate salesperson, so that they could obtain a personal loan from her to pay off Mr. Boquilon's gambling debts. Their first meeting took place in Beckwith's office at Panda Realty, and a number of subsequent meetings also occurred there. Beckwith gave Mr. Boquilon a business card identifying herself as a real estate agent with Panda Realty.

Over the course of several months, Beckwith made two unsecured loans to the Boquilons. Later, when a lender was going to foreclose on the Boquilons' home, Beckwith offered to refinance it for them. Instead of having the Boquilons execute a deed of trust for the refinancing, however, Beckwith simply had them deed the home to her. The plan was for Beckwith to refinance the property under her own name at a lower interest rate than the Boquilons would have been eligible for, then transfer the property back to the Boquilons, who would assume the refinancing loan. In the meantime, the Boquilons would rent the property from Beckwith. But the Boquilons failed to make the rental payments. Eventually Beckwith had the Boquilons and their three children evicted from the home, and Beckwith later sold the property to a third party.

When the Boquilons sued Beckwith for fraud and breach of contract (among other things), they also sued her broker, Panda Realty. Their contention was that Beckwith was acting as Panda's ostensible agent in her dealings with them.

The questions:

Were Beckwith's actions within the scope of her actual or ostensible authority as an agent of Panda Realty? Could Panda be held vicariously liable for Beckwith's actions?

The court's answers:

The trial court ruled that Beckwith was not acting as Panda Realty's agent in these transactions, and the appellate court agreed. "[T]here is no real dispute that the loans made to Mr. Boquilon to pay off his gambling debts were made by Beckwith acting in her individual capacity. The funds came from Beckwith's personal checking account, and the loans were evidenced by a note and… deed of trust executed in favor of Beckwith personally. More importantly, however, it is undisputed that the Boquilons conveyed their residence to Beckwith personally, not to Panda Realty (or to Beckwith in some representative capacity), and that there was no subsequent transfer to Panda Realty as an entity…It is this conveyance to Beckwith…that underlies the Boquilons' successful cause of action for damages. In these circumstances, the trial court did not err in concluding that Beckwith was not an agent of Panda Realty in connection with her dealings with the Boquilons."

The result:

Since Beckwith was not acting within the scope of her authority as an agent of Panda Realty in her transactions with the Boquilons, Panda could not be held vicariously liable for Beckwith's actions.

Chapter Summary

- California's Real Estate Law is found in the Business and Professions Code. Real Estate Law and general agency law work hand in hand to regulate real estate transactions. General agency law applies to all agency relationships; the Real Estate Law imposes special requirements on real estate agents.

- Agency authority is either actual or ostensible. Actual authority is authority the principal gives to her agent, whether express (oral or written) or implied (the authority necessary to carry out the terms of the agency agreement). Ostensible authority is what a principal, negligently or intentionally, allows a third party to believe the agent has.

- When the principal has authorized a listing broker to engage a second broker, the second broker becomes a subagent of the principal. When the principal has not authorized such a delegation of authority, the second broker only becomes an agent of the listing broker.

- Agency relationships are created by express agreement, ratification, estoppel, or implication.

- Renunciation refers to the power an agent has to terminate the agency relationship before the object of the agency has been fulfilled. Revocation refers to the principal's corresponding right. However, the power of the agent to renounce and the power of the principal to revoke do not relieve either party of liability for breach of contract.

- Agency relationships are terminated by fulfillment of purpose, expiration of agency agreement, extinction of subject matter, death, incapacity, or bankruptcy.

Key Terms

- **General agency law** – The body of law dealing with the nature of agency relationships between agent and principal.

- **Special agent** – An agent for a particular act or transaction. Most real estate agents are special agents.

- **General agent** – An agent who is authorized to handle everything for a client in specified areas.

- **Actual authority** – The express or implied authority an agent receives specifically from the principal to act on her behalf.

- **Express authority** – Authority communicated to an agent by an oral or written statement.

- **Implied authority** – Authority to do everything necessary, proper, and usual in the ordinary course of business to effect the purpose of the original agency.

- **Ostensible authority** – Authority that a principal, intentionally or negligently, causes or allows a third person to believe the agent has.

- **Warranty of authority** – A doctrine that protects third parties in their dealings with agents: a person who acts in dealings with third parties as an agent, warrants that he has the authority to perform on behalf of the principal.

- **Imputed knowledge** – A law stating that both principal and agent are assumed to have knowledge of whatever one party ought to have communicated to the other in the exercise of ordinary care.

- **Vicarious liability** – A doctrine that holds principals and brokers liable for their agents' torts.

- **Subagent** – When the principal has authorized a listing broker with express or implied authority to engage a second broker. Under authorized subagency, vicarious liability and imputed knowledge exist between the subagent and the principal.

- **Actual agency** – When a principal appoints someone to act as his agent, and the agent accepts the appointment, they have created an express agreement called an actual agency.

- **Agency by ratification** – When the principal gives verbal or written approval to an agent's actions after the fact, this creates an agency by ratification.

- **Agency by estoppel** – Estoppel is a legal doctrine that prevents a person who has caused a third party to rely upon the person's acts or representations from "going back" on their earlier claims when such reliance caused harm to the third party.

- **Agency by implication** – Agency created when an agent allows a third party to believe that an agency relationship exists between agent and principal.

- **Agency coupled with an interest** – When an agent has a financial interest in the subject matter of an agency, the agency cannot be revoked.

Chapter Quiz

1. California recognizes two types of agency authority:
   a) express and secret
   b) actual and ostensible
   c) practical and impractical
   d) None of the above

2. Seller Juarez hires broker Williams to sell her real property. The authority broker Williams has to show the property to buyers, transmit offers, and place a "for sale" sign on the property is an example of:
   a) implied authority
   b) actual authority
   c) an express agreement
   d) None of the above

3. Which of the following is NOT a reason an agency relationship will automatically terminate by operation of law?
   a) Expiration of the agency agreement
   b) Death of the principal
   c) The seller signs with another agent before the term expires
   d) Destruction of the property

4. Agent Zeller paid seller Alberti $5,000 for the right to be the exclusive agent on Alberti's ocean front property for the period of one year. Seller Alberti will not be able to revoke the agency relationship because Agent Zeller has a/an:
   a) contract
   b) agency coupled with an interest
   c) right to rescind
   d) option

5. A tort is:
   a) a breach of contract
   b) a criminal wrong
   c) a civil wrong for which the law provides a remedy
   d) None of the above

6. The reasonableness of implied authority actions are determined by:
   a) the listing agreement
   b) statute
   c) the custom and practice of the local community
   d) All of the above

7. An agent may:
   a) use an implied authority to carry out the purpose of the agency
   b) act in her own name
   c) define the scope of her agency
   d) None of the above

8. When one broker cooperates with or delegates authority to another broker, the legal relationship between principal, broker, and cooperating broker is determined by:
   a) the listing agreement
   b) statute
   c) whether the principal has authorized the delegation of authority
   d) custom and practice

9. A dual agent must have express written consent to:
   a) tell the buyer that the seller is willing to accept less than the listing price
   b) tell the seller that the buyer is willing to pay more than the listing price
   c) act as an agent for both the buyer and the seller
   d) All of the above

10. Knowledge will be imputed between a subagent and the principal only when:
    a) there is a listing agreement
    b) the principal has authorized the subagency
    c) the subagent works directly for the listing broker
    d) None of the above

Chapter Answer Key

Chapter Quiz Answers:

1. b) California recognizes two types of agency authority: actual and ostensible.

2. a) Implied authority is the authority to do everything necessary, proper, and usual in the ordinary course of business to effect the purpose of the agency.

3. c) Agency relationships will automatically terminate by operation of law only in the following circumstances: achievement of the agency objective; expiration of the agency agreement; destruction of the property; and death, incapacity, or bankruptcy of either party.

4. b) Agent Zeller has an agency coupled with an interest that cannot be revoked.

5. c) A tort is a civil, non-contractual wrong for which the law provides a remedy.

6. c) The reasonableness of actions taken under implied authority are determined by custom and practice of the local community.

7. a) An agent's authority is limited. Regardless of the terms of the agency agreement, an agent may not act in her own name unless it is within the ordinary course of business to do so, and may not define the scope of her agency.

8. c) The legal relationship between principal, listing broker, and cooperating broker is determined by whether the principal authorized the listing broker to delegate some of his authority to another person.

9. d) Before acting as a dual agent, a broker must have the informed written consent of both parties. Furthermore, California law specifically states that a dual agent must have the express written consent of both parties before he can reveal confidential information about one party to the other.

10. b) Knowledge will be imputed between a subagent and the principal only when the subagent has been lawfully appointed.

Cases to Consider... Answers:

Ostensible Authority

Kaplan v. Coldwell Banker Residential Affiliates, Inc. (1997) 59 Cal.App.4th 741. The court ruled in favor of Kaplan, agreeing that there were "triable issues of fact" with regard to ostensible agency. (Summary judgment can only be granted when there are no triable issues of fact—no issues that are appropriate for a jury to decide.) For ostensible agency to exist, the third party dealing with the ostensible agent must have a reasonable belief in the agent's authority. Although Coldwell Banker had made no specific representations to Kaplan personally, it had made representations to the public generally. For that reason, it may have been reasonable for Kaplan to believe that Coldwell Banker "stood behind" Marsh's company. Whether or not Kaplan's belief was reasonable under the circumstances was an issue for a jury to decide, so summary judgment in favor of Coldwell Banker was inappropriate.

Agency by Ratification

Friddle v. Epstein (1993) 16 Cal.App.4th 1649. The appeals court ruled in favor of Friddle. Epstein must accept the burden (paying Friddle a commission) as well as the benefit (the benefit of the purchase and the profit on the subsequent resale) of his agent's unauthorized actions. A principal can't split a transaction into various parts and ratify only those parts that benefit him while rejecting those parts that do not. In this case, the separate agreement authorizing Friddle's 10% commission and referenced in the ratified purchase agreement was part of the whole package and couldn't be separated from the rest. When Epstein ratified part of the transaction, he ratified the whole.

Revocation of Agency Authority

Century 21 Butler Realty, Inc. v. Vasquez (1995) 41 Cal.App.4th 888. When the Vasquezes sent the termination letter to the broker, it ended the agency relationship, and the broker was no longer authorized to act as their representative. However, terminating an agency relationship doesn't terminate any contractual relationship that might also exist. The Vasquezes had agreed to pay the original broker a commission if the property was sold during the listing period, no matter who found the buyer. When the Vasquezes refused to pay the original broker his commission, it was a breach of contract. The court ordered the Vasquezes to pay as agreed.

Agency Termination by Operation of Law

Charles B. Webster Real Estate v. Rickard (1971) 21 Cal.App.3d 612. The court did not enforce the listing agreement or require payment of the broker's commission. An agency relationship is a personal one that depends not only on the agent's promises, but also on the principal's guidance and direction. Death makes those promises and that guidance impossible; therefore, the agency relationship terminated by operation of law when Dr. Moore died, months before the property was sold. There was no breach of contract.

List of Cases

Bernstine v. Jones (1951) 108 Cal.App.2d 135
Boquilon v. Beckwith (1996) 49 Cal.App.4th 1697
Century 21 Butler Realty, Inc. v. Vasquez (1995) 41 Cal.App.4th 888
Charles B. Webster Real Estate v. Rickard (1971) 21 Cal.App.3d 612
Cheda v. Grandi (1950) 97 Cal.App.2d 513
Friddle v. Epstein (1993) 16 Cal.App.4th 1649
Kaplan v. Coldwell Banker Residential Affiliates, Inc. (1997) 59 Cal.App.4th 741

Chapter 7

Duties to Clients and Customers

Outline

I.   Agency Disclosure Requirements
  A.   Agency disclosure form
  B.   Agency confirmation statement
  C.   Acting in accordance with agency disclosures

II. Duties Owed to Clients
  A.   Fiduciary duties
  B.   Utmost care, integrity, honesty, and loyalty
  C.   Fulfilling fiduciary duties
    1.   Obedience
    2.   Confidentiality
    3.   Conflicts of interest
      a.   Relationship between agent and third party
      b.   Self-dealing and secret profits
    4.   Expert advice

III. Duties Owed to All Parties
  A.   Reasonable skill and care
  B.   Honest and fair dealing and good faith
    1.   Actual fraud vs. constructive fraud
    2.   Puffing, opinions, and predictions
  C.   Disclosure of material facts
    1.   Latent defects
    2.   Duty to inspect
      a.   *Easton v. Strassburger*
      b.   Statutory duty to inspect
    3.   Statutorily required pamphlets
    4.   Facts that don't need to be disclosed
    5.   "As is" clauses

Introduction

As we explained in Chapter 6, the relationships between California real estate agents and their clients and customers were once governed almost entirely by general agency law. Over time, however, the California legislature adopted a number of statutory provisions to specifically address agency issues that arise in real estate transactions. These include provisions that describe or define the legal duties that a real estate agent owes to his principal and to third parties. Those duties are the main focus of this chapter.

We'll begin with a discussion of the disclosure law that was developed to address the public's confusion about real estate agency relationships (see Chapter 6). Then we'll examine a real estate agent's fiduciary duties, which are the duties an agent owes only to her clients. After that, we'll look at the duties a real estate agent owes to all parties in a real estate transaction, customers as well as clients.

Agency Disclosure Requirements

A real estate licensee has legal duties to anyone with whom he interacts who is or may become a party in a real estate transaction. The nature and extent of these duties depends on whether an agency relationship has been established; an agent's duties to a client are different from his duties to a customer. That's why it's important for buyers and sellers to understand whether the licensee they're talking to is their own agent or the other party's. In the past, however, considerable confusion has surrounded the issue of real estate agency relationships.

In an effort to reduce that confusion, many states have passed **real estate agency disclosure laws**—laws that require real estate agents to disclose to both the buyer and the seller which party or parties they are representing in the transaction. California's agency disclosure requirements are set forth in Civil Code §§ 2079.14 – 2079.17. These requirements apply to transactions that involve the sale of commercial real property, the sale of residential property with up to four dwelling units, any leasehold interest in such property exceeding one year in duration, and mobile homes.

Agency Disclosure Form

The first step in the disclosure process is providing the parties with a copy of the **agency disclosure form** shown in Figure 7.1. One side of this form explains the duties of a seller's agent, a buyer's agent, and a dual agent, in language specified by Civil Code § 2079.16. The other side of the form presents the text of Civil Code §§ 2079.13 – 2079.24, the statutory provisions concerning real estate agency relationships. An agent must give each party the disclosure form and also have each one sign a copy to acknowledge that they received it. (Note that the agency disclosure form can also be used when an agent is representing a landlord or tenant, although our discussion will focus on buyers and sellers.)

The time frame for providing the agency disclosure form is set forth in Civil Code § 2079.14. The listing agent must give a copy to the seller before the seller signs the listing agreement. The selling agent must give a copy to each party as soon as practicable; the buyer must receive it before signing the offer to purchase, and the seller must receive it before the offer is presented. (If the selling agent is not dealing with the seller directly, the selling agent's disclosure form may be delivered to the seller by the listing agent or by certified mail.)

Fig. 7.1 Agency disclosure form

DISCLOSURE REGARDING REAL ESTATE AGENCY RELATIONSHIP

CALIFORNIA ASSOCIATION OF REALTORS ®

(As required by the Civil Code)
(C.A.R. Form AD, Revised 12/14)

❑ (If checked) This form is being provided in connection with a transaction for a leasehold interest exceeding one year as per Civil Code section 2079.13(k), (l), and (m).

When you enter into a discussion with a real estate agent regarding a real estate transaction, you should from the outset understand what type of agency relationship or representation you wish to have with the agent in the transaction.

SELLER'S AGENT
A Seller's agent under a listing agreement with the Seller acts as the agent for the Seller only. A Seller's agent or a subagent of that agent has the following affirmative obligations:
To the Seller: A Fiduciary duty of utmost care, integrity, honesty and loyalty in dealings with the Seller.
To the Buyer and the Seller:
(a) Diligent exercise of reasonable skill and care in performance of the agent's duties.
(b) A duty of honest and fair dealing and good faith.
(c) A duty to disclose all facts known to the agent materially affecting the value or desirability of the property that are not known to, or within the diligent attention and observation of, the parties. An agent is not obligated to reveal to either party any confidential information obtained from the other party that does not involve the affirmative duties set forth above.

BUYER'S AGENT
A selling agent can, with a Buyer's consent, agree to act as agent for the Buyer only. In these situations, the agent is not the Seller's agent, even if by agreement the agent may receive compensation for services rendered, either in full or in part from the Seller. An agent acting only for a Buyer has the following affirmative obligations:
To the Buyer: A fiduciary duty of utmost care, integrity, honesty and loyalty in dealings with the Buyer.
To the Buyer and the Seller:
(a) Diligent exercise of reasonable skill and care in performance of the agent's duties.
(b) A duty of honest and fair dealing and good faith.
(c) A duty to disclose all facts known to the agent materially affecting the value or desirability of the property that are not known to, or within the diligent attention and observation of, the parties.
An agent is not obligated to reveal to either party any confidential information obtained from the other party that does not involve the affirmative duties set forth above.

AGENT REPRESENTING BOTH SELLER AND BUYER
A real estate agent, either acting directly or through one or more associate licensees, can legally be the agent of both the Seller and the Buyer in a transaction, but only with the knowledge and consent of both the Seller and the Buyer.
In a dual agency situation, the agent has the following affirmative obligations to both the Seller and the Buyer:
(a) A fiduciary duty of utmost care, integrity, honesty and loyalty in the dealings with either the Seller or the Buyer.
(b) Other duties to the Seller and the Buyer as stated above in their respective sections.
In representing both Seller and Buyer, the agent may not, without the express permission of the respective party, disclose to the other party that the
Seller will accept a price less than the listing price or that the Buyer will pay a price greater than the price offered.
The above duties of the agent in a real estate transaction do not relieve a Seller or Buyer from the responsibility to protect his or her own interests. You should carefully read all agreements to assure that they adequately express your understanding of the transaction. A real estate agent is a person qualified to advise about real estate. If legal or tax advice is desired, consult a competent professional.
Throughout your real property transaction you may receive more than one disclosure form, depending upon the number of agents assisting in the transaction. The law requires each agent with whom you have more than a casual relationship to present you with this disclosure form. You should read its contents each time it is presented to you, considering the relationship between you and the real estate agent in your specific transaction. **This disclosure form includes the provisions of Sections 2079.13 to 2079.24, inclusive, of the Civil Code set forth on page 2. Read it carefully. I/WE ACKNOWLEDGE RECEIPT OF A COPY OF THIS DISCLOSURE AND THE PORTIONS OF THE CIVIL CODE PRINTED ON THE BACK (OR A SEPARATE PAGE).**

Buyer/Seller/Landlord/Tenant _____ Date _____

Buyer/Seller/Landlord/Tenant _____ Date _____

Agent _____ DRE Lic. # _____
　　　　　　　　　　Real Estate Broker (Firm)
By _____ DRE Lic. # _____ Date _____
　　　(Salesperson or Broker-Associate)

Agency Disclosure Compliance (Civil Code §2079.14):
• When the listing brokerage company also represents Buyer/Tenant: The Listing Agent shall have one AD form signed by Seller/Landlord and a different AD form signed by Buyer/Tenant.
• When Seller/Landlord and Buyer/Tenant are represented by different brokerage companies: (i) the Listing Agent shall have one AD form signed by Seller/Landlord and (ii) the Buyer's/Tenant's Agent shall have one AD form signed by Buyer/Tenant and either that same or a different AD form presented to Seller/Landlord for signature prior to presentation of the offer. If the same form is used, Seller may sign here:

_____   _____
　Seller/Landlord　　　　Date　　　　　　　Seller/Landlord　　　　Date

Reviewed by _____ Date _____

AD REVISED 12/14 (PAGE 1 OF 2) Print Date

DISCLOSURE REGARDING REAL ESTATE AGENCY RELATIONSHIP (AD PAGE 1 OF 2)

CIVIL CODE SECTIONS 2079.24 (2079.16 APPEARS ON THE FRONT)

2079.13 As used in Sections 2079.14 to 2079.24, inclusive, the following terms have the following meanings: **(a)** "Agent" means a person acting under provisions of Title 9 (commencing with Section 2295) in a real property transaction, and includes a person who is licensed as a real estate broker under Chapter 3 (commencing with Section 10130) of Part 1 of Division 4 of the Business and Professions Code, and under whose license a listing is executed or an offer to purchase is obtained. **(b)** "Associate licensee" means a person who is licensed as a real estate broker or salesperson under Chapter 3 (commencing with Section 10130) of Part 1 of Division 4 of the Business and Professions Code and who is either licensed under a broker or has entered into a written contract with a broker to act as the broker's agent in connection with acts requiring a real estate license and to function under the broker's supervision in the capacity of an associate licensee. The agent in the real property transaction bears responsibility for his or her associate licensees who perform as agents of the agent. When an associate licensee owes a duty to any principal, or to any buyer or seller who is not a principal, in a real property transaction, that duty is equivalent to the duty owed to that party by the broker for whom the associate licensee functions. **(c)** "Buyer" means a transferee in a real property transaction, and includes a person who executes an offer to purchase real property from a seller through an agent, or who seeks the services of an agent in more than a casual, transitory, or preliminary manner, with the object of entering into a real property transaction. "Buyer" includes vendee or lessee. **(d)** "Commercial real property" means all real property in the state, except single-family residential real property, dwelling units made subject to Chapter 2 (commencing with Section 1940) of Title 5, mobilehomes, as defined in Section 798.3, or recreational vehicles, as defined in Section 799.29. **(e)** "Dual agent" means an agent acting, either directly or through an associate licensee, as agent for both the seller and the buyer in a real property transaction. **(f)** "Listing agreement" means a contract between an owner of real property and an agent, by which the agent has been authorized to sell the real property or to find or obtain a buyer. **(g)** "Listing agent" means a person who has obtained a listing of real property to act as an agent for compensation. **(h)** "Listing price" is the amount expressed in dollars specified in the listing for which the seller is willing to sell the real property through the listing agent. **(i)** "Offering price" is the amount expressed in dollars specified in an offer to purchase for which the buyer is willing to buy the real property. **(j)** "Offer to purchase" means a written contract executed by a buyer acting through a selling agent that becomes the contract for the sale of the real property upon acceptance by the seller. **(k)** "Real property" means any estate specified by subdivision (1) or (2) of Section 761 in property that constitutes or is improved with one to four dwelling units, any commercial real property, any leasehold in these types of property exceeding one year's duration, and mobilehomes, when offered for sale or sold through an agent pursuant to the authority contained in Section 10131.6 of the Business and Professions Code. **(l)** "Real property transaction" means a transaction for the sale of real property in which an agent is employed by one or more of the principals to act in that transaction, and includes a listing or an offer to purchase. **(m)** "Sell," "sale," or "sold" refers to a transaction for the transfer of real property from the seller to the buyer, and includes exchanges of real property between the seller and buyer, transactions for the creation of a real property sales contract within the meaning of Section 2985, and transactions for the creation of a leasehold exceeding one year's duration. **(n)** "Seller" means the transferor in a real property transaction, and includes an owner who lists real property with an agent, whether or not a transfer results, or who receives an offer to purchase real property of which he or she is the owner from an agent on behalf of another. "Seller" includes both a vendor and a lessor. **(o)** "Selling agent" means a listing agent who acts alone, or an agent who acts in cooperation with a listing agent, and who sells or finds and obtains a buyer for the real property, or an agent who locates property for a buyer or who finds a buyer for a property for which no listing exists and presents an offer to purchase to the seller. **(p)** "Subagent" means a person to whom an agent delegates agency powers as provided in Article 5 (commencing with Section 2349) of Chapter 1 of Title 9. However, "subagent" does not include an associate licensee who is acting under the supervision of an agent in a real property transaction.

2079.14 Listing agents and selling agents shall provide the seller and buyer in a real property transaction with a copy of the disclosure form specified in Section 2079.16, and, except as provided in subdivision (c), shall obtain a signed acknowledgement of receipt from that seller or buyer, except as provided in this section or Section 2079.15, as follows: **(a)** The listing agent, if any, shall provide the disclosure form to the seller prior to entering into the listing agreement. **(b)** The selling agent shall provide the disclosure form to the seller as soon as practicable prior to presenting the seller with an offer to purchase, unless the selling agent previously provided the seller with a copy of the disclosure form pursuant to subdivision (a). **(c)** Where the selling agent does not deal on a face-to-face basis with the seller, the disclosure form prepared by the selling agent may be furnished to the seller (and acknowledgement of receipt obtained for the selling agent from the seller) by the listing agent, or the selling agent may deliver the disclosure form by certified mail addressed to the seller at his or her last known address, in which case no signed acknowledgement of receipt is required. **(d)** The selling agent shall provide the disclosure form to the buyer as soon as practicable prior to execution of the buyer's offer to purchase, except that if the offer to purchase is not prepared by the selling agent, the selling agent shall present the disclosure form to the buyer not later than the next business day after the selling agent receives the offer to purchase from the buyer.

2079.15 In any circumstance in which the seller or buyer refuses to sign an acknowledgement of receipt pursuant to Section 2079.14, the agent, or an associate licensee acting for an agent, shall set forth, sign, and date a written declaration of the facts of the refusal.

2079.16 Reproduced on Page 1 of this AD form.

2079.17(a) As soon as practicable, the selling agent shall disclose to the buyer and seller whether the selling agent is acting in the real property transaction exclusively as the buyer's agent, exclusively as the seller's agent, or as a dual agent representing both the buyer and the seller. This relationship shall be confirmed in the contract to purchase and sell real property or in a separate writing executed or acknowledged by the seller, the buyer, and the selling agent prior to or coincident with execution of that contract by the buyer and the seller, respectively. **(b)** As soon as practicable, the listing agent shall disclose to the seller whether the listing agent is acting in the real property transaction exclusively as the seller's agent, or as a dual agent representing both the buyer and seller. This relationship shall be confirmed in the contract to purchase and sell real property or in a separate writing executed or acknowledged by the seller and the listing agent prior to or coincident with the execution of that contract by the seller.

(c) The confirmation required by subdivisions (a) and (b) shall be in the following form.

_____(DO NOT COMPLETE. SAMPLE ONLY)_____ is the agent of (check one): ❑ the seller exclusively; or ❑ both the buyer and seller.
(Name of Listing Agent)

_____(DO NOT COMPLETE. SAMPLE ONLY)_____ is the agent of (check one): ❑ the buyer exclusively; or ❑ the seller exclusively; or
(Name of Selling Agent if not the same as the Listing Agent)   ❑ both the buyer and seller.

(d) The disclosures and confirmation required by this section shall be in addition to the disclosure required by Section 2079.14.

2079.18 No selling agent in a real property transaction may act as an agent for the buyer only, when the selling agent is also acting as the listing agent in the transaction.

2079.19 The payment of compensation or the obligation to pay compensation to an agent by the seller or buyer is not necessarily determinative of a particular agency relationship between an agent and the seller or buyer. A listing agent and a selling agent may agree to share any compensation or commission paid, or any right to any compensation or commission for which an obligation arises as the result of a real estate transaction, and the terms of any such agreement shall not necessarily be determinative of a particular relationship.

2079.20 Nothing in this article prevents an agent from selecting, as a condition of the agent's employment, a specific form of agency relationship not specifically prohibited by this article if the requirements of Section 2079.14 and Section 2079.17 are complied with.

2079.21 A dual agent shall not disclose to the buyer that the seller is willing to sell the property at a price less than the listing price, without the express written consent of the seller. A dual agent shall not disclose to the seller that the buyer is willing to pay a price greater than the offering price, without the express written consent of the buyer. This section does not alter in any way the duty or responsibility of a dual agent to any principal with respect to confidential information other than price.

2079.22 Nothing in this article precludes a listing agent from also being a selling agent, and the combination of these functions in one agent does not, of itself, make that agent a dual agent.

2079.23 A contract between the principal and agent may be modified or altered to change the agency relationship at any time before the performance of the act which is the object of the agency with the written consent of the parties to the agency relationship.

2079.24 Nothing in this article shall be construed to either diminish the duty of disclosure owed buyers and sellers by agents and their associate licensees, subagents, and employees or to relieve agents and their associate licensees, subagents, and employees from liability for their conduct in connection with acts governed by this article or for any breach of a fiduciary duty or a duty of disclosure.

Published and Distributed by:
REAL ESTATE BUSINESS SERVICES, INC.
a subsidiary of the California Association of REALTORS®
525 South Virgil Avenue, Los Angeles, California 90020

Reviewed by _____ Date _____

EQUAL HOUSING OPPORTUNITY

AD REVISED 12/14 (PAGE 2 OF 2)

DISCLOSURE REGARDING REAL ESTATE AGENCY RELATIONSHIP (AD PAGE 2 OF 2)

Agency Confirmation Statement

In addition to giving the parties the general disclosure form explaining the different types of real estate agency relationships, each agent is required to disclose whether she is representing only the seller, only the buyer, or both the seller and the buyer in that particular transaction. The agents must make their disclosures to the parties as soon as practicable. Each agent's disclosures must be confirmed in writing by having the parties sign an agency confirmation statement before or at the same time that they enter into a purchase agreement. (See Figure 7.2.) An agency confirmation statement does not have to be a separate document; in many cases, it is included in the purchase agreement form.

Acting in Accordance with Agency Disclosures

The agency disclosures required by California law are fairly straightforward. But merely making the required disclosures is not enough; the agent must also act in accordance with the disclosures. When an agent is representing a seller, her conduct must reflect the fact that the seller, not the buyer, is her client. She must treat the buyer as a customer, not as a client. If the agent fails to do this, there is a danger of inadvertent dual agency, which we discussed in Chapter 6. Civil Code § 2079.24 makes it clear that nothing in the agency disclosure law diminishes the agent's liability to buyers or sellers. Conduct inconsistent with an agency disclosure may result in sanctions by the Bureau of Real Estate, including suspension or revocation of the real estate license and a fine of up to $10,000 (see Chapter 8).

Duties Owed to Clients

As we said earlier, Civil Code § 2079.16 specifically dictates the language that must appear on an agency disclosure form. Among other things, this includes an enumeration of the legal duties real estate agents owe to the buyers and sellers they work with. Some of these duties are owed only to clients, and others are owed to all parties (clients and customers). (See the first page of the form in Figure 7.1.) We'll begin by looking at the special duties an agent owes to clients; the duties owed to all parties will be covered in the next section of the chapter.

Fiduciary Duties

An agency relationship is a **fiduciary relationship**. A **fiduciary** is a person who occupies a place of special trust and confidence in relation to another person. Fiduciaries are expected to act according to the highest standards of care. As a fiduciary, an agent must place the principal's interests above anyone else's—including the agent's own—and the principal has a legal right to rely on the agent to do so.

The duties that an agent owes his principal are called **fiduciary duties**. To avoid lawsuits and disciplinary action, real estate agents must understand and fulfill their fiduciary duties to their clients.

Fig. 7.2 Agency confirmation statement

CALIFORNIA ASSOCIATION OF REALTORS ®

CONFIRMATION OF REAL ESTATE AGENCY RELATIONSHIPS
(As required by the Civil Code)
(C.A.R. Form AC, Revised 04/08)

Subject Property Address _____

The following agency relationship(s) is/are hereby confirmed for this transaction:

LISTING AGENT: _____
(Print Firm Name)

is the agent of (check one):

❏ the Seller/ Landlord exclusively; or

❏ both the Buyer/Tenant and Seller/Landlord

SELLING AGENT: _____
(if not the same as Listing Agent)   (Print Firm Name)

is the agent of (check one):

❏ the Buyer/Tenant exclusively; or

❏ the Seller/Landlord exclusively; or

❏ both the Buyer/Tenant and Seller/Landlord

I/WE ACKNOWLEDGE RECEIPT OF A COPY OF THIS CONFIRMATION.

Seller/Landlord _____ Date _____

Seller/Landlord _____ Date _____

Buyer/Tenant _____ Date _____

Buyer/Tenant _____ Date _____

Real Estate Broker (Selling Firm) _____

By _____ Date _____

Real Estate Broker (Listing Firm) _____

By _____ Date _____

**A REAL ESTATE BROKER IS QUALIFIED TO ADVISE ON REAL ESTATE. IF YOU DESIRE LEGAL ADVICE,
CONSULT YOUR ATTORNEY.**

Published and Distributed by:
REAL ESTATE BUSINESS SERVICES, INC.
a subsidiary of the California Association of REALTORS®
525 South Virgil Avenue, Los Angeles, California 90020

Reviewed by _____ Date _____

EQUAL HOUSING OPPORTUNITY

CONFIRMATION REAL ESTATE AGENCY RELATIONSHIPS (AC PAGE 1 OF 1)

Utmost Care, Integrity, Honesty, and Loyalty

In carrying out her work, an agent owes her principal the fiduciary duties of utmost care, integrity, honesty, and loyalty. As we'll discuss later, an agent also owes duties of care and honesty to third parties (customers), but there's a difference in degree. An agent owes the principal "utmost" care and honesty; this means not just diligence, but the highest degree of care possible.

The duty of utmost care requires an agent to use foresight, caution, and attention to detail in her work for the principal. She must make sure that she has all of the skills necessary to fulfill the terms of her agency, and must let the principal know when another expert should be consulted.

Along with honesty, the principle of integrity should govern an agent's actions in relation to her client. Integrity is sometimes defined as moral or ethical strength. The duty of integrity requires an agent to act ethically, to follow the rules, and to accept responsibility instead of trying to evade it.

Loyalty, the final duty on the list, is the essence of a fiduciary relationship. The agent owes the principal his allegiance. In advising the principal and in negotiations with third parties, the agent should never forget that he must put the principal's interests first.

Fulfilling Fiduciary Duties

Now let's consider some of the issues that may arise in the course of trying to fulfill agency duties towards a client. Specifically, we'll look at the issues of obedience, confidentiality, conflicts of interest, and expert advice.

Obedience. The requirement of **obedience** stems from the duties of utmost care and loyalty. An agent must always make a good faith effort to obey and carry out the principal's instructions. The agent must act in accordance with the purpose and intent of the agency. An agent can be held liable to the principal for losses caused by the agent's failure to comply with the principal's instructions.

But there are limits to an agent's obedience. Specifically, an agent isn't required or allowed to break the law just because a client directs her to do so. For example, an agent should not obey a seller's instructions to show a house only to white people, an act that violates state and federal fair housing laws. Nor should an agent obey a seller's instructions to conceal defects in the house from potential buyers. However, the requirement of a good faith effort to carry out the principal's instructions means that an agent can't simply ignore an illegal request. Instead, the agent must explain to the client that she can't comply because it would be illegal to do so.

Confidentiality. The agency relationship is based on trust and confidence. An agent cannot disclose **confidential information** from the principal to third parties, or use confidential information to the principal's detriment. Any information the agent learns about the client or the property during the course of the agency must be kept confidential unless the client authorizes the disclosure, or unless the information is a material fact that must be disclosed by law. (Material facts will be discussed later in the chapter.)

Example: In negotiations with a prospective buyer, a seller's agent says, "You can offer quite a bit less than the listing price, because my client's in a big hurry to sell." Unless the seller has authorized this disclosure, the agent has breached her fiduciary duties.

Note that the requirement of confidentiality continues after the formal agency relationship has ended. An agent can't disclose confidential information learned from a former client after the transaction has closed.

Confidentiality must be maintained even during a dual agency. A dual agent can't reveal one client's confidences to the other client. Also, Civil Code § 2079.21 specifically states that a dual agent can't tell the seller that the buyer will pay more than the offered price, or tell the buyer that the seller will accept less than the listing price, unless the disclosure has been authorized in writing. The effort to keep information confidential and avoid using it to either party's disadvantage requires a dual agent to walk a fine line.

Conflicts of Interest. As we've said, an agent must put the interests of the principal above the interests of third parties and above the agent's own interests. Therefore, an agent must be on the lookout for situations that involve **conflicts of interest**—situations in which the agent stands to benefit personally while representing his principal. Even if the agent believes that he can remain loyal to the principal in this type of situation, he must disclose the conflict of interest to the principal. An undisclosed conflict is a breach of fiduciary duty.

Once a conflict of interest has been disclosed, it's up to the principal to decide whether to terminate the transaction in question. Alternatively, the principal might decide to continue with the transaction but terminate the agency.

Conflicts of interest may arise in many situations. We'll look first at situations in which the agent has some kind of relationship with a third party, and then at the problem of self-dealing and secret profits.

Relationship between agent and third party. An agent must inform the principal if a third party is a friend, family member, or business associate of the agent's, or if the agent has an interest in a company involved in a transaction with the principal. This should be done before the principal makes a decision about the other party's offer.

Case Example:

Sierra Pacific purchased several pieces of property for a lump sum. Sierra enlisted a real estate broker named Carter to sell one ten-acre parcel known as the Willow Creek property. Based on Carter's recommendation, Sierra listed the property for $85,000. Carter's commission was to be $5,000.

Carter eventually arranged the sale of the property to his daughter and son-in-law and pocketed the $5,000 commission, without informing Sierra of his relationship to the buyers. The court found that this was a breach of Carter's fiduciary duties to Sierra. In consequence, Carter forfeited his commission. *Sierra Pacific Industries v. Carter* (1980) 104 Cal.App.3d 579.

Self-dealing and secret profits. It is a breach of fiduciary duty for an agent to engage in self-dealing or to collect a secret profit in a transaction. **Self-dealing** occurs when a real estate agent purchases her principal's property on her own behalf, while concealing the fact that she's the buyer. For instance, an agent might have a friend pretend to purchase the property for herself, then immediately deed it to the agent after closing.

Case Example:

Estrin was a real estate broker doing business as Rem Realty Company. One of his salespersons, Nicholson, took a listing for two pieces of real property owned by a Mrs. Collins. The listing price was $23,000. Estrin bought the property, describing himself only as "a real estate broker," not as the seller's own broker and Nicholson's employer. Mrs. Collins didn't realize Estrin was Nicholson's boss, or that Estrin was the owner of Rem Realty Company and had collected a commission on the sale.

The transaction came to the attention of the Real Estate Commissioner's office, and Estrin's license was suspended for six months. Estrin brought an action in superior court to have the suspension lifted. He claimed that his salesperson, Nicholson, should have disclosed Estrin's role as the buyer to Mrs. Collins, but Nicholson testified that Estrin had not asked him to make such a disclosure. The court ruled against Estrin and affirmed the license suspension.

When Estrin appealed, the appellate court agreed with the lower court's decision. Whether or not Nicholson should have given Mrs. Collins more information, Estrin himself had a duty to disclose to her that he was the buyer, and he breached that duty. The court also said it considered Estrin's undisclosed commission a "reprehensible" violation of his fiduciary duties. *Estrin v. Watson* (1957) 150 Cal.App.2d 107.

It's a **secret profit** when an agent profits in some way from a principal's transaction without disclosing that to the principal. While it isn't improper for an agent to buy the principal's property and then resell it for a profit, this can be done only with the principal's knowledge and consent. The principal must also be told the true value of the property.

Case Example:

Roberts owned a shopping center and retained Lomanto as his agent to sell the property. In her capacity as trustee for her family's trust, Lomanto offered to buy the shopping center for $11 million. Lomanto told Roberts that the property was not worth more than that, and Roberts relied on her expertise and trusted her as his agent.

While still Roberts' agent, Lomanto assigned the contract to purchase to a third-party buyer. Roberts consented to the assignment, but Lomanto refused to disclose the assignment fee she would receive and the price the buyer had agreed to pay for the shopping center. Lomanto still asserted, however, that the property was worth only $11 million.

After the deal closed and he had paid Lomanto the agreed-upon 2% commission ($110,000), Roberts learned that Lomanto had received $1.2 million as an assignment fee and that the buyer had paid $12.2 million for the property. When he sued, the court found that Lomanto had concealed the true value of the property and that the $1.2 million assignment fee was an undisclosed profit that breached her fiduciary duties to Roberts. *Roberts v. Lomanto* (2003) 112 Cal.App.4th 1553.

Note that an ordinary buyer—an unlicensed person not acting as the seller's agent—is under no obligation to tell the seller that he plans to resell the property at a profit.

Expert Advice. The duty of utmost care doesn't require the agent to be an expert on every aspect of a real estate transaction. It's sufficient if the agent recommends that the client seek expert advice when appropriate. The front of the agency disclosure form states that a real estate agent has expertise in real estate matters, not legal or tax matters: "A real estate broker is the person qualified to advise on real estate transactions. If you desire legal or tax advice, consult an appropriate professional."

Real estate agents should know their limitations and be very careful not to undertake tasks that exceed their skill or ability. Also, claiming expertise in areas beyond their training or knowledge may be considered fraud.

Cases to Consider...

Carleton, an experienced real estate investor, employed Tortosa, a real estate broker, in the sale of two residential rental properties and the purchase of two others. The listing agreements, disclosure statements, and purchase contracts all advised Carleton that Tortosa's responsibilities as a broker did not include giving tax advice. After the deal closed, Carleton was assessed approximately $34,000 in tax liability because the transactions were not properly structured to qualify as tax-deferred exchanges under IRS rules. Carleton sued his broker, alleging that Tortosa failed to fulfill her fiduciary duty of care by neglecting to warn Carleton of the possible adverse tax consequences of the transactions, and by failing to structure the transactions properly as tax-deferred exchanges. Should the court rule in favor of Carleton (the investor) or Tortosa (the broker)? *Carleton v. Tortosa* (1993) 14 Cal.App.4th 745.

The Salahutdins immigrated to California from Korea. Because Shaucat Salahutdin's parents were peasants who fled Russia during the 1917 revolution, the family was considered "stateless" under Korean law, which meant they were unable to own land in Korea. As a result, it was very important to the Salahutdins to be able to buy property in California that they could subdivide and leave to their two children. They explained this to their real estate agent, and the agent told them that to subdivide in that county they would need to purchase at least one acre. That much land would be hard to come by, but the Salahutdins were willing to wait.

The Salahutdins' agent eventually found a piece of property listed as "1+ acres." He assured the Salahutdins that they would have no trouble subdividing the property. Years after the sale, a boundary dispute revealed that the property was actually smaller than one acre and that a fence surrounding the land was not the actual boundary. The Salahutdins could not legally subdivide the property. They sued their agent for breach of the fiduciary duty of care, claiming that he should have investigated the property more diligently. What should the court decide? *Salahutdin v. Valley of California, Inc.* (1994) 24 Cal.App.4th 555.

Duties Owed to All Parties

In addition to a real estate agent's fiduciary duties to her client (utmost care, loyalty, honesty, and integrity), the agent also owes these general duties to all parties:

- diligent exercise of reasonable skill and care,
- honest and fair dealing and good faith, and
- disclosure of material facts.

Again, these duties are listed on the agency disclosure form required by Civil Code § 2079.16. (See Figure 7.1.)

Reasonable Skill and Care

Real estate agents owe their clients utmost care, but they also owe any party they work with the duty to use reasonable skill and care. Even if you don't have an agency relationship with a particular buyer or seller, you must meet this minimum standard.

Essentially, a real estate agent who claims to have certain skills and abilities is expected to act as a competent agent having those skills and abilities would act. Civil Code § 2079.2 specifically states that the standard of care is "the degree of care that a reasonably prudent real estate licensee would exercise…measured by the degree of knowledge through education, experience, and examination, required to obtain a license."

If a real estate agent causes harm to a third party due to carelessness or incompetence, the agent or her employing broker can be held liable, and either or both may have to compensate the injured party. The extent of the liability depends on two things. First, would a competent real estate agent have foreseen that there was an unreasonable risk of harm to the third party? And second, did the agent use reasonable skill and care under the circumstances? In *Norman I. Krug Real Estate Investments, Inc. v. Praszker* (1990) 220 Cal.App.3d 35, the court indicated that the following factors will be considered:

- the extent the transaction was intended to affect the third party,
- the foreseeability of harm,

Fig. 7.3 Real estate agent's duties to buyers and sellers

> **Duties owed to the principal**
> - Utmost care, integrity, honesty, and loyalty
>
> **Duties owed to all parties**
> - Reasonable skill and care
> - Honest and fair dealing and good faith
> - Disclosure of material facts

- the degree of certainty of the injury suffered,
- the moral blame attached to the agent's conduct, and
- the policy of preventing future harm.

We said earlier that real estate agents should encourage their clients to seek the advice of other experts whenever it's appropriate to do so. This is just as important with customers as with clients, if not more so. Giving advice to customers (as opposed to clients) isn't really part of the agent's role; as we discussed in Chapter 6, it can give rise to an inadvertent dual agency.

Honest and Fair Dealing and Good Faith

A real estate agent owes third parties the duty of honest and fair dealing and good faith. Making inaccurate statements or misrepresentations is a breach of this duty, and may also constitute fraud. Most real estate fraud cases involve misrepresentations about the property that are made to prospective buyers by the seller or the seller's agent. In this section, we'll discuss misrepresentations by both sellers and agents, since essentially the same rules apply to both.

While real estate fraud cases are usually based on spoken or written false statements, a claim of fraud can also be based on misleading conduct.

> **Example:** A house for sale has a mold problem in the walls of several bedrooms. The sellers and their real estate agent agree that instead of correcting the problem or telling potential buyers about it, they'll repaint the walls and make sure the windows are open to air out the rooms before showings. This concealment is fraudulent.

Actual Fraud vs. Constructive Fraud. There are two types of fraud: actual and constructive. **Actual fraud** (also called **deceit**) involves intentional misrepresentation or deception, as in the example just given. The perpetrator deliberately misleads the other party. Any of the following intentional actions would be actual fraud or deceit:

1. suggesting or asserting that something is a fact when you don't believe it to be true;
2. positively asserting that something is a fact when you have no reasonable grounds for believing it's true, or when the assertion isn't warranted by the information you have;
3. suppressing information that you know or believe to be true when you're legally required to disclose it, or when suppressing information causes other information you've provided to be misleading;
4. making a promise without any intention of performing it; or
5. performing "any other act fitted to deceive."

Constructive fraud is a misrepresentation resulting from negligence or carelessness, without a fraudulent intent. In other words, a false statement was made or misleading conduct occurred, but there was no intent to deceive the other party. Civil Code § 1573 gives this definition of constructive fraud: "[A]ny breach of duty which, without an actually fraudulent intent, gains an advantage to the person in fault…by misleading another to his prejudice."

Fig. 7.4 Types of fraud

Actual Fraud	**Constructive Fraud**
• Intentional deception • Involves a deliberate action or statement	• Results from negligence or carelessness • Need not involve deliberate act or statement

---

Example: When checking on the zoning that applies to one of his listings, a real estate agent misreads the city zoning map. As a result, the agent ends up giving incorrect information to some buyers, who take the zoning into account when they decide to purchase the property. The agent may have committed constructive fraud.

Note that under the statutory definitions, simply failing to disclose information that you're legally required to disclose can amount to fraud—either actual or constructive, depending on whether the failure to disclose was intentional or negligent. We'll discuss exactly what types of information real estate agents (and sellers) are required to disclose to buyers in the next section of the chapter.

 Cover Your Bases

Misrepresentation violates the Real Estate Law, as well as the Civil Code. (See Chapter 8.) According to the California Bureau of Real Estate, misrepresentation is among the five most frequent violations resulting in disciplinary action. The following is from the CalBRE's publication *Most Common Enforcement Violations*.

Misrepresentation Violations

[Bus. & Prof. Code] Section 10176(a) — Making a substantial misrepresentation in a transaction for which a real estate license is required. The term misrepresentation not only applies to a direct statement regarding a material fact that is untruthful or incorrect, but it also includes the failure of a real estate licensee to disclose material facts that the principal should be made aware of.

Remedy

Real estate licensees should avoid making any statement they do not know to be true to a principal in a transaction. And because failure by licensees to disclose material facts to principals in real estate transactions is a continuing problem, licensees should remember the simple admonition — When in doubt, disclose, and do it in writing.

A buyer who was induced to enter into a contract as a result of either actual or constructive fraud has the right to rescind the contract. In addition, the seller or real estate agent who committed the fraud may be required to pay the victim compensatory damages. With actual fraud, punitive damages are also a possibility. Remember, too, that if an agent commits fraud, her principal could be held liable under the doctrine of vicarious liability (see Chapter 6).

Puffing, Opinions, and Predictions. Not every inaccurate statement can be grounds for a lawsuit. A misrepresentation is "actionable" (a basis for legal action) only if someone relied on the statement and was injured as a result. Also, it must have been reasonable for her to have acted in reliance on the statement.

Some statements that a real estate agent might make to induce buyers to purchase real property aren't actionable, because they're not the type of statements a reasonable person would rely on when deciding whether to buy property. For the most part, the following types of statements have not been considered actionable:

- Puffing: "This house is the nicest one in the whole neighborhood."
- Opinion: "I think this house is a really great buy."
- Prediction: "I'll bet this house doubles in value over the next ten years."

Generally speaking, if a statement is neither specific nor measurable ("this is a super house!") instead of specific and measurable ("this house will appreciate 12% per year for as long as you own it"), it is not actionable.

> **Example:** Sally and Joe are retiring. They tell the selling agent that they want a home near the water where they can relax and enjoy the peace and quiet. The agent shows them a little cottage near the beach and says, "This is the most peaceful, relaxing place on earth!"
>
> After buying the cottage, Sally and Joe discover that the beach is extremely popular during the summer tourist season, and their cottage is subject to a lot of nearby foot traffic and noise from the beach. Contrary to what the agent said, the cottage isn't peaceful or relaxing at all. Even so, it's unlikely that the agent would be held liable for his statement. It was just puffing.

It should be noted, however, that in California there is a growing tendency to treat misleading opinions and predictions as actionable misrepresentations, since unsophisticated buyers sometimes do rely on them. California courts have generally found that a statement couched as an opinion, made by someone having special knowledge of real estate, may be treated as an actionable misstatement of fact. Whether such a statement is a nonactionable opinion or an actionable misrepresentation is a question for a jury. To stay out of trouble, real estate agents should avoid idle sales talk that could be construed as a statement of fact.

Case to Consider...

In 1993, Agent Shore negotiated a sale of residential property between her client, the seller, and an investor named Furla. Furla bought the seller's house for $935,000, which represented an offer of $170 per square foot for 5,500 square feet. Several sources stated that the house was 5,500 square feet: the MLS listing; an oral statement by Agent Shore; and a property profile from a title insurance company. The seller's daughter had told Shore that the architectural plans described the house as 5,500 square feet, although the plans actually said 5,334 square feet. A cost breakdown from the contractor also said 5,334 square feet. Yet during the closing process, an appraisal of the property indicated that the house was only 4,311 square feet—but worth the agreed price of $935,000 even so. However, Furla's lender relayed only the appraiser's conclusion concerning the property's value to Furla; he was never given a copy of the appraisal report that showed the lower square footage figure.

A year later, Furla decided to sell the property he'd bought. During an initial inspection, his listing agent said, "There is no way this house is 5,500 square feet." The agent later stated that a knowledgeable real estate agent should have been able to easily recognize that the house was less than 5,500 square feet.

Furla sued Agent Shore, her broker, and the original seller. In her defense, Shore pointed to the purchase agreement, which stated that the broker made no representation as to boundary size and that the square footage was an "approximation." The trial court granted summary judgment for the defendants on the grounds that Shore had reasonable justification to believe the house was 5,500 square feet, and that it had not been justifiable for Furla to rely on Shore's statements. (To grant summary judgment, a court must decide that there is no triable issue of fact, and therefore no need for a jury to hear the case. See Chapter 2.) Furla appealed. Could Agent Shore and the other defendants be held liable for negligent misrepresentation? Was the trial court right to deny Furla a trial before a jury? *Furla v. Jon Douglas Co.* (1998) 65 Cal.App.4th 1069.

Disclosure of Material Facts

A real estate agent has a duty to disclose **material facts** concerning the property to any party—buyer or seller, client or customer. Specifically, California law requires a real estate agent to disclose information if it:

- is known to the agent and not to the parties,
- is not within the diligent attention and observation of the parties, and
- materially affects the value or desirability of the property.

In effect, an agent must disclose any fact that a reasonable person would want to consider when evaluating the value or desirability of real property, unless it's something the parties can observe for themselves through "diligent attention."

Latent Defects. Problems that are not easily observable in an ordinary inspection of the property are often called **latent defects**. If a real estate agent is aware of a latent defect, the defect is a material fact that the agent must point out to prospective buyers. The same requirement applies to property sellers: sellers are required by law to disclose known latent defects to buyers.

Example: A roof leaks in several places when it rains, but on a dry day you can't see any evidence of the leaks. Naturally, the seller is aware of the problem, and she mentions it to her listing agent. This is a known latent defect, and both the seller and the broker have a legal duty to tell potential buyers about the leaky roof.

In residential transactions, the buyer must be given a transfer disclosure statement, which has sections for the seller, the listing agent, and the selling agent to fill out. Known latent defects should be reported on this form. We'll discuss transfer disclosure statements in Chapter 9.

Duty to Inspect. At one time, disclosing known latent defects—hidden problems that the seller had told the agent about, or that the agent had noticed on his own—was basically all that an agent representing a seller had to do for prospective buyers. The law didn't require the agent to inspect the property and to look for problems. Today, however, California law specifically imposes a duty of inspection on real estate agents in transactions involving residential property with up to four units. Before we examine the modern law, let's look at the development of the inspection duty in California.

The *Easton* case. The California case that ushered in the duty to inspect was *Easton v. Strassburger* (1984) 152 Cal.App.3d 90. Here's a summary of the facts in the case:

> In May 1976, Easton purchased a one-acre residential property from the Strassburgers. The property was improved with a 3,000-square-foot home, a swimming pool, and a guest house.
>
> Soon after Easton bought the home, a large landslide occurred on the property. Subsequent slides in 1977 and 1978 destroyed part of the driveway. Expert testimony later revealed that the slides had occurred because a portion of the property was fill that had not been properly compacted. The slides caused damage to the foundation of the house, large cracks in the walls, and warped doorways. The damage was so severe that, while the property's undamaged value was approximately $170,000, its value in its damaged condition was estimated to be only $20,000. Cost estimates for repairing the damage and preventing further slides added up to more than $200,000.
>
> The Strassburgers had experienced two slides on the property during the time they lived there, but they did not inform their agents or the buyer, Easton, of these earlier incidents.
>
> The agents representing the sellers had inspected the property prior to sale and noticed several "red flags"—such as the cracks in the walls—that raised the possibility of soil problems. The agents did not request soil tests or inform Easton of the potential problems.

The central issue before the *Easton* court was whether a seller's agent is negligent if he fails to disclose defects that should have been discovered through reasonable diligence and the exercise of reasonable care. The court answered in the affirmative. It found that the duty to perform a reasonably competent and diligent inspection of the listed property in order to discover defects for the benefit of the buyer was implicit in the duty of reasonable care. To hold otherwise would have encouraged real estate agents to shield themselves with ignorance and to disregard red flags (based on the theory that as long as they didn't know about a problem, they couldn't be held liable for failure to disclose it). Such a system would be contrary to public policy established in earlier case law, a policy that seeks to protect buyers from unethical real estate agents and sellers, and to ensure that buyers have enough information to make sound purchasing decisions.

So the *Easton* decision expanded on earlier case law to include a duty of diligent inspection for the buyer's benefit. Furthermore, the court held that real estate agents were chargeable with what they should have known had they performed a reasonably competent inspection. The court added, however, that the agent's duty to inspect and disclose does not relieve the buyer of the duty to use reasonable care to protect herself from harm.

Statutory duty to inspect. The California legislature responded to the *Easton* decision with Civil Code § 2079, enacted in 1985. It was the legislature's intent to "codify and make precise" the holding in *Easton v. Strassburger* with this new statute, but not to modify or restrict the existing duties of real estate agents. Here's a summary of the statute:

- **When the duty to inspect applies.** The duty to inspect applies to transactions involving residential property with one to four dwelling units or a manufactured home. (There's an exemption for new homes in subdivisions offered for sale for the first time.) It applies not only to listings and sales transactions, but also to leases with options to purchase, ground leases, and land contracts.
- **Who it applies to.** This is a duty owed to prospective buyers by real estate brokers and their affiliated sales agents who have a contract with the seller (listing agents) or who act in cooperation with the listing broker (selling agents).
- **What's required.** A real estate agent owes a prospective buyer an affirmative duty to conduct a "reasonably competent and diligent visual inspection of the property." If the inspection reveals any material facts affecting the value or desirability of the property, the agent must disclose them to the buyer.
- **What's not required.** The legislature set some limits on the duty to inspect. Agents do not have to inspect any of the following:
  - areas that are not reasonably or normally accessible;
  - areas off the site of the subject property;
  - public records or permits concerning the title or use of the property; or
  - in condominiums or cooperatives, areas outside the individual unit for sale (common areas).
- **Buyer's responsibility.** The statute repeats the *Easton* court's caution that an agent's duty to inspect the property on the buyer's behalf doesn't mean that a buyer has no responsibility to examine the property for herself. Section 2079.5 states, "Nothing in this article relieves a buyer...of the duty to exercise reasonable care to protect himself or herself..." An agent should not be held liable for failure to disclose "facts which are known to or within the observation and diligent attention of the buyer."
- **Statute of limitations.** There's a two-year statute of limitations on legal actions based on a breach of duty under § 2079. The statute of limitations begins to run from the date the buyer takes possession of the property, which is defined in the

law as the date of close of escrow, the date of recordation, or the date of occupancy, whichever comes first.

The results of an agent's visual inspection of the property should be reported to the buyer on the transfer disclosure statement. The listing and selling agents' sections of the form are specifically intended for disclosures based on the agents' inspections.

Here's an important point to keep in mind: although the duty to inspect applies only to residential property with up to four units or to a manufactured home, the duty to disclose known latent defects and other known material facts applies to any real estate transaction, no matter what kind of property is involved.

Statutorily Required Pamphlets. Various California statutes require sellers and real estate agents to provide buyers with information booklets prepared by state agencies. For residential transactions, these include:

- a booklet on common environmental hazards such as radon and asbestos,
- a booklet called *A Homeowner's Guide to Earthquake Safety*, and
- a booklet concerning the dangers of lead-based paint (for homes built before 1978).

Civil Code § 2079 states that giving a buyer these general information booklets does not relieve an agent or seller of the duty to disclose any known problems affecting the property being sold. For example, providing the booklet about environmental hazards does not make it unnecessary to disclose the known presence of asbestos in a home.

Facts that Don't Need to Be Disclosed. Civil Code § 1710.2(a) provides that certain information does not need to be—and sometimes must not be—disclosed. There is no duty to disclose the manner or occurrence of a prior occupant's death on the property if the death occurred more than three years before the buyer's offer. Note, however, that in cases regarding death on the property, sellers and agents may not provide misinformation if they face a direct inquiry from a prospective buyer.

> **Example:** A real estate agent is showing a home to some buyers. The agent knows that the son of the previous owner was killed in the home seven years ago. Because it's been more than three years, the agent is under no obligation to disclose the murder. At the end of the tour, however, one of the buyers says, "You know, this house looks kind of familiar. Is this the place I remember seeing on the news? The one where that kid was killed a long time ago?" The agent is now obligated to disclose the information.

On the other hand, agents should never disclose whether a current or prior owner or resident had AIDS or was HIV-positive. In fact, if a prospective buyer asks whether anyone with AIDS or HIV lived in the house, the agent should refuse to answer the question, explaining to the buyer that answering it could violate fair housing laws that prohibit discrimination based on disability (see Chapter 19).

"As is" Clauses. Here's one final point about disclosure of material facts. Sometimes a purchase agreement includes an "as is" clause, an affirmation that the seller isn't warranting the property's condition and that the seller will not negotiate or make any repairs. Sometimes sellers or real estate agents believe that an "as is" clause is a Get Out of Jail

Free card, making it unnecessary to tell the buyer about specific problems with the property. But it doesn't work that way. Stating that property is for sale "as is" doesn't negate the agent's or the seller's duty to disclose known latent defects.

Also, an "as is" clause will not shield an agent or a seller from liability for fraudulent misrepresentations.

Case to Consider...

Broker Savage represented the sellers in the sale of a building in San Francisco. Lingsch and some other buyers purchased the property. It was an "as is" sale: the purchase agreement stated that the buyers agreed to purchase the property "in its present state and condition." After they'd bought the property, the buyers discovered that the building was in severe disrepair. It had, in fact, been condemned by city officials before the sale. The buyers sued to recover compensatory and punitive damages for fraud. Savage claimed that because the property was purchased "as is," he had no duty to disclose material facts. Since he didn't actually lie to the buyers, but merely kept information about the building's condition to himself, Savage argued that he wasn't guilty of fraud. Could Savage be held liable for fraud? *Lingsch v. Savage* (1963) 213 Cal.App.2d 729.

Whether or not there's an "as is" clause in the contract, whether you're showing property to a customer or advising a client—whatever the situation—remember this dictum from the California Bureau of Real Estate: "When in doubt, disclose, and do it in writing." And always provide accurate information in a straightforward manner, without shading the truth. That's the only way to stay out of trouble in your real estate career.

Case Law in Depth

The following case involves some of the legal issues discussed in this chapter. Read through the facts and consider the questions in light of what you have learned. Then read what the court actually decided.

Brown v. FSR Brokerage, Inc. (1998) 62 Cal.App.4th 766

In 1994, Brown listed a home in Beverly Hills with a broker for $3,950,000. Over the next two years, having no luck finding a buyer, Brown reduced the asking price repeatedly. He eventually listed the property with FSR Brokerage for $2,495,000.

Barbara Tenenbaum, a salesperson employed by FSR, took the listing. Tenenbaum had a partnership agreement with another FSR salesperson, Sid Kibrick, in which they agreed to share each other's listings, both acting as listing agents for all of their listed properties. In May, Kibrick spoke to a lawyer representing a prospective buyer named Lafferty, who told him that Lafferty wanted a new home quickly. When Kibrick learned that the buyer wanted to pay $2.4 million, he promised Lafferty's lawyer that he would try to talk the seller, Brown, down to that figure. Kibrick said that if Lafferty offered $2.4 million, he thought Brown would accept.

On June 1, 1996, Kibrick brought Lafferty to see Brown's property. After the showing, Kibrick told Brown that Lafferty would probably make an offer. The next day, Kibrick took Brown aside and said that Lafferty would offer $2.4 million. Brown wanted to insist on $2,495,000 (the listing price), but Kibrick said that they would lose the buyer if Brown didn't agree to the lower price. According to Brown, Kibrick also repeatedly assured Brown that he was working exclusively for him. Tenenbaum advised Brown to stick with the higher price and consult a lawyer, but Brown decided to follow Kibrick's advice instead.

Because Lafferty was determined to move into the home in less than a week, the closing process progressed very rapidly. On June 4, Tenenbaum told Brown it was time to go to escrow. At that point, there was no signed purchase agreement; in fact, the buyer hadn't even submitted a written offer yet. The first written documents were presented to Brown at the escrow office, when Tenenbaum gave them to Brown to sign. One of the attachments was the agency disclosure form, and an agency confirmation statement in the escrow instructions listed both Tenenbaum and Kibrick as listing agents and Kibrick as the selling agent. But there was no discussion about these provisions; Tenenbaum merely told Brown where to sign.

After closing, Brown finally noticed the references to dual agency in the escrow documents. Claiming this was the first he knew about the relationship between Kibrick and the buyer, Brown sued FSR Brokerage and Kibrick for breach of fiduciary duties. In his defense, Kibrick argued that Brown had signed the agency disclosure statement and agency confirmation provision at closing, and it wasn't Kibrick's fault that Brown couldn't be bothered to read them.

The trial court concluded that Brown didn't have a case and granted summary judgment to the defendants. Brown appealed.

The questions:

Was Kibrick acting as Brown's agent, Lafferty's agent, or a dual agent? Was Tenenbaum a dual agent? Did Kibrick breach any fiduciary duties? What about Tenenbaum's duties to Brown? Did Tenenbaum and Kibrick make the required agency disclosures to Brown in time? Did they fulfill the statutory requirements by merely making sure that Brown signed the forms containing the disclosures?

The court's answers:

Because Kibrick and Tenenbaum had a partnership agreement that made them listing agents on each other's listings, Kibrick was Brown's agent. However, when Kibrick brought the buyer, Lafferty, into the transaction and began serving as his agent, Kibrick became a dual agent. Tenenbaum, by virtue of her partnership agreement with Kibrick, also became a dual agent.

"Even in a consented dual agency situation, the statute specifically forbids the agent from disclosing to the buyer, without express permission from the seller, that the seller will accept less than the listing price. (Civ. Code, § 2079.21.) Based on [the buyer's lawyer's] testimony, that is substantially what Kibrick did.

"Respondents argue that the documents signed or initialed by Brown include adequate disclosures, and that it was his decision not to read them... [However,] the statute and common sense require that the dual agent call attention to the fact of dual agency, and Brown has submitted substantial evidence that [Kibrick and Tenenbaum] failed to do so. He was not on notice that any of the documents he signed or initialed was anything other than a routine instrument technically required for consummation of the sales transaction...[B]y the time the escrow papers were being signed, Brown already had "broken" his price: he could hardly then demand a greater price, particularly since, so far as the record discloses, the buyer was guilty of no impropriety except through his dual agent...

"We end our discussion as we began it: To the degree Brown can prove a monetary loss on account of actions and failures to act by respondents, he is entitled to appropriate monetary recovery."

The result:

The appellate court reversed the trial court's decision granting summary judgment to the defendants. Brown, the seller and plaintiff, was entitled to present his case concerning the agents' breach of fiduciary duties.

Chapter Summary

- In a transaction involving the sale of commercial property or residential property with up to four dwelling units, a leasehold interest in such property exceeding one year, or a mobile home, a real estate agent must give an agency disclosure form to each party before that party signs a contract. The disclosure form explains the duties of a seller's agent, a buyer's agent, and a dual agent. In addition, the parties must sign an agency confirmation statement that indicates which party each agent is representing in the transaction.

- As an agency relationship is a fiduciary relationship, a real estate agent owes her clients the fiduciary duties of utmost care, integrity, honesty, and loyalty. She must always put her client's interests above her own and above those of any third party. She must obey the client's instructions, keep the client's private information confidential, disclose any potential conflicts of interest, and recommend that the client seek another expert's advice when necessary.

- A real estate agent also owes certain duties to all of the parties he works with, whether or not they're his clients. These include the duty to diligently exercise reasonable skill and care, the duty of honesty and fair dealing and good faith, and the duty to disclose material facts.

- Inaccurate statements and misleading actions are violations of the agent's duty of honesty and good faith and may be considered fraud if a party relies on them and is injured as a result. Fraud may be actual (intentional) or constructive (negligent). Puffing, opinions, and predictions have traditionally not been considered actionable misrepresentations, but some may cross the line.

- An agent must disclose known material facts to clients and customers. Information known to the agent is considered material if it is not within the diligent attention and observation of the parties and it materially affects the value or desirability of the property. This includes latent defects (problems with a property that are not easily observable). Both sellers and agents are required to disclose known latent defects to buyers.

- In transactions involving residential property with up to four units, an agent has an affirmative duty to conduct a reasonably competent and diligent visual inspection of the accessible areas of the property. The results of the inspection must be disclosed to the buyer on the transfer disclosure statement.

Key Terms

- **Fiduciary** – A person who occupies a position of special trust and confidence in relation to another. The law requires a fiduciary to place the other person's interests above his own and those of third parties.

- **Self-dealing** – When an agent purchases a client's property on her own behalf but conceals the fact that she's the actual buyer.

- **Secret profit** – A benefit, monetary or otherwise, gained from the sale of property without the knowledge of one's client.

- **Actual fraud** – Making a misrepresentation or taking an action that's intended to deceive another person, if the other person acts in reliance on the misrepresentation.

- **Constructive fraud** – A misrepresentation that results from negligence or carelessness, rather than an intention to deceive.

- **Puffing** – Exaggerated, vague statements made by a real estate agent while showing property to a buyer, such as, "This is the most beautiful house in the neighborhood!" Puffing usually isn't actionable (grounds for a lawsuit), since a reasonable person would know not to rely on this type of statement in deciding whether to purchase property.

- **Material fact** – In the real estate context, any information that a reasonable person would want to consider when determining the value or desirability of real property.

- **Latent defect** – A problem with the property not easily discovered through ordinary inspection.

- **"As is" clause** – A provision in a purchase agreement in which the buyer acknowledges that the property is being purchased in its present condition and the seller isn't warranting that it's in good condition.

Chapter Quiz

1. Stark lists his property with Bell, a licensed broker. Bell shows the property to her cousin, who decides he would like to buy it. Which of the following is true?
   a) Bell can present her cousin's offer to Stark, as long as she tells Stark that the prospective buyer is one of her relatives
   b) Bell violated her fiduciary duties to Stark by showing the property to one of her relatives
   c) It wasn't unethical for Bell to show the property to a relative, but it would be a violation of her fiduciary duties if she presented the cousin's offer to Stark
   d) It is not necessary for Bell to tell Stark that the buyer is related to her, as long as he is offering the full listing price for the property

2. Broker Stevens is helping his client sell some property. The client asks Stevens to give him advice on how to structure the transaction to reduce the amount of income tax he'll have to pay on the proceeds of the sale. Broker Stevens should:
   a) offer to take a look at the tax laws and see what he can come up with
   b) tell the client that he will ask another real estate broker for advice
   c) tell the client to consult an expert qualified to provide advice on income tax matters
   d) None of the above

3. When doing her initial inspection of a client's property, the listing agent notices water stains in the basement. The seller states, "Oh yeah. It leaks sometimes." This is an example of:
   a) confidential information
   b) constructive fraud
   c) a material fact
   d) None of the above

4. Confidential information that an agent receives from his principal:
   a) can be disclosed without consent if it's in the principal's best interests to do so
   b) can be disclosed without consent if the transaction depends on it
   c) must be protected for as long as the agency relationship continues
   d) must be protected for as long as the agency relationship continues and even after it ends

5. Opinions and predictions that turn out to be untrue:
   a) are considered to be constructive fraud rather than misrepresentations
   b) are considered to be actual fraud rather than constructive fraud
   c) have generally not been considered actionable misrepresentations, but are actionable in some cases
   d) were traditionally regarded as actionable misrepresentations, but are no longer actionable under California law

6. A material fact not easily discovered through ordinary inspection is an example of:
   a) constructive fraud
   b) a latent defect
   c) an exculpatory clause
   d) None of the above

7. Jones, the listing agent for a single-family home, gives a potential buyer the statutorily required booklet on common environmental hazards. She doesn't inform the buyer that the seller told her elevated radon levels were detected in the home when it was tested two years ago, and nothing has been done to address the problem. Has Agent Jones breached a duty to the buyer?
   a) No, because she is not the buyer's agent
   b) No, because she provided the required booklet, and that fulfills her duty of disclosure
   c) Yes, because she owes a fiduciary duty to the buyer to disclose material facts
   d) Yes, because providing general information booklets does not relieve an agent of the duty to disclose known material facts about the property

8. An agent owes his principal the duties of:
   a) diligence, duality, adequate care, and confidentiality
   b) utmost care, integrity, honesty, and loyalty
   c) making her the largest profit possible
   d) None of the above

9. A potential buyer asks the selling agent if anyone with AIDS ever lived in the house. The selling agent should:
   a) answer the buyer's question, because she has a duty to disclose material facts to the buyer
   b) answer the buyer's question but explain why it's not a material fact
   c) refuse to answer the buyer's question and explain that disclosing that information might violate state and federal antidiscrimination laws
   d) refuse to answer the buyer's question and withdraw from the agency relationship

10. An "as is" clause in a purchase agreement:
    a) won't relieve an agent of the duty to disclose material facts
    b) relieves the selling agent of the duty to perform a visual inspection
    c) means the listing agent isn't liable for failure to disclose material facts
    d) will protect the listing or selling agent from liability for fraudulent misrepresentations

Chapter Answer Key

Chapter Quiz Answers:

1. a) A seller's real estate agent is required to tell the seller if the prospective buyer is related to or otherwise connected with the agent.

2. c) An agent should never offer information or advice outside his area of expertise; he should recommend to clients and customers that they consult another expert when appropriate.

3. c) The leaky basement is a material fact that must be disclosed to the buyer, since it might affect the property's value or desirability.

4. d) An agent must protect the principal's confidential information during and after the agency relationship. It must not be disclosed without the principal's consent.

5. c) As a general rule, opinions and predictions have not been considered actionable misrepresentations, but courts sometimes hold otherwise. If an opinion or prediction is held to be actionable, it could be either actual or constructive fraud.

6. b) A latent defect is any material fact concerning the property that is not easily discovered through ordinary inspection.

7. d) Providing one of the general information booklets required by statute does not make it unnecessary to disclose specific information about a problem with the property.

8. b) An agent owes the duties of utmost care, integrity, honesty, and loyalty to the principal.

9. c) The agent should refuse to answer the question because to do so could violate laws that prohibit discrimination based on disability. Civil Code § 1710.2 specifically provides that neither an agent nor a seller is required to disclose whether a prior resident had AIDS or was HIV-positive.

10. a) Stating that property is for sale "as is" doesn't negate the agent's duty to inspect the property and disclose material facts about its condition.

Cases to Consider... Answers:

Fulfilling the Duty of Care (Expert Advice)

Carleton v. Tortosa (1993) 14 Cal.App.4th 745. The court sided with Tortosa. A real estate agent's duty of care does not include a duty to offer expert advice on areas outside the field of real estate. Tortosa fulfilled the duty of care when she informed Carleton that he needed to seek the advice of his own accountant or attorney.

Fulfilling the Duty of Care (Diligence)

Salahutdin v. Valley of California, Inc. (1994) 24 Cal.App.4th 555. The court sided with the Salahutdins. The agent knew how important it was to his clients to be able to subdivide the property. While the agent had no duty to investigate public records to confirm the actual boundaries, he did have a duty to disclose to the Salahutdins that he was relying solely upon the seller's description of the property.

Actionable Misrepresentations

Furla v. Jon Douglas Co. (1998) 65 Cal.App.4th 1069. The appellate court overturned the trial court's grant of summary judgment. Ordinarily a buyer is entitled to rely on a seller's representations concerning the property's area, and isn't required to hire an expert to determine whether the seller's representations are accurate. On the other hand, the buyer is expected to exercise reasonable care to protect himself. Whether Furla failed to protect himself appropriately was an issue for a jury to decide. Also, a statement couched as an opinion, made by one holding special knowledge of the subject matter (a real estate agent), may be treated as an actionable misrepresentation. The appellate court found that a reasonable jury might conclude that a grossly inaccurate approximation of square footage amounts to an actionable misrepresentation of fact; therefore, summary judgment was not appropriate. Furla should have been allowed to present his case to a jury.

"As Is" Clauses and Failure to Disclose Material Facts

Lingsch v. Savage (1963) 213 Cal.App.2d 729. The court disagreed with Savage. Keeping back a material fact that affects the value or desirability of the property is just as actionable as an outright lie. Furthermore, an "as is" clause does not relieve a real estate agent of the duty to disclose latent defects and other material facts to third parties.

List of Cases

Brown v. FSR Brokerage, Inc. (1998) 62 Cal.App.4th 766
Carleton v. Tortosa (1993) 14 Cal.App.4th 745
Easton v. Strassburger (1984) 152 Cal.App.3d 90
Estrin v. Watson (1957) 150 Cal.App.2d 107
Furla v. Jon Douglas Co. (1998) 65 Cal.App.4th 1069
Lingsch v. Savage (1963) 213 Cal.App.2d 729
Norman I. Krug Real Estate Investments, Inc. v. Praszker (1990) 220 Cal.App.3d 35
Roberts v. Lomanto (2003) 112 Cal.App.4th 1553
Salahutdin v. Valley of California, Inc. (1994) 24 Cal.App.4th 555
Sierra Pacific Industries v. Carter (1980) 104 Cal.App.3d 579

Chapter 8

Regulation of Real Estate Licensees

Outline

B.   Disciplinary procedures
   1.   Citations
   2.   Accusation and hearing
   3.   Real Estate Recovery Account

Introduction

In this chapter, we'll take a closer look at the Real Estate Law and its requirements. First, we'll discuss the activities that require a real estate license as well as the exemptions from the license requirement. Next, we'll examine the rules that govern the operation of a brokerage business. We'll also consider the broker's role as the client's agent and as the salesperson's principal. Finally, we'll cover the prohibited acts and disciplinary procedures set forth in the Real Estate Law and its accompanying regulations.

Administration of the License Law

In 1917, California passed the nation's first real estate licensing law. After several constitutional challenges, California's supreme court upheld the licensing law as a reasonable use of the state's police power to promote the health, safety, and general welfare of the public. This licensing law, now known as the Real Estate Law, contains the requirements for obtaining and renewing a real estate license as well as the grounds for disciplinary action. Its provisions are contained in Business and Professions Code §§ 10000 – 11506.

The Real Estate Law is administered by the **California Bureau of Real Estate (Cal-BRE)**. The Commissioner of the CalBRE, who is appointed by the Governor, enforces the license law by issuing and denying licenses and by taking disciplinary action in response to license law violations. In addition, the Commissioner can issue regulations to implement the Real Estate Law. These regulations, which have the force and effect of law, are found in Title 10 (Chapter 6, §§ 2705 – 3109) of the California Code of Regulations.

The California Attorney General represents the Commissioner in legal proceedings involving the CalBRE, and advises the Commissioner on license law issues.

Real Estate License Requirement

The cornerstone of the Real Estate Law is the requirement that real estate professionals must be licensed. Licensing is the most common way to regulate the members of any profession.

Section 10130 of the Business and Professions Code states:

> It is unlawful for any person to engage in the business of, act in the capacity of, advertise as, or assume to act as a real estate broker or a real estate salesperson within this state without first obtaining a real estate license from the department...

But what does it mean to act like a real estate broker? What activities fall under "engag[ing] in the business"? It's critical for a licensee to understand which activities require a real estate license. For instance, suppose a broker wants to hire an unlicensed assistant to help with her business. Could this person answer phones, hand out flyers at an open house, or deliver contracts? What about answering a client's finance questions? A thorough understanding of current statutory provisions will help the broker decide which of these tasks may be safely delegated to others.

Activities Requiring a License

The Real Estate Law sets forth a list of activities that require a real estate license. Anyone who engages in any of the following activities, for compensation or the promise of compensation, is considered to be acting as a **real estate broker** and must be licensed:

1. **Sales, purchases, and exchanges.** Selling, buying, or exchanging real property or a business opportunity.
2. **Leases.** Leasing or collecting rents from real property or a business opportunity; or buying, selling, or exchanging leases on real property or a business opportunity.
3. **Advertising and listings.** Soliciting prospective sellers, buyers, or tenants, or listing real property or a business opportunity for sale or lease.
4. **Government lands.** Locating or filing an application for the purchase or lease of lands owned by the state or federal government.
5. **Advance fees.** Charging or collecting an advance fee to promote the sale or lease of real property or a business opportunity (by advertising or listing it, by obtaining financing, or in some other way).
6. **Mortgage loan brokerage.** Soliciting borrowers or lenders for or negotiating loans secured by liens on real property or business opportunities, or collecting payments or performing other services in connection with such loans.
7. **Selling, buying, or exchanging loans or securities.** Selling, buying, or exchanging real property securities, land contracts, or promissory notes secured by liens on real property or business opportunities, and performing services for the holders of contracts or notes.

Anyone who engages in any of these activities on behalf of a broker is considered to be acting as a **real estate salesperson** and must also be licensed.

While not exhaustive, the list shown above illustrates the range of situations and circumstances that require a real estate license. It's important to remember that a license is needed to perform any of these acts even if the promised compensation is never actually paid. If someone promised to give you his boat in exchange for listing his property, the licensing requirements will still apply to you even if he later reneges on that promise.

Note that the licensing requirement also applies to some activities that you may not normally think of as requiring a real estate license. Let's take a brief look at some of these activities.

Business Opportunities. A **business opportunity** is defined as the sale or lease of a business, including the inventory, equipment, goodwill, and other assets. Anyone who handles business opportunities must be licensed, even if the business opportunity does not include the sale of any real property or any interest in real property (such as a long-term lease).

Mortgage Loan Brokerage. A **mortgage broker** is someone who brings real estate buyers and lenders together. A real estate license is required if you engage in any of the following actions in connection with loans secured by real property or business opportunities: soliciting borrowers or lenders, negotiating loans, collecting payments, or performing other services for borrowers, lenders, or note holders.

MLO endorsement. Real estate brokers can't engage in residential mortgage loan brokerage without a **mortgage loan originator endorsement** on their real estate license from the Bureau of Real Estate. The requirements for obtaining an MLO endorsement include becoming licensed through the Nationwide Mortgage Licensing System and Registry.

In addition, no real estate broker can accept compensation from a lender or a mortgage loan originator in a transaction involving a residential mortgage loan unless the broker has an MLO endorsement. (A residential mortgage loan is a loan primarily for personal, family, or household use that is secured by a dwelling with up to four units.)

Any real estate broker or salesperson with an MLO endorsement who engages in residential mortgage loan activities must notify CalBRE by submitting an online notification form within 30 days after starting these activities.

A real estate broker or salesperson may still take certain steps, like providing an application form and collecting information needed to process a loan application, without triggering the MLO endorsement requirements; the MLO requirements apply only to brokers or salespersons who offer or negotiate loans for compensation, or who receive compensation from a lender or mortgage loan originator. Note that a salesperson can obtain an MLO endorsement only if her broker also has an MLO endorsement.

Making or selling loans as a principal. Generally, a broker is someone who acts on behalf of another. However, there is an exception. The broker definition also covers someone in the business of making or selling loans secured by real property. A broker is "in the business" if, during the course of one calendar year, she:

- buys for resale, sells, or exchanges eight or more land contracts or promissory notes secured by real property; or
- makes eight or more loans secured by one- to four-unit residential property using her own funds.

Property Management. The license law's definition of real estate broker isn't limited to sales transactions; it also applies to agents involved in the lease or rental of real property or agents who solicit rental listings for prospective tenants. This means that property managers generally must have real estate licenses. However, as noted in the section below on exemptions from the licensing requirement, employees of property management companies do not need a license to carry out basic leasing activities.

Exemptions from the License Requirement

As is the case with most statutory requirements, there are exemptions from the rule requiring a real estate license. Most of these exemptions fall into two main categories:

exemptions for those who are dealing with their own property, and exemptions for those who are sufficiently regulated by other government agencies (for example, licensed attorneys or financial institutions).

These exemptions are found in Business and Professions Code §§ 10131 – 10133. Specifically, a real estate license is not required under the following circumstances:

- **Someone acting on her own behalf.** A person acting as a principal in relation to her own property does not need a real estate license. (Note, however, that if a licensee is selling or buying her own property, she is still held to a higher standard of care based on her training and expertise. She is not relieved of liability for wrongful acts simply because she is acting as a principal and not an agent.)

- **Partner acting for partnership property.** A partner buying, selling, and negotiating real property transactions for the partnership does not need a real estate license, provided that the partner receives no compensation for his actions other than a share of the partnership's profits. If he receives additional compensation for negotiating the sale, he would be required to have a real estate license.

- **Corporate officer acting for a corporation's property.** Likewise, an officer of a corporation engaging in real estate activities involving the corporation's property need not have a real estate license, provided his only compensation is his salary as a corporate employee.

- **An attorney in fact acting under a power of attorney.** An attorney in fact acting under a power of attorney does not need a real estate license, but the power of attorney cannot be used to circumvent real estate licensing laws. For example, suppose Susan wants to hire you to sell her property, but you don't have a real estate license. You can't ask her to execute a power of attorney making you her attorney in fact to get around the real estate licensing laws.

- **A licensed attorney providing legal services for her client.** An attorney does not need a real estate license when the real estate transaction is incidental to her duties as an attorney, such as when she is administering her client's estate.

- **Someone working under a court order.** A receiver, trustee in bankruptcy, or anyone working under a court order does not require a real estate license when carrying out the specific instructions of the court.

- **A trustee under a deed of trust.** A trustee under a deed of trust does not need a real estate license to sell a foreclosed property. This includes an auctioneer hired by the trustee to oversee the sale. (Deeds of trust and foreclosure sales will be discussed in Chapter 13.)

- **A resident property manager.** Resident managers of apartment buildings do not need a real estate license when performing transactions related to the management of the property.

- **Employees of property managers.** Employees of property managers who merely show rental units, provide lease terms, and accept applications, deposits, and executed rental agreements do not need to be licensed.

- **Clerical staff of licensees.** Employees of real estate licensees who perform purely clerical activities (such as a receptionist or a bookkeeper) do not need a license. Under this exception, a broker may hire an unlicensed person to answer phones, deliver contracts, and perform other administrative tasks. Unlicensed assistants can't show a property or discuss terms of sale.

- **Financial institutions.** With respect to mortgage loan activities, employees of a financial institution, insurance company, pension fund, federally approved housing counseling service, and certain other entities don't have to be licensed.
- **Securities dealers.** With respect to activities related to business opportunities, mortgage loans, or real property securities, a securities broker-dealer (real property securities are investments in real estate where the owners play no active management role).
- **Miscellaneous exemptions.** Other exemptions include managers of hotels, motels, or trailer parks; cemetery authorities and their agents; and those who negotiate the use of properties for photographic purposes (for example, a movie studio employee).

Case to Consider...

From 1983 to 1986, Rose Marie Sheetz managed 23 residential and commercial properties owned by her good friends John and Miriam Lein. Sheetz, who did not hold a real estate license, solicited tenants, negotiated leases, and collected rents. She received 25% of her income from the Leins and spent 10 to 15% of her time managing their properties. On October 6, 1986, the Leins executed a power of attorney that empowered Sheetz to perform the duties mentioned above. An administrative law judge decided that Sheetz performed these acts in the capacity of a broker without a license and ordered her to desist. Sheetz's only defense was the power of attorney exemption of Business and Professions Code § 10133(a)(2). The Commissioner agreed with the decision of the administrative law judge, and Sheetz appealed. Should the power of attorney exemption apply to Sheetz? *Sheetz v. Edmonds* (1988) 201 Cal.App.3d 1432.

Regulation of Brokerage Office Practices

California law not only spells out licensing requirements, it also contains numerous rules governing the operation of a real estate brokerage. It's important to understand these provisions so that you don't become one of the hundreds of licensees who are disciplined each year for violating these rules.

In this section, we'll focus on some of the key requirements for naming a brokerage, setting up an office, and handling records and trust funds.

Business Name and Location

Two common problem areas for brokers are the use of a fictitious business name, and the brokerage office's physical location.

Fictitious Business Name. A **fictitious business name** is a name other than the actual name of the individual doing business. For example, Susan Kim is a broker doing business under the name Sunnyside Properties. Sunnyside Properties is a fictitious business name. A fictitious business name may also be referred to as a **DBA**, which means "doing business as."

Excerpt from CalBRE Publication "Ten Most Common Violations Found in CalBRE Audits"

B & P Code Section 10159.5 and Regulation 2731 – Use of False or Fictitious Name

Business and Professions Code section 10159.5 and Commissioner's Regulation 2731 together state that a licensee shall not use a fictitious name in the conduct of any activity for which a license is required under the Real Estate Law unless the licensee is the holder of a license bearing the fictitious name. Brokers should periodically check their license status with the Bureau to be sure that their license bears the fictitious name(s) they are using. Many brokers cited for violation of this regulation believed that having the DBA registered with the county was sufficient to allow them to use it in their real estate business. Other brokers who are cited for this violation state that they had the fictitious name on their license at one time but may have had their license lapse for a brief period of time and failed to add the DBA back on to their license.

The first step to doing business under a fictitious business name is to file a fictitious business name statement with the county clerk in the county where the broker has her principal place of business. The statement must also be published in a newspaper to notify the general public of the connection between the individual and the fictitious business name.

Once the fictitious business name statement is filed and published, the broker can apply for a real estate license under that name. The Commissioner will issue the license unless the fictitious name:

- is misleading or would constitute false advertising;
- implies a partnership or corporation that does not exist;
- includes the name of a real estate salesperson;
- constitutes a violation of the rules for fictitious business names (BPC §§ 17910, 17910.5, 17913, or 17917); or
- was ever used by someone whose license has since been revoked.

The first person to file for a license under a fictitious name generally receives exclusive rights to that name. Subsequent requests for a confusingly similar name will be denied.

> **Example:** Mike Cheng, a Marina Del Rey real estate broker, is licensed under the fictitious business name "Seashore Properties." Roberta Hess, also from Marina Del Rey, wants to use the fictitious business name "Seaside Properties" for her brokerage. Her request would probably be denied because "Seaside Properties" is confusingly similar to "Seashore Properties."

Problems with fictitious business names are a common reason for disciplinary action, so brokers should be very careful when they use them.

Office Location. The rules regarding business locations are strict. Every broker with an active license in California must maintain a business location in this state. It isn't legal for a California licensee to have her only business office in Nevada or some other state. Furthermore, the broker can conduct her real estate business only from the business address that is shown on her license. If she changes the location of her office, she must notify the Commissioner of the change within one business day. If a broker has one or more branch locations, each location must be separately licensed.

All licensees must provide the Real Estate Commission with a current office or mailing address, phone number, and email address used to conduct real estate activities, and must notify the Commissioner of any changes within 30 days. A broker must keep his own real estate license as well as those of his affiliated licensees (the salespersons and associate brokers who work for the broker) in his main office.

Retention of Records

The law requires thorough recordkeeping. Further, maintaining proper records encourages professional-quality work, and helps prevent disciplinary problems. Finally, a good set of records can help provide a defense in the event of a lawsuit.

Brokers must keep adequate records of all real estate transactions, including transactions that fail to close.

> **Example:** Adam just found out that he's being transferred to his company's new site in North Dakota. He reluctantly lists his house with Sun City Realty. One week later, he finds out that he isn't being transferred after all. Adam immediately—and cheerfully—cancels his listing agreement with Sun City, paying a fee to do so. Sun City must keep records of this transaction, even though it was quickly terminated.

At a minimum, a broker must keep the following records for every transaction:

- listing and buyer agency agreements,
- purchase agreements,
- agency disclosure statements,
- transfer disclosure statements,
- property management agreements,
- trust fund records,

 Recordkeeping Violations

Business and Professions Code section 10148 requires a broker to keep transaction files, trust account records, and any other documents executed or obtained in connection with a real estate transaction for at least three years. Some brokers are cited for violation of this section because they've failed to make records available after the Bureau of Real Estate has made reasonable attempts to examine them. Other brokers are cited because they have destroyed or lost control of records that they were required to maintain.

- bank deposit receipts,
- communications about the transaction (except texts, instant messages, and other electronic communications of an ephemeral nature),
- canceled checks, and
- supporting documents for checks, such as invoices, escrow statements, and receipts.

These records must be retained for at least three years. The three-year retention period begins on the date the transaction closes, or on the listing date if the transaction doesn't close.

The broker must establish an accurate and thorough recordkeeping system. Records may be kept in either paper or digital form. Electronic records are subject to extensive regulations that are designed to ensure the records' accuracy and reliability.

The broker must maintain a reliable method of viewing copies of these documents at his office. All documents (paper or electronic) are subject to inspection and audit by the Real Estate Commissioner at any time during the three-year period.

Note that it's good business practice to keep transaction records for longer than three years, as a broker's tort and contract liability may extend beyond the three-year period.

 WORM Records and Fossilization

By regulation, the Real Estate Commissioner allows brokers to scan documents and to do away with paper copies in favor of digital records.

The state requires recordkeeping partly to provide a basis for resolving client and customer allegations of broker wrongdoing. It might seem that a broker facing investigation or litigation would find altering a paper record harder than tampering with its digital cousin: the computer record doesn't smudge when erased and there's no need to worry about matching ink when forging that missing signature. The law limits this kind of problem by requiring that brokers who go paperless must: 1) establish a regular procedure for making digital copies; 2) scan the documents reasonably promptly; and 3) make the records WORM. WORM stands for Write Once, Read Many. In other words, once scanned, the images can't be rewritten or altered—only viewed.

The digital recordkeeping law also requires a reliable indexing system. Just as a paper file of jumbled transactions is almost useless, so is a chaos of digital images. Brokers must provide a reasonably easy way to search and access their digital records.

Even if the records are WORM, litigants might effectively hide a document simply by deleting any reference to it in the index (most scanned documents aren't text files and can't be searched by key word). Full compliance with the legal requirement of reliable indexing may mean that indexes should be **fossilized**—a term experts use to describe an entry that is locked-in and, like the document images themselves, can't be altered.

Trust Funds

One of the most common causes of disciplinary action is the mishandling of trust funds. Part of the problem is confusion about what trust funds are and what must be done with them. California law is very specific about how to handle trust funds, and it's imperative that licensees learn these rules thoroughly.

Handling Trust Funds. Frequently, a party to a transaction will give the broker funds for safekeeping until the sale closes. These are considered trust funds. For instance, a buyer may turn over her good faith deposit to the real estate broker. To protect the buyer's deposit—and any other funds given to the broker—the license law requires the broker to keep it separate from his own money and to maintain records detailing what he does with it. This makes it less likely that the broker will accidentally or deliberately misuse the funds.

According to the license law, all trust funds received by a broker or salesperson are to be handled in one of three ways. They must be:

1. turned over to the broker's principal,
2. delivered to an escrow agent for deposit into a neutral escrow account, or
3. deposited into a trust account maintained by the broker.

The circumstances will determine which of these actions is appropriate. If trust funds are given to a salesperson instead of directly to the broker, the salesperson must immediately deliver the funds to the broker, or, if so directed by the broker, to one of the three places listed above. Regardless of the manner in which the funds are handled, they must be properly disposed of within **three business days of receipt**. Failure to do so can lead to disciplinary action.

There is an exception to this three-day rule: when a broker is acting as the escrow agent, trust funds must be placed in the hands of the principal, a neutral escrow depository (an escrow account maintained by the escrow agent), or the broker's trust account no later than the **next business day** after receipt.

Good faith deposit. Residential purchase agreement forms often provide that the broker will hold the buyer's check for the good faith deposit uncashed until the seller has accepted the buyer's offer. (If the seller rejects the offer, the broker will simply return the buyer's check.)

It's fine for the broker to hold a buyer's check in this way, as long as the buyer has given written permission to do so and the seller has been informed that the check is being held. Once the offer has been accepted, the check must be placed in the broker's trust account (or into the seller's hands or a neutral escrow depository) within three business days, unless the seller authorizes the broker to continue to hold the check.

Trust Accounts. A broker's trust account must be opened in the broker's name (as licensed) at a recognized financial institution in California. The account must be a non-interest-bearing account and the broker must be named as the trustee. Brokers usually keep only one pooled account because of the fees associated with having multiple accounts. Note that, on the request of the owner of the funds, the broker can open a separate interest-bearing trust fund account just for those particular funds; this enables the owner of the funds to receive interest if an especially large sum of money will be held for a number of months.

Example: Maria Martinez is making an offer on a $3 million house in San Jose, with a good faith deposit of $45,000. She doesn't want to lose interest on the money for the few months it will take to close the transaction, so she asks the broker to deposit the money into a separate interest-bearing trust account.

The broker must disclose to the owner of the funds how the interest will be calculated, who will pay the service charges, and how the interest is to be paid out. The broker cannot retain any of the interest.

Withdrawals. Once trust funds have been deposited into a broker's trust account, they can be withdrawn either by the broker or by someone who has been given written authorization by the broker. Either a licensee or an unlicensed employee of the broker can be an authorized signatory on the trust account. However, if the signatory is an unlicensed employee, she must be covered by a fidelity bond in an amount at least equal to the maximum amount of the trust funds to which she will have access.

Of course, the act of authorizing another person to withdraw funds from the trust account does not relieve the broker of his responsibility for those funds.

Recordkeeping. A broker is required to keep meticulous records of all trust funds that pass through his hands—including trust fund checks that are held uncashed, trust funds that are sent directly to escrow, and trust funds that have been released to the owner.

Accurate and thorough trust fund records allow the broker to calculate the amount owed to any beneficiary at any given time, and to check for imbalances or other red flags that might signal a problem. The broker must reconcile her trust fund records at least once a month.

The accounting system used for trust fund records must comply with generally accepted accounting practices. It may be either a simple columnar system or something more sophisticated. To satisfy CalBRE requirements, the records must show all receipts and disbursements in chronological order. There must be one record for each trust account the brokerage maintains, as well as separate records for each beneficiary or each transaction. Daily running balances must be kept for both the trust account and for each of the separate records. The CalBRE offers forms that can be used to comply with all of these requirements.

In addition to maintaining the trust records themselves, the broker must also keep all supporting documentation, such as canceled checks, bank deposit slips, and receipts.

Advance Fees. An advance fee is money that a real estate broker collects from a client to cover expenses she expects to incur on the client's behalf, or as upfront compensation for services she has yet to provide. Advance fees must be handled in compliance with the trust fund rules we've discussed so far.

Before collecting advance fees, however, a broker must submit all of the materials she's planning to use in advertising or promoting the services to be rendered to the Bureau of Real Estate for approval, along with the advance fee agreement that she will use with her clients. Advance fees generally can't be withdrawn from the trust account until they're actually expended for the client's benefit or until five days after an accounting has been sent to the client. (This may be either a quarterly accounting or a final accounting after the agency has ended.)

Trust Fund Violations. As mentioned, trust fund violations are among the most common causes of disciplinary action. We'll take a brief look at some of the problems that occur most frequently.

Trust fund handling. Not surprisingly, brokers are often cited for failure to deposit trust funds into a trust account by the applicable deadline:

- within three business days after receipt of the funds or acceptance of the buyer's offer, or
- within one business day after receipt of the funds, if the broker is serving as the escrow agent.

Proper designation of trust accounts. A trust account must be designated as a trust account and it must be in the name of the broker, as licensed. If a broker uses an ordinary bank account as her trust account, she can be cited by CalBRE.

Recordkeeping problems. Some brokers are cited by CalBRE for failing to keep any trust fund records at all. Other brokers use a standard checkbook register for their records, which does not comply with CalBRE's requirements.

Sometimes, a broker has an appropriate recordkeeping system in place yet still finds himself in trouble because of inaccuracies in his records (such as incorrect amounts or dates) or for failing to keep running balances.

Shortages. Trust fund shortages are another common problem. A broker's trust account often contains trust funds belonging to several different beneficiaries; a shortage occurs when the account balance is less than the total of the amounts owed to all beneficiaries. The broker must obtain written authorization from all of them before making any disbursement that will reduce the account balance to less than the total trust fund liability (the total amount owed to all beneficiaries).

A shortage could result from the broker's intentional misuse of funds for his own purposes. (This is called **conversion**.) More often, a shortage results from undetected recordkeeping errors and a failure to reconcile the account records with the bank statement on a monthly basis. Of course, even unintentional shortages are violations of the Real Estate Law.

Withdrawal authorizations. Another mistake brokers frequently make is authorizing an unlicensed employee to withdraw funds without making sure she has fidelity bond coverage. Purchasing an inadequate amount of fidelity coverage is a common problem as well.

Commingling. When a broker fails to keep trust funds separate from the broker's own funds, it's called **commingling**. If trust funds are placed in a broker's personal bank account or general business account, this is commingling. Commingling also occurs if the broker's own money is placed in her trust account. (However, a broker is allowed to keep up to $200 of her own money in the trust account to cover bank charges.)

Some commingling violations result from a failure to realize that certain funds are in fact trust funds.

> **Example:** A buyer gives a broker a check to cover the credit report fee and appraisal fee for her mortgage application. The broker doesn't think that these fees are trust funds, so he deposits the buyer's check in his general account, commingling the buyer's money with his own money.

If a broker is entitled to deduct her commission from trust funds, she should immediately transfer the commission out of the trust account into the general brokerage account. The longest a commission can remain in the trust account is 25 days. After that time, commingling has occurred.

The broker who keeps thorough records and handles trust funds conscientiously will avoid many of the most common violations of the Real Estate Law.

Advertising Regulations

Real estate licensees need to be aware of the laws that regulate advertising—not just those that pertain specifically to real estate, but also more general rules, such as the prohibition against false advertising. A violation of state laws against false advertising is a misdemeanor; it's also a violation of the Real Estate Law.

Licensee Designation in Advertising

Advertisements published or distributed by a real estate agent must include a licensee designation (some indication that the advertiser is a licensee). An advertisement that doesn't fulfill this requirement is sometimes referred to as a **blind ad**. A single word such as "broker," "agent," or "Realtor®" is sufficient, or even an abbreviation such as "bro." or "agt."

This rule applies to advertising concerning any matter for which a real estate license is required, but there's an exception for classified ads for rental properties. If the ad gives the phone number or address of the rental property, a licensee designation isn't necessary.

A licensee designation would not have to be included when a licensee advertises his own property for sale or lease, since that isn't an act for which a real estate license is required.

First Contact Solicitation Materials

A real estate agent's license identification number must be included in any solicitation materials that are intended to be the first point of contact with consumers (potential clients or customers). Business cards, stationery, and advertising flyers are examples of first contact materials. The law specifically states that identification numbers are not required on "For Sale" signs or in ads that appear in print or electronic media.

First contact solicitation materials used by a real estate licensee who has a mortgage loan originator endorsement must include the identification number issued by the Nationwide Mortgage Licensing System and Registry, in addition to her real estate license number.

Internet Advertising

Brokers who advertise or provide information about real estate services on the Internet are required to comply with a rule concerning contact with specific customers. There must be procedures in place to ensure that only a real estate licensee (or someone exempt from the licensing requirement) responds to inquiries from customers or otherwise contacts customers.

Advertising Loans and Notes

A licensee engaged in mortgage loan brokerage must comply with additional regulations when preparing advertisements that are addressed to potential borrowers, lenders, or investors concerning loans secured by real property.

For example, these ads may not imply that a loan can or will be approved over the telephone; that any government agency has endorsed the licensee's business activities; or that loans are available on terms more favorable than those generally available in the community, unless the advertiser can show that those terms would be available without undisclosed restrictions or conditions.

Ads concerning loans also may not use words such as "guaranteed" or "safe" to characterize the security of lenders' or investors' funds unless a statement of fact supporting the claim is provided. And an ad for the resale of a promissory note may not guarantee a yield other than the interest rate specified in the note unless the ad also includes the note rate and the amount of the discount. (The discount is the difference between the outstanding note balance and the sales price of the note.)

Inducements

Sometimes a gift, prize, or rebate will be offered as an inducement, either for attending a sales presentation or for purchasing property. (Inducements are always forbidden as part of loan transactions.) If attendance at a sales presentation is required to obtain a gift, that fact must be disclosed in the advertisement or solicitation. Any other conditions for receiving gifts or prizes must also be disclosed. Note that if an inducement is given to one of the parties in a transaction, that's a material fact that must be disclosed to all of the parties.

Do Not Call Registry

Licensees who solicit business by making "cold calls" to strangers must comply with the Federal Trade Commission's telemarketing rules. It's against the law to make this type of call to someone whose name appears on the National "Do Not Call" Registry, so licensees must check the registry before placing calls. Those who engage in ongoing telemarketing are required to check the registry at least once every 31 days. There are also "Do Not Email" and "Do Not Fax" registries.

Broker's Relationship to Principals and Salespersons

This section examines the broker's relationship to clients and salespersons, focusing particularly on the broker-salesperson relationship.

Broker's Relationship to Principal

When a broker becomes an agent for the principal (the client), she is working for the principal, but is not considered the principal's employee. A broker is usually an independent contractor in relation to the principal. An **independent contractor** is someone who is hired to perform a particular job and to use her own judgment as to how the work will be done. In contrast, an employee is hired to perform whatever jobs the employer requires and is given guidelines and instructions as to how to perform each task.

The factors used to determine whether someone is an independent contractor or an employee include the principal's degree of supervision and control, and whether the principal or the licensee sets the work schedule. Courts will also examine who decides how the job will be carried out, and whether the principal withholds taxes and social security from the licensee's commission.

Generally, a real estate broker decides what hours she will work and uses her own judgment about the best way to do her job. She isn't controlled by the seller. Furthermore, the seller does not withhold any income taxes or make any contributions to social security for the broker. Therefore, the broker is generally held to be an independent contractor.

Broker's Relationship to Salesperson

Although some real estate salespersons are employees of a broker or brokerage firm, most are independent contractors. Under the Internal Revenue Service's rules, a real estate salesperson will be considered to be an independent contractor only if:

- the individual is a licensed real estate agent,
- compensation is directly related to sales rather than to hours worked, and
- the services are performed pursuant to a written contract that states the individual will not be treated as an employee for federal tax purposes.

An independent contractor is responsible for paying his own social security and income taxes. State laws differ with regard to the treatment of independent contractors in the area of unemployment and workers' compensation. In California, independent contractors licensed to sell real estate are generally eligible to receive workers' compensation, but not unemployment compensation.

Even though salespeople are typically independent contractors, for some limited purposes they will be considered to be employees. For example, when it comes to complying with the requirements of the Real Estate Law, a salesperson is treated as the broker's employee, not an independent contractor. The broker is responsible for supervising the salesperson's actions, and the broker may be held liable for the salesperson's misconduct.

Case Example:

In 1976, Grubb & Ellis, a brokerage firm, hired Spengler as a salesperson under an "independent contractor agreement" that provided for compensation based solely on commissions. Spengler gave Grubb & Ellis promissory notes totaling $9,100 as draws against future commissions. One year later, Spengler was terminated, and the $6,500 he still owed under the promissory notes became due. Grubb & Ellis sued for payment. Spengler countersued, claiming that he was actually an employee and had been entitled to a minimum hourly wage and social security benefits, and that he was owed back wages, which should offset the promissory notes.

The court disagreed. Under the Real Estate Law, with regard to supervision and liability, the salesperson is an agent and employee of the broker. However, the IRS deems a real estate agent to be an independent contractor for tax purposes. If federal legislation specifically excludes salespersons from the definition of "employee" for the purpose of federal employment taxes, it is unlikely that the government ever intended for salespersons to be employees under the minimum wage laws. *Grubb & Ellis Co. v. Spengler* (1983) 143 Cal.App.3d 890.

As for a state minimum wage law claim, California specifically excludes outside salespeople (those who spend at least half their time outside the office) and workers not under the employer's direct control.

Broker-Salesperson Agreements. California law requires a broker to have a written employment agreement with each licensee who works for him. This **broker-salesperson agreement** must be signed by both parties. The agreement should include all the basic terms of the working relationship, such as the duties of the parties, the amount and type of supervision to be exercised by the broker, the basis for the licensee's compensation, and the grounds for terminating the relationship.

Supervision. Brokers do not exercise the same degree of control over an independent contractor that they would over an employee. But, as noted above, a broker must still supervise each salesperson, and is still liable for each salesperson's actions, since the salesperson is the broker's agent. The broker's legal obligation to supervise her agents also makes good business sense, since better training translates into less negligence liability and fewer disciplinary actions.

Under the Real Estate Law, the broker's obligation to supervise agents includes:

- establishing policies, rules, procedures, and systems to review, oversee, inspect, and manage all transactions and advertising that require a real estate license;
- retaining copies of all documents that have a material effect on parties to a transaction;
- handling trust fund accounts; and
- reviewing the activities of all affiliated licensees, including the review of key transaction documents.

Note that any contract provision that tries to limit or otherwise curtail the broker's duty of supervision is contrary to the law.

Compensation. Broker-salesperson agreements must include information about the salesperson's compensation. Section 10137 of the Business and Professions Code deals with the compensation of both salespersons and unlicensed individuals. It is illegal for a real estate salesperson to accept compensation from anyone other than the broker who holds the salesperson's license. This means that the seller's agent can compensate a licensed cooperating agent only through the cooperating agent's own broker.

Example: Agent Smith works for Broker Jones at ABC Realty and is the listing agent in the sale of a property in San Diego. Agent Williams works for Broker Thomas at XYZ Realty and has found a buyer for Agent Smith's listing. At the close of escrow, Smith's principal cannot pay him directly for selling her property. All commission money must first be turned over to Broker Jones at ABC Realty. Likewise, neither Agent Smith nor Broker Jones can directly split the earned commission with cooperating Agent Williams: all compensation to the cooperating agent must be given to Broker Thomas at XYZ Realty. Broker Thomas will then pay Agent Williams his share of the commission.

It is also unlawful for a broker to employ or compensate any unlicensed individual, either directly or indirectly, for any act that requires a real estate license. Violation of either of these provisions may result in a temporary suspension or permanent revocation of the licensee's real estate license.

Notice of Hiring, Termination, or Relocation. Real estate salespeople frequently move from broker to broker. When this happens, it's up to the broker to notify the CalBRE of the change. A broker has five days to notify the CalBRE in writing whenever a licensee is hired and ten days to notify the CalBRE following the termination of a licensee.

The CalBRE must be notified even when a licensee simply changes offices within the same brokerage. The new supervising broker must notify the CalBRE within five days after the relocating salesperson begins working for her.

Disciplinary Action

Any law designed to regulate an industry will fail if its provisions are ignored by those who are meant to be regulated. So to encourage compliance, the Real Estate Commissioner is empowered to investigate and discipline licensees who violate the Real Estate Law's provisions. The Bureau of Real Estate's website lists the status of every licensee, including accusations, suspensions, and revocations.

Grounds for Discipline

Most of the grounds for suspending, revoking, or denying a real estate license are set forth in §§ 10176 and 10177 of the Business and Professions Code. These sections, with their lists of acts and omissions, set the standard for the licensee's day-to-day behavior.

Remember that a licensee can be subject to disciplinary action while acting as either an agent or as a principal. The fact that a licensee is acting as a principal in a transaction will not relieve her of liability for questionable or illegal conduct.

Acts Prohibited by §§ 10176 – 10177. The grounds for disciplinary action include all of the following actions and conduct, which are listed in Business and Professions Code §§ 10176 and 10177:

1. Making a substantial misrepresentation (deliberately or negligently making a false statement of fact, or failing to disclose a material fact to a principal).
2. Making a false promise that is likely to persuade someone to do or refrain from doing something.
3. Embarking on a continued and flagrant course of misrepresentation or false promises.

4. Acting as a dual agent without the knowledge or consent of all of the parties involved.

5. Commingling your own money or property with money or property you received or are holding on behalf of a client or customer (trust funds).

6. Failing to put a definite termination date in an exclusive listing agreement.

7. Receiving an undisclosed amount of compensation on a transaction (a secret profit).

8. Using a listing agreement that gives you an option to purchase the listed property, and exercising the option without revealing to the principal in writing the amount of profit to be made and obtaining the principal's written consent.

9. Acting in any way, whether specifically prohibited by statute or not, that constitutes fraud or dishonest dealing.

10. Getting a purchaser's written agreement to buy a business opportunity property and to pay a commission, without first obtaining the written authorization of the property owner (a listing agreement).

11. As a lender or mortgage broker, failing to disburse funds in accordance with a mortgage loan commitment.

12. Intentionally delaying the closing of a mortgage loan for the sole purpose of increasing the borrower's interest rate or other charges.

13. Violating any law which provides that a violation of that law by any licensed person is a violation of that person's licensing law if the act is within the scope of the person's duties as a licensee.

14. Acquiring or renewing a license by fraud, misrepresentation, or deceit.

15. Being convicted of (or pleading not guilty or no contest to) a felony charge, or a crime that is substantially related to the qualifications, functions, or duties of a real estate licensee.

16. False advertising, such as a material false statement about property offered for sale, or a misrepresentation of the licensee's credentials.

17. Willfully disregarding or violating the Real Estate Law or the Commissioner's regulations.

18. Willfully using the term "Realtor®" or any trade name of a real estate organization that you are not actually a member of.

19. Having a real estate license denied, revoked, or suspended in another state for actions that would be grounds for denial, revocation, or suspension in California.

20. Performing activities requiring a real estate license negligently or incompetently.

21. As a broker, failing to exercise reasonable supervision over the activities of your salespersons.

22. Using government employment to gain access to private records, and improperly disclosing their confidential contents.

23. Violating the terms of a restricted license.

24. Using "blockbusting" tactics: soliciting business on the basis of statements regarding race, color, sex, religion, ancestry, marital status, or national origin.

25. Violating the Franchise Investment Law, the Corporate Securities Law, or regulations of the Commissioner of Corporations.

26. Violating the laws governing the sale of real property securities.

27. When selling property in which you have a direct or indirect ownership interest, failing to disclose the nature and extent of that interest to a buyer you represent.

28. Violating Article 6 of the license law, concerning qualification and reporting requirements for licensees involved in securities transactions.

29. Violating or failing to comply with state statutes concerning mortgages and foreclosures.

Referral Fees and Kickbacks. A licensee isn't allowed to accept certain types of referral fees. For instance, a licensee can't receive, claim, or demand a commission, fee, or other consideration for referring clients to any escrow agent, structural pest control firm, home protection company, title insurer, controlled escrow company, or underwritten title company. These types of fees, also known as **kickbacks**, are prohibited by state law as well as RESPA. (RESPA, the Real Estate Settlement Procedures Act, is discussed in detail in Chapter 12.)

Agents who violate this rule will be subject to disciplinary action by the Commissioner. In addition, they could be found guilty of **commercial bribery**. The penalty for commercial bribery is significant: imprisonment for up to three years, depending on the amount of the bribe.

Note that a licensee may offer clients or customers discounts on commissions without running afoul of either the Real Estate Law or RESPA. However, a discount or credit on a commission is a material fact, and it must be disclosed to all parties to the transaction.

As we mentioned earlier, § 10137 of the Business and Professions Code makes it illegal for a licensed real estate agent to employ or compensate, directly or indirectly, an unlicensed person for performing acts that require a real estate license. However, it is not illegal for a licensee to pay an unlicensed person a referral fee for introducing him to a potential client or customer.

Catch-all Provisions. Licensees should also be aware of the prohibitions that are included in the catch-all provisions of § 10177(d) (violations of other sections) and § 10177(j) (dishonest dealing).

Violations of other sections. Section 10177(d) prohibits a broad spectrum of activities: basically anything that could be considered to be the willful disregard of the Real Estate Law and the Commissioner's regulations. Examples of behavior that could violate this section include:

- employing or compensating an unlicensed person for any act that requires a license;
- failing to include your licensee designation in your advertising (placing blind ads);
- committing fraud related to a mobile home;
- failing to notify the Commissioner in writing of a salesperson's discharge that was because of her violation of the law;
- failing to notify the buyer and seller of the property's selling price within a month of the closing of a transaction;
- failing to give a copy of a contract to the person signing it at the time of signing (other laws require giving the parties copies of non-contractual documents, such as disclosure and settlement statements); and
- accepting compensation for referring a customer to an escrow, pest control, home warranty, or title insurer.

Dishonest dealing. Section 10177(j) prohibits any conduct that constitutes dishonest dealing or fraud. **Dishonest dealing** is any act that involves betrayal, faithlessness, or an absence of integrity. Suppose a broker issues a check, knowing that there are insufficient funds to cover the amount written. Even if he plans to make a deposit before the check is cashed, this would likely be considered dishonest dealing.

Other grounds for discipline. A licensee may also be disciplined for actions that are not directly related to the practice of real estate, as long as they are substantially related to the licensee's qualifications and suitability to practice real estate. Crimes or other wrongful acts that would qualify as "substantially related" include bribery, fraud, deceit or misrepresentation; sexually related misconduct that causes physical or emotional harm to another; counterfeiting, forgery, or alteration of any instrument; nonpayment of taxes; willful commission of any act that requires a license, without such a license; or any wrongful act for financial gain.

Therefore, in order to avoid discipline or sanctions by the Real Estate Commissioner, agents should carefully consider their actions—not just in relation to real estate transactions, but in all areas of their lives.

Case to Consider...

In 1959, Berg became a practicing attorney and a member of the State Bar of California. In 1988, a civil action was filed against Berg for fraud and deceit based on his practice of bulk billing. The jury found by clear and convincing evidence that Berg had acted with oppression, malice, and fraud. The judgment was affirmed on appeal. In 1994, the State Bar charged Berg with three counts of professional misconduct; one of the counts was based on the civil action involving bulk billing. The State Bar found that Berg's actions were dishonest acts involving moral turpitude and recommended disbarment. In 1998, the California Supreme Court ordered Berg disbarred from the practice of law. In 2002, Berg applied for a real estate salesperson's license. The Department of Real Estate denied Berg a license. Why? *Berg v. Davi* (2005) 130 Cal.App.4th 223.

Knowing or Willful Violations. Under many provisions of the Real Estate Law, a licensee will be held to have violated the law only if he performed a prohibited act "knowingly or willfully." However, this does not mean that the licensee must have intended to break the law. What's required is that the licensee must have intended to commit the act itself. So a licensee may be disciplined for "knowingly" violating a statutory provision even if he wasn't aware that his action was illegal.

The reason for this is straightforward. The disciplinary provisions of the law are intended to protect the public from licensees who are simply ignorant of the law as well as those who are intentionally dishonest. A disciplinary process that applied only to the intentional breaking of the law would encourage agents to remain ignorant of the law in order to escape responsibility for their wrongful actions.

Disciplinary Procedures

If a consumer makes a written complaint against a licensee, the Commissioner is required to investigate it. The Commissioner also has the discretion to investigate licensees on her own initiative. In either case, the investigation usually consists of getting statements from witnesses and the licensee; checking bank records, title company records, and public records; and occasionally calling an informal meeting of everyone concerned. If, after investigation, it appears that a violation of the law has occurred, the Commissioner may either issue a citation without holding a formal hearing into the matter, or file an accusation and schedule a formal hearing.

Citations. Citations are available to the Commissioner in the case of lesser violations of the Real Estate Law where the facts have not been contested. A citation may include a fine of up to $2,500. It may also include an order that directs the licensee to stop an ongoing violation.

A citation is considered a disciplinary action, but is not publicly reported in the same way that a license revocation or suspension (or a monetary penalty in lieu of revocation or suspension) would be. A licensee has 30 days after receiving notice of a citation to request a formal hearing from CalBRE. If the licensee does not request a hearing in this timeframe, the citation becomes final.

Accusation and Hearing. For more serious violations, the Commissioner will usually file an accusation. An **accusation** is a written statement of the charges against the licensee. The accusation must be filed within three years of the allegedly unlawful act, or if the act involved fraud, misrepresentation, or a false promise, then within one year after discovery of the unlawful act by the injured party, or within three years after the act, whichever is later. In no case can the accusation be filed more than ten years after the act.

After an accusation is filed, there may be a **formal hearing**. The procedure for the hearing, as set forth in the Administrative Procedure Act, is as follows:

1. The licensee is served with the accusation, and informed of his rights as an accused. Information about the accusation is posted on CalBRE's website.
2. The Commissioner levies the charges against the licensee; if there was an original complainant (the person who made the complaint), she becomes a witness against the licensee.
3. The licensee is entitled, but not required, to have a lawyer.
4. The licensee has the right to call and examine witnesses, present evidence, and cross-examine opposing witnesses.
5. Testimony is taken under oath and the rules of evidence are followed.
6. An administrative law judge hears the case as presented by the Commissioner's counsel.
7. The administrative judge issues a recommended decision based on the testimony and evidence.
8. The Commissioner accepts, rejects, or modifies the proposed decision.
9. The licensee has the right to petition for reconsideration and to appeal in the court system.

If the charges in the accusation are substantiated, the Commissioner may choose one of three penalties. The accused's license may be either suspended or revoked; in either of these cases, the accused cannot apply for reinstatement for at least one year. Instead of suspension or revocation, a fine may be imposed. The fine can be as high as $250 for each day the license would have been suspended, up to a total of $10,000.

The difference between hearings and court trials. The Commissioner's disciplinary hearing differs in many ways from a regular trial. Though a licensee is entitled to notice and the right to be present at the hearing, significant differences remain. For example, at a hearing a licensee may be called to testify, even over her personal objection. If the licensee is unwilling to testify on her own behalf, she may be called to testify against her will. There is no right to the Fifth Amendment protection from self-incrimination. Likewise, while a licensee has the right to consult an attorney and have one present at the hearing, she is not entitled to have an attorney provided at public expense. Finally, imposition of a fine or other sanction against the licensee by the Commissioner does not protect the licensee from criminal prosecution or additional civil liability.

The Real Estate Recovery Account. Licensing fees are paid into the state treasury, but a portion of them (along with licensee fines) are credited to the Recovery Account. The purpose of the **Recovery Account** is to reimburse someone injured by a real estate licensee when compensation from that licensee is unavailable. To qualify for reimbursement, the injured party must have obtained a civil judgment or arbitration award against the licensee based on the licensee's intentional fraud, misrepresentation, deceit, or conversion of trust funds. If the injured party can establish that the licensee has no assets to pay the judgment, she can ask the Recovery Account to pay the judgment.

The Recovery Account will pay up to $50,000 for losses from a single transaction and up to a total of $250,000 for losses caused by any one licensee. Once payment is made from the Recovery Account on behalf of the licensee, his license is automatically suspended as of the day of payment. The license cannot be reinstated until the amount disbursed from the Recovery Account is fully repaid, with interest. Even bankruptcy does not release the licensee from this obligation.

Most licensees are honest, hard-working individuals who do their best for both clients and customers. Yet some of these licensees will get into trouble simply because they're unaware that their actions are unlawful. Staying up-to-date on the latest license law requirements, as well as handling clients and customers with diligence, will improve any licensee's chances of a complaint-free career.

Case Law in Depth

The following case involves some of the legal issues discussed in this chapter. Read through the facts and consider the questions in light of what you have learned. Then read what the court (or administrative judge, in this case) actually decided.

In re Alberto Puzzy-Trought (Cal. DRE, Mar. 10, 2005) No. H-30941

A Deputy Real Estate Commissioner filed an accusation against Puzzy-Trought, a licensed real estate broker who specialized in mortgage loans. The accusation was based on a judgment that was entered against Puzzy-Trought at the conclusion of a civil suit.

The civil lawsuit resulted from a loan transaction handled by Puzzy-Trought. The plaintiffs were buyers who needed a loan in order to purchase property for about $330,000. The loan amount was $256,800, with a downpayment of $74,238. The buyers deposited $42,238 into escrow and gave Puzzy-Trought a check for the remaining $32,000. They expected this check to be deposited into escrow as well. However, Puzzy-Trought never deposited the check, so the loan was not funded and the buyers could not complete the transaction. As a result, they had to pay $9,600 in liquidated damages to the seller.

Puzzy-Trought claimed that he hadn't deposited the $32,000 check because he had believed it to be for a separate transaction. However, he was unable to adequately explain what he did with the check. A judgment was entered against him for fraud, misrepresentation, and deceit. He was found liable for $41,630 general damages, plus $20,000 punitive damages. Based on this judgment, the Deputy Real Estate Commissioner brought a disciplinary action against Puzzy-Trought.

The DRE (now CalBRE) conducted an audit of Puzzy-Trought's business and concluded that he failed to deposit the $32,000 in question into a trust account. The audit also concluded that he failed to produce records subpoenaed by the Department and that he failed to retain a copy of the Mortgage Loan Disclosure Statements for four unrelated transactions. Furthermore, Puzzy-Trought failed to produce many of the unrelated documents requested by the Department.

The Deputy Commissioner sought to suspend or revoke Puzzy-Trought's license for failure to deposit trust funds into a trust account, failing to properly retain documents, fraud, willfully disregarding the real estate law, and having a civil judgment entered against him for fraud.

The question:

Given the judgment of the civil lawsuit and the Department's audit, what was the appropriate license sanction for Puzzy-Trought?

The court's answer:

The administrative judge found that there was cause to suspend or revoke Puzzy-Trought's license on all the grounds brought by the Deputy Commissioner. According to the administrative judge: "A real estate broker has a fiduciary duty to his clients and must use the utmost care when handling client funds. This duty is breached when a broker deposits client money into his own account, thus misappropriating the funds. Respondent failed to deposit $32,000 of client money into an escrow or trust account, and the Buyers were unable to close their loan.

"Respondent established mitigating circumstances regarding his understanding that the money given to him was [for another transaction]... He further established that this transaction was the first and only complaint against him in 23 years as a broker. However, this evidence was not sufficient to establish that the public interest would be protected if Respondent were to retain his real estate broker's license."

The result:

Puzzy-Trought's real estate license was revoked.

Chapter Summary

- The Real Estate Law contains provisions regarding the licensing requirement, grounds for disciplinary action, and disciplinary procedures. The Real Estate Law is administered and enforced by the California Bureau of Real Estate (CalBRE).

- California law requires a broker to have a written employment agreement with each affiliated licensee. Under the Real Estate Law, salespersons are considered agents of the broker. However, for income tax purposes, they are usually independent contractors rather than employees of the broker.

- A real estate broker must keep adequate records of all real estate transactions (even ones that don't close) and retain those records for at least three years.

- A broker must maintain a trust account to hold funds delivered to the broker for safekeeping. Personal and business funds cannot be commingled with these trust funds.

- The law prohibits deceptive advertising by licensees, and imposes specific rules on a licensee's "first contact" materials, Internet advertising, and certain other types of solicitation.

- It is illegal for a licensed real estate agent to employ or compensate, directly or indirectly, an unlicensed person for performing acts that require a real estate license.

- The Commissioner may discipline a real estate agent even for actions committed when she is acting as the principal in a transaction. A licensee may also be disciplined for any wrongful acts that are related to her truthfulness, honesty, or suitability to practice real estate.

- The Commissioner's disciplinary hearing differs from a court proceeding in many ways, but allows for an appeal to superior court. Sanctions for violations include license suspension, revocation, and fines.

- The purpose of the Real Estate Recovery Account is to reimburse those injured by real estate licensees when the licensees have no assets to pay for a civil judgment against them. The Recovery Account will pay up to $50,000 for losses in a single transaction and up to $250,000 for losses caused by one licensee.

Key Terms

- **California Bureau of Real Estate (CalBRE)** – The entity in charge of administering the Real Estate Law.

- **Fictitious business name** – A name other than the name of the individual doing business. A licensee wishing to use a fictitious business name must follow procedures outlined in the Real Estate Law.

- **Independent contractor** – A person hired to perform a particular job and to use her own judgment as to how the work will be done. Independent contractors are responsible for their own taxes.

- **Employee** – A person hired to perform whatever jobs the employer requires and who is given guidelines and instructions as to how to perform each task.

- **Broker/salesperson agreement** – An agreement that contains all of the basic terms of the employment relationship, such as the duties of the parties, the amount and type of supervision to be exercised by the broker, the basis for the licensee's compensation, and the grounds for terminating the relationship.

- **Kickback** – An illegal commission or fee for referring clients to particular escrow agents, structural pest control firms, title insurers, etc.

- **Dishonest dealing** – Any act that involves betrayal, faithlessness, or an absence of integrity.

- **Recovery Account** – An account set up to reimburse those injured by real estate licensees when the licensees have no assets to pay for a civil judgment against them. The Recovery Account will pay up to $50,000 for losses in a single transaction and up to $250,000 for losses caused by one licensee.

Chapter Quiz

1. The authority of the California Bureau of Real Estate originates from a section of the Business and Professions Code known as the:
   a) Real Estate Law
   b) Real Estate Law and the Licensing Law
   c) Civil Code and the Business and Professions Code
   d) None of the above

2. A licensee cannot do business under a fictitious name, unless:
   a) the licensee is a corporation
   b) the licensee received his license under that name
   c) the licensee is a broker
   d) A licensee can never do business under a fictitious name

3. Which of the following activities requires a real estate license?
   a) A trustee selling foreclosed property
   b) A resident property manager leasing apartments
   c) A partner selling the partnership's real property
   d) A corporate officer selling corporate property for commission

4. In legal proceedings involving the Bureau of Real Estate, the Commissioner is represented by:
   a) the California State Attorney General
   b) a personal attorney
   c) the deputy commissioner
   d) None of the above

5. Which of the following is NOT a factor used to determine whether someone is an independent contractor or an employee?
   a) Principal's degree of supervision and control
   b) Who decides how the job will be carried out
   c) Number of hours worked
   d) Whether the principal withholds taxes and social security contributions

6. The Internal Revenue Service considers a real estate salesperson to be an independent contractor if all of the following conditions are met EXCEPT:
   a) she is a licensed real estate agent
   b) compensation is directly related to sales rather than to hours worked
   c) the services are performed under a written contract stating that she will not be treated as an employee for federal tax purposes
   d) she lists "independent contractor" on her tax return

7. The Real Estate Law requires brokers to keep adequate records of all real estate transactions and to retain those records for at least:
   a) one year
   b) three years
   c) four years
   d) five years

8. Accurate and thorough trust fund records allow the broker to:
   a) provide an exact accounting to clients
   b) calculate the amount owed to any client at a given time
   c) check for imbalances or red flags that might signal a problem
   d) All of the above

9. A broker's trust account doesn't have to be:
   a) at a bank with more than ten branch locations
   b) in the broker's name as it appears on the broker's license, as trustee
   c) maintained at a recognized financial institution in the state of California
   d) a non-interest-bearing demand deposit account

10. A licensee must include what information on her business cards and other first contact solicitation materials?
    a) Broker's name as licensed
    b) License identification number
    c) Business address
    d) Commission rate

Chapter Answer Key

Chapter Quiz Answers:

1. a) The authority of the Bureau of Real Estate originates from Division 4 of the Business and Professions Code. Part I is known as the Real Estate Law.

2. b) A licensee cannot do business under a fictitious name unless she has received a license under that name.

3. d) An officer of a corporation engaging in real estate activity for the corporation need not have a real estate license, provided his only compensation is a salary as a corporate employee. However, a corporate officer selling corporate property for commission must have a real estate license.

4. a) In legal proceedings involving the Bureau of Real Estate, the Commissioner is represented by the California State Attorney General. The Attorney General also advises the Commissioner on license law issues.

5. c) The number of hours worked has nothing to do with whether an agent is an independent contractor or an employee. All of the other choices are factors in making the distinction.

6. d) If the first three requirements are met, the IRS will consider the salesperson an independent contractor for tax purposes. Whether she lists "independent contractor" on her return is irrelevant.

7. b) Brokers are required to retain adequate records of all real estate transactions for at least three years. The retention period runs from the date of closing of the transaction, or from the date of the listing if the transaction does not close.

8. d) The broker should also reconcile her trust fund records on a monthly basis.

9. a) The trust account must have the other listed features, but the number of bank locations isn't important.

10. b) First contact solicitation materials, including business cards, stationery, and flyers, must include the agent's license number.

Cases to Consider... Answers:

Exemptions from License Requirement

Sheetz v. Edmonds (1988) 210 Cal.App.3d 1432. The appeals court agreed with the Real Estate Commissioner. Sheetz argued that the Real Estate Law expressly allowed her to manage the property under the power of attorney exemption of § 10133(a)(2), as Mrs. Lein was ill, Mr. Lein was frequently out of town, and they needed her assistance. Sheetz also pointed out that she only managed property for them and no others. The court found, however, that the power of attorney exemption does not apply where it is used to evade the licensing law. The exemption was meant to apply in those "infrequent circumstances where personal necessity impelled a property owner to appoint another as his attorney in fact." In other words, the legislature intended the power of attorney exemption to apply only when necessary to complete a particular or isolated transaction—not to fulfill the role of property manager on a continuous basis without a real estate license. To hold otherwise would defeat the purpose of the licensing laws, as anyone could get around the requirement with a simple piece of paper giving him power of attorney.

Other Grounds for Discipline

Berg v. Davi (2005) 130 Cal.App.4th 223. The Department of Real Estate denied Berg a license based on Berg's disbarment from the practice of law, citing Business and Professions Code § 10177(f). This section provides that the agency may suspend, revoke, or deny the issuance of a license to any applicant who has had a license denied or revoked by another state or federal licensing agency, if the acts would lead to the same sanctions if they were committed by a real estate licensee in California. Berg had been disbarred for acts that "constitute fraud or dishonest dealing," and this would be grounds for revocation of a real estate license.

List of Cases

Berg v. Davi (2005) 130 Cal.App.4th 223
Grubb & Ellis Co. v. Spengler (1983) 143 Cal.App.3d 890
In re Alberto Puzzy-Trought (2005) (Cal. DRE, Mar. 10, 2005) No. H-30941
Sheetz v. Edmonds (1988) 201 Cal.App.3d 1432

Chapter 9

Real Estate Contract Law

Outline

Introduction

Real estate agents routinely work with a variety of contracts. We'll begin this chapter by reviewing the basics of contract law. Then, in the rest of the chapter, we'll describe the contracts most commonly encountered by agents: listing agreements, buyer representation agreements, purchase agreements, option contracts, land contracts, and leases.

General Contract Law

A contract is an agreement between two or more persons to do or not do a certain thing, for consideration. If created correctly, it's legally binding and can be enforced in court.

As a real estate agent, you're allowed to fill out standard form contracts for your clients and customers, but not allowed to write a contract from scratch, or even draft a special provision. Only lawyers are permitted to write contracts on behalf of the parties. (The parties may draft their own contract, however.) Even so, real estate agents need to be familiar with the basic elements of a valid contract, so that they can recognize situations where legal advice is needed.

Before we explain the elements required for a binding contract, let's take a quick look at the terms used to describe a contract's legal status.

Legal Status of a Contract

From a legal standpoint, a contract may be classified as void, voidable, unenforceable, or valid.

A **void** contract has no legal effect at all, and can't be enforced by either party. In fact, the parties may disregard its existence altogether. In a **voidable** contract, one party has the power to **rescind** (or terminate) the contract; usually this is because that party was forced into the contract or taken advantage of in some way. If that party decides to rescind the contract, she must do so within a reasonable period of time; otherwise the contract will be treated as valid.

An **unenforceable** contract may have all of the required contract elements; nevertheless, it cannot be enforced, either because its contents can't be proved, or because the deadline for enforcement (set forth in the statute of limitations) has passed. Finally, a **valid** contract can be enforced by either party. It contains all of the required elements, which we'll discuss next.

Elements of a Valid Contract

The following four elements are required for a valid contract: 1) legal capacity to contract, 2) mutual consent, 3) a lawful objective, and 4) consideration. In addition, certain types of contracts (including nearly all real estate contracts) must be in writing.

Legal Capacity. Every party to a contract must be at least 18 years old and legally competent. As a general rule, if a **minor** (someone under the age of 18) enters into a contract, the contract will be voidable by the minor. If she chooses to rescind the contract, the other party can't force her to go through with it. If she doesn't rescind the contract, both sides will be legally bound by its terms.

Note, however, that when a minor enters into a real estate contract, the contract generally isn't just voidable; it's completely void, so neither side can enforce it. There's only one exception to this rule: an **emancipated minor** (one who is married, in the military, or has been declared by a court to be an adult) does have the legal capacity to enter into contracts. Therefore, a real estate contract entered into by an emancipated minor won't be void due to the minor's age.

In addition to being at least 18 years of age, a party to a contract must be mentally competent. If a person has been declared mentally incompetent by a court (due to senility, for example), any contract he signs is automatically void. And even without a formal declaration of incompetence, if it can be proved that someone who signed a contract was incompetent at the time, the contract is void. On the other hand, if someone signed a contract while she was only temporarily incompetent (for instance, due to alcohol or drugs), the contract may be voidable if she can prove that the intoxication was involuntary.

Mutual Consent. A valid contract requires a "meeting of the minds," or **mutual consent**, which means that both parties agree to all of the contract's terms and conditions. Mutual consent is reached through the process of **offer and acceptance**, which begins when one person (the **offeror**) makes an offer to another person (the **offeree**).

Offer. A valid offer must meet two requirements. First, it must clearly express an intent to enter into a contract. The evidence of this intent must be objective; in other words, it must be based on the offeror's words and actions. Second, the terms of the offer must be definite. The terms of the offer can't be too vague; "I will buy your property sometime next year for a good price" is too vague to be a valid offer.

Of course, an offer doesn't last forever. The offeror may put a specific time limit on the acceptance ("This offer terminates at midnight on July 2."). When the deadline passes, the offer automatically terminates.

An offer may terminate in other ways as well. First, an offer is terminated if the offeror revokes (withdraws) the offer before it's accepted. The revocation is effective as soon as it is communicated to the offeree. So a revocation over the phone or in person is effective immediately. A special rule applies to a revocation sent by mail; it's effective when the offeror mails the letter, even before the offeree receives it. (See the "Mailbox Rule" sidebar.)

An offer also terminates if the offeree rejects it. Once the rejection is communicated to the offeror, the offer is no longer valid. In other words, once someone rejects an offer, he can't change his mind and accept it later.

Finally, an offer terminates when it is met with a **counteroffer**. A counteroffer is a reply to an offer that contains different or additional terms and conditions. In essence, the counteroffer is a new offer. The new offer constitutes a rejection of the original offer.

> **Example:** Sidney offered to buy Muriel's house for $250,000. Muriel replied, "Make it $275,000 and you have a deal." Muriel didn't accept Sidney's offer; instead, she rejected the offer of $250,000 and made a counteroffer for $275,000. Now it's up to Sidney to accept or reject the counteroffer. Either way, it's too late for Muriel to accept the $250,000 offer.

The Mailbox Rule

Unless otherwise agreed, when the acceptance of an offer is communicated by mail (rather than in person or over the telephone), it's effective when the message is sent. This is true even if the offeror doesn't receive the acceptance for several days. This is known as the mailbox rule: the acceptance forms a binding contract the moment that it's dropped into the mailbox. The mailbox rule applies to faxes and emails as well; in most cases they're effective the moment they're sent. And the mailbox rule applies not only to acceptance of an offer, but also to revocation of an offer. However, note that purchase agreement forms often modify the mailbox rule to require receipt by the party.

Acceptance. A contract is formed as soon as the offer is accepted. But to be valid, the acceptance must meet the following requirements:

- the offer may be accepted only by the offeree (not by anyone else);
- the acceptance must be communicated to the offeror, in the manner specified by the offer; and
- the acceptance must not vary the terms of the offer.

Example: Susan offers to buy Bill's house for $500,000. Only Bill can accept Susan's offer. If Bill rejects the offer, his neighbor Joe can't step in and accept her offer instead.

Susan may revoke her offer at any time until Bill communicates his acceptance to her. If her offer stated: "Acceptance must be faxed to my broker during regular business hours," Bill's acceptance must be communicated in exactly this manner. If he mails her his acceptance, it won't be effective.

Finally, Bill's acceptance can't vary the terms of the offer in any way. If Susan offers "$500,000 with 20% down and the remainder as proceeds of a conventional loan, closing to take place October 9," Bill's acceptance must be on those same terms. If it says, "I accept your offer of $500,000, with 20% down and the remainder as proceeds of a conventional loan, closing to take place October 10," he's not accepting her offer; rather, he's making a counteroffer. Then it will be up to Susan to accept or reject Bill's counteroffer.

One final note on acceptance: since mutual consent is required, the acceptance must be completely voluntary. The contract won't be binding if the acceptance resulted from fraud (misrepresentation), undue influence (one party exerting excessive pressure on another), duress (threats), or mutual mistake (both parties mistaken as to an essential fact of the contract). If any of these negative forces or influences are present, the contract formed will be voidable by the party harmed (the victim of the fraud, for example).

Case to Consider...

Hofer mailed the Youngs an offer to settle a personal injury action for $11,000. The Youngs faxed and mailed their acceptance to Hofer. However, because the envelope was addressed incorrectly, the mailed acceptance was lost. Hofer did receive the faxed acceptance, but subsequently faxed and mailed a revocation of her offer, stating that she was rejecting the faxed acceptance. At trial, the lower court ruled that the faxed acceptance was insufficient and refused to enforce the settlement. The Youngs appealed. Should the court find that a faxed acceptance is binding? *Hofer v. Young* (1995) 38 Cal.App.4th 52.

Lawful Purpose. A contract's objective or underlying purpose must be legal. If a contract has an illegal objective, it is void and a court won't enforce it. To take an obvious example, murder is illegal; therefore, a contract for a "hit" on someone is void. The same rule applies to contract provisions that a court deems to be contrary to public policy or generally accepted moral values.

> **Example:** A company's employment contract includes a provision that prohibits employees from whistle-blowing (reporting corruption or illegal conduct). Since public policy generally encourages whistle-blowing, a court would probably refuse to enforce this provision.

If a contract contains some legal and some illegal provisions, a court may throw out the illegal provisions and still enforce the remaining provisions. This type of contract is said to be **severable**: the court can sever the offending portion and enforce the rest of the contract. In the example above, even if the court won't enforce the provision prohibiting whistle-blowing, it may deem the rest of the employment contract legal and enforceable.

Consideration. The last required contract element is **consideration**: something of value exchanged by the parties. Note that consideration must be given by both parties, not just one; this is what distinguishes a contract from a gift.

> **Example:** Geoff offers to buy Elizabeth's property for $700,000, and Elizabeth accepts. Geoff's consideration is the $700,000; Elizabeth's consideration is the property. If Elizabeth later refuses to follow through with their agreement, Geoff can sue.
>
> On the other hand, suppose Elizabeth offers to give the property to Geoff as a gift, and Geoff accepts. If she changes her mind, Geoff can't sue. Since he didn't offer her any consideration, there's no valid contract to enforce.

Statute of Frauds. In addition to the four requirements discussed so far, which apply to any type of contract, there's an additional requirement that applies only to certain types of contracts—including contracts concerning real estate. Under California's **statute of frauds** (Civil Code § 1624), a real estate contract is not enforceable unless it's in writing and signed by the party or parties to be charged. This law helps prevent fraud and reduce disputes over what the parties agreed to do. Requiring the parties to put their agreement in writing ensures that there will be concrete evidence of the agreement's basic terms.

 Origin of the Statute of Frauds

The term "statute of frauds" comes from a 1677 English law known as the English Act for the Prevention of Frauds and Perjuries. The original act required a contract to be in writing if it involved goods worth a certain amount, or if land was changing hands.

Under the statute of frauds, any agreement authorizing or employing a broker to sell or purchase real estate for compensation (such as a listing agreement or a buyer representation agreement) or any agreement to buy or sell real estate (such as a purchase agreement) must be in writing and signed. The statute of frauds also applies to any contract that by its terms will not be performed within one year after it is made. (Thus, a lease for more than one year must be in writing.)

Note, however, that the statute of frauds doesn't require these agreements to be formal legal documents. A simple signed note or memorandum that references the parties' agreement will be sufficient. In fact, if all of the required terms are included, even notes scribbled on a napkin might be enough to create a valid real estate contract.

Case Example:

When Foulks wanted to sell his ranch, he asked his friend Seck, a licensed real estate broker, for help. Although Foulks didn't want to give Seck a formal listing agreement, he assured Seck that he'd never cheat him out of a commission. Regardless, Seck used the back of a business card to write down details about the listing, including the price per acre, the terms of sale, the commission, and the term and date of the listing. Foulks dated and initialed the back of the card. Seck found a buyer, but the sale later fell through. When Seck sued Foulks for his commission, Foulks claimed that no listing agreement existed, arguing that the notes on the back of Seck's business card didn't meet the requirements of the statute of frauds. However, the court disagreed. The "writing" required by the statute of frauds doesn't need to be a formal contract. *Seck v. Foulks* (1972) 25 Cal.App.3d 556.

Modifying a Contract

Once created, most contracts are performed (or executed) according to their terms: a home buyer and seller enter into a purchase agreement, each party carries out his contractual responsibilities, and the transaction closes smoothly. But sometimes both parties decide they need to change one or more of the terms of the agreement, or even come up with a new agreement altogether. This can be done in a variety of ways.

1. **Amendment.** The parties to a contract can agree to modify its terms with a contract amendment. If the statute of frauds required the original contract to be in writing, the amendment must be in writing (and signed by both parties) as well. For example, if the parties to a real estate sale decide that the seller will reduce the sales price by $7,000 instead of repairing the roof, they can create and sign an amendment to that effect.

2. **Assignment.** One of the parties may want to transfer some of her contractual rights to another person. She can do this by assignment. For instance, a tenant may assign the remainder of her lease to her friend. Even after an assignment, the assigning party remains responsible for fulfillment of the contract, unless released by the other original party. Note that some contracts prohibit assignment without the other original party's consent.

3. **Novation.** The parties may decide to toss out their entire contract and replace it with another one. Or perhaps one party wants to bow out of the agreement completely in

favor of another party. Either of these can be done with a novation. The result of a novation is a new contract. For instance, if the parties to a sales transaction rescind their contract and enter into a lease-option transaction instead, it's a novation. A novation requires the consent of both parties.

4. **Accord and satisfaction.** Occasionally, one party agrees to accept less than full performance from the other party. For example, Johnson has defaulted on his mortgage payments to First Bank. First Bank agrees to accept the deed to the property from Johnson as full repayment of the debt, even though the principal remaining on the mortgage loan is several thousand dollars more than the value of the property. Johnson pays First Bank $1,250 in cash to accept this new arrangement. Once Johnson turns over the deed and the cash, and First Bank accepts the consideration, they've reached an accord and satisfaction. The terms of the original contract are considered to be discharged.

Breach of Contract

What if one party fails to perform his contractual responsibilities? Is the other party entitled to compensation?

In general, when one party **breaches** a contract (fails to perform as promised), the other party no longer has to perform her side of the bargain.

> **Example:** George agrees to build a house for the Alvarez family in exchange for $400,000. If George doesn't build the house, the Alvarez family has no obligation to pay him the $400,000.

Substantial Performance vs. Material Breach. Let's consider what happens if one party meets only some of her contractual obligations. Suppose that by the time his relationship with the Alvarezes went sour, George had built everything except the front steps. Clearly, the contract's main purpose was fulfilled. Even though some tasks haven't been completed, a court would find that **substantial performance** had occurred. The Alvarez family may be able to sue George for failing to finish the steps, but they won't be excused from fulfilling their side of the bargain; namely, paying George the agreed price.

But if George had only gotten around to pouring one small portion of the foundation before he stopped working on the project, a court would likely rule that a **material breach** had occurred. When one party commits a material breach, the other party is excused from fulfilling his side of the bargain. A court will determine whether there has been substantial performance or a material breach by evaluating the circumstances of the individual case.

Remedies for Breach. Let's say George built nothing at all and the Alvarezes sue him for breaching their contract. How might a court handle this issue?

If the court found that there was in fact a valid contract and that the contract had been breached, it would impose an appropriate remedy. The remedies for a breach of contract fall into two general categories: monetary damages and equitable remedies. The most common remedy is **damages**: a sum of money that the breaching party must pay to the nonbreaching party. A damages award is intended to restore the nonbreaching party to the position she would have been in if the breach hadn't occurred.

Fig. 9.1 Remedies for breach

Remedies for Breach of Contract

Damages: A monetary award intended to put the nonbreaching party in the position she would have been in if the other party had performed as agreed; also known as actual damages.

Example: Salazar contracts with Rossi to build a house for $200,000. When Salazar breaches the contract, Rossi is forced to hire another builder. The second builder charges Rossi $225,000. Rossi sues Salazar for breach of contract. The court awards Rossi $25,000, the extra money he had to pay because of Salazar's breach.

Liquidated damages: Damages that the parties agree to in advance (usually in the original contract); either a fixed sum or an amount to be calculated by a specified formula. The nonbreaching party agrees to accept liquidated damages in the event of a breach, instead of suing for actual damages.

Example: Letendre enters into a purchase agreement to buy Cottrell's home. They agree that if Letendre breaches the agreement, she will pay Cottrell $5,000 in liquidated damages and Cottrell won't sue for actual damages.

Injunction: A court order directing a party to do something (or to refrain from doing something); typically used when a breach of contract would cause irreparable harm, and damages would be an inadequate remedy.

Example: A 200-year-old tree is located on the boundary line between Edward's and Sally's properties. Both owners are subject to deed restrictions protecting the tree. Sally learns that Edward plans to cut down the tree. She may be able to obtain an injunction barring him from doing so, since monetary damages would not adequately compensate her for the loss of the tree.

Specific performance: A court order requiring the breaching party to perform according to the contract terms; usually granted only when damages are inappropriate because the subject of the contract is unique, as in the case of a piece of real property.

Example: Alice contracts with Peter to buy Skyline Ranch. Peter breaches the contract. Skyline Ranch (like all real estate) is a unique piece of property and a damages award won't allow Alice to buy an exact substitute. A court might award Alice specific performance, requiring Peter to sell the property to her.

Rescission: A termination of the contract in which the parties return the consideration they exchanged, putting both of them back in the positions they were in before they entered into the contract.

Example: Mary buys a house from Blake for $350,000. When Mary realizes that Blake failed to disclose several serious problems with the home, she sues. The court orders the sale rescinded, so Blake must return the $350,000 and Mary must transfer title back to Blake.

Sometimes damages aren't appropriate or don't fully compensate the nonbreaching party. In these cases, equitable remedies may be available. **Equitable remedies** include injunctions, specific performance, and rescission.

Damages and equitable remedies are summarized in Figure 9.1.

Listing Agreements

Now that we've reviewed the basic principles of contract law, let's look at the types of contracts that real estate agents regularly encounter: listing agreements, buyer representation agreements, purchase agreements, option contracts, land contracts, and leases.

A **listing agreement** is essentially an employment contract between a property seller and a real estate broker. Under the statute of frauds, a listing agreement must be in writing and signed by the seller; otherwise, it won't be enforceable.

Types of Listing Agreements

The three basic types of listing agreements are:

- an exclusive right to sell listing,
- an exclusive agency listing, and
- an open listing.

In an **exclusive right to sell listing**, the property owner agrees to list the property with only one broker. The broker is owed a commission if the property sells during the listing period, regardless of who sells the property. This means that the broker will get paid even if it's the seller herself who finds a buyer. Not surprisingly, this type of listing is the one that's most popular with brokers, and the one most commonly used in residential transactions.

In an **exclusive agency listing**, the owner agrees to list with only one broker, but reserves the right to sell the property herself. If she finds the buyer, she owes the broker nothing. However, if any other agent sells the property during the listing term, the broker is entitled to a commission.

Finally, under an **open listing**, a broker has earned a commission only if he was the **procuring cause** of the sale, meaning that he was primarily responsible for bringing the buyer and seller together. An open listing is nonexclusive, so the owner may give open listings to as many brokers as she likes. (Multiple listing services often don't accept open listings.)

Basic Requirements

A valid listing agreement must meet the basic requirements for a valid contract discussed earlier. In addition, it needs to contain the following information:

- a description of the property to be sold or leased;
- the amount or rate of the broker's commission; and
- if it's an exclusive listing, the date on which the listing will expire.

Although a street address may be enough to identify the property in some situations, it won't always be. It's much better to use a legal description, which you can usually get from a title company. (For more on legal descriptions, see Chapter 11.)

A listing agreement must also state how the broker will be compensated. Both federal and state law require the commission rate to be negotiable; therefore, a broker should never use a listing form with a pre-printed commission rate or amount. The commission must be filled in for every transaction individually. In California, a listing agreement for residential property with up to four units must include the following provision in bold type:

> **Notice: The amount or rate of real estate commissions is not fixed by law. They are set by each Broker individually and may be negotiable between the Seller and the Broker (real estate commissions include all compensation and fees to Broker).**

Finally, any exclusive right to sell or exclusive agency listing must include a termination date. Agents often use standard listing periods of 90 or 120 days, but the parties may negotiate a shorter or longer period. The length chosen may depend on current market conditions (in slower markets, an agent will need more time to sell the home).

Common Legal Issues

Since most brokerages provide their agents with pre-printed listing agreement forms, you probably won't run into too many problems with the elements we've just discussed. But the listing process doesn't always go smoothly. Let's take a look at some common legal issues that can arise in connection with listing agreements.

Agency Duties Without a Contract. You have a 90-day listing agreement with your client, Vera, but your relationship with her isn't going well. She's quite difficult to work with and won't allow her home to be shown at reasonable times. Furthermore, she thinks another agent could do a better job and wants out of her listing agreement. Much to your relief, your broker agrees and the contract is rescinded by mutual consent. Do you still owe Vera agency duties even without the listing agreement?

The answer is yes. Agency duties are based in agency law, not contract law. As you may recall from Chapter 6, terminating an agency relationship doesn't necessarily relieve the parties of any contractual duties they owe each other. Similarly, even without an enforceable employment contract, a real estate agent still owes certain agency duties to a client or former client.

> **Example:** Seller Wu has an oral listing agreement with Broker Carol. During the process of listing and showing the property, Carol learns certain confidential information regarding Wu's finances. Carol finds a buyer and the sale closes, but Wu refuses to pay Carol's commission. Since their listing agreement wasn't in writing, it's unenforceable. Still, even without an enforceable contract, Carol owes Wu the agency duty of confidentiality. Revealing Wu's financial information to another party would violate this duty.

Commission Disputes. Unfortunately, obtaining a written listing agreement and then finding a buyer doesn't guarantee that you'll receive your commission. Let's take a look at some issues that can arise in connection with a real estate agent's compensation.

Ready, willing, and able buyer. Generally, a broker is hired to find a **ready, willing, and able buyer** for the seller's property. A buyer is considered "ready and willing" if she makes an offer that meets all of the seller's terms and conditions. She's considered "able" if she has the financial ability to complete the sale, meaning that she has enough cash on hand to purchase the property outright, or a binding commitment for a loan to finance the purchase, or a strong enough credit rating and sufficient assets to obtain the necessary financing.

> **Example:** Sally's home is on the market for $350,000, and you get a call from a buyer interested in the property. He's been preapproved for a conventional loan to purchase a house worth up to $370,000. After viewing the home, the buyer makes an offer of $350,000. You have found a ready, willing, and able buyer.

Once a broker finds a ready, willing, and able buyer, she's entitled to her commission, even if the seller doesn't accept the offer, or the transaction fails to close because of something the seller does or fails to do. Returning to the example, even if Sally changes her mind and decides not to sell her house, you are still legally entitled to a commission. You did the job that you were hired to do, fulfilling the terms of the listing agreement, so you're entitled to your pay.

However, this, too, is negotiable: for example, the seller may add a provision to the listing agreement, making payment of a commission contingent upon the sale of the property actually closing. In that case, you won't get paid unless the seller does.

Safety clauses. You find out that two days after your listing agreement expired, the seller signed a purchase agreement with one of the buyers you brought to the house. The seller refuses to pay you a commission. Do you have any recourse?

The answer depends on whether your listing agreement had a **safety clause** (also known as an **extender clause**), a provision included in most exclusive listing agreements. A safety clause makes the seller liable for a commission for a specified period after the listing has expired, provided the buyer is someone the broker had contact with during the listing term. Without a safety clause, a buyer and seller could unfairly deprive the broker of a commission by waiting until after the listing term has expired to complete the sale.

> **Example:** Albert listed his Malibu home with Broker Sue. Sue spent months advertising the home, showing the property, and negotiating offers. Eventually, Sue found Mark, a potential buyer. To Sue's disappointment, after extensive negotiations, the sale fell through. Later, it turned out that Albert and Mark had secretly agreed to wait until Sue's listing had expired before entering into a purchase agreement. (That way, Albert would get out of paying the commission, and he'd let Mark have the property for less.) However, since Sue's listing agreement contained a safety clause, she was still entitled to her commission.

Interference with Contractual Relations. You notice that your neighbor Alison has listed her home with ABC Realty, one of your competitors. In your opinion, ABC Realty isn't a very reputable brokerage; in fact, you're positive that you could do a better job. You're on friendly terms with Alison. Can you say something to her?

The answer is no. If you interfere with another real estate agent's listing agreement, you may be committing a tort called **interference with contractual relations**. (As you'll recall from earlier chapters, a tort is a negligent or wrongful act that causes injury to another person.) If you try to convince Alison to list with you instead, ABC Realty could sue you for interference with contractual relations. To win its case, ABC Realty would need to show that you knew about the contract and intentionally interfered with it, causing a breach that resulted in damages for ABC (such as the loss of its commission).

To be on the safe side, many brokers require their agents to include in any general marketing materials a disclaimer that says something like this: "This material is not an attempt to interfere with an established contract. If you are already working with an agent, please disregard."

Of course, the prohibition against interfering with a contract applies not only to a listing agreement, but also to other real estate contracts, such as a binding purchase agreement. It would be illegal to persuade a seller to breach an existing purchase agreement in order to accept a better offer from your client.

Buyer Representation Agreements

A buyer and a real estate broker may enter into an agency relationship by signing a **buyer representation agreement**, sometimes called a "buyer's listing." With this type of contract, a buyer employs a broker to help her find and purchase a suitable property.

Like a listing agreement, a buyer representation agreement can be exclusive or non-exclusive. With an exclusive agreement, the broker will be entitled to compensation if the buyer purchases property during the term of the agreement, whether or not the broker finds the property or helps negotiate the purchase.

A buyer representation agreement usually includes provisions concerning:

- the duration of the agency,
- the general characteristics of the property the buyer wants,
- the acceptable price range,
- the conditions under which the broker's compensation will be earned, and
- how the compensation will be determined and who will pay it.

Basic Requirements

The statute of frauds requires a buyer representation agreement to be in writing and signed by the buyer, or the broker won't be entitled to sue for compensation. A buyer agency relationship can be created by an unwritten agreement, but this agreement can't be the basis for a compensation lawsuit.

Sometimes a buyer isn't hiring a broker to locate suitable property, but to help negotiate the purchase of a specific piece of property that the buyer's already found. In that case, the agreement should include a legal description of the property in question. Otherwise, the representation agreement merely needs to give a general description of the type of property the buyer's looking for (see below).

Like an exclusive listing agreement, in California an exclusive buyer representation agreement must have a definite termination date.

Common Legal Issues

The legal issues that come up in connection with buyer representation agreements are mainly about the agent's compensation. Under what circumstances is the buyer's agent entitled to payment, and who's required to pay him?

Earning Compensation as a Buyer's Agent. A buyer representation agreement usually entitles the broker to compensation if the buyer signs a purchase agreement during the representation period, whether or not the purchase transaction ultimately closes. In addition, the broker can be entitled to compensation even if the buyer doesn't enter into a purchase agreement. If the broker (or, in the case of an exclusive agreement, if anyone) finds property that matches the specifications in the buyer representation agreement during the term of the contract, the buyer may be obligated to pay the agreed compensation.

Because of this, the buyer should give careful consideration to the provision in the buyer representation agreement that describes the type of property she's seeking. The provision should include enough detail about the type of property desired so that it accurately states the buyer's requirements.

Like a listing agreement, a buyer representation agreement may have a safety clause. That would entitle the broker to compensation if, during a specified period after the representation agreement has terminated, the buyer purchases property that the agent introduced him to.

Manner of Compensation. A buyer representation agreement can provide for the broker to be compensated in various ways. The buyer may agree to pay the broker a percentage of the purchase price, a flat fee, or an hourly rate. In some cases, the broker will require a retainer, a sum of money that's paid up front, before services are provided. A retainer is typically nonrefundable, but will be credited against any fee or commission the broker becomes entitled to.

Many buyer representation agreements provide that the buyer will pay the broker if the purchased property was unlisted, but the broker will accept a commission split (a share of the commission the seller pays the listing broker) if one is available. Under California law, when a buyer's agent accepts compensation originally paid by the seller, it doesn't create an agency relationship between the agent and the seller, and it doesn't affect the agent's relationship with the buyer. (See Chapter 6.)

If the buyer is purchasing residential property with up to four units, the representation agreement should include the same notice concerning the negotiability of commissions that's required in a residential listing agreement.

Purchase Agreements

Now let's look at the central contract in a real estate transaction, the **purchase agreement**. The seller and buyer must have a written contract that establishes all of the terms of the sale. In most cases, the form used by the buyer to make the offer will become their contract. The buyer fills out the form and signs it, and if the seller accepts the buyer's offer by signing the form, a binding contract is created.

Although this contract between buyer and seller is commonly called a purchase agreement in California, you may also hear it called a purchase and sale agreement, sales contract, or deposit receipt (since the document may serve as the buyer's receipt for the good faith deposit).

The provisions of a purchase agreement may vary considerably depending on the transaction. However, at a minimum, every purchase agreement should:

- identify the parties;
- describe the property (again, a legal description is not required, but is preferred);
- set forth the terms of sale, such as the sales price, the amount of the downpayment, and the type of financing that will be used;
- identify any contingencies (discussed below); and
- set the date for closing, and also the date when possession of the property will be transferred, if that's going to be different from the closing date.

In addition, many purchase agreements include a reference to the broker's commission and the terms under which the good faith deposit will be returned in the event that the transaction falls through. Real estate agents must also disclose their license number in the purchase agreement if they are representing a party.

Common Legal Issues

The use of standard pre-printed forms eliminates many pitfalls in connection with purchase agreements. Nonetheless, certain legal problems tend to arise with some frequency. Let's take a look at offers, good faith deposits, and the use of contingency clauses.

Offers. As we noted earlier, a contract offer must have definite terms. A purchase agreement that just says "Monica agrees to sell her house to William next year" is too vague. How much will William pay for the house? When, exactly, will they close the sale? If a conflict arises, a court won't want to assume or guess what Monica and William intended to agree to. Instead, the court may simply decide that the mutual consent requirement wasn't met and that the contract is void.

So the buyer's offer must be definite in its terms; in turn, the seller's acceptance cannot change any of the buyer's terms. If it does, the seller's response becomes a counteroffer, not an acceptance. It's then up to the buyer to accept the counteroffer, reject it, or make another counteroffer.

A counteroffer can be made by crossing out a provision on the purchase agreement form and writing in a new one before returning the form to the other party. However, the process of reaching a mutually satisfactory contract may require several rounds of counteroffers. So it's generally preferable to use one of the many pre-printed forms designed for counteroffers, instead of crossing out provisions in the original offer.

Case to Consider...

Roth offered to buy Malson's property. Malson made a written counteroffer on a standard form published by the California Association of Realtors®. Although the form had a signature line in a section labeled "Acceptance," Roth instead signed a section of the form called "Counter to Counter Offer." In a part of the "Counter to Counter Offer" section marked "Changes/Amendments," Roth wrote in terms and conditions substantially the same as those in Malson's original counteroffer. Malson eventually rejected Roth's counter to the counteroffer and took the property off the market. Roth sued, alleging that he'd intended to accept the original counteroffer. Was there a contract? *Roth v. Malson* (1998) 67 Cal.App.4th 552.

Good Faith Deposits. An offer to purchase is typically accompanied by a good faith deposit; if the offer is accepted, the seller keeps the deposit and will apply it toward the purchase price. But what happens if the transaction later falls though? Does the seller have to return the deposit to the buyer?

Many purchase agreements provide that if the sale fails due to a breach by the buyer, the deposit will be treated as liquidated damages. (See Figure 9.1 for more information on liquidated damages.) Civil Code § 1677 requires that a liquidated damages provision in a purchase agreement must appear in boldface type, and it must be initialed by both parties. In a purchase agreement for residential property with up to four units, if the buyer intends to occupy one of the units as her residence, the amount that the seller retains as liquidated damages generally may not exceed 3% of the purchase price (Civil Code § 1675).

As a general rule, a liquidated damages provision is enforceable only if the amount to be forfeited in the event of a breach is reasonable. At the time the contract is made, the amount must be a reasonable estimate of the actual damages a breach would cause.

Contingencies. Purchase agreements often contain one or more conditions, or contingency clauses. A **contingency** makes one party's obligation to perform the contract dependent on the occurrence of a certain event. For example, the buyer might agree to purchase the home only if he is able to obtain financing on specified terms. If the event fails to occur, the party that the contingency clause was intended to protect or benefit may withdraw from the transaction without committing a breach of contract.

> **Example:** Joan signs a purchase agreement with a contingency clause allowing her to back out if she can't obtain a 30-year loan for $280,000 with a 5.5% interest rate. When it becomes clear that she won't be able to obtain a loan on those terms, she decides to withdraw from the sale. She can do so without forfeiting her good faith deposit.

Other common contingencies used in purchase agreements include structural inspection and pest inspection contingencies, and contingencies concerning the sale of the buyer's current home. If a contingency isn't fulfilled and the buyer wants to terminate the transaction, he must inform the seller promptly. Otherwise the buyer will be held to have waived his right to withdraw from the contract.

Sometimes when a transaction has been derailed, the buyer and seller disagree as to whether the seller is entitled to keep the buyer's deposit. In that situation, the escrow agent, broker, or other party who has been holding the deposit will turn the funds over to a court and let the court decide which party is in the right. This is called an **interpleader action** (see Chapter 12).

Disclosures Required in Sales Transactions

State and federal laws require a seller to make certain disclosures about the property and provide certain other information to all potential buyers. Some of these disclosures concern the property's physical condition; others are required because of the property's location, or because of the type of property being sold. It's very important for real estate agents to be familiar with these disclosure requirements, since failure to comply can lead to lawsuits against the seller and the seller's agent.

Transfer Disclosure Statement. As we explained in Chapter 7, sellers and seller's agents have a general duty to disclose problems with the property that they're aware of. To help ensure fulfillment of this duty in residential transactions, California law requires a home seller to provide a buyer with a form called the **real estate transfer disclosure statement** (Civil Code § 1102 *et seq.*). This form must be given to the prospective buyer in most transactions involving residential property with up to four units.

The transfer disclosure statement is filled out by the seller, and it contains information regarding:

- items included in the sale;
- any known defects in the property;
- known environmental hazards, such as lead-based paint, asbestos, or mold;
- shared walls or other structures shared with adjoining property owners;
- encroachments or easements;
- any roof additions or building modifications made without building permits;
- known lateral or subjacent support issues;
- flooding, drainage, or grading problems;
- zoning violations, nearby industry or airports, or neighborhood nuisances;
- any common areas, CC&Rs, or homeowners associations; and
- any lawsuits that might affect the property or common areas.

The transfer disclosure statement form also requires some disclosures from the real estate agents involved in the transaction. Remember, real estate agents are legally required to perform a visual inspection of the property. They're not required to search for hidden defects, but they must report anything they notice.

The disclosure statement form has separate sections to be filled out by the listing and selling agents. Each agent is required to make note of any material facts discovered during the visual inspection. In addition, if the listing agent learned any material facts about the property's condition from the seller, she must disclose these facts—even if the seller fails to mention them in his own disclosure.

The transfer disclosure statement should be given to the prospective buyer as soon as possible. If it is provided after a purchase agreement is signed, the buyer has three days from the time the disclosure statement is received (or five days from the date the statement is deposited in the mail) to rescind the purchase agreement (Civil Code § 1102.3).

Case to Consider...

When Sweat bought a home from the Hollisters, the transfer disclosure statement stated that the property was located in a floodplain. As Sweat later learned, a city zoning ordinance prohibited the enlargement or rebuilding of homes in a floodplain, even after destruction by fire or other calamity. Sweat claimed that this restriction was a concealed defect that decreased the property's value by $215,000, and that it should have been disclosed in the transfer disclosure statement. Were the Hollisters liable for concealing a material fact affecting the property's value? *Sweat v. Hollister* (1995) 37 Cal.App.4th 603.

Natural Hazards Disclosures. California Civil Code § 1103 requires a seller or a seller's agent to disclose the fact that a property is located in one or more of the following six types of natural hazard areas:

- a special flood hazard area,
- an area that could flood if a dam fails,
- a very high fire hazard severity zone,
- a wildland fire area,
- an earthquake fault zone, or
- a seismic hazard zone (or an area subject to landslides).

This requirement applies to most transactions involving residential property with up to four units. The disclosures are typically made on a **natural hazards disclosure statement** form. The statement warns prospective buyers that if a property is located in any of these zones, the hazards may limit the buyer's ability to develop the property, obtain insurance, or receive assistance after a disaster.

In addition, under Government Code § 8897.1, buyers of homes built before January 1, 1960 must receive a copy of *A Homeowner's Guide to Earthquake Safety*. This booklet contains a form for the seller to use to disclose whether the property lies in an earthquake hazard zone and whether the home has had any seismic retrofitting. The booklet also describes earthquake risks and recommends ways to mitigate earthquake damage.

Lead-Based Paint. When a transaction involves a home built before 1978, the federal Residential Lead-Based Paint Hazard Reduction Act requires the owner to provide prospective buyers or tenants with information about lead-based paint. A seller must disclose the location of any known lead-based paint and give a buyer ten days to inspect for lead-based paint or associated hazards. The seller must also provide the buyer with a booklet called *Protect Your Family From Lead In Your Home*.

Sex Offender Information Website. Any real estate contract for the sale of a one- to four-unit residential property must contain a notice that the California Department of Justice has made information about registered sex offenders available to the public on a website at www.meganslaw.ca.gov.

Taxes and Assessments. A seller must disclose the fact that a residential property is subject to special taxes under the Mello-Roos Community Facilities Act or subject to assessments for bonds issued under the

> **More Information**
>
> For a complete list and explanation of California's real estate transaction disclosure requirements, please see the California Bureau of Real Estate's guide *Disclosures in Real Property Transactions* on the Bureau's website.

Improvement Bond Act of 1915. A seller is also required to disclose the possibility of a supplemental property tax bill. (For more on taxes and assessments, see Chapter 14.)

Drug Labs. If a property is known or suspected to be contaminated by methamphetamine laboratory activity, the seller must obtain an order from the local health department stating that the property is clean and needs no further action. The seller must provide the buyer with a copy of this order, and the buyer must acknowledge receipt.

Smoke Detectors. Sellers must give buyers a statement that the property is in compliance with California's law regarding smoke detectors, which requires that there must be at least one installed outside each sleeping area. If a local ordinance is stricter than the state law (for example, requiring an additional smoke detector in the kitchen), then the statement must disclose compliance with the local law.

Option Contracts

Although listing agreements, buyer representation agreements, and purchase agreements are the real estate contracts you're likely to handle most frequently, you should be familiar with other types of real estate contracts as well. For example, suppose your client Manuel is extremely interested in a property listed for sale by Andrea, but he's not quite ready to commit to the purchase. Andrea, however, is anxious to sell as quickly as possible and has made it known that she'll take the first serious offer that comes along. You may want to recommend an option contract.

An **option contract** is an agreement that creates a right to buy or lease a certain property within a set period of time for a fixed price. Returning to our example, Manuel and Andrea could enter into an option agreement that gives Manuel the right to purchase Andrea's property for $1,000,000 during the next two weeks. Of course, to make such a contract enforceable, Manuel must offer Andrea something of value. Manuel could agree to pay $3,000 to Andrea as consideration for leaving the option open for two weeks. Such a payment is called **option money**.

Because an option is a contract, it must meet the usual requirements for validity. Under the statute of frauds, an option concerning real estate must be in writing to be enforceable. The option contract, when exercised, becomes the purchase agreement, so it should spell out all of the terms of the anticipated purchase—not just the price, but financing arrangements, contingencies, closing date, and so on.

Once the parties enter into an option contract, the seller (the **optionor**) is obligated to keep the offer open for the period of time specified in the option contract. This means that the optionor cannot sell or lease the property to anyone other than the buyer (the **optionee**) during that time.

If the optionee decides to exercise the option and buy the property at the agreed price, he must give the optionor a written acceptance, just as with any purchase agreement.

Option Rights

An option contract gives the optionee a contract right—the right to purchase or lease the property within the specified time at the specified price. However, this contract right is not an interest in property and can't be used as security for a mortgage or a deed of trust. Returning to our example, Manuel couldn't obtain a loan using Andrea's property as security.

What rights does an optionee have? If the optionor dies during the option period, the option agreement will remain valid and binding on the optionor's heirs. This means that if Andrea were to die during the two-week option period, Manuel would be able to enforce the option contract against Andrea's husband or other heirs.

Also, the optionee may record the option agreement, which provides constructive notice of the option to any third parties. (Constructive notice means that a third party could find out about the option by checking county records. See Chapter 11 for more about recording and constructive notice.) Recording becomes important if the optionee exercises the option during the option period: his rights will relate back to (become effective as of) the date of recording. This means that his rights will take priority over any other interests or rights that were created after the recording date.

> **Example:** Lyle has an option to purchase Marvin's ranch. The option is good for six months, from May 1 through October 31, and includes the mineral rights. Lyle records the option on May 2. In June, Marvin grants the property's mineral rights to the ABC Mining Company, which records its grant on June 30. On October 30, Lyle exercises his option to purchase Marvin's ranch. Because Lyle recorded his option agreement, his property interest relates back to the day of recording, May 2. Lyle's interest takes priority over ABC Mining Company's interest.

Note that an optionee's rights in regards to the optionor relate back to when the option was granted. The rule set forth above applies only to the optionee's rights in regard to third parties.

Although an option automatically expires at the end of an option term, an unused recorded option will remain a cloud on the property's title. To avoid future problems, the optionor should obtain a release from the former optionee and have it recorded. A quitclaim deed from the optionee to the optionor could serve this purpose.

Option vs. Right of First Refusal

An option is different from a right of first refusal. A **right of first refusal** gives a person the first chance to buy or lease a property if it's put on the market. For example, a lease agreement may give the tenant a right of first refusal to purchase the leased property. This means that if the landlord decides to sell the property, the tenant will be given the opportunity to buy it before it's sold to anyone else.

Suppose the landlord does decide to sell the leased property. He receives an offer to purchase from a third party for $400,000. Under the terms of the lease, the landlord must first give the current tenant the opportunity to match the offered price and buy the property for $400,000. If the tenant doesn't want the property, or can't match the price, the landlord is free to sell the property to the third party.

Although an option and a right of first refusal may appear similar, there's an important difference between them. Under an option, the optionee can force the sale of the property during the option period, even if the optionor has changed his mind. However, a person with a right of first refusal only holds the right to purchase the property if it's put on the market; the property owner has no obligation to sell the property at all. In our example, this means that the tenant cannot force the landlord to sell the property.

Case to Consider...

The Enzlers entered into an exclusive listing agreement with Anthony, a licensed real estate broker, to sell approximately 105 acres of land. The agreement allowed for a 10% commission if the land was sold, exchanged, or conveyed during the listing period, or within three months after the listing expired. The commission could be shared with cooperating brokers.

A cooperating broker showed the property to the Armtrouts, who declined to make an offer. However, the Armtrouts later approached the Enzlers and entered into an option to purchase the property. Neither the optionees nor the optionors were represented by a broker. The option contract was executed one week before the expiration of the listing agreement, although it wasn't recorded or exercised until after the listing agreement had expired. Is Anthony entitled to a commission on the sale to the Armtrouts? *Anthony v. Enzler* (1976) 61 Cal.App.3d 872.

Land Contracts

A **land contract** is also known as a real property sales contract, conditional sales contract, installment sales contract, or contract for deed. Land contracts are sometimes used when buyers can't—or won't—obtain financing from a traditional lending institution.

When a buyer purchases property using a land contract, he pays the seller in installments, rather than all at once. The buyer (known as the **vendee**) takes immediate possession of the property, but the seller (known as the **vendor**) retains legal title to the property until the buyer has paid the full purchase price. In other words, until the land contract is paid in full, the buyer has only possession, not legal title.

While the vendee is making payments on the land contract, he is said to have equitable title to the property. **Equitable title** is the right to possess and enjoy the property while paying off the purchase price. Once the purchase price has been paid in full, the vendor will convey legal title to the vendee.

California has some statutory rules concerning land contracts, which are found in Civil Code §§ 2985 – 2985.6. Civil Code § 2985 defines a land contract as an agreement in which one party agrees to convey property to another on specified terms, but which does not require conveyance within one year after the contract is entered into. The contract must state how many years it will take the vendee to pay off the contract price and obtain legal title, if payments are made as agreed. If the contract is for the purchase of residential property with up to four units, the vendor can prohibit the vendee from making prepayments only during the first 12 months of the contract (Civil Code § 2985.6).

Rights and Responsibilities of the Parties

Both the vendor and the vendee have specific rights and responsibilities under a land contract. The vendor can transfer the property without the vendee's consent, but the land

Using a Land Contract?

Land contracts are more popular when interest rates are high, pricing buyers out of the market. Because the seller is providing the financing, the terms can be more flexible than those offered by a bank or other lender. Land contracts were quite popular in the late 1970s and early 1980s, and then fell out of favor in many parts of the country. (They're still popular in the Midwest, where they are frequently used in the sale of small commercial properties.)

If a buyer and seller decide to use a land contract, the following steps will help keep their relationship running smoothly.

Buyers should:
- get the advice of a real estate attorney,
- have the property appraised,
- purchase title insurance, and
- use an escrow company to hold the executed deed to the property as well as the original documents.

Sellers should:
- check the buyer's credit report (first!),
- put both the buyer's and the seller's names on the insurance policy, and
- use a disbursement company to handle contract collection.

contract must be assigned to the new owner, who will take title to the property subject to the vendee's interest.

> **Example:** Peter sells land to Margaret for $300,000 using a land contract. The terms of the contract require Margaret to make payments over a ten-year period. Five years into the contract, Peter deeds the property to his sister and assigns the contract to her. Peter's sister will have to honor the contract and convey the property to Margaret when she has finished paying for the property.

The vendor may also encumber the property with liens. However, the vendor is required to deliver a clear, marketable title (free from liens or other encumbrances) at the end of the payment term. This means that the vendor must pay off any liens before delivering the deed to the vendee.

Like the vendor, the vendee can encumber the property with liens—although most lenders won't accept a vendee's equitable interest as security for a debt. It is also possible for the vendee to assign his contract rights to a third party, unless that's specifically prohibited in the contract. If the vendee assigns his interest, when the contract price is paid in full, the assignee will receive title.

A vendee's main responsibility is to make regular installment payments until the contract amount is paid in full. The vendee is usually also responsible for making property tax payments and insuring the property.

Remedies for Default

Once the vendee has paid off the full contract price, he's entitled to receive legal title to the property. If the vendor fails to deliver clear legal title, the vendee may be able to sue for specific performance.

At one time, some sellers preferred to use land contracts instead of deeds of trust for seller-financed transactions because it was easier to reclaim the property if the buyer defaulted. That's no longer true in California, where court decisions have placed restrictions on the vendor's remedies for default. A vendor used to be able to declare a forfeiture if the vendee defaulted. In a **forfeiture**, the vendor would terminate the contract, evict the vendee, and retain all the payments the vendee had already made. Now, however, if a vendee defaults and the vendor terminates the contract, the vendor is typically required to reimburse the vendee for the contract payments made, less any damages caused by the breach, and less a reasonable amount of rent for the period of time the property was in the vendee's possession. In addition, a vendee generally has the right to cure the default and reinstate the contract.

Leases

There's one other type of real estate contract to mention: the lease. A lease not only conveys an interest in property, it's also a contract between the property owner (the landlord or lessor) and the tenant (or lessee). A lease is sometimes called a rental agreement.

The statute of frauds requires a lease to be in writing and signed if the term of the lease is longer than one year, or if the lease won't be fully performed within one year of contract formation. Like other types of real estate contracts, a lease should contain an accurate legal description of the property.

A written lease may set out the rights and responsibilities of the landlord and the tenant, stating rules that will govern the tenancy. However, their relationship is governed not only by their contract, but also by landlord-tenant law. A discussion of landlord-tenant law, with more information about leases, can be found in Chapter 20. The different types of leasehold estates are discussed in Chapter 4.

Since contracts play such an important part in real estate transactions, familiarity with the principles of contract law and the different types of contracts is essential for real estate agents. When you fill out a standard form for a listing agreement, a buyer representation agreement, a purchase agreement, an option to purchase, a land contract, or a lease, you're helping the parties create a legally binding contract. Remember that if there's any doubt about the effect of a contract provision, it's best to advise the parties to seek the advice of an attorney.

Case Law in Depth

The following case involves some of the legal issues discussed in this chapter. Read through the facts and consider the questions in light of what you have learned. Then read what the court actually decided.

Franklin v. Hansen (1963) 59 Cal.2d 570

Franklin, a licensed real estate broker, represented Hansen in a sale of property. The original listing price was $115,000 but, after receiving several low offers, Hansen agreed to reduce his price to $100,000. None of this was in writing, since Hansen assured Franklin that a written listing agreement was unnecessary; his word was good.

On January 15, 1960, Franklin got an offer for $100,000. He telephoned Hansen, requesting a telegram authorizing the sale of the property. Hansen sent the following telegram: "Los Angeles, California...D.V. Franklin, 208 Marine Balboa Island California. This is confirm [sic] that I will sell 608 South Bay Front Balboa Island for 100,000 cash this offer good until noon 1–19–60. Chas. P. Hansen." There was no mention of a commission.

On January 19, Franklin called Hansen again, this time to inform Hansen that he'd sold the property and received a check for $5,000 as a downpayment. However, when the standard purchase agreement form (which provided for a 5% commission to Franklin) was presented to Hansen, Hansen refused to sign and wanted out of the deal. Franklin sued for his commission. At trial, Hansen claimed that the telegram could not be considered a memorandum sufficient to satisfy the requirements of the statute of frauds. The trial court disagreed and ruled in favor of Franklin. Hansen appealed.

The question:

Was Franklin entitled to a commission?

The court's answer:

The court began by quoting from California's statute of frauds. "'The following contracts are invalid, unless the same, or some note or memorandum thereof, is in writing:...An agreement authorizing or employing an agent or broker to purchase or sell real estate for compensation or a commission.'"

The court went on to say that a telegram can satisfy the statute of frauds, but the contents of the telegram must contain all the basic elements of the agreement. Every detail isn't necessary, however. For example, if Hansen's telegram had referenced an earlier written agreement to pay Franklin a commission, Franklin might have had a case, even if the commission amount wasn't mentioned. Unfortunately for Franklin, the telegram made no mention of a commission at all, and no promise to pay Franklin anything for his efforts.

The court stated, "The telegram in the instant case fails to use any words in recognition of a contractual obligation for a commission. While it may be a sufficient memorandum of an agreement to sell the property, it is the alleged commission agreement which is sought to be enforced... The meaning of the telegram is clear and definite—it requires no aid in its interpretation, and it does not imply, infer or suggest a commission agreement." Thus, the telegram was "obviously insufficient" to satisfy the requirements of the statute of frauds for a commission agreement.

The result:

The judgment in favor of Franklin was reversed. Hansen wasn't required to pay him a commission.

Chapter Summary

- A contract is a binding agreement between two or more persons that is enforceable by law. To be valid, a contract must have four elements: legal capacity to contract, mutual consent, a lawful objective, and consideration.

- In addition, the statute of frauds requires most contracts relating to real estate to be in writing and signed. This applies to listing agreements, buyer representation agreements, purchase agreements, options to purchase, land contracts, and leases for longer than one year. Another requirement that applies to all of these types of contracts: they all must include a description of the property, preferably a legal description.

- Objective intent to enter into a contract is shown by the process of offer and acceptance. Once a buyer has made an offer, the seller may accept the offer, reject the offer, or make a counteroffer. To be effective, an acceptance can only be made by the offeree; it must be communicated to the offeror; it must be made in the manner specified by the offer; and it must not vary the terms of the offer (otherwise, it's a counteroffer).

- The terms of a contract may be modified by amendment, assignment, novation, or accord and satisfaction.

- Possible remedies for breach of contract include actual damages, liquidated damages, an injunction, rescission, or specific performance. Injunctions, rescission, and specific performance are all equitable remedies.

- A listing agreement is an employment contract between a property seller and a real estate broker. It must state the amount or rate of the broker's compensation, and if it's an exclusive listing, it must have a termination date. Under the terms of most listings, the broker has earned the commission once a ready, willing, and able buyer is found. If the listing has a safety clause, the commission is owed if the property is sold to a buyer the broker introduced to the property within a specified period after the listing expires.

- A buyer representation agreement is an employment contract between a property buyer and a real estate broker. It should include a description of the type of property sought. If it's an exclusive agreement, it must have a termination date. Most agreements provide that the buyer will pay the broker if the property purchased is unlisted, but the broker will accept a commission split if one is available.

- A purchase agreement is the contract between a property seller and a buyer. It typically provides that the buyer's good faith deposit will serve as liquidated damages if the buyer defaults. A purchase agreement often includes a contingency clause, so that the contract will be binding only if a certain event occurs.

- In residential transactions, California law requires the seller and the seller's agent to make numerous disclosures to the buyer. In most cases, the seller must give the buyer a transfer disclosure statement; the form has sections to be filled out by the agents involved in the sale, in addition to the sections filled out by the seller.

- An option contract creates a right to buy or lease property on certain terms during a specified period. The optionee can choose whether or not to exercise the option and enter into a purchase agreement or lease. An unexercised option expires automatically when the option period ends, but if the option was recorded, it creates a cloud on the title.

- Land contracts are used in some seller-financed transactions. The vendee pays the vendor for the property in installments. The vendor deeds legal title to the vendee only when the contract has been paid off.

- A lease is both a conveyance of an interest in property and a contract between the landlord and tenant. It must be in writing if the term is longer than one year, or if it won't be fully performed within one year after it's executed.

Key Terms

- **Contract** – An agreement to do, or refrain from doing, certain things.

- **Voidable contract** – A contract that can be rescinded by one party, usually because that party lacked capacity to contract, or because the contract resulted from fraud, duress, or misrepresentation.

- **Void contract** – A contract that lacks one of the required elements (such as consideration); it's not really a contract at all, so it may be disregarded by either party without court action.

- **Mutual consent** – The "meeting of the minds" that signifies that both parties agree to a contract's terms and conditions, achieved through the process of offer and acceptance.

- **Offer and acceptance** – The process of agreeing to terms and conditions that forms a binding contract.

- **Counteroffer** – A reply to an offer that contains different or additional terms or conditions than the original offer.

- **Mailbox rule** – An acceptance communicated by mail is effective when the message has been sent (put into the mailbox), even though the offeror won't receive it right away. Purchase agreement forms may modify this rule.

- **Consideration** – Something of value exchanged by the parties.

- **Statute of frauds** – A law that requires certain contracts to be in writing and signed in order to be enforceable.

- **Substantial performance** – When a contract has been breached, but the main obligations have been performed.

- **Material breach** – When a party fails to perform one of the basic acts required by the contract.

- **Damages** – A sum of money that a breaching party is ordered to pay to the nonbreaching party.

- **Equitable remedies** – Remedies for breach of contract that are based on fairness and justice, rather than money damages; includes injunctions, rescission, and specific performance.

- **Specific performance** – A court order requiring a party who has breached a contract to fulfill the terms of the contract.

- **Listing agreement** – An employment contract between a property seller and a real estate broker in which the broker agrees to serve as the seller's agent in finding a buyer for the property.

- **Buyer representation agreement** – An employment contract between a buyer and real estate broker in which the broker agrees to serve as the buyer's agent in the search for a property to purchase.

- **Exclusive right to sell listing** – A listing contract that makes one broker the seller's exclusive agent and provides that the broker will receive a commission if the property is sold during the listing term, no matter who finds the buyer.

- **Exclusive agency listing** – A listing contract that makes one broker the seller's exclusive agent and provides that the broker will receive a commission if the property is sold during the listing term, unless the owner finds the buyer himself, without the help of an agent.

- **Open listing** – A listing contract that entitles the broker to a commission only if she is the procuring cause of the sale.

- **Procuring cause** – A broker who is entitled to a commission because he is primarily responsible for bringing buyer and seller together.

- **Ready, willing, and able buyer** – A buyer who makes an offer that meets the seller's terms and has the financial ability to go through with the purchase.

- **Safety clause** – A clause in a listing agreement that makes the seller liable for a broker's commission after the listing has expired, if the property is sold to someone the broker had contact with during the listing term.

- **Interference with contractual relations** – A tort caused when someone wrongfully interferes with the contract of another, causing a financial loss.

- **Purchase agreement** – A contract between a property seller and a buyer, in which the buyer agrees to purchase the seller's property on specified terms. Also called a purchase and sale agreement, a contract of sale, or a deposit receipt.

- **Contingency clause** – A provision in a contract that makes one party's obligation to perform dependent upon the occurrence of a certain event.

- **Option contract** – An agreement that creates a right to buy or lease certain property within a set period of time for a fixed price.

- **Right of first refusal** – A right that gives a person the first chance to buy or lease property if it goes on the market.

- **Land contract** – A contract in which the buyer (vendee) purchases real property on an installment basis, and the seller (vendor) retains legal title to the property until the purchase price is paid in full.

- **Equitable title** – The right to possess and enjoy property while paying off the purchase price in a land contract.

Chapter Quiz

1. The four elements of a valid contract are:
   a) consideration, drawn up by a lawyer, capacity, mutual consent
   b) capacity, mutual consent, a lawful objective, consideration
   c) capacity, mutual consent, a written document, consideration
   d) consideration, a written document, mutual consent, capacity

2. Mutual consent is evidenced by:
   a) offer and acceptance
   b) consideration
   c) a written document
   d) None of the above

3. Abby offers to buy Tyler's house for $200,000. Tyler replies, "How about $210,000?" This is an example of a/an:
   a) acceptance
   b) offer
   c) counteroffer
   d) Both b) and c)

4. The law that requires real estate contracts to be in writing is known as the:
   a) Recording Act
   b) Real Estate Law
   c) statute of frauds
   d) None of the above

5. A contract contains a provision stating that the party who breaches the contract will have to pay the other party $5,000. This is an example of:
   a) an equitable remedy
   b) specific performance
   c) an injunction
   d) liquidated damages

6. Mark signs a listing agreement with XYZ Realty (and no one else), but keeps the right to sell the property himself. If he does, he doesn't have to pay the broker a commission. This is an:
   a) exclusive right to sell listing
   b) exclusive agency listing
   c) open listing
   d) unenforceable listing

7. The purchase agreement contains a condition that makes the contract dependent upon the buyer obtaining a loan at 5% interest. This is an example of a/an:
   a) contingency clause
   b) safety clause
   c) right of first refusal
   d) option

8. A provision in a tenant's contract gives him the right to match any offer by a buyer if the landlord puts the property up for sale. This is known as a/an:
   a) option
   b) right of first refusal
   c) land contract
   d) None of the above

9. In a land contract, the vendee holds:
   a) equitable title
   b) legal title
   c) Both a) and b)
   d) None of the above

10. A married woman who is 17 years old enters into a real estate contract. The contract is probably:
    a) voidable
    b) void
    c) valid
    d) unenforceable

Chapter Answer Key

Chapter Quiz Answers:

1. b) The four elements of a valid contract are legal capacity to contract, mutual consent, a lawful objective, and consideration. In addition, real estate contracts must be in writing.

2. a) For a contract to be valid, there must be a meeting of the minds. This happens when both parties agree to all of the contract's terms and conditions in a process called offer and acceptance.

3. d) When the offeree alters one of the terms of an offer, it becomes a counteroffer. A counteroffer is really a new offer to enter into a contract, one with different terms.

4. c) The law that requires some contracts, including real estate contracts, to be in writing is called the statute of frauds.

5. d) A provision in a contract that specifies an amount of money that will serve as damages in case of a breach of contract is a liquidated damages provision.

6. b) In an exclusive agency listing, the owner agrees to list with only one broker, but keeps the right to sell the property himself.

7. a) A contingency clause makes one party's obligation to perform the contract dependent on the occurrence of a certain event.

8. b) A right of first refusal gives a person the first chance to buy or lease a property if it goes on the market.

9. a) In a land contract, a vendee holds equitable title to the property; the vendor holds legal title until the contract price is paid in full, at which time the vendor will transfer legal title to the vendee.

10. c) A real estate contract entered into by a minor is ordinarily void; however, if the minor is emancipated (married, in the military, or declared by a court to be an adult) the contract will be valid.

Cases to Consider... Answers:

Offer and Acceptance

Hofer v. Young (1995) 38 Cal.App.4th 52. The appeals court sided with the Youngs. Civil Code § 1582 allows any "reasonable and usual mode of communication" for accepting offers unless a specific mode was forbidden by the offer itself. Therefore, the faxed acceptance was sufficient to create a binding contract. Once the acceptance was communicated to the offeror, there was mutual consent between the parties.

Purchase Agreements

Roth v. Malson (1998) 67 Cal.App.4th 552. The court found that there was no contract. Contract formation is governed by "objective manifestations" of the parties' intent (such as the form Roth signed). Courts should not be forced to compare particular terms in contract documents to determine the parties' intent.

Sweat v. Hollister (1995) 37 Cal.App.4th 603. The fact that the house was located in a floodplain was a material fact that had to be disclosed to the buyer, and the sellers made that disclosure. However, the legal and practical effects of this circumstance were not material facts subject to disclosure. If a potential buyer is adequately informed of the property's zoning classification, it's then up to the buyer to investigate the impact of that classification on the property's value.

Option Contracts

Anthony v. Enzler (1976) 61 Cal.App.3d 872. An option is not a sale of property within the meaning of the listing agreement; instead, it's the sale of a right to purchase property. However, when an option to purchase is exercised, the sale of the property relates back to the time the option was granted. Therefore, a broker is entitled to a commission if an option that was granted during the listing period is exercised at some later time by the buyer.

List of Cases

Anthony v. Enzler (1976) 61 Cal.App.3d 872
Franklin v. Hansen (1963) 59 Cal.2d 570
Hofer v. Young (1995) 38 Cal.App.4th 52
Roth v. Malson (1998) 67 Cal.App.4th 552
Seck v. Foulks (1972) 25 Cal.App.3d 556
Sweat v. Hollister (1995) 37 Cal.App.4th 603

Chapter 10

Transfer of Real Property

Outline

Introduction

A person who owns property has title to it. Title may be transferred from the current owner to a new owner in many different ways. Some transfers are voluntary, resulting from an intentional act on the part of the owner; others are involuntary, occurring by operation of law, without action by the owner and sometimes against the owner's will.

We'll begin this chapter with a look at deeds, the legal documents used most commonly to transfer real property, whether or not the owner is still living. Next, we'll discuss transfers that take place after the owner's death (for example, according to the terms of a will). We'll conclude the chapter by addressing involuntary transfers of title, most of which are court-ordered.

Deeds

Ownership of real property begins with the government. Title to land passes from the government to a private party through a document called a **patent**. In the United States, in parts of the country where there were few settlers at the time of statehood, the U.S. sold patents at bargain prices or even gave the land away to encourage settlement.

Once the government has granted land to a private party by patent, later transfers of title to that property usually take place by deed. A **deed** is a legal document in which an owner (the **grantor**) transfers a property interest to another (the **grantee**). A transfer of property by deed is often called a **conveyance**.

In this section, we'll examine the requirements for a valid deed in California. We'll also discuss the common types of deeds and explain when they are used.

Requirements for a Valid Deed

To be valid, a deed must:

- be in writing,
- contain words of conveyance,
- include an adequate description of the property,
- be signed by a competent grantor,
- specify an identifiable grantee,
- be delivered to the grantee, and
- be accepted by the grantee.

In Writing. The first requirement is straightforward. According to Code of Civil Procedure § 1971, any transfer of a real property interest (except a lease for less than one year) must be in writing.

Words of Conveyance. A deed must contain language that actually conveys the property to the new owner, often called a granting clause. For example, the words "convey," "transfer," "sell," or "grant" might be used. Regardless of the specific words used, the language in the granting clause must express the intent to transfer ownership of the property interest.

Property Description. The deed must also contain a legally adequate description of the property being transferred. A description is considered adequate if it makes it possible to identify and locate the property. (See Chapter 11.)

Signature of a Competent Grantor. Next in the list of deed requirements is the signature of a competent grantor. Again, the grantor is the person who grants or transfers an interest in property.

Competence. Like someone entering into a contract, someone conveying property by deed must be legally competent—of sound mind and at least 18 years old. A person younger than 18 can deed property only if she is an emancipated minor (see Chapter 9).

Mental incompetence may be temporary—caused by involuntary intoxication or a passing mental illness—or it may be permanent. If at the time the deed was signed, the grantor had been declared incompetent by a court, or else was entirely unable to understand the transaction, the deed is void and does not transfer title.

Case Example:

Nadine Gamelin, 87 years old, had Alzheimer's disease. One day she was found unconscious in her mobile home, which was filthy and without plumbing or heat. Nadine was suffering from dehydration and her feet had been bitten by rats.

Nadine was quickly hospitalized. Her son was appointed temporary conservator (a type of legal guardian), pending a hearing to make the conservatorship permanent. Four days later, while Nadine was still in the hospital, she deeded her property to the Dudenhoeffers. Susan Dudenhoeffer was a student who had known Nadine for a number of years and visited her occasionally.

Nadine died before the permanent conservatorship hearing. Her son asked the court to set aside the Dudenhoeffer deed. The trial court found that the Dudenhoeffers had not exerted undue influence, and let the deed stand. The appellate court reversed, however, settling title on the son. When a person is placed under any kind of legal guardianship, even temporarily, the court has decided that he or she lacks capacity to make a deed or contract. *O'Brien v. Dudenhoeffer* (1993) 16 Cal.App.4th 327.

Under certain circumstances, a deed signed by a grantor who was only temporarily incompetent may be considered voidable instead of void. In that case, the grantor would have the option of voiding the deed or allowing the transfer of title to be effective.

Signature. The grantor must sign the deed. Illiterate or disabled grantors may use a simple mark if they cannot write their names. Someone must witness the grantor making his mark, and the witness must sign her own name near the mark. The grantor's name should also be written or typed by the mark.

A transfer of community property requires the signature of both spouses or registered domestic partners. (See Chapter 5.)

In contrast to grantors, grantees aren't giving up any rights, so their signatures aren't required on the deed. California's Civil Code imposes one exception to this rule: married grantees taking title as community property with right of survivorship must sign or initial the deed. This helps ensure that the grantees genuinely want this special form of ownership.

Signing by business entities. Corporations and other business entities can transfer property by deed. Who is authorized to sign the deed? That depends on the type of entity and whether the transfer is taking place in the ordinary course of business. (A transfer of all or substantially all of the entity's assets is not considered to be within the ordinary course of business, unless buying and selling real property is the entity's main business activity.)

When property owned by a corporation is transferred in the ordinary course of business, the deed must be signed by corporate officers who have been authorized to do so by the board of directors. Shareholder approval usually isn't required, unless all or substantially all of the corporation's assets are being transferred.

When property owned by a partnership is conveyed in the ordinary course of business, any general partner has authority to sign the deed. If the transaction isn't in the ordinary course of business, the partner signing the deed must be authorized to do so in writing by the other owners.

Similar rules apply to a member-managed limited liability company (LLC): any member can sign a deed if the conveyance is in the ordinary course of business. If the LLC is manager-managed, however, then only the manager has the authority to sign deeds. (See the discussion of LLC structure in Chapter 5.)

Power of attorney. One person may use a written **power of attorney** to give another authority to sign a deed (or other document) on her behalf. The person who is given power of attorney is called the **attorney in fact**. (Despite this term, the person doesn't have to be a lawyer.) The relationship is a form of agency. (See Chapter 6.)

An attorney in fact must sign the deed or other document on behalf of his principal in this fashion:

Example:

> *Phillip K. Montague III*
> by *Gary Booth*, his Attorney in Fact

The principal's name must come first, and California courts are firm on this point. For example, an agent who signs in the format "Gary Booth, attorney in fact for Phillip K. Montague III" has failed to create a valid deed.

Most powers of attorney are general, giving the agent broad powers. A power of attorney may be limited, however. For example, suppose that a married woman will be traveling when the sale of the couple's house will close. She could grant her husband a **limited power of attorney**. This document would give the husband the authority to sign a deed and other documents needed for the closing, but not to do anything else.

Whether general or limited, a power of attorney that authorizes the attorney in fact to convey real property (or enter into contracts concerning real property) must include a legal description of the property and should be recorded in the county where the property is located.

A buyer or other grantee relying on the signature of an attorney in fact needs to make sure that the power is valid at the moment the deed is signed. That's because a power of attorney may be revoked at any time. Furthermore, as with any agency, the death or incompetence of the principal may constitute a revocation. (A **durable power of attorney**, however, is one that is specifically intended to go into effect or remain in effect if the principal becomes disabled or incompetent.)

Acknowledgment. To discourage fraud, county recording offices won't record a deed—or most other documents—unless the signature(s) have been acknowledged. (Recording is discussed in detail in Chapter 11.) In an acknowledgment, the signer declares to an official witness that her signature is voluntary. Most people satisfy this requirement by signing before a notary public. However, state law allows several other officials to take acknowledgments, including judges and court and county clerks.

 A License to Steal

Powers of attorney have been labeled "licenses to steal" by professionals involved in elder care. Most power of attorney forms grant the individual complete power over the principal's finances, leaving some seniors who sign these forms vulnerable.

For example, the San Francisco district attorney's office has reported a number of cases involving financial abuse of elders via a power of attorney. In one case, a woman befriended an elderly alcoholic whom she'd known since childhood. After the inebriated senior was found wandering the streets unable to care for herself, the defendant began "helping" her with financial matters and was soon given a power of attorney. The defendant then deeded the victim's condominium to herself and took out various mortgages. Losses amounted to over $600,000.

There's no easy solution. However, when a person of questionable competence grants a power of attorney, one worthwhile step is to have duplicate statements on all accounts sent to a lawyer or other trusted person who can check for suspicious withdrawals.

Fig. 10.1 Requirements for a valid deed

A VALID DEED

I hereby grant .... words of conveyance
Greenacres Farm .... adequate description of property
To Harry Carter .... identifiable, living grantee
(signed) Sam Smith .... signature of competent grantor

---

The acknowledged signature is accompanied by a certificate of acknowledgment. This is a brief document that states that the grantor was identified and that she admitted signing the document voluntarily. The notary or other official signs the certificate and stamps the document with a notary seal. Note that if the grantee happens to be a notary himself, the grantee should not be the one to take the grantor's acknowledgment. The grantee's interest in the deed would create a conflict of interest, and the acknowledgment would probably be invalid.

A deed without an acknowledged signature is still valid between the grantor and grantee, but since unacknowledged deeds can't be recorded, third parties will not have constructive notice of the grantee's interest in the property. (See Chapter 11.)

Identifiable Grantee. A valid deed requires an identifiable grantee. As long as it's clear who the parties are, merely misspelling a party's name won't invalidate the transfer. Even saying, "To Ben James and his wife" may be enough to identify both grantees.

Grantee competence is not required, since grantees merely receive the property, making their ability to understand the transaction relatively unimportant. This means that property can be deeded to someone who is a minor or mentally incompetent.

Corporations and other legal entities (such as LLCs or trusts) can be grantees. An entity must be validly formed under state law in order to take title in its name.

Delivery and Donative Intent. After signing and acknowledging the deed, the grantor or his agent must physically **deliver** the document to the grantee or her agent (for example, putting a deed in escrow constitutes delivery). Physical delivery isn't enough, however; the grantor must also have **donative intent**: the intent to transfer title. While physical delivery certainly suggests donative intent, it isn't conclusive, as the following case illustrates.

Case Example:

Glen wanted to give his son a ranch, but on the condition that his son live on the ranch and run it. Yet Glen never discussed this with his son—Glen and his wife simply signed a deed and gave it to their attorney for recording. The attorney delivered the deed to the county recording office, but later received a notice that he hadn't paid a sufficient recording fee and the document couldn't be recorded until the necessary additional amount was received.

The day before the recording office received the additional sum, the son and his family were killed in an airplane accident. Hearing of his son's death, Glen immediately asked the attorney to return the deed. The attorney contacted the recording office and the office returned the deed.

The son's estate sued to enforce the gift of the ranch. However, the court ruled that the deed was never delivered, despite its transmission to the recording office. The father intended to condition his gift on his son taking up ranching—something that certainly couldn't happen with his son dead—and thus full intent to deliver did not exist. *Perry v. Wallner* (1962) 206 Cal.App.2d 218.

As a general rule, a deed must be delivered while the grantor is alive. This means that a grantor can't execute a deed with instructions that delivery should take place after his death.

Case Example:

Mr. McClellan signed a quitclaim deed to his wife, which transferred his interest in the family residence. However, the deed was never recorded. Instead, it was kept in a drawer along with a card listing Mr. McClellan's insurance policies. He testified later that the deed was intended to avoid probate of the residence in the event of his death.

The McClellans' marriage dissolved. Mrs. McClellan argued that the deed was valid and thus the residence was her separate property. (Remember, failure to record a deed does not affect its validity between the parties.) However, the court ruled that because the grantor intended delivery to take place after his death—an invalid arrangement—no conveyance ever occurred. The residence remained the joint property of both spouses. *McClellan v. McClellan* (1958) 159 Cal.App.2d 225.

However, California now allows the use of a **transfer on death deed** for residential property. If a grantor records this type of deed, it will transfer title to the grantee automatically, without probate, when the grantor dies. The grantor can revoke the deed at any time before dying.

Acceptance. Last in our list of deed requirements is **acceptance** of the deed by the grantee. Acceptance generally isn't much of an issue, as most people happily accept whatever deed comes their way. Yet sometimes accepting a deed simply doesn't make sense.

Example: Frankie owns a rental house that has sharply declined in market value because of severe neglect. It's now worth only $102,000, and it has tax and other liens against it totaling $114,000. Frankie's daughter is getting married and he wants to make a grand gesture: deeding the house to his child and her fiancé so that they will have a place of their own. The young couple thinks about it and then rejects his gift. The house would be more of a financial burden than a benefit.

Also, only a living grantee can accept a deed. Property cannot be deeded to the dead.

Example: John signs a deed gifting property to his niece, Candace, hoping to surprise her when she returns from trekking in Nepal. He delivers the deed to Candace's 22-year-old son. Unbeknownst to Uncle John, however, Candace had fallen off a cliff a week earlier.

After her death comes to light, Candace's son claims he has inherited the property through the deed to his mother. The son's claim won't hold up, however, because title to the property never transferred to his mother. She couldn't accept the deed because she was dead when it was delivered.

Note that if Uncle John's deed had described the grantee as "Candace and her heirs or assigns," the son would have taken title.

Optional Information in a Deed. Most deeds contain elements that aren't required. Almost every deed is dated, for example, but this isn't legally necessary.

Also not required, but often present, is a "to have and to hold" clause (sometimes called a **habendum** clause), which names the type of interest being conveyed. Is the grantor conveying a fee simple or merely a life estate? Unless specified, the grantor passes everything she owns to the grantee (which is what almost every grantor intends, anyway).

If there is more than one grantee, the deed should clearly state whether the property is being taken as a tenancy in common, a joint tenancy, or community property. Nonetheless, stating this information is optional. If it's not included, the owners will take title as tenants in common, unless they are married, in which case the property will be owned as community property.

Finally, deeds often include a recital of consideration, indicating that the grantee paid the grantor for the property. For example, the following language is typical: "…conveys to Grantee, for $10.00 and other valuable consideration…" Deeds are valid without this recital, but a gift of real property may be subject to claims by the grantor's creditors, so stating that consideration was paid may help refute any argument that the transfer was a gift. (Consideration needn't take the form of money. But if the only consideration is emotional—"love and affection" being the common phrase used in deeds—the courts will consider the transfer a gift.)

Types of Deeds

The requirements we've just discussed apply to every type of deed. Several types of deeds are used in California; the most common are grant deeds and quitclaim deeds.

Let's take a look at the different types of deeds.

Grant Deed. In a **grant deed**, the grantor warrants that:

- she hasn't previously conveyed title to anyone else, and
- she hasn't caused or allowed any encumbrances to attach to the property, other than those already disclosed in the deed.

It is because of these warranties that buyers generally insist on receiving a grant deed in an ordinary private transaction. Both of the warranties apply whether or not they are expressly stated in the deed. And as with any type of deed, the parties may negotiate other warranties.

Case to Consider...

The Faughts leased a portion of their commercial property to the county. The lease had a 25-year term. Two years after executing the lease, the Faughts sold the whole property to Evans, conveying it to him with a grant deed. The lease, which was unrecorded, was not mentioned in the grant deed.

Two years after buying the property, Evans paid the county to give up its lease. He then sued the Faughts (the grantors) to recover the amount of money paid to the county, arguing that the lease was a breach of the warranty against encumbrances in the grant deed. The Faughts claimed that although the lease wasn't recorded, Evans had actual notice of it at the time of conveyance, so there had been no breach of warranty. If the grantee had notice of the lease, could the grantors be required to reimburse him for the money spent on terminating the lease? *Evans v. Faught* (1965) 231 Cal.App.2d 698.

Quitclaim Deed. A **quitclaim deed** conveys whatever interest the grantor has and nothing more. The deed contains no warranties at all. Signing a quitclaim deed means absolutely nothing if the grantor has no interest in the property. A penniless drifter could freely sign a quitclaim deed for some San Francisco real estate and the grantee would have no claim to the property (although he might have a claim against the drifter, if he was convinced to give something of value for the deed).

Grantors use quitclaim deeds when making gifts of property and in other transactions where there's no need to provide the grantee with warranties. Another common use for a quitclaim deed is to cure a **cloud on title**. "Clouds" are potential claims or other problems that cast doubt on the ownership of property.

In a situation where it's uncertain whether someone has an interest in or claim against the property, that person may be asked to execute a quitclaim deed in favor of the property owner. This will release any possible interest and clear away the potential claim against the title.

> **Example:** Kirsten gave Ned a two-month option to purchase her property. Ned recorded the option, but he decided not to exercise it, and it expired. The expired option is a cloud on Kirsten's title. She asks Ned to sign a quitclaim deed transferring any possible interest he might have in the property to her. Kirsten records the deed to clear away the cloud created by Ned's option.

Another type of problem that creates a cloud on title is a minor flaw in an earlier conveyance, such as the misspelling of a party's name or an error in the legal description. A quitclaim deed used to correct these kinds of errors is sometimes called a **reformation deed**.

In a quitclaim deed, conveyance terms like "grant" or "convey," normally used in grant deeds, should be avoided. These words imply that the grantor warrants title. Instead, "release" or "quitclaim" should be used in the conveyance language.

Deeds by Officials and Semi-officials.

Like quitclaim deeds, deeds issued by people acting in an official or semi-official capacity have no warranties. However, different names

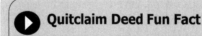

▶ Quitclaim Deed Fun Fact

In 2003, actor Marlon Brando used a quitclaim deed to gift a small plot of land on his private Tahitian island, Onetahi, in Tetiaroa, to his close friend, pop star Michael Jackson.

and slightly differing provisions are used, depending on the situation. For instance, the sheriff's office uses a **sheriff's deed** to transfer property to the highest bidder at a court-ordered execution sale. (See Chapter 13.)

When property is foreclosed under a deed of trust, the trustee conveys the property to the buyer at a foreclosure sale using a **trustee's deed** (again, see Chapter 13). And here's a final example: a **personal representative's deed** is used by an executor in probate proceedings to transfer real property to the beneficiaries named in a will.

Warranty Deeds. In many states, people use a warranty deed in situations where Californians would use a grant deed. The **warranty deed** provides significantly greater protection for the buyer than a grant deed—chiefly, the grantor warrants that if title ever fails from defects that originated before or during the grantor's period of ownership, she will reimburse the grantee for any losses. (In contrast, the grant deed warrants against only those title defects that arose while the grantor owned the property.)

However, practically speaking, California buyers aren't disadvantaged by the lack of warranty deeds. Claims made on title insurance policies have largely replaced suing to enforce a seller's warranties, making the issue of deed warranties moot. (Title insurance is discussed in Chapter 12.)

After-acquired Title. Sometimes a grantor signs a grant deed even though she owns less than complete title (for example, because she has sold off the mineral rights). If she later acquires some rights she previously lacked, perhaps by repurchase or through a lawsuit, this is called **after-acquired title**. In this situation, the grantee automatically owns the after-acquired title—not the grantor.

> **Example:** Marcie sold a house to Phil using a grant deed. Marcie was in hiding from her violent, abusive husband and she kept her married status secret all through closing. But since the house was community property, the deed required the husband's signature. Two months later, Marcie's lawyer arranged for the husband to sign a quitclaim deed of his community interest to Marcie. Marcie's after-acquired title immediately and automatically passed to the buyer, giving him good title.

Case Example:

Lillian Schwenn bought some Long Beach property that generated royalties from an oil and gas lease. Several years later, Lillian deeded the royalty rights to her daughter and son-in-law. Another few years passed and Lillian sold the real estate to the Kayes. The deed of royalty rights had been recorded, but for some reason the deed wasn't discovered by the title company. So the oil company began sending royalty payments to the Kayes, even though Lillian hadn't sold the royalty rights—she had given them away before the sale.

Lillian filed a quiet title action to settle the matter, but she first asked her daughter and son-in-law to gift the royalty rights back to her, "because she did not want them to be involved in litigation." Lillian testified that she hoped to keep the royalty stream in the family. The kids complied with her wishes—but the moment they did so, the doctrine of after-acquired title took effect. Once the rights were back in Lillian's hands, they automatically transferred to her grantees, the Kayes. *Schwenn v. Kaye* (1984) 155 Cal.App.3d 949.

Note that quitclaim deeds transfer only the grantor's current interest; the after-acquired title rule doesn't apply. However, the parties can add language to a quitclaim deed stating that any after-acquired title passes to the grantee.

Transfer of Property After Death

As the saying goes, "You can't take it with you," so when a property owner dies, the property must be transferred to someone else. In this section, we'll focus on how people direct the transfer of property after their deaths using wills, trusts, and community property agreements. We'll also explain what happens when people fail to leave any effective directions regarding their property.

Wills

The topic of wills involves a fair amount of specialized vocabulary. Let's begin our discussion with some basic definitions. The person making a will is the **testator**. (Previously, a female testator was called a **testatrix**—"trix" being a Latin suffix meaning "woman"; however, this term is rarely used today.) Technically, a testator **bequeaths** personal property in a **bequest** to a **legatee**, but **devises** real property in a **devise** to a **devisee**. California's Probate Code has simplified this language, using the term "devise" for any disposition of property made under a will. The courts, however, continue to use the more elaborate vocabulary.

The testator names an **executor** in the will to act as the personal representative (agent) of his estate after his death. When the testator dies, the executor files the will in court and—with court approval—carries out any devises required by the will. This process is called **probate**.

Requirements for a Valid Will. Now that we've defined some key terms, let's look at the requirements for making a valid will. In California, a will generally must be:

- in writing,
- signed by a competent testator 18 years or older, and
- attested to by two or more competent witnesses.

In writing. Wills must be in writing. You cannot create an oral will in California. (And even though some other states allow oral or so-called "nuncupative" wills, they are valid only in very limited circumstances.)

Signed. A will must be signed by the testator. If necessary, the will may be signed with the testator's mark or by someone acting for the testator.

A signature by mark on a will should be witnessed in the same fashion as a mark on a deed. The witness prints or types the maker's name next to the mark along with her own name as witness. Note that the witness to the mark needs to be someone other than the witnesses to the will itself, as in the following case example.

Case Example:

When James McCabe executed his will (15 days before he died), he was too weak to sign his name and instead made a mark above his typewritten name. Two witnesses signed the will. As required, an independent witness witnessed the mark itself, signing her name and writing the date and the word "witness" near the mark. However, the witness failed to write the decedent's name near the mark as California law requires. McCabe's wife was unhappy with the contents of the will and she contested it.

The court agreed that the law had not been followed to the letter. However, while the mark-witnessing requirements help avoid fraud, there's a competing public policy interest in carrying out a decedent's wishes. Given all the witnesses to McCabe's signing, the likelihood of fraud was minimal. Substantial compliance with the statute was sufficient, and throwing out the will would not serve the public interest. *Estate of McCabe* (1990) 224 Cal.App.3d 330.

A testator who is too disabled to write can have someone else sign the will on her behalf. The signer must do so at the testator's request and in the testator's presence. The signer must also sign his own name with a notation that he signed the document at the testator's request.

Competent testator. A person making a will must be at least 18 years old and mentally competent. The testator is competent (has **testamentary capacity**) if he has the mental ability to understand:

1. what the will accomplishes,
2. the nature and extent of his property, and
3. who the members of his family are and whose interests are affected by the terms of the will.

Basically, the testator can't suffer from any delusion-inducing mental disorder that influences his gifts. If the testator was incompetent when the will was signed, the will is invalid, even if the testator regains competency before his death.

The law presumes that a testator is competent: evidence of incompetence must be clear, cogent, and convincing. As a California court remarked of elderly testators in *Estate of Selb* (1948) 84 Cal.App.2d 46, "feebleness, forgetfulness, filthy personal habits, personal eccentricities, failure to recognize old friends or relatives, physical disability, absent-mindedness and mental confusion do not furnish grounds for holding that a testator lacked testamentary capacity."

Witnessed. California requires that two or more competent witnesses sign their names to the will with the testator present (the one exception being the holographic will, discussed below). The witnesses must be able to testify that they knew the testator was signing a will and also that the testator either signed or acknowledged the signature as his own in their presence.

Any competent adult may act as a witness. However, someone who will benefit under the will should not be one of the two witnesses. When a witness is also a beneficiary, the will is still valid, but the witness will not be entitled to any assets under the terms of the will. However, the witness is not entirely out of luck. He will be entitled to receive as much as he would have if the testator had died intestate.

> **Example:** Augustina signs her will and has it witnessed by her chauffeur and her grandson, Franklin. In the will, Augustina leaves half of her estate to Franklin, so Franklin is both a beneficiary and a witness. He won't receive half of her estate as provided for in the will, but he will receive 1/8 of her estate, which is what he would receive under the rules of intestate succession.

Along with about half of the other states, California permits one exception to the witness requirement: a holographic will does not have to be witnessed. A **holographic will** is one that is in the testator's own handwriting and signed by the testator. Dispensing with the witness requirement may appear to streamline the process, but testators who draft their own wills often create difficult-to-interpret provisions, increasing the likelihood of litigation over the estate.

 The Handwriting is on the Will

Holographic wills are sometimes eccentric documents. For instance, there was the so-called "Mormon Will" purportedly written by Howard Hughes and discovered on the desk of a Salt Lake City church official. The beneficiaries of this handwritten will included Melvin Dummar, a gas-station owner, named to receive approximately $156 million. However, a Nevada court rejected the Mormon Will as a forgery; it was one of 40 wills filed by people claiming to be heirs of the billionaire.

Here's an example of a holographic will left by a Texan farmer named John Brugger in 1948. (Note: the misspellings are in the original document.)

Recorded in Volume 150 page 47 et seq. of the Robertson County deed records...

Now as the three boys received Farms...and as Anny received about $2500.00 so far and as Anny maried again, a man I do not aproove of and do not think good for her, I order that she...will get only one hundred dollars. The Rest to be dividet in four parts. One for my wife, and one for each of them three boys...Now, as my wife is geting older and a little fleshy, but having some money, and some sucker will try to ge it, I hope and wish, she will not be a Fool and mary again. Now to the boys, Be peasable among your self, Do not go the Court, and tell nobody how much I left and about Anny I am sory but she told me things, I take from nobody.

JOHN BRUGGER, Sr.

If some provisions of a holographic will are typewritten or pre-printed, the probate court will ignore those provisions. The exception to this rule is general statements of testamentary intent, such as what might be found at the beginning of a commercially printed will form. However, what constitutes a commercially printed will form can be controversial.

Case Example:

Dorothy Southworth never married and had no children. In 1986, at Dorothy's request, North Shore Animal League (NSAL) sent her a letter describing its animal care and bequest program.

In 1989, Dorothy completed a NSAL donor card. She checked a box for "not taking action now," and wrote in a blank space provided on the card that her "entire estate is to be left to North Shore Animal Shelter." She filled out another blank explaining that the shelter would one day receive $500,000. Finally, she checked a box indicating that the bequest should be used for animal food and spaying and neutering.

Later, Dorothy wrote NSAL a letter saying that she intended "to take steps" to make them a beneficiary of her estate. However, she died several years later without having taken further action.

Dorothy's estate entered probate as if she had left no will; NSAL objected, claiming the donor card was a will. The trial court ruled the donor card met the requirements of a holographic will and found in favor of NSAL. On appeal by two of Dorothy's half-siblings, the appellate court reversed. The donor card was not a "commercially printed will form." Also, the boxes that Dorothy checked and the words she wrote did not evidence a present testamentary intent, but merely future plans to make a will. *Estate of Southworth* (1996) 51 Cal.App.4th 564.

Exception for foreign wills. If a will is made by someone in another state and it is valid under the laws of that state, California will recognize the will as valid, even if it doesn't meet California's requirements. The Constitution's Full Faith and Credit Clause requires recognition of other states' judicial acts, such as the admission of a will into probate. (See Chapter 1.)

Example: O'Malley is eaten by an alligator in Houma, Louisiana. His will is a "mystic testament," a type of will unique to Louisiana. The mystic testament was created in accordance with state law: he enclosed the will in an envelope, sealed it in the presence of witnesses and a notary, and announced to those gathered that the document was his testament and that he had signed it.

O'Malley's mystic testament disposes of certain real estate in California. The California probate court will recognize this unusual will, even though it doesn't comply with California's will requirements.

California's Statutory Will. The Probate Code provides a basic statutory will form for use by people who do not face estate tax issues or other complexities. The form is written in simplified language and effectively walks the testator through the steps of making the will. A will made using the statutory will form must meet the same requirements as any other pre-printed will in California. Thus, it must be signed in the presence of two competent witnesses.

Revoking a Will. The testator may revoke an earlier will in a new written will. Alternatively, he may show his intent to revoke the will by burning, tearing, or otherwise destroying the will (or directing another person to do so in his presence). A later inconsistent will also revokes the earlier will, but only as to the inconsistent provisions.

The granting of a decree of marital dissolution automatically revokes any will provisions regarding the testator's ex-spouse. (The same rule applies to the dissolution of a domestic partnership.) Note that a decree of separation, as opposed to dissolution, does not affect will provisions involving a spouse. If a couple separates permanently, but they never actually file their divorce papers, their wills remain effective.

Probate. After the testator's death, the executor files the will in court (referred to as "probate court," although it's a normal county superior court). In probate, the court oversees the distribution of property according to the terms of the will, essentially approving them by court order. As mentioned earlier, the executor makes distributions of real property using a personal representative's deed.

For estates under $100,000 that do not involve real property, California permits a simplified procedure that avoids probate.

Case to Consider...

In her will, Felicitas Worthy left some valuable land to the Kelleys; all the rest of her money and property (the "residual estate") was to go to the Dominican Sisters. But shortly before her death, Ms. Worthy entered into a contract to sell the land. (She needed money to cover medical expenses.) The transaction didn't close until three days after her death, however.

Normally, when a piece of property is willed to a particular person but the testator sells the property before dying, the beneficiary is out of luck. Here, however, the probate court ruled that because closing occurred after death, the land was still part of Worthy's estate when she died, so the proceeds from the sale of the land belonged to the Kelleys.

The Dominican Sisters appealed. They argued that since the land that Worthy had willed to the Kelleys was sold before her death, the land itself was no longer part of her estate when she died; instead, the proceeds of the sale were part of the estate. As a result, the Sisters claimed, they were entitled to the proceeds along with the rest of the residual estate. Were their prayers answered? *Estate of Worthy* (1988) 205 Cal.App.3d 760.

Trusts

The second most common method of directing the disposition of real property after death is a **living trust**. When the creator of a living trust dies, her property is distributed by the trustee according to the terms of the trust. The court plays no role.

Trusts are also used for other purposes, including holding business assets and investment assets, often real estate (these are called real estate investment trusts or REITs). We introduced the topic of trusts in Chapter 5.

Trusts designed to dispose of real property can also be created in a will (these are known as **testamentary trusts**). Our main focus here is on living trusts, the type that real estate agents are most likely to encounter.

Living Trust Mills

California allows probate attorneys to take a percentage of an estate as their fee, instead of charging by the hour. This means that probate can sometimes cost a great deal. To avoid probate, many Californians seek out alternatives to wills such as joint tenancy or living trusts.

Sometimes elderly or unsophisticated consumers get taken in by so-called "living trust mills." These are boiler room sales outfits that use high pressure tactics (including the promise of big tax savings) to push packages that involve generic trust forms and the purchase of overpriced investments or unnecessary annuities.

A State of California website warns:

> These sales agents often pose... as "trust advisors," "senior estate planners," or "paralegals," and schedule initial appointments with seniors in their homes. Under the guise of helping set up or update a living trust, the sales agents find out about seniors' financial assets and investments. They sometimes work in assisted living centers, churches, and other places where seniors gather, hooking elderly victims through free seminars and other sales presentations.

A trust, like a will, works best if it's customized to meet a person's particular needs. Most people will benefit from a lawyer's individualized drafting. And the legal fee charged for this wouldn't necessarily be more than what many of the "mills" bill for a markedly inferior product. Further, lawyers have malpractice insurance backing up their work, something few trust outfits can claim.

Signing. As explained in Chapter 5, a trust is created when the grantor or trustor signs a document containing the various provisions of the trust. The grantor's signing doesn't have to be witnessed—so in this respect, a living trust is slightly more convenient than a will. However, the signature should be notarized, to allow recording of the document after the grantor's death. Recording helps prove that any transfer of real property by the trustee was consistent with the trust's terms.

Trustee. In a living trust, the grantor almost always names herself as the initial trustee. This gives the grantor control of her property during her life. An alternate trustee is also named; this alternate becomes trustee if the original trustee dies or becomes incapacitated. With a living trust, the alternate trustee administers and distributes the property of the **decedent** (the deceased person) according to the trust's terms—acting much like the executor of a will.

Funding. Merely signing a trust document does nothing. The grantor must actually fund the trust by re-titling assets in the trust's name. For example, the trustee of a living trust can't distribute the decedent's property unless the decedent had previously put that property into the trust. For real property, funding usually takes place with a quitclaim deed containing language along the following lines:

> Sarah Jones, a single woman, quitclaims to Sarah Jones, trustee for The Sarah Jones Living Trust, the following described real property…

Thus, while a living trust does avoid probate, setting it up requires an expenditure of some effort. There may also be recording and legal or other professional fees. And even with a trust, experts recommend a backup will to handle any property that the grantor failed to transfer into the trust, which means another expense. On the bright side, California's documentary transfer tax (essentially, a real property sales tax) does not apply; the state exempts a grantor's transfers to his living trust.

Types of Trusts. Many living trusts are **revocable**, meaning that the grantor can transfer any or all of the assets back to herself at any time. However, if the trust does contain assets when the grantor dies, these assets will be distributed according to the trust's terms. When all the assets have been distributed, the trust will terminate.

Note that choosing a revocable living trust over a will has little effect on one's estate tax bill. Property remains in your estate whether disposed of by the living trust or by a will, and if your estate is sufficiently large, it may be subject to an estate tax.

Other living trusts are **irrevocable**. As the name implies, once the grantor signs and funds an irrevocable trust, the transferred property has been given away permanently. Irrevocable trusts are used by people who are wealthy enough to face a considerable amount

 Minor Details

Along with probate avoidance, another benefit trusts can offer is some control over a child's access to assets after the parents' death. In general, the Probate Code provides that gifts and inheritance are automatically held until the minor reaches age 18. Some people, however, worry about turning over large quantities of money to such relatively young people. Trusts can provide a safety check.

To prevent your child from spending your entire life savings foolishly, you can provide that while the custodian (trustee) may use trust assets to pay for your child's medical or educational expenses, your child won't actually have access to the trust property until reaching a specific age. To establish such a trust, California's Uniform Transfers to Minors Act requires specific language to be used in the governing will or trust document.

If the will or trust document contains the required language, the custodian can delay transferring funds to the beneficiary until the age of 25 (but no later). For many parents, this gives them peace of mind that their children will get safely through college before getting full access to their inheritance.

of estate tax and thus want to transfer property out of their estate to help shrink their tax bill (while providing some control over the beneficiaries' access to the assets). IRS rules essentially forbid the grantor of an irrevocable trust from serving as trustee.

Community Property Agreements

The third method of arranging transfer of property after death is the community property agreement (CPA). Spouses and registered domestic partners can use a CPA as a will substitute and avoid probate on the death of the first spouse to die. (We mentioned this in our discussion of community property in Chapter 5.)

Most CPAs contain a provision stating that when one spouse dies, the decedent's one-half interest in the couple's community property automatically becomes the property of the surviving spouse. The CPA is recorded after the spouse's death to prove the transfer of the property's title; no deed is necessary.

Intestate Succession

So far we've discussed ways in which a property owner can arrange for her property to be disposed of after she dies. But what happens when someone dies without making any arrangements concerning her property?

A person who dies without a valid will is said to have died **intestate**. If a decedent left neither a valid will nor a valid will substitute (such as a trust or CPA), her property is distributed to family members as determined by the **intestate succession** statute. California's intestate succession statute is contained in Probate Code §§ 6400 – 6414.

When someone dies intestate, the probate court will appoint an **administrator** to distribute the estate as required by the statute. (An administrator performs essentially the same function as the executor of a will.) The administrator uses an **administrator's deed** to convey any real property. Family members who receive property by intestate succession are known as **heirs**.

As noted in Chapter 5, when a married person dies intestate, his interest in the community property goes to the surviving spouse. The rules involving his separate property are more complex; we'll just summarize some of the main points. Generally speaking, the surviving spouse gets all the property if the decedent had no other family (no surviving children, grandchildren, parents, brothers or sisters, or nieces or nephews). However, if the decedent is survived by one child, the surviving spouse splits the separate property equally with that child. With two or more children, the spouse gets a third and the children share the remainder. If a child predeceased (died before) the intestate decedent, any children of the deceased child take his or her share. If there were no children or grandchildren, but the decedent is survived by other close family members, then the surviving spouse gets half of the separate property, and the other half goes to other family members.

If there's no surviving spouse, the entire estate is divided among the children. (Again, a deceased child's share goes to that child's children.) If there's no spouse and no children or grandchildren, the entire estate goes to other family members (parents, siblings, or nieces and nephews).

Escheat

What happens to the property of someone who dies intestate and has no heirs at all? While this situation isn't common, it does happen.

If no heirs appear within two years of the decedent's death, the attorney general may initiate a court action to vest title to the assets in the state. When the state takes title to unclaimed property, it's called **escheat**. The escheat process applies to any kind of unclaimed property, whether the rightful owner is dead or merely unknown. For example, it applies to unclaimed lottery winnings or forgotten bank accounts.

If another five years passes after the initial court judgment granting escheat, and heirs have still not claimed title, the state can sell the property. Although the state will typically auction escheated property and deposit the proceeds in the general fund, the rightful owner can claim these proceeds at any time.

You can search California's records of unclaimed property at the state controller's website.

Case Example:

McGuigan died intestate in 1990. Six years later, a public administrator filed an order that the estate, worth approximately $160,000, escheat to the state of California for lack of heirs.

Judith Desmond was the daughter of McGuigan's sister. Represented by an attorney who routinely acted as an heir finder, Judith filed a claim for the estate. She was awarded a portion of the money. By statute, claimants to escheated property must give a detailed family history of the decedent and disclose any other possible heirs. Judith failed to disclose that McGuigan had a son, although she knew of the son's existence (in fact, she had met him once). The attorney/heir finder admitted that many heir finders ignored the statutory disclosure requirements. The appellate court declared that this essentially constituted fraud, and reversed the award to Judith. *Estate of McGuigan* (2000) 83 Cal.App.4th 639.

Involuntary Transfers

The transfer of property by deed, will, or will substitute is voluntary; the transfer of property by intestate succession or escheat is involuntary. To conclude the chapter, we'll take a look at some other types of involuntary transfers—ones that, unlike intestate succession and escheat, occur while the property owner is alive.

Court Actions

Many involuntary transfers result from court action. The most common types of actions that can involve a court transferring title against a property owner's wishes are foreclosure, partition, quiet title, and condemnation. (We'll discuss these only briefly here, since they're discussed in more detail elsewhere in the book.)

Foreclosure Actions. Creditors with any kind of lien against a property (for a mortgage loan, construction costs, taxes, judgments, and so on) can force a foreclosure sale of the property and satisfy their debt from the proceeds.

In foreclosure actions, the court orders the sheriff to sell the debtor's property at auction. The successful bidder receives a sheriff's deed, one of the deed types mentioned earlier in the chapter. (Foreclosures are discussed in greater detail in Chapter 13.)

Partition Actions. Co-owners who cannot agree on a division of their property may file a partition action. The court will then either order the property divided or, more commonly, order the property sold and the proceeds shared. Someone called a referee typically conducts the sale and may use a referee's deed or other form of quitclaim deed to transfer title to the property. (Partition actions are discussed in greater detail in Chapter 5.)

Quiet Title Actions. Quiet title actions are used to resolve various questions of ownership, as discussed in Chapter 2. Here, however, we focus on quiet title actions involving either a claim of adverse possession or accession (natural changes in the land). Surprisingly, in either of these quiet title actions, the court can issue an order confirming a person's ownership of land that she neither paid for nor received by gift.

Adverse possession. When someone occupies someone else's land for a period of time, she may be able to acquire ownership of it through **adverse possession**. Many adverse possession claims involve people mistakenly erecting fences or outbuildings on strips of their neighbors' land.

Most states allow adverse possession, though the requirements vary. California imposes five requirements, which are detailed in Chapter 15. Generally, the possessor must be the sole occupier of the land for five years and must pay taxes on the land.

Once the adverse possessor has satisfied the statutory requirements, the land is hers. Practically speaking, however, she must file a quiet title action, secure a court order declaring her the owner, and record the order. No deed is involved.

Natural changes to land (accession). The enlargement of land lying along a river or other body of water, usually by natural means, is called **accession**. Accession processes include accretion, reliction, and avulsion. As with adverse possession, the new owner must bring a quiet title action to settle his ownership of the property.

Accretion occurs when riparian (riverside) or littoral (lakeside) land is slowly enlarged by waterborne sand or soil. The riparian or littoral owner generally acquires title to the new land. (Note: The case example below mentions a narrow exception to this rule.) The buildup of land must be so gradual it isn't readily apparent; otherwise, it constitutes avulsion, discussed below.

When riparian or littoral land is enlarged by the retreat of water, the adjoining landowner acquires title to the newly exposed land. This is referred to as **reliction**. Like accretion, reliction must be quite gradual.

In contrast to the gradual processes of accretion and reliction, **avulsion** occurs when moving water abruptly tears away land and deposits it elsewhere. The original owner still has title to the lost sand or soil, if there is some way to claim it. If unclaimed, it eventually becomes part of the property where it was deposited.

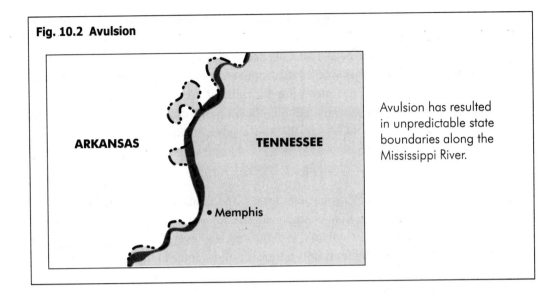

Fig. 10.2 Avulsion

ARKANSAS

TENNESSEE

• Memphis

Avulsion has resulted in unpredictable state boundaries along the Mississippi River.

The rules of avulsion also apply to land exposed by an abrupt change in a river's course. Notable instances of this have occurred along the lower Mississippi River, where storms and other causes have changed the river's course in some places—resulting in Arkansas owning new land on the east side of the river and, conversely, Tennessee owning odd bits of land along the river's west side. (See Figure 10.2.)

Case Example:

California's highest court had to settle the ownership of 12 acres of accreted land along the Sacramento River known as Chicory Bend. Under California law, naturally occurring accretion belongs to private landowners, but accretion resulting from artificial causes (most commonly from dredging and dam-building) belongs to the state.

The court opinion reviewed some California history. Beginning with the Gold Rush of 1849, miners wielding picks and shovels started chewing up the state's rivers and their banks. Eventually, more sophisticated hydraulic mining equipment was used. Hydraulic mining ended within a few decades, but not before it added huge amounts of silt to the Sacramento River and other waterways. By accretion, some of this silt ended up creating Chicory Bend.

The court found that although the silt was human-caused, it had traveled a great distance with the natural flow of the river, over a period of many years. Therefore, it was naturally occurring accretion, and Chicory Bend belonged to the private riparian landowners. *State of Cal. ex rel. State Lands Com. v. Superior Court (Lovelace)* (1995) 11 Cal.4th 50.

Condemnation. Last in our list of court-ordered transfers is **condemnation**. As we discussed in Chapter 1, the Takings Clause in the U.S. Constitution allows the government to take private property for public use without the owner's consent—but only if it pays the owner "just compensation," the fair market value of the property. If the owner isn't properly compensated, the transfer is an unconstitutional taking of private property. (Compensation for a taking of private property is required under the California state constitution as well as the U.S. Constitution.)

When the government determines that it needs a piece of property for public use, it first offers to buy the land. If the owner won't sell, the government files a condemnation action. The court hears expert testimony concerning the value of the property and determines a price. Then the court files an order condemning the property, directing the government to pay the owner, and effecting a transfer of title to the government.

Dedication

To end the chapter, we'll look at one other form of involuntary transfer, one that doesn't require court action: dedication. Like condemnation, dedication involves a transfer of privately owned land to the state; when land is dedicated, however, the government doesn't pay the private owner for it. **Dedication** is a transfer of property to the state without payment of compensation.

Dedication may be voluntary, as when a wealthy philanthropist gives a portion of her urban haven to the city for use as a bird sanctuary. Not surprisingly, voluntary dedication is rare; dedication is usually involuntary. The most common form of involuntary dedication is called statutory dedication. **Statutory dedication** occurs when a developer seeking government approval for a subdivision is required to dedicate land for streets, sidewalks, greenbelts, and other public uses in exchange for the approval.

Public agencies requiring statutory dedication can run into trouble with the federal constitution's Takings Clause. Under this constitutional provision, as currently interpreted by the courts, dedication can only be required in order to mitigate a negative impact caused by the developer's project. For example, since a subdivision development typically involves removing trees and other vegetation, dedication of a greenbelt can be required in order to lessen that impact. But requiring the developer to dedicate land for a public library would presumably be unconstitutional, since the development isn't having a negative impact on the community that would be addressed by construction of a library. If the city wants land for a library, it will have to pay compensation for it.

No deed is necessary with statutory dedication; typically, the plat map and government approvals simply specify that the dedicated land is for public use. Voluntary dedication, on the other hand, is usually accomplished by quitclaim deed.

Finally, there's one other form of dedication. Property owners can end up dedicating property by implication if they allow regular public access to it for at least five years. This is called **implied dedication** or **common law dedication**. Essentially, it's a variant of adverse possession.

> **Example:** Carla owns some lakefront property. For many years, people have been treating a part of her land that's adjacent to the public beach as if it were public property. Carla grouses about this privately, but she's always been too timid to confront the beachgoers. Her acquiescence could be held to constitute an implied dedication, so that the public now has a right to use the property.

In 1971, concerned because a significant number of landowners were refusing people access to recreational lands for fear of losing ownership, the California state legislature passed a statute limiting implied dedication. Under the statute, landowners who post signs at each entrance to their property—or every 200 feet along the boundary—are protected from inadvertent dedication. The signs must say, in essence, "Right to pass by permission, and subject to control, of owner: Section 1008, Civil Code."

As you've seen, there are many ways in which ownership of real property can be transferred. A particular property's history might include not only a long series of transfers by deed, but also transfers by will, intestate succession, foreclosure, partition, or quiet title. Whether voluntary or involuntary, transfers of real property have a great impact on the real estate profession. Understanding the various ways that real property can change hands will help you recognize issues that may make it important for your buyers and sellers to consult an attorney before proceeding with a transaction.

Case Law in Depth

The following case involves some of the legal issues discussed in this chapter. Read through the facts and consider the questions in light of what you have learned. Then read what the court actually decided.

In re Marriage of Broderick (1989) 209 Cal.App.3d 489

In 1973, a married couple bought a house in Petaluma, California. Four years later, the couple separated; the wife planned on moving to Arkansas with the couple's children. To fund her new life, she signed a quitclaim deed transferring all her rights (a community property half-interest) in the house to her husband. The deed was prepared at a title company and signed in the presence of a real estate broker and a notary public. The husband paid the wife only $3,000 for this deed. At the time, the couple had about $27,000 in equity in the house.

Ten months later, the couple reconciled and the family lived together in the California house again. They separated again briefly, then lived together until 1985, when they separated again, finally calling it quits for good in 1987. During the periods of separation, the husband paid the mortgage on the house by himself; during the periods of reconciliation, the wife contributed to the mortgage payments.

In the dissolution of marriage, the wife asked the trial court to void the quitclaim deed. She argued that the deed was invalid because of duress and inadequate consideration, among other reasons. In support of the duress claim, she alleged that a few months before she signed the quitclaim deed, her husband had committed a violent act against her. But the trial court ruled that the quitclaim deed was valid and that it made the house the husband's separate property. The wife appealed.

The questions:

Was there enough duress to justify overturning the deed? Was paying $3,000 for a property interest worth $13,500 so woefully inadequate that the court could void the transfer?

The court's answers:

The appellate court addressed the issue of duress by stating the generally accepted rule that a deed can be set aside for duress only if it was "...obtained by so oppressing a person by threats regarding the safety or liberty of himself, or of his property, or of a member of his family, as to deprive him of the free exercise of his will... [Duress] is more than mere threats or puffing; a party must be shown to have intentionally used threats or pressure to induce action or nonaction to the other party's detriment." The court went on to say that the wife signed the quitclaim deed because she wanted the money to leave, there were no threats of violence by the husband at the time the deed was signed, and the alleged previous act of violence by the husband had taken place months earlier. "Thus, the record demonstrates beyond dispute that at the time of the execution of the deed wife's free will was not overcome by threats, fear or violence, and that she was not induced to sign the document under circumstances which destroyed her free agency and caused her to act against her will..."

The court next addressed the question of whether $3,000 in exchange for an interest worth over $13,000 was so inadequate as to make the deed invalid. The court stated, "...inadequacy of consideration does not defeat the validity of a deed in the absence of fraud...[Here], the record establishes that husband made no representations regarding the value of the home, nor did he make any promises to wife at the time of signing the deed. Wife understood the meaning and effect of the deed and, in exchange for the agreed upon consideration, she voluntarily transferred her title in the home to husband."

The appellate court went on to compare the present case to a previous case that arguably supported the wife's position; but the court held that it did not. In the previous case, a wife who spoke little English had given up rights she didn't understand that she had. "By contrast, wife here was fully aware of both her property right in the home and the legal effect of the quitclaim deed; thus, the conveyance was the result of an informed decision on her part."

The result:

The quitclaim deed was valid. There was no duress. And even though the consideration was much less than the market value of the wife's interest, the husband had not used fraudulent means to persuade her to accept the consideration. (The court did find, however, that the wife had a substantial interest in the property based on the contributions to the mortgage payments she made over the years after she had quitclaimed the house to her husband.)

Chapter Summary

- Voluntary transfers of real property during an owner's lifetime take place by deed. The most commonly used deeds in California are grant deeds and quitclaim deeds. Deeds used by people acting in a public or semi-public capacity include sheriff's deeds and personal representative's deeds.

- To be valid, a deed must: be in writing, contain words of conveyance, include an adequate description of the property, identify the grantee, be signed by a competent grantor, be delivered to the grantee, and be accepted by the grantee. Practically speaking, a deed must also be acknowledged (notarized) so that it can be recorded.

- A property owner can arrange for the transfer of her property after her death with a will. Alternatively, to avoid probate, she could use a will substitute, which might be a living trust or a community property agreement. A revocable living trust avoids probate but has no effect on estate taxes. To reduce estate taxes, the trust must be irrevocable.

- Someone who dies without a valid will dies intestate. Property left by an intestate decedent is distributed to heirs (members of the decedent's family) as determined by the state's intestate succession statute. When there is no valid will and no heirs claim the estate, the property escheats to the state.

- Court actions involving the involuntary transfer of property ownership include foreclosure, partition, quiet title, and condemnation. Quiet title actions are used to confirm change of title resulting from adverse possession or accession.

- Title to real property can also change hands by dedication. Dedication is a transfer of property to the government without payment of compensation, either as a gift or in return for development rights (statutory dedication).

Key Terms

- **Grantor/grantee** – In a deed, the grantor transfers the property to the grantee.

- **Power of attorney** – Full or limited authority to act for another person; this power is granted by a written document.

- **Acknowledgment** – A statement to an official witness, by someone signing a document, that the signing is voluntary.

- **Grant deed** – The most common deed in California, giving the grantee current and any after-acquired title, and warranting ownership and the absence of undisclosed encumbrances.

- **Quitclaim deed** – A deed that transfers whatever interest the grantor currently has in the property, if any, but with no warranties.

- **Testator** – The person who made a will.

- **Executor** – The person named in the will to carry out the distribution of property required by the will.

- **Probate** – Court oversight of the property distribution called for by a will or the intestate succession statute.

- **Living trust** – A type of trust that allows distribution of someone's property after her death without probate.

- **Community property agreement** – An agreement between spouses or registered domestic partners, which typically provides that the community property share of the first spouse to die automatically passes to the surviving spouse without probate.

- **Intestate** – Someone who dies without leaving a valid will.

- **Escheat** – When the state takes ownership of unclaimed property after a certain number of years.

- **Court-ordered transfers** – Various kinds of lawsuits (including foreclosures, partition actions, quiet title actions, and condemnation) that can result in a court ordering transfer of property.

- **Dedication** – The transfer of property to the state without compensation, either philanthropically or in exchange for development rights.

Chapter Quiz

1. Marsha and Martin are married. They accept an offer on their house. Just before closing, Martin is called away by a death in the family. Marsha signs the deed to the buyer for herself and on behalf of her husband. Which of the following is true?
   a) In a community property state, either spouse can sign a deed of real property and obligate the marital community
   b) Unless both spouses are present to sign the deed, the transfer cannot take place
   c) Marsha can sign the deed on behalf of her husband if he has signed a power of attorney giving her authority to do so
   d) So long as a quitclaim deed was used, the buyer takes title

2. Father gifts vacant land in Big Sur to Son using a quitclaim deed. Years earlier, Father had deeded the logging rights to a timber company. One year after the gift to Son, the timber company decides that further logging of the property won't be profitable and quitclaims the timber rights back to Father. Which of the following is true?
   a) Father owns the timber rights
   b) If Father had used a grant deed to gift the property, the son would automatically own the timber rights under the doctrine of after-acquired title
   c) Because a quitclaim deed was used for the transfer, under the doctrine of after-acquired title the son automatically owns the timber rights
   d) Both a) and b)

3. Which of the following are valid deeds in California?
   a) Sheriff's deed, ministerial deed, trustee's deed
   b) Sheriff's deed, personal representative's deed, trustee's deed
   c) Sheriff's deed, personal representative's deed, mediator's deed
   d) None of the above

4. On his deathbed, Juan makes a will leaving all his property to his wife. He signs the document in front of his daughter and acknowledges his signature before a notary. Which of the following is true?
   a) The will is invalid because there was only one witness
   b) The will is valid because the notary counts as a witness
   c) The will is invalid because the daughter is an interested witness
   d) The will is invalid because the daughter has a right to inherit some of her father's estate under the intestacy statute

5. In the previous question, imagine that Juan's wife joins the deathbed signing as a witness. Which of the following is true?
   a) The will is ineffective because people on their deathbed lack competency
   b) The will is ineffective because family members can never serve as witnesses
   c) The will is ineffective because the wife is an interested witness; she receives nothing
   d) The will is ineffective because the wife is an interested witness; however, the wife is still likely to receive some property under the intestate succession statute

6. A living trust:
   a) is a "will substitute"—that is, a method of disposing of one's property after death without probate
   b) usually names the grantor (creator of the trust) to serve as trustee during her life
   c) may be revocable
   d) All of the above

7. Marcus harbors a deep distrust of lawyers. He wants to ensure that when he dies, no lawyer will receive even a dime during probate. He uses a living trust instead of a will. He buys a blank trust form from an office supply store and fills it out and signs it. That very afternoon he gets run over by a car, but he dies happy, knowing his estate is taken care of. Which of the following is true?
   a) Marcus was kidding himself—the probate court administers living trusts after the grantor dies
   b) The trust is without effect, assuming Marcus failed to transfer any assets into it
   c) The trust is invalid because the document requires two witnesses like a will
   d) None of the above

8. Foreclosure, condemnation, and partition actions:
   a) are strictly between private (nongovernmental) parties
   b) all result in either a sheriff's or trustee's deed transferring the property
   c) can result in an involuntary transfer of the property by court order
   d) all result in a voluntary transfer of the property by court order

9. Esmeralda feels she's dying, and she hasn't made a will. She signs a quitclaim deed conveying her residence to her daughter Sue, then puts it in her desk drawer with her other papers, knowing that after her death Sue will find the document. Which of the following is true?
   a) This is a valid will substitute—all Sue has to do is record the deed
   b) This won't accomplish a transfer of the property because the date on the deed won't match the date of death
   c) This won't accomplish a transfer of the property; a deed must be delivered during the grantor's lifetime. Here, delivery isn't intended until after Esmeralda's death
   d) The transfer will be effective between the parties, but since the deed isn't notarized or otherwise acknowledged, Sue can't record it

10. Cruz wants to develop a San Diego hillside. The city states that as a condition of Cruz's proceeding with the project, he must permanently set aside land for use as a public greenbelt to help control runoff along the back of the property. This is an example of:
   a) condemnation
   b) dedication
   c) partition action
   d) escheat

Chapter Answer Key

Chapter Quiz Answers:

1. c) Anyone with the power to sign a real estate agreement or deed can delegate that right to another using a written power of attorney.

2. d) A quitclaim deed conveys only the rights one currently owns; it does not convey after-acquired title. So when the timber company quitclaims the timber rights back to the father, the father keeps those rights. (If the father had deeded the property to the son with a grant deed instead of a quitclaim deed, the timber rights would automatically have passed to the son when the timber company deeded them back to the father.)

3. b) Sheriff's, trustee's, and personal representative's deeds are recognized in California; the mediator's deed and the ministerial deed are imaginary.

4. a) In California and most other states, wills must be witnessed by two people. The notary who takes the acknowledgment does not count as one of the witnesses. The daughter cannot be considered an interested witness since she wasn't named in the will.

5. d) People may very well be competent even though they are dying. Interested witnesses cannot take through a will; however, in such situations, they will still take whatever they are entitled to under the intestacy statute. The intestacy statute provides that the surviving spouse takes all the community property.

6. d) The maker of a living trust usually retains control over her assets and may revoke the trust at any time.

7. b) A living trust does not require witnesses or probate, but the trust can only control the distribution of assets transferred into the trust before the grantor's death.

8. c) In any of these actions, the court may issue an order requiring the transfer of title to the property.

9. c) Courts have repeatedly held that this arrangement doesn't work. Grantors must deliver the deed while they're alive.

10. b) Dedication refers to transferring property to the government as a gift, without compensation. A transfer of property in exchange for development rights is called statutory dedication.

Cases to Consider... Answers:

Deeds

Evans v. Faught (1965) 231 Cal.App.2d 698. With a grant deed, the grantor warrants that he hasn't caused or allowed any encumbrances other than those disclosed in the deed. In this case, where the lease wasn't disclosed in the deed, the grantors breached that warranty, and the grantee was entitled to reimbursement of the money paid to the county. The court reached that result even though it found that the grantee had actual notice of the lease at the time he took title under the grant deed.

Transfers After Death

Estate of Worthy (1988) 205 Cal.App.3d 760. On the date of Ms. Worthy's death, the land was still in her name. True, she was contractually obligated to sell the land, but the court didn't consider that relevant. She still possessed title, and thus title passed under her will to the Kelleys. The Kelleys, not the Dominican Sisters, were entitled to the proceeds of the sale.

List of Cases

Estate of McCabe (1990) 224 Cal.App.3d 330
Estate of McGuigan (2000) 83 Cal.App.4th 639
Estate of Selb (1948) 84 Cal.App.2d 46
Estate of Southworth (1996) 51 Cal.App.4th 564
Estate of Worthy (1988) 205 Cal.App.3d 760
Evans v. Faught (1965) 231 Cal.App.2d 698
In re Marriage of Broderick (1989) 209 Cal.App.3d 489
McClellan v. McClellan (1958) 159 Cal.App.2d 225
O'Brien v. Dudenhoeffer (1993) 16 Cal.App.4th 327
People v. Lapcheske (1999) 73 Cal.App.4th 571
Perry v. Wallner (1962) 206 Cal.App.2d 218
Schwenn v. Kaye (1984) 155 Cal.App.3d 949
State of Cal. ex rel. State Lands Com. v. Superior Court (Lovelace) (1995) 11 Cal.4th 50

Chapter 11

Legal Descriptions and Recording

Outline

Introduction

In the previous chapter, you learned how real property interests are transferred, both voluntarily and involuntarily. Now let's turn our attention to two important elements of any transfer: an accurate description of the property involved, and proper recording of the documents of conveyance.

In this chapter, we'll discuss the types of land descriptions that are used in the various documents associated with the transfer of real property. Next, we'll describe some common solutions to the types of problems that frequently come up in relation to property descriptions. Finally, we'll look at the recording system and the legal consequences of neglected or improper recording.

Of course, the information in this chapter won't replace the need for a lawyer or a survey professional when the adequacy of a land description is in question. However, it should help you identify when to recommend that your clients consult a lawyer or surveyor.

Methods of Land Description

Deeds, mortgages, purchase agreements, and other real estate documents must contain a complete and accurate description of the land involved. This means that the description must identify the property to the exclusion of any other parcel. If a description in a contract or deed is ambiguous or uncertain, the contract will be unenforceable or the deed will be void.

Although technically not required, it's always advisable to describe the property with a legal description. The legal description can be included either within the document itself or attached as an addendum. A **legal description** is a precise description of a parcel of real property that would enable a surveyor to locate its exact boundaries.

The three major types of legal descriptions are:

- metes and bounds,
- government survey, and
- recorded map.

Metes and Bounds

Land was described in England for centuries using the **metes and bounds method** of land description. This method was brought to the United States by the colonists, and used until better, more modern methods were developed. Metes and bounds descriptions are common in the eastern half of the United States; they are not found as often in western states such as California.

The metes and bounds system reads like a unique type of prose. It identifies a parcel of land by referring to the physical features of its surroundings, such as streams, large trees, or dry-stone walls. A metes and bounds description begins by providing a starting point, and then it describes a series of boundaries that would allow a surveyor to trace an outline of the property.

The starting point (referred to as the **point of beginning**) and the boundaries are described by reference to the following:

- monuments (natural or man-made objects);
- directions or courses (compass readings); and
- distances (measured in feet and inches today; old descriptions may refer to poles, rods, or perches).

Point of Beginning. The point of beginning is always described by reference to a monument, such as "the old windmill at Black's Pasture" or "the SW corner of the intersection of Front and Cherry." The point of beginning need not be a monument itself—it may simply refer to a monument (for example, "200 feet east of the old windmill at Black's Pasture").

Courses and Distances. Once the point of beginning is established, courses and distances are provided to form the boundaries of the parcel. For example, "north, 100 feet" describes a distance of 100 feet, heading north from the point of beginning. Both courses and distances may be described in terms of a monument; for example, "north along the eastern edge of Front Street for 100 feet" or "north, 100 feet more or less, to the centerline of Smith Creek." If there is a discrepancy between a monument and a course or distance, the monument will take precedence. For instance, a description that says "100 feet to the center of Smith Creek" would describe a boundary that extends to the center of Smith Creek (the monument) even if that boundary didn't measure 100 feet (the distance).

 Surveying in California

In California, land surveyors must meet experience requirements and pass an examination before receiving a license to practice. Licenses are issued by the California Board for Professional Engineers, Land Surveyors, and Geologists, which is a division of the state's Department of Consumer Affairs.

It is illegal to engage in land surveying without a license. Anyone who attempts to provide such services without a license is subject to fines and discipline by the Board.

A metes and bounds description includes as many courses and distances as are necessary to describe the complete parcel of land. The last course and distance must take the final boundary back to the point of beginning. (A description that doesn't end at the point of beginning is incomplete, as it does not describe an enclosed tract.)

Metes and bounds descriptions tend to be quite lengthy, and they are often confusing. Furthermore, monuments and reference points may change their locations or disappear entirely over time. For instance, a stream may change course or a stone wall may crumble. When a transaction involves a metes and bounds description, an actual survey of the property is often required to re-establish the property's boundaries.

Government Survey

The **government survey system**, also called the **rectangular survey system**, describes land by reference to a series of grids. This system of land description was established after many of the northeastern states were already surveyed; therefore, the government survey method is found mainly west of the Mississippi River.

Meridians and Base Lines. The grids are composed of two sets of lines: one set running north/south; the other running east/west. Each grid is identified by a **principal meridian**, which is the original north/south line established in that grid; and by a **base line**, which is the original east/west line. In California, there are three principal meridians: **Humboldt**, **Mt. Diablo**, and **San Bernardino**. Each has its own base line.

Grid lines run parallel to the principal meridian and the base line at intervals of six miles. The east/west lines are called **township lines**, and they divide the land into rows

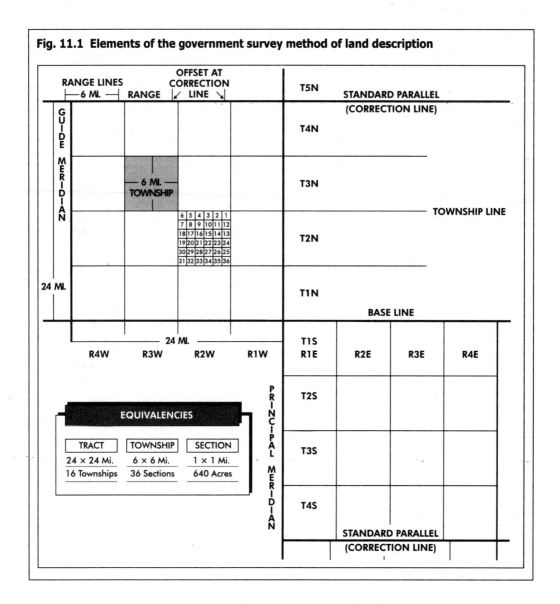

Fig. 11.1 Elements of the government survey method of land description

called **township tiers**. The north/south lines, called **range lines**, divide the land into columns called **ranges**. Every fourth range line is a **guide meridian**.

Townships and Sections. The intersection of a range and a township tier forms a square of land known as a **township**. The township is then identified by its location with reference to the principal meridian and associated base line. For example, the township located in the sixth tier north of the base line and the second range east of the principal meridian would be described as "Township 6 North, Range 2 East" (or "T6N, R2E").

The grids formed by the government survey system are identical all across the United States; therefore, townships are further described by reference to the appropriate principal meridian, as well as to the county and state where the land is located. Thus, to avoid confusion, a complete description of a township might be "T6N, R2E of the Mt. Diablo Meridian, Sacramento County, State of California."

Each township measures 36 square miles and contains 36 sections. Each **section** is one square mile, or 640 acres. These sections are numbered from 1–36, starting in the northeast corner, moving west, then down a row and eastward, snaking back and forth and ending with the southeast corner. Smaller parcels of land are identified by describing partial sections, such as a quarter section or a quarter-quarter section.

Government Lots. Irregularly shaped parcels of land, known as **government lots**, are referred to by lot numbers. Government lots are used when a large body of water or some other obstacle makes it impossible to survey a perfect square-mile section of land. Government lots are also used to compensate for the not-quite square-mile sections that are the result of the curvature of the earth. The earth's curvature causes range lines to converge as they head north and south of the equator, towards the poles. This curvature means that sections along the northern and western boundaries of each township are not completely square; government lots are used along the boundaries.

Recorded Map

The recorded map method (sometimes referred to as the **lot and block** method or the **maps and plats** system) is the method of land description used most frequently in metropolitan areas.

When land is subdivided, the surveyor maps out lots and blocks (groups of lots surrounded by streets) on a subdivision map called a **plat**. Once the plat is recorded in the county where the land is located, simply referring to a numbered lot on the plat will be an adequate legal description of the property.

An example of a recorded map description might look something like this:

> Lot 2, Block 4 of Tract number 455, in the City of Fresno, County of Fresno, State of California, as per map recorded in Book 25, page 92, of maps, in the office of the recorder of said county.

Other Methods of Land Description

We've discussed the three most common methods of land description, but there are a number of other ways to describe real property. For example, when an adequate description of property can be found in an earlier-recorded document, a simple reference to that document will suffice ("All that land described in the grant deed recorded under recording number 1232455677 in Orange County, California."). Reference to survey records or tax assessor's maps also may be used, as long as those records or maps have been recorded in the county where the property is located. In addition, generalized descriptions such as "all my lands" or "the Hernandez Farm" can be adequate, provided that the generalized description makes it clear exactly which property is being described. But it's always best to use the least ambiguous description possible to prevent future problems. This is especially true if the property owner has several properties in one area.

Note, however, that it's not a good idea to use either the street address or the property description found in a property tax bill—neither of these is an adequate legal description.

Air Lots. Some forms of real property, such as condominiums (discussed in Chapter 16) must be described not only as to their location on the ground, but also as to their location (or elevation) above the ground. This type of property is known as an **air lot**. Air lots are described by using datums and benchmarks. A **datum** is a reference point on the Earth's surface that has an established elevation, usually measured in feet above sea level. For instance, a particular datum may be exactly 327 feet above sea level. This datum is then used to measure the elevations of other nearby points. These subsidiary reference points are called **bench marks**. For example, one bench mark may be 20 feet above the nearest datum, and another bench mark may be 14 feet above the same datum.

The use of datums and bench marks increases the accuracy of elevation measurements. Many metropolitan areas have their own datum and bench marks, which surveyors use as a reference point when describing air lots.

> **Example:** Embedded in the ground in Anytown's Central Park is a metal disk with these words engraved on it: "Bench Mark No. 37, located ten feet above Anytown Datum." When a new condominium project is built adjacent to Central Park, a surveyor determines that the building's 12th floor is 172 feet above the bench mark. Since the bench mark is 10 feet above Anytown Datum, the floor of Unit 1260 is located 182 feet above Anytown Datum.

Legal Descriptions in California

Real estate agents in California need to be aware of the state's unique history of land ownership and land grants, since the legacy of these grants survives in today's legal descriptions.

During the 1700s and early 1800s, first Spain and then Mexico controlled the land that would eventually become California. Together, the Spanish and Mexican governments made over 800 huge grants of state land to private individuals. These grants, known as **ranchos**,

 The Treaty of Guadalupe Hidalgo and Its Aftermath

Although the Treaty of Guadalupe Hidalgo acknowledged the land rights of Mexicans in the conquered territory, these rights came with strings attached. Rancho owners were required to prove their private land claims before a newly created Board of Land Commissioners. If an owner was successful, he or she received a final patent from the U.S. government.

In the five years of ownership confirmation hearings, the Board of Land Commissioners heard 813 cases. Of those, 604 claims were confirmed, 190 claims were rejected, and the rest withdrawn. The board actually settled only three of these cases—the other 810 were appealed to the District Court, and most were eventually decided by the Supreme Court.

The confirmation process was long and drawn out, requiring document searches, expensive lawyers, and hearings. The average length of time for a rancho owner to receive a final patent was 17 years—some cases took as long as 40 years. As rancho owners were responsible for the litigation costs, many eventually went bankrupt defending title to the lands that were supposedly protected under the Treaty of Guadalupe Hidalgo.

covered over 10 million acres of the most arable and fertile land in the state. The ranchos were intended to encourage settlement as well as agriculture and industry.

In 1848, a war between the U.S. and Mexico ended with Mexico ceding California (along with much of the southwestern United States) to the United States. In the Treaty of Guadalupe Hidalgo, the U.S. agreed to recognize the legitimacy of the rancho deeds and the land rights of Mexicans living in the newly conquered territory. All of the remaining undeeded land simply became part of the United States public domain.

This public domain land was later surveyed and divided into townships and ranges. As privately held land, ranchos were specifically excluded from the government survey—only the outside boundaries of ranchos were delineated on government maps. Later, as rancho owners sold off or subdivided their lands, they used private surveyors to divide the ranchos into smaller lots (similar to lots on a plat map), numbered accordingly. However, since these lots and subdivisions weren't part of the original government survey, they can't be described simply by referring to the section, township, or range. Any legal description of land that was once part of a rancho must refer to the original rancho by name.

> **Example:** The Kleins purchased a piece of property in Windsor that was once part of the Tzabaco Rancho. The original rancho no longer exists, and recent surveys of the area use the government survey system. The legal description in the Kleins' deed might begin:
>
> *That portion of the Rancho Tzabaco, in the City of Windsor, County of Sonoma, State of California, which is the W ½, SW ¼, SW ¼, SE ¼, Sec. 29 T. 10 N., R. 10 W., M.D.B. & M. [Mount Diablo Baseline and Meridian].*

Descriptions of property once located in a rancho should always use the rancho name, unless the description is by reference to a recorded plat map.

Solving Land Description Problems

Misunderstanding, changes in technology, the passage of time, and human error all contribute to problems with land descriptions. Monuments disappear, rivers change course, surveying equipment becomes more sophisticated, and original land grants are subdivided many times over. A person trying to mark the boundaries of his property using original deeds and records will probably find it quite difficult. Typical problems with land descriptions include:

- incorrect, indefinite, or ambiguous descriptions;
- omission of part of the description;
- adjoining owners who disagree over boundary lines; and
- modern surveys that don't match the original survey lines.

Over the years, courts have developed equitable solutions in response to these issues. Thus, land description problems can often be cured or resolved by:

- reformation,
- possession,
- acquiescence or agreement,
- the practical location doctrine, or
- the intent of the original government surveyor.

Reformation

An error in a land description can often be cured simply by having the party who transferred the property execute a new deed containing the correct description. If this is impossible (for instance, because the transferor is deceased, cannot be found, or is unwilling to execute a new deed), the transferee may obtain a court order to correct the description. This is known as **reformation**.

Possession

Sometimes a description problem can be resolved simply by looking at who is currently in possession of the property.

> **Example:** Alberto Delgado owns property in both Sutter County and in Yuba County. Both pieces of property are referred to as the "Delgado Ranch." Delgado conveys "the Delgado Ranch" to Susan Cartwright, but does not indicate in the deed whether it is the ranch in Sutter County or the ranch in Yuba County. Usually, such an ambiguity in the description would invalidate the conveyance. However, Susan took possession of the Yuba County ranch, so the deed may be valid after all. Her possession of the Yuba property makes it clear which ranch the deed was referring to.

A boundary dispute may also be resolved by adverse possession. Under the doctrine of adverse possession, the exclusive and continuous use and possession of property by a non-owner may result in a transfer of title. We will discuss adverse possession and boundary disputes in much greater detail in Chapter 15.

Acquiescence or Agreement

Boundary disputes may also be resolved under the **agreed boundary doctrine**. Under this doctrine, if neighbors are uncertain as to the true boundary line between their properties, a new boundary may be established by express or implied agreement. The parties must acquiesce to the new boundary for five years before it becomes binding. This five-year period may be shortened if circumstances are such that a change in the boundary position would cause a substantial loss.

Recognizing the accuracy of modern-day surveys, courts are careful to apply the agreed boundary doctrine only to situations of true uncertainty: when the legal records never existed, have been destroyed, or are inaccurate because natural markers have changed or vanished.

A more formal solution that can be used by cooperating parties is a **boundary line agreement**. For example, neighbors may agree to build a fence and use it as the boundary line. This agreement will become binding on both parties and all subsequent owners if it is: 1) put into writing, 2) signed and acknowledged in the same manner as a deed, and 3) recorded in the county where the land is located. The agreement must include a legal description for both properties and a survey map.

Practical Location

Another means for resolving boundary disputes is the **doctrine of practical location**. This doctrine comes into play when an owner of a tract of land conveys part of the property to another party, marking the boundary line between the two properties with a monument such as a fence or a rock wall. If the marked boundary is accepted by the parties, it will be binding on them and on subsequent owners of the property, even if the boundary differs from the one described in the deed.

Case to Consider...

The Frenches' property consisted of lots 52 and 53, with their home and pool situated on lot 53. In 1952, they built a concrete bathhouse and wall on what they believed to be the border between the two lots. They had unsuccessfully searched for the original surveyor's marks, but since they owned both lots, they weren't worried about the exact location and simply guessed. In 1956, the Frenches sold lot 52 to the Brinkmans.

One year later, a contractor for the Brinkmans discovered that the Frenches' wall was 3½ feet over on the Brinkmans' property. Both parties agreed to leave the wall where it was. The Brinkmans did not protest or pay for a later addition to the wall, and the Frenches were assessed the taxes associated with the improvement. When the property was reassessed, the Frenches asked if the Brinkmans wanted to pay the taxes on the wall, but the Brinkmans declined. When the relationship between the parties soured in 1960, the Frenches sued to quiet title to the strip of land and wall. The Brinkmans subsequently demolished the wall and kept the materials. Who should receive title to the strip of land and the wall, the Frenches or the Brinkmans? *French v. Brinkman* (1963) 60 Cal.2d 547.

Intent of Original Government Surveyor

This last method of resolving property description disputes applies only to government survey descriptions. Although the government survey method was an improvement over metes and bounds, it is not problem-free. Modern surveys, using the latest technology and extremely accurate equipment, often uncover mistakes made by the original government surveyors. This is not surprising, since the first surveyors were working in harsh conditions, with tools that would seem crude by today's standards. However, when such errors are discovered today, courts usually try to honor the intentions of the original government surveyor by maintaining the original boundary lines.

Case to Consider...

The boundary between two adjoining properties consisted of the range line established by an 1881 government survey. In 1935, the government commissioned a resurvey of the area and consequently moved the range line further west. Based on this resurvey, the owner of the eastern parcel believed his parcel of land had increased in size. In 1937, he successfully sued the owner of the western parcel to quiet title to the strip of land between the original range line and the new range line. In 1977, the current owner of the western parcel, Casad, sued the current owner of the eastern parcel, Qualls, to get the disputed property back. Who is entitled to the property, Casad or Qualls? *Casad v. Qualls* (1977) 70 Cal.App.3d 921.

Recording

Now that you're familiar with land descriptions, let's take a look at how the documents using those descriptions are recorded. **Recording** is the system by which instruments affecting the ownership or possession of real property are collected and stored in a public place. (An **instrument** is a written and signed document that transfers title, gives a lien, or establishes a right or duty in real property.)

Examples of instruments that can be recorded include:

- deeds;
- land contracts;
- leases exceeding one year;
- lis pendens, mechanic's liens, tax liens, and child support judgments;
- mortgages and deeds of trust;
- assignments or assumptions of deeds of trust;
- contracts of severance for minerals, timber, or crops;
- subdivision maps; and
- easements.

Of course, not all documents can be recorded—only those that actually affect title to or possession of real property, in a format that conforms to recording requirements, can be recorded. Individual parties cannot create a right to record a document simply by contracting to do so. If there is no statutory authorization to record a particular document, the county recorder may refuse to do so.

Procedures for Recording

In general, a recorded document must:

- be reproducible and contain an original signature, unless it is a certified copy or otherwise exempt from this requirement by law;
- be written in English or contain an attached court-certified translation;
- contain the names of all interested parties;
- be signed by the owner (if the document is a conveyance); and
- contain an adequate description of the property.

Civil Code § 1169 states that the document must be recorded by the county recorder in the county where the property is located.

> **Example:** Sarah and David are divorced, with one child. Sarah lives in Ventura County, and David lives in Los Angeles County. When David falls behind in his child support payments, Sarah obtains a court-ordered judgment against him and attaches a lien against his property. The judgment was issued by a Ventura County court. However, to record and preserve her lien against David's property, Sarah must record the judgment with the county recorder in Los Angeles County, since that is where David's real property is located.

A document is submitted for recording by delivering it in the proper, signed format to the county recorder's office. Some documents, such as deeds, must be acknowledged before they can be recorded (see Chapter 10 for a discussion of acknowledgment). In ad-

> ### ▶ Electronic Recording
>
> Reviewing, scanning, indexing, and storing documents is a time-consuming and costly process, especially in larger counties that process millions of documents every year. Electronic document delivery offers significant improvements over the manual recording process: more or less instantaneous recording, and tremendous savings in labor, paper, and postage to both the county and the customer.
>
> In the mid-1990s, the Orange County recorder's office began accepting the electronic delivery of documents for recording; San Bernardino County followed in 2004. However, due to concerns regarding security and technical issues, both counties initially limited electronic delivery to institutional customers, chiefly title companies.
>
> In an effort to improve the workability and security of electronic delivery, California passed the Electronic Recording Delivery Act of 2004. This statute only allows reliable entities to use electronic delivery: title insurers and underwritten title companies, institutional lenders, and the government. Further, the customer's software must be approved by a certified computer security auditor. Finally, individuals at institutions who actually submit the electronic documents must have undergone criminal background checks and also have verified their identities at logon by thumbprint.
>
> Electronic document delivery is now widely used in California. The state's four largest counties, Los Angeles, Orange, Riverside, and San Diego, use a joint electronic recording delivery system known as SECURE; a number of other counties use a system called CERTNA. The paperless submission of documents—that long-cherished dream of county recording officers everywhere—is now a reality.

dition, all of the necessary fees must be paid. The instrument will be considered recorded once it is properly reproduced and indexed in the official county records.

Purpose of Recording

The recording system serves two main purposes. First, recording an instrument provides future buyers (and the public in general) with access to the document's contents. In addition, the recording system helps establish priority when two or more parties claim competing interests in the same property.

Notice. A properly recorded instrument provides the public with **notice** (knowledge) of the interest established in the instrument. There are two types of notice: actual notice and constructive notice. **Actual notice** occurs when a person has actual knowledge of a fact.

> **Example:** Max is interested in buying a home listed for sale in Modoc County. The listing states that the home's roof is in need of repairs. Max has actual notice as to the roof's condition.

Constructive notice, on the other hand, is the legal presumption that a person has knowledge of a fact, whether or not he has actually does. By law, a person has constructive notice of all of the recorded interests in a property. In other words, when someone acquires an interest in a property, he's held to know about all other recorded interests in the property, even if he hasn't actually checked the record.

> **Example:** Max buys the home in Modoc County without bothering to check the public records regarding the property. It turns out that the property has an outstanding judgment lien recorded against it. Max is held to have notice of the lien, even though he wasn't actually aware of its existence.

Case to Consider...

In 1980, the Stevensons bought the Riverview Mobile Home Park from the Baums. The purchase agreement stated that the Baums would provide the Stevensons with title "free of...easements...other than [t]hose of record." The Stevensons did not review any documents before making an offer or signing escrow instructions. They did receive a title report disclosing the existence of an oil company easement in favor of Standard Oil for the purposes of ingress and egress. The Stevensons interpreted the document to mean only that the oil company could enter and travel across their property. In 1993, Chevron Pipe Line Company (Standard Oil's successor in interest) informed the Stevensons that several mobile homes in the park encroached on the easement and would have to be moved to allow Chevron access to their pipeline. The Stevensons sued the Baums for fraud, claiming the Baums knew and did not disclose the existence of the pipeline easement. Should the court find for the Stevensons or the Baums? *Stevenson v. Baum* (1998) 65 Cal.App.4th 159.

Priority. Recording an instrument also helps establish the priority of the recorded interest. This is important if another party later claims a competing interest in the property. Generally, California follows the **race-notice system** ("first in time, first in right") when determining the priority of interests in property. Whoever records first, wins. In other words, the person who records a deed first, with no notice of any competing interest, will have a superior claim to the property, even if someone else actually bought the property at an earlier date.

> **Example:** Returning to our example of Max, let's say he and the seller, Bernadette, close the sale on June 2. Max forgets to record his deed to the home. On June 7, Bernadette executes a second purchase contract, selling the home to Melinda. Melinda, who is unaware of the first sale with Max, records her deed immediately. When Max takes Melinda to court to settle their competing claims to the home, Melinda wins, even though Max purchased the property first.

In this example, Melinda is a **bona fide purchaser**: someone who acquired a later interest in a property, paid value for the interest, and had no notice (actual or constructive) of a prior interest in the property. If the bona fide purchaser records her interest, she holds a superior claim to the property.

Rules of priority. When there are competing claims to a property, priority is determined with a series of court-applied tests. The court will ask four separate questions:

1. When was each interest created?
2. Did the parties record the documents used to create the interests?
3. Did the second party know about the first party's interest?
4. Did the second party pay value for his or her interest?

Once the court has the answers to the above questions, it will apply the rules of priority, as follows:

- If there are two competing interests and neither was recorded, the interest created first will prevail.
- If there are two competing interests and both were recorded, the first to be recorded will prevail.
- If an instrument that is executed second is recorded first, and the party to the second instrument had no knowledge of the first unrecorded instrument, then the second party's recorded interest will prevail. (This rule applies only if the second party paid valuable consideration for her interest in the property; otherwise, the first, unrecorded interest will prevail.)

Example: What if neither Max nor Melinda had recorded their deeds? Between the two unrecorded interests, Max's interest was created first (on June 2). Therefore, his interest would prevail over Melinda's.

Of course, determining the priority of an interest in real property is not something you'll be asked to do. Furthermore, you won't be writing legal descriptions or conducting surveys of your client's property; these tasks are handled by lawyers and professional surveyors. However, you need to be familiar with the legal ramifications of inaccurate or ambiguous legal descriptions and disputed boundary lines. It's also important that you have an understanding of the issues related to the recording system. This knowledge will allow you to identify potential problems and refer clients to the proper professionals.

Case Law in Depth

The following case involves some of the legal issues discussed in this chapter. Read through the facts and consider the questions in light of what you have learned. Then read what the court actually decided.

Verdi Dev. Co. v. Dono-Han Mining Co. (1956) 141 Cal.App.2d 149

The plaintiff, Verdi Development Company, was leasing some land that had been surveyed by government surveyors many years before. The property was the Northeast Quarter of Section 10, Township 9 North, Range 13 West, San Bernardino Base and Meridian. The defendant, Dono-Han Mining Company, had a mining claim to the southeast quarter of that same section of land. The two companies argued over the east/west boundary line that divided the two properties. Verdi claimed that Dono-Han was conducting mining operations on land that it was leasing, and sued the company to get it to stop.

Verdi's surveyor testified that the monument marking the quarter section corner, as set by the original government survey of 1855, could not be found. Therefore, he marked the corner using another method. According to his survey, Dono-Han was using Verdi's property.

Dono-Han's surveyor, on the other hand, claimed that a "pine stake" with surveyor's written marks on it, which was set in a pile of rocks, marked the corner of the quarter section. Dono-Han had witnesses who would testify that they had seen the stake there for many years and that the stake appeared to be 100 years old. Verdi's surveyor admitted that he saw the stake and pile of rocks, but that he did not accept it as the quarter corner because it was in the wrong spot. The trial court found in favor of Verdi, giving preference to the testimony of Verdi's surveyor and dismissing Dono-Han's attempt to prove the monument's authenticity. Dono-Han appealed the trial court's decision.

The question:

Should the court affirm the property boundary as depicted by the stake and pile of rocks, even if its location is inaccurate?

The court's answer:

The court held that if the stake and pile of rocks was a monument marking the quarter corner as set forth in the original government survey, it must be accepted under the law. "A survey of public lands does not ascertain boundaries; it creates them.

"The original government surveys, whether they are mathematically correct or grossly erroneous, control the location and length of the boundaries of sections and parts thereof and the shape and size of tracts granted to patentees."

According to the court, the intention of the original government surveyor is the most important factor to consider. "A government township lies just where the government surveyor lines it out on the face of the earth. These lines are to be determined by the monuments in the field...A line, as shown by monuments...cannot be overturned by measurements alone." Therefore, later, perhaps more accurate lines, such as those of the plaintiff's surveyor, will not trump the original surveyor's lines as determined by the original monument (here, the stake and pile of rocks).

The result:

Because the trial court dismissed the defendant's attempts to prove the authenticity of the corner stake (a ruling that the appellate court called "unquestionably prejudicial"), the decision was reversed.

Chapter Summary

- There are three basic methods of land description. The metes and bounds method describes property by establishing its boundaries using a set of directions and distances. The government survey method (also called the rectangular survey system) describes land by reference to a series of grids. The recorded map method refers to a recorded map that describes plats in a subdivision.

- California's history of land ownership involves large land grants known as ranchos. As private land, ranchos were not included in the original government survey of California. Although the ranchos have long since been subdivided and resurveyed, any legal description of land that was once part of a rancho should include the original rancho's name in the legal description.

- Typical land description problems that may arise in deeds include incorrect, indefinite, ambiguous, or incomplete descriptions; boundary line disagreements; and modern surveys that don't match the original survey lines. These problems are resolved through reformation, determining possession, acquiescence or agreement, the doctrine of practical location, and intent of the original government surveyor.

- Recording an instrument related to real property provides constructive notice of a prior interest. The instrument must be recorded in the county in which the land is situated. In general, an earlier recorded instrument will take precedence over a later recorded instrument. A later interest may prevail over an earlier unrecorded interest if the later purchaser or encumbrancer is a bona fide purchaser (had no notice of the earlier interest, and paid value for the later interest).

Key Terms

- **Metes and bounds** – A method of land description common in the eastern United States; describes a parcel of property by establishing its boundaries using monuments, a point of beginning, courses, and distances.

- **Government survey** – A method of land description common in the western United States; describes a parcel of property in relation to its placement on a grid formed by two sets of lines (the principal meridian and the base line).

- **Township** – A piece of land measuring 36 square miles, formed at the intersection of a range and a township tier; contains 36 one-square-mile sections.

- **Range** – A column of land formed by the north/south lines spaced at six-mile intervals east and west of the principal meridian.

- **Government lot** – Within the government survey system, a parcel of land that is irregular in shape or size, usually because of the curvature of the earth or because of a large body of water or some other obstacle.

- **Recorded map** – A method of land description based on a recorded subdivision plat map; otherwise known as the lot and block method of land description.

- **Reformation** – When a deed contains an incorrect legal description, the process by which the original grantor gives a new deed with the correct description; also the process by which a court orders a correction to a deed's legal description.

- **Agreed boundary doctrine** – A doctrine stating that if uncertainty exists as to a boundary line, the neighbors may agree to a boundary (such as a fence); if they acquiesce to the agreed boundary for a specified period of time, it becomes binding.

- **Doctrine of practical location** – A doctrine stating that if the owner of a larger tract conveys part of his property, marks the boundary with a fixed monument, and the parties accept the marked boundary, the location will prevail over any differing description in the deed.

- **Recording** – The system by which instruments affecting title to or possession of real property are collected and stored in a public place.

- **Actual notice** – When a person has actual knowledge of a fact.

- **Constructive notice** – The legal presumption that a person has knowledge of a fact, whether or not she actually does.

- **Race-notice system** – A "first in time, first in right" recording system; whoever records a property interest first will have priority over all subsequently recorded interests in the same piece of property.

- **Bona fide purchaser** – A person who has no actual or constructive notice of a prior interest, and who acquired a later interest in the property for value.

Chapter Quiz

1. The three most common systems of land description are:
   a) survey, courses and distances, monuments
   b) metes and bounds, government survey, recorded map
   c) metes and bounds, government survey, courses and distances
   d) None of the above

2. In a legal description, T3N, R5W refers to:
   a) Tier 3 North, Row 5 West
   b) Township 3 North, Row 5 West
   c) Tier 3 North, Range 5 West
   d) Township 3 North, Range 5 West

3. A description of property that was once located within a rancho:
   a) must refer to a recorded plat map
   b) must refer to a government survey grid
   c) need not include the original rancho name
   d) should include the original rancho name, unless the description refers to a recorded plat map

4. James sells his property to Mary. In the deed, the property description contains a typo that mistakenly identifies the lot sold as 180 instead of 108. All other details are correct. When the mistake is discovered, James gives Mary a new deed with the correct information. This is an example of:
   a) execution
   b) subrogation
   c) reformation
   d) revision

5. Joe and Fred own adjoining ranches. The boundary between them is the range line established by an 1884 government survey. Recently, Fred had his ranch surveyed with modern equipment and discovered that the range line is actually 25 feet further west, on Joe's side of the fence. Where is a court most likely to place the boundary?
   a) At the true range line, because the modern survey equipment is more accurate
   b) At the original government survey line, because that was the government's intention
   c) Either of the above
   d) Neither of the above

6. In order to serve proper notice on subsequent purchasers, an instrument related to real property must be recorded:
   a) anywhere in the state where the land is located
   b) in the county where the land is located
   c) Both a) and b)
   d) None of the above

7. The two types of notice are:
   a) actual notice and supplemental notice
   b) actual notice and implied notice
   c) actual notice and constructive notice
   d) legal notice and constructive notice

8. A person who acquires a later interest in a property, for value, without actual or constructive notice of a competing prior interest, is known as a/an:
   a) actual owner
   b) legal owner
   c) equitable title holder
   d) bona fide purchaser

9. Two recorded instruments both claim an interest in a piece of property. Which instrument will take priority?
   a) The one executed first
   b) The one recorded first
   c) Either, depending on who gave the most value
   d) None of the above

10. Two unrecorded instruments both claim an interest in a piece of property. Which instrument will take priority?
    a) The one executed first
    b) The one recorded first
    c) Either, depending on who gave the most value
    d) None of the above

Chapter Answer Key

Chapter Quiz Answers:

1. b) The three most common systems of land description are metes and bounds, government survey, and recorded map.

2. d) The description T3N, R5W refers to the third township north of the base line and the fifth range west of the principal meridian.

3. d) If land was once part of a rancho, its description should include the name of the rancho, unless the description refers to a recorded plat map (which would then reference the prior rancho).

4. c) This is an example of reformation to correct a mistake in a legal description.

5. b) The government is likely to honor the original government survey as intended.

6. b) In order to serve proper notice on subsequent purchasers, an instrument related to real property must be recorded with the country recorder in the county in which the real property affected by the instrument is located.

7. c) The two types of notice are actual notice and constructive notice.

8. d) A person who has no actual or constructive notice of a prior interest, and who acquires a later interest in the property for value, is considered a bona fide purchaser.

9. b) Under the rules of priority, if there are two competing interests, both of which have been recorded, the date and time of recordation will establish priority.

10. a) If there are two competing interests, and neither has been recorded, the date of execution will prevail.

Cases to Consider... Answers:

Description Problems

French v. Brinkman (1963) 60 Cal.2d 547. The court found that the Frenches were entitled to the disputed strip of property and the cost of the wall, based on two theories. First, under the doctrine of practical location, when the owner of a large tract conveys part of it with a boundary marked by a fixed monument, and the parties rely on that boundary, it prevails over any different description in the deed. The agreed boundary doctrine also applied, as there was (1) uncertainty as to the true boundary, (2) a wall that the parties had accepted as a boundary, and (3) circumstances under which a change in the boundary would cause substantial loss.

Casad v. Qualls (1977) 70 Cal.App.3d 921. The court reversed the judgment from the 1937 lawsuit, finding that Casad was entitled to the disputed strip of property. When land grants are based on government surveys (as in this case), the property boundaries are determined by the original survey. A resurvey has no effect on the boundaries; thus Casad was entitled to his property as delineated by the original survey.

Recording

Stevenson v. Baum (1998) 65 Cal.App.4th 159. The court found for the Baums. The fact and nature of the pipeline easement was easily ascertainable from the public records, and a reasonable person in the Stevensons' position, knowing of the oil company's easement for pipeline purposes, should have realized that the easement holder may access the pipeline at any time. The recorded easement accurately described where the pipeline was, and the purchase agreement provided notice of the recorded easement. If the Stevensons had failed to investigate the recorded easement, they couldn't blame the Baums for failure to disclose.

List of Cases

Casad v. Qualls (1977) 70 Cal.App.3d 921
French v. Brinkman (1963) 60 Cal.2d 547
Stevenson v. Baum (1998) 65 Cal.App.4th 159
Verdi Dev. Co. v. Dono-Han Mining Co. (1956) 141 Cal.App.2d 149

Chapter 12

Escrow and Title Insurance

Outline

Introduction

There are two main events in a real estate transaction. The first is when the buyer and seller reach an agreement and sign their contract. The second is the closing (or settlement), when the purchase price is paid to the seller and the deed is delivered to the buyer, completing the transaction. Between those two points, however, many tasks must be taken care of. Inspections must be performed, financing arrangements finalized, liens paid off, documents prepared, and funds transferred. This stage of the transaction is known as the closing process or settlement process.

In California and most other states, the closing process is usually carried out through escrow. The first part of this chapter examines the legal aspects of escrow, including the requirements for a valid escrow, the laws governing escrow agents, escrow instructions, termination of escrow, and RESPA (a major federal statute that affects the closing process). The second part of this chapter addresses title insurance, which can play an important role in the closing process. (For example, the preliminary title report may alert the parties to problems that have to be resolved before closing.) We'll look at the function title insurance serves, the types of coverage offered, and how the state regulates the title insurance industry.

Escrow

The parties to a real estate transaction look forward to closing. But no buyer wants to hand over the purchase price without receiving the deed, and no seller wants to let go of the deed without first receiving payment. And the lender certainly doesn't want the loan funds disbursed until the note and deed of trust have been signed. In addition, having all of the parties meet for a simultaneous exchange on the closing date is often inconvenient—one of them might be out of town, for example. Use of a third party, an **escrow agent**, resolves these problems. Buyer, seller, and lender can complete their responsibilities at different times and still achieve a safe exchange.

California Civil Code § 1057 provides the following basic definition of escrow: "A grant may be deposited by the grantor with a third person, to be delivered on performance of a condition…[This arrangement] is called an escrow." The parties to a transaction deposit funds, legal documents, or other items with an escrow agent. At the same time, they give the agent **escrow instructions**. The escrow instructions specify the conditions that must be fulfilled before each party's deposits can be released to the other party.

Escrow is used in many different types of business transactions, but we're concerned only with real estate escrow. Use of escrow in real estate transactions became widespread in the United States during the Depression, when lenders were trying to make home purchases less risky for all parties concerned. Since that time, the role of the escrow agent has expanded; it's now common for the escrow agent to take care of many of the details in the closing process, such as ordering title insurance and preparing documents. Since then, Congress and state legislatures have stepped in with laws intended to make escrow arrangements more secure and to prevent abusive practices in the closing process.

We'll take a brief look at the basic legal requirements for a valid escrow, then consider the laws concerning escrow agents, escrow instructions, and other aspects of escrow.

Requirements for a Valid Escrow

Every escrow must have four basic elements:

- an enforceable contract,
- an escrow agent,
- irrevocable deposits, and
- conditions imposed on those deposits.

Unless all of these elements are in place, a valid escrow does not exist and the legal rules that govern escrow do not apply.

Enforceable Contract. Escrow can't be opened for a transaction unless there is an enforceable contract between the parties. In most cases, this contract is the purchase agreement. Occasionally, usually in a commercial transaction, the parties use just the escrow instructions to express their intentions, rather than using a purchase agreement.

The standard requirements for an enforceable contract apply. Notably, because the statute of frauds applies to the purchase and sale of real estate, the contract must be in writing.

Escrow Agent. The escrow agent must be a third party. A buyer or seller cannot serve as the escrow agent in his own transaction. While the escrow is open, an escrow agent is a dual agent, representing both the buyer and the seller. Even so, if all the parties agree, the buyer's or seller's attorney or real estate agent may act as the escrow agent, but like any escrow agent she must act impartially.

Irrevocable Deposits. A valid escrow requires complete and irrevocable delivery of the deed, purchase price, and other deposits. The depositor cannot retain the right to withdraw a deposit, and the agent is not allowed to return an item deposited by one party without the other party's consent.

> **Example:** After depositing an executed deed into escrow, the seller changes his mind about selling the property. He asks the escrow agent to return the deed. But the escrow agent may not return the deed to the seller without first obtaining the buyer's consent.

Conditions. The parties must impose conditions on their deposits. In other words, the depositor must require that certain events occur before the deposit is transferred to the other party. Without conditions, the other party would be immediately entitled to the deposited item, and escrow wouldn't really exist.

The most basic example of a condition in escrow is the seller's requirement that the deed cannot be delivered to the buyer until the purchase price is deposited in the seller's account.

Escrow Agents

Now let's take a closer look at escrow agents. We'll start with the nature of the agency relationship and the escrow agent's duties to the parties. Then we'll discuss who is allowed to perform escrow services under California law.

Nature of the Agency. In Chapter 6, we explained that general agency law governs many aspects of a real estate agent's relationships with clients and customers. General agency law also applies to escrow agency.

As mentioned above, the escrow agent is a dual agent, owing fiduciary duties to both buyer and seller. The agent's fiduciary duties also extend to any other parties to the escrow. In a real estate transaction, the most common additional party is the buyer's lender. The lender generally gives the escrow agent separate escrow instructions concerning disbursement of the loan funds. (A real estate broker involved in the transaction is not a party to the escrow, despite the fact that he will receive his commission through the settlement process.)

In addition to being a dual agency, an escrow agency is also considered a limited or special agency, as the agent's duties are essentially limited to faithful execution of the escrow instructions. The agent owes the parties a duty to disclose material information, but this duty is generally limited to information gained from carrying out the escrow responsibilities.

> **Example:** A large tract of property is being sold. The escrow agent who's handling the transaction sees a TV news report about a proposed zoning change that could affect the property. The escrow agent need not, and probably should not, disclose this information to the buyer, since it isn't something the agent learned in the course of her escrow duties. On the other hand, if the seller told the agent about a problem with the title, the agent would have an obligation to tell the buyer.

As a fiduciary, the escrow agent cannot disclose confidential information to third parties. Nor can the escrow agent render advice to one party that would disadvantage the other; that would violate the dual agency requirement of neutrality. (Of course, an escrow agent who is not licensed to practice law should never give advice that might be considered legal advice.)

Note that the escrow agent's knowledge is imputed to the principals. This could mean, for example, that if the escrow agent learned of an unrecorded lien and forgot to tell the buyer, the lienholder could nonetheless claim that the buyer knew about the lien. In this situation, the buyer could sue the escrow agent for negligence.

The Escrow Law. In California, an escrow agent's work is governed not only by general agency law, but also by a number of state statutes. The most important of these is the Escrow Law (Financial Code §§ 17000 – 17703). The Escrow Law establishes licensing requirements for escrow agents and also imposes various recordkeeping and financial responsibilities.

Licensing. The Escrow Law provides for the licensing and regulation of escrow agents under authority of the California Department of Business Oversight. Only corporations may be licensed as escrow agents in California. However, certain individuals and entities are allowed to provide escrow services without being licensed as escrow agents.

Financial Code § 17006 exempts the following entities from the licensing requirement and the other requirements of the Escrow Law: banks, trust companies, savings and loans, and insurance companies. Individuals who are similarly exempted from the Escrow Law include a lawyer providing escrow services for a client's transaction (but not carrying on an escrow business generally), and a real estate broker providing escrow services incidental to a real estate transaction in which the broker is either a party or is serving as a real estate agent.

Thus, the Escrow Law applies only to independent escrow businesses, not to the escrow departments of banks, savings and loans, or title insurance companies, and not to lawyers or real estate brokers handling escrow in the course of their usual work. These entities and individuals are exempted from the Escrow Law because they are considered sufficiently regulated by other statutes.

Records and trust accounts. Under the Escrow Law, an escrow company is required to do all of the following:

- keep accurate records, updated daily to reflect any transaction activity (and open to inspection at any time by the Department of Business Oversight);
- maintain an appropriate trust account; and
- supply the Department with independent annual audits.

Financial security requirements. The Department of Business Oversight requires an escrow company to post a surety bond, depending on the size of the business and its liabilities, and maintain $25,000 or more in liquid assets. Escrow companies that process certain types of transactions must also post a fidelity bond covering each officer, director, trustee, and employee, as stated on the California Department of Business Oversight website.

In addition, under Financial Code § 17312, escrow companies must join the Escrow Agents' Fidelity Corporation. Funds collected by the Fidelity Corporation are used to reimburse escrow companies for losses due to fraud, misappropriation, or embezzlement by their employees. For example, if trust funds belonging to a client were stolen by an escrow company employee, the escrow company would have to replace the client's funds. The company could then file a claim with the Fidelity Corporation for reimbursement.

Penalties and remedies. An intentional violation of the Escrow Law may subject an escrow agent to imprisonment and/or a fine of up to $10,000. An unintentional violation may be punished by a civil penalty of up to $2,500. License revocation or suspension typically accompanies these penalties.

Private parties seeking compensation from an escrow agent for a wrongful act have up to two years after the act occurred to file a claim against the agent's bond.

Other Statutory Requirements. In addition to the Escrow Law, various other statutory provisions have an impact on escrow agents and the closing process in California. For example, Civil Code § 1057.3 includes some rules regarding how deposits into escrow must be handled in the event of default; we'll discuss these rules later in the chapter.

Civil Code § 1057.5 prohibits escrow agents from paying referral fees (often called **kickbacks**) to someone who refers clients to them. And Business and Professions Code § 10177.4 prohibits real estate agents from accepting referral fees from escrow agents (or from other settlement service providers such as title companies or pest inspection companies). These rules echo a prohibition in the federal Real Estate Settlement Procedures Act, also discussed later in this chapter.

Under Civil Code § 2995, real estate developers are not allowed to require buyers of single-family homes to use an escrow agent in which the developer has a financial interest (here, an interest means ownership or control equal to 5% or more). Although the statute imposes liability for damages and attorney's fees on the developer, an escrow agent cooperating in a developer-controlled escrow scheme may share liability for having violated the fiduciary duties imposed by the Escrow Law.

Real Estate Brokers Handling Escrow. The Real Estate Commissioner has issued regulations that apply when a real estate broker handles escrow under the exemption from the Escrow Law mentioned earlier. These regulations are §§ 2950 – 2951 of the Regulations of the Real Estate Commissioner. (The Regulations of the Real Estate Commissioner are found in Title 10, Chapter 6 of the Code of Regulations.) The regulations state that the broker must keep records and handle any funds involved in the escrow in accordance with the Commissioner's general rules concerning records and trust funds. They also require the broker to make a written disclosure to the parties if she knows that any of the real estate licensees involved in the transaction has an interest (as a stockholder, officer, partner, or owner) in the brokerage holding the escrow.

The Bureau of Real Estate does not allow a real estate broker to advertise escrow services unless the ad specifies that those services are offered only as an extra brokerage service. Also, the name of a brokerage business may not contain the word "escrow."

Escrow Instructions

As we discussed earlier, one of the requirements for a valid escrow is that deposits into escrow must be subject to conditions. The buyer and seller specify in the escrow instructions what conditions must be met before closing can occur. Although these are the parties' instructions to the escrow agent, in most residential transactions it is the escrow agent who prepares the instructions for the parties to sign.

The escrow instructions must spell out the conditions for release of the deposits to the appropriate parties. Aside from that requirement, the content of the instructions is largely a matter of custom. Typically, the instructions include:

- the details of the transaction (such as the parties, the property, the financing arrangements, and the closing date);
- the encumbrances that the buyer will take title subject to; and
- the allocation between the buyer and the seller of expenses to be paid at closing (closing costs).

Escrow instructions are usually put into writing, but occasionally the parties add oral instructions. These unwritten instructions are valid. In theory, the instructions need not be put into writing at all, as long as there is a written

Escrow North and South

In Southern California, independent escrow companies typically handle escrow. In Northern California, escrow is usually included in the services provided by the title company insuring the property being sold. As a result, home buyers and sellers in the north generally pay less for escrow than their counterparts in the south. Escrow on a transaction in Los Angeles may cost twice as much as the same service in San Francisco. Buyers and sellers should keep in mind that escrow fees are negotiable.

purchase agreement or other writing that satisfies the enforceable contract requirement for a valid escrow. Obviously, however, oral instructions invite disputes over exactly what was said; it's always preferable to have all of the instructions in writing.

The buyer and seller may sign joint escrow instructions (a single document), or each may sign separate instructions. Note that sometimes separate instructions from the buyer and the seller can conflict. For example, the buyer's instructions might say that the seller will pay for a home inspection, while the seller's instructions say that the buyer will pay for it. Joint instructions avoid this problem. (We'll return to the issue of conflicting instructions shortly.)

In some cases, joint escrow instructions are incorporated into the purchase agreement. For example, the residential purchase agreement form published by the California Association of Realtors® includes escrow instructions.

Civil Code § 1057.7 requires that whoever prepares escrow instructions must include a statement explaining under what authority he is operating, his name as licensed, and the department issuing that license.

For a real estate broker handling escrow, Commissioner's Regulation § 2950 includes some rules concerning escrow instructions. It is grounds for disciplinary action if a broker accepts escrow instructions that leave any blanks to be filled in after the parties have signed the instructions. Failure to deliver a copy of the instructions when they're signed to all the parties is also grounds for disciplinary action.

Duty to Obey. The escrow instructions are legally binding on the agent. Escrow agents must guard against even seemingly harmless violations of the instructions.

> **Example:** The escrow instructions require the sellers to replace the external door locksets. After the new locksets have been installed, the buyers aren't satisfied with their quality. They demand that the sellers spend an additional $145. Annoyed, the sellers refuse, and there's a stalemate. The listing broker offers to pay the additional cost out of pocket as a way of getting the transaction closed (and getting her commission check). But the buyers have a right to insist on performance by the sellers as specified in the instructions, and the escrow agent should not accept payment from the broker without the buyers' consent. Deviating from a provision stating who is to pay what could expose the escrow agent to liability.

The escrow agent must obey not only the buyer's and seller's instructions, but also instructions from any other party to the escrow. In the following case, an escrow agent failed to obey instructions from a lender.

Case Example:

> McKinley entered into a contract to buy a chiropractic practice. A bank served as the escrow agent for the transaction. The parties' escrow instructions provided that McKinley would obtain a $497,000 loan. He was to use part of the loan proceeds for the purchase price and part for working capital.
>
> McKinley's lender, the Money Store, wired the loan amount to the escrow agent along with instructions concerning disbursement of the funds. These instructions required the escrow agent to notify the Money Store of any changes in the parties' escrow instructions. There was also a warning that any deviation from the Money Store's instructions without permission would be at the escrow agent's risk.

Later that day, the buyer and seller amended their escrow instructions, changing how the loan proceeds were to be distributed. The escrow agent failed to notify the Money Store and obtain its permission before disbursing the funds as directed in the amended instructions.

McKinley's chiropractic business was unsuccessful; he eventually defaulted on his loan and declared bankruptcy. The Money Store sued the escrow agent over the unpaid loan, claiming that it would never have allowed the funds to be disbursed if the agent had notified it of the amended instructions. The court agreed that the Money Store had properly requested notice of changes. Failure to honor this instruction exposed the escrow agent to liability for the lender's losses. *Money Store Investment Corp. v. Southern Cal. Bank* (2002) 98 Cal.App.4th 722.

Conflicting Instructions. Occasionally, a provision in the escrow instructions conflicts with one in the purchase agreement. Courts try to interpret related contracts together, as a whole, but if conflicts between them can't be resolved, the provisions in the more recent contract control. (Courts presume that the later agreement represents the parties' final intent.) Since escrow instructions are executed after the purchase agreement, the instructions typically prevail if a conflict arises.

> **Example:** The purchase agreement provides that the buyer can occupy the property seven days before closing. But the escrow instructions say nothing about that; they indicate instead that the buyer is to take possession after closing.
>
> The later contract controls. Unless the seller is willing to amend the escrow instructions, the buyer isn't entitled to a house key until after the purchase money and deed are transferred at closing.

As we mentioned earlier, conflicts may also arise if the buyer and seller give the escrow agent separate instructions instead of joint instructions. When an escrow agent receives conflicting or ambiguous instructions, he should immediately ask the parties for clarification. It may be necessary to have them sign amended instructions.

In some cases, however, the parties will be unable to agree on how such a conflict should be resolved, and a lawsuit will result. In this situation, the escrow agent will **interplead** (turn over) the escrowed funds to the court where the lawsuit was filed. The court will hold the funds and decide who is entitled to them. In fact, an escrow agent can file an interpleader action and turn over deposits to the court without waiting for one party to sue the other.

Amending or Waiving Instructions. Rigid adherence to the original escrow instructions may become a problem for the parties as closing nears and circumstances change. Suppose, for example, that the instructions require the seller to repair the chimney before closing, but the parties overlook this condition until three days before the scheduled closing date. The repair cannot be arranged in such a short time. Two options present themselves:

1. the buyer may waive the condition, or
2. the parties may amend or rewrite the condition to accommodate the situation.

Waiver. Under common law, a party to a contract can unilaterally waive a condition that is intended to benefit only that party. Thus, in our chimney example, the buyer could waive the repair condition (with or without the seller's consent) and closing could proceed. The escrow agent should obtain a written waiver from the buyer.

Waiver can also occur unintentionally. For example, if the buyer accepts late performance from the seller on several occasions without objection (perhaps on some minor repair issues), the buyer may be deemed to have waived the "time is of the essence" clause found in many agreements. This implied waiver could prevent the buyer from later insisting on punctuality in the performance of some other, more important, condition.

Amendment. If the party who is intended to benefit from the condition is unwilling to waive it entirely, the buyer and seller may agree to amend their original agreement instead. To return to our chimney example, the seller might agree to credit the buyer $500 towards the purchase price if the buyer releases her from the chimney repair obligation.

When the parties agree to this type of change, both the purchase agreement and the escrow instructions should be amended. Note that the Escrow Law mandates that changes to the escrow conditions require the written approval of every party who signed the original instructions. For a real estate broker handling escrow, failure to obtain the signature or initials of every party when escrow instructions are modified is grounds for disciplinary action.

Ownership of the Deposits During Escrow

Assume we have a valid escrow. The parties have delivered their deposits to the escrow agent along with the escrow instructions. Remember, once funds or other items have been deposited into escrow, they can't be withdrawn. So who owns a deposit in the period before closing? As a general rule, the depositor does. She retains legal title to the deposit until the escrow conditions have been satisfied and the transaction closes.

> **Example:** The buyer has deposited the purchase price into escrow and the seller has deposited a valid deed. Even though these deposits are irrevocable, the buyer retains legal title to the funds and the seller retains legal title to the property until all the escrow conditions have been satisfied and the transaction is ready to close.

The ownership of items deposited into escrow is not an issue in most transactions, but it may be an issue if:

- something happens to a deposited item;
- something happens to one of the parties; or
- the escrow agent makes a premature or wrongful delivery.

We'll look at each of these situations.

Risk of Loss. Exactly when title to property or funds in escrow passes from one party to the other becomes important if the property suffers damage or something happens to the deposited funds. Civil Code § 1662, known as the Uniform Vendor and Purchaser Risk Act, states that if real property under a sales agreement is destroyed or taken by eminent domain, the seller cannot enforce the contract and the buyer is entitled to get any deposits back. The Risk Act also provides, however, that if either title to the property or possession of it was transferred before the loss, the buyer remains liable for any of the purchase price not yet paid.

> **Example:** In the sale of a house, the seller agreed that the buyer could take possession of the property two weeks before closing. The day after the buyer moved in, the house was struck by lightning and burned to the ground. Because possession of the property had

been transferred (and even though title hadn't been transferred yet), the buyer is required to go through with the purchase of the property.

It's important to note that the Risk Act does not apply if the buyer and seller have agreed to a different allocation of the risk of loss in their purchase agreement or escrow instructions. So, for example, a contract could provide that the risk of loss will remain the seller's until title is transferred, even if the buyer takes possession of the property before then. Note, too, that whenever a buyer takes possession before closing, it's advisable for the parties to enter into an interim occupancy agreement and to make sure they are adequately insured against loss.

The Risk Act does not address the loss of money deposits, but California common law does. The rule is that the risk of loss follows legal title (whoever holds title to the deposit bears the risk of loss). And as we discussed earlier, title to each deposited item remains with the depositor until escrow closes. Thus, as the court held in the following case, when an escrow agent makes off with the deposited funds, the buyer bears the loss.

Case Example:

Jose Pagan arranged to sell a lot to the Spencers for $1,500. The downpayment was $700. The balance of the purchase price, with interest, would be paid in $50 monthly installments to an escrow agent named Bowe. Pagan knew Bowe; the buyers did not.

Pagan had purchased the lot at a tax sale, so he and the Spencers agreed that the remaining payments would be held in escrow until he obtained a judgment quieting title and could complete the transaction properly. The Spencers had paid $800 to Bowe when Pagan asked Bowe for $300 to fund a trip to Mexico. Bowe explained he could not release funds without authorization from the Spencers. The Spencers then agreed to the disbursement. But after releasing the $300 to Pagan, Bowe—apparently strict about the legal niceties of escrow only when it came to others—absconded with the remaining $500. He was not heard from again. The rule in such cases was well-established: as long as title to the property remained with the seller, the purchase money still belonged to the buyer. The court ruled that it was the Spencers' loss, and they were required to replace the stolen $500 to complete their purchase of the property. *Pagan v. Spencer* (1951) 104 Cal.App.2d 588.

Relation Back Doctrine. Now let's consider how a transaction is affected when something happens to one of the parties during escrow. If, after a valid deed has been deposited into escrow, the seller loses the ability to convey property or the buyer loses the ability to accept it, then transfer of title is deemed to have occurred on the date the deed was deposited. In other words, the date of title transfer "relates back" to the date of the deposit into escrow. This is called the **relation back doctrine**. It applies if any of the following circumstances arises after the seller has deposited the deed:

- the seller becomes incompetent,
- the seller dies, or
- the buyer dies.

In each of these situations, the transaction will still close if all of the conditions of the escrow are fulfilled. Completion of the transaction wouldn't be possible if it weren't for the relation back doctrine, since a transfer of title ordinarily requires the deed to be delivered to a living grantee during the grantor's lifetime (see Chapter 10). The following case illustrates how the relation back doctrine may be applied after the death of the seller.

Case Example:

Mary Brunoni had her attorney draft a purchase agreement for her son to buy her ranch for less than the market value. The agreement also provided that Mary would be allowed to live on the ranch. The agreement and a deed were signed and left with the attorney on the understanding that the son would bring in the payment price. This was a valid escrow arrangement, because there was an enforceable contract, instructions with conditions, a deposit, and an agent (the attorney).

Three days after signing the documents, Mary died. Her son had not yet paid the purchase price, but a week later he did so.

Some of Mary's other heirs challenged the transfer to the son. The court noted that once a deed is deposited into escrow, the grantor's death does not prevent completion of the transaction, because of the relation back doctrine. Mary's attorney held the documents in a valid escrow, and therefore the son took title to the ranch after tendering the purchase price. *Brunoni v. Brunoni* (1949) 93 Cal.App.2d 215.

The relation back doctrine is also sometimes applied in connection with liens. Suppose a lien attaches to the property after the seller has deposited a valid deed into escrow. If the lienholder was aware that the property was in escrow, a court could hold that the buyer's title related back to the point at which the deed was deposited, so that the lien did not affect the buyer's title. On the other hand, if the lienholder didn't have notice that a sale was pending, the court probably would not apply the relation back doctrine to prevent the lien from attaching. In that situation, however, it would be a breach of the purchase agreement if the seller failed to remove the lien before closing.

Wrongful Delivery. Wrongful or premature delivery occurs when an escrow agent delivers an escrow deposit to a party before she is actually entitled to it. The law regarding wrongful delivery is straightforward. If the escrow agent delivers a deed to the buyer before the buyer has done everything the escrow instructions require, the delivery is legally ineffective: title to the property doesn't pass to the buyer. If the agent delivers the purchase money before the seller satisfies the escrow conditions, the agent will have to reimburse the buyer for any losses incurred.

Tax-related Obligations in Escrow

The laws we've discussed so far are aimed at creating a secure, orderly escrow process. Real estate escrows are also affected by state and federal statutes designed to ensure the collection of certain taxes. We'll look at three statutes that impose reporting and withholding requirements in sales of real property.

Form 1099-S Reporting. The IRS requires an escrow agent to report the gross proceeds from real property sales on Form 1099-S. But the form doesn't have to be filed for the sale of a principal residence if: 1) the seller certifies in writing that none of the gain is taxable; and 2) the sale is for $250,000 or less ($500,000 or less for a married couple filing a joint return).

Form 8300 Reporting. An escrow agent who receives more than $10,000 in cash is required to report the payment on Form 8300, in order to help detect money laundering. This rule applies whether the cash was received in a single transaction or a series of related transactions. The escrow agent must file Form 8300 within 15 days of receiving the cash. A copy of the form should be kept on file for five years.

FIRPTA. Congress passed the **Foreign Investment in Real Property Tax Act (FIRPTA)** because it was concerned that foreign investors were selling U.S. real estate holdings without paying income taxes on their profits. The act requires the buyer to determine if the seller is a "foreign person" (neither a U.S. citizen nor a resident alien). If the seller is a foreign person, the buyer must withhold 15% of the amount realized from the transaction and send it to the IRS (the amount realized is usually the sales price). In practice, the obligation to check the seller's residency status and withhold funds is assumed by the escrow agent. The withheld funds must be paid to the IRS within 20 days after the transfer date (closing).

Some real property sales are exempt from FIRPTA, such as sales of homes under $300,000 to be occupied by the buyer. Sales of homes to be occupied by the buyer where the amount realized is between $300,000 and $1 million require only a 10% withholding amount.

California Withholding Law. California has its own real estate withholding law, sometimes called **Cal-FIRPTA**, designed to prevent non-payment of state income or franchise taxes. Buyers must withhold 3⅓ percent of the total sales price from sellers who reside outside the state but are selling California real property. (Alternatively, the seller can choose to use a withholding amount that is based on her estimated gain from the sale.) The funds must be sent to the state's Franchise Tax Board by the 20th day of the month after the month of closing. Again, these responsibilities are usually assumed by the escrow agent.

Exemptions from Cal-FIRPTA's withholding requirement include:

- sale of the seller's principal residence,
- property selling for less than $100,000,
- sales involving a loss or zero gain on the transaction,
- certain non-recognition transactions as defined by the IRS, and
- sales by certain California-licensed corporations, LLCs, and other business entities.

The state tends to modify this law frequently, so the rules should be checked regularly. Visit the Franchise Tax Board website for more information about the withholding law.

Terminating Escrow

It's time to consider the last stage of an escrow: how it terminates. An escrow can terminate in one of three ways:

1. the transaction closes;
2. the parties agree to terminate; or
3. a party defaults (breaches the purchase agreement).

Closing. Escrow terminates automatically when the transaction closes, with the satisfaction of all conditions and transfer of all deposits. Most escrows end this way. However, some 20 to 30 percent of escrows fail to reach this happy state and terminate instead either by mutual agreement or by default.

Mutual Agreement. The parties can agree to terminate escrow at any time. Changing circumstances may make both parties wish to abandon their transaction.

> **Example:** The Bakers decide to retire, sell their house, and spend the next two years motorcycling from Europe to China. Wanting a bigger place to live, a young couple makes an offer on the Bakers' house. The Bakers accept the offer and escrow is opened. Soon afterwards, however, Mr. Baker dies. Grief-stricken, Mrs. Baker decides she wants to keep the house she shared with her husband.
>
> Meanwhile, the buyers have realized that not even a larger house is going to save their marriage. They decide to divorce. At this point, since neither the seller nor the buyers want to go through with the transaction, they agree to terminate their contract and cancel the escrow.

Note that in a situation like this, the seller could still be liable for the broker's commission. Also, canceling escrow does not automatically cancel the purchase agreement. That is a separate contract and must be expressly rescinded. In *Cohen v. Shearer* (1980) 108 Cal.App.3d 939, a bickering buyer and seller agreed to cancel escrow, but then the buyer turned around and sued for specific performance under the purchase agreement.

When the parties agree to terminate their transaction, the escrow agent will send out a cancellation agreement for them to sign. This agreement should expressly state both that the escrow is canceled and that the purchase agreement is rescinded. It should also state what will happen to any funds already in escrow and who will pay for any costs incurred—for example, the cancellation fee that escrow agents sometimes impose.

An escrow that ends because of a failed contingency (for example, inability to find financing) has effectively terminated by mutual agreement, since the parties agreed in their original contract that the transaction would terminate under these circumstances. Although the failure of a contingency terminates the purchase agreement automatically, the escrow agent should still have the parties sign a cancellation agreement.

Default. Sometimes one party to a purchase agreement wants to go through with the transaction, but the other party breaches the agreement either because she wants out of the deal or because she is simply unable to meet a particular contractual requirement.

Any procedures the escrow instructions specify for handling a default—giving notice of the breach, providing an opportunity to cure, and so on—should be followed closely. As noted earlier, waiver may occur if a party fails to object promptly after a failure to perform; waiver will mean the injured party loses his right to damages.

Ideally, the escrow instructions will state how escrowed funds are to be handled after a default. For example, the instructions may provide that if the buyer does not deposit the remainder of the purchase price in escrow by the closing date, the escrow agent can release the good faith deposit to the seller.

Release of funds requirement. Civil Code § 1057.3 has a special rule concerning release of escrowed funds that applies in transactions involving residential property with up to four units, if the buyer intends to occupy one of the units. If one party refuses in bad faith to release escrowed funds to which the other party is entitled, the one who has acted in bad faith is liable to the other for the escrowed amount, plus a penalty equal to triple the escrowed amount (up to a maximum penalty of $1,000), as well as the other party's attorney's fees.

The statute doesn't require a release when there is a good faith dispute over who is entitled to the funds. In that situation, a lawsuit usually results and the escrow agent will have to interplead the funds.

Case to Consider...

A buyer agreed to purchase two commercial properties from the Salvation Army. Before escrow could close, fire destroyed a building on one of the parcels. The buyer wanted to go ahead and complete the sale—at a reduced price—but the Salvation Army wouldn't agree to take less than the full amount. Could the buyer force the seller to sell at a reduced price, or was rescission of the purchase agreement his only remedy? *Dixon v. Salvation Army* (1983) 142 Cal.App.3d 463.

RESPA

We can't complete our discussion of escrow without examining a significant piece of federal legislation called the Real Estate Settlement Procedures Act (RESPA). In the early 1970s, there was concern about widespread problems in the residential mortgage and escrow industry—problems with fees and services (such as confusing or unexplained charges), mistakes in calculating impound account payments, and failures to notify borrowers when their loans were transferred from one lender to another. Congress enacted reform measures by passing RESPA in 1974. RESPA requires disclosure of closing costs to borrowers and prohibits practices that unnecessarily inflate the cost of settlement services (closing services). Since its passage more than 40 years ago, the act has sparked a considerable amount of industry debate, private litigation, and government enforcement action.

Who needs to worry about RESPA? Everyone who works with residential loans and escrows. If a mortgage falls within RESPA's scope, then the lender and every **settlement service provider** involved in the transaction is subject to the act's prohibitions. This would include the escrow agent, the title company, the credit reporting agency, the appraiser, the pest inspector, and so on. In addition, RESPA's definition of settlement services specifically includes "services rendered by a real estate agent or broker" (12 U.S.C. § 2602(3)). This means the act's rules concerning settlement service providers also apply to real estate agents.

Federally Related Loans. RESPA applies only to transactions involving federally related loans, but this hardly limits the extent of its coverage. A loan is federally related if it meets the following criteria:

1. it is secured by a mortgage or deed of trust against:
   - property on which there is (or on which the loan will be used to build) a one- to four-unit dwelling;
   - a condominium unit or cooperative apartment; or
   - a lot with (or on which the loan will be used to place) a mobile home; AND

2. the lender:
   - is federally regulated;
   - has federally insured accounts;
   - makes loans in connection with a federal program;
   - sells loans to Fannie Mae, Ginnie Mae, or Freddie Mac; or
   - makes more than $1 million in real estate loans per year.

Thus, RESPA applies to the majority of residential mortgage loans made by institutional lenders such as banks and mortgage companies. It covers not only purchase loans, but also assumptions, refinances, reverse mortgages, home improvement loans, and home equity loans and lines of credit.

Exemptions. RESPA does not apply to seller-financed transactions, since sellers aren't federally regulated lenders. And certain types of loans made by institutional lenders are exempted from RESPA. Loans are exempt if used for: 1) the purchase of 25 acres or more; 2) a purpose that is primarily business, commercial, or agricultural; or 3) the purchase of vacant land (unless there will be a one- to four-unit dwelling built on it or a mobile home placed on it). Temporary financing, such as a construction loan, is also exempt from RESPA.

Although loan assumptions are subject to RESPA, there is an exemption for assumptions that don't require the lender's approval (for instance, because the original loan agreement did not include a due-on-sale clause). This type of assumption doesn't involve closing costs or the negotiation of terms with an institutional lender, so there would be little point in imposing RESPA requirements.

Requirements. We've established that RESPA applies to most residential loans. Now let's consider exactly what protections RESPA offers home buyers.

The act imposes the following requirements and prohibitions on lenders and settlement service providers in federally related loan transactions:

1. If the lender or any other provider of settlement services (such as a title company, mortgage broker, or real estate agent) requires the borrower to use a particular appraiser, title company, or other service provider, that requirement must be disclosed to the borrower when the loan application or service agreement is signed.
2. If any settlement service provider refers a borrower to an affiliated provider, that joint business relationship must be fully disclosed, along with the fact that the referral is optional. (This is called an affiliated business arrangement disclosure.) Fee estimates for the services in question must also be given.
3. Required deposits into an impound account (to cover taxes, insurance, and other recurring costs) cannot be excessive—more than necessary to cover the expenses when they come due. (According to RESPA, an excessive deposit is more than two months' worth of payments for recurring costs.)
4. A lender or other settlement service provider may not:
   - pay or receive a kickback or referral fee (a payment from one settlement service provider to another for referring customers);
   - pay or receive an unearned fee (a charge that one settlement service provider shares with another provider who hasn't actually performed any services in exchange for the payment); or

- charge a fee for preparing an impound account statement or any other required disclosure statement.
5. Sellers cannot require buyers to use a particular title company.

Section 8 Violations. Kickbacks and unearned fees (see item number 4 on the list above) are often called "Section 8 violations," since the RESPA rules concerning them are in Section 8 of the act. For RESPA purposes, a kickback is not necessarily a monetary payment. It can be anything of value given in exchange for referrals—a gift, for instance, or services provided without charge or at a discounted rate. Both the person offering the kickback and the person accepting the kickback are in violation of the law. Also, a payment or gift can be illegal even if neither party openly acknowledges that it has anything to do with the referral of business; an unspoken understanding can be enough to violate RESPA.

> **Example:** A real estate agent routinely recommends to all his buyers that they apply to Acme Mortgage for their financing. These referrals aren't illegal, but it would be illegal for loan officers at the mortgage company to pay the real estate agent a fee for each customer referred. It would also be illegal to send the real estate agent concert tickets, restaurant gift certificates, or other presents to encourage more referrals.

Kickbacks were an entrenched practice in the real estate industry before RESPA, and since the law went into effect many people have tried to get around its anti-kickback rules. One common subterfuge is to pay someone a fee that's ostensibly compensation for a service but is actually a disguised kickback for referrals.

> **Example:** A real estate agent recommends Acme Mortgage to his buyers and provides them with a blank copy of the uniform residential loan application form. Acme pays the agent a $100 "application service fee" for each of his buyers who ends up applying for a loan with the company.

The payments in the example run afoul of RESPA's prohibition against unearned fees, so this would be a Section 8 violation. A payment is considered an unearned fee if the recipient has performed no significant service, or if the payment amount does not bear a reasonable relationship to the services provided.

Note that RESPA's rules against kickbacks and unearned fees do not apply to fees paid by one real estate broker to another for the referral of brokerage business. Brokerage referrals don't involve settlement services, and RESPA specifically provides that fees paid for those referrals don't violate the act.

Affiliated Business Arrangements. If a settlement service provider refers a customer to an affiliated service provider, the relationship between the providers must be disclosed to the customer. (This is item number 3 on our earlier list.) The disclosure should take place at or before the time of referral. A relationship between two service providers counts as an affiliated business arrangement if one of them has more than a 1% ownership interest in the other company.

In addition to the disclosure requirement, there are two other rules concerning referrals to an affiliated business. First, the customer can't be required to use the services of the affiliated provider. Second, the first provider can't receive anything of value from the affiliated provider other than a return on his ownership interest.

Example: A real estate broker owns 5% of the stock in Termitron, Inc., a pest inspection business. It's legal for the broker to refer her sellers and buyers to the pest inspection company if she discloses that she has an ownership interest in it. But she may not refuse to provide brokerage services unless they agree to use Termitron instead of another pest inspection company. Termitron may pay corporate dividends to the broker, as long as they do not exceed the appropriate return on her investment in the company.

Required Disclosures. In 2015, Congress imposed new disclosure requirements that satisfy the intent of both RESPA and the Truth in Lending Act (which we will discuss in Chapter 13). These requirements are described in the TILA-RESPA Integrated Disclosure (TRID) rule.

The two most important disclosures under the new rule are the loan estimate form, given after the loan application is received, and the closing disclosure form, given at least three business days before the closing date. These forms replace the two documents that were previously required under RESPA: a good faith estimate of closing costs given after receiving a loan application, and a uniform settlement statement, given shortly before closing.

The closing disclosure, which is prepared by the closing agent or lender, outlines fees and charges associated with closing. The "Closing Cost Details" section of the closing disclosure serves as a settlement statement, listing all of the debits and credits, and the exact amount each party must pay or will receive at closing.

Enforcement. The government agency charged with enforcing RESPA is the Consumer Financial Protection Bureau (CFPB). In recent years, the government has stepped up its rate of RESPA investigations, partly due to complaints by title and escrow companies seeking to stop unfair practices by their competitors. Most of the enforcement activity involves Section 8 violations. Each violation can bring a fine of up to $10,000, as well as up to a year in prison. However, the government typically reaches settlements of its claims rather than imposing fines.

 A Kickback by Any Other Name

Rewarding referrals is a standard way of doing business in many industries, and this may help explain the persistence of the practice in connection with mortgage lending and closing services. More than four decades after RESPA became law, the federal government is still initiating dozens of kickback investigations, and its annual settlements with Section 8 violators add up to millions of dollars. One investigation determined that a real estate brokerage in Atlanta had paid higher sales commissions, offered tickets to Atlanta Braves games, and placed "agent of the month" ads in newspapers to reward its real estate agents for referring business to the brokerage's affiliated title company. This resulted in a $250,000 settlement with the government. In another case, a Detroit title company settled with the government to the tune of $150,000 after paying disguised referral fees in the form of inflated meeting room rental rates.

> **▶ Respite from RESPA?**
>
> Consumer lawsuits over alleged kickbacks are typically brought as class actions, spreading heavy legal costs among a large group of similarly injured individuals. One way the mortgage industry fights these lawsuits is to seek decertification of the plaintiff class, thus breaking up the lawsuit. The industry defendants argue that determining whether a given fee is a kickback or not must be decided on a case-by-case basis, so that a class action is inappropriate. This argument has successfully convinced judges in several cases including, for example, *O'Sullivan v. Countrywide Home Loans Inc.* (5th Cir. 2003) 319 F.3d 732.
>
> All hope is not lost for class action plaintiffs. A few years after *O'Sullivan*, 60,000 Michigan home buyers reached a $27.5 million settlement with four prominent U.S. title companies.

Buyers or sellers who were charged a fee that violates RESPA can sue the violator for treble damages—three times the amount of the illegal fee—plus court costs and attorneys' fees.

Title Insurance

In a typical real estate transaction in California, one of the tasks that the escrow agent performs early in the closing process is ordering a preliminary report on the property from a title insurance company. The report indicates whether the seller's title is marketable and whether there are any unexpected encumbrances or other title issues that need to be resolved before the transaction closes. The report also serves as the basis for the issuance of title insurance policies to protect the buyer and the buyer's lender. In this section of the chapter, we'll look at the purpose of title insurance, the title insurance contract, the preliminary report, the different types of coverage available, and the regulation of the title insurance industry.

The Purpose of Title Insurance

Title insurance was first developed in the post-Civil War era. Recordkeeping in the United States had been relatively poor up to that time and the ravages of the Civil War naturally made matters worse. It was difficult for property buyers to determine whether the seller of a piece of land actually owned it, and whether there were encumbrances or other claims against it. A buyer could hire a lawyer or a specialist called an abstractor to prepare an **abstract of title** based on the public records. The abstract summarized the property's **chain of title** (the series of deeds linking the previous owners to one another and to the current owner) and listed the encumbrances found in the records. But if there were problems with the records, the abstract provided little or no protection for the buyer.

For example, suppose a buyer purchased property in reliance on an abstract of title, only to learn later on that there was a flaw in the seller's title or a claim against the property that hadn't been listed in the abstract. The buyer could sue for compensation only if the lawyer or abstractor had been guilty of negligence in preparing the abstract. There was no protection against hidden problems (a forged signature on a deed in the chain of title, for example) that couldn't be discovered through a careful search of the public records.

It was to provide this type of protection that the first title insurance companies were established. If a property buyer obtained title insurance at the time of his purchase, the title company would pay compensation for losses resulting from certain types of title problems that might be discovered only after the transaction closed—perhaps many years afterward. Title insurance caught on, eventually becoming widely available and widely used. Although there are still some states where abstracts of title are used instead of title insurance, it's currently estimated that about 85 percent of residential property sales in the U.S. are covered by title insurance.

California's Insurance Code § 12340.1 defines title insurance as insurance against "loss or damage suffered by reason of: (a) Liens or encumbrances on, or defects in the title to... property; (b) Invalidity or unenforceability of any liens or encumbrances thereon; or (c) Incorrectness of searches relating to the title..."

In California, title insurance is considered a standard part of a real estate transaction. In fact, in the rare case where a buyer chooses to forego title insurance, Civil Code § 1057.6 provides that the escrow agent must obtain the buyer's signature on a written notice that contains the following warning:

> IMPORTANT: IN A PURCHASE OR EXCHANGE OF REAL PROPERTY, IT MAY BE ADVISABLE TO OBTAIN TITLE INSURANCE IN CONNECTION WITH THE CLOSE OF ESCROW SINCE THERE MAY BE PRIOR RECORDED LIENS AND ENCUMBRANCES WHICH AFFECT YOUR INTEREST IN THE PROPERTY BEING ACQUIRED. A NEW POLICY OF TITLE INSURANCE SHOULD BE OBTAINED IN ORDER TO ENSURE YOUR INTEREST IN THE PROPERTY THAT YOU ARE ACQUIRING.

Most transactions involve two title insurance policies: an owner's policy and a lender's policy. The **owner's policy** insures the title of the buyer (the new owner). The **lender's policy** (also called a **loan policy** or **mortgagee's policy**) insures the lien or security interest of the buyer's lender. Institutional lenders financing real property transactions invariably require title insurance; the buyer, as the party benefiting from the loan, usually pays for the lender's policy. Either the buyer or the seller may pay for the owner's policy protecting the buyer.

The Title Insurance Contract

Like any other insurance policy, a title insurance policy is a contract between the insurer and the insured (the policy holder). More specifically, it's a contract of indemnity. In exchange for a premium payment, the title insurance company promises to indemnify (compensate or reimburse) the policy holder for losses that result from title defects covered by the policy. Covered defects may include liens and other encumbrances and also **clouds on the title**—potential claims that cast doubt on the ownership.

Title companies across the country use policy forms published by the American Land Title Association (ALTA), which is the national trade association for the industry, or by a comparable state association. In California, the state organization is the California Land Title Association (CLTA).

Policy Amount. The title company's liability will not exceed a maximum amount specified in the policy (known as the **policy amount** or the **policy limit**), even if the policy holder's losses do. For instance, if the policy amount is $100,000 and the policy holder suffered $150,000 in damages, the title company's liability is limited to $100,000. The company is liable for the amount of the policy holder's covered losses or for the policy amount, whichever is less.

For an owner's policy, the policy amount is usually the price the insured paid for the property. As a general rule, the policy amount doesn't change during the term of the policy, even though the value of the property may be increasing. In some policies, however, there's an inflation provision that increases the amount of coverage by a certain percentage over a specified period.

For a lender's policy, the original policy amount is the loan amount. As the loan balance is paid down, the lender's coverage decreases.

Whenever a title company has to pay a claim under a policy, the policy amount is reduced by the amount of the claim. For example, if the policy amount is $300,000 and the company pays $50,000 to settle a third party's lawsuit against the insured, then the company's remaining potential liability in case of other claims is $250,000.

Coverage. The policy spells out the extent and limits of the coverage provided. It lists categories of title issues that will be covered and categories that are excluded from coverage. For example, there is generally an exclusion for problems resulting from governmental action, such as zoning or condemnation.

What is and isn't covered by a given policy depends primarily on whether it's a standard coverage, extended coverage, or homeowner's coverage policy; these are distinctions that we'll discuss shortly. In addition, various matters that are known to affect the particular property in question will be listed in the policy as exceptions to coverage.

> **Example:** The title company determines that there's a judgment lien against the title it's about to insure. This lien will be listed in the policy as a known defect and excepted from coverage. As a result, the policy holder (the buyer) won't be able to file a claim based on the judgment lien after the policy is issued.

On the other hand, if the title company failed to list this lien in the policy as an exception—perhaps because the title searcher overlooked it—and the policy holder learned about it only after buying the property, then it could be the basis for a claim.

If the title company fails to list a certain defect, but the insured happens to know the defect exists and doesn't tell the title company, coverage for that defect is excluded. The insured can't hide knowledge of a defect, hoping to later claim coverage.

Duration of coverage. Unlike many other forms of insurance, a title policy requires only a single premium payment, which is paid at closing. The coverage provided by an owner's policy lasts as long as the policy holder or her heirs own the property. There is also limited coverage after the policy holder sells the property, in case she becomes liable to the new owner for a violation of warranties in the deed.

A lender's policy remains in force until the lender's deed of trust or mortgage has been paid off and is no longer a lien against the property.

Duty to Defend. In a title policy, the insurer agrees to defend the insured's title (or security interest) against litigation brought by third parties. This is called the **duty to defend**. Naturally, when a third party raises a claim against the policy holder's title, the appropriate course of action will depend on all of the circumstances. For example, is the claim valid or invalid? How difficult would it be to prove that, one way or the other? Is the claimant reasonable, or hostile and litigious? Depending on the situation, the title company's main options are:

- proving that the claim is invalid (in court or before the case reaches court);
- persuading the claimant to withdraw the claim;
- paying the claimant to settle the claim; or
- paying a judgment to the claimant after a court has granted one.

Even without litigation, if covered title defects come to light, the company may take steps to clear them up. This might involve filing a quiet title action (see Chapter 10) on behalf of the policy holder, or reaching a settlement with a potential claimant. If a covered title defect can't be removed, the company may be required to pay the policy holder compensation for the reduced value of the property, up to the policy amount.

Legal costs. The duty to defend requires the title company to pay all legal costs it incurs in its defense of the title. This is in addition to the policy amount. In other words, with a $300,000 policy, the title company could end up paying $300,000 to settle claims against the title or compensate the insured, and also have to pay whatever attorney's fees, court costs, and other legal expenses it ran up in the course of the litigation or settlement negotiations (which could add up to a considerable sum).

Notification. The policy holder is responsible for notifying the title company in writing when a lawsuit is filed against him or a title problem is discovered in some other way. Most policies simply require the policy holder to notify the company "promptly," instead of setting a deadline for notification. If prompt written notice is not given and the delay affects the title company's ability to defend the title, the company may be relieved of liability under the policy.

Breach of contract. If the title company fails to honor its responsibility for defending the title or breaches the contract in some other way, the policy holder may sue for compensatory damages. She may also be entitled to punitive damages if the company is found to have acted in bad faith. The statute of limitations for a lawsuit based on a title insurance policy is two years. The two-year period begins when the insured discovers she has suffered a loss.

> ▶ **Reissue Rates**
>
> Sometimes a title company is asked to issue a new policy on property that it insured just a few years earlier. This might happen, for example, when owners resell or refinance their home only a couple of years after buying it. In this situation, the company can just update its previous title search (instead of starting from scratch) and then reissue the old policy. Because companies save time and money on reissued policies, they generally charge customers discounted rates for them.
>
> Companies are only willing to reissue their policies within certain time limits, and those limits vary from one company to another. For example, one company might be willing to reissue a homeowner's policy if the property is resold within five years; another might have a shorter time limit. One company might reissue a lender's policy when the mortgage is refinanced up to ten years after the policy was originally issued; another company might be unwilling to do that if it's been more than five years.
>
> How much lower than standard rates are reissue rates? That also varies from one company to another. The reissue premium for a refinance transaction might be 50% or 60% of the usual premium. The premium for a reissued owner's policy might be 80% of the usual premium.
>
> In early 2006, an Ohio couple filed a lawsuit in federal court against a national title company for failing to disclose the availability of a reissued policy at a lower cost when they refinanced their home. Alleging that the company routinely overcharged customers in this way, the couple's lawyers were seeking class action status for the suit.
>
> In California, the Insurance Commissioner's office publishes a consumer brochure that explains various aspects of title insurance, including the availability of discounted rates for certain types of policies. Title companies aren't required by law to give a copy of this brochure to their customers, however.

Case to Consider...

The title policy listed an access easement across the neighbors' land as one of the exceptions from coverage. The buyers assumed that they had a right to use this easement. The neighbors sued to prevent the buyers from using the easement, claiming that it had been terminated by prescription. The buyers asked the title company to defend their right to use the easement. Did the title company have a duty to defend the buyers? *George S. Vorgitch et al. v. Fidelity National Title Insurance* (Cal.App., Jan. 23, 2002) (unpublished) 2002 WL 86870.

The Preliminary Report

Before agreeing to insure a property's title, the title company investigates the condition of the title and, based on that examination, issues a **preliminary report** (sometimes called a preliminary commitment or binder). The first step is a title search performed by an employee of the company. The title searcher looks through recorded documents and other public records to trace the property seller's chain of title and locate liens and other encumbrances affecting the title.

The encumbrances of record that are still in effect are listed in the preliminary report, along with any clouds on the title that the title searcher has discovered. Everything listed in the report will be excepted from coverage if a policy is issued. Depending on the nature of these matters and the terms of the purchase agreement, the buyer and seller may arrange to have some of them resolved before closing. For example, if there's a recorded option to purchase that was never exercised, the seller might obtain a release from the optionee and have it recorded to clear away the cloud. Liens are typically paid off. On the other hand, other types of encumbrances, such as easements or CC&Rs, cannot be removed. The buyer will take title subject to those, and the title policy won't cover them.

Under California law, a preliminary report is merely an offer to issue a title insurance policy on the stated terms. The parties are not entitled to rely on it as a representation as to the condition of the title, in the way that an abstract of title could be relied on. Section 12340.11 of the Insurance Code states that preliminary reports "are not abstracts of title, nor are any of the rights, duties or responsibilities applicable to the preparation and issuance of an abstract of title applicable to the issuance of any report." This means that the title company can't be sued for negligence or inaccuracies in the preliminary report. The company takes on no liability unless and until it actually issues a policy.

If the preliminary report reveals title problems that cannot be fixed and were not disclosed in the purchase agreement, the buyer may waive objection to them, seek concessions from the seller, or rescind the purchase agreement. If the buyer is satisfied with the preliminary report, he purchases the title insurance policy by paying the one-time premium at closing. The title company then issues the policy.

Types of Coverage

In California, as elsewhere, title insurers have traditionally offered two main types of coverage: **standard coverage** and **extended coverage**. In recent years these have been joined by a third type, **homeowner's coverage**. What is and isn't covered by a particular title policy depends first and foremost on which of these types of coverage the policy holder has purchased. Keep in mind, however, that a policy holder may custom-tailor her coverage to a certain degree by purchasing various **riders** (also called **endorsements**) that modify the main contract.

Standard Coverage. The standard coverage policy has traditionally been used to insure the interest of the new property owner (the buyer), so people commonly refer to it as an owner's policy. It is also sometimes called a CLTA policy, after the California Land Title Association.

Standard coverage insures that the title is marketable and vested in the new owner. (A definition of marketable title is usually given in the policy; it essentially means that the condition of the title is such that an informed and reasonably prudent buyer would be willing to accept it.) Standard coverage also insures against encumbrances and title defects that appear in the public record but aren't listed as exceptions in the policy. In addition, it insures against certain latent or hidden defects having to do with invalid deeds in the chain of title (for example, a deed that has an incompetent grantor or a forged signature, or lacks the signature of a spouse).

Standard coverage does not insure against problems that don't appear in the public record but could be discovered by a physical inspection or survey of the property, such as adverse possession or unrecorded easements. To have those types of problems covered, it's necessary to get extended coverage or homeowner's coverage.

Extended Coverage. An extended coverage policy includes the coverage of a standard policy and adds coverage for matters discoverable only by a physical inspection or survey of the property—adverse possession, encroachments, unrecorded easements, and so on. It also insures against unrecorded mechanic's liens for work on projects that began before the closing date.

Many extended coverage policies provide additional coverage, such as coverage for violations of restrictive covenants. They may also cover certain post-policy matters—events that happen after the policy is issued.

> **Example:** When the Carters buy their home, the title company issues an extended coverage policy insuring the lender's interest. Several years later, the Carter's next-door neighbor builds a new garage that encroaches on their property. This encroachment is covered by the lender's title policy, even though it occurred after the policy was issued.

Title insurance generally does not protect against losses resulting from government regulation or other government action. However, extended coverage policies do cover certain limited government-related problems. For example, if there are structures on the property that violate zoning laws or were built without the proper permits and the policy holder is required to remove or modify them, an extended coverage policy may cover the cost of compliance.

Extended coverage costs more than standard coverage, not only because it provides greater protection, but also because it costs the title company more to prepare its preliminary report. Before issuing an extended coverage policy, the title company will usually send an inspector out to look over the property, and in some cases will have it surveyed.

As we said earlier, in transactions with institutional financing, the buyer is required to purchase a title policy to protect the lender's security interest in the property. The lender usually requires this to be an extended coverage policy. Because lenders insist on them, extended coverage policies are often referred to as lender's policies or mortgagee's policies; they're also called ALTA policies, after the American Land Title Association.

Case to Consider...

In connection with the purchase of a house, a title company issued a standard coverage policy to the buyer and an extended coverage policy to the lender. Sometime after closing, the buyer had a survey done, and it revealed that the house was located on a neighboring lot—not the lot described in the buyer's deed. Was the title company liable to the buyer for this problem? *Walters v. Marler* (1978) 83 Cal.App.3d 1.

Homeowner's Coverage. Homeowner's coverage is available only in transactions involving one- to four-unit residences. The property doesn't have to be owner-occupied. Unlike the traditional policies, the homeowner's policy is a "plain language" contract that avoids insurance jargon to make it easier for buyers to understand. In California, most residential purchase agreement forms now provide for this type of policy to be obtained for the buyer, unless the parties specifically agree on another type.

Homeowner's coverage is much broader than standard coverage. It covers most of the same title matters as a traditional extended coverage policy, such as encroachments, unrecorded easements, and certain post-policy matters. The key difference between an extended coverage policy and a homeowner's policy is the party for whom the policy is

Fig. 12.1 Comparison of standard, extended, and homeowner's title insurance coverage

	Standard Coverage	Extended Coverage	Homeowner's Coverage
Unmarketable title	X	X	X
Latent defects in title (forged deed, incompetent grantor)	X	X	X
Incorrect legal descriptions or clerical errors in recorded documents	X	X	X
Undisclosed heirs in improperly probated wills	X	X	X
Nondelivery of deeds or delivery of deeds after grantors' death	X	X	X
Unrecorded liens		X	X
Claims of parties in possession (tenants, adverse possessors)		X	X
Matters discovered by survey (incorrect boundary lines, easements, incorrect area)		X	X
Subdivision regulation violations		X	X
Zoning or building code violations		X	X
Claims that arise post-closing		X	X

intended. Extended coverage is for the benefit of lenders, while homeowner's coverage is for the benefit of buyers who want the same level of protection as lenders.

For homeowner's coverage, the title company usually bases its preliminary report on a visual inspection of the property in addition to a title search. A survey may be ordered, but typically is not.

Regulation of the Title Insurance Industry

Insurance is useless if the insurer has no money to pay claims. The Insurance Code sets out financial requirements that a company licensed to provide title insurance in California must meet, including minimum capital requirements and premium reserve requirements. Each company is required to submit regular financial reports to the Insurance Commissioner. Each company is also required to keep copies of its policy forms on file at the Commissioner's office, along with a schedule of the rates it charges for various types of policies.

Title insurers are prohibited from offering kickbacks or referral fees not only under federal law (RESPA), but also under California law. The California Insurance Code in §12404 prohibits **rebates**. It's an illegal rebate if a title company charges less for a policy than the price indicated on the company's current rate schedule filed with the Commissioner.

It's also illegal in California for a title company to prepare a preliminary report at no charge. (The price of the preliminary report may be, and typically is, applied to the premium if a policy is issued.) The law does allow title companies to provide certain limited services free of charge, however. Specifically, companies aren't required to charge for furnishing someone with a property's legal description, the names of the owners of record, a description of the property's characteristics, or a copy of a recorded deed or map.

Because real estate transactions are complicated, a lot can go wrong in the closing process. The possibility that the sale won't close hangs over some transactions right up to the last minute. While escrow and title insurance prevent many problems, they inevitably raise additional legal issues. Understanding these can help you guide your clients and customers to a successful closing.

Case Law in Depth

The following case involves some of the legal issues discussed in this chapter. Read through the facts and consider the questions in light of what you have learned. Then read what the court actually decided.

Haug v. Bank of America (8th Cir. 2003) 317 F.3d 832

Amy and Peter Haug secured a home purchase loan and were charged $50 for a credit report. Their lender (Bank of America) paid only $15 to obtain the report, however. When they sued the lender in federal court, the Haugs alleged that this and various other overcharges violated RESPA's Section 8(b), which provides:

No person shall give and no person shall accept any portion, split, or percentage of any charge made or received for the rendering of a real estate settlement service in connection with a transaction involving a federally related mortgage loan other than for services actually performed.

The lender moved to dismiss the plaintiffs' claim at trial. In support of its motion, the lender cited earlier federal court decisions holding that it takes two parties to create a kickback. In other words, the defendant and a third party must split the fee to violate Section 8(b).

But the district court denied the defendant's motion for dismissal, citing a HUD policy statement [at the time, HUD enforced RESPA] that prohibited all unearned portions of settlement fees as well as splits. This meant that "a single settlement service provider violates Section 8(b) whenever it receives an unearned fee." Therefore, the plaintiffs could proceed with their claim.

The lender appealed, arguing, among other things, that it was improper for the district court to consider a HUD policy statement when the language of the statute was clear. Various banking associations and escrow companies filed briefs supporting the lender's position. On behalf of HUD, the Department of Justice filed a brief supporting the plaintiffs' position.

To counter the court decisions that the lender cited as precedents, the Haugs pointed to an early RESPA case, *U.S. v. Gannon* (1981) 684 F.2d 433. In the *Gannon* case, a county recording office employee overcharged for recording services and then pocketed the overcharge amount. Ruling that the employee's action violated Section 8, the *Gannon* court said, "Congress' aim was to stop all abusive practices that unreasonably inflate federally related settlement costs . . . [Therefore] a single individual can violate [Section 8] by receiving in his official capacity a 'charge' for the rendering of settlement services, but personally keeping a portion."

The plaintiffs urged that at the very least, Section 8 was ambiguous. A finding of ambiguity would make it appropriate for the court to consider various HUD policy statements that suggested unshared overcharges violated Section 8.

The questions:

Did the appellate court agree that a lender could essentially pay a kickback to itself? If not, how could the court distinguish the *Gannon* case, which found a kickback when a county recording officer acted alone? Finally, was RESPA's Section 8(b) ambiguous enough to allow into evidence HUD policy statements that indicated that a single party could violate the section?

The court's answers:

"We hold that the plain language of Section 8(b) requires plaintiffs to plead facts showing that the defendant illegally shared fees with a third party and the district court erred in relying on the HUD Policy Statement. Accordingly, we reverse..." The court ruled that the language of Section 8(b) was not ambiguous; it was straightforward, at least when applied to this set of facts.

The court also had to distinguish the Gannon case, however. To do so, it relied on *Mercado v. Calumet Fed. Savings & Loan Ass'n* (7th Cir. 1985) 763 F.2d 269, which, addressing *Gannon* a few years later, made it clear that *Gannon* applied to a very limited situation. In *Gannon*, the county employee "was in effect wearing two hats: receiving payments in both his official capacity and his personal capacity, effectively making a kickback to himself." The *Haug* court found that reasoning somewhat stretched and refused to stretch it further to find that RESPA covered all single-party overcharges.

The result:

The trial court's decision was overturned and the Haugs' claim dismissed.

Chapter Summary

- In escrow, money and/or documents are held by a third party for the buyer and the seller until the transaction is ready to close.

- The requirements for a valid escrow include an enforceable contract, an escrow agent, irrevocable deposits, and conditions.

- An escrow agent is a dual agent, owing fiduciary duties to both buyer and seller. California's Escrow Law provides for the licensing and regulation of escrow agents. A real estate broker is exempt from the escrow licensing requirement when providing escrow services incidental to a transaction in which the broker is already acting as a real estate agent.

- Escrow instructions set out the obligations of the parties and the conditions that must be met in order for the transaction to close.

- Legal title and risk of loss stays with the depositor until all the conditions specified in the escrow instructions are satisfied. However, the relation back doctrine provides that in certain situations, the delivery of the deed to the new owner is considered to take place at the initial deposit into escrow.

- Escrow may be terminated when all of the conditions have been met and the transaction closes, by mutual agreement of the parties, or when there is a default.

- Under the Real Estate Settlement Procedures Act (RESPA), lenders must make disclosures concerning closing costs to residential loan applicants. RESPA also prohibits kickbacks to settlement service providers.

- A homeowner's policy is a broader version of an owner's title insurance policy. It covers more title issues than a standard policy and is available only in transactions involving one- to four-unit residences.

Key Terms

- **Escrow** – The placing of funds, deeds, or other items intended for exchange into the custody of a third party until a set of conditions are met.

- **Closing** – The date by which all conditions must be met, the deposits exchanged, and escrow terminated.

- **Escrow instructions** – Directions to the escrow agent, usually written, setting out the conditions for closing.

- **Relation back** – A legal doctrine under which delivery of a deed may be deemed to have occurred on the date a deed was deposited into escrow, if the seller later becomes incompetent or either the seller or the buyer dies.

- **RESPA** – The Real Estate Settlement Procedures Act, a federal law protecting borrowers in the closing process by requiring certain disclosures and prohibiting kickbacks.

- **Kickback** – Illicit compensation paid to the recipient for referring business to the payor.

- **Section 8 violation** – A kickback or unearned fee that violates Section 8 of RESPA.

- **Title insurance** – Insurance against financial losses resulting from undiscovered encumbrances or defects in title.

Chapter Quiz

1. Ed is buying property. He needs more time to secure financing, so he instructs the escrow agent to delay the closing by three days. Which of the following is true?
   a) A three-day automatic extension of escrow is available to any party
   b) A six-day automatic extension of escrow is available to any party
   c) A buyer can unilaterally extend escrow if necessary to obtain financing
   d) No party can unilaterally alter an escrow instruction that benefits another party

2. Under California's Escrow Law, an escrow agent may be a/an:
   a) independent escrow agent
   b) title company
   c) attorney
   d) Any of the above

3. Silver dies suddenly, shortly after depositing a deed into escrow. Which of the following is true?
   a) Under the relation back doctrine, the deed is considered delivered as of the date of deposit into escrow and the transaction can close
   b) Under the dead-hand doctrine, escrow fails and the deed is returned to the seller's estate
   c) The transaction can close, but only if the buyer had deposited the purchase price before the seller's death
   d) None of the above

4. Under RESPA, a loan is considered federally related if:
   a) it will be used to finance the purchase of residential property
   b) it is secured by a mortgage or deed of trust
   c) the lender is federally regulated
   d) All of the above

5. A mortgagee's policy of title insurance insures the:
   a) buyer
   b) seller
   c) lender
   d) escrow agent

6. After a seller deposits a deed into escrow, it comes out that she failed to disclose a latent defect concerning the property to the buyer: the living room fireplace chimney doesn't extend all the way to the roof because of an old remodel. The buyer demands that the chimney be fixed or the purchase price be reduced by $25,000. The seller decides this is a deal-killer and orders the escrow agent to return the deed. Which of the following is true?
   a) The escrow agent must obey the request of a principal
   b) Deposits into escrow are irrevocable, so the escrow agent can only return the deed with the consent of the buyer
   c) Deposits are revocable if a good faith dispute develops over the transaction
   d) The seller gets the deed back, but can't keep the buyer's deposit

7. A preliminary title insurance report:
   a) lists encumbrances that will be excluded from coverage
   b) states the obligations of the parties up to and during closing
   c) is essentially the same as an abstract of title
   d) is a report to the Insurance Commissioner listing the premiums that will be charged for various kinds of policies during the coming year

8. Monique Starr, a top real estate agent, has an unpleasant brother-in-law who owns a title company called TeamOne. Monique strongly encourages her clients to choose TeamOne for all their title insurance needs; in return, the brother-in-law finds himself too busy each summer to come up for the annual Starr family vacation at Mt. Shasta—which makes it a much happier occasion. Which of the following is true?
   a) If the brother-in-law's silent agreement meets the definition of a kickback or reward, Monique could face prosecution under RESPA, but not under any state law
   b) If the brother-in-law's silent agreement meets the definition of a referral fee or reward, Monique could face prosecution under both RESPA and the state law regulating title insurance
   c) Monique's arrangement is fine; title insurers have a right to provide compensation in return for referrals of business
   d) Although RESPA and state law prohibit this type of arrangement, these laws aren't enforced and have no practical meaning

9. Title insurance policies don't typically cover the following types of risk:
   a) easements
   b) mortgages and liens
   c) forged title claims
   d) problems resulting from government regulation

10. When FIRPTA and/or California's withholding law applies to a transaction, the buyer or closing agent must:
   a) withhold a percentage of the purchase price to ensure that the buyer pays taxes
   b) withhold a percentage of the purchase price to ensure that the seller pays taxes
   c) file Form 1099 to report withholding
   d) All of the above

Chapter Answer Key

Chapter Quiz Answers:

1. d) A party may unilaterally alter an escrow condition only if the condition benefits him alone. If the condition benefits any other party, the other party's consent to the change must be obtained.

2. d) Any of these may provide escrow services.

3. a) Under the relation back doctrine, if the seller dies or becomes incompetent after depositing the deed into escrow, delivery of the deed relates back to the date of deposit into escrow.

4. d) A loan is federally related if it will be used to finance the purchase of residential property with up to four units, it is secured by a mortgage or deed of trust, and the lender is federally regulated.

5. c) A mortgagee's policy is also called a lender's policy.

6. b) Deposits into escrow are irrevocable. Escrow wouldn't provide much security if a party could withdraw a deed or a financial deposit whenever a dispute arose.

7. a) The preliminary report lists encumbrances and problems the title insurance company has discovered (and will therefore exclude from coverage).

8. b) Both federal law and California law ban payments and other rewards for referring title insurance business; Monique's arrangement could disadvantage consumers, especially if TeamOne tended to charge high prices.

9. d) As a general rule, title insurance does not protect against financial losses resulting from government regulations and other government actions.

10. b) If the seller isn't a California resident, the buyer must withhold a percentage of the sales price for payment to the state tax authorities. If the seller isn't a U.S. citizen or resident alien, the buyer must withhold an additional share for payment to the federal tax authorities. Generally, the escrow agent fulfills these requirements on behalf of the buyer.

Cases to Consider... Answers:

Escrow

Dixon v. Salvation Army (1983) 142 Cal.App.3d 463. Rescission here was appropriate—the buyer couldn't force the Salvation Army to sell at a reduced price. The Uniform Vendor and Purchaser Risk Act is silent about whether the buyer can enforce the agreement at a discounted price, so the court relied on a California common law rule established after the Great San Francisco Fire of 1906: if neither party was at fault for the destruction, the contract should be rescinded and any money deposited in escrow returned to the parties.

Title Insurance

George S. Vorgitch et al. v. Fidelity National Title Insurance (Cal.App., Jan. 23, 2002) (unpublished) 2002 WL 86870. The title company had no duty to defend the buyer's right to use the easement. The policy listed the easement in the exceptions from coverage, and that meant the company made no warranties concerning it. The nature of the easement or even its existence was not covered by the policy.

Walters v. Marler (1978) 83 Cal.App.3d 1. The title company wasn't liable to the buyer. The buyer's standard policy didn't cover the risk that the house or other improvements weren't on the property purchased. The lender's policy had an endorsement that did cover this risk, however. So the buyer sued the title company for negligent misrepresentation, claiming that issuance of the lender's policy amounted to a representation by the company that the house was in fact on the buyer's lot. The court held that a title policy is not a representation that the risks insured against will not occur. And even if it were, the title company would be liable only to the lender—the party insured by the policy that covered the risk—not to the buyer.

List of Cases

Brunoni v. Brunoni (1949) 93 Cal.App.2d 215
Cohen v. Shearer (1980) 108 Cal.App.3d 939
Dixon v. Salvation Army (1983) 142 Cal.App.3d 463
George S. Vorgitch et al. v. Fidelity National Title Insurance (Cal.App., Jan. 23, 2002)
    (unpublished) 2002 WL 86870
Haug v. Bank of America (8th Cir. 2003) 317 F.3d 832
Kirk Corp. v. First American Title Co. (1990) 220 Cal.App.3d 785
Money Store Investment Corp. v. Southern Cal. Bank (2002) 98 Cal.App.4th 722
O'Sullivan v. Countrywide Home Loans Inc. (5th Cir. 2003) 319 F.3d 732
Pagan v. Spencer (1951) 104 Cal.App.2d 588
Walters v. Marler (1978) 83 Cal.App.3d 1

Chapter 13

Real Estate Financing

Outline

Introduction

The buyer's financing is an important aspect of almost every real estate transaction. The central legal document in real estate financing is the security instrument, either a mortgage or a deed of trust. The security instrument gives the lender a security interest in (in other words, a lien against) real property owned by the borrower. In this chapter, we'll begin with an introduction to liens, then explain how security instruments work. Next, we'll look at some of the most important provisions in a real estate loan agreement. After that we'll describe the procedures that a lender must follow when a borrower fails to pay the debt and the lender decides to foreclose. We'll end with a look at laws that protect borrowers in residential financing transactions, including disclosure laws and predatory lending laws.

Liens (Financial Encumbrances)

As you may remember from Chapter 4, the interest that a real property owner or tenant has in the property is called an estate. An estate is a possessory interest (it includes the right to take possession of the property). In this chapter and some later ones, we'll be discussing **nonpossessory interests**, also called encumbrances. An **encumbrance** is an interest held by someone other than the property owner or a tenant—in other words, an interest held by someone who does not have a right to possess the property.

As the name implies, encumbrances burden (encumber) the property owner's title. They can be classified as financial or nonfinancial. Nonfinancial encumbrances include easements (covered in Chapter 15) and restrictive covenants (covered in Chapter 17). Financial encumbrances, commonly called liens, will be covered in this chapter and the next one.

A **lien** is a creditor's claim against real property that is owned by the debtor. If the debt isn't paid, the lien gives the creditor the right to foreclose on the property. In a foreclosure, the property is sold against the owner's will, and the debt is paid off out of the proceeds of the forced sale. A lien may also be called a security interest, since it secures the payment of a financial obligation. A creditor who has a lien is referred to as a **secured creditor**.

A lien does not keep a property owner from selling his property. Ownership of the property can be transferred whether or not the liens against it are paid off; however, the

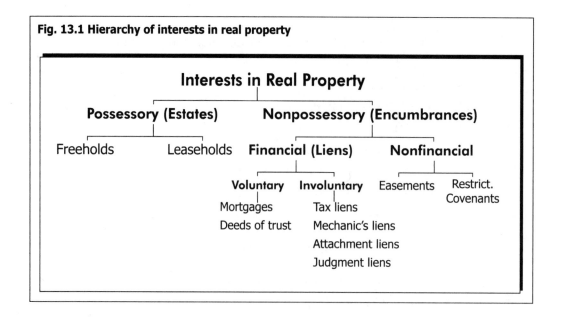

Fig. 13.1 Hierarchy of interests in real property

> ▶ **Lien Classifications**

Every lien is either voluntary or involuntary, and either general or specific.

- A voluntary lien is one that a property owner voluntarily gives to a creditor, usually as security for a loan.
- An involuntary lien (also called a statutory lien) attaches to property without the owner's consent, by operation of law.
- A general lien attaches to all of the debtor's property, real and personal.
- A specific lien attaches only to a particular piece of property.

Mortgages and deeds of trust are voluntary, specific liens. Both are created voluntarily by the borrower, and both attach only to the property offered as collateral for the loan.

new owner will take title subject to the liens that remain. The creditors will still have the right to foreclose on the property if they aren't paid.

When a creditor forecloses on property that's subject to more than one lien, the liens are paid off in order of priority. As a general rule, lien priority is determined by recording date; the earlier the recording date, the higher the priority. (See Chapter 14 for more about lien priority.)

Liens are classified as either general or specific, and as either voluntary or involuntary. (See the Lien Classifications sidebar.) Involuntary liens, which include tax liens, mechanic's liens, attachment liens, and judgment liens, are the topic of Chapter 14. In this chapter, we'll focus on voluntary liens, which are created by either a mortgage or a deed of trust.

Security Instruments

When a real estate loan is made, the lender and the borrower enter into a contract, commonly called a loan agreement. The lender offers to loan money to the borrower on certain terms, and the borrower must accept these terms to obtain the loan. The terms of the loan agreement specify the loan amount, the interest rate, the payment amount, the repayment period, the collateral that the borrower will provide, the borrower's other obligations, the lender's rights in the event of default, penalties for late payment, and many other items. In a real estate loan transaction, the loan agreement is embodied in two main documents: a promissory note and a security instrument.

A **promissory note** is a written promise to pay money. It is the basic evidence of a debt; it shows who owes how much to whom. A **security instrument** is either a mortgage or a deed of trust. While the promissory note establishes the borrower's obligation to repay the loan and sets the repayment requirements, the security instrument turns real property owned by the borrower into the collateral (the security) for the loan.

The security property may be property the borrower already owns, or it may be property the borrower is purchasing with the loan proceeds. The security instrument creates a lien against the property, giving the lender the right to foreclose on the property to satisfy the debt in the event that the borrower defaults. Default includes failing to make the loan payments as agreed, or failing to fulfill some other obligation in the loan agreement.

Hypothecation

A little historical background can make it easier to understand security instruments. In the earliest form of secured lending, personal property was used as collateral. A borrower gave the lender some form of valuable personal property to hold until the loan was repaid. If the loan was not repaid, the lender would keep the collateral. An example of this type of secured lending, still with us today, is the pawnshop.

Transferring possession of personal property to a lender was a relatively straightforward matter. But when land was used as collateral, transferring possession to the lender could be complicated and inconvenient. It was also unnecessary, since the borrower could not move the land or conceal it from the lender. As a result, a process called hypothecation developed. **Hypothecation** refers to offering property as collateral without giving up possession. It became standard practice for a borrower to remain in possession of his land and merely transfer title to the lender. Once the loan had been repaid, title was returned to the borrower.

Eventually, specialized legal documents—security instruments—were developed for use in this type of transaction. Instead of deeding the land to the lender outright, the borrower could execute a mortgage or deed of trust.

There were two ways of viewing how security instruments worked, referred to as title theory and lien theory. Under title theory, a security instrument transferred the property's **legal title** (also called naked title) to the lender or a trustee; the borrower kept possession of the property and had **equitable title** to it. Under lien theory, a security instrument merely gave the lender a lien against the property until the loan was paid off. The borrower retained both possession of the property and legal title to it.

Title theory is associated with the deed of trust, and the terminology reflects that: the borrower deeds the property to be held in trust for the lender. Lien theory is associated with the mortgage. But the distinction between title theory and lien theory has little practical effect nowadays. Both types of security instruments allow the lender to foreclose on the property in the event of default, and outside of very technical legal contexts, both types create a lien against the property.

However, the rights of the lender and the borrower may vary depending on the type of security instrument that's used. Let's look at the differences between a mortgage and a deed of trust.

Mortgages vs. Deeds of Trust

A mortgage and a deed of trust serve the same basic purpose: to secure the debtor's obligation to repay a loan. They just go about it somewhat differently.

A mortgage is a two-party security instrument in which the borrower (called the **mortgagor**) mortgages her property to the lender (called the **mortgagee**).

A deed of trust, sometimes called a trust deed, involves three parties rather than two. The borrower is called the **grantor** or **trustor**; the lender is called the **beneficiary**; and there is an independent third party called the **trustee**. The trustee's role is to arrange for the property to be released from the deed of trust lien when the loan is paid off, or to arrange for foreclosure if necessary.

The most important difference between the two types of security instruments concerns the foreclosure process. The process traditionally required for a mortgage is known as **judicial foreclosure**; it involves a court proceeding followed by a court-supervised auction of the security property. With a deed of trust, **nonjudicial foreclosure** can be used instead. In a nonjudicial foreclosure, the trustee auctions off the property without court supervision. Nonjudicial foreclosure is generally faster and less expensive than judicial foreclosure. (We'll discuss the two procedures in more detail shortly.)

Nonjudicial foreclosure is permitted only if the security instrument contains a **power of sale** clause. This provision, which is standard in a deed of trust, authorizes the trustee to sell the property if the borrower defaults. A mortgage can be foreclosed nonjudicially if it has a power of sale clause, but mortgages don't ordinarily include such a provision.

Because lenders generally favor nonjudicial foreclosure, in many states (including California) deeds of trust have become the most widely used security instrument, eclipsing mortgages. Note, however, that loans secured by real property are commonly called mortgages or mortgage loans even if the security instrument actually used in the transaction is a deed of trust.

Key Provisions in a Loan Agreement

A deed of trust includes a power of sale clause, while a mortgage usually does not. But there are many other provisions that the two types of security instruments have in common. Either type, for example, must identify the parties, include a complete and unambiguous description of the property, indicate that the property is being promised as security for a loan, and reference the promissory note as evidence of the debt.

Together, the promissory note and the security instrument set forth the terms of the loan agreement. The provisions of the promissory note concern repayment of the debt: the amount borrowed, the interest rate, the payment amount, and so on. The provisions of the security instrument generally concern the lender's rights and the borrower's obligations in regard to the security property.

In this section, we'll describe several important provisions that may be included in these documents. Some of these are part of virtually every real estate loan agreement; others are used only for certain types of loans or in special circumstances. Some of the provisions will appear in the promissory note, others in the security instrument; some will appear in both documents.

Taxes, Insurance, and Maintenance Clauses

Various clauses in the security agreement require the borrower to pay the taxes levied on the security property, keep the property insured, and perform adequate maintenance. Because the property serves as collateral for the loan, a tax foreclosure, uninsured destruction of the property, or waste would weaken or even eliminate the lender's security position.

Acceleration Clause

An acceleration clause states that if the borrower defaults, the lender has the right to **accelerate** the loan: to declare the entire remaining loan balance due immediately. (This is also referred to as "calling the note," which is why an acceleration clause is sometimes known as a call provision.) If the borrower doesn't pay off the loan as demanded, along with any interest and penalties owed, the lender may begin foreclosure proceedings.

While acceleration is still part of the foreclosure process in California, state law has limited it. This limitation is discussed later in this chapter.

Alienation Clause

An **alienation clause**, also called a due-on-sale clause, gives the lender the right to demand full payment of the loan if the borrower sells or otherwise transfers the security property, or an interest in it, to someone else. (In this context, alienation refers to any transfer of an interest in real property.)

An alienation clause doesn't actually prohibit the borrower from selling the property; it just allows the lender to force the borrower to pay off the loan if that occurs. Of course, as a practical matter this may in fact prevent the sale of the property.

In some cases, if the borrower wants to sell, the lender may be willing to allow the new owner to assume the loan, instead of requiring it to be paid off. In an **assumption**, the new owner agrees to take on primary liability for repaying the loan. The original borrower will remain secondarily liable unless the lender releases her from the obligation. Before allowing an assumption, the lender will check into the new owner's financial situation; if he meets the lender's standards of creditworthiness, the lender will usually agree to release the original borrower from liability.

California's Civil Code §§ 2924.5 – 2924.6 place some restrictions on the exercise of an alienation clause if the security property is residential property with up to four units. First, the alienation clause is enforceable only if it is set forth in its entirety in both the promissory note and the security instrument. Also, certain types of transfers can't be used to trigger acceleration of the loan. For example, the lender can't exercise the alienation clause if the borrower's spouse becomes a co-owner of the property, or if the property is encumbered with a junior lien (a lien that has lower priority than the lender's lien).

Late Payment Penalty Provision

A lender can charge a penalty for late payment only if the loan agreement provides for that. California's Civil Code § 2954.4 limits the penalties that can be charged if the security property is a single-family, owner-occupied residence. In that case, a late payment penalty can't exceed 6% of the overdue principal and interest payment or five dollars, whichever is more. And the penalty can't be charged unless the payment is at least ten days overdue.

In addition, there are federal provisions concerning late payment penalties. For federally insured or guaranteed mortgages, such as FHA and VA loans, the late payment fee generally cannot exceed 4% of the overdue amount and cannot be charged unless the payment is more than 15 days overdue. The same restrictions apply to high-cost loans (loans with total points and fees that exceed a specified threshold), as defined in HOEPA, a federal law we'll discuss later in this chapter.

Prepayment Provision

It's called **prepayment** when a borrower repays all or a portion of the loan before payment is due. A loan agreement may allow the borrower to prepay the loan in full at any time, or it may place restrictions on prepayment.

Some loan agreements provide that the lender can impose a penalty if the borrower prepays the loan.

> **Example:** A promissory note includes this provision: "Borrower may prepay up to 10% of the original loan amount in any 12-month period without penalty. If the prepayment exceeds 10%, then a prepayment fee equal to one year's interest on the excess will be charged."

A prepayment penalty is designed to partially compensate the lender for the loss of the additional interest it would have collected had the prepayment not occurred.

California law limits the prepayment penalties that can be charged on loans secured by owner-occupied residential property with up to four units. For these loans, the lender can charge prepayment penalties only during the first five years of the loan term. The borrower must be allowed to prepay 20% of the original loan amount in any 12-month period without penalty. If the prepayment exceeds 20%, a penalty can be charged on the excess, but the penalty can't be more than six months' interest on the excess. (Civil Code § 2954.9.) The prepayment penalty provision in the example above would be illegal in a residential loan covered by this rule.

In addition to those California rules, there are federal limits on prepayment penalties; they apply to nearly all consumer loans secured by a dwelling. Under the federal rules, prepayment penalties are prohibited in adjustable-rate mortgages and in high-cost and higher-priced loans (see the discussion of HOEPA). And even for mortgage loans in which prepayment penalties are allowed—referred to as "qualified mortgages" in the law—a penalty may be charged only during the first three years of the loan term. During the first two years, the penalty cannot exceed 2% of the total outstanding principal balance; during the third year, it can't exceed 1% of the balance. (See 12 CFR 1026.43(g).)

The federal legislation provides that either state or federal provisions may apply; the law that provides the greater protection to the consumer controls. An attorney specializing in real estate finance should always be consulted when issues such as these arise.

Subordination Clause

A subordination clause in a security instrument gives it lower priority than another security instrument that will be recorded later. Since lien priority is determined by recording date, the earlier instrument would ordinarily have higher priority than the later one. The subordination clause reverses that.

Subordination clauses are most common in loans for the purchase of vacant land when the purchaser intends to obtain a construction loan later. Lenders generally require a construction loan to have **first lien position** (highest priority), and the subordination clause in the earlier land purchase loan makes that possible.

Defeasance Clause

A defeasance clause requires the lender to release the property from the lien when the debt has been fully repaid. When a mortgage is paid off, California law requires the lender to record a document called a **certificate of discharge** (or satisfaction of mortgage) within 30 days. With a deed of trust, the beneficiary (the lender) must submit a **request for reconveyance** to the trustee within 30 days after the loan is paid off, and the trustee then has 21 days to record a **deed of reconveyance**. If these requirements aren't fulfilled, the responsible parties can be fined and ordered to pay damages to cover any loss resulting from the failure to record the lien release document promptly. (Civil Code § 2941.)

Foreclosure

When a borrower defaults on a mortgage or deed of trust, the lender can foreclose. To do so, the lender must follow procedures prescribed by law. As we said earlier, the main difference between mortgages and deeds of trust concerns foreclosure procedures. A mortgage ordinarily does not have a power of sale clause, and therefore requires judicial foreclosure. A deed of trust has a power of sale clause, giving the lender the option of nonjudicial foreclosure.

For the sake of convenience, we'll refer to mortgages when discussing judicial foreclosure, and to deeds of trust when discussing nonjudicial foreclosure. Keep in mind, however, that a mortgage can be foreclosed nonjudicially if it includes a power of sale clause, and a deed of trust can be foreclosed judicially if the lender chooses to do so.

Judicial Foreclosure

As explained earlier, when a mortgagor defaults—either by failing to repay the loan or by breaching covenants in the mortgage—the mortgagee can accelerate the loan. The mortgagee's next step is to initiate a lawsuit, called a **foreclosure action**, in the county where the security property is located. The purpose of this legal proceeding is to ask a judge to order the seizure and sale of the property. Most of the rules concerning judicial foreclosure in California can be found in the Code of Civil Procedure §§ 725a – 730.5.

In addition to the mortgagor, any **junior lienholders** are made parties to the lawsuit. These are creditors who have liens against the property with lower priority than the foreclosing lender's mortgage. The junior lienholders are included in the lawsuit because their liens will be eliminated by the foreclosure sale.

At the same time that the lawsuit is started, the mortgagee records a document called a **lis pendens**. A lis pendens states that the property is subject to a foreclosure action. By recording the lis pendens, the mortgagee provides constructive notice to anyone who might consider buying the property from the mortgagor (or acquiring some other interest in it) that the title may be affected by the pending lawsuit.

Cure and Reinstatement. In some states, once a mortgagee accelerates a loan and begins foreclosure proceedings, the only way that the mortgagor can stop the foreclosure and keep the property is by asserting the **equitable right of redemption**. This is the right to redeem the property by paying off the entire outstanding loan balance (not just the delinquent payments), plus interest, penalties, and costs incurred as a result of the foreclosure, such as court costs and attorneys' fees. Equitable redemption stops the foreclosure, satisfies the debt, and terminates the mortgagee's interest in the property.

California law has replaced the equitable right of redemption with a right to **cure** the default and **reinstate** the loan. The default can usually be cured by paying the delinquent amount, plus interest, penalties, and costs. (If the default involved a breach of covenants, as opposed to failure to make loan payments, the breach must be rectified. For example, overdue taxes must be paid, or insurance must be obtained.) Once the default is cured, the foreclosure is terminated and the loan is reinstated; the parties are back to where they were before the default.

A default can be cured at any time while the judicial foreclosure action is pending, up until the court issues a decree of foreclosure (see below). It can be cured either by the mortgagor or by a junior lienholder who wishes to preserve a junior lien.

Decree and Sale. Unless the mortgagor reinstates or pays off the loan beforehand, the foreclosure action will proceed to trial. In most cases, after reviewing the note and mortgage and the facts concerning the default, the judge issues a court order directing the sheriff or a court-appointed receiver to take charge of the property and sell it. This court order is called a **decree of foreclosure**.

The sheriff records a **notice of levy** and serves it on the mortgagor and other parties. The next requirement is the **notice of sale**. (In some cases, 120 days must elapse between the notice of levy and notice of sale.) At least 20 days before the sale date, the notice of sale must be posted on the property and also in a public place, published in a newspaper of general circulation once a week for three weeks, and mailed to the parties and to anyone else who has submitted a request for notification.

The **sheriff's sale** (sometimes called an execution sale) is a public auction. It is usually held at the county courthouse, and anyone who wants to bid on the property can do so. The property is sold to the highest bidder, who is given a **certificate of sale**.

Post-sale Redemption. Following the sale, the mortgagor may be allowed an additional period of time to redeem the property. To redeem it at this stage, the mortgagor usually must pay the highest bidder the amount that the highest bidder paid for the property, plus interest accrued from the time of the sale. The mortgagor will regain title to the property, now free of the foreclosed mortgage and any junior liens, but still subject to any liens senior to the mortgage. This right to redeem the property following the sheriff's sale is called the **statutory right of redemption**. (This is in contrast to the equitable right of redemption mentioned earlier, which refers to redeeming the property before the sale.)

In California, post-sale redemption is not allowed in certain circumstances. (See the discussion of deficiency judgments, below.) In cases where it is allowed, the length of the redemption period varies. It lasts for three months after the sale if the sale proceeds turned out to be enough to pay off the debt, plus interest, costs, and fees. It lasts for one year after the sale if the proceeds weren't enough to fully pay off the amounts owed.

The mortgagor is entitled to remain in possession of the property during the redemption period, provided that she pays a reasonable rent to the holder of the certificate of sale. Only at the end of the redemption period is the certificate holder given a **sheriff's deed**, which transfers title and the right of possession to the new owner.

Deficiency Judgments. A foreclosure sale may not bring in enough money to completely pay off the debt and costs. A **deficiency judgment** is a personal judgment against a borrower to recover the difference between the amount owed and the foreclosure sale proceeds.

> **Example:** Susana's property is being foreclosed on by Acme Mortgage. Susana owes Acme $300,000. In the foreclosure sale, Susana's property nets only $265,000. Acme may ask the court for a $35,000 deficiency judgment against Susana.

To obtain a deficiency judgment, the lender must apply to the court within three months after the foreclosure sale. The court will determine the amount of the deficiency and enter a judgment in favor of the lender.

Anti-deficiency rules. To ease some of the financial burden on defaulting property owners, California's **anti-deficiency rules** prohibit deficiency judgments in certain types of foreclosures. (See Code of Civil Procedure §§ 580a – 580e.) First of all, a deficiency judgment is never allowed in a nonjudicial foreclosure. And in a judicial foreclosure, the anti-deficiency rules prohibit deficiency judgments under the following circumstances:

- when the property's fair market value is greater than the amount of the debt;
- when the security instrument is a purchase money mortgage given to the seller for all or part of the purchase price (seller financing);
- when the security instrument is a mortgage given to a third-party lender to finance the purchase of owner-occupied residential property with up to four dwelling units; or
- after a residential short sale has been completed with the lender's consent. (In a short sale, the mortgagor sells the property for less than the remaining amount of indebtedness due at the time of sale.)

As you can see, a lender wouldn't be able to sue for a deficiency judgment after foreclosing on a typical home purchase loan, even if it was a judicial foreclosure.

Also, provisions in the federal Mortgage Reform and Anti-Predatory Lending Act include disclosure requirements that apply when a borrower applies for any new loan that would cause her to lose the protections of state anti-deficiency rules applicable to her existing mortgage.

Nonjudicial Foreclosure

When a trustor defaults on a loan secured by a deed of trust, the beneficiary (the lender) is not required to file a lawsuit and obtain a court order to foreclose. Instead, the beneficiary can ask the trustee appointed in the deed of trust to arrange for the property to be sold at a **trustee's sale**. Like a sheriff's sale, a trustee's sale is a public auction. The trustee sells the property to the highest bidder on the beneficiary's behalf. The rules governing nonjudicial foreclosure in California are set forth in Civil Code §§ 2923.5 – 2924(l).

Because court supervision is not required, nonjudicial foreclosure is less expensive and faster than judicial foreclosure. Remember, however, that nonjudicial foreclosure is

Fig. 13.2 Comparison of mortgages and deeds of trust

Security Instruments	
Mortgage	**Deed of Trust**
• Mortgagor and mortgagee • Judicial foreclosure • Reinstatement before decree of foreclosure • Redemption after sheriff's sale • Deficiency judgment allowed (subject to limitations)	• Trustor, beneficiary, and trustee • Nonjudicial foreclosure • Reinstatement before trustee's sale • No post-sale redemption • No deficiency judgment

permitted only if the security instrument contains a power of sale clause. A power of sale clause is standard in a deed of trust, and one can be included in a mortgage.

Although we're describing the nonjudicial foreclosure of a deed of trust, essentially the same procedures would apply to a mortgage with a power of sale clause, if the mortgagee chose nonjudicial foreclosure.

Notices of Default and Sale. To foreclose a deed of trust nonjudicially, the trustee must follow steps similar to those taken by the sheriff in a judicial foreclosure. The trustee must record a **notice of default and election to sell** and mail a copy to the trustor, junior lienholders, and anyone who has requested notification. The notice of default accelerates the loan and explains the right of reinstatement (see below). A **notice of trustee's sale** is issued three months after the filing of the notice of default. The three-month waiting period is mandatory, but the notice of sale can be filed up to five days before the lapse of the three-month period as long as the date set for the sale is no earlier than three months plus twenty days from the filing of the notice of default. The notice of trustee's sale must be: 1) recorded, 2) sent to everyone who received the notice of default, 3) posted on the property and also in a public place, and 4) published in a newspaper once a week for three weeks.

As a result of the foreclosure crisis that began in 2007, the California legislature instituted due diligence requirements aimed at encouraging loan workout agreements, which can help avoid foreclosures. These requirements apply only to loans secured by owner-occupied residences. Under the rules, a series of additional pre-foreclosure communication requirements must be met before the foreclosure process can begin.

For instance, before filing the notice of default, a trustee or other authorized agent must make several attempts to contact the defaulting homeowner by phone to discuss foreclosure alternatives. If the specified number of attempts at telephone contact fail, certain requirements for notice by mail are triggered. The mailed notices must give the homeowner an opportunity to contact the lender to discuss the borrower's financial situation and options to avoid foreclosure. These notices must also give the borrower information on the availability of a HUD-certified counseling agency, as well as a toll-free number for reaching that agency. These notification requirements, set forth in Civil Code §2923.5, will expire on January 1, 2018, unless extended by the legislature. Any notice of default that is filed under this provision must contain a declaration by the mortgagee or other authorized agent that the mortgagee has complied with these due diligence requirements.

Reinstatement. As in a judicial foreclosure, the borrower (or a junior lienholder) in a nonjudicial foreclosure has a right to cure the default and reinstate the loan, stopping the foreclosure. The default may be cured at any time up until five days before the trustee's sale. And in the five-day period before the sale, right up until bidding at the trustee's sale ends, the trustor or a junior lienholder may redeem the property by paying off the loan balance at the time of default, plus interest, penalties, costs, and fees.

The statutory right of redemption that may follow the sheriff's sale in a judicial foreclosure does not apply to a trustee's sale. The successful bidder at the sale receives a **trustee's deed**. The trustor is immediately divested of title and may be given only a short time to vacate the property. As in a judicial foreclosure, the purchaser takes title subject to senior liens but free of the foreclosed lien and junior liens.

Choosing Between Judicial and Nonjudicial Foreclosure

As we said earlier, deeds of trust are used instead of mortgages in nearly all California real estate loan transactions. Since nonjudicial foreclosure saves time and money, and since there's no statutory redemption period afterwards, lenders almost always choose to foreclose nonjudicially. Usually, judicial foreclosure is chosen only when the lender believes the foreclosure sale will result in a deficiency (because the property's value is less than the debt) and a deficiency judgment would be allowed (because the anti-deficiency rules do not apply).

> **Example:** Zenith Savings is going to foreclose on its deed of trust against Winston's commercial property. Because the property's value has declined sharply in the past few years, the foreclosure is likely to result in a deficiency. In other words, the sale proceeds probably won't cover the full amount of the debt.
>
> Zenith decides to foreclose judicially. This will allow Zenith to ask the court for a deficiency judgment if necessary. Since the loan isn't seller financing or for owner-occupied residential property, a deficiency judgment will be allowed if the sale results in a deficiency, as long as Zenith uses the judicial foreclosure process.

Protecting the Borrower

To close the chapter, we'll look at some laws intended to help home buyers avoid getting in over their heads when they obtain financing. Real estate agents often work with mortgage brokers and lenders, so they need to understand the laws regarding lending practices.

Truth in Lending Act

The Truth in Lending Act (TILA), a federal law that went into effect in 1969, is designed to help consumers compare the cost of financing offered by competing lenders. The statute (15 U.S.C. §§ 1601 et seq.) is implemented by **Regulation Z** (12 C.F.R. §§ 226 et seq.) and enforced by the Consumer Financial Protection Bureau. TILA does not

Real Estate Financing **367**

set limits on interest rates or other finance charges, but it requires the disclosure of those charges to the consumer.

Types of Loans Covered. TILA applies to **consumer loans**, which are loans used for personal, family, or household purposes. More specifically, it applies to consumer loans if they are to be repaid in more than four installments, or are subject to finance charges. Also, the loan must be for $54,600 or less (the dollar limit is adjusted annually based on the Consumer Price Index), or secured by real property.

Under these rules, a mortgage loan for any amount is covered by TILA, as long as the proceeds are used for personal, family, or household purposes, such as buying or remodeling a home, consolidating personal debt, or sending children to college.

Loans for business, commercial, or agricultural purposes are exempt from the Truth in Lending Act. (The law does not apply to loans made to corporations or organizations.) Also, TILA does not apply to seller financing, unless the seller is a developer or investor who routinely extends credit in the ordinary course of business.

Disclosure Requirements. TILA has always required lenders to provide a residential mortgage loan applicant with a disclosure statement about the proposed financing. However, as we explained in Chapter 12, the combined TILA-RESPA Integrated Disclosure (TRID) rule has imposed disclosure requirements that generally supplant the earlier rules and required forms.

TRID disclosure requirements apply to most home purchase, home equity, and refinance loans. Home equity lines of credit, reverse mortgages, mortgages secured by any dwelling not attached to land, and loans made by creditors who make five or fewer mortgage loans per year are exempt. Transactions exempt from TRID requirements are still subject to the original TILA disclosure requirements.

The two essential disclosures required by the TRID rule are the **loan estimate** and the **closing disclosure** forms. (We discussed the closing disclosure form in Chapter 12.) The loan estimate form, which is provided after receiving a loan application, helps applicants understand the features, risks, and costs of the loan they have chosen. The information given in the loan estimate depends on the specifics of the loan, but two of the most important disclosures are the annual percentage rate and the total interest percentage.

The **annual percentage rate** (APR) is the cost of the financing expressed as an annual percentage of the loan amount. It states the relationship of the finance charges to the amount financed. The finance charges include the interest, plus any origination fee, discount points, mortgage insurance costs, servicing fees, or mortgage broker's compensation. Because interest is rarely the only charge a borrower is required to pay for a mortgage, the APR of the loan is almost always higher than the quoted interest rate.

> **Example:** First Savings offers a loan with an interest rate of 7%. Because the APR takes into account the origination fee and mortgage insurance, as well as the interest on the loan, this loan has an APR of 7.32%.

The **total interest percentage** (TIP) expresses the total amount of interest that the borrower will pay over the loan term as a percentage of the loan amount. It includes only interest, without the other finance charges that are reflected in the APR. The TIP gives the prospective borrower a clearer picture of how interest impacts the total amount paid over the life of the loan.

The lender must give the loan applicant the loan estimate form within three business days after receiving the loan application. The lender can't require the applicant to pay any fees (such as an application fee, appraisal fee, or underwriting fee) until the loan estimate has been provided and the applicant has indicated an intent to proceed with the loan transaction. One exception: the credit report fee can be collected beforehand.

Adjustable-rate mortgages (ARMs) require additional disclosures. Lenders must give applicants a government brochure about ARMs (the *Consumer Handbook on Adjustable-Rate Mortgages*), follow guidelines for calculating and disclosing the annual percentage rate, and disclose information about the particular ARM program applied for.

Right of Rescission. TILA provides for a right of rescission in connection with certain types of mortgage loans. When the security property is the borrower's existing principal residence, the borrower may rescind the loan agreement any time within three days after signing the loan documents, receiving a disclosure statement, or receiving notice of the right of rescission, whichever happens last. Note that the right of rescission will last for three years if the borrower never receives the disclosure statement or the rescission notice.

The borrower has no right to rescind a loan agreement when the proceeds are for the purchase or construction of the borrower's principal residence. In addition, the right of rescission does not apply to a refinance of the principal residence when the refinance lender is the same one that made the original loan.

Advertising under TILA. In addition to requiring disclosure statements for loan applicants, the Truth in Lending Act has rules that govern the advertising of credit terms. These rules apply to lenders, mortgage brokers, and anyone else who advertises consumer credit. For example, a real estate broker advertising financing terms for a listed home must comply with TILA.

It's always legal to state the cash price or the annual percentage rate in an ad. But if the ad mentions any other specific loan terms commonly known as triggering terms (the downpayment amount or percentage, the repayment period or number of payments, the amount of any payment, or the amount of any finance charge), then the APR and other loan terms must also be disclosed in the ad.

> **Example:** A newspaper ad says, "Assume VA loan—only $1,350 a month!" Because it specifies the monthly payment amount, the ad will violate the Truth in Lending Act if it doesn't also state the APR, the downpayment, the repayment period, and other loan terms.

Note, however, that while the reference in the example to the specific monthly payment triggered the full disclosure requirement, a general statement such as "low monthly payment" or "easy terms" would not.

Mortgage Acts and Practices Rule

The Mortgage Acts and Practices Rule is a federal regulation, adopted in 2011, that is intended to limit deceptive mortgage advertising. The rule, also known as **Regulation N**, applies to all entities who advertise residential mortgage financing to consumers, except for banks and similar supervised financial institutions. For instance, the rule applies to independent mortgage companies and mortgage brokers, and it also applies to real estate agents if they advertise home financing.

The rule prohibits misrepresentations concerning loan features or the lender and the deceptive use of certain terminology. In addition to avoiding these practices, advertisers must comply with recordkeeping requirements. Marketing materials, training materials, sales scripts, and other communications that describe mortgage products must be retained for at least two years.

California Financing Disclosure Laws

In addition to the federal Truth in Lending Act, there are some California laws that help ensure that home buyers get the information they need to make sound financing decisions. These include the Mortgage Loan Broker Law and the seller financing disclosure law.

Mortgage Loan Broker Law. Real estate agents often help buyers obtain financing, and this assistance may go beyond simply helping a buyer submit a loan application. In California, an agent who negotiates a loan for compensation is considered to be acting as a mortgage broker.

Real estate agents acting as mortgage brokers must comply with the Mortgage Loan Broker Law, also known as the Real Property Loan Law (Business and Professions Code §§ 10240 et seq.). This law requires an agent acting as a mortgage broker to give a disclosure statement to borrowers. And for loans secured by residential property, the law restricts the size of the mortgage brokerage commission and the costs that the borrower can be charged.

Disclosure statement. The required disclosure statement lists all the charges associated with the loan, as well as the amount of the loan proceeds that will be left after all of these charges have been deducted. The disclosure statement must be delivered to the borrower no later than three days after the lender's receipt of the loan application, or before the borrower signs the loan agreement documents—whichever comes first.

Real estate agents must use a disclosure statement whenever negotiating a loan or performing any other services for borrowers or lenders in connection with financing. This applies to loans for commercial property too, not just residential property. Real estate agents must keep a copy of the statement on file for at least three years.

A special form of disclosure statement is required if the loan is considered a nontraditional mortgage product. This covers loans where the borrower can defer repayment of the principal or interest. Examples include interest-only loans, where the borrower doesn't pay any of the principal balance, or loans that allow for negative amortization, where interest goes unpaid and is added to the principal balance.

Commissions and costs. The Mortgage Loan Broker Law places limits on the total commissions and other fees a real estate agent may charge for helping arrange certain kinds of residential financing. These limits apply to loans secured by residential property with up to four units where the lien is either a first position deed of trust (for under $30,000) or a junior deed of trust (for under $20,000). California law does not impose commission limits on larger loans.

The commission limits are tiered: for a loan in first lien position, with terms under three years, the commissions and charges together can't exceed 5% of the principal. The maximum is 10% for first position loans with longer terms.

For loans in a junior position, the rules are more generous. The 5% limit applies only to loans with terms of less than two years. For loans with terms of at least two years but less than three years, the maximum commission is 10%. The ceiling on commissions for loans with terms of three years or more is 15%.

The borrower's costs for these loans (such as the appraisal and escrow fees) cannot exceed $390 or 5% of the loan amount, whichever is greater, up to a maximum of $700 (not counting commissions). In addition, the charges cannot exceed the actual costs incurred or compensation reasonably earned.

Balloon payments. A **balloon payment** is a loan payment that is significantly larger than the regular loan payment. For the purposes of this law, it is a payment that is more than twice the size of the smallest required loan payment. The Mortgage Loan Broker Law makes it illegal to require balloon payments in short-term loans (loans with terms of less than three years) that are secured by real property. If the property is owner-occupied, the rule applies to loans with terms of less than six years. The balloon payment prohibition doesn't apply to seller financing.

Seller Financing Disclosure Law. A number of borrower protection laws we've discussed so far exempt seller financing. However, under Civil Code §§ 2956 – 2967, if a seller finances all or part of the purchase price for a one- to four-unit residential property, and an **arranger of credit** (such as a real estate broker) is involved in negotiating or setting up the transaction, the borrower is entitled to loan disclosures similar to those available in more conventional financing.

Some of the disclosures that are required to be made include:

- a copy or description of the promissory note and security agreement,
- a warning concerning the difficulties balloon payments may cause (if such a payment is required),
- an explanation of title insurance and a recommendation to purchase it, and
- a statement that a tax service has been or will be retained to report to the vendor whether property taxes are being paid by the purchaser.

These disclosures are made in a **seller financing disclosure statement**. It's the responsibility of the arranger of credit to make sure that both the buyer and the seller receive the disclosure statement before signing the offer, the acceptance, or any other binding documents.

The Civil Code does not require a seller financing disclosure statement if the transaction is already covered by other disclosure laws such as the Truth in Lending Act, the Mortgage Loan Broker Law, or RESPA (see Chapter 12).

Predatory Lending

Predatory lending refers to practices that unscrupulous mortgage lenders and mortgage brokers use to take advantage of unsophisticated borrowers for their own profit. Real estate agents sometimes participate in predatory lending schemes and, in some cases, a buyer or seller may play a role in deceiving the other party.

Predatory Practices. Some predatory lending practices involve tactics that are always abusive; others involve ordinary lending practices and loan terms that can be misused for a predatory purpose. Some of the more common predatory practices are listed below.

- **Predatory steering:** Steering a buyer toward a more expensive loan (one with a higher interest rate and/or fees) when the buyer could qualify for a less expensive loan.
- **Fee packing:** Charging interest rates, points, or processing fees that far exceed the norm and are not justified by the cost of the services provided.
- **Loan flipping:** Encouraging borrowers to unnecessarily and repeatedly refinance (and profiting off the loan fees for each refinance).
- **Fraud:** Misrepresenting or concealing unfavorable loan terms or excessive fees, falsifying documents, or using other fraudulent means to induce a prospective borrower to enter into a loan agreement.
- **Property flipping:** Purchasing property at a discount (because the seller needs a quick sale) and then immediately reselling it to an unsophisticated buyer for an inflated price. This isn't automatically illegal, but it is illegal when a real estate agent, appraiser, or lender commits fraud to make the buyer believe the property is worth substantially more than it actually is.
- **Loan in excess of value:** Loaning a home buyer more than the appraised value of the property. This usually involves a fraudulent appraisal. It may occur when a lender and an appraiser collude in a property flipping scheme; or it may occur when a mortgage broker and an appraiser collude to deceive a lender, victimizing both the lender and the borrower.
- **Unaffordable payments:** Making loans to borrowers without using appropriate qualifying standards, so that they can't afford the payments and will probably default and lose their homes. In this situation, the predator is likely to be someone who won't be affected when the borrower eventually defaults, such as a mortgage broker.

  In some cases, the payments are unaffordable because the predator persuaded the borrower to commit **mortgage fraud**, providing inaccurate information to the lender in order to get a larger loan. The fraud ultimately backfires for the borrower, who winds up in foreclosure because she can't afford the payments.
- **Impound waivers:** Not requiring a borrower to make monthly deposits for property taxes and insurance into an impound account, even though the borrower is unlikely to be able to pay the taxes and insurance when they are due. Waiving the impound requirement encourages a home buyer to borrow more, because it reduces the monthly payment, making the mortgage seem more affordable.

Targeted Victims. Predatory lenders and mortgage brokers deliberately target prospective borrowers who:

- aren't able to understand the transaction they're entering into, and/or
- don't know that better alternatives are available to them.

> ▶ **Foreclosure Epidemic**
>
> Starting in early 2007 and continuing during the severe recession that followed, there was a drastic increase in foreclosure rates around the country. Many of the loans in question were subprime, and the surge in foreclosures led a number of prominent subprime lenders to declare bankruptcy.
>
> While the foreclosed loans weren't necessarily predatory, many had features that enabled less-qualified buyers to purchase "more house"—as it turned out, more house than the borrower could actually afford. For example, these loans often allowed very low payments during an initial "teaser" period, but the payment amount would rise sharply when that period ended.
>
> In response to the crisis, politicians and consumer advocates called upon subprime lenders to restructure existing loans to help borrowers keep their homes. Fannie Mae and Freddie Mac also took steps to discourage risky lending.

Potential borrowers are especially likely to be targeted if they are elderly, have a limited education, or speak limited English. Also, targeted borrowers often have a low income, a poor credit history, or no credit history; in other words, predatory lending is most likely to occur in the subprime market. **Subprime lenders** make riskier loans than prime lenders. While the majority of subprime lenders are legitimate, some profit by taking advantage of vulnerable borrowers.

Predatory lending concerns overlap with fair lending issues (see Chapter 19), because racial and ethnic minority groups are disproportionately represented in the ranks of predatory lending victims.

Predatory Lending Laws. There are both federal and state laws that are intended to put a stop to predatory lending.

Federal law. The main federal predatory lending law is called the Home Ownership and Equity Protection Act (HOEPA). Although it's usually discussed as a separate law, HOEPA actually consists of provisions that were added to the Truth in Lending Act in 1994, together with additional amendments contained in the Mortgage Reform and Anti-Predatory Lending Act. (See 15 U.S.C. § 1639. This law was Title XIV of the 2010 Dodd-Frank Act, comprehensive financial reform legislation.)

To be covered by HOEPA, a loan must be used for consumer purposes and must be secured by the loan applicant's principal dwelling. Originally HOEPA covered only **high-cost loans**. This category includes home equity and refinance loans, but not purchase loans, construction loans, or reverse mortgages. A home equity or refinance loan secured by a principal dwelling is classified as a high-cost loan if the APR exceeds the prime rate for comparable transactions by more than 6.5% for most first-position loans, or 8.5% for junior-position loans. Those thresholds are actually quite high, so relatively few loans fall into the high-cost category.

To provide consumers with greater protection, new provisions were added to TILA and Regulation Z in 2008 and 2010. These provisions created a broader category of mortgage loans, known, confusingly, as **higher-priced loans**. Although loans in this category are more expensive (have higher points and fees) than standard loans, they are less expensive than loans in the high-cost category.

The higher-priced category includes not just home equity and refinance loans, but also home purchase loans. (Again, the loans must be secured by the borrower's principal residence.) The category also has much lower APR thresholds than the high-cost category; for example, a first-position loan is higher-priced if the APR is 1.5% higher than the prime rate (2.5% for larger loans). These rules mean that, compared to the high-cost category, the higher-priced category covers many more loans. Nearly all loans that would be considered subprime are included in this broader category.

Certain rules apply to both high-cost and higher-priced loans. As mentioned earlier, prepayment penalties are not allowed. For a first-lien loan, the lender must set up an escrow

 Protecting Borrowers from Predators

Here is some of the advice that experts offer borrowers to help them avoid being victimized by predatory lenders:

1. Don't let a real estate agent, a mortgage broker, or anyone else steer you to one particular lender.

2. Don't assume that you won't be able to qualify for a loan on reasonable terms from a legitimate lender.

3. Don't let anyone persuade you to make false statements on a loan application or in other aspects of the transaction.

4. Don't let anyone persuade you to borrow more money than you can afford to repay.

5. Don't let anyone convince you that you've committed yourself to a transaction before you actually have. For example, signing a disclosure form does not obligate you to proceed with the loan.

6. Don't sign documents that have blanks that haven't been filled in. In provisions that don't apply in the current transaction, the blank lines should have "N/A" (for "not applicable") written in them.

7. Don't sign documents without reading them first and asking questions about provisions you don't understand.

8. If you don't speak English fluently, try to arrange for a translator to accompany you to the loan interview and help you review documents before signing.

9. Even if you are fluent in English, get the assistance of a lawyer, a housing counselor, a trusted real estate agent, or even a trusted friend or relative who has some experience in financial matters. Two pairs of eyes are better than one.

account (an impound account) and require the borrower to make deposits adequate to cover property taxes and insurance as part of the monthly mortgage payment.

There are additional rules for high-cost loans that do not apply to higher-priced loans. A high-cost loan with a term of less than five years can't be structured to require a balloon payment. Negative amortization is not allowed in high-cost loans, and the interest rate cannot be raised after a default.

One of the most important federal anti-predatory lending provisions is known as the **ability to repay rule**. It applies not just to high-cost and higher-priced loans, but to almost any consumer loan secured by the borrower's principal residence. A lender may not make such a loan without evaluating the borrower's ability to afford the monthly payments and repay the loan. Unverified income or assets cannot be taken into account during this underwriting process.

State law. California's predatory lending law (Financial Code §§ 4970 – 4979.8) also applies to both home purchase loans and home equity loans. The loan must be secured by residential property with no more than four dwelling units, and it must be the applicant's principal residence.

Like HOEPA, California's law applies only to expensive loans, so it sets specific thresholds for the APR and the total points and fees. For instance, the state law applies to a loan if the total points and fees exceed 6% of the loan amount. The California law has an additional limitation: it applies only if the loan amount is less than the conforming loan limit (a limit set by the Federal Housing Finance Agency that is adjusted annually).

California's law prohibits many of the same things that the federal law does, and it includes quite a few additional rules. Here are some of the prohibitions and requirements for loans covered by the state law:

- loan applicants may not be steered toward a subprime loan if they could qualify for a standard loan, or toward a loan with a higher interest rate and fees if they could actually qualify for a less expensive loan;
- loan applicants must be given a disclosure statement entitled *Consumer Caution and Home Ownership Counseling Notice*;
- the loan agreement can't include an acceleration clause that allows the lender to accelerate the loan at its discretion (even if the borrower hasn't defaulted);
- prepayment penalties are prohibited during the first three years of the loan, and limited in amount throughout the loan term;
- a prepayment penalty can't be charged if the loan is accelerated due to default; and
- refinancing isn't allowed if it doesn't result in an identifiable benefit to the consumer.

The California predatory lending law gives enforcement authority to the Department of Business Oversight for lenders and mortgage brokers, and to the Bureau of Real Estate for real estate agents. Anyone who willfully and knowingly violates the law will be liable for a civil penalty of up to $25,000 per violation, and also must pay damages to the consumer. A real estate agent who participates in a predatory lending scheme may be subject to disciplinary action and lose his license, in addition to facing monetary penalties under the predatory lending law.

Case Law in Depth

The following case involves some of the legal issues discussed in this chapter. Read through the facts and consider the questions in light of what you have learned. Then read what the court actually decided.

Nguyen v. Calhoun (2003) 105 Cal.App.4th 428

Harbor Financial Corporation (Harbor) held a deed of trust against Chavez's home. Chavez became unable to make the payments and defaulted on the loan. Harbor instituted a foreclosure action, recording a notice of default and election to sell. Meanwhile, Chavez listed his property in an attempt to sell it before Harbor's foreclosure sale. A buyer (Nguyen) was found, and Chavez asked Harbor to postpone the foreclosure sale. Harbor refused to postpone the sale unless they received proof that Nguyen's loan had been funded and put into escrow. (In other words, Harbor wanted proof that Nguyen would be able to pay Chavez, who would then be able to pay Harbor).

Nguyen's loan was funded on the morning of the day (a Friday) the foreclosure sale was to take place. The escrow company sent the check to Harbor, who didn't receive it until the following Monday. That same Friday morning, several hours before the trustee's sale, the escrow company also faxed a certified copy of the escrow settlement statement to Harbor. Due to a faxing error, Harbor didn't receive the proof of funds until the following Monday. By then, Harbor had already gone ahead with the foreclosure sale. The property was sold at the foreclosure sale to Calhoun. In other words, at the end of the day, both Nguyen and Calhoun thought that they owned the property.

Nguyen brought a quiet title action against Calhoun, claiming that his escrow took place before the trustee's sale and thus had priority. The trial court found for Nguyen, and Calhoun appealed.

The question:

Who owns the property? Nguyen, who bought the property from Chavez? Or Calhoun, who purchased the property at the trustee's sale?

The court's answer:

The court stated that the lower court decided that title passed to Nguyen because the escrow company had enough funds to pay off Harbor before the foreclosure sale. However, that alone was not enough. Nguyen "took title to the property subject to Harbor's preexisting deed of trust. Thus, in order to protect his interest in the property from the pending foreclosure, [Nguyen] had to ensure that the underlying obligation to Harbor was satisfied.

"We therefore consider this critical question: Was the debt paid prior to the foreclosure sale?... [Calhoun and the other defendants] rely heavily on the fact that payment was not received until after the foreclosure sale.

"We agree with defendants...[A]s a general rule, depositing a check in the mail (or, in this case, with a courier) does not constitute payment...Here, the payment sent by the escrow holder via Federal Express was not received until three days after the foreclosure sale. Thus, the debt remained unsatisfied as of the time of the foreclosure sale.

"Given the undisputed facts of this case, there is no basis for invalidating the foreclosure sale. The debt giving rise to the lender's lien was not satisfied prior to foreclosure; the foreclosure sale thus cannot be set aside on the ground that the lien was extinguished prior to the sale."

The result:

The judgment was reversed and Calhoun, the purchaser at the trustee's sale, prevailed.

Chapter Summary

- A promissory note is a written promise to pay a debt. For a real estate loan, the borrower is required to sign a promissory note along with a security instrument, which makes the borrower's property collateral for the loan.

- The two main types of security instruments are mortgages and deeds of trust. The central difference between the two is that a deed of trust includes a power of sale clause, which allows the trustee to foreclose nonjudicially in the event of a borrower's default. The borrower has the right to cure the default and reinstate the loan before the trustee's sale.

- A mortgage is foreclosed judicially. The borrower has the right to cure the default and reinstate the loan before the sheriff's sale. In addition, the borrower may have a statutory right of redemption for a period of time afterwards. If the foreclosure sale proceeds aren't enough to pay off the debt and sale costs, the lender may be able to obtain a deficiency judgment against the borrower.

- The Truth in Lending Act (TILA) is a federal consumer protection law intended to help borrowers compare the cost of different financing alternatives. TILA requires certain disclosures to loan applicants and regulates lender advertising. California's Mortgage Loan Broker Law and the seller financing disclosure law also require lender disclosures.

- Predatory lending refers to unscrupulous practices by lenders and mortgage brokers who profit by taking advantage of unsophisticated borrowers. Laws designed to help eliminate these practices include the federal Home Ownership and Equity Protection Act (HOEPA) and California's predatory lending law.

Key Terms

- **Promissory note** – A written promise to pay money.

- **Security instrument** – An agreement such as a mortgage or deed of trust, that makes a property collateral for a loan.

- **Hypothecation** – Pledging property as collateral without giving up possession of the actual property.

- **Foreclosure action** – Under a judicial foreclosure, the mortgagee's lawsuit to initiate foreclosure on a loan.

- **Lis pendens** – A recorded document that gives notice to subsequent purchasers and encumbrancers that a property is subject to a legal action.

- **Equitable right of redemption** – In a judicial foreclosure, the right of the borrower in default to redeem the property before a sheriff's sale by paying off the entire outstanding loan balance, plus costs incurred as a result of the foreclosure.

- **Statutory right of redemption** – In a judicial foreclosure, the right of the borrower in default to redeem a property following a sheriff's sale by paying the amount paid for the property, plus accrued interest from the time of sale.

- **Regulation Z** – Implements the Truth in Lending Act.

- **Annual percentage rate** – The cost of a loan expressed as an annual percentage of the loan amount, taking into account not only the interest charges, but also other financing costs such as an origination fee, discount points, and mortgage insurance.

- **Total interest percentage** – The amount of interest paid over the life of the loan, expressed as a percentage of the loan amount.

- **Predatory lending** – Abusive lending practices used to take advantage of unsophisticated borrowers.

Chapter Quiz

1. The practice of offering property as collateral for a loan without giving up possession of the property is known as:
   a) hypothecation
   b) a promissory note
   c) a voluntary lien
   d) a general lien

2. Provisions in a security instrument typically require the borrower to:
   a) pay the property taxes
   b) keep the security property insured
   c) maintain the security property
   d) All of the above

3. A borrower defaults on his loan; under the _____, the lender has the right to declare the entire remaining balance due immediately.
   a) due-on-sale clause
   b) subordination clause
   c) defeasance clause
   d) acceleration clause

4. Under California law, a lender may charge loan prepayment penalties during the first _____ years of the loan term.
   a) two
   b) three
   c) five
   d) ten

5. A lender may ask a judge to order the seizure and sale of property in a legal proceeding called a:
   a) power of sale clause
   b) foreclosure action
   c) request for reconveyance
   d) lis pendens

6. The main difference between a mortgage and a deed of trust as a security instrument is the:
   a) length of the loan
   b) interest rate
   c) foreclosure process
   d) recording process

7. What clause, standard in a deed of trust, allows the trustee to sell the property if the borrower defaults?
   a) Power of sale clause
   b) Habendum clause
   c) Transfer clause
   d) None of the above

8. The Truth in Lending Act (TILA):
   a) sets limits on interest rates
   b) applies to commercial loans as well as consumer loans
   c) is implemented by Regulation Y
   d) requires lenders to disclose information to loan applicants

9. Which of the following phrases in an advertisement would trigger TILA's disclosure requirements?
   a) "Low downpayment"
   b) "Affordable interest rate"
   c) "Only $1,800 a month"
   d) All of the above

10. Predatory lending practices may involve which of the following?
    a) Fee packing
    b) Fraud
    c) Unaffordable payments
    d) All of the above

Chapter Answer Key

Chapter Quiz Answers:

1. a) Hypothecation refers to offering property as collateral without giving up possession.

2. d) A security agreement usually requires the borrower to fulfill all of these obligations.

3. d) If a borrower defaults, an acceleration clause allows the lender to declare the entire remaining loan balance due immediately. If the borrower fails to pay off the loan, the lender may begin foreclosure proceedings.

4. c) Under California law, prepayment penalties may be charged on loans secured by owner-occupied residential property with up to four units, but only during the first five years of the loan term. Federal law allows prepayment penalties only during the first three years of the loan term.

5. b) A foreclosure action is the legal proceeding in which a lender asks a judge to order the seizure and sale of real property to satisfy the debt.

6. c) The key difference between mortgages and deeds of trust concerns the procedures the lender is required to follow in order to foreclose. Generally, mortgages are foreclosed judicially; deeds of trust, nonjudicially.

7. a) Nonjudicial foreclosures are permitted if the security instrument contains a power of sale clause, which allows the trustee to sell the property if the borrower defaults.

8. d) The Truth in Lending Act requires lenders to make disclosures about loan costs and terms to consumer loan applicants. It does not set limits on interest rates or other charges, and it does not apply to loans for a commercial purpose. The statute is implemented by Regulation Z.

9. c) It's always legal to state the cash price or the annual percentage rate in an ad. But if certain other specific terms (such as the monthly payment amount) are stated in the ad, additional information must also be disclosed.

10. d) Predatory lending refers to practices that unscrupulous mortgage lenders and mortgage brokers use to take advantage of (prey upon) unsophisticated borrowers.

List of Cases

Nguyen v. Calhoun (2003) 105 Cal.App.4th 428

Chapter 14

Involuntary Liens

Outline

Introduction

In the last chapter, we examined voluntary liens—mortgages and deeds of trust. In this chapter, we turn to involuntary liens: liens that attach to and encumber property without the owner's consent. We'll begin with mechanic's liens, which are designed to protect contractors and subcontractors from property owners who fail to pay for improvements to their property. Next, we'll discuss liens associated with judicial actions, both before and after judgment. Then we'll discuss liens that the government uses to enforce collection of property taxes, special assessments, and income taxes. After that, we'll explain the lien priority rules. The final section of the chapter covers the homestead law, which gives homeowners limited protection against lien foreclosure.

Mechanic's Liens

A person who provides materials, labor, or other professional services for the improvement of real property may be entitled to a mechanic's lien, to help ensure that he gets paid for his labor or materials. A **mechanic's lien** (also known as a **construction lien**) is an involuntary, specific lien that attaches only to the property that is improved by the work or materials. (The distinction between specific and general liens is explained in Chapter 13.)

A mechanic's lien is intended to prevent the **unjust enrichment** of a property owner who benefits from labor or materials but fails to pay for them. If a contractor, subcontractor, or supplier isn't paid, she has a right to place a lien against the improved property for the reasonable value of the labor or materials provided. If necessary, the lienholder can force a sale of the property to satisfy the debt.

California lawmakers considered mechanic's liens so fundamental that they provided for them in the state constitution. Article XIV, Section 3 of the constitution states:

> Mechanics, persons furnishing materials, artisans, and laborers of every class, shall have a lien upon the property upon which they have bestowed labor or furnished material for the value of such labor done and material furnished; and the Legislature shall provide, by law, for the speedy and efficient enforcement of such liens.

Although mechanic's liens have a constitutional basis, the procedures for filing and enforcing them have been established by statute. The main provisions concerning mechanic's liens are in Civil Code §§ 8400 – 8494.

Mechanic's Lien Claimants

A construction or improvement project often involves a number of different workers and suppliers, and many of them may have the right to file a mechanic's lien. Civil Code § 8400 specifies the parties who can claim this type of lien. The list includes, but is not limited to, contractors, subcontractors, material suppliers, equipment lessors, laborers, and design professionals.

A potential lien claimant's work and/or materials must have been incorporated into or installed onto the property, or the lien will not be valid. (The property owner hasn't received any benefit unless her property has actually been improved with the materials or labor she ordered.) So a contractor, for example, won't have a valid lien if work never actually began on the project.

The property owner must have agreed—either directly or through an authorized agent—to pay for the materials or labor before a mechanic's lien can be filed. This isn't as much of a limitation as it might seem, however. For the purposes of creating a mechanic's lien, any contractor, subcontractor, architect, builder, or other person who has charge of all or part of the construction project is considered to be the owner's agent.

> **Example:** Contractor Jim hires a subcontractor, Flooring Specialists, to install hardwood floors in Mary's home. Flooring Specialists purchases the lumber for the hardwood floors from the Good Earth Lumber Company.
>
> After the floors are finished, Mary refuses to pay her bill. As a result, Contractor Jim isn't able to pay Flooring Specialists, and Flooring Specialists isn't able to pay the Good Earth Lumber Company.
>
> Contractor Jim (who has a contract directly with Mary) and Flooring Specialists (which has a contract with Mary's agent, Contractor Jim) are both eligible to file mechanic's liens against Mary's home. The Good Earth Lumber Company is also eligible for a mechanic's lien, even though its contract is with a subcontractor (Flooring Specialists), since the subcontractor is also considered to be Mary's agent in this context.

Creating a Mechanic's Lien

The statutory requirements for creating a mechanic's lien are detailed. If a claimant fails to follow all the rules, the right to a lien will be lost.

However, it's important to note that mechanic's liens aren't the only legal remedy available to contractors and suppliers who aren't paid for their work. If a lien is invalid because the claimant failed to meet a deadline or some other statutory requirement, she still may be able to sue the property owner for breach of contract. If she wins the suit, she may obtain a judgment lien (discussed later in this chapter) and foreclose on the property to satisfy the debt. But a mechanic's lien is a quicker and more efficient way to achieve the same result.

Notice Requirements. The rules concerning mechanic's liens involve several notice requirements and deadlines—some that apply to potential lien claimants and some that apply to the property owner.

Preliminary notice. Contractors who work directly for the property owner aren't required to provide the owner with any sort of formal notice of their status as a potential lien claimant. But eligible subcontractors and material suppliers are required to provide a **preliminary notice** of the right to claim a lien.

A subcontractor or supplier must serve the property owner, the original contractor, and any construction lender with the preliminary notice within 20 days after first providing labor or materials. The preliminary notice preserves the right to a mechanic's lien. It doesn't matter how many days the project takes, or how many times a supplier delivers materials to the site: the lien right is preserved as long as notice was given within 20 days of first providing the labor or materials.

Notices of completion and cessation. Sometimes work on a project stops because one of the parties involved is unhappy with the way things are going. A contractor might walk off a project because the owner hasn't been paying his bills. Or an owner might tell a contractor to stop working because of a disagreement over how the job is being carried out. Of course, another reason for stopping work may simply be that the job is finished.

Once work on a project has stopped (for any reason), the property owner may sign either a notice of completion or a notice of cessation and file it at the recorder's office in the county where the property is located. Both of these documents offer some protection to the property owner.

A **notice of completion** states that a project is finished. It must be filed within 15 days of the project's completion. A **notice of cessation** states that work had stopped on a project for at least 30 continuous days before the date the notice of cessation was recorded. These notices, if properly recorded, shorten the time contractors, subcontractors, and other potential mechanic's lien claimants have to file a claim of lien (see below).

Claim of Lien. To create a mechanic's lien, a **claim of lien** must be recorded in the county where the property is located. A contractor ordinarily has 90 days from the date the entire project was completed to file a claim of lien. However, if the property owner has recorded a notice of completion or notice of cessation, a direct contractor's window for filing a claim of lien is reduced to 60 days (30 days for a subcontractor).

Note that if a subcontractor or material supplier who served a preliminary notice on the property owner also filed a copy of that preliminary notice with the county recorder, the recorder's office will notify him if a notice of completion or notice of cessation is recorded.

Foreclosure

Within 90 days after filing a claim of lien, the holder of a mechanic's lien must do one of two things: 1) file a lien foreclosure action, or 2) grant a written extension of credit to the property owner.

If a foreclosure action is not brought within 90 days of filing the claim of lien and there is no extension of credit, the lien automatically becomes void and has no further effect. When a foreclosure action is filed, the lienholder should also have a lis pendens recorded. The lis pendens will give notice of her claim to any subsequent purchasers or encumbrancers of the property. (Foreclosure is discussed in Chapter 13.)

If the lienholder chooses to grant the owner an extension of credit rather than foreclosing on the lien, she must prepare and record a document that states all the terms of the extension. At the end of the credit term, if the amount owed is still outstanding, the lienholder must file a lien foreclosure action within 90 days.

Although the lienholder may grant more than one extension of credit, she must ultimately bring a foreclosure action within one year of completion of work on the project or the lien becomes void.

Terminating a Mechanic's Lien

A valid mechanic's lien is terminated when the debt underlying the lien is paid. Terminating an invalid lien, on the other hand, can be more complicated. Mechanic's liens are often invalid, because the contractor or subcontractor failed to meet one of the statutory requirements, such as filing the claim of lien by the applicable deadline. As noted above, any lien becomes void if the lien claimant fails to pursue foreclosure within 90 days of recording the lien claim (unless there's an extension of credit).

A void or invalid mechanic's lien will remain a cloud on the property owner's title until she takes some action to remove it. The first step in removing an invalid lien is sending a written request for removal to the claimant by certified mail. If the claimant refuses to

Evolving Law

Although California's mechanic's lien law is constitutionally based and long-established, it's still evolving. Proposed changes to the law would address a variety of issues, such as the problem of owners having to pay twice for contracted work. For example, a property owner may pay his contractor on time, but if the contractor fails to pay his subcontractors, the subcontractors are legally entitled to put liens on the property—even though the owner has already paid for the improvement. The owner then has to choose between paying for the work twice or having his property encumbered. (An owner who paid twice would be entitled to sue the contractor for reimbursement; but like most litigation, this would be time-consuming and expensive, and even after winning a judgment it might be difficult to collect the money.)

Another concern is that certain types of workers who add value to real property aren't eligible for mechanic's liens, which leads to some inequities. For instance, a landscaper who plants trees and shrubs is entitled to a mechanic's lien, but a landscaper who maintains the trees and shrubs generally is not.

In considering these and other issues, the legislature tries to balance the interests of contractors and material suppliers against the interests of property owners.

act or fails to respond, the owner may file a petition with the court for a decree to release the property from the mechanic's lien. In the case of a void lien, the owner does not need to send a request for removal before petitioning the court for a release decree, but a copy of the petition and supporting documents must be served on the lien claimant, either by process service or by registered mail. Whoever prevails at the hearing is entitled to reasonable attorney's fees.

Design Liens

A **design lien** is a type of lien available to design professionals—architects, engineers, and surveyors—who provide services under written contract during a construction project's planning phase. Design liens are very similar in function and purpose to mechanic's liens; the key difference is that a design lien is claimed before construction on the project starts and can be foreclosed only if construction never starts. Although the labor that a design professional puts into a project seems intangible, it can increase the property value significantly, and allowing design professionals to go unpaid would unjustly enrich the property owner.

Design liens are available only in certain situations. First, the lien must be placed on the property that was the subject of the design plans. Second, design liens cannot be used for single-family, owner-occupied homes that will cost less than $100,000 to build. Third, a design lien may not be recorded unless a building permit or other official project approval has been obtained in connection with the services provided by the design professional. A copy of the permit or approval document must be recorded along with the claim of lien.

Once a design professional knows (or has reason to know) that the project will not be built, she has 90 days to file a claim of lien for recording. She must have given the defaulting property owner a written demand for payment at least ten days before filing the claim of lien.

A design lien will automatically expire if:

- the lienholder hasn't filed a suit to enforce the lien within 90 days of recording the claim of lien, or
- construction work actually begins on the project.

Once construction work actually begins, the design lien terminates, but the design professional can then obtain a mechanic's lien to ensure that he's compensated for his work.

Case to Consider...

D'Orsay International Partners, a developer, owned property that it planned to develop into a 176-room hotel and retail complex. In 2001, D'Orsay entered into an agreement with Summit, a licensed general contractor. Over the next two years, Summit provided design-related services worth almost $850,000. However, construction on the D'Orsay project never started, because the financing fell through. No building permit was obtained, and no supplies were ever delivered to the property. In 2003, Summit recorded a mechanic's lien for $850,000 against D'Orsay's property. D'Orsay sought to have the mechanic's lien removed, because Summit never actually did any work on the property itself. Was the mechanic's lien valid? Was Summit entitled to a design lien instead of a mechanic's lien? *D'Orsay Internat. Partners v. Superior Court (Jeffrey C. Stone, Inc.)* (2004) 123 Cal.App.4th 836.

Attachment Liens

There are two types of involuntary liens that can arise in connection with litigation: attachment liens and judgment liens. We'll look at attachment liens first, and then at judgment liens.

An **attachment lien** is a general lien against the real or personal property of a defendant in a lawsuit. The lien is used to prevent the defendant from selling or giving away his property before it can be used to satisfy the claim on which the lawsuit is based. The property may be attached—an attachment lien may be created—even before the trial begins.

When Attachment is Allowed

Attachment liens are available only in connection with claims for more than $500 that arise out of a dispute over a business contract, as specified in California Code of Civil Procedure § 483.010. They aren't available for suits brought in small claims court.

The defendant in an attachment lien situation is often a business entity. However, an attachment lien may be allowed against a natural person if the underlying claim results from the person's conduct in connection with a business, trade, or profession.

An attachment lien is created by means of a **writ of attachment** issued by the court. Before issuing the writ, the court will hold a formal hearing to make sure that:

- the claim is one for which an attachment lien may be used,
- the property to be attached is not exempt from attachment, and
- the plaintiff's underlying claim is probably valid.

Once issued, a writ of attachment is recorded by the plaintiff. This creates a lien against any property owned by the defendant in the county in which the writ is recorded.

Property Subject to Attachment

Attachment liens are frequently placed on bank accounts and securities. Other types of property subject to attachment liens include:

- any interest in real property, except leasehold estates with less than one year remaining in the term;
- crops, uncut timber, and other farm products; and
- minerals, oil, or gas not yet extracted from the ground.

Note that California courts can attach only property located within California.

Terminating an Attachment Lien

Once an attachment lien has been created, the property remains attached even if it is sold or otherwise transferred or if the defendant dies. (As with other liens, the new owner takes title subject to the attachment lien.) However, an attachment lien may be terminated for a number of reasons. If the lawsuit ends with a judgment in the plaintiff's favor, the attachment lien will terminate by merging into the judgment lien. On the other hand, if the defendant receives a judgment in her favor—in other words, if the plaintiff loses the case—then the lien will be released.

Unless it is merged or released earlier, an attachment lien will expire three years from the date it is issued. However, the court may extend the lien term for up to one year if the plaintiff can show good cause for doing so. This one-year extension may be granted up to five times, so the attachment lien may last for up to eight years.

Judgment Liens

A **judgment lien** is an involuntary, general lien that is placed against property to secure the payment of a money judgment awarded by a court. While an attachment lien is used to secure property before a trial, a judgment lien is used to secure property after a trial.

Child Support Liens

California, like many states, has become quite aggressive in its efforts to collect child support from "deadbeat" parents who fail to fulfill their responsibilities, as this statement on the website of the San Mateo County Department of Child Support Services suggests: "The San Mateo County DCSS aggressively enforces all child support obligations within our county. One effective method of assuring that child support is paid is the recording of liens on real property owned by the obligor parent. A real property lien is recorded in all child support cases enforced by the Department. Property liens are a security for any past due child support debt that has accrued as a result of non-payment of the child support obligation."

A judgment lien is created when a judgment creditor records a document called an **abstract of judgment** in a county where the judgment debtor owns property.

> **Example:** Claire owns property in Los Angeles County. John sues Claire for personal injuries sustained in a car accident and wins a judgment for $18,000. Claire has very little money in the bank and can't pay the judgment right away. So John files an abstract of judgment for recording in Los Angeles County. If John forecloses on his lien, John's judgment will be paid from the proceeds of the sale of Claire's property.

Judgment liens are also available to enforce awards of spousal or child support. In that situation, a judgment lien is created by recording a certified copy of the support order.

Property Affected by Judgment Liens

Because it is a general lien, a judgment lien attaches to all of the debtor's property in the county where an abstract of judgment (or support order) is recorded. If the debtor owns property in more than one county, an abstract must be recorded in each county separately.

A judgment lien attaches to any interest in real property, including present or future interests, vested or contingent, legal or equitable. (See Chapter 4 for a discussion of interests in real property.) And once an abstract has been recorded, the lien will also attach to any property in the county that the debtor might acquire in the future, while the lien remains in effect.

> **Example:** Let's return to Claire and John. A few years after John's judgment lien attaches to Claire's property in Los Angeles County, Claire's rich uncle dies and leaves her a remainder interest in some other property in Los Angeles. John's lien automatically attaches to Claire's newly acquired remainder without any other action on John's part.

What if the judgment creditor lives in one state, and the judgment debtor lives in another state? The Full Faith and Credit Clause of the U.S. Constitution (Art. IV, § 1) requires that a judgment issued by a court in another state be given the same effect and consideration as a judgment rendered in California. As long as the other state's court had jurisdiction over the parties and the subject matter, and all parties were given reasonable notice and a chance to be heard, the judgment will be honored in California.

Example: Now let's suppose that Claire lives in Los Angeles and John lives in Las Vegas, Nevada. The lawsuit stems from a car accident that occurred while Claire was driving a car in Las Vegas on vacation. The lawsuit was eventually heard and decided in Clark County, Nevada. Claire doesn't own any property in Nevada but, thanks to the Full Faith and Credit Clause, John can obtain a judgment lien against Claire's property in California. However, he will need to record an abstract of judgment in Los Angeles County—not in Nevada.

A judgment creditor can foreclose on a judgment lien by obtaining a **writ of execution** from the court. The foreclosure process is similar to the judicial foreclosure of a mortgage (see Chapter 13). There must be a notice of levy and a notice of sale, and unless the debtor prevents foreclosure by paying off the judgment, the property will be auctioned to the highest bidder at a sheriff's sale.

Renewal and Termination

Once created, a judgment lien remains valid even if the property is transferred. Under California Code of Civil Procedure § 697.310, the lien will last for ten years from the date that the court clerk entered the judgment into the public record, unless the lien is released. The judgment debtor may get her property released from the lien by paying the amount owed and obtaining a certificate of satisfaction from the judgment creditor.

After at least five years, but before the ten-year period is up, the judgment creditor may file an application to renew the judgment lien. This will renew the lien for another ten years from the date the application was filed. The priority of the lien will continue to relate back to the date of the original entry of judgment.

There's an important exception to these rules. Judgment liens based on child support obligations are exempted from expiration and renewal requirements. In other words, this type of lien never expires and will remain attached to the property until the debt has been paid.

Tax Liens

Federal, state, and local governments may place liens against real property to ensure collection of various types of taxes. The most common tax liens you'll encounter are those based on annual property taxes and special assessments. Unpaid federal income taxes will also create liens against a taxpayer's property.

Property Taxes

Annual **property taxes**, also called **general real estate taxes**, are the largest single source of income for local governments. All real property is taxable unless specifically exempted. Property owned by churches, hospitals, or other charitable organizations is usually entirely exempt, and there are various other full and partial exemptions as well.

Property is taxable in the county where it is located, regardless of where the owner resides.

> **Example:** Peter owns property in San Diego County but lives in Orange County. The San Diego property will be taxed based on San Diego County's tax rates. Peter is obligated to pay those property taxes, even though he lives in Orange County.

Assessment. The amount a property owner must pay in annual property taxes depends on the value of the property. For this reason, property taxes are sometimes referred to as **ad valorem** taxes. ("Ad valorem" means "according to value" in Latin.) Valuing a property for tax purposes is known as **assessment**. Assessments are carried out by the county assessor in accordance with the state constitution, the Revenue and Tax Code, and other state and local property tax rules.

When property is assessed, it is placed on the **assessment roll**, which is a county's official list of all taxable property within its boundaries. The assessed value is then multiplied by the annual tax rate to determine the amount the property owner must pay in property taxes for the year in question.

In 1978, California voters approved Proposition 13, which amended the state constitution to limit both tax rates on real property, and annual increases in the assessed value of real property.

As a result of Proposition 13, ad valorem property tax rates generally cannot exceed 1% of a property's assessed value. (Actual tax rates may be slightly over 1%, since certain kinds of bonded indebtedness aren't subject to the 1% limit.) And a property's assessed value generally cannot be increased by more than 2% per year, except:

- when the property is transferred to a new owner, or
- when new construction is completed.

In other words, as long as ownership doesn't change hands and there's no new construction on the property, the assessed value can't go up more than 2%, even if the market value increases much more than that in the course of the year. However, when there is a change in ownership, or when new construction occurs, the property is assessed at its **full cash value**, which is essentially the fair market value. A property's **base year value** is its full cash value as of the last date it changed owners (or when construction was completed, if it's a new or remodeled home).

> **Example:** Helen bought her property at the beginning of the fiscal year. She paid $500,000 for it, which is the base year value. It's also the assessed value for her first year of ownership. Helen ends up paying about 1% of the assessed value ($5,000) in property taxes that year.
>
> Over the course of the year, Helen's property appreciates dramatically. Its market value goes from $500,000 to $600,000, a 20% increase. But because of Proposition 13, the assessed value can't increase more than 2%, which means that Helen's assessed value only rises from $500,000 to $510,000. Therefore, $510,000 is the figure that will be used to determine how much Helen must pay in property taxes for her second year of ownership.
>
> If property values continue to increase, the longer Helen owns the property, the greater the difference between the assessed value and the market value will be. If Helen sells the property, it will be reassessed at its fair market value again, and the new owner's tax bill will be based on this significantly higher assessment.

Certain types of transfers don't trigger reassessment of the property at its full cash value. For example, some transfers between parents and children are exempt from reassessment.

Supplemental assessments. When property is reassessed upon transfer, a supplemental assessment is added to the tax roll, and a supplemental bill is sent to the new owner. If the supplemental assessment takes place between January 1 and May 31, two supplemental bills will be sent. If the supplemental assessment takes place between June 1 and December 31, one supplemental bill will be sent. (This supplemental tax bill must be paid in addition to the regular annual property tax bill.)

Change in Ownership Statement. A person who acquires an interest in real property must file a **change in ownership statement** with the county recorder or assessor at the time the transfer is recorded, or within 45 days of the change in ownership if the transfer is not recorded. Failure to file a change in ownership statement may result in fines.

Lien Foreclosure. In California, anyone who owns taxable property on the lien date is liable for annual property taxes. The **lien date** is the previous January 1; for example, the lien date for the fiscal year running from July 1, 2016 through June 30, 2017 was January 1, 2016. On that date, at 12:01 AM, a lien for the 2016 – 2017 property taxes automatically attached to all taxable property.

Property tax bills are due in two equal installments, one on November 1 and one on February 1, becoming delinquent on December 10 and April 10. If a property owner fails to pay her bill on time, the state will impose a penalty. If the taxes and penalties remain unpaid, the state will eventually foreclose on the property to pay the debt.

California taxpayers are given a five-year grace period before property is foreclosed on because of delinquent property taxes. After taxes have been delinquent for five years, the property is considered to be **tax-defaulted**, and the foreclosure process begins. The owner must receive notice of the impending foreclosure sale at least 45 days before the sale takes place. The tax collector's office must also attempt to personally contact the owner at least 10 days before the sale takes place, and if that attempt is unsuccessful, must attempt to serve written notice on the owner at least five days before the sale.

The taxpayer has the right to redeem the property up until the time of sale by paying the delinquent amount, any accrued interest, and other costs and penalties. Once the property has been sold at auction, the purchaser takes title immediately. At that point, the former owner has no more redemption rights in the property.

Special Assessments

Local governments may levy taxes known as **special assessments** to pay for specific improvement projects such as street paving, sidewalks, drainage systems, and sewers. The government entity issues bonds and sells them to investors to raise money for the project, and it repays the investors out of the special assessment funds collected from local property owners. In California, certain types of special assessments can be imposed only with local voter approval.

As a general rule, special assessments are levied only against the properties that actually benefit from the improvements. The assessments are **apportioned**, meaning that they are divided proportionately between the property owners, based on the value or benefit that each property receives.

California has several statutes that authorize special assessments, including the Vrooman Street Act, the Improvement Act of 1911, and the Improvement Bond Act of

1915. One statute, the **Mello-Roos Community Facilities Act of 1982**, was enacted after Proposition 13's limitations on ad valorem taxes made it necessary for local governments to find new ways to fund infrastructure development and community services.

Mello-Roos assessments can be used for a greater variety of improvements, facilities, and services than traditional special assessments. Also, Mello-Roos assessments are not apportioned and need not directly benefit the taxed properties. As long as a two-thirds majority of district residents has approved the assessment, every property within the boundaries of the district will be subject to it.

Special assessments, including assessments levied under the Mello-Roos Act, create involuntary, specific liens against the taxed properties. If a property owner fails to pay a special assessment, the property can be foreclosed on to collect the money owed.

Mello-Roos liens and some other special assessment liens have an accelerated foreclosure process. Foreclosure may begin after a payment has been delinquent for 180 days—a much shorter grace period than the five years allowed for delinquent general property taxes (see above). Because of this, Civil Code § 1102.6(b) requires sellers to make a good faith effort to provide buyers with a "Notice of Special Tax." This disclosure explains that the property lies within a special taxing district and may be subject to Mello-Roos liens or other special assessment liens for which accelerated foreclosure is allowed.

Federal Tax Liens

Income tax liens are involuntary, general liens. If a taxpayer fails to pay his federal income taxes, it creates a lien for the unpaid amount against all of his personal and real property. The lien also attaches to any property that the taxpayer may acquire in the future.

Although the income tax lien arises automatically, the Internal Revenue Service (IRS) will file a **notice of tax lien** with the county recorder in the county where the property is located. This notice establishes the IRS's lien position (see the discussion of lien priority, below).

To remove the lien, the taxpayer must pay the entire delinquent tax amount, along with any penalties and interest that may have accrued. The IRS will then issue a certificate of discharge.

Unpaid estate or gift taxes also create liens. Unlike income tax liens, these are specific liens that attach only to the estate property or gift property.

Lien Priority

A single piece of real property may have several different liens against it at the same time. For example, a home might be encumbered by a mortgage, a mechanic's lien, a special assessment, a property tax lien, and a judgment lien. If the homeowner defaults on any of these liens, and the property must be sold to satisfy the debt, which creditors will be paid first from the proceeds of the forced sale? And what happens if the sale proceeds aren't enough to satisfy all of the liens against the property?

The order in which creditors will be paid is known as **lien priority**. As a general rule, lien priority is determined by the date of recording; in other words, the first lien recorded is paid first, the second lien recorded is paid second, and so on. However, the priority of certain types of liens is not based on recording date. Property tax and special assessment liens typically have priority over all other liens. (In relation to each other, property tax liens and special assessment liens are equal in priority.) Also, the priority of mechanic's liens depends on the date work was actually started on the project, rather than the date the claim of lien was recorded.

> **Example:** Bill's property has the following liens against it:
>
> - a mortgage recorded February 15, 2005;
> - a judgment lien recorded August 10, 2011;
> - a second mortgage recorded April 27, 2012;
> - a property tax lien that attached January 1, 2016;
> - a lien for child support recorded March 6, 2016; and
> - a mechanic's lien recorded on March 13, 2016, for work begun on February 14, 2016.
>
> When Bill fails to pay his mortgage, the mortgage company decides to foreclose on his property. The liens will be paid from the sale proceeds in the following order:
>
> 1. the property tax lien,
> 2. the 2005 mortgage,
> 3. the judgment lien,
> 4. the 2012 mortgage,
> 5. the mechanic's lien, and
> 6. the child support lien.

The proceeds of a foreclosure sale aren't prorated so that each lienholder receives at least partial payment. If the sale proceeds aren't sufficient to pay off the costs of foreclosure and all of the liens against the property, a lienholder with lower priority may be left empty-handed. The proceeds are applied first to the foreclosure costs, and then to the lien with highest priority. If there are any proceeds left over after the first lien is paid off, they're applied to the lien with next highest priority, and so on.

The Homestead Law

California's homestead law (Code of Civil Procedure §§ 704.710 – 704.995) gives homeowners limited protection against foreclosure by judgment creditors. The homestead law protects the equity in a debtor's principal residence, or **homestead**, up to a specified amount.

In California, the homestead exemption amounts are as follows:

- $75,000 generally; or
- $100,000 if the debtor or resident spouse of the debtor is a member of a family unit and, at the time of the sale, at least one member of the family unit owns no interest or only a community property interest in the property; or
- $175,000 if the debtor or resident spouse of the debtor is unable to work due to a mental or physical disability, is 65 or older, or is 55 or older with less than $25,000 in income ($35,000 if married).

A judgment creditor cannot foreclose on a homestead unless the property is worth enough to cover all of the liens against it and the homestead exemption amount.

Example: Halbrook Construction sues McLaughlin over a contract dispute and wins a $44,000 judgment. When McLaughlin fails to pay the judgment, Halbrook records an abstract of judgment and a judgment lien attaches to McLaughlin's home. Although the home is worth $630,000, it is now encumbered by $614,000 in liens (a $570,000 mortgage and the $44,000 judgment lien). The $75,000 homestead exemption and the $614,000 in liens total $689,000. Since that total exceeds the home's value of $630,000, Halbrook won't be allowed to foreclose on its judgment lien.

The homestead exemption provides protection only against judgment liens. It does not offer protection against:

- mortgages or deeds of trust,
- mechanic's liens,
- tax liens,
- liens for child support or spousal maintenance obligations, or
- liens imposed by a condominium or homeowners association.

> ### ▶ Homestead Sweet Homestead
>
> A homeowner can easily obtain a homestead declaration form from a stationery store, fill it out, sign it before a notary, and then file it with the county recorder. Alternatively, a homeowner can have a homestead filing service prepare the document and take care of the filing. A consumer protection statute added to the Business and Professions Code limits the maximum charge for this service to $25.
>
> Before this statute, some homestead filing services made exaggerated claims about the value of a homestead declaration. For example, they stated or implied that a declaration was a requirement for homestead protection, or that a declaration would prevent foreclosure. California law now bans misleading promotional materials and requires a statement that the homestead declaration is optional and can't prevent a forced sale.
>
> The statute exempts attorneys who provide filing services. But state bar rules forbid lawyers from making misleading representations, so the statutory exemption doesn't have much effect. A case in point: From early 1988 until the end of 1992, attorney Ivan O.B. Morse mailed about four million "homestead information sheets" to homeowners with offers to prepare declarations for them. Morse failed to make the kind of disclosures required by the statute.
>
> Morse's return on his mass mailing was pretty good. He prepared upwards of a hundred thousand declarations and took in almost $2,000,000. In an action brought against him by the state attorney general, Morse claimed that only $150,000 to $200,000 of that amount was profit. Still, not a bad haul—until one factors in the $800,000 fine the court assessed him for misleading the public.

In California, a homeowner is automatically protected by the homestead law; it isn't necessary to record a document or take other formal steps to establish protection. This means that a debtor may claim the homestead exemption after the property has already become the subject of a judgment lien foreclosure proceeding. However, the debtor must reside in the home at the time the automatic exemption is claimed. In addition, the automatic exemption is available only in a forced sale of the property; it does not protect the proceeds of a voluntary sale.

Instead of relying on the automatic homestead exemption, a debtor may choose to record a **declaration of homestead** in the county where the property is located. A declaration of homestead provides greater protection than the automatic exemption, since it applies to a voluntary sale of the property as well as a forced sale. If the debtor voluntarily sells her home, the declaration of homestead will protect the sale proceeds for up to six months, which will give her a chance to reinvest the money in a new home.

In addition, there is no residency requirement with a declared homestead. Although the homeowner must reside on the property when the declaration is recorded, the exemption will be effective later even if he isn't currently living there.

A person may have only one homestead at a time. If she's already recorded a declaration of homestead on one property and wishes to make a new property her homestead, she can simply record a declaration of homestead for the new property (with or without first recording a **declaration of abandonment** for the first property).

A declaration of homestead may be filed by any person living on the homestead property who owns an interest in the property. The interest need not be fee simple ownership.

Case to Consider...

Mr. and Mrs. Appel hired the Fisch law firm (Fisch) to help them with their estate planning. In 1989, following their lawyers' advice, the Appels established a revocable family trust, with the Appels themselves as trustees; they also quitclaimed their home to the trust, so that the trust held title to it. A year later, the Appels, in their capacity as trustees, recorded a declaration of homestead on the property.

In 1991, the Fisch law firm (which apparently hadn't been paid) obtained a judgment against the trust. In 1992, the law firm foreclosed on the home to collect its judgment. The Appels claimed that they were entitled to the $75,000 homestead exemption. Fisch argued that a trust was not a natural person and therefore was not entitled to protection under the homestead law. The Appels argued that because they could revoke the trust, they were trustors as well as trustees. As trustors, they had a contingent reversionary interest in the property. Were the Appels entitled to the homestead exemption? *Fisch, Spiegler, Ginsburg & Ladner v. Appel* (1992) 10 Cal.App.4th 1810.

Although the homestead law is an important safeguard for families, its reach is quite limited. On the whole, involuntary liens are an effective collection tool for creditors. Unlike other assets, land can't be concealed or moved, and that makes a lien against real property one of the best forms of security available. Whether the underlying debt is a contractor's bill, a court judgment, or taxes owed, the lien makes it more likely that the money will ultimately be paid.

Case Law in Depth

The following case involves some of the legal issues discussed in this chapter. Read through the facts and consider the questions in light of what you have learned. Then read what the court actually decided.

Lambert v. Superior Court (MacEwen) (1991) 228 Cal.App.3d 383

In June 1988, the Lamberts hired contractor MacEwen to make some major alterations to their home in San Rafael. The contract was for $327,705, and the work was to be finished within a year. Instead, two years passed and there were several change orders. (A change order is official authorization by the property owner to change the price, timing, or construction requirements outlined in the original contract.) Eventually, the Lamberts fired MacEwen and hired another contractor to finish the job.

In 1990, MacEwen filed a mechanic's lien against the Lamberts' property for $117,328, which represented unpaid change orders of over $28,000 and nearly $89,000 in delay and interest damages. According to the parties' contract, MacEwen was entitled to bill delay damages as "extra work."

While MacEwen was waiting for the arbitration required under the contract to begin, the Lamberts filed a motion to remove the mechanic's lien on the grounds that they had already paid the contractor over $361,000—more than the original contract price, and more than enough to cover the change orders and all finished work.

The trial court denied the Lamberts' motion to remove the lien, and they appealed.

The questions:

Under California's mechanic's lien law, did MacEwen have a right to a mechanic's lien against the Lamberts' property for unpaid delay and interest penalties? Why or why not?

The court's answers:

"This petition presents novel and substantive questions about recording and removing mechanic's liens.

"Article XIV, section 3, of the California Constitution provides that '[m]echanics, persons furnishing materials, artisans, and laborers of every class, shall have a lien upon the property upon which they have bestowed labor or furnished material for the value of such labor done and material furnished...'

"Had the [lower] court probed the contractor's arguments, as we have done in this proceeding, it would have seen that validity of the lien turns not on accounting, but on a legal issue of first impression in California: whether contractor's lien could include almost $89,000 in 'delay/interest damages.'... [Contractor] directed us to a provision of the contract which permitted delay damages to be billed as extra work.

"Civil Code section 3123 permits a mechanic's lien for 'the reasonable value of the labor, services, equipment, or materials furnished...' At least for almost $89,000 of the mechanic's lien, the court could have decided probable validity of the lien by answering one question: may delay damages be considered part of the reasonable value of labor and services?

"Contractor has presented no authority for recording a mechanic's lien to recover damages based on delay.

"We agree that Civil Code section 3123 does not permit a lien for delay damages, whether or not the contract describes them as extra work. The function of the mechanic's lien is to secure reimbursement for services and materials actually contributed to a construction site, not to facilitate recovery of consequential damages..."

The result:

The lower court erred in dismissing the Lamberts' motion to remove the lien.

Chapter Summary

- A person who provides construction materials, labor, or other professional services may be entitled to a mechanic's lien against the property if he isn't paid. Potential lien claimants who don't contract directly with the owner must give the owner a preliminary notice of the right to claim a lien. A claim of lien must be filed by the applicable deadline.

- A design lien is available to architects, professional engineers, and land surveyors who provide services during the planning stage of construction. A design lien can only be claimed after a building permit is issued, but before actual construction has started.

- A plaintiff may request an attachment lien against a defendant's property. The lien prevents the defendant from transferring the property before it can be used to satisfy a judgment against the defendant.

- When a court awards a money judgment in a lawsuit, the winning party may record an abstract of judgment to create a judgment lien against the losing party's property. The lien will also attach to any property the debtor acquires in the county in the future.

- Property taxes are ad valorem taxes (based on the taxed property's value) that create a lien against the taxed property. California's Proposition 13 limits property taxes to approximately 1% of the property's assessed value and limits increases in assessed value to 2% per year (except when ownership changes hands or new construction occurs).

- Local governments use special assessments to fund certain improvements. Most special assessments are levied only against property that benefits from the improvements. A special assessment creates a lien on the property it's levied against.

- Unpaid federal income taxes create a general lien against all of the taxpayer's personal and real property.

- When property is foreclosed on to satisfy a debt, the lienholders are paid according to lien priority, which is generally determined by the date of recording. However, the priority of mechanic's liens depends on when work on the project began, and property tax and special assessment liens take priority over all other liens.

- California's homestead law protects homeowners from creditors by exempting a certain amount of equity in the homestead (principal residence) from judgment lien foreclosure.

Key Terms

- **Mechanic's lien** – A lien available to a person who provides materials, labor, or other professional services that improve the value of real property.

- **Design lien** – A lien available only to architects, professional engineers, and land surveyors who provide services during the planning phase of construction. Once construction begins, the design lien terminates, but it can be replaced with a mechanic's lien.

- **Attachment lien** – A lien available to a plaintiff in a pending lawsuit against the defendant's property, which prevents the defendant from transferring the property before it can be used to satisfy a possible judgment for the plaintiff.

- **Writ of attachment** – A court order creating an attachment lien, granted only after a hearing to determine the amount and validity of the attachment.

- **Judgment lien** – A lien against property to secure payment of a court-awarded judgment, such as money damages from a civil trial; also available to enforce awards of spousal or child support.

- **Abstract of judgment** – A document recorded to create a judgment lien.

- **Ad valorem taxes** – Taxes that are based on the value of the taxed property.

- **Full cash value** – Under Proposition 13, the fair market value of a home or new construction used to determine its assessed value for taxation purposes.

- **Supplemental assessment** – An additional assessment of property taxes a new owner is required to pay because of the reassessment triggered by the change in ownership.

- **Special assessment** – A tax levied by a local government against properties that benefit from a specific improvement such as street paving, sewers, or irrigation.

- **Mello-Roos lien** – A lien based on a type of special assessment allowed under the Mello-Roos Community Facilities Act, which allows communities to create special districts to finance certain kinds of improvements or services.

- **Lien priority** – The order in which lienholders will be paid from the proceeds of a forced sale.

- **Homestead** – A dwelling occupied by the owner or the owner's spouse as a principal residence.

- **Homestead exemption** – The amount of a homeowner's equity that the homestead law protects against lien foreclosure.

- **Declaration of homestead** – A document recorded to provide more protection than the automatic homestead exemption; it protects the proceeds of a voluntary sale as well as a forced sale, and the homeowner does not have to reside on the property when the exemption is claimed.

Chapter Quiz

1. To be the basis for a valid mechanic's lien, the labor or materials must be:
   a) delivered to the property
   b) incorporated into the property
   c) valued at more than $500
   d) None of the above

2. AJ Siding Company makes three deliveries to a construction project. To preserve its right to a mechanic's lien, AJ Siding must serve a preliminary notice to the property owner, original contractor, and construction lender:
   a) each time it delivers materials to the construction site
   b) only once
   c) within 20 days of first providing the materials
   d) Both b) and c)

3. A homeowner files a notice of completion when construction on his property is finished. This means that a subcontractor who has had direct contact with the owner must file a claim of lien, if necessary, within:
   a) 90 days
   b) 60 days
   c) 30 days
   d) 10 days

4. A judgment lien will ordinarily expire after ten years unless it is renewed. However, this rule does not apply to a lien:
   a) for money awarded in a civil trial
   b) to enforce child support
   c) against residential property
   d) All of the above

5. In California, the lien date for property taxes is:
   a) June 1
   b) July 1
   c) January 1
   d) None of the above

6. A tax imposed by the local government on properties that benefit from a road improvement project is a:
   a) levy tax
   b) value-added tax
   c) supplemental assessment
   d) special assessment

7. Assessments levied under the Mello-Roos Community Facilities Act are different from other special assessments in that they:
   a) are ad valorem taxes
   b) do not have to directly benefit the taxed property
   c) are apportioned
   d) do not create liens

8. A piece of property has the following liens against it. Which lien will have first priority if the property is foreclosed on?
   a) A mortgage recorded on January 12, 2007
   b) A mechanic's lien recorded on December 4, 2015
   c) A property tax lien that attached on January 1, 2016
   d) A judgment lien recorded on March 2, 2016

9. The homestead exemption may provide protection against foreclosure of a:
   a) judgment lien
   b) mortgage
   c) lien for child support
   d) property tax lien

10. In California, the general homestead exemption is:
    a) $25,000
    b) $50,000
    c) $75,000
    d) $150,000

Chapter Answer Key

Chapter Quiz Answers:

1. b) Until labor or materials have actually been incorporated into the property, the contractor or supplier cannot create a valid mechanic's lien.

2. d) To preserve its right to a mechanic's lien, AJ Siding must serve the preliminary notice within 20 days after first delivering materials to the site. Additional notices are unnecessary, even if there are multiple deliveries.

3. c) Generally, if the owner files a notice of completion, contractors have 60 days in which to file a claim of lien; subcontractors have 30 days.

4. b) Judgment liens based on child support obligations do not expire and are exempted from renewal requirements. A child support lien will remain in effect until the support is paid.

5. c) In California, the property tax lien date (the date the lien attaches to property) is January 1 of each year.

6. d) Taxes levied by municipalities against certain properties or neighborhoods that benefit from specific improvements to roads, sidewalks, sewers, irrigation, and similar items are called special assessments.

7. b) Mello-Roos allows communities to finance certain types of capital projects by creating a special district and taxing all of the properties within it, whether or not they benefit from the project directly.

8. c) A lien for delinquent property taxes will have first priority, even over liens that attached earlier.

9. a) The homestead exemption does not apply to the foreclosure of a mortgage or deed of trust, a mechanic's lien, a tax lien, a lien for child or spousal support, or a lien imposed by a condominium or homeowners association.

10. c) In California, the general homestead exemption is $75,000. The exemption is $100,000 if the debtor or the debtor's resident spouse is a member of a family unit and, at the time of the sale, at least one member of the family owns no interest or only a community interest in the property. It's $175,000 if the debtor or the debtor's resident spouse is physically or mentally disabled, is 65 or older, or is 55 or older with less than $25,000 in income ($35,000 if married).

Cases to Consider... Answers:

Mechanic's Liens

D'Orsay Internat. Partners v. Superior Court (Jeffrey C. Stone, Inc.) (2004) 123 Cal.App. 4th 836. The court ruled that Summit's lien was invalid. Mechanic's liens can be obtained only in connection with projects on which construction actually begins, and in this case that never happened. Design liens can be claimed for planning work if construction never begins, but in this case the Summit had recorded a mechanic's lien. The court did not rule on whether Summit would have been entitled to a design lien, but it did note that exceptions to the construction commencement requirement previously available under the mechanic's lien statute had been rendered moot by the addition of the design lien statute. In order to force D'Orsay to pay for the planning work, Summit would have to sue D'Orsay for breach of contract.

Homestead Law

Fisch, Spiegler, Ginsburg & Ladner v. Appel (1992) 10 Cal.App.4th 1810. The court ruled in favor of the Appels. The homestead law applies to any interest in real property, "whether present or future, vested or contingent, legal or equitable." Even though the homestead law only protects natural persons, and the title to the property was held by the trust, the Appels had interests in the property sufficient to allow homestead protection.

List of Cases

D'Orsay Internat. Partners v. Superior Court (Jeffrey C. Stone, Inc.) (2004) 123 Cal.App. 4th 836
Fisch, Spiegler, Ginsburg & Ladner v. Appel (1992) 10 Cal.App.4th 1810
Lambert v. Superior Court (MacEwen) (1991) 228 Cal.App.3d 383

Chapter 15

Rights and Duties of Landowners

Outline

I. Protecting Rights of Possession and Use
- A. Trespass
  - 1. Types of trespasses
  - 2. Signs and fences
  - 3. Remedies and penalties
  - 4. Premises liability and trespassers
- B. Nuisance
- C. Encroachments

II. Adverse Possession
- A. Requirements for adverse possession
- B. Adverse possession and government property
- C. Adverse possession and encroachments

III. Easements
- A. Distinguishing easements from other interests
- B. Types of easements
  - 1. Appurtenant easements
  - 2. Easements in gross
- C. Creation of easements
- D. Maintenance and repair
- E. Termination of easements
- F. Easements vs. licenses

IV. Disputes Between Neighbors
- A. Trees
  - 1. Trees owned by one neighbor
  - 2. Boundary trees

Introduction

As we said in Chapter 3, real property ownership includes a "bundle of rights": the rights to possess, use, enjoy, encumber, will, sell, or do nothing at all with the land. But a landowner's rights aren't absolute; they're limited by the rights of other property owners and the general public, and that often causes conflicts. Landowners frequently clash with their neighbors and other parties over fences, rights-of-way, encroachments, and similar issues.

In this chapter, we'll consider the legal rules used to resolve these types of disputes. We'll begin by discussing a landowner's rights of possession and use, and related property law concepts such as trespass. Next, we'll explain some limitations on the landowner's rights, including adverse possession and easements. Then we'll examine some of the problems that arise between neighboring landowners, such as conflicts over trees and liability for damage caused by water.

Protecting Rights of Possession and Use

There are two rights that are fundamental to real property ownership: the right to the **use and enjoyment** of the property, and the right to **exclusive possession**. Within the property's boundaries, the landowner has dominion, like the monarch of a very small kingdom. She can prevent others from entering the property or otherwise interfering with her possession and use of it.

Of course, every landowner is also a neighbor to others, and thus has responsibilities that correspond to her rights. She has a duty to refrain from interfering with her neighbors' use and enjoyment of their property, and with their exclusive possession of it.

In this section of the chapter, we're going to examine the basic rules that protect a landowner's possession of the property against intrusion and interference. Specifically, we'll consider the rules concerning:

- trespasses,
- nuisances, and
- encroachments.

As you'll see, these three legal concepts overlap to a certain extent. A trespass may involve a nuisance, a nuisance may involve a trespass, and an encroachment may be either a trespass or a nuisance.

Trespass

A **trespass** is an unlawful entry onto another person's land. It's an entry without permission or legal authority, violating the landowner's right to exclusive possession. (In the case of leased property, it violates the tenant's right to exclusive possession.)

A trespass is considered to be a tort, which is an injury against a person or property (see Chapter 1). Under certain circumstances, a trespass may also be considered a criminal act.

Types of Trespasses. Of course, the term trespassing is familiar from "No Trespassing" signs that are often posted on property to discourage intruders. Climbing over a fence and walking around or engaging in other activities on someone else's land is a clear example of a trespass.

> **Example:** Mark owns some industrial property with a warehouse on it. One night some teenagers sneak onto the property and have a party in the warehouse. The teenagers have committed a trespass against Mark, violating his right of exclusive possession.

While we've described the most obvious type of trespass, the legal concept is broader than that. Trespass also includes the physical invasion of property with an object or a substance.

> **Example:** Glen keeps his gigantic RV parked behind his house. He doesn't realize that the vehicle is straddling the property line, so that the back end is on his neighbor's property. The presence of the RV on the neighbor's property is a trespass.

A trespass may be a one-time event, like the party in the warehouse, or it may be a **continuing trespass**, which occurs when a person fails to remove himself or an object from another's land. The RV parked on the neighbor's property is an example of a continuing trespass.

Signs and Fences. A property owner doesn't have to post "No Trespassing" signs or put up a fence to be entitled to protection against trespassers. That doesn't mean that signs and fences serve no purpose, however. As a practical matter, they make people less inclined to trespass. And as a legal matter, they can affect how a judge or jury views the relative rights and obligations of the trespasser and the landowner (see the discussion of premises liability, below). Signs and fences can also affect whether a trespasser is subject to criminal prosecution (again, see below).

Remedies and Penalties. Tort liability for trespass generally doesn't require physical damage to the property. The trespass itself, the violation of the right of exclusive possession, is a harm. Trespass is actionable *per se*, which means that the act itself is wrong and may be the basis for a lawsuit, even if no physical damage occurs.

> **Example:** Let's go back to the earlier example involving Glen, whose RV is parked on his neighbor's property. The RV is on a part of the neighbor's property that she's not currently using in any way, and it's not causing any harm. Even so, if Glen refuses to move the RV, the neighbor can sue him for trespass.

If a one-time trespass didn't cause any actual harm, it probably wouldn't be worth it to the landowners to sue, because the court would order the trespasser to pay only nominal damages (a small sum) to the landowner. But in the case of a continuing trespass, like the one in the RV example, the landowner could ask the court for an injunction ordering the trespasser to take whatever steps are necessary to end the trespass. The court could also impose a fine for each day that the trespasser or the object remains on the property unlawfully, even though it's not causing harm.

When a trespass has in fact harmed the property or caused a financial loss, then the trespasser may be ordered to pay compensatory damages to the landowner.

> **Example:** Glen has been keeping a large barrel of corrosive chemicals in the back of the RV he's parked on his neighbor's property. The chemicals corrode the barrel, leak out of the RV, saturate the soil, and end up killing the neighbor's plants and destroying $10,000 worth of landscaping. In addition to issuing an injunction ordering Glen to move the RV and fining him if he fails to do so, the court could require Glen to pay damages to cover all of the costs related to cleaning up the chemical spill and restoring the landscaping.

Criminal penalties. Certain types of willful trespasses are crimes (see California Penal Code §§ 602–602.8). For these acts, a trespasser can face fines and imprisonment in addition to being sued by the landowner.

The Penal Code's list of criminal trespasses includes many activities, ranging from vandalism to clam digging. In some cases, whether a particular trespass is a criminal act may depend on the presence of fencing or signs. For example, Penal Code § 602.8 makes it a criminal infraction to willfully enter land without written permission if the land is either under cultivation or enclosed with a fence, or if there are "No Trespassing" signs posted (three signs for each mile of exterior boundary, plus a sign on each road or trail serving as an entrance).

Premises Liability and Trespassers. As you've seen, a trespasser can be held liable to the landowner and required to pay damages. Perhaps surprisingly, there are also circumstances in which a landowner can be liable to a trespasser.

 Attractive Nuisances

You may have heard the term "attractive nuisance." This relates to trespassing and premises liability, rather than to the rules concerning nuisances. An attractive nuisance is a dangerous structure or condition on property that may be especially interesting to children, who may not fully understand the danger. For example, an unfenced swimming pool may be considered an attractive nuisance. Under common law, landowners generally weren't liable for injuries to trespassers, but an exception was made for trespassing children injured by an attractive nuisance. Since California landowners can be held liable to trespassers, a special rule for attractive nuisances is unnecessary in this state.

However, many California communities have ordinances that require landowners to take specific steps to protect children from hazards such as swimming pools, abandoned refrigerators, and derelict cars.

When someone enters another person's land and is injured there, the landowner can be held liable if the injury was caused by conditions on the property that resulted from the landowner's negligence. This is called **premises liability**. In California, premises liability applies to a landowner if the injured person was on the property legitimately (as in the case of a mail carrier delivering the mail), and also if the injured person was a trespasser.

> **Example:** A trespasser is severely injured by a bear trap on Rachel's property. Rachel could be held liable for the trespasser's injuries if this type of accident was foreseeable. If it was foreseeable, then Rachel could be considered negligent for not taking steps to prevent it—for instance, by putting up a warning sign near the trap.

A judge or jury deciding the case in the example might be more likely to hold the landowner liable if the trespasser could claim he entered the property unintentionally (without realizing he was trespassing), than if the trespasser climbed over a fence and ignored "No Trespassing" signs. Also, under the rule of comparative negligence, a property owner's liability for negligence is reduced if the injured person did something reckless, foolish, or careless that contributed to the accident. That rule is more likely to apply to willful trespassing than to unintentional trespassing.

Nuisance

Now let's examine another basic property law concept that's a counterpart to trespass: nuisance. A **nuisance** is any activity or conduct that substantially interferes with an owner's use and enjoyment of her property, or with the general welfare of the community. A **public nuisance** affects a community or neighborhood, or a large number of people. A **private nuisance** affects only one person or just a few people.

> **Example:** Anthony loves to practice the drums in his garage for hours, often late into the evening. However, since the houses in his neighborhood are very close together, his neighbors can hear every drumbeat. While he's practicing, they can't sleep, read, or watch television. Anthony's drumming could be considered a private nuisance.

It's possible for an activity to be completely legal and nevertheless have the effect of creating a nuisance. As long as Anthony's drumming doesn't violate any laws (such as noise ordinances) or other restrictions, it's not illegal—but it still may be a nuisance. The neighbors could sue and ask the court for an injunction ordering Anthony to stop or limit his drumming.

On the other hand, according to Civil Code § 3482, if an activity is specifically authorized by law, it won't be considered a nuisance. For example, if a municipal ordinance authorizes a street sweeper to operate before morning commute hours, any early morning noise created by the sweeper won't be considered a nuisance.

Nuisance vs. Trespass. Nuisance and trespass are overlapping, but distinguishable, concepts. A particular activity may be a trespass, a nuisance, or both. A trespass is an invasion (an unlawful entry) that violates a landowner's right to exclusive possession; it may or may not actually interfere with the owner's use and enjoyment of the land. A nuisance, on the other hand, is an interference with the owner's use and enjoyment; it may or may not involve an unlawful entry and violation of the right to exclusive possession. Returning to our earlier example, Anthony's drumming interferes with the neighbors' use and enjoyment of their property but doesn't involve an invasion of their property, so it's a nuisance and not a trespass. In contrast, an activity that floods a neighbor's property with runoff water involves both an invasion and an interference with use and enjoyment, so it's both a trespass and a nuisance.

Nuisances *Per Se.* An activity or condition on property may be declared by law to be a **nuisance *per se***. A nuisance *per se* is automatically actionable (cause for legal action), even without proof of injury or any damaging effect.

Some examples of nuisances *per se* under California statutes include:

- fire hazards;
- hazardous weeds or rubbish;
- breeding places for mosquitoes;
- street and sidewalk obstructions;
- open pits or excavations (such as mining shafts) without proper fencing; and
- buildings used for gambling, prostitution, drug sales, or criminal gang activity.

> **Example:** Bob has huge piles of trash in his yard that are creating a fire hazard. His neighbor, Ellen, may bring an action against Bob for nuisance, even though she can't show that the trash is causing an actual injury.

Local ordinances may also make certain conditions or conduct nuisances *per se*. For example, many city ordinances state that abandoned and inoperable motor vehicles are nuisances *per se*.

Over time, the courts have declared a number of other activities to be nuisances *per se*, even though they aren't mentioned in any statute or ordinance. For instance, courts have held that discharging water across another person's property is a nuisance *per se*. Another example of a court-declared nuisance *per se* is using explosives near heavily populated business and residential areas.

Remedies. A landowner who is subjected to a substantial interference with the use and enjoyment of her property may sue for abatement of the nuisance. **Abatement** refers to stopping, reducing, or removing a nuisance. A court can issue an injunction directing the party responsible for the nuisance to stop or remove it, and may also order him to pay damages for any harm already caused.

In some circumstances, a court won't order the abatement of a nuisance, because abatement would be unreasonably expensive or cause unreasonable hardship. In that case, the nuisance may be considered a **permanent nuisance**. The party responsible for a permanent nuisance may be required to pay damages, even though the activity causing the nuisance is allowed to continue.

Instead of taking the matter to court, someone who is being harmed by a private nuisance may have the right to use "self-help" to abate it. In other words, she may remove or destroy the thing that's causing the nuisance, even though it belongs to someone else. Section § 3502 of the Civil Code provides that self-help abatement is allowed only if it can be carried out without committing a breach of the peace or causing an unnecessary injury. Anyone who removes or destroys a nuisance in an unreasonable manner could be held liable to the landowner for negligence.

Encroachments

An **encroachment** is an object or structure that extends over a property boundary onto neighboring land or into neighboring airspace, without the neighbor's permission. The most common examples of encroachments are fences, buildings, and tree branches. In many cases, an encroachment is unintentional and simply results from a mistake as to the exact location of the boundary between the neighboring properties.

> **Example:** Alexi and Amanda are neighbors. When Alexi builds an addition to his garage, he inadvertently extends the structure over the boundary line and onto Amanda's property. That portion of the garage is an encroachment.

A court may classify an encroachment as either a trespass or a nuisance, or both, and the reasoning behind the classification isn't always clear. An encroachment that physically rests on the land (such as the garage in the example) is generally treated as a violation of the landowner's right of exclusive possession, and therefore a trespass. On the other hand, an encroachment that intrudes into the airspace (such as an overhanging tree branch) is more likely to be regarded as a substantial interference with use and enjoyment, and therefore a nuisance. Although this distinction can affect the parties' rights in some cases, for the most part it's a technicality.

A landowner who sues a neighbor over an encroachment needs to show only that the encroaching structure or object extends over the legal boundary line, without any legal right and without the owner's consent. It doesn't matter whether the encroachment was intentional, or whether it presents any danger.

Remedies. A court may order an encroachment to be removed, or allow the encroachment to remain if compensatory damages are paid to the landowner. In determining a remedy, the court may weigh the relative hardships of the landowner and the encroacher. Factors the court may consider include:

- whether the encroachment was intentional or unintentional,
- the expense and difficulty of removing the encroachment,
- the damage that may result from the encroachment's continued existence, and
- the effect of the encroachment on the landowner's use and enjoyment of her property.

Case Example:

The Leues' house was built in 1946 by the prior owners, who believed they were placing the house about five feet from the property line. Actually, it was mere inches from the line. In fact, the eaves (the lower edge of the roof), which were twenty feet off the ground, extended over the property line by about a foot. However, the Bagliones' house was 50 feet from the property line, and the Leues' encroachment did nothing to interfere with the Bagliones' use or enjoyment of their property.

> When a 1954 survey revealed the true boundary, the Bagliones (the owners of the property next door) sought an injunction to force the Leues to remove the encroaching eaves. Removal would have cost the Leues approximately $3,500. The trial court denied the request and instead awarded an easement to the Leues and $330 to the Bagliones. (That was $300 as payment for the easement and $30 in damages.) The Bagliones appealed.
>
> The appellate court affirmed the lower court's decision. The hardship and cost to the Leues from an injunction would have far outweighed the hardship to the Bagliones from the encroachment. An injunction was inappropriate under the circumstances, and the $330 was adequate compensation for the slight injury suffered by the Bagliones. *Baglione v. Leue* (1958) 160 Cal.App.2d 731.

Adverse Possession

Now that you're familiar with the concept of trespass and the rules protecting a landowner's right to exclusive possession of the property, we'll consider a legal doctrine that cuts in the other direction, favoring trespassers over landowners.

Suppose you live in a development where the houses are fairly close together. Between your house and your neighbor's, there's a strip of lawn ten feet wide divided down the middle by the property line. Although you and your neighbor each own half of the strip of lawn, your neighbor is in the habit of mowing the entire strip when he mows the rest of his yard. This is a trespass, but you don't mind at all, because it saves you the trouble of mowing.

You should know, however, that under the right (or wrong) circumstances, this type of trespassing can actually bring about a change in ownership. The statutory process by which unauthorized possession and use of property can ripen into ownership of the property is known as **adverse possession**.

Adverse possession may be raised as a defense in a lawsuit brought by the owner of the property against a trespasser. Or it may be asserted in a quiet title action brought by the adverse possessor (the trespasser) to formally establish her ownership of the property. This is called "perfecting" title gained by adverse possession.

The rules concerning adverse possession are intended to promote productive use of property. Courts and lawmakers reason that it's better to have title vested in someone who wants to make use of the property, rather than someone who leaves the property unused for a long period of time.

Still, it takes more than just trespassing to gain title to another's property. Let's examine the requirements for adverse possession in California.

Requirements for Adverse Possession

In California, a person claiming adverse possession of someone else's real property must be able to prove all of the following in court:

- possession of the property under claim of right or color of title;
- actual, open, and notorious possession;
- possession that is exclusive and hostile to the owner;

- possession that is continuous and uninterrupted for five years; and
- payment of all property taxes during the five-year period.

Claim of Right or Color of Title. The first requirement is that the adverse possessor must have possession of the property either under a claim of right or under color of title. A key distinction between these two alternatives is that under color of title, the adverse possessor has a bona fide (good faith) belief that he owns the land; under a claim of right, he does not necessarily have that good faith belief. Let's take a closer look at what this means.

A person who has possession of property under **color of title** holds a document (a deed, a court order, or some other type of instrument) that appears to give her title to the property, but actually fails to do so. She has a bona fide belief that she owns the property; she isn't trying to take it from anyone, and doesn't even realize that she's a trespasser.

> **Example:** Sharon has lived on some property known as the Sloan Ranch for over 20 years. She bought the property in 1987, and she has a recorded deed showing the transfer of ownership. What she didn't know is that the grantor's signature on the deed was forged. When the fraud is discovered, Sharon claims adverse possession based on color of title. The forged deed couldn't give her title to the property, but it gave her color of title.

On the other hand, a person claiming adverse possession under a **claim of right** doesn't have a deed or any other document that seems to give him ownership. He doesn't necessarily have a bona fide belief that he owns the property; he may strongly suspect or even fully realize that he's trespassing. To establish title by adverse possession, he must be able to prove that during his possession of the property he intended to claim ownership of it, and that his actions and conduct demonstrated that intention.

> **Example:** Rob built a cottage and planted a large vegetable garden on some abandoned property at the edge of town. He knew the land wasn't his, but he'd never seen anyone else using it.
>
> Years go by; eventually the true owner comes forward to claim the property. Rob doesn't have a deed or any other document that gives him color of title, so his adverse possession claim will have to be based on a claim of right. To prove to a court that he intended to claim title, he'll essentially be required to show that he has consistently acted as if he were the owner, even though he knew he was not.

Whether an adverse possession claim is based on color of title or a claim of right matters for two reasons.

First, it may affect the amount of property the adverse possessor will receive if the claim is successful. Someone claiming adverse possession under color of title will, if successful, receive title to all of the land described in her faulty instrument. Going back to our earlier example, if Sharon is successful in her adverse possession claim, she'll receive title to all of the property known as the Sloan Ranch, as described in the forged deed, even if she's only lived on a small portion of it.

On the other hand, an adverse possessor under a claim of right will receive title only to the portion of the property that he actually took possession of. In our second example, no matter how big the abandoned property is as a whole, Rob will get title only to the part he has used—the cottage, yard, and vegetable garden. The rest will still belong to the true owner.

Fig. 15.1 Distinguishing claim of right from color of title

Claim of Right	Color of Title
• Intent to claim title	• Faulty deed or other instrument
• Claimant may know he's trespassing	• Claimant has good faith belief in ownership
• Successful claim gives title only to the portion enclosed, cultivated, or improved	• Successful claim gives title to the entire property described in the instrument

---

Whether the adverse possessor has color of title or claim of right is important for another reason: there's a different burden of proof for claim of right than for color of title. In general, it's harder to prove adverse possession under a claim of right; the evidence showing that the other requirements for adverse possession have been met must be stronger.

Actual, Open, and Notorious Possession. The next requirement—actual, open, and notorious possession—concerns constructive notice. The trespasser must occupy the property in a way that puts the true owner on notice that his property interest is threatened.

This means the trespasser must take actual possession of the property; simply walking around on it, for example, wouldn't be enough to give the owner constructive notice. Depending on the type of property in question, actions that count as actual possession include enclosing the property (for example, putting up a fence), growing crops, or making substantial improvements (for example, building a cabin). If the true owner were paying attention to the property, these actions would give him plenty of notice that someone else was using his land.

Also, an adverse possessor's use of the property must be open, not hidden or secret.

> **Example:** Jack has been living for several years in a shack on a far corner of the Juarezes' land. The shack is well hidden by trees, and Jack comes and goes in secret. If anyone comes near the shack, Jack hides. His possession doesn't fulfill the actual, open, and notorious requirement, so an adverse possession claim would fail.

Exclusive and Hostile Possession. To prove adverse possession, a claimant must show exclusive use. This means she must be using the property to the exclusion of everyone else, not sharing possession. With a claim under color of title, the exclusive use rule applies to all of the land described in the faulty deed. With a claim of right, the rule applies only to the property being claimed by the adverse possessor.

It's also necessary for the claimant's possession of the land to be **hostile** to the true owner, which means that the possession is adverse to the owner's interests and in disregard of his rights. Possession can be considered hostile only if it's unauthorized. So the true owner can defeat a trespasser's adverse possession claim by granting him permission to use the property.

Example: Cal owns 500 acres of rural property. One day he discovers Ben and Roberta, two trespassers who have been living on a half-acre piece of the property for three years. After meeting them and hearing their story, Cal decides to let them stay, since he doesn't use that part of the property anyway. Cal drafts a document giving Ben and Roberta permission to live on the half-acre plot, rent free, for 20 years. Cal's permission automatically defeats any adverse possession claim Ben and Roberta might have been able to make, since their possession of his property is no longer hostile.

Continuous and Uninterrupted Possession. The next requirement for adverse possession is that possession must be continuous and uninterrupted for five years. It's interrupted if the true owner takes possession even briefly during that period, and even if the adverse possessor remains in possession while the owner is there. Suppose someone intending to claim adverse possession has had exclusive possession of the property for four years, and then the true owner shows up and stays for two months; after that, the adverse possessor has exclusive possession again. The owner's two-month interruption stopped the adverse possession clock, and the claimant has to start over from scratch. The four years of possession that she logged before the interruption no longer count.

However, the requirement of five years of continuous possession doesn't mean that the same person must be in possession for the entire five-year period. The periods of possession of a series of adverse possessors can be added together, as long as they aren't interrupted by the true owner. This is called **tacking**.

Example: When the Harpers bought their property, they were given a deed signed by an incompetent grantor, so they have only color of title. After two years, they sell the property to the Wongs; and after another two years the Wongs sell it to the Fitzgeralds. If the Fitzgeralds remain in exclusive possession for a year, their period of possession can be tacked together with the Harpers' and the Wongs' to make up a continuous five-year period of possession. If all of the other requirements have been met, the Fitzgeralds will be entitled to claim ownership by adverse possession.

Note that a sale of the property by the true owner doesn't automatically interrupt an adverse possession claim. The buyer (the new true owner) takes title with the adverse possession clock already running. The clock will stop only if the buyer actually takes possession of the property.

There's one more point about the continuity requirement. In some cases, an adverse possessor can fulfill this requirement even if she's only using the property periodically, as long as that periodic use is how an owner would ordinarily use the type of property in question. For example, suppose the property is enclosed pasture land that's used only for grazing sheep, and it's only suitable for grazing in the summer months; if the adverse possessor grazes her sheep there from June through August every year for five years, that could be considered continuous use.

Payment of Taxes. In California, an adverse possessor must pay all of the taxes on the property that are assessed during the five-year period of possession. This includes the regular property taxes and any other assessments.

But what if the true owner has been receiving the tax bills and paying them regularly? That won't prevent the adverse possession claim, as long as the adverse possessor pays the taxes, too. If both the owner and the adverse possessor are assessed (billed) for the taxes, then it doesn't matter which one pays the taxes first. If only the owner is assessed, however, then the adverse possessor must be the first to pay to satisfy the tax requirement. The adverse possessor must have records that prove the taxes were paid in a timely manner in each of the five years; he cannot simply pay the entire five years' worth of taxes in a lump sum in order to make an adverse possession claim.

You may be wondering how two different people could be assessed for the taxes on the same property. According to Revenue Code § 610, anyone can have her name added to the assessment roll for a particular property, if she submits a request to the assessor's office with a sworn statement declaring that she currently has possession of the property and wants to be assessed for the purposes of an adverse possession claim.

Adverse Possession and Government Property

There is an important exception to the rules concerning adverse possession: property owned by the government or a public entity cannot be adversely possessed. For instance, if someone builds a cabin in a state or national park, they can never acquire title to the property, no matter how long they remain in possession.

Adverse Possession and Encroachments

Most of the examples in our discussion of adverse possession have involved trespassers who are actually residing on a piece of property they don't own. But not all adverse possession claims are that dramatic; some involve only a strip of land along a property line and a problem with an encroachment.

> **Example:** When the Perlmans bought their property, it was their understanding that it extended all the way to a certain stand of trees. Actually, the true property line was three feet closer than that.
>
> The Perlmans put up a fence where they believed the boundary to be and built a patio next to the fence. The fence and part of the patio are encroachments on the three-foot strip of land that's really part of the neighboring property.
>
> It's now six years after the Perlmans built the fence and patio, and the property next door has recently been sold. A survey reveals the encroachments, and the new neighbor sues the Perlmans, demanding that they take down the fence and tear up the patio. The Perlmans refuse, claiming that they've acquired title to the three-foot strip by adverse possession.

An adverse possession claim can be based on an encroachment like the one in the example, but claims like this generally don't succeed. One requirement in particular is usually a stumbling block: the payment of the property taxes. The Perlmans would have to be able to prove that they've paid the taxes on the three-foot strip for five years.

If the Perlmans haven't paid the taxes, they haven't acquired ownership of the strip of land by adverse possession. However, they might still be able to claim a prescriptive easement that would allow them to keep their fence and patio in place. (We'll discuss prescriptive easements in the next section of the chapter.) If not, a court could either require the Perlmans to remove the encroachments or else order them to pay the neighbors for an easement, as occurred in *Baglione v. Leue*, a case we looked at earlier.

Adverse Squatters

In cities all over the world, millions of poor people have created unauthorized communities by a process called squatting: taking up residence in abandoned, dilapidated buildings without the permission of the property owners. In some places, like the slums of Rio de Janeiro, tiny areas of land contain a large percentage of the city's population, and many of those residents are squatters.

Squatting isn't as common in the United States as in some other parts of the world, but one group in San Francisco, Homes Not Jails (HNJ), has advocated squatting in abandoned buildings as a way for homeless people to obtain shelter and use civil disobedience to protest their plight. The group regularly tried to use adverse possession as a way to address the problem of homelessness.

In 1993, HNJ took over a vacant building in the Haight-Ashbury district. During the course of the next five years, at least 14 otherwise homeless squatters lived in the building for various periods ranging from six months to the full five years. Having met all of the other requirements for adverse possession in California, HNJ paid five years of delinquent property taxes and filed a claim to quiet title. While a superior court judge ultimately denied the squatters' adverse possession claim for technical procedural reasons, San Francisco and other California cities may see similar claims in the future.

Easements

In the first part of this chapter, we examined the basic legal rules that apply when someone enters another person's land without a legal right to do so. In this section, we're going to look at what happens when someone does have the right to enter and use another's land. In particular, we'll address these questions: how does such a right arise, and how does it limit the property owner's rights?

The right to enter and use land owned by another person for a particular, limited purpose is called an **easement**. The most common easement is one that allows someone to drive across another person's land to reach her own.

Distinguishing Easements from Other Interests

Easements are a type of encumbrance, a nonpossessory interest in real property, like the liens we discussed in Chapters 13 and 14. Liens (security interests) are financial encumbrances; easements are nonfinancial encumbrances. Nonfinancial encumbrances not only encumber a landowner's title but also affect use of the property.

In addition to easements, there are two other categories of nonfinancial encumbrances: restrictive covenants and profits. Before discussing easements in detail, we should briefly explain the relationship between easements and these other nonfinancial encumbrances.

While an easement gives someone else the right to use a landowner's property in a specified way, **restrictive covenants** limit how the landowner herself can use her own property. For example, a restrictive covenant might prohibit a landowner from cutting down certain trees on her own lot. Sometimes restrictive covenants are called "negative easements," but that terminology is probably more confusing than helpful. We'll be examining restrictive covenants in Chapter 17.

The other type of nonfinancial encumbrance is a **profit**, also called a *profit à prendre*. (Profits were mentioned in Chapter 3.) A profit allows someone to take something away from another person's land. For example, if you had the right to enter someone's property, pick apples, and take the apples away with you, that would be a profit. Although profits are technically a separate type of nonfinancial encumbrance, it's simpler to view them as a kind of easement. Essentially the same legal rules that apply to easements also apply to profits, so we'll set aside the distinction. We'll call the right to enter another person's land for a specified purpose an easement, whether or not it includes the right to take something away from the land.

Types of Easements

Some easements are tied to the ownership of particular property, and some are not. This is the fundamental difference between the two main categories of easements: appurtenant easements (also called easements appurtenant) and easements in gross.

Appurtenant Easements. As you'll recall from Chapter 3, appurtenant rights are rights that go along with ownership of real property. An **appurtenant easement** is an easement that goes along with ownership of real property. It burdens or encumbers one piece of land for the benefit of another piece of land.

The piece of land benefited by the easement is called the **dominant tenement**, and its owner is called the **dominant tenant**. The piece of land burdened by the easement is called the **servient tenement**, and its owner is called the **servient tenant**. (In this context, the term "tenement" refers to the land and all of the rights that go along with the land.)

The type of easement we mentioned earlier—an easement across someone else's land for access to one's own land—is an example of an appurtenant easement.

> **Example:** George owns a piece of land that has no access to or from the main road except by way of a driveway across the neighboring property, owned by the Smiths. George has an easement that allows him to drive across the Smiths' property to reach his property. This easement gives George the right to use part of another person's property (the Smiths' driveway) for a particular purpose (access to and from the main road). George's property is the dominant tenement, because it benefits from the easement. The Smiths' property is the servient tenement, because it is burdened by the easement.

This type of appurtenant easement is often called a **right-of-way**, or sometimes an **easement for ingress and egress**. ("Ingress and egress" means entering and exiting.) Though that's the most common type, someone could have an appurtenant easement for any number of other purposes. Here are some of the examples listed in Civil Code § 801:

- the right of pasturing livestock;
- the right of fishing or taking game;
- the right of taking water, wood, minerals, and other things;
- the right of transacting business upon land;

- the right of conducting lawful sports upon land;
- the right of flooding land; and
- the right of burial.

An appurtenant easement **runs with the land**. This means that when either the dominant tenement or the servient tenement is transferred (sold, inherited, or given away), the benefit or the burden of the easement is transferred along with it—even if the easement isn't specifically mentioned in the deed. An appurtenant easement is appurtenant to the dominant tenement and cannot be sold separately from it; whoever owns the dominant tenement also owns the easement. And whoever owns the servient tenement must allow the easement to be used.

Easements in Gross. An **easement in gross** is an easement that benefits an individual or a company, rather than a piece of land. With an easement in gross, there is no dominant tenement; there's only a servient tenement, the piece of land burdened by the easement.

> **Example:** Mary grants Sam an easement in gross that allows him to enter her land and fish in her pond. Mary's land is the servient tenement, but because this is an easement in gross, there is no dominant tenement. Ownership of the easement isn't tied to ownership of a parcel of land.
>
> Sam may have this easement in gross even if he doesn't own any land. And even if he does—for example, if he owns the property next door to Mary's—since this is an easement in gross, it isn't appurtenant to Sam's land. If he were to sell his land, the new owner would not automatically have the right to fish in Mary's pond. The easement in gross would still be Sam's.

The burden of an easement in gross can run with the land, however. Depending on the circumstances, if Mary were to sell her land (the servient tenement), the new owner might be required to allow Sam to go on fishing in the pond.

Note that it isn't the purpose of the easement that determines whether it's appurtenant or in gross. For example, whether an easement for a right to fish is appurtenant or in gross would depend on the intentions of the parties and the circumstances in which it was created. If it was created with a deed, the deed could state that it was an easement in gross, or that it was appurtenant to property described in the deed. (We'll be discussing creation of easements shortly.) Of course, if the easement holder didn't own any land, then it could only be an easement in gross.

Personal vs. commercial easements in gross. There are two types of easements in gross: personal and commercial. An easement in gross is personal if the easement holder is an individual rather than a business. Returning to our earlier example, Sam's fishing easement was a personal easement in gross.

Most easements in gross are commercial (related to a business) rather than personal, however. The most common commercial easements in gross are those owned by utility companies. For example, a power company or telephone company typically has a commercial easement in gross that allows its employees to enter private property to install and maintain wires and other equipment.

Commercial easements in gross are freely assignable and transferable. If a large power company purchases a smaller one, the smaller company's commercial easements can be transferred to the larger one as part of the sale. But the purpose of the easement can't change. For example, if the power company has an easement on your property for power lines, the easement can't be sold to the sewer district for installation of pipes and sewer mains.

In many states, personal easements in gross can't be assigned or transferred. In California, however, a personal easement in gross may be assignable, transferable, and inheritable.

Creation of Easements

Whether they're appurtenant or in gross, easements can be created in a number of ways, some that involve the consent of the landowner (the servient tenant) and some that don't. The most important methods of creation are:

- express grant or reservation,
- implication from prior use or necessity, and
- prescription.

Express Easements. An express easement is one that's created expressly and deliberately by the servient tenant. Express easements must be created in writing, so they're ordinarily created in a deed. An easement may be included in a deed transferring title to property, or there may be a separate deed that grants only the easement. In either case, the purpose, extent, and location of the easement is usually described in the document; for example, "an easement over the west 20 feet of Lot 16 to be used for automobile parking during regular business hours."

An easement may be created by express grant or by express reservation. When an easement is created by **express grant**, a property owner grants someone else a right to use his property in a particular way.

> **Example:** Joe sold the west half of his farm to Cindy. In the deed, he expressly granted Cindy the right to use the private road located on the east half of the farm, the property that Joe still owned.

An **express reservation** is similar to an express grant, except that the property owner keeps an easement for himself rather than granting it to another person.

> **Example:** Joe sold the east half of his farm to Cindy. In the deed, he expressly reserved to himself the right to use the private road located on the east half of the farm, the property transferred to Cindy.

Express easements can also be created by recording a plat map. If a developer subdivides land and records a plat of the subdivision, purchasers of lots in the subdivision acquire easements to use the roads, alleys, and all common areas shown on the plat.

Implied Easements. An easement by implication can be either an implied grant or an implied reservation. This type of easement can arise only when a property is divided into more than one lot, and the grantor neglects to grant or reserve an easement on one lot for the benefit of the other. The easement is implied by law instead of created through a deed. For an easement to be created by implication, two requirements must usually be met:

- it must be reasonably necessary for the enjoyment of the property, and
- there must have been apparent prior use.

The second requirement is fulfilled if use of the access was established before the property was divided, and would have been apparent to prospective purchasers from an inspection of the property.

> **Example:** John has owned and lived on a piece of property in the mountains for 20 years. He divides the property into two parcels, Parcel A and Parcel B, and sells Parcel A to Sarah. Parcel A is only accessible by two roads. One road is impassable during the winter; the other road is located on what is now Parcel B. When John owned the whole property, he used both roads.
>
> After selling Parcel A to Sarah, John refuses to let her use the road on Parcel B during the winter. If Sarah sues and the court decides that wintertime use of the road on Parcel B is reasonably necessary for the use and enjoyment of Parcel A, Sarah will have an easement implied from prior use.

However, different rules apply if one of the parcels would be entirely landlocked without an easement. When an easement for ingress and egress is strictly necessary (not merely reasonably necessary) because there is no other way to reach the landlocked parcel, then a court may declare that there is an easement even though there was no apparent prior use. This type of easement is called an easement by necessity. Note that technically this is not considered an implied easement.

Case to Consider...

The Kelloggs owned a landlocked parcel accessible only by private road over several of their neighbors' properties. Some of the neighbors wanted to deny the Kelloggs the use of the road, but the Kelloggs claimed an easement by necessity. Although the Kelloggs and the neighbors had acquired their properties from various different grantors over the years, the original conveyances that landlocked the Kelloggs' parcel were all grants from the federal government in 1878. In the quiet title action, did the court rule in favor of the Kelloggs or their neighbors? *Kellogg v. Garcia* (2002) 102 Cal.App.4th 796.

Easements by Prescription. An **easement by prescription** (or prescriptive easement) is established when someone makes use of another's property for a long time without permission. Prescription is quite similar to adverse possession, in that the prescriptive use must be open and notorious, hostile or adverse to the owner's interests, and continuous for a certain length of time—in California, five years. And just as government property can't be acquired by adverse possession, a prescriptive easement can't be created on government property.

However, a prescriptive easement is distinguished from adverse possession because it only gives the easement holder the right to use another's property; it doesn't give her title to it. Also, there's no need to pay property taxes on the land in question, and exclusive use is not necessary. A prescriptive easement can be established while the landowner is still in possession of the property.

> **Example:** Cecilia has been cutting across her neighbor's backyard for more than five years, wearing a little dirt path through the grass. The neighbors have never raised any objection, but they've never given her permission to do this. She has acquired an easement by prescription, and the neighbors can no longer prevent her from crossing that part of their yard.

The particular circumstances involved will determine whether a prescriptive easement is an appurtenant easement or an easement in gross, and whether it will run with the land, so that new owners of the servient tenement will be required to allow the use.

Note that a continuous use by the general public may create an easement that can be used by anyone, not just a specific individual. This type of public easement is called an easement by implied dedication. (See Chapter 10.)

To prevent individual or public use of her property from ripening into an easement, a landowner can post signs that say, "Right to pass by permission, and subject to control, of owner: Section 1008, Civil Code." Alternatively, she can record a notice declaring that any use is by permission and is subject to the owner's control. However, under Civil Code § 813, to be effective against a particular individual (as opposed to the general public), the notice must also be served on that individual.

Once an easement by prescription has been established, its scope or range will be limited to the same use of the property made during the five-year prescriptive period. In other words, an easement established by gardening on another's land for five years gives the easement holder the right to go on gardening there; it doesn't give him the right to build a shed or park his car there. The scope of an easement by prescription was the issue in the following case.

Case Example:

Plaintiffs had been raising cattle on their land since the 1800s. Their property was physically divided into two parcels by the defendants' property. A rugged mountain road connected the plaintiffs' two parcels, crossing over the defendants' property about ten feet from the defendants' vacation cabin.

The plaintiffs, on horseback or on foot, used the road approximately 40 times a year to drive 150 head of cattle from one of their parcels to the other. The plaintiffs' individual parcels were accessible by motor vehicles at points that didn't involve the defendants' property. The plaintiffs sued for a prescriptive easement to use the road across the defendants' property for their cattle drives, by foot, by horseback, or by motorized vehicle. The trial court granted the plaintiffs a prescriptive easement for their cattle and horses only, not cars or other motorized vehicles. The plaintiffs appealed.

The appellate court agreed with the lower court. The scope of a prescriptive easement is determined by the use through which it was acquired. The plaintiffs sometimes used the road for motorcycles, but admitted trying to hide that use from the defendants. Such secretive use did not meet the "open and notorious" requirement for establishing an easement by prescription. In addition, allowing motorized vehicles would constitute an increased burden on the servient tenement. The plaintiffs established a prescriptive easement over the years for their horses and cattle, and could continue to use the road on the defendants' property in that way only. *Connolly v. McDermott* (1984) 162 Cal.App.3d 973.

Maintenance and Repair of Easements

You just bought a summer home near a popular lake. The property comes with a right-of-way easement to use an old dirt road across the neighbors' property to get to the beach.

The neighbors are at their summer cottage only a few weeks of the year, and the road usually gets overgrown with weeds. What right or responsibility do you have to maintain the road on their property? Suppose you want to pave the road; can you? And if so, can you ask the neighbors to help you pay for it?

These issues are addressed both by statutes and by court decisions. The general rule is that the servient tenant (the owner of the property being used) has no duty to maintain or repair the easement. In other words, your neighbors don't have to maintain the dirt road on their property for your benefit.

However, under Civil Code § 845, the easement holder has both the right and the duty to repair and maintain the easement. There's also an implied right to enter the property to perform all necessary maintenance. So, in the case of a right-of-way, you can enter your neighbors' land to clear vegetation from the road or to fill in potholes, for example. Also, an easement holder generally has the right to make improvements to the easement that are reasonably necessary for safety reasons, or even just for the easement holder's convenience. An example would be paving a road (depending on the circumstances).

Shared Use. When a private road is used by both the landowner and the easement holder, or is used by more than one easement holder, the parties must share both the maintenance responsibilities and the cost in proportion to their respective uses. However, while the parties have the duty to maintain and repair the shared road, there's no duty to improve it. In our example, if some of your neighbors share use of the dirt road to the beach, you're all required to help maintain it and share the maintenance costs. However, none of you could require the others to help pay for having the road paved.

Maintenance Agreements. Instead of following the standard legal rules concerning maintenance of an easement, the parties may enter into an agreement that provides for a different division of responsibilities. For example, you and your neighbors could agree that you'll be the one to keep the vegetation cleared from the road, but they'll hire someone to fill in the potholes once each spring.

Keep in mind that such agreements apply only to the current owners. If your neighbors sell their property, you'll still have your easement, but any agreement to modify the maintenance responsibilities will have to be renegotiated. In other words, someone who buys your neighbors' property doesn't have to honor the agreement to fill in the potholes once a year.

Case to Consider...

The Herzogs owned property in a steep, hilly area. They had an easement that allowed them to use a road over neighboring properties, Parcels 2 and 3, for access to their property, Parcel 1.

Grosso bought Parcel 3 and soon afterward graded his portion of the road, dumping fill dirt across the Herzogs' access and putting up a gate that prevented them from using the road. Grosso eventually agreed to cut a new access road through the fill to Parcel 2, but he put the new road along a very steep, muddy bank; it was narrow and dangerous. Grosso refused to let the Herzogs put up a guardrail and reflectors on the edge of the steep bank and also prevented them from having the road paved.

When the Herzogs sued, the trial court ruled in their favor, ordering Grosso to remove the gate, to stop interfering with the Herzogs' right to use and improve the easement, and to pave the Herzogs' portion of the road. Grosso was also ordered to pay damages to the Herzogs. He appealed. On appeal, should the court uphold the trial court's orders? *Herzog v. Grosso* (1953) 41 Cal.2d 219.

Termination of Easements

Now let's look at the various ways in which easements terminate. These can be grouped into three main categories: express termination, implied termination, and termination by prescription. (As you'll notice, these roughly correspond to the ways in which easements can be created.)

Express Termination. An easement is expressly terminated if the termination is specified in the deed or some other legal document.

Expiration. When an easement was granted, the parties may have agreed to a specific termination date. For example, a deed granting an easement might state that it will last until June 30, 2020. Most easements do not have an expiration date, however.

Release. The owner of the dominant tenement may agree at any time to relinquish the easement and give the owner of the servient tenement a written release. The release should be recorded.

Automatic termination. A grant of easement may specify that the easement will terminate automatically when or if a specified event occurs. For example, if an easement is granted "for life," it will terminate automatically when the person who is the measuring life dies. (See the discussion of life estates in Chapter 4.)

Condemnation. Another way in which an easement may be expressly terminated is through condemnation, when the state takes private property for public use. (See Chapter 10.) The easement holder must be compensated for the value of the lost easement.

> **Example:** Mary Jane has a right-of-way easement across Karl's property. The state decides to put in a new freeway, and Karl's property is condemned. Mary Jane's easement terminates when Karl's property is condemned. Not only must the state compensate Karl for the value of his condemned property, it must also compensate Mary Jane for the value of her easement across Karl's property.

Implied Termination. Easements may be created by implication, and they may also be terminated by implication. An easement may terminate because of the actions of the parties, or because of events that are beyond the parties' control. An easement may terminate by implication as a result of merger, the end of necessity, abandonment, failure of purpose, or destruction of the servient tenement.

Merger. Let's say that you own a property burdened by an easement, which gives the neighboring property owner the right to cross your land to reach a public beach. When the neighboring property is put up for sale, you buy it. What happens to the easement?

Because an easement is defined as an interest in another person's land, you can't have an easement in your own property. So when the easement holder (the dominant tenant) also becomes the owner of the servient tenement, the easement is extinguished. This is called termination by **merger**; the dominant and servient tenements are merged in common ownership.

Necessity ends. If an easement was created by necessity and the necessity ends, the easement terminates. That would happen, for example, if an easement by necessity provided access to a landlocked property and the county built a new road so that the property was no longer landlocked.

Abandonment. What if the easement holder just stops using the easement? Under certain circumstances, it may be held to have been terminated by **abandonment**.

The rules concerning when an easement can be considered abandoned are different for prescriptive easements than for other types of easements. A prescriptive easement will be considered abandoned if it is simply not used for a five-year period. (Civil Code § 811.)

In contrast, other types of easements (easements created by express grant, express reservation, or implication) generally can't be considered abandoned unless there is a clear, direct expression of the owner's intent to abandon the easement, such as a statement in writing, or the construction of a permanent barrier that makes it impossible to use the easement. Non-use alone is not sufficient evidence of intent to abandon, if the easement was created by express grant, express reservation, or implication.

That said, however, Civil Code §§ 887.010 – 887.090 provides a procedure for terminating an easement that hasn't been used for 20 years. Under this statute, the owner of property subject to an easement can bring a quiet title action to have the easement declared abandoned and terminated. The easement (no matter how it was created) will be considered abandoned if, during the 20 years preceding the quiet title action:

- the easement has not been used at any time;
- property taxes separately assessed against the easement (if any) haven't been paid; and
- no document creating, transferring, or otherwise evidencing the easement has been recorded.

The court won't rule that the easement has been abandoned if a notice of intent to preserve the easement has been recorded within the 20-year period preceding the action. And once a quiet title action has begun, the easement holder can stop it by recording a notice of intent to preserve at any time before the court enters a judgment of abandonment. If the notice isn't recorded until the action has begun, however, the easement holder will be required to pay the servient tenant's legal costs.

Case Example:

In 1953, Anna Jonas purchased a lot that shared a nonexclusive driveway easement with several other property owners. The easement had been created by express grant at some earlier time. Jonas used the easement to enter and exit from her property. In 1954, she planted a hedge on part of the easement to beautify the neighborhood. Although the hedge partially blocked Jonas's access to the easement, it didn't prevent her from using it, and she continued to do so.

In 1959, the Buechners bought some of the land that was subject to the easement. They wanted Jonas to stop using the portion of the easement that was on their property, Jonas refused to stop, and the dispute ended up in court. The Buechners asserted that Jonas had no right to use that portion of the easement because she had abandoned it when she planted the hedge.

The court disagreed. For an easement by express grant to be abandoned, there must be an actual intention to abandon it. The hedge Jonas planted did not prevent use of the easement, and in fact Jonas continued to use it as she always had. The mere planting of an ornamental hedge was not enough evidence of intention to abandon a portion of the easement, and Jonas's easement rights had not terminated. *Buechner v. Jonas* (1964) 228 Cal.App.2d 127.

Failure of purpose. An easement will also be terminated when the reason for which it was created has ceased.

> **Example:** A railroad has an easement over Fred's property where the train tracks pass through town. Recently, the railroad stopped serving that line and ripped up its tracks. The railroad's easement will terminate, because the reason for the easement no longer exists.

Destruction of servient tenement. Sometimes an easement exists in a building rather than in land. In that case, if the building is involuntarily destroyed, the easement will terminate.

Termination by Prescription. The last method of termination we'll mention is termination by prescription. This can happen if the servient tenant interferes with the easement holder's use of the easement. The interference must be open, continuous, and uninterrupted for five years.

> **Example:** Mark has an easement across his neighbor Kim's property. Kim builds a fence across the easement. The fence remains in place, blocking Mark's use of the easement, for five years. Mark's easement has probably been terminated by prescription.

Easements vs. Licenses

We'll end our discussion of easements by explaining the difference between an easement and a license.

If I give you permission to come onto my property to pick wild blueberries, I haven't necessarily granted you an easement. Instead, I may simply have given you a **license**.

A license entitles the holder to enter someone else's property for a specific purpose, just like an easement. Unlike an easement, however, a license doesn't create an interest in real property. It is not an encumbrance on the landowner's title.

An easement may last indefinitely and run with the land, so that future owners of the servient tenement must allow the specified use. In contrast, a license can be revoked by the landowner at any time. If I've given you only a license, I can change my mind tomorrow and revoke your permission to enter my land and pick berries.

A grant of easement must be in writing to be enforceable, but a license doesn't have to be. Spoken permission to pick blueberries creates a license. Written permission will also create a license, unless the document clearly indicates an intention to create an easement and meets all of the requirements for a valid deed.

A license isn't assignable. The license holder doesn't have the right to transfer the license to a third party without the landowner's consent. On the other hand, easements are transferable in California.

Note that because a license represents permission from the landowner, a license holder's use of property can never be hostile or adverse to the owner's interests. So a license holder can never claim a prescriptive easement or adverse possession of the property based on the licensed use.

Disputes Between Neighbors

Now let's consider some common types of conflicts that arise between neighbors. We'll look at disputes concerning trees, fences, the right to farm, and liability for water damage. Note that public or private restrictions often address these types of conflicts. For example, in a particular neighborhood, either a local ordinance or a subdivider's declaration of restrictions (or both) may impose rules concerning fence height and fencing materials. However, here our focus is on common law rules that govern landowners in the absence of land use ordinances or private restrictions (we'll discuss public and private restrictions in Chapter 17).

Trees

Trees are frequently the subject of disputes between neighbors. Neighbor A might regard the flowering cherry tree in the backyard as the most beautiful thing for miles around, yet Neighbor B might see it as nothing but an annoying source of petals and leaves that fall into her yard from overhanging branches. What are their respective rights? What can Neighbor A do to protect the tree from Neighbor B? What can Neighbor B do to defend her yard from the tree?

Trees Owned by One Neighbor. The rights of neighbors in regard to a tree depend on whether the tree is owned by only one of them, or owned in common by both of them. Ownership of a tree is determined by the location of the trunk. In general, a property owner owns any trees that have trunks that are wholly on his land, even if the branches and roots extend over the property line. (Civil Code § 833.)

> **Example:** Javier and Peter are neighbors. A large oak tree grows near the boundary between their properties. Several of the big roots and many of the branches extend onto Javier's property. But the trunk itself is completely on Peter's side of the property line. Thus, the tree belongs to Peter, no matter how many of the roots and branches cross the line into Javier's yard.

Still, in this situation, the tree owner's neighbor does have some rights. Overhanging branches may be considered a nuisance, and the neighbor has the right to abate the nuisance by trimming the branches to the property line, no matter how ugly or unbalanced it makes the tree look. This is generally true even if the branches aren't causing any damage to the neighbor's property.

But what about the tree roots invading the neighbor's lawn? Encroaching roots can be considered both a trespass and a nuisance, but they may be trimmed to the property line only if they are causing damage to the neighboring property (this is because trees generally have more difficulty recovering from root disturbance than from branch trimming). This rule represents a balancing of interests: the right of the neighbor to protect her property balanced against the right of the tree owner to protect his tree.

> **Example:** Let's go back to the previous example. Although Peter's tree roots cross the property line onto Javier's land, they aren't causing damage. Under these circumstances, Javier probably doesn't have the right to trim the roots. However, if the roots eventually started to lift up and crack the paving stones on Javier's patio, he would then be within his rights to trim them.

A neighbor is allowed to use self-help to deal with an offending tree—that is, she may fix the problem herself, instead of taking the tree owner to court. But there are limits to this right. When a neighbor trims either the roots or the branches of the tree, she can cut them back only to the property line, and she must carry out the trimming in a reasonable manner, so that the health of the tree is not injured. If it's necessary to go onto the tree owner's property to do the trimming, she should obtain his permission; otherwise it could be considered a trespass.

The law gives tree owners an incentive to keep their trees trimmed. A tree owner may be held liable for any damage to neighboring property caused by damaged or sickly trees or branches. If a rotting branch from Peter's tree falls on Javier's car, Peter will be liable.

Boundary Trees. Now let's consider the rules that apply if a tree's trunk is partly on one property and partly on another. A tree that straddles a property line is called a **boundary tree** or **line tree**.

According to Civil Code § 834, a boundary tree is owned by both neighbors in common. It doesn't matter what percentage of the trunk is on one side of the property line or the other. If even an inch of trunk is over the line, both neighbors own the tree. Note that a tree can start out belonging to one neighbor, but become common property over time if the trunk grows over the boundary line as its girth increases.

When a tree is owned in common, both neighbors share equally in maintenance responsibilities and liability. But one owner can't trim any part of the boundary tree without the other owner's permission, even if the tree is causing damage to his yard.

There is one exception: boundary trees that are diseased, have dangerous limbs, or exceed legal height limits are the responsibility of both property owners. If one owner performs maintenance that is required by law (clearing away a dead tree, for example), she can demand a contribution from the other property owner to cover part of the cost.

Fences

According to a proverb made famous by the poet Robert Frost, "Good fences make good neighbors." While that may be true in many cases, neighbors often end up fighting over fences.

Division Fences. If a fence is entirely on one person's property, it belongs to that property owner. If a fence is on the boundary line between two properties, it may be a **division fence**. A division fence is the responsibility of both neighbors.

Under Civil Code § 841, adjoining landowners are presumed to benefit equally from a fence that divides their properties. Accordingly, they are equally responsible for the costs of construction and maintenance of the fence, unless it can be shown that equal responsibility would be unjust to one of the property owners.

Spite Fences. A **spite fence** is one that is built to bother or inconvenience a neighbor. Under Civil Code § 841.4, a fence that unnecessarily exceeds ten feet in height and was erected to annoy the neighbor is a private nuisance and may be considered a spite fence.

To decide whether a fence is a spite fence, a court will consider whether there was a conflict between the neighbors before the fence was built. The court will also evaluate the intentions of the fence builder, taking into account the height and the appearance of the fence. If it's very tall and unusually ugly (for example, a 15-foot purple fence painted with orange stripes), the court is likely to conclude that it's a spite fence.

On the other hand, a court will also consider whether the fence is serving a reasonable purpose: whether it creates privacy, helps protect children against a hazard, or is needed to keep trespassers out, for example.

Resolving a spite fence situation doesn't necessarily require a lawsuit. In many places, the rules concerning fence heights and materials in the local building code or the subdivision restrictions make a spite fence unlawful, and the rules can be enforced by building inspectors or homeowners associations.

Livestock Fences. Fences that keep livestock on the owner's property or off other people's property are an issue in agricultural areas. In California, the rules concerning livestock fences differ depending on what county you're in. Specifically, they depend on whether you're in a county or a portion of a county that's been designated as "devoted chiefly to grazing" in the Food and Agricultural Code (see sidebar).

Most of the state is not devoted chiefly to grazing and, as you might expect, farmers and cattle ranchers are expected to fence their livestock in, to prevent animals from straying and damaging other people's property.

But in counties that have been declared to be devoted chiefly to grazing, the cows have the right of way, so to speak. Farmers and ranchers aren't required to fence their animals in; other property owners are expected to fence other people's animals out.

In fact, in grazing counties, a farmer or rancher won't be liable for any damage caused by a stray animal unless the property owner can prove that his premises were enclosed with a "good and substantial fence." Food and Agricultural Code § 17121 specifies the requirements for a good and substantial fence, including the materials, construction standards, and minimum height.

Right to Farm

As suburbs have pushed further and further into what were once rural and farming areas, new types of conflicts between neighbors have developed. After buying a home in a new subdivision in an apparently idyllic rural community, former city dwellers may be in for a shock when the odor of manure from nearby farms fills the air in the heat of summer.

Usually, such an offensive odor would meet the statutory definition of a nuisance, but protective statutes, known as **right to farm laws**, try to balance the needs of farmers and homeowners.

California's right to farm law is contained in Civil Code § 3482.5. Under this statute, if a commercial farm was not a nuisance when it began, then after three years of operation it cannot be considered a nuisance due to any later change in circumstances (such as the development of a residential subdivision nearby). In essence, the right to farm law gives farmers the right to say, "I was here first."

Liability for Water Damage

Water can be a very destructive force, so another common issue between neighbors is liability for damage caused when water flows from one person's property onto another's. There are different liability rules depending on whether the water is from a man-made source, such as pipes or sprinklers, or from a natural source, such as rainfall or an underground spring.

Water from Man-Made Sources. Suppose a neighbor uphill from you leaves the sprinklers on all day, and the runoff washes away part of your garden. Is your neighbor responsible for the damage?

Fig. 15.2 Livestock fencing rules

Most counties: farmers responsible for fencing animals in

Grazing counties: property owners responsible for fencing animals out

Devoted Chiefly to Grazing

California Food and Agricultural Code § 17123 proclaims that the following areas are "devoted chiefly to grazing." In these areas, landowners must enclose their land to keep other people's stray livestock out.

- A portion of Trinity County, as delineated by statute.

- A portion of Shasta County, as delineated by statute.

- All of Siskiyou, Lassen, and Modoc Counties.

In addition, § 17124 authorizes the board of supervisors of any county to pass an ordinance declaring the county (or a portion of the county) to be devoted chiefly to grazing. If you're working in a rural area, check local ordinances to see whether your clients may need to erect or maintain a livestock fence.

In general, landowners are liable for water damage to neighboring property when the source of the water is man-made, even if the discharge of water was accidental. So a landowner can be held liable if he leaves the sprinklers on too long, or if his pipes freeze and burst, or if the pipes just start leaking because they're worn out. And, of course, he can be held liable for deliberately discharging water over a neighbor's property—by emptying his hot tub onto the neighbor's land, for example.

Water from Natural Sources. Water that accumulates on land from rain, snow, and natural springs (instead of flowing in a river channel or watercourse) is called **surface water**. Many cases concerned with liability for damage from a natural source of water involve surface water. What steps can an "upper" landowner—one whose property is on higher ground—take to protect his property from an excessive accumulation of surface water, if it results in the drainage or discharge of water onto a "lower" landowner's property?

Some states follow the **common enemy rule**. This rule holds that excessive surface water is the common enemy of every landowner, and an owner has the right to protect his own land without regard for the neighbors. In other words, you have a right to divert surface water from your property, even if your efforts end up harming your neighbors' property.

Other jurisdictions follow the **civil law rule**, which makes upper landowners responsible for damage they cause by diverting natural runoff away from their property. A lower landowner is required to accept drainage onto her property that occurs naturally, but if the upper landowner has interfered with the natural drainage, he's liable for the resulting damage.

The California supreme court established this state's rule for liability for damage from surface water in *Keys v. Romley* (1966) 64 Cal.2d 396. It's based on the civil law rule, but it requires both upper and lower landowners to act reasonably. In California, according to the *Keys* decision, an upper landowner must "take reasonable care in using his property to avoid injury to adjacent property through the flow of surface waters." At the same time, a lower landowner whose property is threatened by the flow of surface waters has a duty

---

Fig. 15.3 Liability for damage from surface water under California law

If:	If:	If:
• Lower landowner acted reasonably • Upper landowner acted either reasonably or unreasonably	• Lower landowner acted unreasonably • Upper landowner acted reasonably	• Both parties acted unreasonably
Then: Upper landowner is liable	*Then: Upper landowner is not liable*	*Liability rule not yet decided by courts*

"to take reasonable precautions to avoid or reduce any actual or potential injury." What is considered reasonable depends on all of the circumstances in the case.

If the lower landowner has acted reasonably, then the civil law rule applies: the upper landowner is liable for damage to the lower landowner's property caused by interference with the natural flow of surface water. That's true even if the upper landowner's conduct was also reasonable. But if the upper landowner has acted reasonably and the lower landowner has not, the upper landowner won't be liable.

California courts have not yet decided whether the upper landowner can be held liable if both parties have acted unreasonably. One possible result in such a case would be to hold the upper landowner liable, but award compensation to the lower landowner only for the damage that would have occurred even if she had taken reasonable steps to protect her property. She would not receive money for any damage that was the result of her failure to take reasonable protective action.

The rights and duties of landowners are complicated, and they can lead to bitter and long-running disputes with neighbors and other parties. Property buyers should take the possibility of conflict or liability into account when they're considering a purchase, and real estate agents should keep an eye out for encroachments and other red flags. Of course, not all problems have visible signs. In residential transactions, the transfer disclosure statement asks sellers to disclose encroachments, easements, neighborhood noise problems, and other nuisances they're aware of. And in every transaction, whether or not a disclosure statement is required, the seller can be a very important source of information about conflicts with neighbors and related problems. In some cases, asking the right questions will help a buyer avoid years of aggravation or misery.

Case Law in Depth

The following case involves some of the legal issues discussed in this chapter. Read through the facts and consider the questions in light of what you have learned. Then read what the court actually decided.

Tract Development Services, Inc. v. Kepler (1988) 199 Cal.App.3d 1374

The recorded map for the Temescal Gardens subdivision showed a 40-foot strip of land that was called "Diplomat Avenue" and designated as a right-of-way easement for the lots in the subdivision.

The Keplers purchased several lots, and also purchased the western half of Diplomat Avenue. Tract Development Services ("Tract") purchased several lots to the east of the Keplers, along with the eastern half of Diplomat Avenue. The initial deeds conveying the subdivision lots from the subdivider to the first purchasers back in the 1920s referenced the subdivision map, but the 1984 deed granting Tract its property made no mention of the map. Instead, the property was described by reference to a survey.

The Diplomat Avenue easement had never been used as a road. For 17 years, the previous owners of the Kepler property had maintained a fence and an unlocked gate across the northern end of the strip. The previous owners of Tract's property had planted trees on the easement. But after learning of the right-of-way, Tract began grading the entire 40-foot width of Diplomat Avenue as part of its plans to develop and build. In response, the Keplers began building a fence right down the middle of the easement to section off the western half.

The questions:

Did Tract acquire easement rights over the western half of Diplomat Avenue even though their deed made no reference to the subdivision map? When Tract's predecessors planted trees, did they abandon the easement? Or was the easement terminated by prescription after the Keplers' predecessors fenced off the northern edge of the strip? Could Tract demand that the Keplers help pay for grading and paving the shared easement?

The court's answers:

The court rejected the argument that Tract did not acquire the easement because its deed failed to mention the subdivision map. The court stated, "...once such easements for rights-of-way have been created by initial reference to a subdivision map, they pass without subsequent reference unless they are specifically excepted."

The court also rejected the abandonment argument, stating that "[An] easement created by grant is not lost by mere nonuse, no matter how long, and may be lost by abandonment only when the intention to abandon clearly appears...Trees planted on a way may indicate nothing more than the property owners' intent not to use the way as a way until some time in the distant future, e.g., not until the lots fronting on the way are developed."

And finally, the court rejected the termination by prescription argument, stating, "...not every act which appears, at first blush, to be adverse to the rights represented by the easement will suffice to extinguish it by prescription...Here, the evidence showed that the [Keplers' predecessors] erected a fence...which bisected Diplomat Avenue...and remained in place from 1943 to 1960. However, the evidence also indicated that there was a gate in the fence where it crossed Diplomat Avenue, from which it could be inferred that some person or persons used, or could use, if they desired, the right-of-way." The court concluded that the act of building the fence was "...not sufficiently hostile, open, notorious or under claim of right to constitute a prescriptive extinguishment, nor even so incompatible with the easement's nature or use as to constitute a prescriptive extinguishment."

The result:

The Keplers lost. The easement had not been terminated by prescription, nor was it abandoned, so Tract had the right to use it. Note: Although it was not specifically mentioned in the opinion, Tract could not demand that the Keplers pay for half of the cost of grading and paving the road. The Keplers had a duty to maintain and repair a shared easement, but not to improve it.

Chapter Summary

- A trespass, the unlawful entry onto another's land without permission or authority, can lead to adverse possession or to a prescriptive easement. Under adverse possession, if the possession meets the statutory requirements, a trespasser may gain title to the property in question. A prescriptive easement, on the other hand, will grant the trespasser only the right to use the underlying land for a particular, limited purpose; the original owner still retains title to the property.

- Laws against nuisances are based upon the general rule that one property owner may not use his property in such a way as to cause unnecessary damage to, or interfere with, another's use and enjoyment of her land. A nuisance *per se* is one that has been declared a nuisance by law. A public nuisance is one that affects an entire neighborhood or a large number of people. A private nuisance is one that only affects an individual or just a few people.

- To prove adverse possession, a claimant must show that the unlawful possession was by claim of right or color of title; actual, open, and notorious; exclusive and hostile; and uninterrupted and continuous. In California, an adverse possessor must also prove that she paid the property taxes on the disputed property that were assessed during the statutory period (five years).

- Easements may be created by grant, reservation, implication, or prescription. Easements may be terminated in analogous ways by express writing, implication, or prescription.

- Boundary trees and boundary fences are owned in common, and one owner may not harm or destroy such a tree or fence without the other owner's permission. Care and maintenance of such trees and fences are the shared responsibility of both owners, unless they agree to other arrangements.

- In counties declared by statute to be devoted chiefly to grazing, a property owner will not be able to claim damages for harm caused by stray livestock unless they have built a good and substantial fence (one that meets statutory specifications). In areas not devoted chiefly to grazing, it is the responsibility of ranch owners to fence their animals in.

Key Terms

- **Trespass** – The unlawful entry onto another's land without permission or lawful authority.

- **Adverse possession** – The acquisition of title to property by continuous possession for a prescribed period of time.

- **Color of title** – In adverse possession, refers to a person who holds some sort of defective instrument that appears to convey title to property.

- **Claim of right** – Refers to a person trying to claim adverse possession by showing that she had the intent, evidenced by actions and conduct (rather than a document), to claim title to property to the exclusion of all others.

- **Encroachment** – The extension of a building or other structure from land on which it was rightfully constructed onto neighboring land where it doesn't belong.

- **Nuisance** – Anything that is injurious to health, is indecent or offensive to the senses, or is an obstruction to the free use of property that interferes with an owner's comfortable use and enjoyment of life or her property. A nuisance may be public or private.

- **Nuisance *per se*** – Conduct that has been declared a nuisance by law and can be shown without proof of injury or damaging effect to another.

- **Easement** – The right held by one party to use land owned by another person for a particular, limited purpose.

- **Easement by prescription** – An easement that is established when someone makes use of another's property for a long time without permission.

- **Appurtenant easement** – An easement that attaches to and benefits a particular piece of property.

- **Runs with the land** – When land is transferred, sold, inherited, or given away, the easement is also transferred in the deed, even if the easement isn't specifically mentioned.

- **Easement in gross** – An easement that benefits a person or company, rather than a piece of land.

- **Condemnation** – A process in which the state takes private property for public use.

- **Attractive nuisance** – A dangerous structure or condition on property that is or may be particularly attractive to children.

Chapter Quiz

1. Edward holds a forged deed that purports to give him title to a farm. If all other requirements are met, Edward may still be able to claim adverse possession by:
   a) claim of right
   b) color of title
   c) possession
   d) None of the above

2. By California law, to prove adverse possession, possession must be continuous and uninterrupted for:
   a) 20 years
   b) 15 years
   c) 10 years
   d) 5 years

3. A person seeking to claim adverse possession in California must also prove that she paid the taxes that were assessed on the property for:
   a) at least two of the five years
   b) only if they were levied in her name
   c) only if the true owner hasn't paid them
   d) all five years

4. When weighing the relative hardships between a landowner and an encroacher, the court may consider:
   a) whether the encroachment was intentional or unintentional
   b) the expense and difficulty of removing the encroachment
   c) the damage that may result from the encroachment's continued use
   d) All of the above

5. Depending on local ordinance, an inoperable vehicle on residential property maybe considered a/an:
   a) nuisance *per se*
   b) encroachment
   c) trespass
   d) None of the above

6. Adverse possession and prescriptive easements are similar in all of the following ways EXCEPT:
   a) use must be open and notorious
   b) property taxes must be paid during the statutory period
   c) use must be hostile and adverse
   d) use must be continuous and uninterrupted for the statutory period

7. In general, tree ownership is determined by:
   a) the placement of the trunk
   b) the proportion of trunk on each property
   c) the placement of branches and roots
   d) None of the above

8. A large branch from Mary's tree is hanging over Bill's fence and leaning on his roof. Bill has the right to:
   a) enter Mary's property and cut off the branch near the trunk
   b) cut down the tree
   c) trim the branch back to the property line
   d) None of the above; it's against the law for Bill to touch Mary's tree

9. Susan lives in a county that California has declared devoted chiefly to grazing. Her property is unfenced, and a steer from a neighboring ranch wanders onto her property, trampling her prize-winning roses. Susan can:
   a) claim the animal as her own
   b) sue the ranch owner for damages
   c) do nothing, as the ranch owner's property was properly fenced
   d) do nothing, as her own property wasn't property fenced

10. The Jones family builds a large house down the road from the Clearview Farm, in operation since 1910 as a dairy farm. On hot summer days, the smell of manure pervades the neighborhood. The Joneses sue. At court, the law finds for Clearview Farm based on:
    a) lack of nuisance *per se*
    b) the right to farm law
    c) weighing relative hardships
    d) the cost to Clearview Farm to abate the nuisance

Chapter Answer Key

Chapter Quiz Answers:

1. b) If all other conditions are met, Edward may be able to prove adverse possession by color of title, which refers to a person who holds some sort of defective document that claims to convey title to property.

2. d) By California law, possession must be continuous and uninterrupted for a period of five years.

3. d) In California, an adverse possessor must pay taxes during the statutory period (five years). If both owner and adverse possessor are assessed, it doesn't matter who pays first. However, if only the owner is assessed, the adverse possessor must pay first to meet the requirement.

4. d) In addition, the court may consider the effect of the encroachment on the landowner's use and enjoyment of her property.

5. a) Depending on local ordinance, an inoperable vehicle on private property may be considered a nuisance *per se*.

6. b) A person may acquire an easement by prescription even if he hasn't paid the property taxes during the statutory period.

7. a) In general, a property owner owns any trees whose trunks are wholly on her land, even if branches and roots extend over and under neighboring property. Proportion of trunk placement is irrelevant: any tree that straddles a property line is owned in common.

8. c) Bill has the right to self-help to deal with Mary's encroaching tree limb. However, he is limited to trimming the branch back to the property line.

9. d) Susan is out of luck. In counties devoted chiefly to grazing, property owners are expected to fence other people's animals out. Susan lacked a good and substantial fence; therefore, she has no right to damages.

10. b) California has developed laws, known as right to farm laws, which declare that existing agricultural activities cannot be nuisances.

Cases to Consider... Answers:

Easement by Necessity

Kellogg v. Garcia (2002) 102 Cal.App.4th 796. The court ruled in favor of the Kelloggs. An easement by necessity arises when the requirement of strict necessity is met, and when the dominant and servient tenements were under common ownership at the time of the conveyance that created the necessity. In this case, the neighbors asserted that the second requirement wasn't fulfilled, because the dominant and servient tenements were never under common ownership. But the court looked all the way back to the original 1878 conveyances by the federal government. It was those original conveyances that landlocked the Kelloggs' parcel, making an easement strictly necessary, and the easement became appurtenant at that time.

Maintenance of Easements

Herzog v. Grosso (1953) 41 Cal.2d 219. On appeal, the court upheld most of the lower court's decision, but overturned the order requiring Grosso to pave the road. The appellate court found that Grosso could not interfere with the Herzogs' use of the easement or prevent them from maintaining it and putting up a guardrail. It was also within the trial court's power to order removal of the gate. But as the owner of the servient tenement, Grosso had no duty to maintain or improve the road. The Herzogs had the right to pave their section, but Grosso could not be ordered to pay for it.

List of Cases

Baglione v. Leue (1958) 160 Cal.App.2d 731
Buechner v. Jonas (1964) 228 Cal.App.2d 127
Connolly v. McDermott (1984) 162 Cal.App.3d 973
Herzog v. Grosso (1953) 41 Cal.2d 219
Kellogg v. Garcia (2002) 102 Cal.App.4th 796
Keys v. Romley (1966) 64 Cal.2d 396
Tract Development Services, Inc. v. Kepler (1988) 199 Cal.App.3d 1374

Chapter 16

Common Interest Developments

Outline

Introduction

This chapter surveys the laws surrounding common interest developments (CIDs). "Common interest development" is California's term for subdivisions in which the homeowners share title to certain aspects of the subdivision property. Almost all subdivisions developed today are CIDs.

We'll start by describing the various types of common interest developments. Next, we'll consider two state statutes that have an impact on subdivision developers: the Subdivision Map Act and the Subdivided Lands Law. We'll also briefly examine the laws regulating subdivision units and timeshares sold through interstate commerce. Finally, we'll discuss the Davis-Stirling Common Interest Development Act, which provides rules for forming and operating the homeowners associations that manage CIDs.

Types of Common Interest Developments

California subdivisions that date back to the 1950s and 1960s are typically **standard subdivisions**: groups of traditional houses built more or less simultaneously by a single developer. Since the 1970s, however, smaller families and increasing land costs have made common interest developments far more common than standard subdivisions.

In standard subdivisions, the homeowners are usually governed by a set of restrictions or rules, but they don't share ownership of any of the subdivision property. In a **common interest development**, on the other hand, homeowners share title to at least some aspects of the property. Examples of shared elements—known as **common elements**—include parking lots, recreational facilities, golf courses, parks, and even roads.

The housing units in many CIDs are clustered together; they are built far closer together than more traditional housing. This allows the development to have more surrounding open space, an added benefit to homeowners.

There are four main types of common interest developments: condominiums, planned developments, community apartments, and cooperatives.

Condominiums and Planned Developments

A common interest development is almost always either a condominium or a planned development. Here's the distinction between the two. A **condominium** owner owns her unit

---

 CIDs: the Dark Side?

CIDs have been the fastest-growing form of housing for quite some time. Indeed, over 47,000 CIDs are currently listed in a California registry. But is the tremendous growth of this form of housing entirely a good thing?

CIDs are sometimes criticized for privatizing parks and streets and other amenities that have been traditionally enjoyed by the general public. To some, the security gates at the entrance of many CIDs represent strength and security; to others, they create a sense of exclusion and mark a decline in community. Should the government be putting traditionally public tasks (such as road construction and maintenance) in private hands, even if it means saving tax dollars?

Another controversial aspect of CIDs is their frequent exemption from certain zoning requirements. Local governments claim that these zoning exemptions help to protect rural areas by encouraging high-density development instead of sprawl.

from the walls in, but shares ownership of the hallways, the roof, and the land beneath the building. In a **planned development** (sometimes referred to as a planned unit development or PUD), owners take title to their individual homes and lots, as in a standard subdivision.

The deed to a condominium unit or a house in a planned development gives the grantee sole ownership of the unit or house, along with an undivided partial interest in the CID's common elements. The common elements are owned by all of the homeowners in the development as tenants in common.

Townhouses. The units in either a condominium or a planned development may take the form of townhouses. The term **townhouses** is often used to describe multi-story homes that share common walls with other units (as in a condominium) and yet have private yard areas (like the houses in a planned development).

When a townhouse development is created as a condominium, then the private yard area of each townhouse is classified as a limited common area. A **limited common area** is owned by all of the owners in the development as tenants in common, but the possessory rights to it are assigned to a particular owner. So the private yard of a townhouse may be owned by all of the owners in the development, but only the owner of that townhouse has the right to use its yard. (If townhouses are created as a planned development instead of a condominium, then the yards are owned separately, as in a planned development with regular houses.)

Community Apartments and Cooperatives

Two much less common forms of CIDs are the community apartment and the stock cooperative (or "co-op"). In each case, ownership of the whole development is shared, and the entire subdivision may be thought of as a single common element.

In a **community apartment**, all of the owners own the entire development as tenants in common. Each owner receives a deed for an undivided partial interest in the development, along with a lease to their individual unit (or lot). Most multi-unit buildings that were originally formed as community apartments have long since been converted to condominiums. Mobile home parks, however, are often organized as community apartments.

With a **cooperative**, residents don't receive deeds. Instead, they own stock in a corporation that holds title to the entire development, and they have a lease for their individual unit. Although co-ops are more common on the east coast, there are some co-ops in California, mainly in urban areas. Most of them were created to provide lower-cost housing for students or workspace for artists.

Subdivision Laws

In this section, we'll examine four statutes that affect the subdivision and sale of real property in California. These statutes are the:

- Subdivision Map Act,
- Subdivided Lands Law,
- Vacation Ownership and Timeshare Act of 2004, and
- Interstate Land Sales Full Disclosure Act.

The Subdivision Map Act and the Subdivided Lands Law are state laws regulating the subdivision of land and the sale of subdivided parcels. Another state law, the Vacation Ownership and Timeshare Act, regulates the sale of timeshare interests. Finally, the Interstate Land Sales Full Disclosure Act is a federal statute that applies when subdivision lots are sold or advertised across state boundaries.

Subdivision Map Act

California's Subdivision Map Act was originally passed in 1907 to help standardize subdivision procedures and to keep track of titles to lots. The law requires developers to create and record detailed plans or maps of their subdivisions. These maps show lot lines, roads, grading, utility easements, and numerous other subdivision elements.

The Subdivision Map Act was subsequently amended to include a number of provisions designed to address problems caused by the state's burgeoning growth. Now the law also requires developers to design subdivisions to conform to city or county land-use goals, pay fees for the use of public services, and prepare environmental impact reports. (This last requirement is discussed in Chapter 18.)

Although the Map Act is a state law, contained in Government Code §§ 66410 – 66499, local governments are responsible for enforcing its provisions. City and county agencies will review a subdivision map in its early stages and may require the developer to make certain changes to the project to lessen its impact on the community and environment.

A developer can't enter into any binding purchase agreements with home buyers until he has filed the required map and complied with the requirements of the local government agencies. If a subdivision property is sold but no map has been recorded, the buyer has one year to void her purchase. Developers who ignore the Map Act requirements may also be subject to criminal penalties.

Application of the Map Act. The Subdivision Map Act applies to every subdivision of a parcel of property, even to the simple act of dividing one parcel into two. (The term "parcel" is interpreted broadly; for example, a condominium project meets the definition of a subdivision and requires a map.) However, some of the Map Act's provisions apply only when land is divided into five or more parcels.

Map Approval Process. The first step in the approval process for those dividing land into five or more parcels is filing a tentative map. The **tentative map** is a draft of the **final map** that the developer must eventually record. The local agency charged with evaluating subdivision maps (often called the planning department) circulates the tentative map to other city or county departments, so they can study any issues relating to such things as flood control, utility supply, public amenities, and impact on schools. The developer can argue its case to these departments—for example, by filing an expert's opinion that the proposed roads are adequate to meet the anticipated traffic demands generated by the new development.

Once the tentative map has been recorded, the developer may sign conditional purchase agreements for subdivision properties. However, these presales aren't binding on purchasers until the final map is filed. (The Subdivided Lands Law, discussed next, also imposes conditions that these developers must meet before selling property.)

Eventually each department that received a copy of the tentative map makes its report to the planning department regarding the proposed project. Based on these reports, the planning department either accepts or rejects the tentative map. Most commonly, the map receives qualified acceptance: acceptance with remedial conditions imposed on the developer based on recommendations from the reviewing departments. The subdivider may have to dedicate land for open space, reduce the height of structures, or change grading. It's not uncommon for a planning department to impose dozens of conditions. Getting a tentative map approved may take years. And once approved, the subdivider must satisfy all the conditions (widening a street, adding drainage, and so on) before filing the final map.

Generally, the tentative map expires within 24 to 36 months, although developers may seek extensions under certain conditions. If a tentative map expires before the developer can file the final map, the developer will have to begin the process all over again: re-filing a tentative map and seeking planning department approval.

Property owners who are subdividing a parcel into fewer than five parcels typically have an easier time; they usually just need to file a **parcel map**. The procedure is somewhat simplified, and the planning department usually imposes fewer conditions on these smaller subdivisions.

Condominium Conversions. Developers who want to convert an apartment building into a condominium must file a subdivision map under the Subdivision Map Act. If the conversion creates five or more condominium units, the developer must also meet the report requirements of the Subdivided Lands Law, which we'll discuss shortly.

Tenants displaced by a condominium conversion may have trouble finding other rental units, and the Subdivision Map Act tries to address this problem. The act requires the developer to give tenants 180 days' written notice that their tenancy is terminating due to a conversion. Further, tenants must receive at least 90 days' notice before their unit is actually put on the market. For the 90 days that follow this notice, tenants have the exclusive right to buy their unit on the same or more favorable terms than will be offered to the public.

Some local governments impose additional requirements on conversions to help protect tenants from displacement. These local ordinances can be fairly tough. San Francisco, for example, strictly limits the size and number of buildings that may be converted in any given year and conducts a lottery to determine which conversion applications will receive permits.

Conversion laws can apply to other types of residential rental property besides apartment buildings. For instance, the following case involved conversion of a mobile home park.

Case Example:

El Dorado Palm Springs, Ltd., the owner of a 377-lot mobile home park, sought approval under the Subdivision Map Act to subdivide the park into individual units and sell them to the current renters, thereby converting the park into a resident-owned mobile home park.

When a mobile home park is converted, the government can require the owner to help displaced residents obtain a berth at another mobile home park. Citing this law, the city of Palm Springs required El Dorado to come up with over one million dollars in aid to help existing tenants purchase their mobile home lots. But the court ordered the city to lift this requirement. The law was intended to help only those who were being displaced, not those who were purchasing their lots. *El Dorado Palm Springs, Ltd. v. City of Palm Springs* (2002) 96 Cal.App.4th 1153.

Subdivided Lands Law

The Subdivided Lands Law (also known as the Subdivided Lands Act) requires the sellers of residential subdivided parcels or interests to make detailed disclosures to any potential buyers. These disclosure requirements are intended to protect the public from fraud or misrepresentation in the purchase or lease of a subdivision property. The statute was enacted in 1943, partly in response to several land swindles that involved fraudulent marketing. Its provisions are contained in Business and Professions Code §§ 11000 – 11200.

The Subdivided Lands Law applies to sales, financing, and leases of property in residential subdivisions containing at least five lots or units. (In contrast, the Subdivision Map Act applies to every subdivision, regardless of size.)

If a subdivision project is covered by the Subdivided Lands Law, its developer must obtain a **public report** from the California Bureau of Real Estate (CalBRE) before offering any lot or unit for sale or lease. To obtain a public report, the developer files an application with the CalBRE that contains a notice of intent, a completed questionnaire with information regarding the project, and attached documentation.

The Real Estate Commissioner reviews each application, checking for misrepresentations and seeking evidence that buyers will get what they pay for. The developer must demonstrate that it has a reliable procedure for removing blanket financing and construction liens from sold properties. It must also have a trust account in place for securing buyer deposits. If the application is approved, the Commissioner will issue a public report.

Public Reports. The public report is intended to help consumers make informed decisions about the subdivision. To that end, it contains a number of disclosures about the subdivision properties, including descriptions of any:

- taxes and assessments,
- private restrictions,
- unusual charges to buyers,
- hazards or environmental issues, or
- potentially harmful financing terms.

The Subdivided Lands Law prohibits making any arrangement for the sale of a subdivision property before the Commissioner issues either a preliminary report, a conditional report, or a final report.

Case Example:

Sidebotham pled guilty to subdividing land in Solano County and offering the lots for sale without first notifying the Commissioner as required by law.

Sidebotham was sentenced to one year in jail. After his sentencing, he challenged the constitutionality of the law he'd been convicted of violating. He argued that the requirement that he obtain and distribute a public report was an unconstitutional infringement of his property rights. The court disagreed. Protecting consumers from "sharp practices" was a reasonable exercise of the state's police power and not unconstitutional. (Note: Although this is an old case, it's still frequently cited in current court decisions.) *In re Sidebotham* (1938) 12 Cal.2d 434.

Each type of subdivision public report (preliminary, conditional, and final) plays a distinct role in the sales process. Let's consider each of them individually.

Preliminary subdivision public report. Developers may apply to the Commissioner for a **preliminary report** in advance of the final report. This allows a developer to get the selling process underway by taking buyer "reservations." The preliminary report is printed on pink paper and is frequently referred to as a "pink report" (as opposed to the "white report"—the final report). A buyer can back out of a reservation that is made based on a pink report and get her full deposit back; she isn't locked into the purchase until after she receives the final report. Developers can use a preliminary report for one year. After that, it expires and a new one must be obtained from the Commissioner.

The preliminary report contains initial versions of most or all of the disclosures that will make up the final report. The Commissioner won't issue the pink report unless it's reasonably certain that the requirements for issuing the final report will be met in due time.

Conditional subdivision public report. As a subdivision project nears completion, a developer may want to stop taking buyer reservations and begin entering into conditional purchase contracts. Before it can do this, though, the developer must be able to give potential buyers a **conditional report** before they sign the conditional contract. To obtain a conditional report, the developer must provide evidence that (among other things) the project will be completed as promised and that buyers' deposits will be handled properly.

Conditional purchase contracts are binding only for a certain period of time, during which the seller/developer must obtain the final report. Until recently, developers had only six months after issuance of a conditional report to obtain the final report. Developers complained that the Commissioner was taking years to issue final reports and approve final maps. Responding to industry lobbying, the legislature expanded the life of a conditional report from half a year to 30 months, though only for condominiums.

Final subdivision public report. When the Commissioner determines that the subdivision project meets the requirements of the Subdivided Lands Law, a **final report** will be issued. Once the final report is distributed to buyers and the final map is recorded, subdivision home sales can be finalized.

A prospective buyer must receive a copy of the final report before signing a purchase agreement. (A copy must also be given to anyone else who requests one.) Sellers need to get signed statements from buyers acknowledging receipt of this report, and must keep these statements for at least three years. (Similar receipts also must be kept for any conditional and preliminary reports that have been given to buyers.)

The final report is valid for five years. After five years, the seller must obtain a fresh report from the Commissioner to give to buyers. A new report is also required if the subdivision undergoes **material changes**, such as: 1) the addition of new streets; 2) alteration

Subdivision Advertising

Summarized below are some of the Real Estate Commissioner's more interesting regulations on subdivision advertising.

- A subdivider cannot advertise using a name that incorrectly implies that the subdivider is a research organization, public agency, or nonprofit organization.
- Illustrations of the subdivision must accurately portray the land as it exists and the proposed improvements as they will be built.
- A subdivider cannot advertise that a facility exists for the exclusive use of subdivision owners if the public has a right to use the facility.
- A subdivider cannot advertise a "discounted purchase price" unless the subdivider has established a base price through a substantial number of sales.
- Offers of travel, accommodations, meals, or entertainment at no or reduced cost to promote sales cannot be described as "awards" or "prizes."
- The approximate value of any gift or premium offered to purchasers must be stated in the advertisement.

of lot sizes; or 3) restructuring of sales (either in terms of financing or the method of conveyance). Also, if a buyer takes a significant stake in the project by purchasing five or more parcels, a new report must be issued disclosing this information. For a detailed list of conditions requiring a new report, see California Code of Regulations, Title 10, § 2800.

Sales Not Requiring Public Reports. Before concluding our discussion of the Subdivided Lands Law, let's look at three situations where the act does not require a public report (although the last one—out-of-state sales—requires something very similar).

Exemptions based on size or type of subdivision. As noted, the Subdivided Lands Law doesn't apply to developments involving fewer than five parcels. Nor does it apply to subdivisions with big lots: the statute exempts subdivisions where each parcel is 160 acres or larger. Presumably, people buying such large pieces of land are reasonably sophisticated investors—or have the funds to hire lawyers, surveyors, and other professionals.

Case to Consider...

Developers have attempted to escape the requirements of the Subdivided Lands Law through a process known as "four-by-fouring." A developer divides a large property into four lots that are then conveyed to people controlled by the developer. Since this subdivision involves only four lots, the Subdivided Lands Law doesn't apply. The new owners (called "strawman grantees") then divide their pieces into four more parcels each and deed them to associates. This cycle repeats itself until a normal residential-sized lot is reached.

A subdivider named Byers tried this "four-by-four" scheme, using a real estate broker as one of the strawman grantees. Did Byers violate the Subdivided Lands Law by failing to apply for a public report? *People v. Byers* (1979) 90 Cal.App.3d 140.

Note that although it is certainly possible (and common) for land to be subdivided for commercial purposes such as an industrial park, the Subdivided Lands Law doesn't apply to commercial subdivisions.

Resale of properties. If a private homeowner sells her subdivision property, the buyer has no right to a public report. However, the buyer usually receives many of the same disclosures through the real estate transfer disclosure statement (discussed in Chapter 9). The seller must also provide the buyer with other materials, including:

- copies of the homeowners association's governing documents,
- a summary of restrictions affecting the property, and
- disclosures regarding financial matters such as homeowner dues and assessments for major repairs.

Homeowners associations, restrictions, dues, and assessments are discussed in the next section of this chapter.

Out-of-State Subdivision Sales. We'll conclude our discussion of the Subdivided Lands Law with a note about the consumer protection extended to California residents who buy property in a subdivision located outside the state if the developer conducts sales activity in California.

Someone who develops a subdivision outside of California, but who markets the subdivision properties within California does not need a public report. However, she must obtain permits from the Real Estate Commissioner, and the permit process is similar to the process for obtaining a public report. As part of the permit process, buyers must receive disclosures like those required by the Subdivided Lands Law for in-state sales.

Note that the federal Interstate Lands Sales Full Disclosure Act, discussed below, also requires these kinds of disclosures for interstate sales.

Vacation Ownership and Timeshare Act of 2004

With a timeshare, a buyer purchases the right to occupy a property—usually a condo in a vacation area—for one or more periods every year. Traditionally, California treated timeshares as subdivisions under the Subdivided Lands Law. However, consumer complaints about timeshare sales helped convince legislators that separate statutory treatment was needed. The **Vacation Ownership and Timeshare Act of 2004** (Business and Professions Code §§ 11210 – 11288) now governs many aspects of the timeshare business.

Under the act, buyers must receive a public report making numerous disclosures about the timeshare property. The statute also provides buyers with a seven-day right of rescission after they sign a timeshare purchase agreement. The seller must include a prominent statement over the contract signature line that advises the buyer of this rescission right.

> ▶ **Timeshare or Crimeshare?**

Most buyers report reasonable satisfaction with their timeshare property. Others, however, have found timeshares to be an over-priced, over-hyped product deserving of the nickname "crimeshares." Based on recommendations from the Federal Trade Commission, here are some questions that potential timeshare purchasers should ask themselves:

- Are you buying under impulse or pressure? Any incentives (such as discounts on vacation accommodations or activities) should be evaluated carefully. Review all of the purchase documents carefully, preferably outside of the presentation setting, or have someone familiar with timeshares review them.

- Are you counting on an easy resale? Local real estate brokers may not want to include timeshares in their listings. Also, be aware that significant appreciation is rare. It's not uncommon for people to end up selling their timeshares for less than half what they paid.

- Are you relying on a salesperson's oral statements? Make sure everything promised is written into the contract.

- Are you counting on vacationing in a more desirable destination by using an exchange program? Exchange programs typically offer no guaranty of availability. In addition, you may need to request exchanges far in advance. Check the timeshare plan's flexibility: some are better than others at accommodating a last-minute change of plans.

- Have you researched the track record of the seller, developer, and management company? Visit the facilities and try to talk to other owners. Local real estate agents, Better Business Bureaus, and consumer protection offices may also be good sources of information.

- Are all facilities complete? If any amenities remain unfinished, get a written commitment that the work will be completed. Consider requiring that some of your money be held in escrow in case the developer defaults.

Interstate Land Sales Full Disclosure Act

The federal **Interstate Land Sales Full Disclosure Act** (ILSA) applies to the interstate sale and advertising of unimproved residential lots in medium- or larger-sized subdivisions (at least 25 lots). The law is intended to prevent fraud and deceptive practices in the sale of vacant lots by providing potential buyers with important information about the properties offered for sale. Congress passed ILSA partly in response to interstate land development scams that took place during the 1960s. The Consumer Financial Protection Bureau enforces the act.

Any development covered by ILSA must be registered with the Bureau, and the developer must prepare a **property report** containing certain disclosures about the project. A potential buyer must receive a copy of the property report before signing a sales agreement. The buyer has seven days to withdraw from a sale after receiving the disclosure report.

Note that the disclosures required by California's permitting process for out-of-state subdivisions also meet ILSA's requirements; therefore, interstate sellers involved in California projects only have to produce a single report.

Homeowners Associations

Now that we've covered the laws that regulate the development of a CID, let's turn our attention from the developers to the subdivision homeowners. Under the **Davis-Stirling Common Interest Development Act** (Civil Code §§ 4000 – 6150), every residential common interest development in California must form a **homeowners association** to manage the subdivision and handle disputes between owners. The Davis-Stirling Act governs the creation and operation of these associations.

Note that although associations may go by various names—for example, condo residents typically belong to a "condominium association"—any group of property owners that's formed to manage a CID is a homeowners association for the purposes of the Davis-Stirling Act.

Association Membership

Every homeowner in a CID automatically becomes a member of the CID's homeowners association. The association must hold regular meetings. At these meetings, the unit owners vote on various issues, with either one vote per unit or with voting power determined by unit square footage or some other factor. This means that developers retain some voting power until they've sold all of the units.

The homeowners association is generally responsible for maintaining and repairing the CID's common areas and structures; in addition, the association sometimes makes improvements to the development (building a recreational facility, for example). Funds for repairs, maintenance, and improvements are raised through member assessments.

Assessments. The homeowners association levies regular fees on its members, typically on a monthly basis. These **homeowner dues** cover routine expenses such as the maintenance of hallways and grounds and other common elements. The association may also levy **special assessments** to make major repairs to roofs, sewers, and other common elements. Special assessments may also be used to pay for outright improvements, such as the addition of a tennis court or playground.

The association may impose fees on individual homeowners for some services—for example, when an owner sells a unit, the association may impose a **transfer fee**. The Davis-Stirling Act forbids associations from imposing transfer fees that exceed the actual costs incurred in performing the required tasks (for instance, preparing copies of the association's governing documents, which the seller must provide to the buyer).

Associations must follow detailed notice procedures laid out in the Davis-Stirling Act when making assessments or pursuing collection. Homeowners who dispute an assessment

Special Assessments

Homeowners associations facing major repairs can hit their members with some pretty big special assessments—as high as $25,000 or more per unit. Huge assessments like these can impose serious hardships for owners and may even lead to a forced sale of the home.

To avoid this kind of situation, an association should steadily accumulate a reserve fund for repairs and improvements. Yet many boards are reluctant to impose homeowner fees for anything other than immediate needs. As a result, reserves are often underfunded. One survey determined that over half the state's homeowners associations lack enough funding to meet reasonably foreseeable expenses.

Home buyers should ask what major repairs or improvements loom ahead and determine how well the reserve fund can handle these costs.

must be informed of their right to meet with the board, and their right to use a method of alternative dispute resolution (such as mediation or arbitration) instead of filing a lawsuit.

The federal **Fair Debt Collection Practices Act** applies to an association's assessment collection actions. The act imposes restrictions on where and when a debtor may be called on the phone. This law also limits fees and provides various other debtor protections.

Board of Directors

In most associations of any size, the homeowners elect a **board of directors** from among the members. This board makes most of the management decisions.

Boards hold regular public meetings, but they also conduct executive or "closed" sessions to consider private matters, such as litigation strategy, personnel matters, bids from contractors, and how to handle owners who ignore rules or assessments.

Homeowners who are disgruntled by a board's decision may sue the association. However, courts won't reverse a board's decision as long as there was a reasonable basis for it. As this is a fairly lenient standard, most association actions are upheld.

Case to Consider...

A La Jolla condominium complex suffered from termites. Lamden was one of the unit owners affected. The condo board chose spot treatment instead of fumigation. They cited numerous reasons for this decision, including cost, toxicity, resident relocation difficulty, anticipated breakage by the fumigators, and the likelihood that termite infestation would recur despite fumigation. The termite problem continued for several years. Lamden sued the association over its failure to fumigate. Was the association's decision to spot treat unreasonable? *Lamden v. La Jolla Shores Clubdominium Homeowners Assn.* (1999) 21 Cal.4th 249.

Governing Documents

Homeowners associations are also governed by a set of documents that includes a **declaration** (a recorded document that contains rules affecting the entire subdivision, discussed in the next chapter), **articles of incorporation** (or articles of association, if the group doesn't incorporate), and, usually, **bylaws**.

The governing documents must include a great deal of information, including:

- a property description;
- rules affecting ownership;
- the method of calculating and collecting assessments;
- disciplinary procedures;
- notice, voting, and quorum requirements; and
- powers of the board (if a board is created).

Recordkeeping and Inspection Rights. The association must keep minutes of all its board meetings and general meetings. It must also maintain financial books and other records. All members have a right to inspect these records, with the exception of the board's executive session minutes. The votes cast by homeowners are also entitled to some protection, as the court held in the following case.

Case Example:

A homeowners association director wanted to examine the ballots from a recent board election, believing the votes that were cast for him had been undercounted. The association refused, citing the members' right to keep their votes private.

The trial court balanced the right to privacy against the right of inspection by ruling that the director's lawyer could view the ballots, and take notes, but neither write down nor reveal to his client how any particular homeowner had voted. Rather than accept this arrangement, the director appealed.

The appellate court rebuffed the director and upheld the trial court's decision. The limited inspection approach would reveal whether fraud or error had taken place and yet preserve voter privacy. *Chantiles v. Lake Forest II Master Homeowners Assn.* (1995) 37 Cal.App.4th 914.

Since common interest developments account for a significant share of the residential real estate in California, you'll probably deal with CIDs, homeowners associations, and their governing documents quite often in your career. You're also likely to see a fair number of subdivision public reports and subdivision maps. Familiarity with the state's laws governing common interest developments and other subdivisions should be useful in many transactions.

Case Law in Depth

The following case involves some of the legal issues discussed in this chapter. Read through the facts and consider the questions in light of what you have learned. Then read what the court actually decided.

Ostayan v. Nordhoff Townhomes Homeowners Assn., Inc. (2003) 110 Cal. App.4th 120

The 1994 Northridge earthquake damaged the Nordhoff townhouse complex in North Hills. Three years later, Ostayan purchased an uninhabitable Nordhoff unit from HUD for $25,000.

When Ostayan bought his unit, the homeowners association was embroiled in a dispute with its insurer over payment for earthquake damage. In the summer of 1997, the association wrote a notice to the homeowners describing meetings with the insurance company over its failure to pay for a $100,000 electrical vault repair. That fall, two similar notices followed. Ostayan admitted receiving all three notices, but pointed out that none specifically mentioned litigation.

In 1998, Ostayan sold the unit to the Estradas for $53,500. A week after the sale closed, the association wrote its members that it had sued the insurer. In 2000, the association settled its lawsuit for $20 million. The association distributed these settlement funds to its current members. The Estradas received $180,000—almost three times what they paid for the townhouse. Ostayan sued the association, claiming that he wouldn't have sold if he'd known the association was contemplating litigation.

The questions:

Must a homeowners association notify its members of an intention to sue an insurer? If so, do notices simply stating that a dispute exists, without mentioning litigation, meet this duty?

The court's answers:

The court stated that a homeowners association has a fiduciary relationship with its members similar to the relationship of a corporation to its shareholders. When an association is planning to use its funds for litigation, it must tell its members so in the next available mailing. But while it's true that homeowners associations are sometimes legally obligated to give written notice of intended litigation to association members, this rule applies only when the lawsuit concerns construction defects.

The court stated, "There is no allegation or evidence that the board's decision...was made in bad faith or was not in the interest of the Association. The Association cannot be expected to make disclosures so as to impart information in relation to every possible sale of a unit within the development. Were there such a requirement, the Association's time could be consumed with the preparation of disclosure statements. Any such rule would also render redundant the procedure of annual reports, meetings, and the disclosures of budgets established by statute.

"If Ostayan had wanted information concerning the dispute with the Association's insurer, he could have exercised his right to inspect the Association's records—or even queried a director. Then he would have been armed with all the information he now claims he needed before selling his unit...

"[Even if] the Association had some duty to Ostayan of disclosure of the litigation, the Association satisfied that duty with its disclosures of its dispute with the insurer...With this information, Ostayan had his own responsibility to ascertain 'the precise nature and scope' of the status of the dispute with the insurance carrier if such information was 'material to [his] decision to [sell the] unit.'"

The result:

The court ruled in the homeowners association's favor.

Chapter Summary

- A common interest development is a subdivision containing at least some common elements—parts of the property that are owned in common, such as a lobby or a parking area. There are four main types of common interest developments: condominiums, planned developments, community apartments, and cooperatives.

- The Subdivision Map Act requires a developer to create and record an official plan or map of its subdivision. The map shows lot lines, roads, drains, utility and public easements, and other information. The act applies to every subdivision of property. The local planning authority typically imposes a number of conditions on the developer before allowing recording of the final subdivision map. Sales of subdivision properties don't become absolutely binding until a final map is recorded.

- The Subdivided Lands Law applies to subdivisions containing five or more lots (or units). Properties can't be sold, financed, or leased until the Real Estate Commissioner reviews the project and issues a public report. The public report contains disclosures about property taxes and assessments, restrictions, unusual charges to the buyer, environmental issues, and potentially harmful financing terms. A buyer must receive a copy of the report before signing a purchase agreement.

- With a timeshare, a buyer purchases the right to occupy a property—usually a condo in a vacation area—for one or more periods every year. The Vacation Ownership and Timeshare Act of 2004 governs many aspects of the timeshare industry. The act requires that buyers be given a public report containing numerous disclosures about the timeshare property; the act also gives buyers a seven-day right of rescission.

- The Interstate Land Sales Full Disclosure Act (ILSA), a federal law, applies to interstate sales and advertising of unimproved residential lots in medium to large subdivisions (at least 25 lots). Buyers must receive a property disclosure report before signing a sales agreement. The buyer has seven days to withdraw from a sale after receiving the disclosure report. ILSA is enforced by the Consumer Financial Protection Bureau.

- The Davis-Stirling Common Interest Development Act governs the management of subdivisions by homeowners. The act requires every common interest subdivision developer to create a homeowners association. The association maintains the common elements and otherwise manages the development. Every subdivision homeowner automatically becomes a member of the association. The association must hold regular meetings and each unit gets one vote.

Key Terms

- **Common interest development** – A subdivision containing commonly owned elements such as hallways, green space, or streets.

- **Condominium** – A subdivision in which the owner owns her unit from the walls in, but shares ownership of the hallways, the roof, and the land beneath the building. All of the unit owners own the common elements as tenants in common.

- **Planned development** – A common interest development in which an owner owns both a home and the land on which it's located, but also owns common elements with all of the other homeowners as tenants in common.

- **Community apartment** – A subdivision in which each owner owns an undivided partial interest in the entire development and has an individual lease to his unit or lot. The owners own the development as tenants in common.

- **Cooperative** – A subdivision in which an owner holds stock in a corporation that holds title to the entire development, and also has a lease to her unit.

- **Subdivision Map Act** – A state law requiring that everyone who subdivides land must record a map or plan of the subdivision before selling properties.

- **Tentative and final maps** – Developers who divide land into five or more lots must file a tentative map for review by various city or county agencies; upon approval, they record a final map.

- **Subdivided Lands Law** – A state statute requiring consumer protection disclosures to buyers of property in subdivisions containing five or more lots.

- **Subdivision public report** – A disclosure report provided to the buyer of a subdivision property in compliance with the Subdivided Lands Law.

- **Vacation Ownership and Timeshare Act of 2004** – A state law requiring that timeshare buyers receive certain property disclosures and have a seven-day right of rescission after agreeing to purchase a timeshare.

- **Timeshare** – A timeshare buyer purchases the right to occupy a unit for a certain period each year.

- **Interstate Land Sales Full Disclosure Act (ILSA)** – A federal law that provides protections to interstate buyers of vacant lots in subdivisions containing 25 or more lots.

- **Davis-Stirling Common Interest Development Act** – A state law that requires any residential subdivision containing property owned in common to have a homeowners association.

- **Homeowners association** – An association that includes every homeowner in a subdivision; the association maintains any common elements and otherwise manages the development.

- **Board of directors** – In most homeowners associations, the members elect a board of directors to make management decisions.

- **Assessments** – Homeowners associations levy regular assessments to pay for routine maintenance; they may also levy special assessments for major repairs and improvements.

Chapter Quiz

1. Which of the following is a list of the different types of common interest developments?
   a) Condos, common elements, high-rises, co-ops
   b) Condos, planned developments, community apartments, co-ops
   c) Libraries and other public facilities, community apartments, co-ops
   d) None of the above

2. Mother dies, leaving her dilapidated house to her children, James and Karla. James and Karla don't get along and decide to tear down the house and divide the land in half so that each will legally own a separate parcel. Which of the following is true?
   a) The Subdivision Map Act applies and the siblings will have to obtain a public report
   b) The Subdivision Map Act applies and the siblings will have to file a tentative map and a final map
   c) The Subdivision Map Act applies, but the siblings can simply file a simple parcel map
   d) The Subdivided Lands Law applies and the siblings will have to obtain a public report

3. The chief purpose of the Subdivision Map Act is to:
   a) protect purchasers of subdivided properties by requiring financial and other disclosures about the development
   b) protect the general public by requiring local agencies to analyze and impose conditions that will mitigate the impact of the proposed subdivision
   c) protect those people who buy undeveloped subdivision lots
   d) All of the above

4. Referring to the fact pattern in question 2, as James oversees the demolition of his childhood home, a neighbor casually states that he and his sister will have to comply with the Subdivided Lands Law since they're subdividing the property. This is:
   a) false; this law does not apply to intra-family subdivisions
   b) true; this law, like the Subdivision Map Act, applies to all subdivisions
   c) false; this law does not apply to the subdivision of vacant land
   d) false; this applies only to subdivisions with five or more lots

5. Barbara, a developer, receives a final subdivision report from the Commissioner. But while waiting for this report, Barbara made some changes to her project: 1) each lot size was reduced just enough to create space for one additional lot; 2) Barbara took on a partner who bought ten lots; and 3) a road underwent a name change from Shady Street to Shady Lane.
   a) Using the final report, Barbara can sign binding purchase agreements with any buyer
   b) Using the final report, Barbara can sign binding purchase agreements with any buyer whose lot is not affected by these changes
   c) Barbara must apply for a new report because some of these project changes are material
   d) Barbara does not have to apply for a new report because none of these changes are material

6. A developer needs additional financing to complete her subdivision. She wants to prove the viability of her project to a lender by arranging sales of units before the Commissioner issues the final subdivision report. Which of the following is true?
   a) No sales activity can take place before the final subdivision report is issued
   b) The developer may enter into conditional sales contracts before the final report is issued
   c) The developer may enter into nonbinding reservation agreements for units as soon as the preliminary report is issued
   d) Both b) and c) are true

7. Jolene and Perry visit Palm Springs to stay at a friend's resort timeshare. They enjoy their stay, and on their last night the resort management talks the couple into signing a purchase agreement for a one-bedroom unit with a pool view. When the couple returns home, however, they have second thoughts. Can Jolene and Perry get out of their timeshare purchase?
   a) No; the law gives timeshare buyers only three days to rescind a purchase agreement
   b) Possibly, if they deliver their notice of rescission promptly; the law allows rescission on a case-by-case basis, with proof of economic hardship
   c) No; the law does not provide a right of rescission for timeshare purchases
   d) Yes, if they deliver their notice of rescission promptly; the law provides timeshare buyers with seven days to rescind a purchase agreement

8. The Davis-Stirling Common Interest Development Act:
   a) allows homeowners to elect a board to make decisions concerning subdivision operation
   b) requires formation of an association composed of all homeowners in the subdivision
   c) gives homeowners a vote concerning subdivision operation and provides a right to inspect most association records
   d) All of the above

9. The Shangri-La Condominiums homeowners association passes a special assessment to pay for resurfacing the tennis courts. Which of the following is true?
   a) A member of a homeowners association can't be forced to pay a special assessment; these assessments are voluntary
   b) The homeowners will have to pay the assessment
   c) The Davis-Stirling Act now prohibits homeowner assessments
   d) The special assessment is invalid: associations may only pass special assessments to pay for repairs involving safety issues

10. The tennis court resurfacing mentioned in the previous question is completed. However, a Shangri-La homeowner named Jane suspects that the association board president has kept some of the special assessment money for himself. Jane asks to look at the financial records to see how much the association paid to repair the courts.
    a) Since Jane is not a board member, she has no right to view the association's financial records
    b) Homeowners have a right to review every kind of association record
    c) Homeowners have a right to review association records except for the board's executive session minutes; here, a court would probably uphold Jane's right to inspect
    d) None of the above

Chapter Answer Key

Chapter Quiz Answers:

1. b) Condos, planned developments, community apartments, and co-ops are all forms of subdivisions in California in which some or all of the property is owned in common.

2. c) The Map Act does apply, but James and Karla will only need to file a parcel map. The Map Act doesn't require a tentative map for a subdivision with less than five lots, nor does it involve a public report. The Subdivided Lands Law doesn't apply to a subdivision with fewer than five lots.

3. b) Requiring disclosures about the property to protect purchasers is a function of the Subdivided Lands Law, not the Map Act. Under the Map Act, the planning board and other local agencies analyze a proposed subdivision and usually impose conditions on the developer.

4. d) The Subdivided Lands Law does not apply to small subdivisions.

5. c) Sellers of subdivision lots can't form binding sales agreements using a final report that has become outdated due to material changes. While the street name change is minor, a buyer purchasing five or more lots and the redrawing of lot lines are material changes.

6. d) Limited forms of sales activity are allowed before the Final Subdivision Report, though sales do not become absolutely binding until that time.

7. d) California timeshare buyers have seven days to rescind a timeshare purchase agreement.

8. d) The Davis-Stirling Common Interest Development Act provides for the formation of a homeowners association, the election of a board of directors, and the right of owners to vote and inspect association records.

9. b) Homeowners associations may levy special assessments for recreational amenities.

10. c) Homeowners may inspect the association's books and records, though not the board's executive session minutes.

Cases to Consider... Answers:

Subdivided Lands Law

People v. Byers (1979) 90 Cal.App.3d 140. Evading the Subdivided Lands Law requirements by using a series of small subdivisions to mask a larger subdivision into five or more lots is illegal. Byers and others in the scheme received criminal convictions.

Homeowners Associations

Lamden v. La Jolla Shores Clubdominium Homeowners Assn. (1999) 21 Cal.4th 249. The trial court concluded that the association had acceptable reasons for failing to fumigate. The appellate court reversed and found in favor of the unit owner, Lamden. The association appealed. The state supreme court reversed the appellate court decision, holding that the association had acted in good faith and had a right to choose the form of termite treatment it considered best.

List of Cases

Chantiles v. Lake Forest II Master Homeowners Assn. (1995) 37 Cal.App.4th 914
El Dorado Palm Springs, Ltd. v. City of Palm Springs (2002) 96 Cal.App.4th 1153
In re Sidebotham (1938) 12 Cal.2d 434
Lamden v. La Jolla Shores Clubdominium Homeowners Assn. (1999) 21 Cal.4th 249
Ostayan v. Nordhoff Townhomes Homeowners Assn., Inc. (2003) 110 Cal.App.4th 120
People v. Byers (1979) 90 Cal.App.3d 140

Chapter 17

Private and Public Restrictions on Land

Outline

Introduction

Restrictions on land use weigh individual rights against community needs—a difficult balancing act, and one that leads to many interesting conflicts. It should come as no surprise that this is a particularly contentious area of real estate law.

We've divided our discussion of restrictions into two sections. The first deals with private restrictions on land use, which are restrictions imposed by private parties such as sellers or homeowners associations. The second section addresses public restrictions, which are imposed by the government through zoning and other means.

Private Restrictions on Land Use

Private restrictions—also known as **restrictive covenants**—are land use limitations imposed on property by a private party, as opposed to a governmental agency. For example, a subdivider selling a lot to a builder might impose restrictions concerning building height, setbacks, and minimum construction costs, to help ensure a certain level of quality in the subdivision. Or the owner of a forest lot who's giving the property to a conservation group might impose a restriction that requires the land to remain undeveloped.

Private restrictions are used to address all sorts of land use issues. They may limit a property to residential use, prevent it from being subdivided into lots smaller than a specified size, prohibit certain types of trees from being planted, require certain types of shrubbery or fencing, set maintenance standards, and so on. Restrictions are typically imposed for the benefit of neighboring properties; for instance, building height restrictions often protect a neighbor's view.

If certain requirements are met, private restrictions (like easements) can **run with the land** and last indefinitely. In other words, all future owners of the property in question will have to comply with the restrictions. And all future owners of properties that benefit from the restrictions will have the right to enforce them. We'll explain the requirements for making restrictions run with the land later in this chapter.

Private restrictions are by no means unusual; it's estimated that one in six American homeowners are subject to private restrictions on the use of their land. Now let's discuss how these restrictions are created, enforced, and terminated.

Creating Private Restrictions

Private land use restrictions can be created in one of three ways: by deed, by declaration, or by contract. We'll look at each of these methods, and then we'll examine the requirements for making private restrictions run with the land. We'll also discuss illegal types of restrictions.

By Deed. Restrictions affecting a single piece of property are usually created in a deed, when ownership of the property changes hands. For example, the owner who's donating her forest lot could impose a restriction preventing development simply by including the restriction in the deed that transfers title to the conservation group: "The property described herein is to be preserved as undeveloped wilderness…" (or words to that effect).

Covenants vs. conditions. A restriction imposed in a deed may be either a covenant or a condition. A condition makes the grantee's title conditional, so that the grantee owns the property in fee simple defeasible rather than fee simple absolute. (See Chapter 4.) If the condition is violated, the grantee's title may be terminated by the grantor. In contrast, a covenant does not make the grantee's title subject to termination. A grantee who violates a covenant in his deed may be ordered to stop the violation and pay damages, but will not lose title to the property. (The same rules apply to the heirs and assigns of the grantor and grantee.)

Whenever possible, courts interpret restrictions in deeds as covenants rather than conditions. They will allow termination of title only when the wording is unambiguous and the restriction is plainly intended to make the grantee's title conditional and subject to termination. Our focus in this chapter will be on restrictive covenants, not conditions. For more information about conditions in deeds, see Chapter 4.

By Declaration. Most restrictions apply not just to a single property, but to an entire neighborhood. Instead of being created by deed, these restrictions are created with a **declaration of restrictions**, also called **CC&Rs** ("covenants, conditions, and restrictions"). This is a document prepared and recorded by a subdivision developer who wants a blanket set of restrictions to affect all of the lots in the subdivision. As an example, Figure 17.1 shows some excerpts from the CC&Rs of a fictitious subdivision.

As we said, CC&Rs stands for "covenants, conditions, and restrictions." The phrase is redundant, since the term "restrictions" is generally understood to encompass covenants and conditions. Also note that even though the phrase includes the term "conditions," CC&Rs virtually never make title conditional in the sense that we discussed above. The restrictions in CC&Rs are interpreted as restrictive covenants, not as conditions.

When a developer first begins selling lots, the deed to each individual lot simply references the recorded declaration ("subject to declaration of restrictions, recording no. 99100801326"), instead of actually giving the text of the restrictions. When the original lot owners resell their lots, the deeds will also typically mention the declaration, though that isn't required, since the information has already entered the chain of title. A title search will alert prospective buyers to the existence of the restrictions.

Purpose of CC&Rs. In most parts of the country, recording a declaration of restrictions is now a standard step in residential subdivision development. By setting certain standards and preventing conduct that might have a negative impact on the community, CC&Rs are intended to protect property values in a subdivision. The CC&Rs often require homeowners to maintain the physical condition of their properties (for instance, by repairing broken windows or unsafe porch railings), and they may impose purely aesthetic rules (for instance, limiting the colors that houses may be painted or the type of siding that can be used). In a subdivision with a homeowners association, owners may be required to submit plans to an **architectural review committee** before remodeling their home or changing the landscaping.

Changing the CC&Rs. Buyers purchasing property in a development with CC&Rs should be aware that their fellow homeowners have the power to impose new restrictions, some of which may be unwelcome. Procedures for adding restrictions or otherwise modifying the CC&Rs may be included in the declaration itself or in the homeowners association bylaws. Changes typically require a majority vote of the homeowners. However, in some cases the declaration or bylaws may state that a particular type of change requires approval by a supermajority (more than a simple majority of the homeowners). For example, changing restrictions concerning allowable building heights might require approval by 70% or 80% of the homeowners.

Note that certain kinds of rules governing a subdivision may be imposed without a vote of the homeowners. Usually the bylaws or other governing documents for a homeowners association allow the association's board to create **operating rules** without homeowner approval. Like the CC&Rs, operating rules can address matters such as property use or aesthetic and architectural review of proposed alterations. In the early 2000s, the California legislature began reining in the power of homeowners association boards to a certain

---

Fig. 17.1 Excerpts from a declaration of restrictions

Orange County Clerk-Recorder's Office: #04660968

Covenants, Conditions & Restrictions for
Valley Heights Homes

The owner of the lots described in Exhibit A declares that these lots shall be held and transferred to all subsequent owners subject to the conditions, covenants, and restrictions set forth below and subject to any additional restrictions lawfully adopted by the Valley Heights Homeowners Association.

1. **Residential use.** All lots are restricted to single-family residential use.

* * * *

10. **Outbuildings.** No structure may be added to a home or its lot, except for a single modest shed for gardening or similar quiet noncommercial activities.

* * * *

14. **Building height.** No building may be built or addition added if the resulting structure will exceed 25 feet in height. Additions of any height that block a neighbor's view are prohibited.

* * * *

27. **Nuisance.** No owner shall maintain any condition which constitutes an unreasonable nuisance to his or her neighbors.

* * * *

30. **Fines.** The association may fine any owner who violates any provision herein $35.00 per day for each violation.

* * * *

34. **Attorneys' fees.** The party prevailing in an action concerning any provision herein is entitled to attorneys' fees and costs.

extent. For example, the law now provides that homeowners can repeal a board-passed rule by vote (Civil Code § 4365). The board can't readopt a repealed rule for at least one year after the vote.

By Contract. In addition to using deeds and declarations, people occasionally create private land use restrictions by contract.

> **Example:** Morgan lives next to Tom. Cedar trees on Morgan's property are blocking Tom's view of the ocean. The neighborhood is not a subdivision and there are no restrictions created by deed or declaration that protect property owners' views or limit the height of trees. However, in return for a cash payment, Morgan signs an agreement with Tom to cut down the cedars and keep any new trees from interfering with Tom's view.

Will subsequent owners of Morgan's property be bound by this tree height restriction? That depends on several factors. The requirements for creating restrictions that run with the land is our next topic.

Requirements for Restrictions that Run with the Land

Restrictions that protect views or provide other benefits can add significantly more to property values if future owners must honor them. Thus, most people want restrictions to run with the land. Under Civil Code § 1468, a restriction that burdens subsequent owners of a property must meet these requirements:

1. It must include a legal description of the properties affected (both the property burdened by the restriction and the property benefited by it).
2. It must express an intent that subsequent owners of the burdened land be bound by the restriction.
3. It must relate to the:
    *   use, repair, maintenance, or improvement of the property;
    *   suspension of co-owners' partition rights; or
    *   payment of taxes and assessments.
4. It must be recorded.

> **Example:** Returning to Morgan and Tom, if the neighbors put their agreement in writing, with the legal descriptions of both of their properties and a statement of intent to bind future owners, and then record the document, they would satisfy the statute. Future owners of Morgan's property would have to honor the tree height agreement, and future owners of Tom's property would have the right to enforce the agreement.

Illegal Restrictions

Private restrictions concerning certain matters are illegal and unenforceable. For example, at one time restrictions against selling property to African-Americans and Jews were common, especially in wealthy areas such as Beverly Hills and Bel-Air. The U.S. Supreme Court ruled that this type of discriminatory covenant was unenforceable in the 1948 case *Shelley v. Kraemer* (see Chapter 19). Even so, the restrictive language lingered on in older deeds. In the 1980s, HUD instructed title companies to strike these offensive provisions out of title documents, and California lawmakers passed a similar requirement that went into effect in 2001 (Government Code § 12955(l)). Currently, California law prohibits not only restrictions that discriminate on the basis of race or religion, but also any that discriminate on the basis of sex, gender, gender identity, gender expression, sexual orientation, marital status, familial status, national origin, ancestry, disability, genetic information, or (to protect those receiving public assistance) source of income.

State law imposes a requirement concerning illegal covenants on those who provide copies of recorded documents to others in the course of their work. This includes county recorders, title company employees, escrow agents, homeowners association representatives, and real estate agents. Whenever someone is given a copy of a previously recorded deed or declaration of restrictions that contains a discriminatory covenant, the person providing the copy must stamp the document or attach a cover page stating that the restriction is void and may be removed by recording a Restrictive Covenant Modification.

A number of other statutes also limit private restrictions. As of 2001, every California homeowner has the right to keep at least one pet. (That rule isn't retroactive, however; bans on pet ownership in CC&Rs established before 2001 are still enforceable.) Restrictions prohibiting installation of solar energy systems are illegal, although reasonable requirements concerning the systems can be imposed. It's also illegal to prohibit display of noncommercial signs and flags (a rule mainly intended to protect political free speech), as long as they don't exceed a certain size. "For Sale" and "For Rent" signs can't be prohibited, either. In addition, a homeowners association can't restrict owners to the use of a particular real estate brokerage when selling their homes.

Federal communications law makes it illegal to prohibit residents from erecting satellite dishes and antennas. This law protects renters as well as homeowners.

More generally, under both common law and statutory law, the courts will not enforce unreasonable or unfair restrictions. Numerous websites are devoted to homeowner complaints of unreasonable CC&Rs enforced by "out-of-control" condo boards and homeowners associations. Although the courts presume reasonableness and rarely rule against the enforcement of a restriction, it does happen occasionally, as in the following case.

Case Example:

Cunningham, a senior citizen, a veteran, and a sufferer from Hodgkin's disease, owned an attached home in Fountain Valley. Neighbors complained to the homeowners association that his home's cluttered interior posed a fire hazard. The association demanded that Cunningham allow an inspection. Under the threat of litigation, Cunningham agreed.

After the inspection, the association's attorneys wrote Cunningham a letter claiming that his housekeeping violated CC&Rs related to cleanliness and safety. They ordered him to clear his bed of all papers and books, remove boxes from around his bed and dresser, and stop using his downstairs bathroom for storage. The letter also stated, "The Association suggests that all outdated clothing that has not been worn in the last five years be removed and/or donated to the Salvation Army or similar organization...Books that are currently in book shelves, and which are considered standard reading material, can remain in place."

The association was dissatisfied with Cunningham's attempts to comply, and they sued. A fire department inspection determined that none of the messiness constituted a fire hazard, and eventually the jury returned a verdict in favor of Cunningham. But the trial judge rejected the jury's verdict and ordered a new trial. An appeal followed.

The appellate court called the association's letter "presumptuous," and found "particularly galling" the directive to Cunningham regarding his clothing. The homeowners association had gone too far; its interpretation and enforcement of the CC&Rs was unreasonable. *Fountain Valley Chateau Blanc Homeowner's Assn. v. Dept. of Veterans Affairs* (1998) 67 Cal.App.4th 743.

Enforcing Restrictions

Property owners can sue a fellow property owner who violates a private restriction. In a subdivision with a homeowners association, a homeowner seeking to enforce the CC&Rs against a troublesome neighbor actually has three options. She can:

1. sue the neighbor for violating the restriction(s);
2. ask the homeowners association to sue or to take other enforcement action; or
3. sue the association, if the board refuses to act.

The primary remedy in lawsuits concerning private restrictions is an **injunction**, a court order directing the defendant to stop or cure the violation.

Case Example:

The Ezers lived just up the hillside from the Fuchslochs in a Pacific Palisades development. Every lot was subject to a restriction prohibiting plantings that blocked a neighbor's view.

The Fuchslochs allowed their backyard pine tree to reach 25 feet—tall enough to partly block the Ezers' ocean view. The Ezers won a trial court injunction ordering the Fuchslochs to trim their tree down to the same height as their house. The Fuchslochs appealed, arguing that the tree blocked only one percent of the Ezers' 175-degree view, making the injunction unreasonable. The appellate court disagreed, finding that losing even one percent of a view wasn't completely trivial.

The Fuchslochs also argued that their tree had a right to exist without trimming—citing the U.S. Supreme Court case *Sierra Club v. Morton*, in which Justice William O. Douglas suggested in the dissent that trees should have standing to sue in their own defense. However, the California appellate court refused to adopt this line of reasoning. The Fuchslochs were ordered to comply with the injunction and have the tree topped. *Ezer v. Fuchsloch* (1979) 99 Cal.App.3rd 849.

If violation of a restriction has caused a financial loss, the court will order the defendant to pay the plaintiff compensatory damages, in addition to issuing an injunction.

Example: In their backyard, the Cornwalls planted a type of bamboo that spreads rapidly and is extremely difficult to eradicate. This violated a restriction in the CC&Rs that prohibits planting potentially invasive vegetation without the approval of the homeowners association.

The bamboo took over the yard of the neighbors, the Ochoas, who ended up spending a considerable amount of money digging up their lawn and trying to get rid of the bamboo. Not only that, the Cornwalls still refused to remove the bamboo from their own yard, meaning that the problem was likely to recur.

Association Lawsuits: Footing the Bill

Homeowners associations often get involved in legal action of one sort or another. Associations sue, and are sued by, both developers and homeowners.

When homeowners sue associations, it's usually to fend off the enforcement of a restriction. Recent lawsuits brought by homeowners have involved such matters as fence heights, Christmas lights, and even whether a spider is a pet.

The presence of an attorneys' fees provision in the bylaws or CC&Rs may influence whether a homeowner decides to sue. If the homeowner has confidence in her case, she might count on having her attorneys' fees paid by the association. But fee provisions are a double-edged sword. Since courts favor enforcing restrictions, the homeowner could very well wind up paying the association's legal fees as well as her own. That could add tens of thousands of dollars if the case goes through trial and appeal.

When the Ochoas and the homeowners association sued, the court issued an injunction ordering the Cornwalls to remove the bamboo from their yard. It also awarded damages to the Ochoas, requiring the Cornwalls to reimburse them for the expenses they'd incurred in removing the bamboo.

Many declarations of restrictions have an attorneys' fees provision, which requires the losing party to pay the winning party's attorneys' fees and other legal costs involved in the dispute.

Terminating Restrictions

A restriction running with the land typically continues indefinitely unless the owners of the properties involved agree to terminate it. (For CC&Rs that apply to an entire subdivision, this would generally require a vote of the homeowners.) A restriction can also terminate without voluntary action on the part of the owners through waiver, changed conditions, or expiration.

Waiver. If homeowners routinely fail to enforce a particular restriction—for example, by ignoring hedges that stayed untrimmed or RVs that were parked in side yards—they may be held to have **waived** their right to enforce that restriction. Association boards often use the possibility of waiver to justify a seemingly petty enforcement of a restriction, arguing that failure to object to minor violations might prevent the board from protesting later, more serious violations of that restriction.

The fear of an unintentional waiver may not really be justified. Courts interpret the doctrine of waiver narrowly, and are reluctant to invalidate a restriction if it's still serving a community interest.

Example: Homeowners in a subdivision are subject to a view protection restriction that includes a clause banning rooftop flags. However, several residents have been flying such flags for some time, and the homeowners association has never taken any action to make them take the flags down.

Now a homeowner has built an addition that interferes with a neighbor's view. When the homeowners association orders the homeowner to remove the addition, the homeowner argues that the right to enforce the view protection restriction has been waived. However, when the matter ends up in court, the judge rules that only the flag ban has been waived. Waiver of one clause in a view protection restriction does not prevent enforcement of other unrelated clauses.

Case to Consider...

Mistaken about the boundaries of his subdivision lot, Mittal built a deck and breakfast nook addition that encroached five feet into a city park. The project had been approved by the homeowners association. Almost 20 years passed before the encroachment was discovered. At that point, the homeowners association also decided that Mittal's deck and addition violated the setback requirements in the CC&Rs. Yet over the years, the association had granted exceptions to the setback rules to a number of other homeowners whose property abutted the park, allowing them to count some of the park's open space as part of their setbacks. The city settled with Mittal regarding the encroachment, but the homeowners association went to court to enforce the setback rules. What was the result? *Palos Verdes Homes Assn. v. Arun K. Mittal* (Cal.App., Nov. 13, 2002, No. B152448) 2002 WL 31518878.

Changed Conditions. A court may refuse to enforce a restriction because of **changed conditions** in a neighborhood. In *Bard v. Rose* (1962) 203 Cal.App.2d 232, for example, a Palm Springs development became so hemmed in over the decades by commercial and multi-family dwellings that it lost its single-family character. When a lot owner sought to lift the single-family residence restriction and build commercially, two neighbors objected; however, the court found that conditions had changed so much that the restriction served no real purpose.

Proving changed conditions can be challenging, though. There are many residential neighborhoods where commercial development has made inroads. Property owners in these areas often bring suit, arguing that because of the changed conditions, they should be allowed to develop their property commercially and reap a higher return. But if allowing the commercial use would cause the remaining homeowners to suffer any loss in property value, a court is unlikely to find the conditions have changed sufficiently to justify overturning the restriction.

Expiration. Although modern CC&Rs usually don't contain an expiration date, many older sets of CC&Rs do. There's no real reason for CC&Rs to have an expiration date, but developers of early subdivisions tended to include one. However, it soon became apparent that permanent restrictions protect property values better, so that practice fell out of favor. It's generally recommended that a homeowners association vote to renew restrictions that are set to expire.

Case to Consider...

Terifaj, a veterinarian and an animal lover, bought a vacation unit at Villa De Las Palmas in 1995. She knew the CC&Rs prohibited pet ownership, but she brought her dog to her villa numerous times anyway. She attempted to have the pet restriction removed from the CC&Rs, but failed to win enough votes. The homeowners association warned Terifaj and then fined her. Finally, the association sought an injunction.

By this time, the California legislature had passed a law prohibiting complete bans on pets. Since the law allowing homeowners at least one pet wasn't retroactive, it didn't help Terifaj directly. However, she argued that the legislature clearly considered bans on pet ownership to be against public policy. If pet bans were against public policy, this suggested that the Villa De Las Palmas restriction was unreasonable and thus unenforceable under common law. Was a ban on pet ownership inherently unreasonable? *Villa De Las Palmas Homeowners Assn. v. Terifaj* (2004) 33 Cal.4th 73.

Public Restrictions on Land Use

Up to this point, we've been discussing private restrictions on land use. Now let's focus on the other half of the equation: public restrictions (restrictions imposed by the government). Most public restrictions are laws passed by city or county governments. However, as you'll see, state law limits the types of land use restrictions that cities and counties may pass.

Constitutional Requirements for Land Use Laws

The government's goals in restricting land use rights sometimes overlap with the goals of homeowners associations and other private parties, but they aren't identical. Public restrictions must serve a public purpose. The basis for the government's ability to impose restrictions on land use is the **police power**, which is the power to adopt laws and regulations to protect the public's health, safety, morals, and general welfare. A land use law that isn't reasonably related to these goals is unconstitutional and unenforceable.

> **Example:** In Summerville, one of the members of the town council owns a painting business. He convinces the other members of the council to pass an ordinance requiring everyone in town to paint their houses once every two years. This requirement isn't reasonably related to the protection of the public's health, safety, morals, or general welfare, so a court would be very likely to rule that the ordinance is unconstitutional.

However, the constitutional requirement that public land use restrictions protect health, safety, morals, or general welfare is given a broad interpretation. Courts have upheld land use laws that address aesthetic considerations instead of practical ones. For example, many communities have zoning ordinances that regulate the size, location, and appearance of billboards and other signage. Junkyards and ham radio towers are among the other uses that have been regulated to protect a community's visual appeal.

Public restrictions must meet other constitutional requirements, as well. Not only must the prohibited use harm the public in some way, the restrictions must apply in the same manner to all property owners who are similarly situated. Otherwise, the restrictions will violate the Equal Protection Clause of the Fourteenth Amendment. Also, the restrictions must not reduce a property's value so much that it amounts to an uncompensated taking of private property, in violation of the Fifth Amendment. (See Chapter 1 for more information about the Fifth and Fourteenth Amendments.)

We're going to discuss three areas of land use regulation most commonly encountered by real estate agents: comprehensive planning, zoning, and building codes.

Comprehensive Planning

Over the last several decades, much of the U.S. population has moved away from cities and into suburbs. This shift has caused a host of problems—chiefly, the loss of agricultural land and open space, but also increasing automobile congestion and pollution. In most parts of the country, cities and counties have enacted **general plans** to control how and where local development takes place. A general plan—which may also be called a master plan, city plan, or comprehensive plan—is typically designed by a local **planning commission** and adopted by the city or county council or board of supervisors. Public hearings are held before a plan is adopted, giving the public a chance to make suggestions or objections.

In California, state law requires every local government to have a general plan. The plan must address seven issues: land use, transportation, housing, conservation of natural resources, open space, noise, and safety (protection against natural hazards).

Local efforts to manage sprawl have been vigorous in California; examples include the **urban growth boundary** (UGB) laws imposed in Ventura County, Sacramento, and the Bay Area. Those laws either limit or ban significant development outside a designated boundary line, focusing development in the urban areas.

Zoning

Zoning ordinances—one type of public restriction—are enacted by a city or county council, usually after one or more public hearings. Zoning laws split a city or other governmental unit into zones that are limited to particular uses. The basic categories in a zoning scheme (agricultural, residential, commercial, and industrial) contain many subcategories. For example, within a residential category, zoning ordinances will typically provide for areas where only single-family homes are allowed (usually called R-1 zones), where duplexes are also allowed (R-2), and where condominiums and apartment buildings are also allowed (R-3).

Zoning preserves the basic character of neighborhoods. Few people want to live next to a pig farm or a rubber factory. Few retail businesses want to share a street with smokestack factories. Zoning helps keep incompatible uses from bumping up against each other.

The Ugly Side of UGBs?

At first many developers supported urban growth boundaries as a way to concentrate their building efforts and reward large-scale projects close to the city. But as the supply of buildable land dwindled, developers began to complain. Mostly, they pointed to an unintended consequence of UGBs: buildable land inside the boundary rapidly becomes scarce, driving up land costs and driving out low-income home buyers.

While this argument stems from self-interest, it may have merit. However, proving the claim is difficult, since home prices have risen dramatically even in areas that don't have UGBs.

Some developers confronted by UGBs have leapfrogged over the out-of-bounds areas into the remote countryside. This "solution" creates long commutes, traffic pollution, and a strain on road infrastructure.

In some areas with UGBs, developers have lobbied to expand the boundary lines to accommodate fresh development, but these efforts have largely failed. Voters are generally inclined to protect open space.

In addition to separating different types of uses, zoning regulates many aspects of development within each zone. Commonly regulated building elements include setbacks, square footage, and height. In commercial areas, zoning may also regulate issues such as business hours of operation, noise levels, and parking. In residential areas, the zoning rules promote neighborhood uniformity in a manner similar to the private restrictions of a subdivision.

Zoning and the General Plan. Zoning ordinances must be consistent with, and further the goals of, the community's general plan. To that end, zoning may encourage density in certain areas. On the flip side, zoning may also preserve open space and agricultural land. And inside areas zoned for density, zoning often creates strips of open land called "green belts." Sometimes, this open land serves as a buffer between zones.

Zoning laws help carry out the goals of the general plan by concentrating growth, protecting wetlands and other open spaces, and supporting the plan's transportation scheme.

Exceptions to Zoning Rules. Zoning laws aren't completely rigid. Property owners who want to use their land in a way prohibited by the local zoning ordinance may find relief in one of three ways: by qualifying as a nonconforming use, by obtaining a conditional use permit, or by obtaining a variance.

Nonconforming uses. Often when an area gets zoned for the first time, or rezoned, an existing use falls outside the new restrictions. It doesn't conform to the new rules, so it's considered a **nonconforming use**. For example, when a rural area gets zoned for residential development, an existing gravel pit in the zone becomes a nonconforming use.

These nonconforming uses are almost always "grandfathered in," as the expression goes. That means they can remain in operation, although usually subject to limits. Often the law requires that nonconforming uses must cease within a certain period—for example, 20 years. At the very least, most zoning ordinances state that nonconforming uses can't be enlarged or replaced if destroyed. For instance, suppose a lumberyard is a nonconforming use in the middle of several residential subdivisions; if the lumberyard burns down, it can't be rebuilt, and the owners will probably end up selling the property to residential developers.

Conditional uses. Churches, schools, hospitals, and other community uses sometimes want to locate in a neighborhood that's zoned strictly for residential use. The organization involved may apply to the zoning authority for a conditional use permit. (Depending on the community, the zoning authority might be the board of zoning adjustment, the office of the zoning administrator, or the planning commission.) If the proposed use satisfies an unmet community need, the permit may be granted—conditionally. For example, in an area underserved by hospitals, the planning board might issue a conditional use permit to a hospital, provided that the facility builds underground parking to minimize impact on

 Zoning for Health

Some people have suggested that as part of the nation's campaign against obesity, communities use zoning laws to restrict how and where fast-food restaurants operate. This idea may sound a little strange, but perhaps less so when you consider that for many years urban communities have used zoning to restrict the location, number, and hours of businesses selling alcohol.

The legality of zoning bans on fast food hasn't been thoroughly tested, but some communities already have bans in place. For example, the municipal code of Carlsbad prohibits new drive-through restaurants in the city. Fast food outlets are limited by zoning laws in south Los Angeles, a relatively poor area with high obesity rates.

An ordinance restricting fast-food restaurants must define "fast food" in a clear and rational manner to survive court scrutiny. One town, Concord, Massachusetts, met the definitional challenge as follows:

> "A drive-in or fast-food restaurant is defined as any establishment whose principal business is the sale of foods or beverages in a ready-to-consume state, for consumption within the building or off-premises, and whose principal method of operation includes: (1) sale of foods and beverages in paper, plastic or other disposable containers; or (2) service of food and beverages directly to a customer in a motor vehicle."

the neighborhood. The conditions imposed must be related to relieving the burden caused by the project.

Variances. Property owners seeking relief from specific zoning requirements concerning matters such as setbacks, building height, or parking may apply to the zoning authority for a **variance**. As a general rule, variances are used only to allow fairly minor departures from the zoning requirements.

To receive a variance, a property owner usually must show that failure to grant the variance would deprive her of privileges available to most other property owners in the zone. Also, her property must have some special characteristic—an unusual lot size, shape, topography, location, or unusual surroundings—that justifies the variance. In addition, the variance should not violate general planning goals or reduce the value of neighboring property.

Whether or not these factors are present, the court may grant a variance if a property owner relied on a zoning authority error made during the permitting process.

Case Example:

La Mesa's zoning ordinance generally required at least a five-foot setback from sideyard lot lines in residential zones. The city granted Leona Anderson a building permit for a house that would have a seven-foot sideyard setback. During the construction process, the city inspected the house six times. Before the final inspection, however, the city decided that a special zoning provision applied to the project, and this required a ten-foot setback for Anderson's sideyards. Rebuilding a portion of her house to conform to this requirement would have cost her over $6,000.

The city refused to grant Anderson a variance, so she sued. The court ruled in her favor. Because a variance would not seriously harm Anderson's neighbors, and because she had relied on the city's permitting decisions, fairness required granting the variance. *Anderson v. City of La Mesa* (1981) 118 Cal.App.3d 657.

While state law allows local governments to grant variances concerning physical aspects of the property, Government Code § 65906 forbids **use variances**. A zoning authority can't grant a variance to allow a use or activity that's prohibited by the zoning ordinance. So, for instance, a variance could not be granted to allow an industrial use—even a completely clean manufacturing plant—in a residential zone. Property owners who want to use their land in a way that's prohibited by the zoning law generally must seek a rezone.

Rezones. A **rezone** is not merely a permit or an exception to the rules, but an actual change in the zoning ordinance. For example, a property owner who wants to put a business in a residential zone might seek to have the whole neighborhood rezoned for commercial use.

A rezone that imposes requirements on a particular property that are different (either stricter or looser) from the ones that apply to the surrounding properties is called **spot zoning**. Spot zoning is illegal, because it violates the constitutional requirement of equal protection, discussed earlier. The same zoning rule would not apply to all similarly situated property owners.

Property owners may claim spot zoning if a law's impact on their land is more severe than its impact on neighboring properties. For example, in *Echevarrieta v. City of Rancho Palos Verdes* (2001) 86 Cal.App.4th 472, a homeowner subject to a city's view protection ordinance was ordered to cut some trees. Arguably, the ordinance had a much greater impact on his park-like property than on surrounding lots. But since the law hadn't been aimed specifically at his property, it wasn't spot zoning.

Occasionally a business requests a rezone that could be considered spot zoning. For example, a chain of warehouse stores might request the rezone of a well-located piece of agricultural land for a new store. Whether the zoning authority rejects this application as illegal spot zoning may depend more on community attitudes than on strict legal principles.

Zoning Conflicting with Private Restrictions. Since zoning sometimes addresses the same issues that private restrictions do, a property may be subject to both. But what if the zoning rule and the private restriction conflict? The private restriction may impose stricter limits on property than the local zoning ordinance, or it may be the other way around. As a general rule, a property owner must comply with the more restrictive requirement.

> **Example:** The zoning law covering a subdivision allows buildings up to 30 feet in height. However, the subdivision's CC&Rs prohibit buildings over 25 feet in height. Subdivision homeowners must comply with the 25-foot limit set in the CC&Rs, since that restriction is stricter than the 30-foot limit set in the zoning law.
>
> If the situation were reversed (so that the zoning law had a 25-foot limit, while the CC&Rs had a 30-foot limit), then the owners would have to comply with the limit set by the zoning law.

Building Codes

Building codes are another type of public restriction. These laws govern all aspects of building construction: design, materials, construction methods, electrical wiring, plumbing, and so on. They have several purposes. They protect the public's health and safety by setting minimum construction standards, which, among other things, help prevent buildings from collapsing and fires from spreading. Building codes also promote energy efficiency, and help make buildings accessible to the disabled.

Statewide Standards. Although in some states building codes are strictly local laws, California sets statewide building requirements. These are contained in California Code of Regulations, Title 24, known as the California Building Standards Code. The state law is based on national and international model building codes.

A local government may establish more restrictive construction standards than those found in the California Building Standards Code. But any local modifications must be reasonably necessary due to local climatic, geological, or topographical conditions. The modifications must be filed with the state Building Standards Commission.

Permitting Process. Both new construction and most remodeling projects require a building permit. When a property owner applies for a building permit, the planning or building department reviews the plans and specifications to determine whether they comply with the zoning ordinances and building codes. (For some larger projects, a public comment period may be required before a permit is issued.) Building inspectors will also inspect the construction at various points before finally issuing a **certificate of occupancy**.

New Requirements. Building codes change periodically to take into account new and improved construction materials or methods. Usually, these new rules apply only to new construction. However, sometimes a new rule involves such an important safety concern that it is made retroactive. This means that existing buildings must comply with the new rules, not just new construction. Generally, property owners have a certain period of time

 Planning and Building Department, Mill Valley, CA 94942
www.cityofmillvalley.org

Excerpts from City of Mill Valley
Residential Design Review Handbook

Helpful Tips for Applicants:

8. Maintain a Good Attitude. It is generally counterproductive to have an adversarial attitude or resist the process as you are going through it. It usually only results in delaying your project.

* * * *

Design Guidelines:

2. Relationship of Building Size to Slope. Slope conditions can exaggerate height, bulk and mass. A building shall be in scale with its surroundings. Special attention shall be given to minimize the height, bulk and mass on steep sites. When a lot has steep slopes, the maximum permitted floor area may be substantially reduced to mitigate impact (see Mill Valley Municipal Code Section 20.66.045).

* * * *

4. Plant Material Selection and Compatibility with Setting. Plans should focus on restorative efforts to replenish native species and complement preserved, existing vegetation. In more natural locations, the design should be integrated with the natural setting.... Plants that are pyrophytic or tend to spread rapidly, crowding out natives, should not be planted.

* * * *

19. Windows, Roofs and Skylights and Roof Mounted Equipment. Window and skylight size, placement and design should be selected to maximize the privacy between adjacent properties. To the extent consistent with other design considerations, the placement and size of windows and skylights should minimize light pollution and/or glare.

to bring their buildings "up to code." These types of retroactive requirements rarely apply to single-family homes, however.

Building codes are just one of the ways in which local or state governments use public restrictions to protect the public's health, safety, morals, and general welfare. As we've seen, zoning and planning laws also play a significant role. Taken together with the private restrictions that homeowners associations and private owners use to maintain property values and to minimize conflicts between neighbors, it's easy to understand why almost all land is subject to some form of land use restriction. Understanding how these limitations affect real property will help you advise your clients in the sale and purchase of real estate.

Case Law in Depth

The following case involves some of the legal issues discussed in this chapter. Read through the facts and consider the questions in light of what you have learned. Then read what the court actually decided.

Elysium Institute, Inc. v. County of Los Angeles (1991) 232 Cal.App.3d 408

Starting in the 1960s, the Elysium Institute ran a "private clothing-optional recreational and educational facility" on seven acres in Topanga Canyon. (The facility closed in 2000.) The septic system was inadequate for the attendees, who occasionally numbered several hundred, and the nudist camp also created some traffic and noise burdens. A Los Angeles County zoning ordinance passed in 1971 limited nudist camps to A-2 zones (heavy agriculture). Elysium was in an A-1 zone, making it a nonconforming use, and the ordinance required that the use end within five years unless extended by permission. (Other types of recreational uses were allowed to remain in the A-1 zone if they obtained a conditional use permit, but not nudist camps.)

Elysium eventually applied for an extension of its nonconforming use status. Initially the application was denied, but on reconsideration it was granted—with 27 conditions attached. Then, after Elysium protested these conditions, the application was denied again. The camp would be required to shut down when the five-year deadline was reached.

Elysium sued. After losing at the trial level, it appealed. The appellate court found no merit in Elysium's argument that the county was violating the nudists' constitutional right to freedom of expression. But Elysium was also making other constitutional arguments. It claimed that the county's exclusion of nudist camps from A-1 zones wasn't rationally related to a public need. It argued that the county was singling out nudist camps and restricting them more than other uses, thus violating their right to equal protection of the laws. Finally, Elysium claimed that requiring the camp to cease operations after five years was an uncompensated taking of its property.

The questions:

Was Los Angeles County violating the nudists' right to equal protection, or were the county's zoning rules fair and rational? Did the ordinance's five-year limit on nonconforming uses result in a taking of land without just compensation?

The court's answers:

On the taking of property question, the court stated, "California cases have firmly held zoning legislation may validly provide for the eventual termination of nonconforming property uses without compensation if it provides a reasonable amortization period commensurate with the investment involved." Thus, the court rejected Elysium's argument. Five years was not unreasonable.

On the equal protection questions, the court stated, "[The County argues] that the recreational uses permitted in the A-1 zone...are for the most part designed to serve the local neighborhood and/or are open in character (athletic fields, playgrounds)." But all the various recreational uses that are currently permitted (such as health retreats and airports) simply do not serve local neighborhoods, nor can they be characterized as predominantly "open." While some of the permitted uses (such as campgrounds and athletic fields) are comprised of "open space," many of the other permitted uses are highly developed in nature.

The county maintained that a "motley throng" of "curiosity seekers and voyeurs," caused traffic problems in the surrounding residential neighborhood. However, the court stated that this "secondary effect" of nudist camps could not, under this particular ordinance, justify the different treatment of nudist camps from the other permitted uses. The ordinance "already subjects all similar uses to a conditional use permit procedure in which the County can consider...whether the site is adequately served by highways or streets sufficient to carry the kind and quantity of traffic such use would generate, and whether the use would adversely affect the health, peace, comfort or welfare of persons residing in the surrounding area."

The result:

The requirement that a nonconforming use cease after five years wasn't a taking. But exclusion of nudist camps from A-1 zones (when comparable uses were allowed) violated Elysium's right to equal protection and was unconstitutional.

Chapter Summary

- Private restrictions on land use may be created by deed, by contract, or, most commonly, in a declaration recorded by a subdivision developer. A developer's declaration of restrictions is often referred to as the CC&Rs (covenants, conditions, and restrictions). CC&Rs may be enforced by a homeowner or the homeowners association. The association may amend or delete the restrictions or add new ones.

- Violation of CC&Rs can result in homeowners association fines, court-ordered damages, or an injunction halting the violation. Restrictions may terminate by a vote of the homeowners, waiver, changed conditions, or expiration.

- Public restrictions on land use—including a city or county's general plan, zoning ordinances, and building codes—must be reasonably related to protection of the public's health, safety, morals, or general welfare.

- Zoning ordinances separate incompatible land uses. Most zoning ordinances classify uses as agricultural, residential, commercial, or industrial, with subcategories such as light industry and heavy industry. Zoning ordinances also impose building height limits, setback requirements, parking requirements, and other rules.

- Zoning ordinances allow for three types of exceptions to their requirements: nonconforming uses, conditional uses, and variances. Nonconforming uses—existing uses that don't comply with a new zoning law—are usually allowed to continue, but there may be a time limit, and the structures can't be enlarged or replaced if destroyed. A conditional use permit allows an entity that serves a public need to operate in a zone that doesn't allow the use, as long as specified conditions are met. Variances allow exceptions to setback requirements and other minor zoning rules. Property owners may also seek to have an area rezoned to allow a use that is currently prohibited.

- Building codes require construction to meet certain standards. In most cases, a building permit must be obtained before construction begins, and the project will be inspected during the construction process. A certificate of occupancy will be issued if the completed project complies with the building code.

Key Terms

- **Declaration of restrictions** – A document recorded by a subdivision developer that lists restrictions that apply to all of the lots in the development; also called the CC&Rs.

- **Covenants that run with the land** – Private restrictions that future owners of a property will be required to comply with; the restrictions must be recorded and must state that they burden future owners.

- **General plan** – A plan created by a city or county that spells out its land use goals; also called a comprehensive plan, city plan, or master plan.

- **Zoning** – Ordinances governing what land uses are permitted in certain areas (zones) and specifying requirements for building height, setbacks, and so on.

- **Nonconforming use** – An existing use that does not comply with the requirements of a new zoning law but is allowed to continue.

- **Conditional use permit** – A permit for a use not otherwise allowed in a zone, in order to meet a community need.

- **Variance** – A permit allowing a minor deviation from the zoning requirements.

- **Rezone** – A change in a zoning ordinance that applies a new zoning classification to an area.

- **Spot zoning** – Zoning that imposes either stricter or easier requirements on a particular property than the ones that apply to surrounding properties; spot zoning is usually illegal.

- **Building code** – A set of rules establishing minimum construction standards.

- **Certificate of occupancy** – A document issued by the local planning or building agency, certifying that a completed building complies with building codes and may be occupied.

Chapter Quiz

1. The Waverly Creek CC&Rs ban political signs in yards and also prohibit the use of the color purple on houses in the development. Are these restrictions legal?
   a) The first restriction is illegal, the second is not
   b) The second restriction is illegal, the first is not
   c) Neither restriction is illegal
   d) Both restrictions are illegal

2. The Altoa neighborhood isn't a planned development and no declaration of restrictions affects the area. At an informal neighborhood meeting, the homeowners agree they will never build fences between their lots, hoping to maintain an open, neighborly feel. For many years, the homeowners honor this oral agreement. But finally, when one of the houses is sold, the new owner promptly builds a fence around his yard. Which of the following is true?
   a) The restriction runs with the land, so the new owner is bound by it and must remove the fence
   b) The new owner is not bound by the restriction; it wasn't put into writing and recorded, so it doesn't run with the land
   c) The new owner isn't bound by the restriction unless most of the owners vote to approve it again
   d) The city can enforce the private restriction against the new owner

3. The homeowners association demands that an owner cease making homemade beer in his basement, stating that the activity violates a morals clause in the CC&Rs. The homeowner sues. Which of the following arguments might help him win his case?
   a) State law allows home brewing, so the private restriction is invalid
   b) A homeowners association cannot enforce any restriction that concerns activities inside an owner's house
   c) The restriction and/or the association's enforcement action is unreasonable
   d) None of the above

4. A zoning ordinance:
   a) must be consistent with the general plan
   b) cannot regulate building heights
   c) must provide for spot zoning
   d) All of the above

5. The four basic zoning classifications are:
   a) rural, industrial, school, religious (church)
   b) agricultural, industrial, residential, commercial
   c) light entertainment, red zone, transportation, rezone
   d) single-family, multi-family, governmental, commercial

6. A drug treatment facility wants to locate in a rundown area that's zoned for residential use only. They should apply to the zoning authority for a:
   a) rezone
   b) variance
   c) conditional use permit
   d) nonconforming use license

7. A lot owner in a struggling part of downtown would like to reopen an empty storefront. The current zoning requires new businesses to provide off-street parking. But the cost of adding parking is prohibitive, and this area has plenty of on-street parking. The property owner should probably seek a/an:
   a) rezone
   b) variance
   c) injunction
   d) private restriction

8. Some property owners in a turn-of-the-century abandoned industrial area would like to reuse the old brick factories for a mix of retail stores and condos. However, this area is zoned for heavy industry; residential and commercial construction aren't allowed. The property owners should seek a:
   a) rezone
   b) variance
   c) conditional use permit
   d) nonconforming use

9. Under the terms of most zoning ordinances, a nonconforming use:
   a) must be allowed to continue for at least twenty years
   b) must be brought into compliance within two years
   c) cannot be continued without a conditional use permit
   d) cannot be enlarged or rebuilt if destroyed

10. In connection with a construction project, the procedures for enforcing building codes generally require:
    a) a building permit
    b) inspections during construction
    c) a certificate of occupancy
    d) All of the above

Chapter Answer Key

Chapter Quiz Answers:

1. a) A state statute protects political and other noncommercial signs, but CC&Rs may impose restrictions on paint colors and other design elements.

2. b) Restrictions don't run with the land unless they are in writing, state that they bind subsequent owners of the property described, and are recorded.

3. c) Courts will not enforce an unreasonable restriction. If the owner can convince the court that this restriction is unreasonable, or that the association is applying it in an unreasonable manner, he won't be required to comply with it.

4. a) Zoning laws must be consistent with the general plan. They usually include restrictions on building heights. Spot zoning is illegal.

5. b) Agricultural, industrial, residential, and commercial are the four basic zoning classifications.

6. c) Entities hoping to provide a service that is prohibited by the zoning classification may seek a conditional use permit from the zoning authority. Rezones change the zoning for an entire area and are hard to get. Variances are permits for minor exceptions to the zoning requirements for matters such as setbacks, but use variances are not allowed.

7. b) Variances are sometimes granted for parking requirements.

8. a) The parties want an industrial zone to be reclassified for mixed residential and commercial use; seeking a rezone would be appropriate.

9. d) As a general rule, a nonconforming use cannot be enlarged or expanded, and if the buildings are destroyed, they can't be rebuilt.

10. d) A property owner undertaking a construction project generally must obtain a building permit, allow inspections during construction, and obtain a certificate of occupancy after the final inspection.

Cases to Consider... Answers:

Waiver of Private Restrictions

Palos Verdes Homes Assn. v. Arun K. Mittal (Cal.App., Nov. 13, 2002, No. B152448) 2002 WL 31518878. The homeowners association lost. The numerous exceptions to the setback requirements that the association had granted constituted a waiver of the restriction, unless they could show that Mittal's lack of a setback caused harm to the development's residents. Concluding that there was no proof of harm, the court refused to enforce the setback requirements against Mittal.

Private Restrictions: Changing Conditions

Villa De Las Palmas Homeowners Assn. v. Terifaj (2004) 33 Cal.4th 73. The California supreme court ruled that the statute guaranteeing homeowners the right to keep a pet did not imply that the legislature considered pet bans inherently unreasonable. After all, the legislature itself had failed to make the law retroactive. Terifaj could not keep a pet, because the Villa De Las Palmas restriction banning pets had been established before the statute went into effect.

List of Cases

Anderson v. City of La Mesa (1981) 118 Cal.App.3d 657

Bard v. Rose (1962) 203 Cal.App.2d 232

Echevarrieta v. City of Rancho Palos Verdes (2001) 86 Cal.App.4th 472

Elysium Institute, Inc. v. County of Los Angeles (1991) 232 Cal.App.3d 408

Ezer v. Fuchsloch (1979) 99 Cal.App.3rd 849

Fountain Valley Chateau Blanc Homeowner's Assn. v. Dept. of Veterans Affairs (1998) 67 Cal.App.4th 743

Palos Verdes Homes Assn. v. Arun K. Mittal (Cal.App., Nov. 13, 2002, No. B152448) 2002 WL 31518878

Villa De Las Palmas Homeowners Assn. v. Terifaj (2004) 33 Cal.4th 73

Chapter 18

Environmental Law

Outline

Introduction

Dealing with an environmental problem of any size typically involves a complex mix of state and federal laws and agencies. In this chapter, however, we've narrowed our focus to a few environmental statutes and agencies that the average real estate agent may have to deal with at some point. The first section of this chapter provides an overview of environmental law. Next we'll examine environmental impact assessments and endangered species protection. Finally, we'll take a look at the laws and processes that govern the cleanup of properties contaminated with toxic waste.

To help illustrate the interplay between environmental laws and enforcement agencies, we'll drop in from time to time on a hypothetical property owner negotiating his way through the environmental law maze. Randy Todd recently purchased a 160-acre former ranch in Big Sur on a slope high above the sea. The land is undeveloped except for a caretaker's cabin on a corner of the property, and Randy plans to build an impressive estate house. However, several environmental laws have thrown up roadblocks he wasn't really expecting.

Environmental Law: Past and Present

The U.S. didn't really pay much attention to environmental problems until the 1960s, and the concern was limited at first. For example, Congress passed a version of the Clean

Air Act in 1963, but this law didn't even mention automobile emissions, one of the largest sources of air pollution in the United States. Water pollution also received some early legislative attention, but the effort was weak; during this period, some U.S. waterways (such as the Cuyahoga River) grew so contaminated that they became fire hazards.

By 1969, public anxiety over the environment had grown. Worries about air and water pollution, unchecked growth, and species loss prompted the federal and state governments to pass a number of environmental laws. One of the first and most important of these laws is the federal **National Environmental Policy Act** (NEPA), which was passed in 1970 and lays out a good deal of U.S. environmental policy. NEPA's statement of purpose reads in part:

> To…encourage productive and enjoyable harmony between man and his environment; to promote efforts which will prevent or eliminate damage to the environment and biosphere and stimulate the health and welfare of man; to enrich the understanding of the ecological systems and natural resources important to the Nation…

NEPA (which appears in the United States Code at 42 U.S.C. § 4321 *et seq.*) implements these goals chiefly by requiring the federal government to assess and possibly mitigate the environmental impact of all federally related projects.

A number of states soon followed suit with laws designed to lessen the impact of projects falling under state or local jurisdiction. California's law is the **California Environmental Quality Act of 1970**, known as CEQA (Public Resources Code §§ 21000 – 21177). The goals of the state law echo the idealistic language of the national law.

Also in 1970, President Nixon created a powerful new federal agency to address problems caused by pollution: the **Environmental Protection Agency** (EPA). The EPA's main goal was to clean up toxic waste left by decades of industrial dumping. Since the EPA's creation, all 50 states and the District of Columbia have formed environmental agencies of their own. California's state agency (created in 1991) is called the California Environmental Protection Agency, or **CalEPA**.

In 1973, a Congress alarmed by the dwindling biodiversity of the U.S. enacted the **Endangered Species Act** (16 U.S.C. §§ 1531 – 1544), which protects plants and animals and their habitats. California again followed the federal lead and passed statutes protecting species within the state's boundaries.

In the next few years, Congress also strengthened the Clean Air Act and Clean Water Act. (Again, California and most other states have their own versions of these laws.) Finally, at both the state and federal level,

 Acronym Guide

Environmental law is full of acronyms, but you don't have to keep track of all of them. These are the most important:

NEPA – National Environmental Policy Act (requires an environmental impact statement, or EIS)

CEQA – California Environmental Quality Act (requires an environmental impact report, or EIR)

EPA – Environmental Protection Agency

CalEPA – California Environmental Protection Agency

legislatures passed numerous laws regulating cleanup and disposal of toxic waste. Chief among these is the federal Superfund statute, CERCLA.

The rest of this chapter looks at the requirements of some of these environmental statutes in greater detail.

Environmental Impact Assessments

As we mentioned, one of NEPA's most important aspects is that it requires environmental impact assessments. An **environmental impact assessment** is a report prepared before a development or other project is undertaken, describing ways to limit the project's environmental impact. Certain state environmental protection laws, including California's CEQA, also require impact assessments.

Whether required by state or federal law, the environmental impact assessment is the chief tool for limiting environmental damage from new developments and other projects. ("Projects" here has a broad meaning; it even includes a new law or regulation that may negatively affect the environment.) An assessment evaluates a proposed project's effect on the environment and, if the effect is significant, suggests alternatives and modifications that lessen the harm.

The assessment considers the project's environmental impacts to:

- water (supply, runoff, etc.);
- biology (endangered species, etc.);
- services (public safety, transportation, etc.);
- health (pollution, cleanup, etc.); and
- culture (archeological, historical, and aesthetic issues).

 The Birth of Environmental Protection

In the late 1960s, Vietnam, race relations, and other issues divided the United States politically. But public support for environmental action had grown to be quite widespread. A *New York Times* editorial in 1969 declared, "Call it conservation, the environment, ecological balance, or what you will, it is a cause more permanent, more far-reaching, than any issue of the era..."

Toward the end of 1969, President Nixon appointed a committee to consider the formation of a national environmental agency. At the same time, Congress sent the president a bill called the National Environmental Policy Act.

In response to the public's mounting "eco-awareness," Nixon signed the NEPA bill on New Year's Day, 1970. Later that year, he ordered the creation of the Environmental Protection Agency.

Who prepares these studies and who bears the cost? An impact assessment is produced either by a government agency or by an independent consultant hired specifically for the task. Preparing an assessment can take months, if not years, and often involves paying for outside experts. As a result, the studies can be quite costly: an environmental assessment for even a small project will typically cost several thousand dollars; for major projects, the cost will be a great deal more.

Federal and State Assessments

Federal and state environmental impact assessments share similar characteristics, though the reports go by different names. The National Environmental Policy Act calls for an **environmental impact statement** (EIS) for all significant federal projects. This includes private projects that require some sort of federal agency involvement or simply receive some federal funding. An EIS must describe the proposed project and its impacts, and list and evaluate possible alternatives. The study is prepared and funded by the federal agency involved with the proposed project.

California, under CEQA, requires an **environmental impact report** (EIR) for any public or private project likely to have a significant effect on the environment. An EIR is similar to an EIS but its list of alternatives must include a "no project at all" option. The cost of preparing an EIR falls on the project applicant, whether it's a public entity (such as a city seeking to build a new park) or a private party (for example, a developer with plans to construct a shopping center).

Many federal projects also have a state component, so both an EIS and an EIR may be required. If so, the agencies involved typically combine the assessments into a single document.

The studies play somewhat different roles despite their similar content. The federal law doesn't require the government to implement the alternatives suggested by the EIS, but merely to consider the information presented. Still, if only for political reasons, the federal employees must pay at least some heed to their own analysis.

CEQA, on the other hand, imposes stricter requirements. It generally requires that California projects adopt whatever changes the EIR suggests for mitigating environmental harm. That said, however, an EIR can't ask for unreasonable changes: the suggestions must follow "the rule of reason," balancing cost against benefits. Of course, builders and birdwatchers have different views of what is reasonable.

The Assessment Process

The assessment process begins with the government making an initial evaluation of whether the project will cause significant environmental harm. If significant harm appears

 Earth Day

On April 22, 1970, a few months after Nixon signed the National Environmental Policy Act, some 20 million Americans went out in the spring sunshine and celebrated the first Earth Day. Community events featured music, street theater, and speeches. In 2016, over one billion people in 190 countries celebrated Earth Day worldwide.

likely, the government requires an impact assessment. Once the initial draft is completed, it is reviewed by environmental and other government agencies, interested members of the public, and the applicant (for instance, a subdivision builder or a port authority). Any of these parties may suggest revisions or corrections. After this review period, a final draft is prepared.

Let's examine this process more closely.

Determination of Significant Impact. Under NEPA, the federal agency that is planning to build or fund a proposed project (a dam, for example) is responsible for the initial evaluation concerning possible environmental impact. If the agency determines that significant impact is likely, an EIS must be prepared. Alternatively, the agency may issue a **finding of no significant impact** (FONSI). However, the standards for determining significance are a bit murky. When an agency decides that a significant impact is unlikely, neighbors, environmental groups, and competing commercial interests can sometimes successfully challenge the decision.

The procedure is similar at the state level. Under CEQA, the local agency in charge of approving building projects performs an evaluation and either requires an EIR or issues a **negative declaration** (the equivalent of a FONSI).

Would our hypothetical estate-builder, Randy Todd, need to obtain an EIR? That decision would be made by the Monterey County Resource Management Agency, which includes the county's planning department. In California, agencies can't require an EIR for single-family residential projects, unless the unique location of the house may result in environmental harm. In Randy's case, not surprisingly, the Monterey planning department determines that a relatively undeveloped wilderness area by the sea is unique and that such an enormous residence will have some environmental impact. Randy must pay for an environmental impact report.

The following case illustrates some factors a local agency may have to consider when deciding whether to require an EIR.

Case Example:

One method of disposing of sewage sludge (a wastewater treatment by-product) is applying it to farmland as a fertilizer. In 1999, roughly one million tons of sludge were applied to Kern County's farmlands—about one-third of the total applied throughout the state. Sewage sludge isn't harmless; problems include odor, runoff, and heavy-metal pollution from factory waste entering the sewage stream.

Later that year, Kern County passed an ordinance restricting the application of sewage sludge on local farmland. The county saw little downside to cutting back on sludge, so it issued a negative declaration regarding the ordinance. However, various state sanitation agencies sued, asking the court to require an EIR evaluating the potential impact of the ordinance.

The court declared that local governments have to look beyond their immediate borders when deciding if a project has a significant environmental impact. Here, if the Kern County ordinance went into effect, some of the unused sludge would instead be disposed of in already-burdened landfills elsewhere in the state. That would shift some of the runoff problem from Kern County to other state residents.

In addition, the county had overlooked some actual local impact. Farmers giving up sludge would have to use other types of fertilizers, and these would bring their own problems. Furthermore, the sludge provided a stabilizing effect on soil that lessened erosion and decreased water use. All of these considerations made an EIR analyzing the sludge-limiting ordinance necessary. *County Sanitation Dist. No. 2 v. County of Kern* (2005) 127 Cal.App.4th 1544.

Draft and Final Assessment. After preparing its evaluation, the local agency circulates the draft EIS or EIR to other agencies and experts. The draft will also be made available to the public (possibly via public hearings, depending on the number of interested parties). If important new information comes to light during this process, the agency will publish a redraft assessment. Again there is more comment and possibly another draft. Clearly, reaching the final draft stage can take some time. Often, the process is drawn out even further by legal challenges regarding the adequacy of the EIS or EIR.

In addition, information occasionally comes to light after final publication, and then the agency may require a supplemental EIS or EIR. The call for a supplemental EIS or EIR after the final assessment is published can cause difficulties for property owners such as Randy Todd.

Case to Consider...

In 1980, Nichols Institute Reference Laboratories (Nichols) applied for a use permit to build a medical research and laboratory complex on a 100-acre site located adjacent to Caspers Wilderness Park. Following publication of a final EIR, the Orange County Board of Supervisors permitted rezoning of the site to allow the development.

Nichols didn't begin development immediately and its use permit eventually expired. In 1985, more land was added to Caspers Wilderness Park, so that the proposed development site was now completely enclosed within the park.

In 1986, Nichols filed a new use permit application. The county planning commission approved the permit, based on the previous EIR. An environmental group, Fund for Environmental Defense, appealed the permit approval to the Board of Supervisors, claiming that a supplemental EIR was required. The group argued that the site was now completely enclosed by the park and that the proposed project was now larger than initially planned. When the Board denied the appeal, the environmental group sued. How did the court rule? *Fund for Environmental Defense v. County of Orange* (1988) 204 Cal.App.3d 1538.

As you can see, NEPA and CEQA can seriously impact plans to develop a property. Although a real estate agent won't be directly involved in the preparation of an environmental impact assessment, it's important for agents to understand when these assessments are required and what the assessment process generally entails.

Endangered Species Protection

Initially, it may be difficult to see how endangered species protection relates to the real estate profession. However, endangered species laws extend their protection to include not just the plants and animals themselves, but also to any land designated as their habitats.

> ### ▶ Making the List
>
> The benefits to an at-risk species of getting officially classified as endangered appear to be quite real: a good number of species have died out while waiting to be listed, yet only a few have gone extinct after actually making it safely onboard.
>
> Here's the average number of species listed as endangered or threatened per year, by administration:
>
> > Ford administration: 15
> >
> > Carter administration: 31
> >
> > Reagan administration: 32
> >
> > Bush I administration: 59
> >
> > Clinton administration: 64
> >
> > Bush II administration: 9
> >
> > Obama administration (through mid-2016): 41
>
> Note that a listed species can also be de-listed, if it is established that the population has recovered and no longer needs Endangered Species Act protection.

Because the endangered species laws are quite strict and contain few exemptions, they can have grave implications for a developer who finds that his property serves as habitat for a protected species.

Federal Law

The federal **Endangered Species Act** (ESA) is administered by the U.S. Fish and Wildlife Service and NOAA's Marine Fisheries Service. (NOAA is the National Oceanic and Atmospheric Administration.) Plant and animal species are added to the endangered list only after a process of nomination, study, and public comment. (A species that is not yet endangered may be listed as threatened.) Litigation to fight or force the listing of a species is not uncommon. As you might imagine, citizen and environmental groups typically request species listings; industry and trade associations generally oppose listings.

As we mentioned, the ESA's requirements are fairly strict: the law forbids any action that might harm a listed species or adversely affect its habitat. This means that it's illegal to do anything that kills, injures, or harasses a listed plant or animal. It also means that it's illegal to do anything that reduces or modifies the natural habitat of a listed species. A violation of the ESA is referred to as a "take" and may result in stiff fines and prison time.

> **Example:** Kenneth, a developer, is building a condominium near a breeding site of the endangered Santa Cruz long-toed salamander. One day, while Kenneth is driving to the construction site, he accidentally runs over one of the endangered salamanders. Obviously, Kenneth has committed a take by killing the salamander. Less obvious is the fact that Kenneth has probably also committed a take simply by building close to the breeding site, thereby impacting the salamanders' habitat.

It's been estimated that half of the species listed as endangered by the federal government have at least 80% of their habitat on privately owned land. As a result, the federal government has created certain incentive-based permits and programs intended to encourage landowners to protect species and habitat. For example, under the Safe Harbor Agreement program, a landowner may agree to maintain or enhance habitat for a particular endangered species that is found on her land. In return, the federal government agrees not to impose any future ESA-related development restrictions on her property.

State Law

The **California Endangered Species Act** (Fish & Game Code §§2050 – 2115.5) is administered by the state Department of Fish and Wildlife. The state law parallels the federal ESA: it prohibits the same actions (harming a listed species or adversely affecting its habitat) and establishes a similar process for listing a species as endangered. However, the amount of protection offered by the state law does vary from its federal counterpart in a few significant ways.

First, the state endangered species act protects only those species that are native to California; in other words, a non-native species cannot be listed. Second, the state law extends protection to species that are merely candidates for listing and that haven't actually been listed as endangered.

Finally, the federal ESA protects endangered animal species on all land within the U.S., but the protection of endangered plants generally applies only to federal land. By contrast, endangered species protection under California law covers both plant and animal life equally. Thus, if an endangered plant species were found on Randy Todd's Big Sur property, it would be protected under state law, but not under federal law.

For example, it's the California Endangered Species Act that protects Hickman's potentilla, a wildflower whose cheery yellow blossoms can be seen in a few spots on the slopes of Big Sur each spring. In 1973, California classified this species as endangered. Randy Todd is aware of Hickman's potentilla and its protected status. When Monterey County circulates the draft EIR for his project, and Randy gets his copy, he quickly turns to the section on biological resources. Skimming the pages, he breathes a sigh of relief to find no mention of Hickman's potentilla or any other protected species.

Cleanup of Toxic Waste

This section of the chapter addresses toxic waste cleanup (often referred to as **remediation**). We'll introduce this subject by taking another look at Randy Todd's project.

Although Randy's property got a clean bill of health regarding endangered species, the EIR process did result in some bad news. We mentioned at the beginning of the chapter that the property contained a caretaker's shack. When Randy bought the property, the shack was occupied by a squatter who claimed to be there as a tenant of the former owner. To avoid any trouble, Randy paid him to move out. Later, during a property inspection by Monterey County's building inspection department, a small trash dump was discovered behind the caretaker's shack, full of discarded buckets, cans of drain cleaner, and other suspicious debris. Lab analysis confirmed the presence of chemicals used in the manufacturing of methamphetamine.

The California Department of Toxic Substances Control, under guidelines from CalEPA, handles meth lab cleanups, and they moved in promptly to dispose of the contamination on Randy's property. The department's work isn't limited to meth labs: they also deal with more significant California cleanups. Various California statutes, including the Land Reuse and Revitalization Act of 2004 and the Land Environmental Restoration and Reuse Act, guide this cleanup work.

But what about the really big jobs—who handles those? Larger scale remediation projects, such as those involving commercial properties, are typically handled under federal law.

CERCLA

If the EPA decides a location requires a major cleanup, it adds the site to the National Priorities List (NPL). The federal statute that authorizes federal cleanups and lays out rules for making polluters pay for remediation is the **Comprehensive Environmental Response, Compensation, and Liability Act** (CERCLA).

CERCLA casts a broad net when looking for parties to pay the cleanup bill; the goal is to avoid burdening taxpayers with the cost. Not only will the actual polluting parties be liable for remediation—but so will the subsequent owners of the polluted property. Under CERCLA, anyone who's owned the land since the contamination occurred can be considered a **potentially responsible party** (PRP) and charged cleanup costs. This rule of strict liability extends even to an owner who took possession long after the land became polluted.

 A Local Cleanup Success Story

From 1968 to 1981, Fairchild Semiconductor in Silicon Valley used huge quantities of solvents to clean materials used in semiconductor chip making. The company's underground solvent storage tanks leaked at some point, polluting portions of Fairchild's 56-acre site. The solvents reached a drinking water aquifer.

The nearby middle-class neighborhood of Los Paseos, which used the aquifer, suffered an increased rate of birth defects. (Community advocates claimed that miscarriages were five times the average rate.) Residents blamed Fairchild's leaking of trichloroethane and dichloroethylene into the drinking water. The EPA put Fairchild on the National Priorities List in 1991.

Fairchild undertook the cleanup. It was successful, and the drinking water eventually tested clean. The property was then sold to a developer, with the EPA agreeing not to hold the developer responsible if further contamination was discovered. Netscape Communications leased the bulk of the site and completed building an office campus on the location in 1998. Currently, the EPA is monitoring some low-level vapor intrusion into some of these buildings.

Dealing with Contaminated Soil

Some kinds of contaminated soil can be safely incinerated. Another method of disposal consists of simply trucking the dirt off for burial in some dry, remote spot that no one cares about. This is not a great solution, obviously.

A happier approach is bioremediation—the use of enzymes, fungus, or other life forms to treat the contamination. Certain organisms can break down pollutants into harmless components. In the case of more stubborn contamination (certain heavy metals, for example), the bioremediant simply bonds with the pollutant, allowing it to be removed for further treatment, usually incineration. In at least one case, the government has used a certain type of fern to remove arsenic.

A relatively recent cleanup technique is soil washing. A machine "scrubs" the polluted soil with a mixture of water and detergent. The waste water is then transported to a treatment plant.

Defenses to CERCLA's Strict Liability. The law does provide several important exceptions to this strict liability for certain parties that own or acquire property that has been contaminated through no fault of their own. If a party can prove that she qualifies as an innocent landowner, a contiguous property owner, or a bona fide prospective purchaser, she cannot be forced to pay for remediation.

An **innocent landowner** is someone who acquires contaminated property but didn't know (and had no reason to know) about the contamination when the property was acquired.

A **contiguous property owner** is someone whose property has been contaminated by an adjacent property owned by someone else. To qualify for this exception, the owner cannot have a relationship or affiliation with the party responsible for the contamination. And the owner can't have known (or had reason to know) about the contamination when the property was purchased.

A **bona fide prospective purchaser** is someone who purchases a property knowing (or having reason to know) that the property is contaminated. A bona fide prospective purchaser can't have a relationship or affiliation with the party responsible for the contamination.

Anyone asserting one of these three defenses must have made **all appropriate inquiries** (AAI) to discover if the property is contaminated. The inquiries must have been completed *before* the property is purchased. If the AAI reveals problems, the party must take reasonable steps to prevent further environmental damage from the contamination. An owner who fails to complete the AAI process won't be able to claim the defense against CERCLA liability.

Residential Exception to CERCLA Liability. Although CERCLA applies to both residential and commercial property, the EPA generally won't take enforcement action against a residential owner, unless the owner:

- causes a release (or a threat of a release) of hazardous substances;
- fails to cooperate with an EPA or state cleanup effort, or
- develops or improves the property in any manner that is inconsistent with residential use.

Superfund Sites. When a site is seriously contaminated, if the EPA can't identify any potentially responsible parties, or the parties somehow avoid paying the bill (commonly by declaring bankruptcy—cleanup costs can be huge), the cleanup contractors are paid out of the **Superfund** created under CERCLA. The Superfund consists of money raised by taxes on the petroleum and chemical industries, businesses that have historically profited from polluting activities.

Obviously, CERCLA's requirements can impose serious financial burdens on purchasers of polluted properties, and make selling such properties quite difficult. Anyone buying commercial property should conduct a thorough environmental investigation before putting their money down.

Case to Consider...

The city of Lodi, California enacted what the federal appeals court labeled an "innovative" ordinance—a town version of CERCLA called MERLO (Municipal Environmental Response and Liability Ordinance). MERLO allowed Lodi to conduct environmental investigations and impose liability for contamination of its soil and groundwater. In an effort to rid its drinking water of various cancer-causing chemicals, Lodi attempted to impose remediation liability on a nameplate-etching company, among others. This company was insured by Fireman's Fund, which sued to avoid liability. CERCLA contains a provision allowing states to pass toxic cleanup acts, but says nothing about the right of a municipality to do so. Fireman's Fund argued that this statutory silence implicitly barred Lodi's effort at lawmaking. Can local governments enforce CERCLA-like ordinances? *Fireman's Fund Insurance Co. v. City of Lodi* (9th Cir. 2002) 302 F.3d 928.

CERCLA is just one of the federal and state environmental statutes to be aware of when helping your clients evaluate the purchase or sale of property. The possibility of significant cleanup costs or the presence of an endangered species, for example, can radically alter the desirability or usefulness of a particular piece of land. Knowing when an environmental impact assessment is needed and understanding how it might affect your clients are important, especially when your clients are looking to invest significant money and resources in a project. However, while these state and federal laws may seem to complicate development, they play an important role in preserving and protecting environmental quality.

Case Law in Depth

The following case involves some of the legal issues discussed in this chapter. Read through the facts and consider the question in light of what you have learned. Then read what the court actually decided.

Bakersfield Citizens for Local Control v. City of Bakersfield (2004) 124 Cal.App.4th 1184

Following the preparation and publication of two EIRs, the city of Bakersfield approved the construction of two massive shopping centers totaling 1.1 million square feet of retail space. Each center included a Wal-Mart Supercenter. The EIRs failed to address concerns about the projects' impacts on existing businesses and the possibility of urban decay in downtown Bakersfield. The city considered this topic to be outside the scope of the EIRs. A citizens group, Bakersfield Citizens for Local Control (BCLC), challenged the EIRs.

The question:

Was the possibility of urban decay resulting from two major shopping center projects an issue that the EIRs were required to analyze?

The court's answer:

The court stated that its role in this case was "...to ensure that the public and responsible officials are adequately informed of the environmental consequences of their decisions before they are made.

"Water contamination and air pollution, now recognized as very real environmental problems, initially were scoffed at as the alarmist ravings of environmental doomsayers. Similarly, experts are now warning about land use decisions that cause a chain reaction of store closures and long-term vacancies, ultimately destroying existing neighborhoods and leaving decaying shells in their wake...

"There is a great deal of evidence in the record supporting the validity of concerns that the shopping centers could cause a ripple of store closures and consequent long-term vacancies that would eventually result in general deterioration and decay within and outside the market area of the two shopping centers. Although much of BCLC's evidence specifically applied to the Supercenters, the administrative records as a whole contain sufficient indication that addition of 1.1 million square feet of retail space in the shopping centers' overlapping market areas could start the chain reaction that ultimately results in urban decay to necessitate study of the issue with respect to the entirety of the shopping centers.

"Accordingly, we hold that the omission of analysis on the issue of urban/suburban decay and deterioration rendered the EIRs defective as informational documents. On remand, the EIRs must analyze whether the shopping centers, individually and/or cumulatively, indirectly could trigger the downward spiral of retail closures and consequent long-term vacancies that ultimately result in decay."

The result:

The court ordered Bakersfield to void its publication of the EIRs and to void its approval of the retail projects. The city had to prepare new EIRs in accordance with CEQA standards and procedures. Note: In a 2010 case, the court clarified that an EIR doesn't have to consider urban decay in every circumstance, merely because a project involves a certain type of building (such as a "supercenter"). "The inquiry is not whether the project...is of a certain type. To the extent that this court's decision in *Bakersfield Citizens*...might be interpreted as saying that whenever a project includes something called a supercenter, the project becomes a type of project which necessarily triggers an examination of some particularized theoretical environmental effect or effects, we expressly decline to adopt such an interpretation..." *Melom v. City of Madera* (2010) 183 Cal.App.4th 41.

Chapter Summary

- During the early 1970s, the U.S. government began taking significant steps to protect the environment. Congress passed the National Environmental Policy Act and the Endangered Species Act, and President Nixon created the Environmental Protection Agency.

- California and many other states have state environmental laws and agencies like those at the federal level. California has an environmental protection act (CEQA) and an endangered species act. CalEPA is the state's environmental protection agency.

- An environmental impact assessment lists steps that could be taken to mitigate or lessen a proposed project's harmful impact. Federal law requires an environmental impact statement (EIS) for all federal government or federally financed projects likely to have an environmental impact. California requires a similar impact assessment, known as an environmental impact report (EIR), for public and private projects within the state that are likely to have an environmental impact.

- The agency in charge of a federal project evaluates a proposed project's environmental impact; if the impact is significant, the agency will have to produce an EIS. A decision that an EIS is unnecessary is called a finding of no significant impact. In California, the local planning department decides whether to require an EIR for a project. A local agency's decision that an EIR isn't necessary is called a negative declaration.

- If an EIS or EIR uncovers the existence of critical plant or animal habitat, or the danger of harming a protected species, the federal and state endangered species acts require certain mitigating steps.

- The EPA handles cleanup of major contaminated sites, making the responsible parties pay for the work or, if this isn't possible, using Superfund money (acquired through a tax on the petroleum and chemical industries). The statute authorizing the Superfund and creating rules for assessing liability is called the Comprehensive Environmental Response, Compensation, and Liability Act (CERCLA). The California agency that also handles cleanups is the Department of Toxic Substances Control.

Key Terms

- **National Environmental Policy Act (NEPA)** – A federal statute requiring an environmental impact statement for every federal project likely to have a significant impact on the environment.

- **California Environmental Quality Act (CEQA)** – A state law requiring an environmental impact report for every public or private project in California that is likely to have a significant environmental impact.

- **Environmental impact assessment** – An analysis of the environmental impact of a proposed project, including suggested ways to mitigate the harm; a federal assessment (to comply with NEPA) is called an EIS (environmental impact statement), while a state assessment (to comply with CEQA) is called an EIR (environmental impact report).

- **Finding of no significant impact/Negative declaration** – A determination by a federal agency or local planning department that a proposed project will not have significant environmental impact, so that no environmental impact assessment is required.

- **EPA** – The Environmental Protection Agency, a federal agency charged with oversight of toxic waste cleanups and other environmental matters.

- **CalEPA** – The California Environmental Protection Agency.

- **Endangered Species Act (ESA)** – A federal law that prohibits harming or adversely affecting the habitat of any species that has been listed as endangered by the federal government.

- **California Endangered Species Act** – A state law that prohibits harming or adversely affecting the habitat of any species that has been listed as endangered (or is a candidate for listing) by the state government.

- **CERCLA** – The Comprehensive Environmental Response, Compensation, and Liability Act, a federal statute that authorizes the Superfund, creates rules for cleanup of polluted sites, and imposes liability on responsible parties.

- **Superfund** – A federal fund built up from taxes on the chemical and petroleum industries and used to pay for cleanup of toxic waste sites if the responsible parties can't be identified or are bankrupt.

Chapter Quiz

1. The early 1970s saw the creation of which federal environmental agency and which environmental laws?
   a) NOAA and state and federal mandatory recycling laws
   b) The EPA, NEPA, and the Endangered Species Act
   c) EarthFirst, Earth Day Proclamation Act, and the Ozone Elimination Act
   d) CalEPA, MERLO, and CEQA

2. True or false? The EPA administers the federal Endangered Species Act.
   a) False; species protection is left to state law
   b) True; the U.S. EPA administers the Endangered Species Act along with Superfund cleanups
   c) False; the U.S. Fish and Wildlife Service and NOAA administer this law
   d) None of the above

3. An endangered species of rabbit that lives in marshy areas is found in a Florida swamp that the U.S. Army Corps of Engineers wants to isolate with levees for flood control. Which of the following is correct?
   a) The levee project won't be allowed; the federal government can't undertake construction projects that may harm an endangered animal species
   b) As long as there is habitat for the rabbit species elsewhere in the country, the project is permissible
   c) Endangered species protection doesn't apply to projects related to public health or safety, so the project can proceed
   d) None of the above

4. The National Parks Service decides it wants to add a roller coaster behind the lodge at Yellowstone. Which of the following is correct?
   a) The Parks Service must apply to the EPA for a finding of no significant impact
   b) Since minimal land is involved, and a roller coaster causes little air pollution, the Parks Service can probably proceed without an EIS
   c) It's solely up to the county planning department to decide whether to require an EIS for the roller coaster project
   d) The Parks Service must make a preliminary analysis of whether the roller coaster is likely to have a negative environmental impact; if harm is likely, the agency must produce an EIS

5. Suppose that in the Yellowstone situation described above, an EIS is eventually completed. A local hiking club sues, claiming that the EIS failed to fully consider the noise the roller coaster would make. Which of the following is correct?
   a) If the EIS failed to consider noise impact, a court will probably order a new or supplemental EIS
   b) If the EIS gave substantial consideration to noise impact, it's unlikely that a court will order a new or supplemental EIS
   c) Noise could have an adverse impact on animals and the human environment, and is a legitimate subject for an environmental assessment
   d) All of the above

6. An EIR for a hillside condominium development offers three proposals for mitigation: 1) building 42 fewer units (reducing the builder's profit to nearly zero); 2) using deeper foundation posts to decrease the risk of landslides; and 3) instead of paving the parking lot, using concrete tiles with openings that allow some grass to grow and thus decrease rain runoff (costing 26% more than simple paving and requiring periodic grass mowing). Which of the following is correct?

a) Proposal #1 is economically unreasonable, which means the agency can't require the builder to comply

b) There is no flexibility; if the EIR mentions a possible mitigation, the court will require the builder to comply

c) Because the rain-absorbing tile costs more (although not enough to render the project unfeasible), the agency cannot require the builder to use the tile

d) None of the above

7. CERCLA:
a) created the state Superfund
b) created the federal Superfund
c) is an international protocol to impose limits on greenhouse gases
d) is better known as the Clean Air Act

8. Who or what typically covers the cost of cleanup for sites placed on the National Priorities List?
a) U.S. taxpayers
b) Superfund
c) Potentially responsible parties (PRPs)
d) Either b) or c)

9. Martina is considering buying a large commercial property. She asks the seller a few casual questions about environmental issues and then walks around the land. Martina buys the property, only to later discover that under a harmless-looking grassy area lies a network of rotting chemical tanks and pipes. Which of the following is correct?

a) As long as Martina did nothing to cause the pollution, she won't have to pay for the cleanup

b) Martina may have to pay for some or all of the cleanup, because she failed to make a thorough environmental inquiry

c) There is no defense for buyers of contaminated property; strict liability applies, and Martina will have to help pay for the cleanup

d) As long as Martina does nothing to aggravate the pollution, she won't be liable

10. A buyer of contaminated property will be considered a bona fide prospective purchaser and therefore exempt from CERCLA's strict liability if:

a) the buyer isn't responsible for the contamination

b) the buyer makes all appropriate inquiries to determine whether the property is contaminated

c) problems are revealed, the buyer takes reasonable steps to prevent further environmental damage from contamination

d) All of the above

Chapter Answer Key

Chapter Quiz Answers:

1. b) The federal Environmental Protection Agency, the National Environmental Policy Act, and the federal Endangered Species Act all came into existence during the early 1970s.

2. c) Responsibility for administering the Endangered Species Act belongs to the Fish and Wildlife Service and the National Oceanic and Atmospheric Administration.

3. a) Species and habitat covered by the Endangered Species Act receive very strict protection.

4. d) The federal agency funding a project, not the EPA, decides whether to produce an environmental assessment. Here, impact on the environment is likely, so an EIS is required.

5. d) Noise, especially in a national park, clearly has an impact on the environment. The assessment must address noise, but can reach any conclusion about it that is based on substantial evidence—even if significant contrary evidence exists.

6. a) The government can't require economically unreasonable mitigation. However, if the required mitigation merely makes a project somewhat less profitable, a court won't overturn the requirement.

7. b) CERCLA created the federal Superfund for cleanup of toxic sites.

8. d) The EPA tries to get responsible parties to pay for toxic waste cleanup; failing that, the agency dips into the Superfund.

9. b) Martina failed to make a thorough inquiry as to whether the property was contaminated, so she cannot avoid liability.

10. d) A buyer who meets all three requirements will be considered a bona fide prospective purchaser and cannot be forced to pay for cleanup of the property.

Cases to Consider... Answers:

Environmental Assessment

Fund for Environmental Defense v. County of Orange (1988) 204 Cal.App.3d 1538. The court found for the county. A supplemental EIR is only required when major revisions to the EIR are required due to: (1) substantial proposed project changes, (2) substantial changes in circumstances, or (3) new information that wasn't known at the time the final EIR was published. Here, the changes weren't substantial enough to require a supplemental EIR. Although the site was now completely enclosed by the park, the additional environmental impact wasn't significant. And although the project's total square footage had increased, it was primarily due to an increase in two-story buildings (so that the increase in developed land was only marginal). The development's number of employees, work output, and traffic impacts all remained the same.

Cleanup

Fireman's Fund Insurance Co. v. City of Lodi (9th Cir. 2002) 302 F.3d 928. Municipalities have a long history of passing laws regulating matters of health. Absent evidence of congressional intent to the contrary, the court declared that CERCLA's authorization of state toxic cleanup laws also included political subdivisions of the state, such as the city of Lodi. The city was entitled to pass MERLO and collect cleanup costs from polluters.

List of Cases

Bakersfield Citizens for Local Control v. City of Bakersfield (Panama 99 Properties) (2004) 124 Cal.App.4th 1184

County Sanitation Dist. No. 2 v. County of Kern (2005) 127 Cal.App.4th 1544

Fairchild Semiconductor Corp. v. EPA (9th Cir. 1993) 984 F.2d 283

Fireman's Fund Insurance Co. v. City of Lodi (9th Cir. 2002) 302 F.3d 928

Fund for Environmental Defense v. County of Orange (1988) 204 Cal.App.3d 1538

Chapter 19

Civil Rights and Fair Housing Laws

Outline

Introduction

Over the last 150 years, the federal and state governments have enacted various civil rights laws to help protect the rights of certain groups of people. In the context of real estate, these laws are meant to ensure that all types of people with similar financial resources have equal access to the same types of housing. Anyone with the requisite income, net worth, and credit history should be able to choose a home or an apartment in any affordable neighborhood, regardless of race, national origin, gender, or other similar characteristics.

Today, compliance with civil rights laws is an integral part of the real estate profession. Real estate agents must be familiar with these laws and understand what activities and practices are prohibited as discriminatory. In this chapter, we'll examine both federal and California antidiscrimination laws. We'll also look at the effects of antidiscrimination laws on the real estate business—specifically in the areas of selling and renting, MLS membership and practices, employment by brokers, advertising, and lending.

State Action vs. Private Action

The earliest civil rights laws were originally interpreted to forbid only discrimination that resulted from **state action**: action by federal, state, or local government officials or entities. For example, say a city law prohibited loitering, but only African-Americans were arrested for violating the law, even though whites were loitering as well. This uneven enforcement of the law would be considered both state action and discriminatory.

Discriminatory state action includes discriminatory laws and regulations, discriminatory enforcement of the law by the courts, and court orders to enforce discriminatory private covenants or restrictions.

Case Example:

A party brought suit to enforce private covenants that restricted ownership of property to members "of the Caucasian race." The U.S. Supreme Court, however, held that it was unconstitutional to enforce such restrictive covenants. Although the covenants themselves were not unlawful, the government could not enforce them (by issuing orders prohibiting their violation or by hearing lawsuits for damages based on their violation). Such enforcement would be discriminatory state action. *Shelley v. Kraemer* (1948) 334 U.S. 1.

However, since the 1960s, both legislatures and the courts have extended antidiscrimination laws to prohibit discriminatory action by private parties as well as the state. This means that activities by private citizens—including real estate sellers, buyers, and their agents—are now subject to these laws as well.

Federal Antidiscrimination Laws

The first legislative efforts to eliminate discrimination began on the federal level with the Thirteenth and Fourteenth Amendments to the Constitution. These amendments, passed after the Civil War, abolished slavery and guaranteed equal protection under the law. Subsequently, Congress enacted the following federal laws, all of which contain provisions prohibiting discrimination in real estate transactions:

- the Civil Rights Act of 1866,
- Title VIII of the Civil Rights Act of 1968 (usually referred to as the federal Fair Housing Act),

- the Equal Credit Opportunity Act,
- the Home Mortgage Disclosure Act, and
- the Americans with Disabilities Act.

During our discussion of federal laws, keep in mind that California has its own anti-discrimination laws. Some of these state laws are stricter than their federal counterparts. When state and federal antidiscrimination laws differ, the stricter law will apply. For example, many federal laws contain exemptions that don't exist under the comparable state law; this will mean that particular exemption isn't available in California.

Civil Rights Act of 1866

Suppose Mr. and Mrs. Jones try to buy a home in a subdivision. Because they are African-American, their offer is refused. What recourse do Mr. and Mrs. Jones have? What can the agent representing the Joneses do? What kind of liability, if any, would the sellers and their agent have?

The **Civil Rights Act of 1866** prohibits discrimination based on race or color, giving all citizens of the United States the same rights to own and enjoy property as those held by white persons. The 1866 Act applies to all real estate transactions, without exception.

The constitutionality of the 1866 Act was challenged and upheld in a landmark case decided by the U.S. Supreme Court just a few weeks after Congress passed the Civil Rights Act of 1968 (discussed in more detail below).

Case Example:

Mr. and Mrs. Joseph Jones tried to buy a home, or have one built for them, in a subdivision being developed by the Mayer Company. When the Mayer Company rejected their offer, the Joneses brought suit, claiming that the refusal was evidence of racial discrimination in violation of the Civil Rights Act of 1866. The Mayer Company argued that the law was unconstitutional. The court sided with the couple: the 1866 Act was constitutional. *Jones v. Alfred H. Mayer Co.* (1968) 392 U.S. 409.

In addition to declaring the 1866 Act constitutional, the *Jones* ruling established three important points. First, because the right to buy or to lease property can be hindered just as much by private citizens as by governments, the 1866 Act prohibits all racial discrimination in the sale or rental of property—not just discrimination that results from state action.

Second, Congress has the power to enforce the Thirteenth Amendment (which abolished slavery) using "appropriate legislation." The 1866 Act addresses one of the "badges of slavery" (the inability to own or to exchange property) and is therefore an example of such appropriate legislation.

Third, the 1866 Act is supplemented—not replaced—by the Civil Rights Act of 1968. The 1866 Act isn't a comprehensive fair housing act, as it only addresses racial discrimination and is enforceable only by private parties. (This is quite different from the fair housing provisions of the 1968 Civil Rights Act, which cover many types of discriminatory practices and give federal agencies broad powers of enforcement.)

Enforcement of the 1866 Act. A person who is discriminated against in violation of the 1866 Act may bring a lawsuit in federal district court. Injunctive relief, actual damages, and punitive damages are possible remedies. (For a review of remedies and damages, see Chapters 2 and 9.)

Federal Fair Housing Act

Title VIII of the Civil Rights Act of 1968 (commonly known as the **Fair Housing Act**) is a federal law that prohibits a wide range of discriminatory practices related to housing. The act declares that "It is the policy of the United States to provide, within constitutional limitations, for fair housing throughout the United States."

The Fair Housing Act prohibits discrimination on the basis of **race**, **color**, **national origin**, **religion**, **sex**, **disability**, or **familial status** (families with minor children) in the sale or lease of residential property or vacant land intended to be used for residential purposes. (Note: The groups of persons protected under the Fair Housing Act and other antidiscrimination laws are referred to as **protected classes**.) In addition, the act prohibits discrimination in advertising, lending, real estate brokerage, and certain other services in connection with residential transactions.

Application of the Fair Housing Act. The federal Fair Housing Act covers most sales, rentals, or exchanges of residential property involving buildings or portions of buildings occupied, or intended to be occupied, as a residence. Also covered is vacant land, offered for sale or lease, that will be the site of a residential building.

The Fair Housing Act, however, does contain several exemptions from its coverage. Here are the details of those exemptions:

1. **Sale or Rental by Private Owner.** The law doesn't apply when a private individual sells or rents a single-family home, as long as the owner has less than four homes, doesn't use any discriminatory advertising, and doesn't employ a real estate broker. This exemption is available only once every 24 months, unless the owner is the occupant (or the most recent occupant).

2. **Rental in an Owner-Occupied Dwelling.** The law doesn't apply to the rental of a room or unit in a dwelling with up to four units if the owner lives in one of the units, doesn't use any discriminatory advertising, and doesn't employ a broker.

3. **Accommodations Owned by Religious Organization or Private Club.** A private club or religious organization that provides accommodations incidental to its primary purpose may limit occupancy of the accommodations to its own members (or give preference to members). However, a religious organization can't use this exemption if the religion restricts membership based on race, color, or national origin. Finally, this exemption does not apply to commercial transactions. So, for example, a private club running a motel as a for-profit venture could not favor its members when renting rooms.

4. **Housing for Older Persons.** Children may be excluded from housing that is expressly designated for the elderly, provided that the housing is:
   - developed or provided through a program to assist older persons,
   - intended for and occupied only by people over 62, or

All in the Family

The federal Fair Housing Act makes it illegal to discriminate based on "familial status"—but what does this term mean, exactly? Generally, it's illegal to discriminate against someone based on the fact that he or she has legal custody of a child under 18 years of age, intends to adopt or otherwise obtain custody of a child, or is pregnant.

In its original form, the Fair Housing Act did not include familial status as a protected class. This meant, for example, that an apartment building could exclude families with children, and that landlords were permitted to refuse rental applications from pregnant women. But in 1988 the Fair Housing Act was amended to add familial status as a protected class. (Disability was also added at the same time.)

Note, though, that the law still provides an exemption for housing that is specifically intended for older persons.

- intended to meet the needs of people age 55 or older and at least 80% of the units are occupied by at least one person who is 55 or older.

Case to Consider...

In 1985, Colony Cove Mobile Home Park instituted a new rule restricting residency in the park to persons 55 years of age or older. Current residents under age 55 were permitted to stay, but the rule was enforced against any children born to residents after that point. When two families in the park later had children, they were evicted. The families sued, stating that the Fair Housing Act prohibits discrimination based on familial status. Should the court find for the families or for Colony Cove? *Colony Cove Associates v. Brown* (1990) 220 Cal.App.3d 195.

Remember, however, that these exemptions apply very rarely. The Civil Rights Act of 1866 prohibits discrimination based on race or color in any property transaction, regardless of any exemption under the Fair Housing Act. In addition, there are no exemptions for any transaction involving a real estate licensee.

Prohibited Acts. Under the federal Fair Housing Act, it is unlawful to engage in the following acts if they are based on race, color, national origin, religion, sex, disability, or familial status:

- to refuse to sell or rent after the making of a bona fide offer, or to refuse to negotiate for the sale or rental of, or otherwise make unavailable or deny, a dwelling;
- to discriminate against any person in the terms, conditions, or privileges of sale or rental of a dwelling, or in the provision of services or facilities in connection with those dwellings;

- to make, print, or publish any notice, statement, or advertising that indicates any preference, limitation, or discrimination in the sale or rental of a dwelling;
- to represent that any dwelling is not available for inspection, sale, or rental when the dwelling is in fact available;
- to induce or attempt to induce, for profit, any person to sell or rent any dwelling by representations regarding the entry or prospective entry into the neighborhood of a member or members of any protected class (blockbusting, discussed below);
- to discriminate in the making of a loan for buying, building, repairing, improving, or maintaining a dwelling, or in the terms of such financing, by a commercial lender;
- to deny access to a multiple listing service (or similar organization) or to discriminate in the terms or conditions for access to such a service;
- to coerce, intimidate, threaten, or interfere with anyone on account of her enjoyment, attempt to enjoy, or encouragement or assistance to another in enjoying the rights granted by the Fair Housing Act.

We'll take a closer look at three discriminatory activities that are specifically prohibited by the Fair Housing Act: redlining, steering, and blockbusting.

Redlining. Refusal to make a loan will be considered illegal **redlining** if the refusal is based on the racial or ethnic composition of the neighborhood in which the property is located. Redlining occurs when lenders assume that property values in minority-owned neighborhoods are more likely to decline and, for that reason, refuse to make loans in those areas (or only make loans on unfavorable terms). The inability to secure financing makes it harder for owners to renovate, repair, or improve their properties—thus contributing to the predicted decline in values.

Although redlining is now prohibited, it's not illegal for lenders to refuse to make loans in areas where property values are declining. But refusals must be based on purely objective economic criteria, such as the value of the property and the values of other properties in the neighborhood—not the racial composition of the area's population.

▶ **Housing and Security in the Wake of 9/11**

Since September 11, 2001, Muslims and persons who are (or appear to be) of Middle Eastern or South Asian descent have reported acts of discrimination and harassment in connection with housing. In 2016, the refugee crisis is raising similar issues. Some landlords may wonder if it's legal to screen tenants based on their citizenship status.

The federal Fair Housing Act makes it unlawful to screen tenants based on national origin. However, under the federal law it's not illegal to screen applicants based on citizenship or immigration status, provided ALL applicants are required to provide proof of their status, not just those who appear to be Muslim, Middle Eastern, or South Asian.

In California, however, the Unruh Civil Rights Act—discussed later in this chapter—does make it illegal to ask applicants for proof of citizenship or immigration status.

The History of Redlining

The practice of redlining can be traced back to the 1930s, when a federal government agency known as the Home Owners' Loan Corporation surveyed nearly 240 American cities and created color-coded maps showing the areas and neighborhoods in which real estate investments were believed to be the most secure. These areas were predominantly homogenous, white neighborhoods.

Conversely, the maps indicated the areas in which loans and insurance were believed to be high-risk. These neighborhoods, populated primarily by African-Americans and other ethnic minorities, were literally circled on the maps in red ink—hence the term "redlining."

Many banks and insurers relied on these maps, avoiding business in the high-risk areas. Even the Federal Housing Administration encouraged this practice: its 1938 Underwriting Manual warned appraisers of areas with "inharmonious racial groups" and promoted the use of racially restrictive covenants to maintain segregation between neighborhoods.

Steering. Channeling prospective buyers or renters into or away from specific neighborhoods, based on race or some other protected class, is known as **steering**. For instance, if an agent shows white clients homes only in white neighborhoods, and shows Asian clients homes only in Asian neighborhoods, the agent is steering.

Although it's usually not a problem for an agent to answer a buyer's question about a neighborhood's racial, ethnic, or religious composition, an agent cannot direct or advise a buyer to buy (or not to buy) in a certain neighborhood based on those characteristics.

Blockbusting. Blockbusting occurs when a real estate agent tries to convince a property owner to sell by creating the impression that the neighborhood is declining due to an influx of minority owners. The agent might predict that lower property values, higher crime rates, or a decline in school quality will result from the neighborhood's changing racial composition. These predictions can cause property owners to panic and list their properties with the agent, who profits from the resulting sales.

Some examples of blockbusting include:

- selling homes on contract to minority buyers to create the impression that the neighborhood is changing;
- distributing literature or other types of advertising that states that a member of a minority group has purchased a home nearby;
- obtaining numerous listings in the area and placing "For Sale" signs on the properties, to try to frighten neighbors into selling while they still can; and
- telling owners that the changing neighborhood will adversely affect the local schools.

Enforcement. If someone believes she has been discriminated against in violation of the Fair Housing Act, she may file a complaint with the Office of Fair Housing and Equal

Opportunity. (This office is a division of the Department of Housing and Urban Development, or HUD.) HUD may also file a complaint on its own initiative. HUD will investigate the complaint and attempt to negotiate an agreement between the parties; if this is unsuccessful, the dispute will be resolved by HUD or by a federal court. HUD may also refer discrimination complaints to the state agency equivalent of HUD: California's Department of Fair Employment and Housing (we'll discuss this agency later in the chapter).

As an alternative to filing a complaint with HUD, an individual may file a lawsuit directly, either in federal or state court. A complaint must be filed with HUD within one year of the discriminatory conduct; a lawsuit must be filed within two years.

The Fair Housing Act authorizes compensatory damages, injunctions, and civil penalties for violations of the act. The civil penalty amounts range from a maximum of $16,000 for a first offense to $70,000 for a third offense.

The Fair Housing Act may be enforced by the U.S. attorney general, if it appears that someone is routinely engaging in discriminatory acts or that an issue of general public importance exists. In these situations, the attorney general may bring a civil suit in federal district court seeking temporary or permanent injunctions, or other court orders as necessary. The court may award civil penalties of up to $75,000 for a first violation and up to $150,000 for a third violation.

Fair Lending Laws

Federal law also prohibits discriminatory activities by mortgage lenders. As we mentioned earlier, the federal Fair Housing Act prohibits discrimination in home loans and other aspects of residential financing. In addition, you should be familiar with two other federal laws that require fair lending practices: the Home Mortgage Disclosure Act and Equal Credit Opportunity Act.

 Discrimination by Proxy

In 2006, the National Fair Housing Alliance published *Unequal Opportunity—Perpetuating Housing Segregation in America*, a report on fair housing trends. The report revealed that many real estate agents are knowingly engaging in steering, substituting a discussion of schools for a discussion of a neighborhood's racial or ethnic composition.

For example, the report cited cases in which agents would define schools as either "good" or "bad" based simply on the client's race. White clients were told that schools in a predominantly Latino area were "bad," while Latino clients were told that those very same schools were "good." The agents were clearly attempting to discourage white clients from considering the area, while encouraging the Latino clients to consider it. Although the agents never actually mentioned race or ethnicity, their actions constituted illegal steering.

Various reports indicate that this kind of problem continues today.

Equal Credit for Everyone

The Equal Credit Opportunity Act states that it is unlawful for creditors to discriminate against applicants. But what does this actually mean for someone applying for a home loan? The agency in charge of enforcing the ECOA, the Federal Trade Commission, has published a list of specific requirements that apply to lenders. Here are some of these requirements:

A lender may not:
- ask an applicant whether she is divorced or widowed;
- ask an applicant whether he intends to have children;
- discount an applicant's income based on sex or marital status, or assume that a woman of childbearing age will stop working to raise children;
- consider whether an applicant has a telephone listing in his name; or
- require a cosigner if the applicant meets the lender's standards.

A lender must:
- consider credit acquired under a birth name (Mary Smith), when the applicant is now married (Mary Jones); and vice versa, consider credit acquired under a married name when the applicant is now single;
- consider alimony, child support, part-time income, or retirement benefits, when evaluating income;
- either accept or reject a loan application within 30 days of receiving it; and
- provide definite and specific reasons for rejecting an application.

The **Home Mortgage Disclosure Act** was enacted in 1975 to help enforce federal laws against redlining. The law requires large institutional lenders to report annually on the residential mortgage loans that they make or purchase each year. By studying the loan data contained in these reports, government investigators can identify the areas and communities in which few or no home loans are being made, and check for any discriminatory lending patterns.

The **Equal Credit Opportunity Act (ECOA)**, passed in 1974, is intended to provide consumers with equal access to credit. To that end, the law prohibits lenders from discriminating against a potential borrower based on race, color, religion, national origin, sex, marital status, or age (provided the borrower is of legal age). It also bars a lender from discriminating on the basis that the applicant's income is wholly or partly derived from public assistance. The ECOA applies to residential real estate loans, as well as all other credit transactions.

Equal Access to Facilities

An important element of federal antidiscrimination law is the promotion of equal access to facilities and services. To help guarantee this access, federal law now includes disabled persons as a protected class. In 1988, the federal Fair Housing Act was amended to prohibit housing discrimination on the basis of disability. The Americans with Disabilities Act (ADA), which became effective in 1992, prohibits discrimination on the basis of disability in any business or other facility that is open to the public. Under both laws, a **disability** is defined as any physical or mental impairment that substantially limits one or more major life activities.

Fair Housing Act Requirements. As discussed earlier in this chapter, the Fair Housing Act prohibits discrimination in the terms, conditions, or privileges of sale or rental of housing, or in the provision of services or facilities related to the housing. This provision requires landlords to permit any reasonable accommodations or modifications that a disabled person needs in order to be able to use and enjoy a housing unit.

Reasonable accommodations and modifications. Under the law's reasonable accommodations requirement, a landlord must make reasonable exceptions to his rules, policies, practices, or services if a disabled person needs those to use and enjoy a residence like everyone else. This requirement applies to public and common use areas as well as individual living areas.

> **Example:** Bert is blind and uses a guide dog for assistance. His apartment building does not allow pets. However, the landlord must allow Bert to keep his guide dog because the dog is necessary for Bert to have an equal opportunity to use and enjoy the apartment.

Under the Fair Housing Act's **reasonable modifications** requirement, a landlord must permit a disabled person to make reasonable modifications to existing housing if such modifications are necessary for the disabled person's full enjoyment. The landlord may require the tenant to pay for the modifications. The landlord may also require the tenant to return the premises to their original condition, as long as it is reasonable to do so.

> **Example:** Terry and Lisa Landon rent a house. When they move in, they realize that Terry's wheelchair won't fit through certain doorways. They ask the landlord for permission to widen the doorways, at their expense. This is a reasonable modification and the landlord must allow it. When the Landons move out, the landlord can't require them to change the doorways back to their original width, unless the wider doorways somehow interfere with the landlord's (or a future tenant's) use and enjoyment of the home.

New multi-family construction. The Fair Housing Act contains several specific design and construction requirements that apply to multi-family dwellings (buildings with four or more residential units) built after 1991.

- All public and common use areas must be accessible and usable by disabled persons.
- Doors must be wide enough for wheelchairs to pass through.
- There must be an accessible route into and through the covered dwelling unit.
- Light switches, outlets, and thermostats must be placed in accessible locations.
- Bathroom walls must be reinforced, to allow for the installation of grab bars.
- Kitchens and bathrooms must be designed so that a person in a wheelchair can maneuver about the space.

These requirements apply to the ground floor units in buildings without elevators, and to all units in buildings with elevators (in other words, to those units accessible by wheelchairs).

Americans with Disabilities Act. While the Fair Housing Act's requirements apply only to housing, the ADA's coverage is more expansive, prohibiting discrimination on the basis of disability in any place of public accommodation or commercial facility. A place of **public accommodation** is defined to include any nonresidential place that is owned, operated, or leased by a private entity, and open to the public, as long as the operation of the facility affects commerce.

As you can see, the definition of public accommodation is quite broad. It encompasses hotels, restaurants, retail stores, banks, schools, and professional offices—including real estate brokers' offices. This means that real estate brokerages themselves must comply with the ADA. It also means that real estate agents working with commercial owners and landlords should be prepared to advise their clients of the ADA's requirements.

ADA requirements. The ADA requires each of the following to be accomplished, as long as they are readily achievable:

- Reasonable modifications must be made in policies, practices, and procedures in order to make goods or services accessible to individuals with disabilities.
- Architectural barriers, structural communication barriers, and transportation barriers must be removed so that goods and services are accessible to the disabled.
- Auxiliary aids and services must be provided so that no disabled person is excluded, denied services, segregated, or otherwise treated differently from other individuals.
- All new construction of places of public accommodation and commercial facilities must be accessible to the disabled, unless structurally impractical.

The ADA defines **readily achievable** as action that can be easily accomplished, without much difficulty or expense. Some examples of readily achievable modifications would be:

- The owner of a commercial building with no elevator installs automatic entry doors and a buzzer at street level so that customers of a second-floor business can ask for assistance.
- A commercial building owner alters the height of a counter to make it accessible to someone in a wheelchair, adds grab bars to restroom stalls, and takes a variety of other steps to make the building's facilities accessible.

Exemptions. Private clubs and religious organizations are exempt from the accessibility requirements of the ADA.

Enforcement of the ADA. An individual who is being discriminated against (or who reasonably believes that she is about to be discriminated against) in violation of the ADA may bring a civil action and obtain a temporary or permanent injunction or a restraining order from the court. An individual may also file a complaint with the U.S. attorney general, who will investigate the alleged violation.

If the attorney general finds that a case of general public importance exists, or that a person is engaging in a pattern or practice of discrimination under the ADA, the attorney general may file a lawsuit seeking injunctive relief, monetary damages for the victim(s), and civil penalties payable to the government.

California Antidiscrimination Laws

Real estate agents, sellers, and landlords must comply not only with the federal anti-discrimination laws discussed above, but also with state laws that prohibit discriminatory behavior. California's antidiscrimination laws are often much stricter than their federal counterparts, containing a broader range of protected classes and allowing few, if any, exemptions.

In California, the state laws designed to prohibit discrimination and promote fair housing include:

- the Fair Employment and Housing Act,
- the Unruh Civil Rights Act,
- the Housing Financial Discrimination Act, and
- the Real Estate Law.

Fair Employment and Housing Act

The **Fair Employment and Housing Act** (sometimes referred to as the **Rumford Act**) prohibits discrimination in the sale or lease of housing in California. The law was passed in 1963 and is contained within Government Code §§ 12900 – 12996. It imposes many of the same requirements as the federal Fair Housing Act; however, as you'll see, it protects a much wider range of classes and contains fewer exemptions.

Application. The Fair Employment and Housing Act makes it illegal for any owner, landlord, assignee, managing agent, real estate broker or salesperson, or any business establishment to discriminate based on race, color, religion, sex, gender, gender identity, gender expression, sexual orientation, marital status, national origin, ancestry, familial status, source of income, disability, or genetic information.

The law prohibits the use of discriminatory terms when advertising housing for sale or rent. For example, a landlord can't use any advertising that suggests she would prefer married couples or single women as tenants.

The law specifically prohibits a seller or landlord from even asking about a prospective buyer's or tenant's race, color, religion, sex, gender, gender identity, gender expression, sexual orientation, marital status, national origin, ancestry, familial status, disability, or genetic information. If a real estate licensee is asked such a question regarding a buyer or a tenant, the agent should refuse to supply the information.

Discrimination in the financing of housing is also prohibited. Banks, mortgage companies, and other financial institutions cannot discriminate against anyone based on one of the protected characteristics mentioned above.

Reasonable accommodations and modifications. Landlords are required to make reasonable accommodations in rules, policies, practices, or services if a disabled tenant requests it and the accommodations are necessary to allow the tenant to use and enjoy a

Agency Hearing on Discriminatory Act

State of California, Department of Fair Employment and Housing

In April 2003, a woman rented a room from New Beginnings, a board and care home in San Jose. When the tenant informed the manager that she had just ended a four-year relationship with her female partner, the manager responded by declaring that "homosexuality is an abomination...I don't want any of 'that' in my house." Subsequently, the manager subjected the tenant to special conditions, including restrictions on her access to the women's dorm room. Later investigation by a housing rights organization showed that the manager also clearly indicated a preference for heterosexual tenants when renting out rooms. The Department of Fair Employment and Housing brought suit against the manager and New Beginnings.

The manager argued that her comments conformed to her religious beliefs and were constitutionally protected free speech, but this argument was rejected. Under California law, religious beliefs don't allow a landlord to violate the Fair Employment and Housing Act and discriminate based on sexual orientation. The manager and New Beginnings were required to compensate the tenant for emotional pain and suffering, pay a civil penalty, adopt and post an antidiscrimination policy, and undergo training on state and federal antidiscrimination law.

housing unit. The landlord may ask for medical verification of the disability and the need for an accommodation.

Service animals. Under the reasonable accommodation requirement, a landlord with a "no pets allowed" policy must make an exception for disabled persons who require the use and companionship of service animals. The landlord cannot charge the tenant any extra fees for keeping a service animal, but the tenant will be liable for any damages caused by the animal. The same rules apply to persons who are licensed to train such service animals, even if the trainer is not himself disabled.

In California, an animal does not need to be trained as a service animal to qualify as a reasonable accommodation; animals prescribed as companion animals for those with mental illness or depression, or to help alleviate the psychological impact of physical disabilities, are also covered by the law.

Case to Consider...

The Elebiaris sought permission from their condominium association, Auburn Woods, to keep a small dog, even though the development had a no-dogs policy. A serious car accident had left Mr. Elebiari permanently disabled, and both Mr. and Mrs. Elebiari suffered

Agency Hearing on Discriminatory Act

State of California, Department of Fair Employment and Housing

In 1997, a tenant diagnosed with AIDS moved into a Los Angeles apartment building; subsequently, his ill health forced him to stop working. He received state disability benefits and rental assistance from an organization that provides rent subsidies to persons with AIDS. The checks from the organization could only be made payable to the rental housing's owner, not the individual tenant.

In 2002, a new landlord took over management of the building. He refused to accept these third-party checks from the aid organization, even after the tenant formally requested a reasonable accommodation based on his disability. The landlord eventually evicted the tenant for failure to pay rent. The tenant filed a complaint with the Department of Fair Employment and Housing, who agreed that accepting a third-party check to pay the rent of a person with AIDS is not an economic hardship on the landlord and is, therefore, a reasonable accommodation.

The parties eventually reached a settlement: the landlord agreed to pay the tenant $80,000 and get out of the business of renting or managing housing.

from severe depression. They found that keeping a dog helped alleviate their symptoms. They provided Auburn Woods with a letter from their doctor that described their condition and recommended they be allowed to keep the dog. Auburn Woods denied the request. At trial, Auburn Woods argued that since the dog was not trained as a service animal, Auburn Woods was not required to make an exception to its policy. Should the Elebiaris be allowed to keep their dog? *Woods I Homeowners Assn. v. Fair Employment & Housing Com. (Elebiari)* (2004) 121 Cal.App.4th 1578.

Exemptions. The Fair Employment and Housing Act contains a few fairly limited exemptions. First, the act doesn't apply to accommodations operated by nonprofit religious, fraternal, or charitable organizations. It also doesn't apply when a portion of a single-family owner-occupied home is rented out. Further, when the rental involves shared living space, the advertising may limit the vacancy to only men or only women. Finally, the act's familial status protections do not apply to housing for senior citizens.

Enforcement. Complaints of discrimination are handled through the court system. Until recently, complaints under the Fair Employment and Housing Act were adjudicated by the state Fair Employment and Housing Commission in administrative hearings. Now, however, such cases are filed in court. The Department of Fair Employment and Housing or the state Attorney General may bring action on the aggrieved person's behalf. The department may require the parties to participate in mandatory dispute resolution before it files a suit. However, an aggrieved person may file suit under the act on her own, without previously filing a complaint with the department.

In a suit brought under the act, the court may award both actual and punitive damages to the injured party. It may also issue a temporary restraining order or other injunctive relief to prevent the defendant from continuing to violate the law. The court may also award the prevailing party attorney's fees and costs, even if the department is the party who brought the suit. In suits brought by the Attorney General, it may also impose a civil penalty of up to $50,000 for a first violation or $100,000 for subsequent violations.

> **Example:** Shirley Carper, a long-time tenant of a San Francisco apartment building, had a severe degenerative joint disease that made walking up and down stairs very difficult. She requested a parking space that was accessible via the elevator and an extra building key for her caregiver. She provided the landlord with written documentation from her doctor as to her disability. The landlord denied her request, questioning whether her disability even existed. Carper sought help from a nonprofit housing rights organization and the city's Human Rights Commission. Over the next three years, the landlord continued to deny Carper's requests, even though suitable parking spaces became available. Eventually, the Department of Fair Employment and Housing brought a disability discrimination lawsuit against the landlord.
>
> Following an eight-day trial, a jury found the landlord liable for discriminatory harassment and denial of a reasonable accommodation. Before the jury began to deliberate as to punitive damages, the parties settled. The landlord agreed to pay the tenant $1 million, to distribute a written policy to tenants regarding their right to reasonable accommodation, to undergo training, and to post publicly the court order stating that the landlord had violated the law.

Unruh Civil Rights Act

California's **Unruh Civil Rights Act**, contained in §§ 51 – 52 of California's Civil Code, prohibits discrimination by business establishments. Specifically, the law states that all persons are entitled to "full and equal accommodations, advantages, facilities, privileges, or services in all business establishments," regardless of sex, race, color, religion, ancestry, national origin, disability, medical condition, genetic information, marital status, sexual orientation, citizenship, primary language, or immigration status. In addition, business establishments are prohibited from discriminating in housing transactions based on age.

Since a brokerage firm is a business establishment, the Unruh Act prohibits brokers from discriminating in the performance of their duties. A broker cannot refuse a listing or turn away a prospective buyer for discriminatory reasons.

Apartment houses, condominiums, and other types of real estate developments are also considered business establishments under the Unruh Act. Generally, this means that apartment and condominium complexes cannot enforce "No children" rules. However, the act does make an exception for housing intended for senior citizens.

Expanded Protection. Although the Unruh Act specifically mentions only the classes listed above, California courts have long interpreted the list of protected classes to be "illustrative rather than restrictive." In fact, the courts have repeatedly stated that the Unruh Act prohibits all arbitrary and intentional discrimination by businesses. Discrimination is considered arbitrary when it is based on individual characteristics, traits, or beliefs similar to those listed in the act. For example, although familial status isn't specifically mentioned in the Unruh Act, families with children are nevertheless a protected class under the law.

Case Example:

The owner of an apartment complex refused to rent units to families with minor children, contending that children are "rowdier, noisier, more mischievous and more boisterous than adults." When the owners were sued, the superior court found that the landlords had not discriminated against families with children, because familial status wasn't specifically listed in the Unruh Act. The appeals court disagreed, stating that the list of protected classes is "illustrative rather than restrictive." It pointed to language and history that indicated the legislature's intent to prohibit all arbitrary discrimination by business establishments. The landlord could institute rules and regulations that addressed issues of particularly noisy or rowdy children ("No running in hallways," for example), but could not discriminate against an entire class of persons merely because they are children. *Marina Point, Ltd. v. Wolfson* (1982) 30 Cal. 3d. 721.

Similarly, marital status and sexual orientation were also considered to be protected classes, even before a 2005 amendment expressly added them to the Unruh Act.

It's important to understand that the Unruh Act doesn't prohibit all discrimination whatsoever. For example, the law doesn't prohibit discrimination based on economic status, as long as the discrimination isn't simply a way of masking discrimination against a protected class. This means, for example, that a landlord may institute a policy of denying rental units to applicants based on insufficient income—as long as the policy applies to all applicants and isn't used simply to exclude minority applicants.

Housing Financial Discrimination Act

California's **Housing Financial Discrimination Act** (Health and Safety Code §§ 35800 – 35833, also known as the **Holden Act**) targets the illegal practice of redlining. According to the law, it's against public policy to deny mortgage loans (or to impose stricter loan terms) based on neighborhood conditions that are unrelated to the borrower's creditworthiness or to the security property's value. For example, a lender cannot refuse to make a loan simply because the borrower plans to purchase a home in a predominantly Latino or Asian neighborhood.

Specifically, the Housing Financial Discrimination Act makes it illegal to:

- discriminate in providing financial assistance to purchase, construct, rehabilitate, improve, or refinance housing on the basis of the characteristics of the neighborhood surrounding the property, unless the lender can show that consideration is required to avoid an unsound business practice;
- consider the racial, ethnic, religious, or national origin composition of the neighborhood surrounding the property; or
- discriminate in providing financial assistance for housing on the basis of race, color, religion, sex, marital status, national origin, or ancestry.

Complaints that a lender has violated the Housing Financial Discrimination Act may be filed with the state Department of Business Oversight. Following an investigation and a hearing, the Department may require the violator to make the loan or to pay damages to the injured party.

Real Estate License Law and Regulations

In addition to the federal and state laws we've discussed, real estate licensees must be aware of the antidiscrimination provisions contained in the Real Estate Law and the Real Estate Commissioner's regulations. Both the statute and the regulations prohibit discriminatory behavior by licensees.

Under the Real Estate Law, a licensee who engages in discriminatory behavior may be disciplined by the Bureau of Real Estate, and sanctions may include license suspension or revocation. (For more on the disciplinary process, see Chapter 8.)

The Real Estate Commissioner's regulations prohibit real estate licensees from discriminating based on race, color, sex, religion, ancestry, physical handicap, marital status, or national origin.

The regulations also include examples of actions that constitute discriminatory conduct. The following activities are illegal if they involve discrimination against a protected group:

- refusing to negotiate for the sale, rental, or financing of the purchase of real property;
- refusing or failing to show, rent, sell, or finance the purchase of real property;
- channeling or steering a person away from real property;
- discriminating in the terms, conditions, or privileges of the sale, rental, or financing of the purchase of real property;
- providing differing services or facilities in connection with the sale, rental, or financing of real property (such as handling applications, showings, or referrals differently);
- representing to any person that a property is not available for inspection, sale, or rental when it is in fact available;
- processing an application more slowly, or otherwise acting to delay, hinder, or avoid the sale, rental, or financing of a property;
- performing any acts, making any notes, asking any questions, or circulating any material that seems to express or imply a limitation or preference for certain races or classes of people;
- soliciting sales, rentals, or listings from some persons, but not others;
- refusing to accept a rental or sales listing or application for financing of the purchase of real property;
- using any advertising or making any statements that indicate any preference or limitation; and
- assisting or aiding in any way, any person in the sale, rental, or financing of the purchase of real property when there is a reasonable belief that such a person intends to discriminate.

Note that the above examples do not represent all of the discriminatory conduct for which an agent may be disciplined.

All licensees have an affirmative duty to familiarize themselves with the requirements of both federal and state antidiscrimination laws. In addition, brokers have the duty to supervise their affiliated licensees and to take reasonable steps to make sure their licensees are familiar with the requirements of those laws.

The Right to Sue

As you've seen, federal and state civil rights laws apply to a broad range of parties and situations, and penalties for violations can be severe. So who has the right to sue under these laws? A housing discrimination case may involve many more parties than simply a single plaintiff and a single defendant. For example, the plaintiffs in a discrimination case may include testers (discussed below), fair housing organizations, the U.S. and California attorneys general, the Department of Fair Employment and Housing, and HUD. Depending on the nature of the incident, those sued may include property managers, real estate salespersons and their brokers, and owners. Liability can be based on someone's own discriminatory acts or on the basis of agency liability. (For more on vicarious liability, see Chapter 6.)

Testers

One of the most common methods of proving fair housing law violations involves the use of **testers**. For example, if a person feels that he has been lied to about the availability of housing, she will complain to a community fair housing organization. In turn, the organization will send testers out to the housing. Many testers are volunteers; others are paid expenses and a nominal fee.

The most frequent type of test is the so-called **sandwich test**. In this test, a white tester asks to see available housing, followed by a minority tester, and then another white tester. If the white tester is shown available units, the minority tester is told there are no vacancies, and then the second white tester is shown units, there is probably sufficient evidence to prove in court that the property owner or agent is discriminating based on race.

Obviously, in such a case, the original applicant (the one who complained to the organization) would be entitled to damages upon proving that the discrimination occurred. What might not be so obvious is that the white testers, the minority testers, and the fair housing organization may also be entitled to sue and recover damages from the landlord and/or property owner.

Case Example:

When an African-American man inquired about available apartments in a complex near Richmond, Virginia, he was told by the owner that there were no apartments available. A fair housing organization sent two testers (one African-American, one white) to the apartment complex. On four separate occasions, the white testers were shown apartments while the African-American testers were told none were available.

The original applicant, the African-American tester, the white tester, and the fair housing organization all sued the apartment complex owner. The court allowed all of these plaintiffs to proceed for the following reasons:

- The original applicant's suit was based on a straightforward claim of denial of housing and racial steering.
- The African-American tester's claim was based on the Fair Housing Act, which makes it unlawful for someone to pretend that housing is not available when it is, in fact, available.

- The claim of the white tester, who was truthfully told that apartments were available, was based on the right to enjoy an integrated society.
- The fair housing organization's claim was based on the theory that the defendant's discriminatory actions interfered with the organization's abilities to provide its services, which resulted in a drain on its financial resources.

Havens Realty Corp. v. Coleman (1982) 455 U.S. 363.

As this case illustrates, many parties may be permitted to sue based on an act or practice of illegal discrimination. It's even possible for a broker to be a plaintiff—a broker may be able to sue for his commission if the seller backs out of a deal simply because the buyer is a minority.

Antidiscrimination Law and the Real Estate Profession

Now that we've examined both federal and state antidiscrimination laws, let's look at how these laws impact the real estate profession and your day-to-day business activities. In this section, we'll provide some examples of violations in:

- advertising,
- selling or renting real property,
- lending,
- zoning and other regulatory actions,
- brokers' employment and business practices, and
- MLS membership and practices.

Note that although many of the cases we'll be discussing are from other jurisdictions, they would likely be decided in the same way under California law.

Advertising

It is illegal under both federal and California state law to use advertising that indicates a preference, restriction, or intent to discriminate. Sometimes such discrimination is unintentional; however, even unintentional discrimination may be a violation.

> **Example:** A flyer that describes a house as "Near local church and synagogue" may seem to indicate that Muslims are unwelcome.

Many brokers send advertisements to the neighbors of listed homes in search of potential buyers. While such solicitations are not necessarily discriminatory, they can have a discriminatory effect when:

1. the solicitations are used only in neighborhoods where the residents are predominantly of the same race and/or religious or ethnic background;
2. persons in the neighborhood of a particular race or ethnic background are not sent copies of the solicitation; or
3. the solicitation suggests that the recipient can control the type or character of the person who will buy the property. For example, if the solicitation suggests that a

neighbor can, by referring potential buyers, "uphold the standards of the community" (when the standards are unspecified), the neighbor is likely to infer that he can control the race or ethnic background of the buyer.

Solicitations used under those circumstances are considered an unfair practice and a violation of licensing regulations, as are solicitations that invite or provoke discriminatory feelings or actions.

Case Example:

A real estate brokerage in Detroit advertised listed properties in two metropolitan area newspapers, a number of community newspapers, and in a weekly newspaper circulated primarily in African-American neighborhoods. However, the company had a policy of advertising listings in "changing areas" of the city only in the African-American newspaper. The listings in the "changing areas" were not generally advertised in the newspapers of wider distribution.

The court found the brokerage's advertising practice to have a steering effect, since only readers of the African-American newspaper (usually African-Americans) would know about the homes for sale in the "changing" neighborhoods. The end result of this practice would be to speed up the neighborhood's change from a mixed or diverse neighborhood to one that was all or mostly African-American. In other words, it would speed up the segregation of African-Americans into separate neighborhoods, in violation of the state's policy to encourage integration. *U.S. v. Real Estate One, Inc.* (E.D. Mich. 1977) 433 F. Supp. 1140.

The type of models used in advertising can also lead to charges of discrimination.

Example: A broker is the listing agent for a large, exclusive housing development. He advertises homes in the development by putting display ads in the local paper. (Display ads are larger than the average classified ad and typically include illustrations or photos.) In every ad placed by the broker, the buyers and sellers depicted are white, even though 30% of the city's population is non-white. The use of only white models could be the grounds for a discrimination suit.

Selling and Renting

Refusing to sell or rent after receiving a bona fide offer (that is, an offer that meets all of the seller's or landlord's terms, including the price) is prohibited if it can be shown that race (or some other characteristic such as religion, national origin, or disability) is a factor in the decision. Refusal to negotiate for a sale or rental may be a straightforward refusal to talk to or deal with a potential purchaser or renter. Or the lessor or seller simply may refuse to answer the door.

Example: An actual case in Washington involved an apartment building manager who could see the front steps of her building from the door of her own unit. When prospective tenants rang the buzzer, she was able to observe them without actually opening the building door. If they were African-American, she simply went back inside her unit and ignored the door buzzer.

Property managers may also discriminate against minorities by ignoring rental applications, or by failing to service the rental applications the same way for all classes.

> **Example:** The owner of an apartment building only processes rental applications that are accompanied by a deposit. White applicants are told of this procedure, ensuring compliance with the owner's rule. Latino applicants are not informed of the deposit requirement. As a result, they don't include deposits with their applications, and those applications are thrown away.

Lending

Although the most common type of discriminatory lending practice is redlining, discrimination in financing can take many other forms. A lender might use different foreclosure procedures for different parties, or use discriminatory criteria when determining application fees or other finance charges.

Zoning

Civil rights laws prohibit zoning practices that have the effect of denying housing to minorities. Zoning that prohibits or unreasonably restricts permits for multi-family or low-income housing may result in charges of discrimination based on **exclusionary zoning**, as such zoning may impact some classes more than others.

With so many antidiscrimination laws currently in place, it's unlikely that any state or municipality would enact an obviously racist zoning ordinance. So most charges of discrimination in zoning are based upon the concept of **disparate impact**. This means that even though the ordinance or regulation may appear to be neutral, its effect is nevertheless discriminatory, because the impact of the law falls more heavily on one particular class than it does on others.

Case Example:

A city approved low-income housing in only one (predominantly African-American) section of the city. The court held this zoning practice to be discriminatory. The court reasoned that the lack of low-income housing in other parts of the city prevented African-Americans from moving into predominantly white neighborhoods, since there was little or no housing available for low- or middle-income residents in these areas. *U.S. v. Yonkers Board of Education* (S.D.N.Y. 1985) 624 F. Supp. 1276.

Employment by Brokers

In California, a broker may not discriminate based on race or any other protected class when hiring sales associates, determining commission splits or other compensation, assigning work, or determining other terms and conditions of employment. Such discriminatory practices violate not only state and federal antidiscrimination laws, but also the state Real Estate Law.

MLS Practices

Charges of discrimination have also come up in connection with the denial of access to a multiple listing service.

Case Example:

In 1973, a multiple listing service operating in an Indiana city served the local Board of Realtors. The Board of Realtors consisted of 40 white brokers and four African-American brokers. The MLS itself had 26 broker members, all white. The four African-American members of the Board of Realtors repeatedly applied for membership in the MLS but were continually denied.

After a year, the original MLS went out of business and was replaced by a new MLS made up of 18 white brokers and three African-American brokers. At the same time, eight of the white brokers in the city MLS joined a suburban MLS and a local board in a neighboring area. Even though they continued doing most of their business in the city, the eight white brokers began directing all of their listings to the suburban MLS (whose members were all white). The African-American brokers were unable to access those listings, because they were not members of the suburban MLS. By 1977, all of the white brokers had withdrawn from the city MLS and were operating solely out of the all-white suburban MLS.

The drop in the city MLS's membership caused it to go out of business. Seven of the African-American brokers then tried to join the suburban MLS but were unable to do so, because membership in the suburban MLS required membership in the local board. To gain membership in the local board, brokers were required to have an office in the suburban area.

The African-American brokers tried to rent office space in the suburb, but they alleged that discriminatory practices and racial attitudes in the area prevented them from doing so. Consequently, they were refused access to the only operating MLS in the area; as a result, they were also denied access to a majority of the real estate listings.

The African-American brokers sued the MLS, the local board, and eight white brokers. Eventually they were able to get a consent order from a federal district court in which the local board waived the suburban office requirement. *U.S. v. South Suburban MLS, and Wilkes Realty, Inc. v. South Suburban MLS* (N.D. Ind. 1984) No. H77-417 and No. 80-307.

Damages awarded in fair housing lawsuits can run into hundreds of thousands of dollars, and licensees who violate these laws may be subject to license suspension or revocation. It is extremely important for all real estate licensees to understand the application, effect, and consequences of state and federal antidiscrimination laws, both for their own protection and to provide more professional service to their clients and customers.

Case Law in Depth

The following case involves some of the legal issues discussed in this chapter. Read through the facts and consider the questions in light of what you have learned. Then read what the court actually decided.

Harris v. Capital Growth Investors XIV (1991) 52 Cal.3d 1142

The plaintiffs were two females, each the head of her household. Each family was a low-income family whose income consisted solely of public assistance benefits. The defendants owned and operated apartment buildings, and had a written policy that required sufficient income in order to rent an apartment. "Sufficient income" was defined as income that was equal to or greater than three times the amount of rent charged. While the two women could afford the monthly rent, they did not have enough income to meet the defendant's minimum income policy.

The two plaintiffs filed a lawsuit, claiming that the landlord's minimum income policy was arbitrary economic discrimination in violation of the Unruh Act. The defendants claimed that the Unruh Act did not apply to economic criteria, and the plaintiffs claimed that it did, because economic criteria is an arbitrary and unreasonable distinction. While the trial court dismissed the plaintiffs' complaint, an appeals court reversed the decision, finding that the allegation that the defendant's practice was arbitrary raised factual issues. The apartment building owners appealed the reversal.

The question:

Does a landlord's minimum income policy violate California's Unruh Act based upon arbitrary economic discrimination?

The court's answer:

The court stated that the classes listed in the Unruh Act "...involve personal as opposed to economic characteristics...Conspicuously absent from the list is any reference to financial or economic status, although the Legislature could not have been unaware throughout the history of the Unruh Act that businesses make charges for goods and services and impose financial conditions on access to their establishments." The court decided that this omission strongly suggested a limitation on the scope of the Unruh Act.

Furthermore, "...the California appellate cases have also recognized that legitimate business interests may justify limitations on consumer access to public accommodations.

"The minimum income policy is no different in its purpose or effect from stated price or payment terms [in a store]. Like those terms, it seeks to obtain for a business establishment the benefit of its bargain with the consumer: full payment of the price.

"In summary, we hold that defendant's minimum income policy does not violate the Unruh Act. The policy does not make distinctions among persons based on the classifications listed in the Act (e.g., race, sex, religion, etc.) or similar personal traits, beliefs, or characteristics that bear no relationship to the responsibilities of consumers of public accommodations. It is a financial criterion of customer selection that applies uniformly and neutrally to all persons regardless of personal characteristics. Moreover, on its face, it makes permissible distinctions among persons that are justified by the landlord's legitimate business interest in assessing the capability of prospective tenants to pay rent on a continuing basis. As such, it does not offend the language, policy, or purpose of the Act."

The result:

The court found for the defendants. A minimum income policy does not violate the Unruh Act; those affected by economic discrimination are not a protected class, and an income policy serves a legitimate business interest.

Chapter Summary

- Federal laws prohibiting discrimination include the Civil Rights Act of 1866, Title VIII of the Civil Rights Act of 1968 (usually referred to as the federal Fair Housing Act), the Equal Credit Opportunity Act, and the Home Mortgage Disclosure Act.

- California laws prohibiting discrimination include the Unruh Civil Rights Act, the Fair Employment and Housing Act, the Housing Financial Discrimination Act, and the Real Estate Law.

- Three specifically prohibited acts under the federal Fair Housing Act are blockbusting, steering, and redlining. Blockbusting is attempting to obtain listings or to arrange sales by predicting the entry of minorities into the neighborhood and implying that this will cause a decline in property values. Steering is the channeling of buyers or renters to specific neighborhoods based on race or other protected characteristics. Redlining is the refusal to make loans on properties located in a particular area because of its racial or ethnic makeup.

- The Americans with Disabilities Act guarantees equal access to public accommodations regardless of physical or mental disability. Under the ADA, a property owner may be required to modify the property to make its facilities accessible to the disabled, provided such modifications are "readily achievable."

- The Unruh Civil Rights Act prohibits arbitrary discrimination against any class of people based on physical or inherent characteristics. However, the act does not preclude economic discrimination (such as a minimum income policy for renting).

Key Terms

- **Federal Fair Housing Act** – Title VIII of the Civil Rights Act of 1968; prohibits discrimination in the sale or lease of residential property or vacant land intended to be used for residential purposes.

- **Steering** – Channeling prospective buyers or renters into specific neighborhoods based on race or some other protected class; a form of discrimination.

- **Blockbusting** – An illegal practice in which someone (such as a real estate agent) predicts the entry of minorities into a neighborhood and forecasts lower property values, higher crime rates, a decline in schools, or some other undesirable consequence as a result.

- **Redlining** – The refusal by a lender to make a loan on property in a certain neighborhood for discriminatory reasons (as opposed to creditworthiness).

- **Equal Credit Opportunity Act (ECOA)** – A fair lending law that prohibits discrimination in credit transactions, including residential real estate loans.

- **Home Mortgage Disclosure Act** – Requires large institutional lenders in metropolitan areas to make annual reports on residential mortgage loans (both purchase and improvement loans) that were originated or purchased during the fiscal year so that investigators can look for possible redlining or patterns of discrimination.

- **Americans with Disabilities Act (ADA)** – A federal law that ensures disabled persons have equal access to public accommodations and commercial facilities.

- **Disability** – Any physical or mental impairment that substantially limits one or more of the individual's major life activities.

- **Public accommodation** – Any place owned, operated, or leased by a private entity that is open to the public, as long as the operation of the facility affects commerce.

- **Readily achievable** – Under the ADA, any action that can be easily accomplished without much difficulty or expense, such as adjusting shelving or counter heights to make them more accessible to a person in a wheelchair.

- **Unruh Civil Rights Act** – A California law that states that all persons are entitled to the full use of any services provided by a business establishment, regardless of sex, race, color, religion, ancestry, national origin, disability, medical condition, genetic information, marital status, sexual orientation, citizenship, primary language, or immigration status.

- **Fair Employment and Housing Act** – Also known as the Rumford Act; generally prohibits all housing discrimination in California based on race, color, religion, sex, gender, gender identity, gender expression, sexual orientation, marital status, national origin, ancestry, familial status, source of income, disability, or genetic information.

- **California Housing Financial Discrimination Act** – Also known as the Holden Act; states that it is against state public policy to deny mortgage loans or to impose stricter terms on loans because of neighborhood characteristics unrelated to the creditworthiness of the borrower or the value of the real property.

- **Disparate impact** – Occurs when a law or ordinance appears neutral on its face (seems to apply to everyone, equally), but actually affects some protected class of people more than other classes of people, thus having a discriminatory effect.

- **Exclusionary zoning** – Zoning practices that unreasonably restrict permits for multi-family or low-income housing in such a way as to have a discriminatory effect on minorities.

- **Sandwich test** – A test to determine discrimination; for example, a white tester asks to see available apartments and is shown available space, followed by a minority tester who is told that there are no vacancies. Finally, a second white tester appears. If he is shown space, the test can be used to prove that the property owner or agent is discriminating based on race or some other protected class.

Chapter Quiz

1. The Civil Rights Act of 1866 prohibits discrimination based on race or color and applies to all property and real estate transactions:
   a) with limited exemptions
   b) with no exemption
   c) owned by the state
   d) None of the above

2. A person unlawfully discriminated against under the Civil Rights Act of 1866 may be entitled to:
   a) injunctive relief
   b) actual damages
   c) punitive damages
   d) All of the above

3. An agent shows Hispanic buyers homes only in predominantly Hispanic neighborhoods. This is an example of:
   a) steering
   b) blockbusting
   c) redlining
   d) None of the above

4. Data shows that a major lender has made 95% of its loans in white neighborhoods. This may be an example of:
   a) steering
   b) blockbusting
   c) redlining
   d) None of the above

5. To comply with the Americans with Disabilities Act, a restaurant owner may be required to:
   a) allow service animals in the dining area
   b) move tables apart to provide access to wheelchairs
   c) install handrails and widen doors in restrooms
   d) All of the above

6. A landlord has several application policies in place to screen potential tenants. Which of the following is illegal under California's Unruh Act?
   a) Requiring a minimum income of three times the unit rental rate
   b) Requiring proof of citizenship from all applicants
   c) Performing a credit check on all applicants
   d) All of the above are legal under the Unruh Act

7. A city ordinance that requires all firefighters to be at least six feet tall is an example of:
   a) a legal public policy regulation
   b) a law that applies to everyone equally
   c) possible discrimination based upon disparate impact
   d) Both b) and c)

8. The Home Mortgage Disclosure Act helps to enforce the prohibition against:
   a) redlining
   b) steering
   c) blockbusting
   d) None of the above

9. Under the Americans with Disabilities Act:
   a) real estate firms are exempt
   b) real estate firms may discriminate against the disabled when taking listings, if applicable
   c) real estate firms must be accessible to the disabled
   d) only individual real estate agents are prohibited from discriminating against the disabled

10. Rental of a room in an owner-occupied dwelling is exempt from the federal Fair Housing Act if the dwelling contains:
    a) two or more units
    b) three units or less
    c) less than five units
    d) six units or more

Chapter Answer Key

Chapter Quiz Answers:

1. b) The Civil Rights Act of 1866 prohibits discrimination based on race or color and applies to all property and real estate transactions, with no exemption.

2. d) A person unlawfully discriminated against under the Civil Rights Act of 1866 may be entitled to injunctive relief, actual damages, and punitive damages.

3. a) Channeling prospective buyers or renters into specific neighborhoods, based on race or some other protected class, is known as steering.

4. c) A lender's refusal to make a loan on property in a certain neighborhood, when based on discriminatory reasons, is considered redlining. A pattern of loans made only to white neighborhoods may be proof of such practice.

5. d) Under the ADA, all persons must have equal access to public facilities. To meet this requirement, the restaurant owner is required to make all physical, architectural, or policy changes necessary, so long as they are readily achievable. Allowing service animals in the dining area, removing transportation barriers, and modifying restroom facilities so as to be accessible to disabled patrons are all examples of readily achievable modifications.

6. b) Income requirements and credit checks are both acceptable, so long as they aren't arbitrary. However, it is illegal under the Unruh Act for landlords to require proof of citizenship or immigration status.

7. d) An ordinance that requires all firefighters to be six feet tall may apply to everyone equally (be neutral on its face) but have a disparate impact on certain minorities and women and, therefore, be discriminatory.

8. a) The Home Mortgage Disclosure Act helps to enforce the prohibition against redlining by requiring large institutional lenders to file an annual report of all mortgage loans made during that year. Loans are categorized according to location, alerting investigators to areas of possible redlining.

9. c) Under the provisions of the ADA, real estate firms must take reasonable actions necessary to make their accommodations accessible to the disabled.

10. c) The Fair Housing Act exemption for rentals applies to owner-occupied dwellings with up to four units.

Cases to Consider... Answers:

Federal Fair Housing Act

Colony Cove Associates v. Brown (1990) 220 Cal.App.3d 195. The court found for Colony Cove. While it is true that the Fair Housing amendments prohibit discrimination based on familial status, the law also creates an exemption for "housing for older persons." The mobile home park met all the statutory requirements to create such an exemption; therefore, the park's policy wasn't discriminatory against the evicted families. The court noted that the need for adequate and affordable housing for families with children must be balanced against society's legitimate interest in providing adequate and affordable housing for seniors.

Fair Employment and Housing Act

Auburn Woods I Homeowners Assn. v. Fair Employment & Housing Com (Elebiari) (2004) 121 Cal.App.4th 1578. The court disagreed. The Elebiaris were disabled and had requested a reasonable accommodation. In addition, a companion animal need not be trained as a service animal in order to fulfill its role.

List of Cases

Auburn Woods I Homeowners Assn. v. Fair Employment & Housing Com. (Elebiari) (2004) 121 Cal.App.4th 1578
Colony Cove Associates v. Brown (1990) 220 Cal.App.3d 195
Jones v. Alfred H. Mayer Co. (1968) 392 U.S. 409
Harris v. Capital Growth Investors XIV (1991) 52 Cal.3d 1142
Havens Realty Corp. v. Coleman (1982) 455 U.S. 363
Marina Point, Ltd. v. Wolfson (1982) 30 Cal.3d. 721
Shelley v. Kraemer (1948) 334 U.S. 1
U.S. v. Real Estate One, Inc. (E.D. Mich. 1977) 433 F.Supp. 1140
U.S. v. South Suburban MLS (N.D. Ind. 1984) No. H77-417
U.S. v. Yonkers Board of Education (S.D.N.Y. 1985) 624 F.Supp. 1276
Wilkes Realty, Inc. v. South Suburban MLS (N.D. Ind. 1984) No. 80-307

Chapter 20

Landlord-Tenant Law

Outline

Introduction

In this chapter, we'll discuss the legal rules that govern the relationship between a landlord and a tenant. For the most part, landlord-tenant law is intended to protect tenants, who generally have less power in the relationship than landlords. To that end, the law imposes quite a few restrictions and duties on landlords; but it also gives them some protection against troublesome tenants.

Many of the rules that we'll cover apply only to residential tenancies. The law provides fewer protections for commercial tenants than for residential tenants, because commercial tenants are considered better prepared to protect their own interests. The rules for residential tenancies generally apply to the rental of any type of dwelling, whether it's a studio apartment, a penthouse, or a single-family home. (There are some special rules for mobile homes and houseboats that we won't cover here, but most of the general rules for residential tenancies apply to those, too.)

We'll begin with a quick review of the different types of leasehold interests. The rest of the chapter is structured around the various stages of a tenancy. First we'll review the requirements for creating a lease; then we'll look at issues surrounding rent, security deposits, and the condition of the premises. Finally, we'll examine how a tenancy can be transferred and how it may terminate.

Leasehold Interests

A lease is a type of contract; it's also a conveyance of a real property interest from the landlord to the tenant. This property interest is known as a **leasehold** or **leasehold estate**. (Note that the terms "leasehold estate," "leasehold," and "tenancy" tend to be used more or less interchangeably.) We discussed leaseholds in Chapter 4, but we'll review them here briefly.

A **term tenancy** has fixed beginning and ending dates. The landlord and tenant agree in advance on when the tenancy will end. Although this type of leasehold is sometimes called an **estate for years**, any period of time may serve as the term. In residential tenancies, three-month, six-month, and one-year terms are common.

Fig. 20.1 Types of leasehold estates

Term Tenancy	Fixed-length term, usually a certain number of months or years
Periodic Tenancy	No fixed term; tenancy continues week-to-week, month-to-month, or year-to-year
Tenancy at Will	Tenant is in possession with landlord's consent, but neither a term nor a periodic tenancy exists
Tenancy at Sufferance	Tenant is holding over without landlord's express or implied consent

In contrast, a **periodic tenancy** has no fixed ending date. It continues from week to week, month to month, or even year to year, until either the landlord or the tenant gives the other party proper notice of termination. (Notice of termination is discussed later in the chapter.)

A periodic tenancy may be arranged at the outset, before the tenant moves in, or it may arise after a term tenancy ends. When a term tenancy expires, if the tenant "holds over" (remains in possession of the property) and the landlord continues to accept rental payments, a periodic tenancy is established by implication. For example, acceptance of one month's rent creates a month-to-month tenancy. When this occurs, Civil Code § 1945 provides that the old lease provisions will remain in force during the periodic tenancy—except, of course, the provision regarding the length of the lease.

In a term tenancy, the parties can't change the provisions of the lease during the term, unless the lease agreement permits the change in question or both parties consent to it. In a periodic tenancy, on the other hand, the landlord is free to raise the rent or require an increased security deposit, as long as she gives the tenant the proper amount of notice. We will discuss notice periods shortly.

The third type of leasehold, the **tenancy at will**, refers to possession of property with the landlord's express or implied consent when neither a term tenancy nor a periodic tenancy has been established. This most commonly occurs when a tenant holds over after a term tenancy has ended and no new lease has been agreed upon. In that situation, a tenancy at will is usually brief; as we said, when the landlord accepts a rent payment from the tenant, that creates a periodic tenancy.

Finally, a **tenancy at sufferance** refers to possession by a tenant who holds over after the tenancy has ended without the landlord's express or implied consent. This isn't really a leasehold estate at all, since the tenant no longer has the right of possession. Not surprisingly, the law gives tenants at sufferance less protection than other types of tenants.

The Lease Agreement

A tenancy begins with a lease, also called a rental agreement. Since the lease is a contract, all of the usual contract requirements apply (see Chapter 9). For example, the landlord and tenant both must have the legal capacity to form a contract—that is, they must be at least 18 years old and of sound mind.

If a lease has a term longer than one year, the statute of frauds requires it to be in writing. A lease for a shorter term may be created by oral agreement. Most landlords rarely forego a written agreement, however. Putting the details of the lease agreement on paper lessens the chance of a dispute with the tenant.

If a written lease is used, it must contain an adequate description of the leased property and it must be signed by the landlord. The tenant usually signs the lease as well, but this isn't technically required. Once the tenant has moved into the unit and paid rent, she's considered to have accepted the lease terms. In a residential tenancy, the tenant must be given a copy of the lease within 15 days after the lease is executed.

Payment of Rent

The lease should state the rent amount, when it is due, and how and where it should be paid. If the lease doesn't specify a due date, Civil Code § 1947 provides that the rent is due at the end of each period. For example, the rent for a month-to-month tenancy will be due at the end of the month. Most leases require payment at or near the beginning of the period, however.

Under Civil Code § 1962, a residential lease must contain the name, address, and telephone number of the property owner or her representative, and also of the property manager, if there is one. If rent is to be paid to someone other than the manager or owner, that party's contact information must be provided as well. The lease must also state any restrictions on how and when the rent is to be paid.

In a residential tenancy, if the parties aren't using a written lease agreement, the landlord has 15 days to provide all of this information to the tenant in writing. Alternatively, the landlord may post this information in the building's elevators and in one other conspicuous place (or, in a building without elevators, in two conspicuous places).

If the tenant requests it, the landlord must give the tenant a written receipt each time rent is paid.

Cash Payments

Under Civil Code § 1947.3, a landlord can't require a tenant to pay rent in cash or electronic funds transfer unless the tenant's rent check has been returned either: 1) for insufficient funds, or 2) because the tenant stopped payment on it. In this situation, if the landlord wants to require cash payments, she must give the tenant written notice of this requirement and attach a copy of the dishonored check to the notice. The landlord can require cash payments only for a period of three months following the date the check was returned.

Late Fees

A landlord may charge fees for late rent payments or dishonored checks, provided the lease agreement authorizes the fees. State law doesn't set fee limits (although local rent control ordinances may contain restrictions), but the fees must be reasonable (that is, they must reflect actual costs).

Rent Increases

With a term tenancy, the landlord can't increase the rent during the term unless the lease agreement specifically permits it. Residential fixed-term leases rarely allow rent increases; commercial leases sometimes do.

For a periodic tenancy, state law places no limit on the amount or frequency of rent increases (although a local rent control law may apply—see below). But a rent increase is a modification of the parties' agreement and therefore requires advance written notice. As a general rule, a landlord must give a month-to-month tenant 30 days' notice of the increase. For a residential month-to-month tenancy, if the rent increase will mean that the rent has risen more than ten percent in the last 12 months, the landlord must give the tenant 60 days' notice of the increase. (Civil Code § 827(b).)

Rent Control Laws. While there are no state restrictions on rent increases, some cities limit a residential landlord's ability to raise rents. During the 1970s, a number of California cities enacted rent control ordinances that strictly limit the size of rent increases (although, under constitutional principles, they must allow a "reasonable return" on the landlord's investment). Currently, 15 California cities have rent control laws; in addition, more than one hundred cities provide rent control for mobile home park residents.

In the 1990s, the state legislature placed significant restrictions on rent control laws with the **Costa-Hawkins Rental Housing Act** (Civil Code §§ 1954.50 – 1954.535), which prohibits any locality from enacting new rent control ordinances. The act also excludes from rent control any building completed after early 1995. With single-family home or condo rentals, rent control doesn't apply to any tenancy that began after 1995 (regardless of when the building was built). And in buildings that are still rent-controlled, if a tenant moves out through no fault of the landlord, rent control no longer applies to that unit.

Many rental property owners in rent-controlled areas are understandably impatient for their units to escape rent control restrictions. A landlord might even be tempted to demolish the structure and put up a new building free from rent control. However, provisions in the **Ellis Act** (Government Code §§ 7060 – 7060.7) limit this strategy. If an owner demolishes a rent-controlled building and then replaces it within five years with a new rental building, the new building simply continues with the old building's rent control restrictions. Converting the rental property to a condominium can be another way to escape rent control laws. However, many rent control communities limit the number of apartments that may be converted to condominiums in any given year. If conversion from rent control is allowed, the landlord must usually pay the tenants some relocation assistance money. Payment amounts and eligibility requirements are left up to local governments and vary by jurisdiction.

Security Deposits

Most residential lease agreements require the tenant to pay a **security deposit** before moving in. This gives the landlord some protection against the risk that the tenant will damage the property or default on the rent. California law limits the size of residential security deposits, and also regulates the circumstances in which the landlord can withhold money from the deposit when the tenant moves out.

Size of Deposit

For a residential tenancy, the total amount of the security deposit can't exceed two months' rent for an unfurnished unit, or three months' rent for a furnished unit. However, there's a special rule for a deposit that's designated as an advance payment of rent: if the lease term is six months or longer, the landlord can require a deposit of six times the monthly payment (or more) as an advance payment of rent. (Civil Code § 1950.5.)

A tenant might wonder whether she's entitled to the interest that accrues on her security deposit; after all, the landlord may hold thousands of dollars of the tenant's money for years. Generally, the answer is no: state law doesn't require a landlord to pay interest on security deposits. However, tenants in rent-controlled cities are more fortunate than tenants elsewhere in the state; these cities have ordinances requiring the payment of interest.

Increasing Deposit During Tenancy. At some point during a tenancy, a landlord may decide that a tenant's security deposit is too small to cover the expense of a possible default. Regardless, a tenant with a fixed-term lease can't be forced to add money to the deposit unless the lease agreement provides for increases.

During a periodic tenancy, in contrast, the landlord can require an additional deposit. The landlord must give the tenant the same amount of notice that's required for any other change to the lease agreement. Note that the two- or three-month limit on the size of the deposit may preclude a residential landlord from increasing the deposit amount, if the original deposit was already the maximum allowed.

Refunds and Deductions

Unless the tenant breaches the lease agreement, the landlord must fully refund the security deposit. Landlords can't get around this requirement by labeling the deposit a nonrefundable "cleaning fee" or "key fee."

However, the landlord is permitted to deduct from the security deposit an amount equal to losses caused by a tenant's breach. For example, if a tenant owes the landlord $1,340

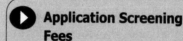

Application Screening Fees

Some landlords charge a non-refundable fee for screening rental applicants. This fee isn't considered part of the security deposit.

California law limits the size of screening fees. They can't exceed the landlord's actual expenses (the cost of checking the applicant's credit and completing any other screening tasks), and they also can't exceed a certain maximum set by law. The maximum was originally $30, but since 1998 the amount has been increased annually to reflect inflation as measured by the Consumer Price Index. Currently, the limit works out to be about $49.50.

in back rent and fees when the tenancy is terminated, the landlord can keep $1,340 out of the deposit. In addition, the landlord may deduct the cost of:

- cleaning the unit (to the state of cleanliness it was in when the tenancy began),
- repairing damage to the unit (not counting normal wear and tear), and
- repairing items in a furnished unit (if the lease allows this deduction).

After a tenant vacates the premises, the landlord has 21 calendar days to return the security deposit to the tenant, less any lawful deductions. The landlord must itemize the deductions in writing. If deductions for repairs and cleaning total more than $125, the landlord must also provide copies of invoices or receipts (or at least good faith estimates) for all expenditures.

Civil Code § 1950.5(l) provides that if a residential landlord withholds security deposit funds in bad faith, the tenant is entitled to actual damages plus a penalty of up to double the amount of the security deposit.

Note that if a landlord is selling or transferring the leased premises to another party, the landlord has two choices: he can return the security deposits to the tenants, or he may give them to the new owner, who will then keep them under the same rules that applied to the original landlord. Either way, the original landlord is allowed to make appropriate deductions from the deposits before parting with them.

Inspection of the Premises

In some states, the landlord and tenant are required to go over the premises together at the start of the tenancy and fill out an inventory describing the condition of the property. Although California law doesn't require this type of inspection, it's an excellent practice. An initial inventory can prevent both parties from making unfair claims at the end of the tenancy.

California law does provide that, at the tenant's request, the landlord must inspect the premises shortly before the end of the tenancy, to identify cleaning or repairs that the landlord considers the tenant's responsibility. This gives the tenant time to correct any problems the landlord identifies. By law, the landlord must notify the tenant in writing of the right to this inspection within a reasonable time either: 1) before the lease term expires, or 2) after either party has given a notice terminating the tenancy. The landlord's inspection must occur no longer than two weeks before the end of the tenancy. (Civil Code § 1950.5(f).)

After the inspection, the landlord must give the tenant a written list of the charges that will be deducted if damaged items remain unfixed or soiled items remain uncleaned. This may work to the tenant's advantage, since the landlord can't deduct for items omitted from the list. However, this rule doesn't apply if the tenant's possessions hid the soiled or damaged item, or the tenant caused the problem after the inspection.

Use and Condition of the Premises

The law imposes duties on both the landlord and the tenant as to the use and condition of the leased premises. The tenant is prohibited from damaging or misusing the premises; the landlord cannot unreasonably disturb the tenant's use of the property and must keep the premises in good repair. Both parties have financial and judicial tools for enforcing the other party's obligations.

We'll begin our discussion with a duty that arises before the tenancy even begins: the landlord's obligation to disclose certain negative facts about the premises to potential tenants.

Landlord's Disclosures

Since California law requires the landlord and tenant to act in good faith, a landlord can't hide material facts about the premises from a potential tenant. In addition, under federal and state law, the landlord is required to make some specific disclosures.

The most elaborate of these disclosure requirements concerns lead-based paint. Before a tenant signs a lease for a dwelling built before 1978, the landlord must disclose the presence of any lead-based paint hazards by:

- including a "Lead Warning Statement" in the lease,
- giving the tenant a pamphlet on lead hazards, and
- giving the tenant a completed lead hazard disclosure form.

The contents of the warning statement, pamphlet, and disclosure form are mandated by federal law.

Another disclosure specifically required by law is information concerning the manufacture of drugs on the property. If the premises have been contaminated by methamphetamine or other illegal drug manufacturing, the landlord must inform prospective tenants.

A landlord of a one- to four-unit residential rental property who has received a notice of default regarding an underlying mortgage or deed of trust must disclose the default notice to any prospective tenants before they sign a lease. This is to protect tenants from renting a property that the landlord knows is in danger of foreclosure.

Also, if an occupant died on the premises in the preceding three years, the landlord must disclose this fact to any tenant who offers to rent the property. The manner of death must also be disclosed, unless the occupant died of, or was ill with, AIDS or HIV. (Civil Code § 1710.2.)

Tenant's Responsibility for the Premises

Statutory and common law, as well as provisions in most leases, require tenants to take reasonable care of the premises. Civil Code § 1941.2 spells out this responsibility in some detail, stating that tenants must:

- refrain from damaging the premises or allowing guests to do so (except for reasonable wear and tear);
- keep the dwelling unit clean and sanitary and free of rubbish and garbage;
- use all gas, electrical, and plumbing fixtures properly; and
- use the various parts of the premises as intended (for example, cooking only in the kitchen and not in the bedrooms).

If a tenant's violation of any of the duties listed above causes significant damage, the landlord has no duty to repair the damage (we'll discuss the landlord's general duty to repair shortly).

Alterations. Most residential leases prohibit a tenant from remodeling or otherwise altering the premises without the landlord's consent. However, Civil Code §§ 54.1 – 54.3 protects the right of a disabled tenant to make any alterations that are needed to accommodate her disability. (This statute is part of the Unruh Civil Rights Act, discussed in greater detail in Chapter 19.) The tenant must pay for these alterations, and the landlord can require her to restore the premises to their original condition at the end of the tenancy. The landlord can also require her to deposit a reasonable estimate of restoration costs into an escrow account. This deposit is separate from the security deposit.

Landlord's Responsibility for the Premises

Every lease includes an implied promise by the landlord called the covenant of quiet enjoyment. Residential leases also carry a second implied promise, the warranty of habitability. These obligations originated in the common law and have since been codified in the Civil Code. They apply even though they aren't actually stated in the lease, and they can't be waived. Any provision in a lease stating that the tenant waives these implied promises will have no legal effect.

Covenant of Quiet Enjoyment. With the **covenant of quiet enjoyment**, the landlord guarantees that she has title to the property and that the tenant's use and enjoyment of the property won't be interfered with, either by the landlord herself or by others making claims against the landlord's title.

Entry by landlord. Among other things, the covenant of quiet enjoyment means that the landlord can't enter the leased premises except with good reason. Civil Code § 1954 allows a residential landlord to enter the premises only in order to:

- investigate or remedy an emergency;
- make repairs or agreed upon alterations;
- show the apartment to prospective tenants, purchasers, or lenders;
- investigate the tenant's abandonment of the premises; or
- comply with a court order.

Entry should take place only between 8:00 A.M. and 5:00 P.M. on weekdays, unless there is an emergency, the tenant has abandoned the premises, or the parties have agreed otherwise.

The landlord has to give the tenant advance written notice of the intended entry. The amount of advance warning isn't much: generally, 24 hours is sufficient. The notice must provide the following details: date of entry, approximate time, and reason for entry. The landlord may deliver the notice: 1) to the tenant, 2) to someone at the unit who is of reasonable age (a teenager, for example), 3) by posting it at the entry to the unit, or 4) by mailing it to the tenant at least six days before the scheduled entry.

The statute carves out a couple of exceptions to the written notice requirement. A landlord may give the tenant oral notice that he plans to show the unit to a potential purchaser. Also, the landlord can obtain oral permission for entry to make repairs or to provide services. This can't serve as a blanket permission for entry, however; the entry must take place within a week of the conversation.

In some cases, neither oral nor written notice is necessary. The landlord is excused from providing notice when responding to an emergency (for example, a broken water pipe). The same is true when a tenant abandons the premises, since requiring notice of entry to a tenant who's no longer in residence wouldn't make much sense.

Of course, a tenant can waive the notice requirement at any time, simply by opening the door and letting the landlord in.

Warranty of Habitability. With the **warranty of habitability**, a residential landlord gives an implied promise to provide a dwelling that is weatherproof, pest-free, reasonably safe, and served by the standard utilities. Although the implied warranty of habitability is now statutory in California, it was originally established in the following case.

Case Example:

A landlord started eviction proceedings against a tenant for failure to pay rent. In his defense, the tenant argued that the landlord had failed to maintain the premises in habitable condition. At trial, the tenant described a number of serious defects in the premises, including a collapsed bathroom ceiling, vermin, lack of heat, plumbing blockages, faulty wiring, and a dangerous stove. Setting aside prior California case law, the state supreme court held that the common law implied a warranty of habitability in residential leases. Although leased premises need not be in perfect condition, "bare living requirements" must be maintained. Here, the landlord clearly had breached the implied warranty of habitability. *Green v. Superior Court* (1974) 10 Cal.3d 616.

The statutory provisions concerning habitability are quite detailed. Civil Code § 1941.1 begins, "A dwelling shall be deemed untenantable...if it substantially lacks any of the following..." The list includes:

- effective waterproofing and weather protection of roof and exterior walls, including unbroken windows and doors;
- plumbing in good working order producing hot and cold running water;
- heating facilities;
- electric lighting, with wiring and electrical equipment;
- building and grounds kept clean and free of debris, filth, rubbish, garbage, rodents, and vermin, with adequate garbage receptacles provided; and
- floors, stairways, and railings maintained in good repair.

Other sections of the Civil Code require deadbolts, smoke detectors, window locks, and bathroom ventilation. In addition, the Health and Safety Code imposes some basic requirements, such as carbon monoxide detectors.

Constructive Eviction. Sometimes a landlord interferes so thoroughly with the tenant's quiet enjoyment of the premises or allows them to become so uninhabitable that a tenant is effectively forced to move out. This is called **constructive eviction**. Constructive eviction could result from any number of things: for example, negligently failing to repair a roof leak or shutting off the utilities. A tenant's rent obligation ceases at the point when the landlord makes or allows the premises to become unusable.

Commercial tenants must physically abandon the premises in order to claim constructive eviction. The law has loosened this requirement for residential tenants. A residential tenant may remain on the premises and still bring a claim for constructive eviction against the landlord. Finding an affordable rental unit can be difficult, and forcing a tenant to move before she can sue a landlord tends to punish the victim.

Injuries to Tenants and Guests. Generally, owners of any type of property—including rental property—are liable for personal injuries that are caused by unsafe property conditions that result from their negligence. (See the discussion of premises liability in Chapter 15.) Thus, a landlord is potentially liable for injuries suffered by tenants and tenants' guests. If anything, the law tends to impose a slightly higher standard of care on landlords than on property owners who aren't renting their property to others.

The responsibility to maintain safe premises for the tenant isn't limited to the property's physical condition. It can also include liability for assaults or other wrongful acts committed by neighboring tenants or even outside parties.

Case Example:

When Mr. and Mrs. Andrews leased a spot in a Covina mobile home park, the rental agreement stated, "The park is an average residential neighborhood, it is not perfect. We will try to maintain the peace and quiet, but there may be times when whatever we do won't work." Mr. and Mrs. Andrews developed a contentious relationship with Mr. Molyneux, another park resident. They claimed that Molyneux had deliberately splashed mud on their freshly washed cars, aimed a video camera into their living room, subjected them to verbal abuse, and tried to run Mr. Andrews off the road.

Mr. and Mrs. Andrews complained to the park manager, who suggested they call the police. The Covina police department received about 50 calls over the course of seven months, some from Mr. and Mrs. Andrews, some from Molyneux. Eventually, a dispute over fencing erupted into physical violence between Molyneux and Mr. Andrews, and Andrews accused Molyneux of battery.

In addition to suing Molyneux, Mr. and Mrs. Andrews sued the mobile home park for failing to evict Molyneux. The trial court granted summary judgment for the mobile home park, finding the contractual language in the lease didn't constitute a promise to handle dangerous tenants. Mr. and Mrs. Andrews appealed.

The appellate court ruled that even if the express contract provisions didn't require the park to deal with troublemakers, the implied covenant of quiet enjoyment did. The court overturned the summary judgment in favor of the mobile home park. *Andrews v. Mobile Aire Estates* (2005) 125 Cal.App.4th 578.

There are limits to a landlord's liability for tenants' injuries, however. In the following case, the court was asked to decide whether the landlord was liable for injuries to a tenant that took place off the leased premises.

Case Example:

A gang known as the Westsiders made a particular apartment complex its base for criminal activity, gathering in and around the grounds. Both the police and tenants had complained, so the property owner was aware of the problem.

Several gang members noticed the son of a tenant walking by the apartments. Mistaking this person for a rival gang member, they chased him down a nearby street and shot and killed him. While the court termed this death "tragic," it found in favor of the property owner. The court refused to expand premises liability to areas outside of a landlord's immediate control, such as neighboring streets. *Medina v. Hillshore Partners* (1995) 40 Cal. App.4th 477.

Remedies for Landlord's Violations. If a landlord fails to provide habitable premises or unreasonably interferes with a tenant's quiet enjoyment, the tenant must give the landlord notice of the problem and an opportunity to correct it. Although the notice need not be in writing, using a written document is recommended; it provides tangible evidence that the landlord knew about the problem and had a chance to fix it. Ideally, the tenant should describe the problem in a letter, send it to the landlord by certified mail, and keep a photocopy. However, sending a notice by fax or email also provides some record.

After receiving this notice, the landlord is permitted a reasonable amount of time (in most cases, 30 days) to remedy the problem. However, for genuine emergencies, such as lack of heat in the winter, the landlord will have to act more quickly. If the landlord fails to remedy the situation after being given notice and time to repair, state law offers the tenant three basic remedies. These are:

- repair and deduct,
- rent withholding, and
- a lawsuit for damages.

In some situations, these remedies can be combined. We'll look at the advantages and disadvantages of each remedy.

Repair and deduct. If a landlord fails to repair a defect that violates the implied warranty of habitability, the tenant may perform the repair herself and deduct the expense from the rent. (Civil Code § 1942.) This remedy, known as **repair and deduct**, is subject to several restrictions. First, tenants can't repair and deduct if they themselves (or their guests) caused the damage. Second, the tenant can't undertake a repair that costs more than one month's rent. Finally, a tenant can only use the repair and deduct remedy twice in any 12-month period.

Rent withholding. If the tenant doesn't want to arrange for repair work, or can't use the repair and deduct remedy because of the scope or cost of the repairs, she can consider withholding rent until the landlord fixes the problem. The tenant can choose to withhold only a portion of the rent; the amount withheld should reflect the degree to which the premises are unusable.

Tenants should approach this remedy cautiously. In contrast to the repair and deduct remedy, withholding rent requires the habitability defect to be fairly serious. The tenant must show that the problem directly affects her health and safety.

A tenant who opts to withhold rent should consider depositing the unpaid rent into an escrow bank account that has been opened for this purpose. Although the law doesn't require withheld rent payments to be placed in escrow, it helps demonstrate to the court that the tenant was acting in good faith, not merely trying to get out of paying the rent.

Lawsuit for damages. The tenant's last resort against a landlord is usually a lawsuit. A tenant with premises that are uninhabitable may sue in small claims court or superior court to force a repair and/or seek damages. Civil Code § 1942.4 requires the tenant to prove several elements:

- the defect is substantial (for example, a roof leak);
- the problem wasn't caused by the tenant or the tenant's guest;
- a housing inspector gave the landlord written notice to repair the problem;
- at least 35 days have passed since the housing inspector mailed the notice; and
- the landlord continues to collect or demand rent.

If the tenant wins her case, she is entitled to actual damages, plus up to $5,000 in special damages for costs incurred while the premises were uninhabitable (for example, the cost of staying in a motel). The prevailing party is awarded reasonable attorneys' fees.

If the landlord has acted willfully or maliciously to force a tenant out, he may be subject to civil penalties. For example, if a landlord tries to make a tenant leave by threats or harassment (as has been known to happen in some rent-controlled buildings), the law provides for a statutory penalty of up to $2,000 per act, in addition to actual damages (Civil Code § 1940.2).

Retaliatory Acts. Civil Code § 1942.5 prohibits a landlord from raising the rent or starting an eviction action to retaliate against a tenant for making a habitability complaint or asserting certain other lawful rights. A court will presume that a rent raise or eviction was **retaliatory** if it occurred within 180 days after a tenant:

- complains about the condition of the premises, either to the landlord or a public agency;
- causes a public agency to inspect the property or issue a citation against the landlord;
- starts a lawsuit or arbitration based on the condition of the premises;
- claims a civil rights violation by the landlord; or
- participates in forming a tenant's union.

The tenant's action must have been taken in good faith, not merely to stall rent increases or eviction. And the landlord can rebut the court's presumption of retaliation. For example, the landlord could show that the rent raise was building-wide and didn't single out the complaining tenant for punishment.

A tenant who proves that a retaliatory act occurred may collect actual damages and up to $2,000 in punitive damages.

Transferring a Tenancy

We've surveyed many of the legal rules that govern an ongoing tenancy. In this section, we'll look at a tenant's ability to transfer a leasehold interest: to grant another person all or part of the leasehold for all or part of the remaining term. Depending on the extent of the interest transferred, such a transfer is either an assignment or a sublease.

Assignment and Subleasing Distinguished

In an **assignment**, the original tenant (the assignor) transfers the entire leasehold to a new tenant (the assignee). The assignee takes over the lease and is responsible for paying rent directly to the landlord.

> **Example:** Nancy, an accounting student at Pepperdine University, signs a one-year lease that begins on January 1. Midway through the spring semester, she drops out of school and moves home. She assigns the lease for her apartment to Alison, who moves in and begins making the rent payments to the landlord. Alison occupies the apartment and pays the rent for the rest of the term, through the end of the year.

By contrast, transferring an interest that is less than the entire leasehold—only a portion of the remaining lease term, or only a portion of the leased premises—is **subleasing**. The new tenant (the sublessee or subtenant) almost always pays rent to the original tenant (the sublessor), who then in turn pays rent to the landlord.

> **Example:** Returning to our previous example, let's say Nancy isn't dropping out of school; instead, she's simply returning home for the summer to work on the family farm. Before she leaves, she arranges for Karl to sublease her apartment from June through September. During those months, Karl pays rent to Nancy; in turn, Nancy makes her usual rent payments to her landlord. At the end of September, Karl moves out and Nancy moves back in. She occupies the apartment for the rest of the year, through the end of the lease term.

Assignor and Sublessor Liability

It's important to realize that despite the transfer, an assignor or sublessor still remains liable to the landlord. So, for example, if an assignee or sublessee damages the leased premises or fails to pay rent, the landlord can and often does sue the original tenant for compensation.

The only way for the original tenant to completely avoid liability for a lease is through **novation**. In the novation of a contract, a new party steps into the shoes of one of the original parties, and the other original party releases the withdrawing party from the obligation. Typically, a landlord won't agree to the novation of a lease unless the original tenant pays the landlord some consideration for releasing her from liability.

Landlord's Consent

If a lease says nothing about the tenant's transfer rights, the tenant can freely sublet or assign the leasehold. However, most leases limit or prohibit transfer, using a provision similar to the following example.

SUBLEASING AND ASSIGNMENT. Tenant cannot assign this agreement, or sublet all or part of the premises, without the landlord's prior written consent.

Some leases provide that the landlord can't unreasonably withhold consent to a sublease or assignment. In other words, if a tenant finds a comparably responsible and fiscally sound replacement tenant, then the landlord must consent to the transfer. And even if the lease doesn't address the issue, the common law nevertheless may require the landlord to consent to a reasonable transfer.

Case to Consider...

A commercial lease prohibited the tenant from assigning or subletting without the landlord's prior written consent. The tenant sought consent to a reasonable assignment, but the landlord "demanded increased rent and other more onerous terms" in exchange. The landlord claimed that the right to withhold consent was absolute. The case reached the California supreme court, which had never decided this issue before. Courts in most other jurisdictions had ruled in favor of the landlord, finding that refusal to consent to a transfer required no justification. However, courts in a few other jurisdictions had held that a leasehold transfer was a type of property sale, and that since the common law frowns on restraints on alienation, landlords could object only to unreasonable transfers. The California supreme court noted this reasoning, and also questioned whether withholding consent to a reasonable transfer served any useful commercial purpose. Which way did the California court go? *Kendall v. Ernest Pestana, Inc.* (1985) 40 Cal.3d 488.

 Danger Ahead

Transferring a tenancy can pose certain risks. For example, many college students sublease their campus-area apartments when they return to their hometowns for the summer. However, their subtenants (also college students) often view the summer rentals as party pads—leaving behind cigarette burns on counter tops, filthy appliances, and beer-soaked carpets. The original tenants return to their fall classes to find themselves facing damage claims or even eviction actions.

Some authorities recommend that anyone subleasing or assigning a unit take "before" pictures of the premises, perhaps even shooting a walk-around video with the new tenant. This provides evidence of the current condition and helps remind the new tenant that reasonable care is expected.

The original tenant should be sure to transfer the utilities to the new tenant's name. Assignors or sublessors, like any other landlords, should also require a security deposit. Of course, like other landlords, they will have to justify in writing any funds withheld from this deposit.

Termination of a Tenancy

To end the chapter, we'll look at four ways in which a tenancy can terminate: expiration, notice of termination, abandonment, or eviction.

Expiration of Lease

With a lease for a fixed term, it isn't necessary for either party to give notice of termination. The leasehold simply ends when the term expires, on the date originally agreed to. After expiration, if the tenant remains in possession of the property without the landlord's consent, the landlord can begin eviction proceedings (see below).

Notice of Termination

With a periodic tenancy, either the landlord or the tenant can terminate the tenancy by giving the other party advance notice in writing. The required notice period is usually the same as the lease period. So seven days' notice is required to end a week-to-week tenancy, and 30 days' notice is required to end a month-to-month tenancy. There's one exception to this rule: residential landlords must give a more generous 60 days' notice of termination to tenants who have lived on the property for a year or more. (Civil Code § 1946.1.)

Just Cause Exception. As a general rule, either party can terminate a periodic tenancy for any reason. But in some cases, the landlord's power to terminate the tenancy is limited. This is true for tenancies in government-assisted housing (such as Section 8 housing), and also in some cities that have "just cause" eviction ordinances. In these situations, a landlord generally can't terminate a periodic tenancy unless the tenant has committed a material breach of the leasehold agreement. A material breach (the just cause for termination) exists if the tenant does any of the following:

- fails to pay rent,
- materially damages the rented property,
- substantially interferes with another tenant's quiet enjoyment,
- uses the premises illegally, or
- otherwise materially breaches the lease agreement.

Even in a community with a just cause eviction ordinance, exemptions apply to certain types of property and in certain situations. Anyone who may be affected by this type of ordinance should obtain more detailed information from local sources.

Abandonment

Abandonment occurs when a tenant leaves the premises before a fixed lease term expires, or departs without giving the 30-day notice required to properly end a month-to-month tenancy. Common reasons for tenant abandonment include financial problems, job relocation, and constructive eviction by the landlord.

A tenant who abandons without good cause (such as constructive eviction) has breached the lease agreement and is liable for the remaining rent payments as they come due under the terms of the lease. However, contract law gives the landlord a duty to **mitigate** (lessen) the damages by re-renting the property as soon as possible. In a reasonably active rental market, re-renting may be easy; in that case, the landlord may not even bother to pursue the abandoning tenant for damages.

The landlord must start trying to re-rent the property as soon as it's clear the tenant has abandoned it. Although a tenant often leaves without any warning, it's better to give the landlord notice of abandonment. The tenant will have to pay less in damages if the landlord was able to re-rent promptly.

Without a notice of abandonment from the tenant, the landlord can presume abandonment if: 1) rent becomes overdue by 14 days, and 2) the landlord reasonably suspects the tenant has abandoned. Civil Code § 1951.3 provides an abandonment confirmation procedure for the landlord to follow. The statute includes a notice form the landlord must mail to the tenant at the leased premises, as well as to any other address where the landlord has reason to believe the tenant will receive the notice.

A landlord can enter the abandoned premises without notifying the tenant. If the landlord finds personal property left behind by the tenant, he must store it safely. If the tenant fails to reclaim this property within 15 days after a notice from the landlord was personally delivered to the tenant (or within 18 days after the notice was mailed), the landlord can freely dispose of the property, provided it appears to be worth less than $700. If the property is worth $700 or more, the landlord must sell the belongings in a public auction. (Civil Code § 1983 and following sections.) The landlord can use the sale proceeds to reimburse himself for storage costs, but must forward any remaining amount to the tenant or to the county.

Eviction

If a tenant's act or omission provides just cause for termination—or the tenant stays on without consent after the leasehold has terminated—the landlord can legally force the tenant out through a process called **eviction**.

Notice to Quit. The landlord begins an eviction by serving the tenant with a three-day notice to quit the premises. The landlord must attempt to serve the notice on the tenant personally. If the tenant evades service or the process otherwise proves unreasonably difficult, the notice may be mailed. When using mail service, however, the landlord must also post the notice on the tenant's door or in a similarly conspicuous place. This secondary form of service is sometimes referred to as "nailing and mailing."

If the landlord is serving this notice because of a breach of the lease terms (and not for holding over without consent), the tenant has the right to cure certain types of defaults. For example, the tenant could pay any overdue rent; or, if the lease prohibited pet ownership, find a new home for the cat. Curing the default ends the eviction process and allows the tenant to remain in possession and continue the tenancy. However, there are three types of default that the landlord doesn't have to allow the tenant to cure:

- damage to the premises (waste);
- substantial interference with other tenants' enjoyment of the premises; and
- illegal use of the premises (for example, for drug sales or manufacturing).

Eviction Options

It is said that as a lawyer, Abraham Lincoln occasionally advised landlord clients to change the locks on the doors of non-paying tenants. This advice was legal in Lincoln's day, but virtually every state has long since made lockouts and all other forms of self-help eviction illegal.

Over half a century ago, in *Sanders v. Allen* (1948) 83 Cal.App.2d 362, a California court called it "well-established law" that acts designed to make a tenant's life unbearable were wrongful and illegal. The landlord in the *Sanders* case engaged in a campaign of window-breaking, "door rapping," hourly phone calls, sugaring the tenant's gas tank, soaking him with a garden hose, and finally, when all else had failed to dislodge him, beating him up.

Landlords who want a tenant evicted, but prefer not to tackle the task personally, can hire a company to handle the process. A typical eviction service in California charges anywhere from $700 to $1,000 for an uncontested eviction. However, if the tenant appears in court to argue that the eviction is retaliatory or otherwise improper, the additional attorney time will add several hundred dollars to the base fee.

Tenants have been known to damage a unit after being named in an unlawful detainer action. Landlords who are afraid of such unpleasantness, or simply want the speediest resolution possible, sometimes negotiate a so-called "cash for keys" deal. Paying a tenant several hundred dollars to move on can avoid a stressful, drawn-out eviction process.

If the tenant fails to cure, or has no right to cure, he must leave the premises by the end of the third day. The three-day clock begins running the day after the tenant receives the notice to quit. If the third day falls on a weekend or holiday, the next regular business day is treated as the third day.

Note that the three-day notice to quit requirement doesn't apply to tenants at sufferance. Landlords must still follow other eviction procedures (discussed below), but notice to quit is not required.

Unlawful Detainer Action. If the tenant ignores the three-day notice to quit, the landlord's next step is to file a lawsuit called an unlawful detainer action. (Some leases or some local ordinances may require arbitration instead.) In an **unlawful detainer** action, the plaintiff (the landlord) alleges that the defendant (the tenant) has illegally "detained" the premises—in other words, has remained on the property without the right to be there. Unlawful detainer cases proceed relatively quickly: tenants have only five days to respond to the complaint, and a court usually renders judgment on the matter within a month.

Tenants may raise various defenses in an unlawful detainer action. For example, a tenant might claim that the landlord's eviction action was illegal retaliation for a habitability complaint, or that the eviction violates the tenant's civil rights (see Chapter 19). A tenant who remains on the premises despite an eviction proceeding and without a good faith defense may be penalized up to $600, in addition to being required to pay the landlord's actual damages. (Code of Civil Procedure § 1174(b).)

Writ of Possession. If a tenant refuses to move after losing an unlawful detainer action, the landlord must again seek help from the court, this time requesting a **writ of possession**. The writ is a pre-printed form stating that the tenant has five days to leave the premises. Once the landlord obtains a judge's signature on the writ, a sheriff must serve the document on the tenant. Then, after five days, the sheriff can physically remove the tenant and his possessions from the premises.

Of course, writs of possession, unlawful detainer actions, and other aspects of the eviction process are usually handled by lawyers. But leases are very common real estate contracts, and you're likely to encounter them frequently. State and local laws carefully regulate the residential landlord-tenant relationship, seeking to respect the landlord's property rights while protecting the tenant from unsafe living conditions and unreasonable eviction practices. Understanding the issues that may arise regarding security deposits, landlord responsibilities, assignment and subleasing, and termination of tenancies can be helpful not only when your client is a landlord or a tenant, but also when you're working with buyers or sellers.

Case Law in Depth

The following case involves some of the legal issues discussed in this chapter. Read through the facts and consider the questions in light of what you have learned. Then read what the court actually decided.

Hyatt v. Tedesco (2002) 96 Cal.App.4th Supp. 62

The owner of a rental property filed an unlawful detainer action against a tenant for nonpayment of rent. The tenant, Nora Tedesco, properly answered the complaint within five days. She raised breach of the warranty of habitability as a defense, citing a leaking roof, missing bathtub tiles, rotten window frames, carpet holes, security bars without release latches, water damage, and bad drains.

The landlord testified that these conditions didn't exist when he bought the property five years earlier. He also stated that he'd repaired the roof the previous year, but hadn't been told of the other problems before the lawsuit started. Tedesco produced copies of letters she'd sent to the landlord describing the problems, but he denied receiving them.

Although the trial court found that the problems described by Tedesco didn't constitute a "substantial" violation of the statutory habitability requirements, it awarded her a rent reduction of $200 because of the problems. On the other hand, the court granted the landlord possession of the property and ordered Tedesco to pay the landlord $629 in rent, $70 in damages, and $119 in legal costs. Tedesco appealed.

The questions:

Was there a substantial violation of the habitability requirements? Was the landlord entitled to prevail in the unlawful detainer action and evict the tenant?

The court's answers:

The court first reviewed what trial courts are supposed to do if they find proof of a substantial breach of the warranty of habitability: 1) reduce the rent to reflect the breach; 2) give the tenant the right to possession as long as the tenant pays the reduced rental rate; 3) order that the rent remain reduced until the repairs are made; and 4) award costs and attorney's fees to the tenant if that's permitted under the law and the contract between the parties. On the other hand, if the trial court determines that there has not been a substantial breach of the habitability requirements, the court must rule in the landlord's favor.

The court then addressed the issue of whether there had been a substantial violation of the habitability requirements in this case. "Civil Code section 1941.1 defines a dwelling as untenantable for human occupancy 'if it substantially lacks...(a) Effective waterproofing and weather protection of roof and exterior walls, including unbroken windows and doors. (b) Plumbing... maintained in good working order...(d) Heating facilities...maintained in good working order...(h) Floors...maintained in good repair.'...

"As previously stated, the evidence was undisputed that the premises were not properly waterproofed from the outside elements, that the roof leaked to the extent that the rain damaged the inside walls of the property, that the windows were not waterproofed, that portions of the wall were visible in the bathroom, and that the thermostat was inoperative. These conditions are clearly visible in the photographs entered into evidence at the trial. Furthermore, these conditions are not merely cosmetic or aesthetic, but affect the health and safety of the tenant."

The result:

Disagreeing with the trial court's conclusion that the problems with the premises were non-substantial, the appellate court found that they clearly violated the statutory requirements for habitability. Since there had been a substantial violation, Tedesco had a legitimate defense against the landlord's claim of unlawful detainer. She was entitled to remain in possession of the property and continue her tenancy.

Chapter Summary

- A lease is both a contract and a conveyance. The lease agreement or contract conveys a real property interest known as a leasehold. The statute of frauds requires that leases with a term greater than one year must be in writing.

- Residential fixed-term leases usually don't allow rent increases. In a month-to-month tenancy, however, the landlord can raise the rent by any amount and with any frequency, unless a rent control law applies. However, the landlord must give the tenant at least 30 days' notice of the proposed increase, and 60 days' notice if the rent has risen more than ten percent in the last 12 months.

- A few California cities have rent control ordinances that strictly limit rent increases. In the 1990s, state-wide legislation prohibited localities from passing any new rent control ordinances and exempted new buildings and new tenancies in single-family homes and condo units from rent control.

- Residential landlords generally can't require a security deposit greater than two or three months' rent. A landlord can't keep any of the deposit except to cover unpaid rent or expenses actually incurred in repairing tenant damage. The landlord must provide a written statement accounting for any money withheld from the deposit.

- Under common law and statute, the landlord promises the tenant quiet enjoyment of the premises. The landlord can't enter the premises without the tenant's consent except to address an emergency, repair damage, investigate abandonment, show the unit, or comply with a court order. Generally, the landlord must give the tenant at least 24 hours' notice of an intended entry, except in an emergency.

- Under common law and statute, the landlord must keep the premises habitable. A habitable dwelling is weatherproof, reasonably safe and sound, pest-free, and served by the standard utilities, including heat, electricity, telephone, and water.

- An assignment is a transfer of the entire remaining lease term; a sublease is a transfer of only part of the leasehold (either part of the premises or part of the term). A lease may require the landlord's consent for an assignment or sublease, but this consent cannot be unreasonably withheld. Despite the assignment or sublease, the original tenant remains liable if the new tenant breaches the terms of the lease.

- A term tenancy generally can't be terminated early by either party except for a material breach. A month-to-month tenancy generally can be terminated by either party without cause by giving 30 days' notice, except that residential landlords must give 60 days' notice if the tenant has lived on the premises for a year or more.

- Tenants who materially breach a leasehold agreement can be evicted. The landlord begins the process by serving the tenant with a three-day notice to quit the premises. If the tenant fails to remedy a curable breach and refuses to leave, the landlord can bring an unlawful detainer action. The landlord cannot evict the tenant by cutting off utilities or otherwise making the unit uninhabitable.

Key Terms

- **Leasehold** – The property interest acquired by a tenant under the terms of a lease.

- **Rent control law** – A local ordinance that limits or prohibits rent increases in residential tenancies under certain circumstances.

- **Covenant of quiet enjoyment** – An implied guarantee (included by law in every lease) that the landlord won't interfere with, or allow others to interfere with, the tenant's quiet enjoyment of the leased property.

- **Warranty of habitability** – An implied guarantee (included by law in every lease) that the property is fit for human habitation.

- **Constructive eviction** – When a tenant is forced to leave the premises due to serious interference with her quiet enjoyment of the property, or due to substantial property defects affecting habitability.

- **Repair and deduct** – One of the remedies available to a tenant if the landlord fails to repair a defect in the rented premises after reasonable notice; subject to certain conditions, the tenant may perform the repair and then deduct the cost from the rent.

- **Security deposit** – A refundable deposit that a tenant is required to give the landlord at the beginning of the tenancy as security against damage to the premises or failure to pay rent.

- **Assignment** – A tenant's grant of the entire leasehold to another person for the remaining lease term.

- **Subleasing** – A tenant's grant of part of the leasehold (either a portion of the term or a portion of the premises) to another person.

- **Notice of termination** – Advance written notice that a landlord or tenant who wants to terminate a periodic tenancy must give to the other party.

- **Termination for just cause** – Termination of a tenancy because of the tenant's material breach of the terms of the lease.

- **Three-day notice to quit** – A notice that a landlord serves on a tenant who has breached the lease agreement; the first step in the eviction process.

- **Unlawful detainer action** – A lawsuit filed by a landlord against a tenant who fails to move out after receiving the three-day notice to quit (or who has stayed on without consent after the tenancy has ended).

- **Writ of possession** – A court order that a landlord may request after winning an unlawful detainer action, which directs the sheriff to forcibly remove the tenant and her belongings from the leased property if she refuses to leave voluntarily within five days.

Chapter Quiz

1. In September, Linda phones James and agrees to rent his two-bedroom house for two years for $4,000 per month, beginning in January. Shortly thereafter, she finds out that James rented the house to someone else. Which of the following is true?
   a) Linda will have trouble winning a lawsuit because a lease for over one year must be in writing
   b) Leases are not deeds and do not convey a real property interest, so a writing isn't necessary; Linda's oral lease agreement is enforceable
   c) $4,000 for a two-bedroom house probably violates California's rent control statute, making Linda's lease agreement unenforceable
   d) None of the above

2. When Jolinda pays her rent two days late, the landlord assesses her a $125 late fee. Which of the following is true?
   a) The late fee is illegal: state law limits late fees to $30
   b) The late fee is legal: state law doesn't regulate late fees
   c) While no state statute regulates late fees, these fees are a form of liquidated damages and must be a reasonable estimate of actual damages; a court might find $125 unreasonable
   d) State law doesn't allow late fees unless the rent is at least three days late

3. California law limits the landlord's ability to enter the leased premises as follows:
   a) landlords must generally give tenants three days' notice of an intention to enter the premises
   b) landlords can't enter the premises without the tenant's permission
   c) landlords must generally give tenants 24 hours' notice of an intention to enter the premises
   d) since landlords own the property, they can enter it freely; notice is a courtesy, not a requirement

4. Kylie writes her tenant Ohno a letter raising the rent 15% ($200) in 30 days. Ohno has a month-to-month tenancy. Ohno calls Kylie and says "You have to give me 60 days' notice of a rent increase of over 10%." Kylie replies, "Okay. Then let's just make it $100 a month more instead." Which of the following is true?
   a) Ohno is wrong: the landlord can raise the rent by any amount with 30 days' notice
   b) Ohno is right: all rent increases require 60 days' notice; but the $100 increase is effective because small increases need not be in writing
   c) The $100 increase is effective because Kylie gave 30 days' notice
   d) Kylie is entirely out of luck because a 15% rent increase requires 60 days' notice, and the notice of any rent increase must be in writing

5. Terri rents a house. Her landlord drops by unannounced to mow the lawn, pull a few weeds, and occasionally enter the house to make sure that Terri is keeping the place clean. Although Terri has complained about a leaking bedroom window and a broken upstairs toilet, the landlord never finds time to fix those problems. Which of the following is true?
   a) The landlord has violated both the covenant of quiet enjoyment and the warranty of habitability
   b) The landlord has not violated the covenant of quiet enjoyment: his intrusions are reasonable and minor
   c) The landlord has not violated the warranty of habitability: the problems with the premises do not make the premises completely unlivable
   d) The landlord has violated neither the covenant of quiet enjoyment nor the warranty of habitability

6. Rent control:
   a) is widespread in California
   b) is available in only a few communities in California
   c) was significantly cut back by the state legislature in the 1990s
   d) Both b) and c)

7. Pearl accidentally starts a small fire in her apartment that burns the bottom corner of a wall through to the studs. The landlord pays $450 to have the wall repaired and deducts this amount from Pearl's security deposit. He also decides it's time to replace the ten-year-old bedroom carpet. He charges Pearl $125, labeling it a prorated share of the carpet replacement. Which of the following is true?
   a) The statute allows the landlord to deduct the cost of wall repairs from the security deposit ($450), plus the $125 for the prorated carpet replacement
   b) The statute allows the landlord to deduct only $450 from Pearl's security deposit; the carpet replacement is normal wear and tear
   c) The landlord can't deduct anything from Pearl's security deposit because he failed to use a competitive bidding process for the wall repair
   d) None of the above

8. Now suppose that after the fire described above, the landlord mailed Pearl a three-day eviction notice, and then four days later he set her belongings on the sidewalk. Which of the following is true?
   a) The three-day notice is inadequate; the landlord can't physically evict a tenant without giving a 30-day notice to quit the premises
   b) The three-day notice for breach is correct; however, if the tenant refuses to move out after the notice, the landlord must bring a court action
   c) The eviction itself is permissible, but leaving someone's belongings on a public sidewalk is illegal littering
   d) The fire damage was less than $1,000—not enough to constitute a material breach of a lease agreement and justify an eviction

9. Pearl leaves and a new tenant named Alejandro moves in. The landlord promises to replace three broken overhead light fixtures, but fails to do so. Which of the following is true?
   a) If Alejandro gives the landlord three days' notice, he can have the repair done himself and then subtract the amount of the repair from the rent
   b) If Alejandro gives the landlord notice and two weeks to act, he can have the lights repaired himself and then subtract the amount of the repair, provided it is no more than half of the monthly rent
   c) If Alejandro gives the landlord notice and 30 days to correct the problem, he can have the lights repaired himself and then subtract the amount of the repair, provided it is no more than one month's rent
   d) If Alejandro gives the landlord notice and a reasonable amount of time to act, he can have the lights repaired himself; no cost limit applies since the repair involves safe lighting, a habitability concern

10. A commercial tenant wants to leave the building and assign the remaining ten months of his lease to another company. However, the lease says the landlord must give prior written consent to any assignment. The second company has a bad credit rating. Which of the following is true?
   a) If the landlord consents to the assignment, the original tenant will have no further liability on the lease
   b) The landlord probably has the right to withhold consent to the assignment, even for a reasonable substitute tenant
   c) The landlord probably does not have the right to withhold consent from a reasonable substitute tenant; however, the second company could be rejected as financially risky
   d) California law guarantees a tenant's right to sublease or assign a tenancy; lease provisions to the contrary have no effect

Chapter Answer Key

Chapter Quiz Answers:

1. a) The statute of frauds requires that leases with a term of over one year must be in writing. Rent control is not statewide; further, a rent control ordinance would not deprive a tenant of the right to enforce a lease, though it might limit the rent she has to pay.

2. c) California does not limit late fees by statute; under the common law of contracts, however, the fee would probably have to be reasonable.

3. c) Generally, the landlord must give tenants 24 hours' notice before entering the premises, except in an emergency.

4. d) Notice of a rent increase must be in writing; an increase of ten percent or less requires 30 days' notice; a larger increase requires 60 days' notice.

5. a) Landlords can't enter the premises without adequate notice: the covenant of quiet enjoyment provides no exception for a brief entry to "check on things." Leaks and plumbing problems violate the warranty of habitability: the premises don't have to be rendered completely unlivable.

6. d) Only a limited number of California communities ever passed rent control ordinances, and the state legislature has limited their application.

7. b) The landlord can deduct the cost of the wall repairs. The statute doesn't require competitive bidding. Landlords can't deduct from security deposits for damage caused by normal wear and tear.

8. b) Starting a fire may be sufficiently negligent to justify eviction. However, the landlord can never physically evict a tenant; only a sheriff, following a successful unlawful detainer action, and further notice, can remove a tenant.

9. c) Tenants can deduct up to one's month rent for a repair, but the law requires the tenant first allow the landlord 30 days to take care of the problem unless it's an emergency.

10. c) Many leases prohibit an assignment or sublease without the landlord's consent; however, at least in the commercial setting, a landlord can't withhold consent to a responsible new tenant. Even if the transfer is allowed, the original tenant remains liable under the lease.

Cases to Consider... Answers:

Assignment and Subleasing

Kendall v. Ernest Pestana, Inc. (1985) 40 Cal.3d 488. Allowing a landlord to withhold consent to a reasonable transfer is an unreasonable restraint on alienation and serves no valid commercial purpose. The court created new law in California by ruling that, at least in commercial settings, a landlord can't unreasonably withhold consent to an assignment or sublease. It's likely that residential landlords must also consent to reasonable transfers, but California courts haven't settled that issue yet.

List of Cases

Andrews v. Mobile Aire Estates (2005) 125 Cal.App.4th 578
Green v. Superior Court (1974) 10 Cal.3d 616
Hyatt v. Tedesco (2002) 96 Cal.App.4th Supp. 62
Kendall v. Ernest Pestana, Inc. (1985) 40 Cal.3d 488
Medina v. Hillshore Partners (1995) 40 Cal.App.4th 477
Sanders v. Allen (1948) 83 Cal.App.2d 362

Chapter 21

Antitrust Law

Outline

Introduction

The typical real estate professional is aware of the dangers of violating license laws or fair housing laws, but she may overlook the very real risk of running afoul of antitrust laws. Real estate agents are fiercely competitive, but also have to work in cooperation with one another. Because of this, the profession is under close watch for antitrust violations. Even the most casual of conversations—"talking shop" or networking with an agent from another company—can raise questions of anticompetitive behavior.

In this chapter, we'll examine both federal and California antitrust laws. We'll start by exploring the reasons for antitrust laws and then explain the types of actions and activities these laws prohibit. Next, we'll look at the civil and criminal penalties for violating antitrust laws. Finally, we'll take a more in-depth look at the specific real estate practices that are barred by antitrust laws, and provide some tips on how to avoid antitrust violations.

Antitrust Law

Antitrust laws are aimed at preventing business agreements and practices that have the effect of restraining trade. Monopolies, price fixing, and anticompetitive agreements are all examples of prohibited antitrust activities or arrangements.

The enforcement of antitrust laws has evolved over the years, due to shifts in public policy and an evolving marketplace. Initially, antitrust scrutiny was primarily focused on oil, gas, and tobacco companies; later, the laws were used to break up large communication and transportation companies. Nowadays, antitrust actions often focus on software companies and Internet-related services.

We'll begin our discussion of antitrust law by examining the policy behind the laws. We'll also take a brief look at the history of the federal and state antitrust laws.

Purpose of Antitrust Law

Antitrust laws were designed to protect a free enterprise system that encourages competition between businesses. When businesses work together to control prices or limit supply, customers typically end up paying higher prices and the economy suffers. A competitive marketplace, on the other hand, leads to better products and better prices for consumers. The antitrust laws were created to support this type of competition.

Antitrust laws are also intended to encourage entrepreneurs and small businesses to compete in the marketplace. In other words, the antitrust laws seek to create a level playing field, without the unreasonable restrictions on free trade that can be created by big businesses.

History of Antitrust Law

In the late 1800s, businesses in several different industries (oil, tobacco, and steel, for example) began merging and consolidating into huge corporations known as **trusts**. As mergers and buyouts eliminated the competition from smaller businesses, companies like Standard Oil and American Tobacco grew in

 Another Opinion

Some economists argue that antitrust laws actually punish innovation and reward less efficient business practices. These critics ask why companies should strive to be innovative and do well, when that very success may lead to charges of unfair business practices. They claim that the government's constant attempt to level the playing field encourages poor business practices and rewards incompetence. As a result, consumers are denied both the lower costs and innovative new products that are the by-product of a truly competitive marketplace.

size and power until they essentially monopolized their respective industries. (A **monopoly** occurs when one seller of goods or provider of services has exclusive control over the market—a situation characterized by a lack of competition, with no reasonable substitutes. In other words, in a monopoly, there are many buyers but only one seller—and that single seller wields an inordinate amount of control over its industry and market.)

In response to these growing monopolies, state governments began enacting antitrust legislation. But while these state laws prohibited restraints of trade, they did so only within each respective state's borders. In 1890, the federal government stepped in with the Sherman Antitrust Act, which regulates interstate restraints of trade (that is, restraints of trade between the various states). Under the Sherman Act, "Every contract, combination in the form of trust or otherwise, or conspiracy, in restraint of trade or commerce among the several States, or with foreign nations, is declared to be illegal." Congress has since passed additional antitrust statutes (such as the Clayton Act in 1914), but the Sherman Act remains the foundation of federal antitrust law.

By the early 1900s, the federal government was using the Sherman Act as a powerful tool to break up monopolies in the industries mentioned above. Over time, courts expanded the Sherman Act's definition of "trade" to include not just the production and sale of goods, but also the provision of services. In 1950, the U.S. Supreme Court held that federal antitrust laws apply to the real estate industry.

Case Example:

The Washington Real Estate Board adopted standard commission rates and required its real estate broker members to charge these rates. When the board was sued for price-fixing, the case eventually reached the U.S. Supreme Court. The court made it clear that the Sherman Antitrust Act applies to real estate brokerage services. The business of a real estate broker is a trade, carried on for profit and commercial purposes. Therefore, the competitive standards addressed by the Sherman Act apply to real estate brokerages, just as to any other commercial activity. The court found that the board's practices constituted a price-fixing scheme within the meaning of the Sherman Antitrust Act. *United States v. Real Estate Boards* (1950) 339 U.S. 485.

Then in 1976, California's supreme court took up the same issue: whether the state's antitrust law (the **Cartwright Act**) applied to services provided by real estate brokers.

Case Example:

Eugene Palsson, a licensed real estate agent, was denied membership to the Marin County Board of Realtors because he was also a flight engineer and didn't meet the board's requirement that members be "primarily engaged in the real estate business." The board enforced this requirement by sanctioning any member that employed (or shared an office with) someone who had been denied membership. As a result, Palsson was denied employment by 75% of the brokers in Marin County and denied access to the multiple listing service. In support of the board, the California Association of Realtors® argued that the Cartwright Act doesn't apply to the sale of services, only to goods. But the court disagreed, stating that although the Cartwright Act excluded "labor" as a commodity, this provision was merely intended to exclude labor unions from the act's coverage. It was never meant to shield services, including brokerage services. *Marin County Bd. of Realtors, Inc. v. Palsson* (1976) 16 Cal.3d 920.

Federal and state antitrust laws are very similar in California. In this chapter, we'll be focusing on issues related to the federal antitrust law. However, keep in mind that for the most part, the concepts discussed are true of both the Sherman Antitrust Act and the state's Cartwright Act.

Prohibited Acts

As we've just discussed, antitrust laws apply to the provision of real estate brokerage services. But before we examine some of the specific real estate practices that may lead to antitrust violations, let's look at the general nature of the acts prohibited by antitrust laws.

Not all business decisions that increase profits or **market share** (the amount of business a company does in a particular area) violate antitrust laws. If a business's competitive practices and lower prices take business away from a less efficient competitor, that's probably not an antitrust violation; it's simply good business. This is how a free market is designed to work. On the other hand, a business activity will violate antitrust laws if it:

- is the result of a conspiracy,
- is an unreasonable restraint of trade, and
- creates an impact on competition.

Conspiracy

A **conspiracy** is an agreement between two or more people to commit an illegal act, or to use illegal methods to achieve a legal purpose. For example, it's perfectly legal to profit from selling widgets. However, it's illegal to conspire with a competitor to profit from selling widgets by making it impossible for anyone else to sell widgets in the same area.

Individual vs. Group Action. One person acting alone cannot be a conspirator—group action is required. It is the involvement of two or more competitors (or groups) that makes the agreement a conspiracy.

> **Example:** Broker Sue owns Mountain Realty, which is located in Alpineville, a small town in a remote area in the Sierras. The only competition in town is another small brokerage, Town Realty. Sue decides that she would like to raise her commission rates from 6% to 7%, but worries about losing business to Town Realty if her rates appear too high.
>
> While having lunch one day with Broker Michael from Town Realty, Sue proposes that Town Realty should also raise its standard rate to 7%. "If you do the same thing," she says, "we could both get away with higher rates. What are people going to do, drive 30 miles to Valley City to list with Mega Brokers?" Broker Michael replies, "Great idea. I'm in." This meets the definition of group action and would probably be considered a conspiracy.

It's important to understand that a real estate brokerage is considered a single entity under the antitrust laws. This is true even if a single brokerage is quite large, with many branches and many salespeople working for each branch as independent contractors.

Example: Let's return to Broker Sue and Mountain Realty. Mountain Realty has ten full-time salespersons. At a meeting, Broker Sue tells her salespersons that the company policy will now be to list properties at 7%. She does not discuss this with anyone from any other brokerage. Since Mountain Realty is considered a single entity, Broker Sue's actions do not constitute a conspiracy. Her company business plan will not violate the antitrust laws.

There's one exception to the group action requirement: suppose a company has already achieved a monopoly position in its industry through legal means, because of innovation or simple luck. If it takes steps to prevent new competitors from entering the market, it may, in unusual circumstances, be found in violation of antitrust laws even though it acted unilaterally.

Agreement to Act. An important component of a conspiracy is an agreement to act. However, many people don't understand that an agreement to act doesn't need to be spoken or explicit. In fact, it can be as simple as a nod or a wink; it can even be listening to a conversation in silence, or giving in to pressure from competitors.

Example: Returning once more to Broker Sue and Broker Michael, let's say that when she encourages him to adopt her business plan, Broker Michael says nothing in response and simply changes the subject. Nonetheless, Broker Michael later institutes the very same 7% commission plan at his brokerage. He could still be found guilty of conspiracy.

You can see that competitors must be careful to avoid any situations or conduct that may appear to be part of a larger conspiracy to restrain trade.

Unreasonable Restraints of Trade

To constitute an antitrust violation, an act must also be an unreasonable **restraint of trade**. A restraint of trade is any act that prevents an individual or company from doing business in a certain area or with certain people. In other words, it is an act that hinders free trade. Not every restraint of trade is illegal, however; courts have interpreted the Sherman Act to prohibit only unreasonable restraints.

So what types of business activities constitute unreasonable restraints of trade? Courts use three tests for answering this question:

- the *per se* rule,
- the rule of reason, and
- the "quick look" test.

Per Se Rule. *Per se* is a Latin term meaning "by itself." An action that is illegal *per se* is one that is automatically illegal, regardless of the circumstances. (The term *per se* is used in many areas of the law; for example, in Chapter 15 we discussed nuisance *per se*.)

Courts have determined that certain activities, such as price-fixing, are unreasonable restraints of trade and unlawful *per se*. It doesn't matter whether the parties had any intent to break the law. If they are found to have engaged in an unreasonable restraint of trade, they are guilty of an antitrust violation.

Rule of Reason. The rule of reason is a balancing test that is applied when an act isn't a *per se* violation, but might still constitute an illegal restraint of trade. Under this rule, a court weighs the activity's impact on competition and decides whether the activity's negative effects outweigh the positive effects.

Applying the rule of reason test requires the court to consider the individual circumstances of each case, such as the reason for adopting the practice and how it affected the defendant's position in the market. If the questionable activity resulted in higher prices, a deterioration of services, or stifled innovation, it's likely to be considered an unreasonable restraint of trade.

> **Is Everything Unlawful?**
>
> "Ronald [Coase] said he had gotten tired of antitrust because when the prices went up the judges said it was monopoly, when the prices went down they said it was predatory pricing, and when they stayed the same they said it was tacit collusion."
>
> – William Landes, "The Fire of Truth: A Remembrance of Law and Econ at Chicago," JLE (1983) p. 193.

Example: Mega Software Company ships its product with samples of other software programs that complement its system. These samples are not owned or produced by the software company, but the company does pick and choose which of the smaller software companies it will feature in its product. Mega Software Company usually packages its software with GoFind Internet search software, because Mega Software feels that GoFind puts out a superior product. Smaller Internet search companies complain. Mega Software's conduct may not be *per se* illegal, but a court may still apply a "rule of reason" test to determine whether Mega Software's actions violate antitrust law. Specifically, the court will weigh the company practice's positive effect on the marketplace and consumers against the practice's negative effect on the marketplace and consumers.

Case to Consider...

Derish sold his current home and bought a new home with the assistance of Atwater, a real estate broker. Atwater received a $3,780 commission from the sale of Derish's home; Atwater also received a commission when he represented Derish in the purchase of the new home. After the sales closed, Derish sued Atwater, the San Mateo-Burlingame Board of Realtors®, the California Association of Realtors®, and the National Association of Realtors®, claiming antitrust law violations. Derish asserted that the MLS should be open to the public; since it wasn't, he was forced to work with a broker and pay a commission. Does the practice of allowing only licensed real estate brokers and agents to use the MLS violate the antitrust laws? *Derish v. San Mateo-Burlingame Bd. of Realtors* (1982) 136 Cal.App.3d. 534.

"Quick Look" Test. A court may choose to use a shortened version of the rule of reason test, known as the **quick look** test. This test is appropriate when there is not a *per se* violation of the law, but the anticompetitive effects of the restraint of trade are plainly obvious to a casual observer. This can expedite cases where there is clearly a restraint of trade, because proving a violation under the rule of reason test requires detailed and time-consuming analysis by experts in economics.

Impact on Competition

The third requirement for a violation of antitrust law is that there must be an actual injury to a competitor or consumer. A competitor or consumer who is simply unhappy about a changed business landscape does not have a claim. On the other hand, the plaintiff doesn't have the burden of actually producing evidence that the offender's actions resulted in higher prices; he needs to show only that the action is likely to adversely affect other participants in the market and reduce competition.

Enforcing the Law

Actions to enforce federal antitrust laws may be brought by the Federal Trade Commission or the Antitrust Division of the U.S. Department of Justice. The Department of Justice investigates complaints of antitrust violations through its own investigation division or through the Federal Bureau of Investigation (FBI). Depending on the results of its investigation, the Department of Justice may initiate criminal proceedings, civil enforcement proceedings, or both.

The Federal Trade Commission, on the other hand, may initiate civil or administrative antitrust proceedings, but cannot impose criminal sanctions. To avoid duplicating any investigative or procedural efforts, the Department of Justice and the Federal Trade Commission consult each other before opening a case.

In California, the Cartwright Act is enforced by the state attorney general. The attorney general's office may initiate civil actions and criminal actions against violators, or it may recommend that local district attorneys bring enforcement actions in their respective counties.

Finally, both federal and state laws grant individual citizens and businesses the right to pursue damages for antitrust violations in civil court.

 Penalty Enhancement

When the Sherman Act was enacted in 1890, the maximum penalties for federal antitrust violations were a $5,000 fine and up to one year in prison. To say that they've increased considerably since then would be putting it mildly.

The most recent increase came in June 2004, when President George W. Bush signed the Antitrust Criminal Penalty Enhancement and Reform Act into law.

Under the 2004 act, the maximum fine for an individual convicted of an antitrust violation increased to $1 million per offense, and the maximum prison term went from three years to ten years per offense. The maximum fine for a corporation jumped from $10 million per offense to $100 million per offense.

Penalties

The penalties for violating federal antitrust laws vary depending on whether the offender is an individual or a corporation, and whether the case is criminal or civil. In criminal cases, individual violators may be fined up to $1 million and sentenced to up to ten years in federal prison for each offense. Corporations can be fined up to $100 million for each offense.

In addition, parties injured by federal antitrust violations may sue violators for treble damages (three times the amount of their actual damages), plus attorney's fees and costs.

Under California law, an individual found guilty of an antitrust violation may be fined up to $250,000 and sentenced to prison for up to three years. A corporation can be fined up to $1 million, or up to two times the gain received from the illegal act, whichever is greater.

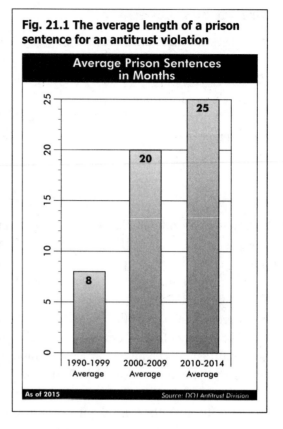

Fig. 21.1 The average length of a prison sentence for an antitrust violation

Average Prison Sentences in Months

- 1990-1999 Average: 8
- 2000-2009 Average: 20
- 2010-2014 Average: 25

As of 2015   Source: DOJ Antitrust Division

Antitrust Law and the Real Estate Profession

Now that you're familiar with antitrust laws and the general nature of the acts they prohibit, let's look at some specific real estate practices that may lead to antitrust violations. In particular, real estate agents must be aware of the potential dangers of:

- price and commission fixing,
- group boycotts,
- tie-in arrangements, and
- market allocation.

Price and Commission Fixing

Price fixing is defined as the cooperative setting of prices or price ranges by competing firms. You'll recall our earlier case example involving the fixing of standard commission rates. Price fixing, in any industry, is a *per se* antitrust violation.

Commission Rates. To avoid the appearance of price fixing, two agents from different brokerages should never discuss their commission rates. Remember, it is a discussion between competing agents that is dangerous; a broker can freely discuss commission rates with his own salespeople.

Even a casual announcement that a broker is planning to raise her commission rates could lead to antitrust problems.

Example: Broker Wood goes to a dinner given by her local MLS. She is called on to discuss current market conditions and, in the middle of her speech, she announces that she is going to raise her commission rate. This statement could be viewed as an invitation to conspire to fix prices. If any other MLS members raise their rates in response to her announcement, they can be held to have accepted Wood's invitation to conspire.

Brokers must understand that they do not have to actually consult with each other to be charged with conspiring to fix commission rates. The kind of scenario described in the above example is enough to lead to an antitrust lawsuit.

 An Internet Revolution

The advent of the Internet has raised some new and interesting questions about anti-trust practices and the real estate profession. An issue that has come under particular scrutiny involves "discount" or "limited service" brokers, who charge reduced or flat fees for simply listing properties on the MLS, without offering any additional advertising or negotiating services. Brokerages who have only an online presence are sometimes called VOW or "virtual office website" brokers. These online-based services appeal to an increasingly Internet-savvy public: many sellers and buyers are happy to place their own advertising and do their own online searching in exchange for reduced brokerage fees.

Of course, many traditional real estate brokers are less enthusiastic about limited service brokers. They claim that these discount brokers ultimately harm the public, since the result is often inexperienced consumers handling and negotiating their own sales. Pressure from traditional brokers (and their trade associations) has caused a handful of states to enact minimum service laws: laws that limit discount brokerage by requiring all licensees to provide a minimum level of service.

Opponents of these laws claim that the real estate profession is simply attempting to maintain its monopoly on information and, in the process, is limiting competition and violating antitrust prohibitions against price fixing and group boycotting. The Department of Justice (DOJ) and the Federal Trade Commission (FTC) appear to agree, advocating against the adoption of minimum service laws and, in some cases, even bringing antitrust actions against the state agencies enacting them.

In the early 2000s, the National Association of Realtors® enacted a policy that allowed member-brokers to prevent their listings from appearing during Internet MLS searches performed by clients of VOWs (virtual brokerages). The DOJ filed suit in 2005, arguing that the policy reduced consumer choice and drove up costs in violation of the Sherman Act. In 2008, the court approved a settlement against NAR® in which NAR was required to repeal the challenged policies and replace them with rules that don't discriminate against Internet-based limited service brokers.

Publications that appear to fix prices are prohibited as well. Any MLS or other association that tries to publish "recommended" or "going" rates for commissions could be sued.

California law requires any standard form (such as a listing agreement) that establishes or changes a broker's compensation to contain the following disclosure in boldface, ten point type:

> **NOTICE: The amount or rate of real estate commissions is not fixed by law. They are set by each Broker individually and may be negotiable between Seller and Broker (real estate commissions include all compensation and fees to Broker).**

Commission Splits. One exception to this general prohibition is that two competing brokers may discuss a commission split (the split between the listing broker and the selling broker) in a cooperative sale for a specific transaction. However, competing brokers should never form an agreement regarding a uniform or standard commission split that applies to all transactions. It is a *per se* violation of antitrust laws to fix commission splits between competing real estate companies.

Group Boycotts

A **group boycott** is an agreement between two or more real estate brokers to exclude other brokers from fair participation in real estate activities. Because the purpose of group boycotts is to hurt or destroy a competitor, they are illegal *per se* under the antitrust laws.

> **Example:** Becker and Jordan are both brokers. They have lunch together and begin discussing the business practices of a third broker, Harley. Becker grumbles that Harley is just a "discount broker" and is lazy and dishonest. "I refuse to do business with the guy," Becker says. Jordan laughs and agrees. She says that she never returns any of Harley's calls when he is inquiring about a listed property. "I'm not going to make it easy for him to undercut us," she says. They both nod in agreement. Becker and Jordan could be found guilty of a conspiracy to boycott.

If a broker feels that another broker is dishonest or unethical, she may choose not to do business with him. However, the unhappy broker cannot tell other brokers (or agree with other brokers) to do the same. This is the distinction between individual and group action. Individual brokers have the right to do business with whomever they choose, but they may not join with other brokers to make those decisions.

Here's something else to consider: as you know, a broker has a fiduciary duty to do what's best for her client. Let's return to the above example. When Jordan refuses to return Harley's calls regarding listed properties, is she really doing what is best for her clients? In this situation, a broker like Jordan could find herself in violation of not only the antitrust laws, but of the real estate licensing law.

Case to Consider...

Feldman, a real estate broker who practiced throughout the state of California, wanted to use various local multiple listing services on a per-use basis, even though he wasn't a

Banning Rebate Bans

Certain brokers discount their services by providing commission rebates. For example, one web-based brokerage returns 20 percent of its commission to buyers or sellers, and another provides a flat rebate via $1,000 gift cards. Attempting to eliminate this form of discount brokerage, a number of states banned commission rebates (California was not among them, however).

The government views these rebate bans as favoring established players at the expense of the consumer and free market competition—a violation of antitrust law. In the mid-2000s, the Department of Justice (DOJ) began investigating the real estate commissions of several states, including those of West Virginia, South Dakota, and Kentucky, all of which had passed rebate bans. Following the initial investigation, the West Virginia and South Dakota commissions withdrew their anti-rebate rules. Kentucky also repealed its regulation, but only after the DOJ filed suit.

The government's campaign against the anti-rebate rules remains unfinished. Ten states still have bans in place.

member of any of the local real estate boards or associations that operated the local listing services. The boards and associations, who usually charge a membership fee and/or a quarterly fee for use of the MLS, declined Feldman's requests. Feldman, stating that he could not afford to pay all of the membership fees requested by the boards and associations across the state, filed suit, alleging violations of the state antitrust act. Feldman asserted that the various boards and associations' refusals to let him use local listing services on a per-use basis constituted a group boycott. Did Feldman have a case? *Feldman v. Sacramento Bd. of Realtors, Inc.* (1981) 119 Cal.App.3d 739.

Tie-in Arrangements

A **tie-in arrangement** (also known as a tying arrangement) occurs when a buyer is required to purchase one product or service in order to purchase another product or service. A tie-in arrangement is illegal *per se* under the antitrust laws.

> **Example:** Brown is a subdivision developer. Tyson, a builder, wants to buy a lot. Brown tells Tyson that he will sell him a lot only if Tyson agrees that, after Tyson builds a house on the lot, he will list the improved property with Brown.

The above is an example of a **list-back agreement**. List-back agreements violate the antitrust laws if the listing requirement is a condition of the original sale. Note, though, that two parties may mutually agree on a list-back agreement without violating antitrust laws.

Market Allocation

Another business practice that is *per se* illegal under the antitrust laws is known as **market allocation**. It's illegal for competing businesses to agree not to sell products or services in specified areas, or to agree not to sell to certain customers in specified areas.

Market allocation between competing brokers is prohibited because it limits competition. Brokers should be free to do business in whatever area—and with any customer—they wish.

As with group boycotts, it is the collective action that makes market allocation illegal. It's perfectly acceptable for an individual broker to determine the specific market area that will be serviced by his company. It is also acceptable for a broker to allocate territory to the salespersons who work for her company. However, all territory allocations must be made within one firm, not between two competing firms. Allocation between competing firms is group action and is therefore illegal under the antitrust laws.

The same is true with regard to allocating customers. Competing firms may not agree to allocate business from certain types of customers; however, an individual broker may allocate the types of incoming customers within her brokerage.

> **Example:** Based on their training and specialties, Broker Joan of ABC Realty assigns Salesperson Mary to handle all incoming customers in the luxury home market, and assigns Salesperson Bill to all incoming customers in the vacant land market. This practice does not violate the antitrust laws.
>
> However, if Broker Joan of ABC Realty and Broker Jim of XYZ Realty agree to allocate customers so that ABC Realty will handle all luxury homes, and XYZ Realty will handle all vacant land, this would be a violation of the antitrust laws.

Avoiding Antitrust Violations

There are certain steps brokers can take to prevent possible antitrust violations. Brokers should:

- always establish their fees and other listing policies independently, without consulting competing firms;
- never use listing forms that contain pre-printed commission rates;
- never imply to a client that the commission rate is fixed or non-negotiable, or refer to a competitor's commission policies when discussing commission rates;
- never discuss their business plans with competitors;
- never tell clients or competitors that they won't do business with a competing firm, or tell them not to work with that firm because of doubts about its competence or integrity; and
- train their licensees to be aware of what may constitute an antitrust law violation.

As you've seen, real estate agents and brokers who ignore federal and state antitrust laws can face serious penalties and even prison time. Because brokers are competitors who also work in cooperation with each other, the real estate industry is under continuous and close scrutiny by government agencies on the lookout for antitrust violations. It's easy to violate the antitrust laws inadvertently with merely a nod, a wink, or a casual comment. Therefore, brokers should be very careful to train their licensees to recognize potential antitrust situations and to know how to avoid them.

Case Law in Depth

The following case involves some of the legal issues discussed in this chapter. Read through the facts and consider the questions in light of what you have learned. Then read what the court actually decided.

Classen v. Weller (1983) 145 Cal.App.3d 27

Smith hired Classen to build a home on a lot in an exclusive development known as "Tobin-Clark." The lot was owned by HDC. The president of HDC, Weller, told Classen that the lots would be sold only to builders and that the sale had to go through the development's broker, Fox. When Classen protested that he didn't need a broker (since he already had Smith as a buyer), he was told that he couldn't buy the lot to build Smith's house unless he agreed to employ Fox as the exclusive broker. On March 17, 1977, Classen, Weller, and Fox signed a purchase agreement which expressly provided that Fox would have "an exclusive authorization to sell listing contract by the buyer, at a commission of 6% for a term of 3 years from date of acquisition of property by the buyer or one year after completion of any home that is constructed."

Classen built a home on the lot and then conveyed the property to Smith in April of 1977, but did not pay Fox the 6% commission. Fox then sued for its commission. Classen cross-complained, alleging antitrust violations; namely, that Weller, HDC, and Fox were conspiring to sell lots in Tobin-Clark by tying a builder's purchase of lots to the additional purchase of real estate services from Fox, in violation of the California Cartwright Act. The lower court granted Weller's, HDC's, and Fox's motions for summary judgment. Classen appealed.

The question:

Were Weller, HDC, and Fox guilty of a tie-in arrangement in violation of California's antitrust act? Is Classen entitled to damages?

The court's answer:

Allowing a seller to tie the sale of a limited, desired product to the sale of a second product shields the second product from competitive market forces, creating a restraint of trade.

A tie-in arrangement will be held illegal if (1) the sale of the tying product was linked to the sale of the tied product, (2) the seller had enough power in the tying market to coerce the purchase of the tied product, (3) a substantial sale of the tied product took place, and (4) the plaintiff suffered damages.

In this case, the first three requirements were met: the two sales were linked, the limited supply of the tying product (the Tobin-Clark lots) placed the seller in a position to coerce the purchase of the tied product (Fox's brokerage services), and the sale of the tied product was substantial. Only the fourth requirement (damage to the plaintiff) was in dispute.

"Underlying the illegality of tie-ins is the assumption that the buyer is coerced into taking a product or service he does not want...Since Classen faced the adverse alternatives of losing his customer [Smith] or signing the agreement to obtain the lot, [he suffered damages].

"We conclude that the injury Classen alleged was the direct result of the restriction, i.e., of the tied fee.

"The focus of the antitrust laws is not upon the intentions of the actor, but rather upon the effect of the actions on commerce."

The result:

Reversed. Weller, HDC, and Fox were not entitled to summary judgments. If Classen later prevailed at trial, he would be entitled to damages.

Chapter Summary

- Antitrust laws are intended to protect a free enterprise system that encourages competition between businesses. Antitrust laws also encourage entrepreneurs and small businesses by leveling the playing field and allowing them to compete with bigger businesses. The main federal antitrust law is the Sherman Antitrust Act; California's state antitrust law is the Cartwright Act.

- To be prohibited under the antitrust laws, a questionable activity must be the result of a conspiracy, create an unreasonable restraint of trade, and result in an accompanying injury. A conspiracy is an agreement between two or more people to commit an illegal act, or to use illegal methods to achieve a legal purpose. The conspiracy must be based on group action, and there must be an agreement to act. For purposes of the antitrust law, a brokerage is considered an individual entity.

- A restraint of trade is any act that prevents an individual or company from doing business in a certain area, or with certain people. Some restraints of trade (such as price fixing) are illegal *per se*: automatic violations of the antitrust laws, regardless of intent or the circumstances. Other restraints of trade are evaluated under the "rule of reason" or "quick look" tests to determine whether they are unreasonable and therefore illegal.

- The federal antitrust laws are enforced by the Antitrust Division of the U.S. Department of Justice and by the Federal Trade Commission. California's state antitrust laws are enforced by the state attorney general. Both federal and state antitrust laws also recognize the right of individual citizens and businesses to pursue damages from antitrust violations in civil court.

- Under federal law, individual violators can be fined up to $1 million and sentenced to up to 10 years in federal prison for each offense. Corporations can be fined up to $100 million for each offense. In civil cases, victims may be entitled to receive treble damages, plus attorney's fees and costs. Under California law, an individual guilty of an antitrust violation can be fined up to $250,000 and sentenced to prison for up to three years. A corporation can be fined up to $1 million, or up to two times the gain received from the illegal act, whichever is greater.

- Real estate activities that are *per se* violations of state and federal antitrust laws include: fixing commission rates and commission splits; group boycotts (usually involving the MLS); tie-in arrangements (such as list-back agreements); and market allocation of areas or customers by competing brokerages.

Key Terms

- **Sherman Antitrust Act** – The main federal antitrust law, passed in 1890, which makes it illegal to conspire to create an unreasonable restraint of trade.

- **Monopoly** – When one seller of goods, or provider of services, has exclusive control over a market, resulting in lack of competition and higher prices for consumers.

- **Cartwright Act** – California's antitrust statute.

- **Conspiracy** – An agreement between two or more people to commit an illegal act or to use illegal methods to achieve a legal purpose.

- **Restraint of trade** – Any act that prevents an individual or company from doing business in a certain area, or with certain people, which hinders free trade. The antitrust laws apply only to unreasonable restraints of trade.

- ***Per se* illegal** – An action that is automatically illegal, regardless of the circumstances surrounding the activity or whether there was any intent to commit a crime.

- **Rule of reason** – A balancing test that courts use to determine whether a practice or activity constitutes an unreasonable restraint of trade. The court weighs the action's positive impact on competition against its negative impact on competition. Used when no obvious *per se* violation has occurred.

- **Quick look test** – A shortened version of the rule of reason test that is applied by courts when anticompetitive effects of a restraint of trade are plainly obvious, but no *per se* violation has occurred.

- **Price fixing** – The cooperative setting of prices or price ranges by competing firms.

- **Group boycott** – An agreement between two or more real estate brokers to exclude other brokers from fair participation in real estate activities.

- **Tie-in Arrangement** – Otherwise known as a tying arrangement; occurs when a buyer is required to purchase one product or service in order to purchase another product or service.

- **List-back agreement** – A tie-in arrangement that requires a builder, in order to buy a lot, to agree to list the completed property with a particular broker. Illegal under the antitrust laws.

- **Market allocation** – Dividing certain areas or customer types amongst competing businesses.

Chapter Quiz

1. California's antitrust law is known as the:
   a) Cartwright Act
   b) Sherman Antitrust Act
   c) Law Against Competition
   d) None of the above

2. The purpose(s) of antitrust laws is/are to:
   a) protect a free enterprise system by encouraging competition
   b) encourage better prices and better products
   c) level the playing field for entrepreneurs and small businesses
   d) All of the above

3. To be prohibited under the antitrust laws, an act must be:
   a) the result of a conspiracy
   b) profitable
   c) an unreasonable restraint of trade
   d) Both a) and c)

4. The broker of ABC Realty tells her salespersons not to take listings with less than a 5% commission. This activity is:
   a) prohibited under the Sherman Act as a restraint of trade
   b) an example of a conspiracy
   c) an example of group action
   d) legal

5. An act that is not illegal *per se* under the antitrust laws, but that causes a restraint of trade, may still be a violation under the:
   a) rule of reason
   b) law of restraint
   c) conspiracy test
   d) None of the above

6. The agency in charge of enforcing the Sherman Act is the:
   a) Federal Bureau of Investigation
   b) Antitrust Division of the U.S. Department of Justice
   c) Federal Trade Commission
   d) Both b) and c)

7. City Realty and Country Realty agree to charge a 6% commission on listings. This is an example of:
   a) price fixing
   b) a conspiracy
   c) group activity
   d) All of the above

8. Builder Jones wants to buy a lot from a developer, but the developer insists that Builder Jones list the completed home with the developer's broker. This is an example of a:
   a) tie-in arrangement
   b) list-back agreement
   c) Both a) and b)
   d) None of the above

9. There are only two real estate brokers in the town of Little Village. They agree that one of them will take all the listings on the east side of town, and that the other broker will take all the listings on the west side of town. This is:
   a) legal, because they are the only two brokers in town
   b) illegal, because it is an example of market allocation
   c) legal, so long as they don't fix prices
   d) None of the above

10. To avoid antitrust violations, brokers should:
    a) never use listing forms that contain pre-printed commission rates
    b) never discuss commissions or business plans with competitors
    c) train their licensees to be aware of the antitrust law
    d) All of the above

Chapter Answer Key

Chapter Quiz Answers:

1. a) California's antitrust law is known as the Cartwright Act.

2. d) When businesses conspire to control prices or to limit products by reducing competition, consumers usually end up paying higher prices and innovation is reduced. In addition, there is less incentive for entrepreneurs and small businesses to enter and compete in the market.

3. d) To be prohibited under the antitrust laws, an action must be the result of a conspiracy that unreasonably restrains trade.

4. d) For purposes of the antitrust law, a brokerage is considered to be an individual entity; therefore, the broker's action is legal. To be a violation of the antitrust law, there must be a conspiracy to restrain trade. A conspiracy is an act by two or more persons, not an individual.

5. a) The rule of reason is a balancing test that courts apply to determine whether an activity or practice creates an unreasonable restraint of trade.

6. d) The Sherman Antitrust Act is enforced by both the Antitrust Division of the U.S. Department of Justice and by the Federal Trade Commission. Both agencies may pursue civil cases against violators, but only the Department of Justice may pursue criminal charges.

7. d) The conspiracy between competitors to set commissions at 6% is a group action to commit price fixing, which is an illegal act under the antitrust laws.

8. c) A tie-in arrangement occurs when a buyer is required to purchase one product or service in order to purchase another product or service. If a list-back agreement is a required condition of a transaction, it is a tie-in arrangement.

9. b) Market allocation is an illegal activity under the antitrust laws. It doesn't matter that there are no other brokers in town, or that the brokers haven't agreed to fix prices. Under the antitrust laws, it is automatically illegal for competing brokers to agree not to sell in specified areas.

10. d) To avoid antitrust violations, a broker should never use listing forms with pre-printed commission rates; never discuss commissions or business plans with competitors; and should always train their licensees to be aware of federal and state antitrust laws and how they impact the real estate business.

Cases to Consider... Answers:

Unreasonable Restraints

Derish v. San Mateo-Burlingame Bd. of Realtors (1982) 136 Cal.App.3d 534. Allowing only licensed real estate brokers and agents to use the MLS does not violate antitrust laws. The MLS facilitates an exchange of information among competitors that increases economic efficiency and makes the market more competitive. It aids buyers and sellers by increasing the access to and exposure of a greater number of homes. Under a rule of reason analysis, it is reasonable to limit access to licensed professionals, because the real estate commission cannot guarantee the same level of competence and regulation over non-licensees. Without some assurance that everyone on the MLS is capable and qualified to act as a subagent, with professional standards, brokers would stop using the MLS to exchange information—and the pro-competitive benefits of the MLS would be lost.

Group Boycotts

Feldman v. Sacramento Bd. of Realtors, Inc. (1981) 119 Cal.App.3d 739. The court found that Feldman had the burden of proving that the defendant's MLS practices had a substantial or serious effect on the real estate market, not just on an individual broker. The purpose of the antitrust laws is to protect consumers and the public by encouraging healthy competition; protecting an individual competitor (Feldman) is only of secondary concern. The fact that Feldman chose to practice statewide, and couldn't afford the associated MLS fees and dues or meet the local board requirements for membership, is not proof of a monopoly or group boycott on the part of the local multiple listing services.

List of Cases

Classen v. Weller (1983) 145 Cal.App.3d 27
Derish v. San Mateo-Burlingame Bd. of Realtors (1982) 136 Cal.App.3d 534
Feldman v. Sacramento Bd. of Realtors, Inc. (1981) 119 Cal.App.3d 739
Marin County Bd. of Realtors, Inc. v. Palsson (1976) 16 Cal.3d 920
United States v. Real Estate Boards (1950) 339 U.S. 485

Glossary

Abandonment—Failure to occupy and use property, which may result in loss of rights.

Absolute Fee—*See:* Fee Simple.

Abstract of Judgment—A summary of the provisions of a court judgment which, when recorded, creates a lien on all of the real property of the debtor within the county where recorded.

Abstract of Title—A brief, chronological summary of the recorded documents affecting the title to a particular piece of property.

Abut—To touch, border on, be adjacent to, or share a common boundary with.

Acceleration Clause—A provision in a promissory note or a security instrument allowing the lender to declare the entire debt due immediately if the borrower breaches one or more provisions of the loan agreement. Also referred to as a call provision.

Acceptance—1. Agreeing to the terms of an offer to enter into a contract, thereby creating a binding contract. 2. Taking delivery of a deed from the grantor.

Accord and Satisfaction—An agreement to accept something different than, and usually less than, what was called for in the original agreement.

Accretion—A gradual addition to dry land by the forces of nature, as when waterborne sediment is deposited on waterfront property.

Acknowledgment—When a person who has signed a document formally declares to an authorized official, such as a notary public or county clerk, that he or she signed willingly. The official can then attest that the signature is voluntary and genuine.

Acre—An area of land equal to 43,560 square feet; or 4,840 square yards. There are 640 acres in a section of land in the government survey system.

Actual Notice—Actual knowledge of a fact, as opposed to knowledge imputed by law.

ADA—*See:* Americans with Disabilities Act.

Adjacent—Nearby, next to, bordering, or neighboring; may or may not be in actual contact.

Adjustable-Rate Mortgage—A mortgage loan with an interest rate that is periodically increased or decreased during the loan term.

Administrator—A person appointed by the probate court to manage and distribute the estate of a deceased person when no executor is named in the will, or there is no will.

ADR—*See:* Alternative Dispute Resolution.

Ad Valorem—A Latin phrase meaning "according to value," used to refer to taxes assessed on the value of property. Ad valorem taxes are also known as general real estate taxes.

Adverse Possession—Acquiring title to real property owned by someone else, by means of open, notorious, exclusive, continuous and uninterrupted possession of the property, in a manner hostile to the title of the owner, for five years. In California, an adverse possessor must also prove that she paid the property taxes on the disputed property during the prescribed period.

Affirm—1. To confirm or ratify. 2. To make a solemn declaration that is not under oath.

After-Acquired Title—Title acquired by a grantor after he attempted to convey an interest in property that he did not own.

Agency—A relationship of trust created when one person, the principal, delegates to another, the agent, authority to represent the principal in dealings with third parties.

Agency, Actual—When a principal appoints someone to act as his agent, and the agent accepts the appointment, they have created an express agreement called an actual agency.

Agency, Apparent—*See:* Agency, Ostensible.

Agency, Dual—When an agent represents both parties to a transaction, as when a broker represents both the buyer and the seller.

Agency, Exclusive—*See:* Listing, Exclusive Agency.

Agency, Ostensible—When third parties are given the impression that someone who has not been authorized to represent another is that person's agent, or else given the impression that an agent has been authorized to perform acts which are in fact beyond the scope of his or her authority. Also called apparent agency.

Agency by Implication—Agency created when an agent allows a third party to believe that an agency relationship exists between agent and principal.

Agency by Ratification—When the principal gives verbal or written approval to an agent's actions after the fact, this creates an agency by ratification.

Agency Coupled With an Interest—When an agent has a claim against the property that is the subject of the agency, so that the principal cannot revoke the agent's authority.

Agent—A person authorized to represent another (the principal) in dealings with third parties.

Agent, Dual—*See:* Agency, Dual.

Agent, General—An agent authorized to handle all of the principal's affairs in one area or in specified areas.

Agent, Special—An agent with limited authority to do a specific thing or conduct a specific transaction.

Agent, Universal—An agent authorized to do everything that can be lawfully delegated to a representative.

Agreed Boundary Doctrine—If uncertainty exists as to a boundary line, the neighbors may agree to a boundary (such as a fence); if they acquiesce to the agreed boundary for a specified period of time, it becomes binding.

Agreement—*See:* Contract.

Air Lot—A parcel of property above the surface of the earth, not containing any land; for example, a condominium unit on the third floor.

Air Rights—The right to undisturbed use and control of the airspace over a given parcel of land; may be transferred separately from the land.

Alienation—The transfer of title, ownership, or an interest in property from one person to another, by any means.

Alienation, Involuntary—Transfer of an interest in property against the will of the owner, or without action by the owner, occurring by operation of law, through natural processes, or by adverse possession.

Alienation, Voluntary—Voluntary transfer of real property from one person to another.

Alienation Clause—A provision in a security instrument that gives the lender the right to declare the entire loan balance due immediately if the borrower sells or otherwise transfers the security property. Also called a due-on-sale clause.

Alluvion—The solid material deposited along a river bank or shore by accretion. Also called alluvium.

Alternative Dispute Resolution (ADR)—Using mediation or arbitration to resolve a legal dispute as an alternative to a courtroom trial.

Americans with Disabilities Act (ADA)—A federal law that prohibits employment discrimination based on disability, and mandates equal access to public accommodations for the disabled.

Amortize—To gradually pay off a debt with installment payments that include both principal and interest.

Annexation, Actual—When personal property is physically attached to real property, so that it becomes part of the real property.

Annexation, Constructive—When personal property becomes associated with real property in such a way that the law treats it as a fixture, even though it is not physically attached; for example, a house key is constructively annexed to the house.

Annual Percentage Rate (APR)—All of the charges the borrower will pay for the loan (including the interest rate, origination fee, discount points, and mortgage insurance fees), expressed as an annual percentage of the loan amount.

Answer—In a lawsuit, the defendant's response to the plaintiff's complaint.

Anticipatory Repudiation—When one party to a contract informs the other before the time set for performance that he or she does not intend to fulfill the terms of the contract.

Anti-Deficiency Rules—Laws that prohibit a secured lender from suing the borrower for a deficiency judgment in certain circumstances (for example, after nonjudicial foreclosure of a deed of trust).

Appeal—When one of the parties to a lawsuit asks a higher court to review the judgment or verdict reached in a lower court.

Appellant—The party appealing a decision or ruling. Also called the petitioner.

Appellee—In an appeal, the party who did not file the appeal. Also called the respondent.

Apportionment—A division of property (as among tenants in common when the property is sold or partitioned) or liability (as when responsibility for closing costs is allocated between the buyer and the seller) into proportionate, but not necessarily equal, parts.

Appraisal—An estimate or opinion of the value of a piece of property as of a certain date. Also called a valuation.

Appraiser—One who estimates the value of real or personal property, especially an expert qualified to do so by training and experience.

Appreciation—An increase in value; the opposite of depreciation.

Appropriation—Taking property or reducing it to personal possession, to the exclusion of others.

Appropriation, Prior—A system of allocating water rights, under which a person who wants to use water from a certain lake or river in a way that will diminish the quantity or flow is required to apply for a permit. The permit will have priority over other permits that are issued later. *Compare:* Riparian Rights.

Appropriative Rights—The water rights of a person who holds an appropriation permit.

Appurtenances—Rights that go along with ownership of a particular piece of property, such as air rights or mineral rights; they are ordinarily transferred with the property, but may, in some cases, be sold separately.

Appurtenances, Intangible—Rights that go with ownership of real property which do not involve physical objects or substances; for example, an access easement (as opposed to mineral rights).

Arbitration—Submitting a disputed matter to a private party (rather than to the judicial system) for resolution.

Area—1. Locale or region. 2. The size of a surface, usually stated in square units of measure, such as square feet or square miles.

Artificial Person—A person created by law, with legal rights and responsibilities, such as a corporation, as distinguished from a natural person (a human being). *Compare:* Natural Person.

Assessment—1. The valuation of property for taxation. 2. A non-recurring specific charge against property for a definite purpose, such as curbs or sewers (usually called a special assessment) 3. A regular or special charge by a homeowners association to pay for routine maintenance or major repairs and improvements.

Assessor—An official who determines the value of property for purposes of taxation.

Asset—Anything of value that a person owns.

Assets, Liquid—Cash, and other assets that can readily be turned into cash (liquidated). Real estate holdings are not considered to be liquid assets.

Assign—To transfer rights or interests to another.

Assignee—One to whom rights or interests have been assigned.

Assignment—1. A transfer of contract rights from one person to another. 2. In the case of a lease, when the original tenant transfers his or her entire leasehold estate to another. *Compare:* Sublease.

Assignor—One who has assigned his or her rights or interests to another.

Assumption—When a buyer takes on personal liability for paying off the seller's existing mortgage or deed of trust.

Assumption Fee—A fee paid to the lender, usually by the buyer, when a mortgage is assumed.

Attachment—Court-ordered seizure of property belonging to a defendant in a lawsuit, so that it will be available to satisfy a judgment if the plaintiff wins. In the case of real property, attachment creates a lien.

Attachment Lien—*See:* Attachment Lien.

Attachments, Man-Made—*See:* Fixture.

Attachments, Natural—Plants growing on a piece of land, such as trees, shrubs, or crops.

Attestation—The act of witnessing the execution of an instrument (such as a deed or will).

Attorney in Fact—Any person authorized to represent another by a power of attorney; not necessarily a lawyer (an attorney at law).

Attractive Nuisance—A dangerous structure or condition on property that is or may be particularly attractive to children.

Authority, Actual—Authority actually given to an agent by the principal, either expressly or by implication.

Authority, Express—Authority that is specifically communicated from the principal to the agent, either orally or in writing.

Authority, Implied—An agent's authority to do everything reasonably necessary to carry out the principal's express orders.

Authority, Ostensible—Authority that a principal, intentionally or negligently, causes or allows a third person to believe the agent has.

Avulsion—1. When land is suddenly (not gradually) torn away by the action of water. 2. A sudden shift in a watercourse.

Balance Sheet—A summary of facts showing the financial condition of an individual or business, including a detailed list of assets and liabilities. Also called a financial statement.

Balloon Payment—A payment on a loan (usually the final payment) that is significantly larger than the regular installment payments.

Bankruptcy—1. When the liabilities of a person, firm, or corporation exceed its assets. 2. When a court declares a person, firm, or corporation to be insolvent, so that the assets and debts will be administered under the bankruptcy laws.

Bargain and Sale Deed—A deed that conveys title but does not make the same promises as a full warranty deed.

Base Line—In the government survey system, a main east-west line from which township lines are established. Each principal meridian has one base line associated with it.

Bench Mark—A surveyor's mark on a stationary object at a known point of elevation, used as a reference point in calculating other elevations in a surveyed area; often a metal disk set into cement or rock.

Beneficiary—1. One for whom a trust is created and on whose behalf the trustee administers the trust. 2. One entitled to receive real or personal property under a will; a devisee or legatee. 3. The lender in a deed of trust transaction.

Bequeath—To transfer personal property to another by will.

Bequest—Personal property (including money) that is transferred by a will.

Bilateral Contract—*See:* Contract, Bilateral.

Bill—A proposed law introduced in either house of the legislature.

Bill of Sale—A document used to transfer title to personal property from one person to another.

Binder—1. An instrument providing immediate insurance coverage to an insured person until the regular policy is issued. 2. Any payment or preliminary written statement intended to make an agreement legally binding until a formal contract has been drawn up.

Blanket Mortgage—*See:* Mortgage, Blanket.

Block—In a subdivision, a group of lots surrounded by streets or unimproved land.

Blockbusting—Attempting to induce owners to list or sell their homes by predicting that members of another race or ethnic group, or people suffering from some disability, will be moving into the neighborhood, with the suggestion that this will lower property values. Also called panic selling.

Board of Directors—A board elected by the members of a homeowners association to make management decisions.

Bona Fide—In good faith; not fraudulent.

Bona Fide Purchaser—A person who has no actual or constructive notice of a prior interest, and who acquired a later interest in the property for value.

Boundary—The perimeter or border of a parcel of land; the dividing line between one piece of property and another.

Bounds—Boundaries. *See:* Metes and Bounds Description.

Branch Manager—An associate broker designated by a firm's primary broker to manage the operations of a branch office.

Breach—Violation of an obligation, duty, or law.

Breach, Material—A breach of contract serious enough that the other party is excused from performing his or her side of the bargain.

Breach of Contract—The unexcused failure to perform according to the terms of a contract.

Broker—A natural or artificial person that is licensed to represent members of the public in real estate transactions for compensation.

Broker, Associate—A person who has qualified as a real estate broker, but is affiliated with another broker.

Broker/Salesperson Agreement—A broker/ salesperson agreement contains all of the basic terms of the employment relationship, such as the duties of the parties, the amount and type of supervision by the broker, the basis for the licensee's compensation, and the grounds for terminating the relationship.

Brokerage—A real estate broker's business.

Brokerage Fee—The commission or other compensation charged for a real estate broker's services.

Building Codes—Rules set up by local governments regarding minimum construction standards.

Building Restrictions—Rules concerning building size, placement, or type; they may be public restrictions (in a zoning ordinance, for example) or private restrictions (CC&Rs, for example).

Bundle of Rights—The rights inherent in ownership of real property, including the right to use, lease, enjoy, encumber, will, sell, or do nothing with the property.

Bureau of Real Estate (CalBRE)—The state agency in charge of administering the Real Estate Law in California.

Business Opportunity—A business that is for sale.

Buyer Representation Agreement—An employment contract between a buyer and real estate broker in which the broker agrees to serve as the buyer's agent in the search for a property to purchase.

Call—In a metes and bounds description, a specification that describes a segment of the boundary; for example, "south 15° west 120 feet" is a call.

CalEPA—The California Environmental Protection Agency.

California Endangered Species Act—A state law that prohibits harming or adversely affecting the habitat of any species that has been listed as endangered (or is a candidate for listing) by the state government.

California Environmental Quality Act (CEQA)—A state law requiring an environmental impact report for every public or private project in California that is likely to have a significant impact on the environment.

California Housing Financial Discrimination Act—*See:* Holden Act.

Cancellation—Termination of a contract without undoing acts that have already been performed under the contract.

Capacity—The legal ability or competency to perform some act, such as entering into a contract or executing a deed or will. *See:* Competent.

Capture, Rule of—A legal rule that grants a landowner the right to all oil or gas produced from wells on his or her land, even if the oil or gas migrated from underneath land belonging to someone else.

Cartwright Act—A California antitrust law.

Case Law—*See:* Common Law.

CC&Rs—A declaration of covenants, conditions, and restrictions; usually recorded by a developer to place restrictions on all lots within a new subdivision.

CERCLA—The Comprehensive Environmental Response, Compensation and Liability Act; a federal law that established the Superfund to clean up hazardous substances, and a process for determining liability for the cleanup costs.

Certificate of Occupancy—A statement issued by a local government verifying that a newly constructed building is in compliance with all building codes and may be occupied.

Chain of Title—*See:* Title, Chain of.

Civil Law—The body of law concerned with the rights and liabilities of one private party in relation to another, as distinguished from criminal law. Contract law is an example of civil law.

Civil Rights—Fundamental rights guaranteed to a person by the law. The term is most often used in reference to constitutional and statutory protections against discrimination or government interference.

Civil Rights Act of 1866—A federal law guaranteeing all citizens the right to purchase, lease, sell, convey, and inherit property, regardless of race or color.

Civil Wrong—*See:* Tort.

Claim of Right—Refers to a person trying to claim adverse possession by showing that she had the intent, evidenced by actions and conduct (rather than a document), to claim title to property to the exclusion of all others. *Compare:* Color of Title.

Clean Air Act—A federal law passed to maintain and enhance air quality.

Clean Water Act—A federal law passed to maintain and enhance the quality of the nation's water resources.

Client—One who employs a broker, a lawyer, or an appraiser. A real estate broker's client can be the seller, the buyer, or both, but is usually the seller.

Closing—The final stage in a real estate transaction, when the seller delivers the deed and the buyer pays the purchase price. Also called settlement.

Closing Costs—The expenses incurred in the transfer of real estate in addition to the purchase price. A typical list might include the appraisal fee, title insurance premium, real estate commission, excise tax, etc.

Closing Date—The date by which the terms of a contract must be met, or else the contract is terminated.

Closing Disclosure Form—Under TRID, a disclosure given to residential loan applicants at least three business days before closing that outlines all the fees and charges associated with closing.

Closing Statement—*See:* Settlement Statement.

Cloud on Title—Any claim, encumbrance, or apparent defect that makes title to real property unmarketable. *See:* Title, Marketable.

Codicil—An addition to or revision of a will. It must be executed with the same formalities as a will.

Codification—The collection and organization of piecemeal laws into a systematic, comprehensive statute called a code.

Collateral—Anything of value used as security for a debt or obligation.

Collusion—An agreement between two or more persons to defraud another.

Color of Title—Title that appears to be good title, but which in fact is not; commonly based on a defective instrument, such as an invalid deed. *Compare:* Claim of Right.

Commercial Bank—A type of financial institution that has traditionally emphasized commercial lending (loans to businesses), but which also makes many residential mortgage loans.

Commercial Property—Property zoned and used for business purposes, such as restaurants, hotels, retail stores, and office buildings; distinguished from residential, industrial, or agricultural property.

Commingling—1. Illegally mixing trust funds held on behalf of a client with personal or general business funds. 2. When separate and community property interests have been mixed so thoroughly that a court cannot trace the asset's origins; the separate property interest is usually treated as community property.

Commission—1. The compensation or fee paid to a broker for services rendered in a real estate transaction. 2. A group of people organized for a particular purpose or function.

Common Areas—1. In a condominium, planned unit development, or cooperative housing project, the land and improvements that are owned and used collectively by all the residents. Common areas usually include driveways, recreational facilities, and stairwells. Also called common elements. 2. In a building with leased units or space, the areas that are available for use by all of the tenants.

Common Interest Development—A subdivision containing commonly owned elements such as hallways, green space, or streets.

Common Elements, Limited—In a condominium, areas outside of the units (such as balconies or assigned parking spaces) that are designated for the use of particular unit owners, rather than all of the residents.

Common Law—The body of law based on the decisions of judges, developed in England and incorporated into the American legal system. Also called case law or decisional law.

Community Apartment—A subdivision in which each owner owns an undivided partial interest in the entire development and has an individual lease to his unit or lot. The owners own the development as tenants in common.

Community Property—Property owned jointly by a married couple in California and other community property states; generally, any property acquired during marriage through the labor or skill of either spouse (but not through gift or inheritance) belongs to both spouses equally. *Compare:* Separate Property.

Community Property Agreement—An agreement between spouses or registered domestic partners; allows the community property share of the first spouse to die to pass automatically to the surviving spouse without probate.

Community Property with Right of Survivorship—Community property that automatically passes to the surviving spouse without probate when a spouse dies.

Competent—1. Of sound mind. 2. Legally qualified to enter into a contract, by virtue of being of sound mind and having reached the age of majority.

Complaint—Legal papers that outline a dispute, which must be filed to start a lawsuit.

Comprehensive Environmental Response, Compensation, and Liability Act—*See:* CERCLA.

Comprehensive Plan—*See:* General Plan.

Concurrent Ownership—A form of ownership in which two or more people share title to one property at the same time. Also called a co-tenancy.

Condemnation—1. The taking of private property for public use (for streets, sewers, airports, railroads, etc.) through the government's power of eminent domain. 2. A declaration that a structure is unsafe and must be closed or destroyed.

Condition—A provision in an agreement or contract, limiting the rights and obligations of the parties or making them contingent on the occurrence or nonoccurrence of a specified event.

Conditional Fee—An ownership estate that may be terminated by the previous owner if specified conditions are not met. Also called a fee simple subject to condition subsequent. *See:* Fee Simple Defeasible.

Conditional Use Permit—A permit that allows a special use, such as a school or hospital, to operate in a neighborhood where it would otherwise be prohibited by the zoning. Also called a special exception permit.

Condominium—Property developed for concurrent ownership, where each co-owner has a separate interest in an individual dwelling unit, combined with an undivided interest in the property's common areas.

Condominium Association—*See:* Unit Owners Association.

Condominium Bylaws—The rules governing the operation of a condominium development.

Consent—To agree, to give permission or assent.

Conservation—1. Regarding real estate, preservation of structures or neighborhoods in a sound and favorable condition. 2. Regarding natural resources, preserving or using them in a way that provides the most long-term benefit.

Consideration—Anything of value given to induce another person to enter into a contract, such as money, services, goods, or a promise. Sometimes called valuable consideration.

Conspiracy—An agreement or plan between two or more persons to perform an unlawful act (or to use illegal methods to achieve a legal purpose).

Construction Lien—*See:* Mechanic's Lien.

Constructive Annexation—A doctrine holding that some moveable items are so strongly connected with real property that they are considered fixtures.

Constructive Eviction—When a landlord's actions interfere with a tenant's rights seriously enough to force the tenant to vacate the premises.

Constructive Severance—Constructive severance occurs when an interest in the land has been sold or transferred separately from the real property, but the interest in question still remains in, on, or attached to the land itself.

Consumer Credit—All credit given to individuals, rather than businesses, for personal, family, or household use.

Consumer Financial Protection Bureau—A federal agency that oversees financial institutions and enforces federal consumer finance laws.

Contiguous—Physically adjoining, abutting, or in close proximity.

Contingency Clause—A provision in a contract that makes one party's obligation to perform dependent upon the occurrence of a certain event.

Contour—The surface shape or configuration of land. A contour map depicts the topography by means of lines, called contour lines, which connect points of equal elevation.

Contract—An agreement, for consideration and between competent parties, to do or not do a certain thing. It is an agreement enforceable at law.

Contract, Bilateral—A contract in which each party promises to perform something in exchange for the other's promise to perform.

Contract, Executory—A contract in which one or both parties have not yet completed performance. (An executed contract, on the other hand, is one in which both parties have completely performed their obligations under the contract.)

Contract, Express—A clear and definite contract set forth in words.

Contract, Implied—One implied by the actions of the principals; in contrast to an express contract, in which the words forming the agreement are stated, orally or in writing.

Contract, Oral—A spoken agreement.

Contract, Real Estate—*See:* Real Estate Contract.

Contract, Unenforceable—A contract that will not be enforced by a court because its contents can't be proven (usually an oral contract); or because it is of a type required to be in writing (such as a real estate contract), but is not.

Contract, Unilateral—A contract that is accepted by performance. The offeror is not required to perform his part of the contract until the offeree has performed.

Contract, Valid—A binding, legally enforceable contract.

Contract, Void—A "contract" that is really not a contract because it lacks one of the key elements, such as consideration or a lawful objective.

Contract, Voidable—A valid contract that may be terminated without liability by one or both of the parties (because of fraud, undue influence, duress, or mistake, or because the party seeking to terminate the agreement is a minor).

Contract of Sale—*See:* Purchase Agreement.

Contractor—One who contracts to provide labor or materials, or construct a building, or do other work for a certain price.

Conversion—1. Misappropriating property or funds belonging to another; for example, converting trust funds to one's own use. 2. The process by which an existing building is turned into a condominium.

Conveyance—The transfer of title to real property from one person to another by means of a written document, such as a deed.

Cooperating Agent—A member of a multiple listing service who helps find a buyer for property listed by another brokerage company within the same multiple listing service.

Cooperative—A building or project owned by a nonprofit corporation. In a cooperative, the residents purchase shares in the corporation that owns the building. A resident receives a proprietary lease on a living unit and the right to use the common areas.

Corporation—An association organized according to certain laws, in which individuals may purchase ownership shares; regarded by the law as an artificial person, separate from the individual shareholders.

Correction Lines—Adjustment lines used in the government survey system to compensate for curvature of the earth. They occur at 24-mile intervals, every fourth township line, where the distance between north and south range lines is corrected to six miles.

Co-Tenancy—*See:* Concurrent Ownership.

Counteroffer—A new offer made by the offeree in reply to an offer to enter into a contract. It constitutes a rejection of the first offer, and the roles of the two parties are now reversed. The original offeror is the offeree and can accept or reject the counteroffer.

County—An administrative subdivision of the State, created by the State and deriving all of its powers from the State.

Course—In a metes and bounds description, a direction, stated in terms of a compass bearing.

Covenant—1. A written agreement or promise to do or not do something. 2. A stipulation that a property will be used or will not be used for a particular purpose or purposes. 3. A guarantee that some state of facts exists (such as the fact that a grantor has good title to real property).

Covenant, Restrictive—A promise to do or refrain from doing an act relating to real property, especially such a promise that runs with the land; usually imposed by a grantor on all subsequent owners of the property. Also called deed restrictions.

Covenant of Quiet Enjoyment—A promise that a buyer or tenant's possession of the property will not be disturbed by the previous owner, the landlord, or anyone else making a lawful claim against the property; implied promise that is included by law in every lease agreement.

Credit—A payment that is receivable (as opposed to a debit, which is a payment due).

Creditor, Secured—A creditor who has a lien on specific property, such as a mortgagee.

Customer—In real estate, usually a prospective purchaser.

Davis-Sterling Common Interest Development Act—A state law that requires any subdivision containing property owned in common to have a homeowners association.

Damage Deposit—*See:* Security Deposit.

Damages—The amount of money one can recover as compensation for an injury to his or her person or property resulting from an act or failure to act.

Damages, Compensatory—The amount of money awarded for an injury, or a loss incurred.

Damages, Liquidated—A sum that the parties to a contract agree in advance (at the time the contract is made) will serve as full compensation in the event of a breach.

Datum—A reference point used by surveyors to determine elevation.

Debit—A charge listed on a settlement statement, showing a debt or payment owed by one of the parties.

Debtor—One who owes something (usually money) to another.

Decedent—A person who has died.

Decisional Law—*See:* Common Law.

Declaration of Abandonment—A recorded document voluntarily releasing a property from homestead protection.

Declaration of Homestead—A document claiming homestead protection for a property.

Declaration of Restrictions—*See:* CC&Rs.

Dedication—An appropriation or granting of private property for public use; may be a grant of the entire fee simple interest or just an easement (such as an easement for sidewalks or streets).

Dedication, Implied—Transfer of land from private to public ownership or use by virtue of the private owner's acquiescence to public use of the land for an extended period of time. Also known as common law dedication.

Dedication, Statutory—Transfer of land from private to public ownership as required by law, as a prerequisite to subdivision approval, for example.

Deed—A written instrument that, when properly executed and delivered, conveys title to real property from the grantor to the grantee.

Deed, Correction—A deed used to correct minor mistakes in an earlier deed, such as misspellings of names or errors in description of the parcel.

Deed, Grant—The most common deed in California, giving the grantee current and any after-acquired title and warranting ownership and the absence of undisclosed encumbrances.

Deed, Partial Reconveyance—The document used to release a portion of the secured property from the lien of a blanket deed of trust.

Deed, Quitclaim—A deed that operates to convey and release any interest in a piece of real property that the grantor may have. It contains no warranties of any kind, but does transfer any right, title, or interest the grantor has at the time the deed is executed.

Deed, Sheriff's—A deed delivered by the sheriff, on court order, to the holder of the Certificate of Sale following the period of redemption after a mortgage foreclosure.

Deed, Trustee's—A deed given to the successful bidder at a trustee's sale in the nonjudicial foreclosure of a deed of trust.

Deed, Warranty—A deed with greater protections than a grant deed; the grantor also warrants against defects in title that originated before or during the grantor's period of ownership.

Deed Executed Under Court Order—A deed, such as a sheriff's deed or tax deed, that is the result of a court action, such as foreclosure.

Deed in Lieu of Foreclosure—A deed given by a borrower to a lender to satisfy the debt and to avoid a foreclosure suit.

Deed of Partition—A deed used by co-owners, such as joint tenants or tenants in common, to divide up the co-owned property so that each can own a separate portion.

Deed of Release—A deed used to release property (or part of it) from a lien created by a land contract. Most often used when the contract covers more than one parcel of land.

Deed of Reconveyance—The instrument used to release the security property from the lien created by a deed of trust when the debt has been repaid.

Deed of Trust—One of the two main types of security instruments used to finance the purchase of real estate, the other being a mortgage. Under the deed of trust, the power to sell the secured property in the event of default by the trustor (the borrower) is given to an independent third party (the trustee) to protect the interests of the beneficiary (the lender) and the trustor. A deed of trust can be foreclosed at a trustee's sale. Unlike foreclosure of a mortgage, judicial intervention is not required, and there is no period of redemption following the trustee's sale. A trustee's deed is issued after the sale.

Deed Restrictions—Limitations in a deed restricting the use of the property, such as "Residential use only" or "No building over 35 feet in height." Also called restrictive covenants.

Default—Failure to fulfill an obligation, duty, or promise, as when a borrower fails to make loan payments or a tenant fails to pay rent.

Default Judgment—*See:* Judgment, Default.

Defeasance Clause—A clause in a mortgage, deed of trust, or lease that cancels or defeats a certain right upon the occurrence of a certain event.

Defeasible Fee—*See:* Fee Simple Defeasible.

Defendant—In a lawsuit, the individual or entity being sued.

Deficiency Judgment—*See:* Judgment, Deficiency.

Degree—In surveying, a unit of circular measurement equal to 1/360th of one complete rotation around a point in a plane.

Delivery—The legal transfer of an instrument evidencing title or ownership. A valid deed does not convey title unless it has been delivered (actually or constructively) to the grantee.

Density—The number of buildings or the number of occupants per unit of land (square mile, acre, etc.).

Deposit—1. Money offered as an indication of good faith in regard to the future performance of a contract to purchase real property. Also called earnest money. 2. A security deposit given to a landlord by a tenant.

Deposit Receipt—A written instrument used as a receipt for the good faith deposit and as an offer to purchase real property, which becomes a binding contract if accepted by the seller. Also called a purchase and sale agreement or contract of sale.

Deposition—Formal out-of-court testimony of a witness taken before trial, for possible use later in the trial. Testimony taken either for discovery, to determine the facts of the case, or when a witness will be unable to attend the trial, or both.

Depreciation—A loss in value. For appraisal purposes, depreciation results from physical deterioration (such as cracks in the foundation), functional obsolescence (such as old-fashioned plumbing or lighting fixtures), or economic obsolescence (such as deterioration in the neighborhood).

Design Lien—A lien available to architects, professional engineers, and land surveyors who provide services during the planning phase of construction. Once construction begins, the design lien terminates, but it can be replaced with a mechanic's lien.

Detached Residence—A home physically separated from other houses; not connected to another house by a common wall.

Detrimental Reliance—*See:* Estoppel.

Developed Land—Land that has been improved by man-made additions, such as buildings, roads, or sidewalks.

Developer—Someone who makes changes to bring land to its most profitable use by subdividing and/or improving it.

Devise—1. A gift of real property transferred by will. The donor is the testator and the recipient is the devisee. 2. To transfer real property by will. *Compare:* Bequest.

Devisee—A recipient of real property under a will. *Compare:* Beneficiary; Legatee.

Disability—According to the Americans with Disabilities Act and the Fair Housing Act, a physical or mental impairment that substantially limits a person in one or more major life activities.

Disaffirm—To ask a court to terminate a voidable contract.

Discount—1. An amount paid to the lender or withheld from the loan amount at the time a loan is made, to increase the lender's yield on the loan. 2. To sell a note at a reduced value or less than face value.

Discovery—The stage of a lawsuit in which each party is required to provide information about the case to the other party, in response to interrogatories (written questions), depositions (formal interviews of witnesses), and requests for the production of documents.

Discrimination—Unequal treatment, either favorable or unfavorable, based on the class, race, or other group to which a person or persons belong.

Disparate Impact—Occurs when a law or ordinance appears neutral on its face (seems to apply to everyone, equally), but actually affects some protected class of people more than other classes of people, thus having a discriminatory effect.

Diversity Jurisdiction—The federal courts' power to hear cases in which a citizen of one state sues a citizen of another state (or country).

Doctrine of Emblements—The right of a tenant farmer, under a lease of unspecified length, to re-enter a property to harvest the first crop that matures after termination of his lease.

Doctrine of Practical Location—A doctrine holding that if the owner of a larger tract conveys part of his property, marks the boundary with a fixed monument, and the parties accept the marked boundary, the location will prevail over any differing description in the deed.

Dominant Tenement—Property that receives the benefit of an appurtenant easement.

Downzoning—Rezoning land for a more restricted use.

Dual Agent—An agent who represents both the buyer and the seller in the same transaction.

Due-on-Sale Clause—*See:* Alienation Clause.

Due Process—A fair hearing by an impartial judge. Under the U.S. Constitution, no one may be deprived of life, liberty, or property without due process of law.

Duress—Unlawful force, constraint, threats, or other actions used to compel someone to do something (such as sign a contract) against his will.

Dwelling—A building or part of a building used or intended to be used as living quarters.

Earnest Money—*See:* Good Faith Deposit.

Easement—A right to use some part of another person's property for a particular purpose; for example, as a driveway, or for installing and maintaining a water line.

Easement, Implied—An easement created by law (not by express grant) when a property is divided into more than one parcel, when there was apparent prior use of the easement and it is reasonably necessary for the enjoyment of the dominant tenement. Also called an easement by implication.

Easement, Negative—An easement that prevents the landowner from using the land in a certain way; essentially the same thing as a restrictive covenant.

Easement, Positive—An easement that allows a landowner to use another's land for a specific purpose.

Easement Appurtenant—An easement for the benefit of a particular piece of property (the dominant tenement). *Compare:* Easement in Gross.

Easement by Express Grant—An easement granted to another by means of a deed or other document.

Easement by Express Reservation—An easement created by deed in favor of the grantor, who transfers the property (or part of the property) but reserves an easement for her own use.

Easement by Implication—*See:* Easement, Implied.

Easement by Necessity—An easement implied by law when a property is divided into more than one parcel if the dominant tenement would be completely useless without an easement, even though it was not a long-standing, apparent use.

Easement by Prescription—An easement that is established when someone makes use of another's property for a long time without permission. The use must be open and notorious, hostile, and continuous for five years.

Easement in Gross—An easement for the benefit of a person instead of a piece of land. *Compare:* Easement Appurtenant.

Egress—A passageway leading from property; a means of exiting. It is the opposite of ingress (entry). The terms ingress and egress usually refer to easements.

Emancipated Minor—A person under 18 who is or has been married, is on active duty in the military, or has a declaration of emancipation from a court.

Emblements—Crops, such as wheat or corn, that are produced annually through the labor of the cultivator.

Emblements, Doctrine of—The right of an agricultural tenant to enter land after termination of the lease for the purpose of harvesting crops.

Eminent Domain—The power of the government to take (condemn) private property for public use, upon payment of just compensation to the owner.

Employee—Someone who works under the direction and control of another. *Compare:* Independent Contractor.

Encroachment—Unlawful physical intrusion onto the property of another, usually as the result of mistake.

Encumber—To place a lien or other encumbrance against the title to a property.

Encumbrance—A nonpossessory interest in property; a lien, easement, or restrictive covenant burdening the property owner's title.

Endangered Species Act (ESA)—A federal law that prohibits harming or adversely affecting the habitat of any species that has been listed as endangered by the federal government.

Enjoin—To prohibit an act, or command performance of an act, by court order; to issue an injunction.

Environmental Impact Report (EIR)—An environmental impact assessment required by CEQA for all public and private projects within California that are likely to have a significant environmental impact.

Environmental Impact Statement (EIS)—An environmental impact assessment required by NEPA for all federal projects likely to have a significant environmental impact.

Environmental Protection Agency (EPA)—The federal agency in charge of overseeing toxic waste cleanups and other environmental matters.

Equal Credit Opportunity Act (ECOA)—A federal law prohibiting providers of credit from discriminating based on race, color, religion, national origin, sex, marital status, age, or because the applicant receives public assistance.

Equal Protection—Under the U.S. Constitution, all citizens are entitled to the equal protection of the laws; no law may arbitrarily discriminate between different groups, or be applied to different groups in a discriminatory manner.

Equitable Redemption Period—The period between the initial complaint and the sale of a foreclosed property, during which time a borrower may redeem the property by paying the amount of the debt plus costs.

Equitable Remedy—A remedy granted to a plaintiff that is something other than an award of money (damages), when money alone cannot adequately correct the problem, such as an injunction or an order of specific performance.

Equitable Title—The right to possess and enjoy property while paying off the purchase price in a land contract.

Equity—1. The difference between the value of a piece of property and the liens against it; an owner's unencumbered interest in his or her property. 2. In law, a judge's power to soften or set aside strict legal rules, to bring about a fair and just result in a particular case.

Erosion—Gradual loss of soil due to the action of water or wind.

Escheat—The reversion of property to the State when a person dies without leaving a will and no heirs entitled to the property can be located.

Escrow—An arrangement in which something of value (such as money or a deed) is held by a disinterested third party, called an escrow agent, until certain conditions specified in the escrow instructions have been fulfilled.

Escrow Agent—1. A neutral third party who holds money and documents in trust and carries out the closing process. 2. A company (not a natural person) that is licensed to engage in the escrow business.

Escrow Instructions—A written document that tells the escrow agent how to proceed and states the conditions each party must fulfill before the transaction can close.

Estate—1. A possessory interest in real property; either a freehold or a leasehold. 2. The property left by someone who has died.

Estate, Fee Simple—*See:* Fee Simple.

Estate at Will—*See:* Tenancy at Will.

Estate for Life—*See:* Life Estate.

Estate for Years—*See:* Tenancy, Term.

Estate in Remainder—*See:* Remainder.

Estate in Reversion—*See:* Reversion.

Estate of Inheritance—An estate that can be inherited by the owner's heirs, such as a fee simple estate.

Estoppel—A legal doctrine that prevents a person from asserting rights or facts that are inconsistent with his earlier actions or statements.

Eviction—Dispossession, expulsion, or ejection of a person from real property.

Eviction, Actual—Physically forcing someone off of property (or preventing them from re-entering), or using the legal process to make someone leave.

Eviction, Constructive—When a landlord's act (or failure to act) interferes with the tenant's quiet enjoyment of the property, or makes the property unfit for its intended use, to such an extent that the tenant is forced to move out.

Eviction, Retaliatory—When a landlord evicts a tenant in retaliation for requesting repairs, filing a complaint against the landlord, or organizing or participating in a tenants' rights group.

Eviction, Self-Help—When a landlord uses physical force, a lock-out, or a utility shut-off to get rid of a tenant, instead of using the legal process. (This is generally illegal.)

Excise Tax—*See:* Tax, Excise.

Exclusionary Zoning—Zoning practices that unreasonably restrict permits for multi-family or low-income housing in such a way as to have a discriminatory effect on minorities.

Exclusive Right to Sell—*See:* Listing, Exclusive Right to Sell.

Execute—1. To perform or complete. 2. To sign a document and take any other formal steps that may be necessary for its validity (such as acknowledgment).

Execution—A legal process in which the court orders the sheriff or another official to seize and sell the property of a debtor to satisfy a judgment lien or other lien.

Executor—A person named in a will to carry out the provisions of the will. (If it is a woman, she may be referred to as the executrix, although that term is passing out of use.)

Exemption—A provision holding that a law or regulation does not apply to a particular person or group. For example, a person entitled to a property tax exemption is not required to pay property taxes. An exemption can be full or partial.

Express—Stated in words, spoken or written (rather than merely implied by actions). *Compare:* Implied.

Extender Clause—*See:* Safety Clause.

Failure of Purpose—An excuse for rescinding a contract; if the contract cannot achieve its intended purpose, the parties are released from their obligations.

Fair Employment and Housing Act—*See:* Rumford Act.

Fair Housing Act—Title VIII of the Civil Rights Act of 1968; makes it illegal to discriminate in the sale or rental of residential property or vacant land that will be used for residential construction.

Fannie Mae—A popular name for the Federal National Mortgage Association (FNMA).

Fed—The Federal Reserve.

Federal Deposit Insurance Corporation (FDIC)—A federal agency that insures deposits in state and federally chartered banks and savings and loan associations.

Federal Home Loan Mortgage Corporation (FHLMC)—One of the three major secondary market entities. Commonly called Freddie Mac.

Federal Housing Administration (FHA)—An agency within the Department of Housing and Urban Development that provides mortgage insurance to encourage lenders to make more affordable home loans.

Federal National Mortgage Association (FNMA)—One of the three major secondary market entities. Commonly called Fannie Mae.

Federal Question—A legal question involving the U.S. Constitution, a treaty, or a federal statute. Federal question cases may be heard in federal court.

Federal Reserve System—The government body that regulates commercial banks and implements monetary policy in an attempt to control the national economy.

Federal Trade Commission (FTC)—A federal agency responsible for investigating and eliminating unfair and deceptive business practices.

Fee Simple—The greatest estate one can have in real property; of indefinite duration; with no conditions on the title; freely transferable or inheritable. Also known as a fee or a fee simple absolute.

Fee Simple Defeasible—A fee estate in real property that is subject to being defeated or undone if a certain event occurs or a certain condition is not met. Also known as a defeasible fee.

Fee Simple Determinable—A defeasible fee that is terminated automatically if certain events occur; abolished by California statute.

Fee Simple Subject to Condition Subsequent—A defeasible fee that may be terminated by the grantor after breach of a condition specified in the grant. The grantor has a power of termination.

FHA—Federal Housing Administration.

Fictitious Business Name—A fictitious business name is a name other than the name of the individual doing business. A licensee wishing to use a fictitious business name must follow procedures outlined in the Real Estate Law.

Fiduciary Relationship—A relationship of trust and confidence, in which one party owes the other (or both parties owe each other) loyalty and a higher standard of good faith than they owe to third parties. For example, an agent is a fiduciary in relation to the principal; husband and wife are fiduciaries in relation to one another.

Finance Charge—Any charge a borrower is assessed, directly or indirectly, in connection with a loan.

Financing Statement—A brief document that, when recorded, gives notice of a creditor's security interest in an item of personal property.

Finder's Fee—A referral fee paid to someone for directing a buyer or seller to a real estate agent.

Finding of Non-Significance (FONSI)—A determination by a federal agency that a proposed project will not have significant environmental impact, so that no environmental impact statement is required.

First Lien Position—The position held by a mortgage or deed of trust that has higher lien priority than any other mortgage or deed of trust against the property.

First Refusal, Right of—*See:* Right of First Refusal.

Fiscal Year—Any 12-month period used as a business year for accounting, tax, and other financial purposes, as opposed to the calendar year.

Fixed Term—A period of time which has a definite beginning date and ending date.

Fixture—An item that was personal property, but which has become affixed to or associated with real property in such a way that it has legally become part of the real property.

Fixture, Trade—Article of personal property annexed to real property by a tenant for use in his or her trade or business, which the tenant is allowed to remove at the end of the lease.

Foreclosure—When a lienholder causes property to be sold, so that the unpaid lien can be satisfied from the sale proceeds.

Foreclosure, Judicial—A lawsuit filed by a mortgagee or deed of trust beneficiary to foreclose on the security property when the borrower has defaulted.

Foreclosure, Nonjudicial—Foreclosure by a trustee under the power of sale clause in a deed of trust.

Forfeiture—Loss of a right or something else of value as a result of failure to perform an obligation or condition.

Fraud—An intentional or negligent misrepresentation or concealment of a material fact, which is relied upon by another, who is induced to enter a transaction and harmed as a result.

Fraud, Actual—Intentional deceit or misrepresentation.

Fraud, Constructive—Negligent misrepresentation, or a breach of duty that misleads the person the duty was owed to, without an intention to deceive.

Freddie Mac—A popular name for the Federal Home Loan Mortgage Corporation (FHLMC).

Free and Clear—Title to real property that is completely free of encumbrances such as mortgages, liens, and so forth.

Freehold—An ownership estate in real property; either a fee simple or a life estate. The holder of a freehold estate has title, whereas the holder of a less-than-freehold estate (leasehold estate) is merely a tenant, having a temporary right to possession, but no title.

Full Cash Value—Under California's Proposition 13, the fair market value of a home or new construction used to determine its assessed value for taxation purposes.

Future Estate—An interest in property that will or may become possessory at some point in the future, such as an estate in remainder or an estate in reversion.

Garnishment—A legal process by which a creditor may gain access to a debtor's personal property or funds that are in the hands of a third party. Items that may be garnished include wages, debts owed, security interests, and goods or personal effects concealed in the possession of third parties.

General Agent—*See:* Agent, General.

General Lien—*See:* Lien, General.

General Partnership—*See:* Partnership, General.

General Plan—A plan created by a city or county that spells out its land use goals and is used as a guide for the development of zoning regulations. Also called a comprehensive plan, city plan, or master plan.

Ginnie Mae—A popular name for the Government National Mortgage Association (GNMA).

Good Faith Deposit—A deposit made by a prospective purchaser of real estate as evidence of a good faith intention to complete the purchase. Also called an earnest money deposit.

Goodwill—An intangible asset of a business resulting from a good reputation with the public, serving as an indication of future return business.

Government Lot—In the government survey system, a parcel of land that is not a regular section (one mile square), because of the convergence of range lines, or because of a body of water or some other obstacle; assigned a government lot number.

Government National Mortgage Association (GNMA)—A government entity within HUD, popularly known as Ginnie Mae; one of the major secondary market entities, along with Fannie Mae and Freddie Mac.

Government Survey System—A system of land description in which the land is divided into squares called townships, each approximately six miles square (containing 36 square miles), which are divided into 36 sections, each approximately one mile square and containing approximately 640 acres. Also called the rectangular survey system or section, township, and range system.

Grant—To transfer or convey an interest in real property by means of a written instrument.

Grantee—One who receives a grant of real property.

Granting Clause—Words in a deed that indicate an intent to transfer an interest in land.

Grantor—One who grants an interest in real property to another.

Grantor/Grantee Indexes—Indexes of recorded documents maintained by the recorder, with each document listed in alphabetical order according to the last name of the grantor (in the grantor index) or the grantee (in the grantee index); the indexes list the recording number of each document, so that it can be located in the public record.

Group Boycott—An agreement between two or more real estate brokers to exclude other brokers from fair participation in real estate activities.

Guardian—A person appointed by a court to administer the affairs of a minor or a mentally incompetent person.

Guide Meridian—*See:* Meridian, Guide.

Habitability—*See:* Warranty of Habitability.

Heir—Someone entitled to inherit another's property under the laws of intestate succession.

Highest and Best Use—The use that is most likely to produce the greatest net return from the property over a given period of time.

Historic Preservation—The protection of historic buildings from destruction or unauthorized modifications.

Holden Act—A California law stating that it's against state public policy to deny mortgage loans or to impose stricter terms on loans because of neighborhood characteristics unrelated to the borrower's creditworthiness or the property's value. Also known as the California Housing Financial Discrimination Act.

Holder in Due Course—A person who obtains a negotiable instrument for value, in good faith, and without notice of any defenses against it.

Holdover Tenant—A tenant who fails to surrender possession of the premises at the end of the tenancy.

Home Mortgage Disclosure Act—A federal law requiring institutional lenders to make annual disclosures of all mortgage loans made, as a means of enforcing prohibitions against redlining.

Homeowners Association—A nonprofit association made up of every homeowner in a subdivision, responsible for enforcing the CC&Rs, maintaining any common elements, and managing other community affairs.

Homestead—A dwelling occupied by the owner or the owner's spouse as a principal residence.

Homestead, Declaration of—A document recorded to provide more protection than the automatic homestead exemption; it protects the proceeds of a voluntary sale as well as a forced sale, and the homeowner does not have to reside on the property when the exemption is claimed.

Homestead Exemption—The amount of a homeowner's equity that the homestead law protects against lien foreclosure.

Homestead Law—A state law that provides limited protection against creditors' claims for homestead property.

Housing Codes—Local regulations setting minimum standards for aspects of housing that affect health and safety.

HUD—The Department of Housing and Urban Development.

Hypothecate—To give real or personal property as security for an obligation without giving up possession of it. *Compare:* Pledge.

Implied—Not expressed in words, but understood from actions or circumstances. *Compare:* Express.

Impound Account—A bank account maintained by a lender for payment of property taxes and insurance premiums on the security property; the lender requires the borrower to make regular deposits, and pays the expenses out of the account. Also called a reserve account.

Improvements—Man-made additions to real property.

Imputed Knowledge—A legal doctrine stating that a principal is considered to have notice of information that the agent has, even if the agent never passed that information on to the principal.

Incompetent—1. Not legally qualified to enter into contracts, as in the case of a minor or a mentally ill person. 2. Not of sound mind.

Independent Contractor—A person who contracts to do work for another person, agreeing to achieve a certain result but retaining control over how she will carry out the task, rather than submitting to the control of the other person. Real estate brokers are usually independent contractors. *Compare:* Employee.

Indexing—A means of cataloging deeds and other documents in the recording office; deeds are indexed according to grantor and grantee, and sometimes according to the location of the land.

Ingress—A means of entering a piece of property, such as a driveway. The opposite of egress.

In-House Transaction—A sale in which the buyer and the seller are brought together by salespeople working for the same broker.

Injunction—A court order prohibiting someone from performing an act or commanding performance of an act.

Instrument—A legal document, usually one that transfers title (such as a deed), creates a lien (such as a mortgage), or establishes a right to payment (such as a promissory note or contract).

Insurance, Hazard—Insurance against losses on property caused by fire, flood, theft, or other disaster. Also called casualty insurance.

Insurance, Homeowner's—Casualty insurance that covers the homeowner's personal property as well as the real property.

Insurance, Title—Insurance that protects against losses resulting from undiscovered title defects. An owner's policy protects the buyer, while a mortgagee's policy protects the lien position of the buyer's lender.

Insurance, Title, Extended Coverage—A policy of title insurance that covers problems which should be discovered in an inspection of the property, such as adverse possession or encroachments.

Insurance, Title, Homeowner's Coverage—Like a standard coverage title insurance policy but with broader coverage; available only in transactions involving one- to four-unit residences.

Insurance, Title, Standard Coverage—Title insurance that protects against latent title defects (such as forged deeds) and undiscovered recorded encumbrances, but does not protect against problems that would only be discovered by an inspection of the property, such as adverse possessors or unrecorded easements.

Interest—1. A charge a borrower pays to a lender for the use of the lender's money. 2. A right or share in something (such as a piece of real estate).

Interest, Future—An interest in property that will or may become possessory at some point in the future, such as an estate in remainder or an estate in reversion.

Interest, Prepaid—Interest on a new loan that must be paid at the time of closing; covers the interest due for the first month of the loan term. Sometimes called interim interest.

Interest, Simple—Interest that is computed on the principal amount of the loan only. (This is the type of interest charged in connection with real estate loans.)

Interest, Undivided—A co-owner's interest, giving him or her the right to shared possession of the whole property, rather than exclusive possession of a particular section of it.

Interference with Contractual Relations—A tort caused when someone wrongfully interferes with the contract of another, causing a financial loss.

Interpleader—A court action filed by someone who is holding funds that two or more people are claiming. The holder turns the funds over to the court; the court resolves the dispute and delivers the money to the party who is entitled to it.

Interrogatories—A discovery tool similar to a deposition but conducted by mail instead of in person. One party sends a series of questions to the other and the other party must send back answers.

Interstate Land Sales Full Disclosure Act (ILSA)—A federal law that provides protections to interstate buyers of vacant lots in subdivisions containing 25 or more lots.

Intestate—Without a valid will.

Intestate Succession—Distribution of the property of a person who died intestate to his or her heirs.

Inverse Condemnation Action—A court action by a private landowner against the government, seeking compensation for damage to property caused by government action.

Investment Property—Unimproved property that produces no income, but is held in the expectation that it will appreciate in value.

Involuntary Lien—*See:* Lien, Involuntary.

Joint and Several Liability—*See:* Liability, Joint and Several.

Joint Tenancy—*See:* Tenancy, Joint.

Joint Venture—Two or more individuals joining together for one specific project as partners. A joint venture is of limited duration; if the members of the venture undertake another project together, the association may become a partnership.

Judgment—1. A court's binding determination of the rights and duties of the parties to a lawsuit. 2. A court order requiring one party to pay damages to the other.

Judgment, Default—A court judgment in favor of the plaintiff due to the defendant's failure to answer the complaint or appear at a hearing.

Judgment, Deficiency—A personal judgment entered against a borrower in favor of the lender if the proceeds from a foreclosure sale of the security property are not enough to pay off the debt.

Judgment Creditor—A person to whom money is owed by virtue of a judgment in a lawsuit.

Judgment Debtor—A person who owes money by virtue of a judgment in a lawsuit.

Judgment Lien—*See:* Lien, Judgment.

Judicial Foreclosure—*See:* Foreclosure, Judicial.

Jurisdiction, Personal—A trial court's authority to order a particular defendant into the court and pass judgment on him.

Jurisdiction, Subject Matter—A trial court's authority to hear the kind of case being brought.

Just Compensation—The compensation that the Constitution requires the government to pay a property owner when the property is taken under the power of eminent domain.

Kickback—An illegal commission or fee for referring clients to particular escrow agents, structural pest control firms, title insurers, etc.

Land—In a legal sense, the solid part of the surface of the earth (as distinguished from water), everything affixed to it, by nature or by human beings, or anything on it or in it, such as minerals and water.

Land Contract—A contract in which the buyer (vendee) purchases real property on an installment basis, and the seller (vendor) retains legal title to the property until the purchase price is paid in full. Also known as a real property sales contract, conditional sales contract, installment sales contract, or contract for deed.

Landlocked—A parcel of land without access to any type of road or highway. The owner of landlocked land may be able to obtain an easement by necessity from the court.

Landlord—A landowner who has leased his property. Also called a lessor.

Landmark—A monument, natural or artificial, set up on the boundary line of two adjacent estates in order to mark the boundary.

Latent Defects—Defects in property that are not visible or apparent.

Lateral Support—*See:* Support, Lateral.

Lawful Purpose—An objective of a contract that is not against the law.

Lease—A contract in which a landlord (lessor) grants a tenant (lessee) the possession of real estate in exchange for rent.

Leasehold Estate—The possessory interest that a tenant has in the leased property during the term of the lease.

Legal Description—A method of describing a parcel of real estate that is recognized by law, including the recorded map (lot and block) method, the government survey method (also called the township and range or rectangular survey method), or the metes and bounds method.

Legal Person—*See:* Artificial Person.

Legatee—A recipient of personal property under a will.

Lender, Institutional—A bank, savings and loan association, life insurance company, or similar organization that invests others' funds in mortgages and other loans; as distinguished from individual or private lenders who invest their own money.

Lessee—One who possesses or occupies property owned by another under the terms of a lease. Also called a tenant.

Lessor—One who has leased property to another. Also called a landlord.

Leverage—The effective use of borrowed money to finance an investment such as real estate.

Liability, Joint and Several—A form of liability in which several persons are responsible for a debt both individually and as a group. Any one of the individuals can be required to pay the entire debt if the others fail to pay their shares.

Liability, Vicarious—A legal doctrine stating that a principal can be held liable for harm to third parties resulting from an agent's actions.

Liable—Legally responsible.

License—1. Official permission to perform certain acts that the law does not allow everyone to do. 2. Revocable, non-assignable permission to enter land owned by someone else for a particular purpose. *Compare:* Easement.

Lien—A nonpossessory interest in property, giving the lienholder the right to foreclose if the owner does not pay a debt owed to the lienholder; a financial encumbrance on the owner's title.

Lien, Attachment—A lien on property intended to prevent transfer of the property pending the outcome of litigation.

Lien, Design—*See:* Design Lien.

Lien, Equitable—A lien arising as a matter of fairness, rather than by agreement or by operation of law.

Lien, General—A lien against all of the property of a debtor.

Lien, Involuntary—A lien that arises by operation of law, without consent of the property owner.

Lien, Judgment—A general lien against all of the property of a judgment debtor, making it possible for the judgment creditor to have the property sold to satisfy the debt.

Lien, Materialman's—Similar to a mechanic's lien, but it refers specifically to sums owed suppliers, as opposed to laborers, for materials provided in connection with a construction project.

Lien, Mechanic's—*See:* Mechanic's Lien.

Lien, Mello-Roos—*See:* Mello-Roos Lien.

Lien, Property Tax—A specific lien on property to secure payment of the property taxes.

Lien, Specific—A lien that attaches only to a particular piece of property, as opposed to a general lien, which attaches to all of the debtor's property.

Lien, Statutory—A lien created by operation of law, rather than by contract, such as a tax lien.

Lien, Tax—A lien on property to secure the payment of taxes.

Lien, Voluntary—A lien placed against property with the consent of the owner.

Lienholder, Junior—A secured creditor whose lien has lower priority than another lien against the same property.

Lien Priority—The order in which liens are paid off out of proceeds of the foreclosure sale.

Lien Theory—A legal theory holding that upon giving a mortgage or deed of trust as security for a debt, the borrower does not transfer title to the lender. The lender has a security interest during the period of indebtedness, but not title. *Compare:* Title Theory.

Life Estate—A freehold estate that lasts only as long as a specified person lives. That person is referred to as the measuring life.

Life Tenant—Someone who owns a life estate; the person entitled to possession of the property during the measuring life.

Limited Liability Company (LLC)—A business entity that combines the management and tax advantages of a partnership with the limited liability of a corporation.

Limited Partnership—A partnership in which the liability of some of the partners (the limited partners) is limited to the amount they invested.

Liquidated Damages—*See:* Damages, Liquidated.

Lis Pendens—A recorded notice stating that there is a lawsuit pending that may affect title to the defendant's real estate. Also called a notice of pendency.

List-Back Agreement—An arrangement that requires a builder, in order to buy a lot, to agree to list the completed property with a particular broker.

Listing—A written contract between a principal and an agent stipulating that the agent will be paid a commission for finding or attempting to find a ready, willing, and able buyer to purchase the seller's property on terms acceptable to the seller. Also called a listing agreement.

Listing, Exclusive—Either an exclusive agency listing or an exclusive right to sell listing.

Listing, Exclusive Agency—A listing agreement that entitles the broker to a commission if anyone other than the seller finds a buyer for the property during the listing term.

Listing, Exclusive Right to Sell—A listing agreement that entitles the broker to a commission if anyone—including the seller—finds a buyer for the property during the listing term.

Listing, Open—A nonexclusive listing, given by an owner to as many different brokers as he or she chooses. If the property is sold, a broker is only entitled to a commission if he or she is the procuring cause of the sale.

Litigants—The parties to a lawsuit; the plaintiff and defendant.

Living Trust—A type of trust that allows distribution of someone's property after her death without probate.

Loan, Conventional—A loan that is not insured or guaranteed by any government agency (such as the FHA or VA).

Loan Assumption Fee—A fee charged to the buyer by the existing lender in return for permission to assume an existing loan.

Loan Estimate Form—Under TRID, a disclosure given at the time of a residential loan application that states the best estimate of closing costs.

Loan-to-Value Ratio—The relationship between the loan amount and either the sales price or the appraised value of the property (whichever is less), expressed as a percentage.

Lock-In Clause—A clause in a promissory note or an installment sales contract prohibiting full payment of the debt before a date specified in the contract.

Lot—A parcel of land in a subdivision.

LTV—*See:* Loan-to-Value Ratio.

Mailbox Rule—A common law rule under which an acceptance communicated by mail is effective when the message has been sent (put into the mailbox), even though the offeror won't receive it right away.

Majority, Age of—Age at which a person becomes legally competent to enter into contracts and transactions; usually 18 years old.

Marketable Title—*See:* Title, Marketable

Market Price—The price actually paid for property. *Compare:* Value, Market.

Material Breach—*See:* Breach, Material.

Material Fact—Information that has a substantial negative impact on the value of the property, on a party's ability to perform, or on the purpose of the transaction.

Measuring Life—*See:* Life Estate.

Mechanic's Lien—A specific lien claimed by someone who performed work on the property (construction, repairs, or improvements) and has not been paid. Also called a construction lien.

Meeting of the Minds—*See:* Mutual Consent.

Mello-Roos Lien—A lien based on a type of special assessment allowed under the Mello-Roos Community Facilities Act, which allows communities to create special districts to finance certain kinds of improvements or services.

Merger—Uniting two or more separate properties by transferring ownership of all of them to one person.

Meridian—An imaginary line running north and south, passing through the earth's poles. Also called a longitude line.

Meridian, Guide—In the government survey system, one of the north-south lines, spaced 24 miles apart.

Meridian, Principal—In the government survey system, the main north-south line in a particular grid, used as the starting point in numbering the ranges.

Metes—Measurements. *See:* Metes and Bounds Description.

Metes and Bounds Description—A method of legal description that starts at an easily identifiable point of beginning, then describes the property's boundaries in terms of courses (compass directions) and distances, ultimately returning to the point of beginning.

Mill—One-tenth of one cent; the measure used to state the property tax rate. A tax rate of one mill on the dollar is the same as a rate of one-tenth of 1% of the assessed value of property.

Mineral Rights—Rights to the minerals located beneath the surface of a piece of property.

Minor—A person who has not reached the age at which the law recognizes a general contractual capacity (usually 18 years old).

Misrepresentation—An incorrect or false statement. *See:* Fraud.

Mitigation—When the nonbreaching party takes action to minimize the losses resulting from a breach of contract.

MLO Endorsement—An endorsement on a real estate license that allows a licensee to broker mortgage loans.

MLS—Multiple Listing Service.

Monetary Policy—The Federal Reserve Board's effort to control the supply and cost of money in the United States.

Monopoly—When one seller of goods, or provider of services, has exclusive control over a market, resulting in lack of competition and higher prices for consumers.

Monument—A visible marker, natural or artificial, used in a survey or a metes and bounds description to establish the boundaries of a piece of property.

Mortgage—1. An instrument that creates a voluntary lien on real property to secure repayment of a debt. The parties to a mortgage are the mortgagor (borrower) and mortgagee (lender). 2. The term is often used more generally, to refer to either a mortgage or a deed of trust.

Mortgage, Assumption of—Taking over the primary liability on an existing mortgage from the original borrower, usually in connection with the purchase of the security property.

Mortgage, Balloon—A mortgage that provides for payments that do not fully amortize the loan by the loan's maturity date. The balance of the mortgage is then due in one lump sum (called a balloon payment) at the end of the term.

Mortgage, Blanket—A mortgage or deed of trust that covers more than one piece of real estate.

Mortgage, First—The mortgage or deed of trust that has higher lien priority than any other on a property. Without a subordination agreement, this will be the one that is recorded first. Also called a senior mortgage.

Mortgage, Junior—A mortgage or deed of trust that has lower lien priority than another mortgage or deed of trust against the same property. Sometimes called a second mortgage.

Mortgage, Satisfaction of—The document a mortgagee gives the mortgagor when the mortgage debt has been paid in full, acknowledging that the debt has been paid and the mortgage is no longer a lien against the property.

Mortgage, Senior—*See:* Mortgage, First.

Mortgage Broker—An intermediary who brings real estate lenders and borrowers together and negotiates loan agreements between them.

Mortgage Company—A type of real estate lender that originates and services loans on behalf of large investors or for immediate resale on the secondary market.

Mortgagee—The one who receives a mortgage; the lender.

Mortgaging Clause—A clause in a mortgage that describes the security interest given to the mortgagee.

Multiple Listing Service—An organization of real estate brokers who share their exclusive listings.

Mortgagor—A property owner (usually a borrower) who gives a mortgage against the property to another (usually a lender) as security for payment of an obligation.

Mutual Consent—When all parties freely agree to the terms of a contract, without fraud, undue influence, duress, menace, or mistake. Mutual consent is achieved through offer and acceptance. Sometimes called mutuality or "a meeting of the minds."

Mutuality—*See:* Mutual Consent.

National Environmental Policy Act—*See:* NEPA.

Natural Person—A human being, an individual (as distinguished from an artificial person, such as a corporation).

Negative Declaration—A determination by a local planning department that a proposed project will not have significant environmental impact, so that no environmental impact report is required.

Negligence—Conduct that falls below the standard of care that a reasonable person would exercise under the circumstances; carelessness or recklessness.

Negotiable Instrument—An instrument containing an unconditional promise to pay a certain sum of money, to order or to bearer, on demand or at a particular time. It may be a check, a promissory note, a bond, a draft, or stock.

NEPA—The National Environmental Policy Act; federal legislation requiring the preparation of an environmental impact statement (EIS) before any government action that would have a significant effect on the environment.

Nominal Interest Rate—The interest rate stated in a promissory note.

Nonconforming Use—A property use that does not conform to current zoning requirements, but is allowed because the property was being used in that way before the present zoning ordinance was enacted.

Nonpossessory Interest—An interest in property that does not include the right to possess and occupy the property; an encumbrance, such as a lien or an easement.

Non-Recourse Provision—A promissory note provision in which a lender agrees to limit its recovery on a loan default to proceeds from a foreclosure sale.

Notary Public—An official whose primary function is to witness and certify the acknowledgment made by someone signing a legal document.

Note, Promissory—A written promise to repay a debt.

Notice, Actual—Actual knowledge of a fact, as opposed to knowledge imputed by law.

Notice, Constructive—Knowledge of a fact imputed to a person by law. A person is held to have constructive notice of something when he should have known it, even if did not actually know it.

Notice of Cessation—A notice recorded by a property owner when construction on the property has ceased, although the project has not been completed; it limits the period during which mechanic's liens can be filed.

Notice of Completion—A recorded notice that announces the completion of a construction project and limits the period in which mechanic's liens may be filed.

Notice of Default—A notice sent by a secured creditor to a debtor, informing the debtor of a breach of the loan agreement.

Notice of Sale—A notice sent to a defaulting borrower, to junior lienholders, and to other interested parties, setting the date for a foreclosure sale.

Notice of Termination—Advance written notice that a landlord or tenant who wants to terminate a periodic tenancy must give to the other party.

Notice to Quit—A notice given to a tenant by a landlord, demanding that the tenant cure a default (e.g., by paying overdue rent) or else vacate the leased property.

Novation—1. When one party to a contract withdraws and a new party is substituted, relieving the withdrawing party of liability. 2. The substitution of a new obligation for an old one.

Nuisance—Anything that is injurious to health, is indecent or offensive to the senses, or is an obstruction to the free use of property that interferes with an owner's comfortable use and enjoyment of life or her property. A nuisance may be public or private.

Nuisance *Per Se*—Conduct that has been declared a nuisance by law and can be shown without proof of injury or damaging effect to another.

Nuisance, Attractive—*See:* Attractive Nuisance.

Obligatory Advances—Disbursements of construction loan funds that the lender is obligated to make (by prior agreement with the borrower) when certain phases of construction have been completed.

Offer—When one person (the offeror) proposes a contract to another (the offeree); if the offeree accepts the offer, a binding contract is formed.

Offeree—One to whom an offer is made.

Offeror—One who makes an offer.

Officer—In a corporation, an executive authorized by the board of directors to manage the business of the corporation.

Off-Site Improvements—Improvements that add to the usefulness of a site but are not located directly on it, such as curbs, streetlights, and sidewalks.

Open Listing—*See:* Listing, Open.

Option—A contract giving one party the right to do something, without obligating him or her to do it.

Optionee—The person to whom an option is given.

Optionor—The person who gives an option.

Option to Purchase—An option giving the optionee the right to buy property owned by the optionor at an agreed price during a specified period.

Ownership—Title to property, dominion over property; the rights of possession and control.

Ownership, Concurrent—Any form of ownership in which two or more people share title to a piece of property, holding undivided interests; includes joint tenancy, tenancy in common, and community property.

Ownership in Severalty—Ownership by one person alone.

Panic Selling—*See:* Blockbusting.

Parcel—A lot or piece of real estate, especially a specified part of a larger tract.

Parol Evidence—Evidence concerning negotiations or oral agreements that were not included in a written contract, often altering or contradicting the terms of the written contract.

Partial Release Clause—A clause in a blanket mortgage or deed of trust which allows the borrower to get part of the security property released from the lien when a certain portion of the debt has been paid or other conditions are fulfilled.

Partial Satisfaction—The instrument given to the borrower when part of the security property is released from a blanket mortgage under a partial release clause.

Partition—The division of property among its co-owners, so that each owns part of it in severalty; this may occur by agreement of all the co-owners (voluntary partition) or by court order (judicial partition). In many cases, the property is sold and the sale proceeds are divided among the former co-owners.

Partner, General—A partner who has the authority to manage and contract for a general or limited partnership, and who is personally liable for the partnership's debts.

Partner, Limited—A partner in a limited partnership who is primarily an investor and often does not participate in the management of the business. A limited partner is not personally liable for the partnership's debts.

Partnership—According to the Uniform Partnership Act, "an association of two or more persons to carry on, as co-owners, a business for profit."

Partnership, General—A partnership in which each member has an equal right to manage the business and share in the profits, as well as equal responsibility for the debts of the business.

Partnership, Limited—A partnership made up of one or more general partners and one or more limited partners.

Patent—The instrument used to convey government land to a private individual.

Patent Defect—A problem that is readily observable in an ordinary inspection of the property (as opposed to a latent defect, which is not readily observable).

***Per Se* Illegal**—An action that is automatically illegal, regardless of the circumstances surrounding the activity or whether there was any intent to commit a crime.

Personal Jurisdiction—*See:* Jurisdiction, Personal.

Personal Property—Any property that is not real property; movable property not affixed to land. Also called chattels or personalty.

Personalty—Personal property.

Physical Life—An estimate of the time a building will remain structurally sound and capable of being used.

Plaintiff—The party who starts a civil lawsuit; the one who sues.

Planned Unit Development (PUD)—A subdivision in which an owner owns both a home and the land on which it's located. Usually a residential development with small, clustered lots, designed to leave more open space than traditional subdivisions have.

Planning Commission—A local government agency responsible for preparing the community's master plan for development.

Plat—A detailed survey map of a subdivision, recorded in the county where the land is located. Subdivided property is often called platted property.

Plat Book—A book containing the subdivision plat maps of all the subdivided property in the county, maintained at the county recorder's office.

Pledge—When a debtor transfers possession of property to the creditor as security for the repayment of a debt. *Compare:* Hypothecate.

Plottage—The consolidation of several parcels of land into one, resulting in greater utility and consequently higher value. The additional value that results is called the plottage increment.

Point of Beginning—The starting point in a metes and bounds description; a monument or a point described by reference to a monument.

Points—An amount equal to 1% of the principal amount of a loan, paid to the lender at the time the loan is made to give the lender an additional yield above the interest rate. Because of the points paid at the outset, the lender is willing to make the loan at a lower interest rate.

Police Power—The power of state and local governments to enact and enforce laws to protect or promote the public's health, safety, morals, and general welfare.

Possession—1. The holding and enjoyment of property. 2. Actual physical occupation of real property.

Possessory Interest—An interest in property that includes the right to possess and occupy the property. The term includes all estates (leasehold as well as freehold), but does not include encumbrances.

Possibility of Reverter—The possibility that a defeasible fee estate may revert to the grantor (or the grantor's heirs or assigns) if a condition is not met or if a particular event occurs.

Power of Attorney—An instrument authorizing one person (the attorney in fact) to act as another's agent, to the extent stated in the instrument.

Power of Sale Clause—A clause in a deed of trust that gives the trustee the right to foreclose nonjudicially (sell the debtor's property without a court action) if the borrower defaults.

Power of Termination—In connection with a fee simple defeasible, a power of termination is the right to sue for return of the real property if the condition attached to the grantee's estate has been broken.

Precedent—A published judicial opinion that serves as authority for deciding a similar issue in a later case. A binding precedent is a precedent that a particular court is required to follow.

Predatory Lending—Lending practices used to take advantage of unsophisticated borrowers.

Prepayment—Paying off all or part of a loan before payment is due.

Prepayment Penalty—A penalty charged to a borrower who prepays.

Prepayment Provision—A provision in a promissory note that gives the borrower the right to pay off the loan before it is due.

Prescription—A method of acquiring an interest in real property (usually an easement) by using it openly and without the owner's permission for the period of time required by statute (in California, five years). *Compare:* Adverse Possession.

Primary Mortgage Market—The market in which loans are originated, where lenders make loans to borrowers. *Compare:* Secondary Mortgage Market.

Price Fixing—The cooperative setting of prices or price ranges by competing firms.

Principal—1. One of the parties to a transaction (such as the buyer or seller of a home), as opposed to those who are involved as agents or employees (such as a broker or escrow agent). 2. One who grants another person (an agent) authority to represent him or her in dealings with third parties. 3. In regard to a loan, the amount originally borrowed, as opposed to the interest.

Principal Meridian—*See:* Meridian, Principal.

Prior Appropriation—*See:* Appropriation, Prior.

Private Restrictions—*See:* Restrictions, Private.

Probate—A judicial proceeding in which the validity of a will is established and the executor is authorized to distribute the estate property; or, when there is no valid will, in which an administrator is appointed to distribute the estate to the heirs.

Probate Court—A court that oversees the distribution of property under a will or by intestate succession.

Procedural Law—A law that establishes the legal procedure for enforcing a substantive right. *Compare:* Substantive Law.

Profit à Prendre—The right to enter another's land to remove the soil or a product of the soil, such as oil, gas, crops, or timber. A profit à prendre is a property interest, but it is not a form of ownership of real property.

Procuring Cause—The real estate agent who is primarily responsible for bringing about a sale; for example, by negotiating the agreement between the buyer and the seller.

Promissory Note—*See:* Note, Promissory.

Property—1. The rights of ownership in a thing, such as the right to use, possess, transfer, or encumber it. 2. Something that is owned.

Property Manager—A person hired by a property owner to administer, merchandise, and maintain property, especially rental property.

Property Tax—*See:* Tax, Property.

Proprietary Lease—A lease of a unit in a cooperative building, held by a tenant who has purchased stock in the cooperative corporation.

Proprietorship, Individual or Sole—A business owned and operated by one person.

Proration—The process of dividing or allocating something (especially a sum of money or an expense) proportionately, according to time, interest, or benefit.

Public Accommodation—Any private entity that owns, operates, leases, or leases to, a place open to the public, as long as the operation of the facility affects commerce.

Public Record—The official collection of legal documents that individuals have filed with the county recorder in order to provide constructive notice to the public of the information contained in them.

Public Report—A disclosure report provided to the buyer of a subdivision property; required by the Subdivided Lands Law.

Public Restrictions—*See:* Restrictions, Public.

Public Use—A use that benefits the public. For a condemnation action to be constitutional, it must be for a public use.

Puffing—Superlative statements about the quality of a property that should not be considered assertions of fact.

Punitive Damages—Damages awarded to a plaintiff in a civil suit as a punishment to the wrongdoer (the defendant) and as a deterrent to others.

Pur Autre Vie—For another's life. A life estate based on the life of someone other than the holder of the life estate is called a life estate pur autre vie.

Purchase Agreement—A contract in which a seller promises to convey title to real property to a buyer in exchange for the purchase price. Also called a purchase and sale agreement, earnest money agreement, deposit receipt, sales contract, purchase contract, or contract of sale.

Qualified Acceptance—*See:* Counteroffer.

Qualifying Standards—The standards a lender requires a loan applicant to meet before a loan will be approved. Also called underwriting standards.

Quick Look Test—A shortened version of the rule of reason test that is applied by courts when anticompetitive effects of a restraint of trade are plainly obvious, but no per se violation has occurred.

Quiet Enjoyment—Use and possession of real property without interference from the previous owner, the lessor, or anyone else claiming title.

Quiet Title Action—A lawsuit to determine who has title to a piece of property, or to remove a cloud from the title.

Quitclaim Deed—*See:* Deed, Quitclaim.

Ranchos—Large land grants deeded to private owners by the Spanish and Mexican governments, in what is now California and other western states.

Range—In the government survey system of land description, a strip of land six miles wide, running north and south.

Range Lines—In the government survey system of land description, the north-south lines (meridians) located six miles apart.

Ratification—The later confirmation or affirmation of an act that was not authorized when it was performed.

Readily Achievable—Under the ADA, any action that can be easily accomplished without much difficulty or expense, such as adjusting shelving or counter heights to make them more accessible to a person in a wheelchair.

Ready, Willing, and Able—A buyer is ready, willing and able if he makes an offer that meets the seller's stated terms, and has the contractual capacity and financial resources to complete the transaction.

Real Estate—*See:* Real Property.

Real Estate Brokerage—A real estate broker's business; the business of bringing a buyer and seller together and negotiating a sales contract between the two parties.

Real Estate Contract—1. A contract for the sale of real property in which the buyer (the vendee) pays in installments; the buyer takes possession of the property immediately, but the seller (the vendor) retains legal title until the full price has been paid. Also called a land contract, installment sales contract, or contract for deed. 2. An earnest money agreement. 3. Any contract having to do with real property.

Real Estate Investment Trust (REIT)—A real estate investment business that has a minimum of 100 investors and meets other requirements to qualify for tax advantages.

Real Estate Recovery Account—The purpose of the Real Estate Recovery Account is to reimburse those injured by real estate licensees when the licensees have no assets to pay for a civil judgment against them.

Real Estate Salesperson—A person who is licensed to work for and represent a broker in real estate transactions.

Real Estate Security—An arrangement in which someone invests money in an enterprise involving real estate with the expectation of earning profits from the efforts of another party.

Real Estate Settlement Procedures Act—*See:* RESPA.

Real Property—Land and everything attached or appurtenant to the land. Also called realty or real estate. *Compare:* Personal Property.

Realtor®—A real estate agent who is an active member of state and local real estate boards that are affiliated with the National Association of Realtors®.

Realty—*See:* Real Property.

Reconveyance—Releasing the security property from the lien created by a deed of trust, by recording a deed of reconveyance.

Recorded Map Description—A type of legal description; a piece of land is described by reference to a lot and block appearing on the subdivision plat map recorded by the county auditor or county recorder. Sometimes called a lot and block description or a maps and plats description.

Recording—Filing a document at the county auditor's or county recorder's office so that it will be placed in the public record, providing constructive notice to the public of the contents of the document.

Rectangular Survey—*See:* Government Survey System.

Redemption—1. When a defaulting borrower prevents foreclosure by paying the full amount of the debt, plus costs. 2. When a mortgagor regains the property after foreclosure by paying whatever the foreclosure sale purchaser paid for it, plus interest and expenses.

Redemption, Equitable Right of—The right of a mortgagor to redeem property prior to the foreclosure sale, by paying off the debt, plus costs.

Redemption, Statutory Right of—The right of a mortgagor to get the property back during a specified period after a foreclosure sale, by paying whatever the foreclosure sale purchaser paid for it, plus interest and expenses.

Redemption Period, Statutory—The period of time (set by statute) after a judicial foreclosure sale during which the debtor can reclaim foreclosed property by paying the full amount of the debt plus costs.

Redlining—When a lender refuses to make loans secured by properties in a certain neighborhood because of the racial or ethnic composition of the neighborhood.

Regulation Z—The Federal Reserve's regulation that implements the Truth in Lending Act.

Reinstatement—When foreclosure proceedings are stopped and the loan agreement is restored after the borrower cures the default (for example, by paying the delinquent payments, plus costs).

Relation Back—A legal doctrine holding that, under certain circumstances, title acquired by deed relates back to the point at which the deed was delivered to the escrow agent.

Release—1. To give up a legal right. 2. A document in which a legal right is given up.

Release Clause—1. A clause in a blanket mortgage or deed of trust that allows the borrower to have certain parcels of land released from the lien when a certain portion of the debt has been paid off. 2. A clause in a real estate contract providing for a deed to a portion of the land to be delivered when a certain portion of the contract price has been paid. Also known as a deed release provision.

Reliction—When a body of water gradually recedes, exposing land that was previously under water. Also called dereliction.

Remainder—A future interest that becomes possessory when a life estate terminates, and that is held by someone other than the grantor of the life estate (as opposed to an estate in reversion, which is a future interest held by the grantor or the grantor's successors in interest).

Remainderman—The person who has an estate in remainder.

Remand—To send back. When an appellate court remands a case, it is sent back to the lower court for additional proceedings or a new trial.

Remise—To give up; a term used in quitclaim deeds.

Rent—Compensation paid by a tenant to the landlord in exchange for the use and possession of the leased property.

Rent Control Laws—Local ordinances that restrict the amount of rent a residential landlord can charge.

Renunciation—When someone who has been granted something or has accepted something later gives it up or rejects it; as when an agent withdraws from the agency relationship. *Compare:* Revocation.

Repair and Deduct—A remedy available to a tenant if the landlord fails to repair a defect in the rented premises after reasonable notice; subject to certain conditions, the tenant may perform the repair and then deduct the cost from the rent.

Rescission—When a contract is terminated and each party gives anything acquired under the contract back to the other party, restoring the parties, as nearly as possible, to the positions they were in before entering into the contract.

Reservation—A right retained by a grantor when conveying property; for example, mineral rights, an easement, or a life estate can be reserved in the deed.

Reserve Account—*See:* Impound Account.

Resident Manager—A salaried manager of an apartment building or complex, who resides on the property.

Res Judicata—The legal doctrine holding that once a lawsuit between two parties has been tried and a final judgment has been issued, neither one can sue the other over the same dispute again.

RESPA—The Real Estate Settlement Procedures Act, a law that requires lenders making loans secured by residential property to provide disclosures concerning closing costs to loan applicants, and prohibits kickbacks to settlement service providers.

Restitution—Restoring something to a person that he was unjustly deprived of.

Restraint of Trade—Any act that prevents an individual or company from doing business in a certain area, or with certain people, which hinders free trade. The antitrust laws apply only to unreasonable restraints of trade.

Restrictions—Limitations on the use of real property. Restrictions may be private (such as restrictive covenants) or public (such as zoning ordinances).

Restrictions, Private—Restrictions on the use of land that have been imposed by private parties in deeds or contracts (as opposed to public restrictions, which are imposed by law).

Restrictions, Public—Law or governmental regulations limiting or restricting the use of real property.

Restrictive Covenant—*See:* Covenant, Restrictive.

Retainer—A fee paid up front to a licensee when entering into a real estate agency (usually a buyer agency) relationship.

Reversion—A future estate that becomes possessory when a life estate terminates, and that is held by the grantor (or his or her successors in interest). *Compare:* Remainder.

Revocation—When someone who granted or offered something withdraws the grant or offer; as when a principal withdraws the authority granted to the agent. *Compare:* Renunciation.

Rezone—A revision of a zoning ordinance, usually changing the uses allowed in a particular zone. Also called a zoning amendment.

Right of First Refusal—A right that gives the holder the first opportunity to purchase or lease a particular piece of property, should the owner decide to sell or lease it.

Right of Survivorship—A characteristic of joint tenancy; surviving co-tenants acquire a deceased joint tenant's interest in the property.

Right of Way—An easement that gives the holder the right to cross another person's land.

Riparian Rights—The water rights of a landowner whose property is adjacent to or crossed by a body of water. *Compare:* Appropriation, Prior.

Rumford Act—A state law that generally prohibits all housing discrimination in California based on race, color, religion, gender, gender identity, gender expression, sexual orientation, marital status, national origin, ancestry, familial status, genetic information, medical condition, source of income, or disability. Also known as the Fair Employment and Housing Act.

Rule of Capture—*See:* Capture, Rule of.

Rule of Reason—A balancing test used to determine whether a practice or activity constitutes an unreasonable restraint of trade. The court weighs the action's positive impact on competition against its negative impact on competition. Used when no obvious per se violation has occurred.

Running with the Land—Binding or benefiting the successive owners of a piece of property, rather than terminating when a particular owner transfers his or her interest. Usually used in reference to an easement appurtenant or a restrictive covenant.

Safety Clause—A clause in a listing agreement providing that the broker will still receive the commission if the property is sold during a specified period of time after the listing expires to someone who was a prospect during the listing term. Also called a carryover clause or extender clause.

Sandwich Test—A test to determine whether a property owner or agent is discriminating.

Satisfaction of Mortgage—*See:* Mortgage, Satisfaction of.

Savings and Loan Association—A type of financial institution that emphasizes consumer loans and home mortgages.

Secondary Financing—Money borrowed to pay part of the required downpayment or closing costs for a first loan, when the second loan is secured by the same property that secures the first loan.

Secondary Mortgage Market—The market in which investors (including Fannie Mae, Freddie Mac, and Ginnie Mae) purchase real estate loans from lenders; also called the national market.

Secret Profit—A financial benefit that an agent takes from a transaction without informing the principal.

Section—In the government survey system of land description, a section is one mile square and contains 640 acres. There are 36 sections in a township.

Section 8 Violation—A kickback or unearned fee that violates Section 8 of RESPA.

Security—A real estate security is an arrangement in which people invest money in an enterprise involving real estate, with the expectation of earning profits from the efforts of a promoter or some other third party.

Security Deposit—Money a tenant gives a landlord at the beginning of the tenancy to protect the landlord in case the tenant defaults; the landlord may retain all or part of the deposit to cover unpaid rent or repair costs at the end of the tenancy. Also called a damage deposit.

Security Instrument—A document that creates a voluntary lien on real property to secure repayment of a loan; either a deed of trust or a mortgage.

Security Interest—The interest a creditor may acquire in the debtor's property to ensure that the debt will be paid; if the debt is not paid as agreed, the creditor may foreclose (force the sale of the property) and collect the amount owed from the sale proceeds.

Security Property—The collateral for a loan; the property that a borrower gives a lender a voluntary lien against, so that the lender can foreclose if the borrower defaults.

Seisin—The possession of a freehold estate; ownership.

Selling Broker—The broker responsible for procuring a buyer for real estate; may represent either the seller or the buyer.

Separate Property—Property owned by a married person that is not community property; includes property acquired before marriage, or by gift, devise, or inheritance after marriage.

Service of Process—Hand delivery to the defendant of the plaintiff's complaint, along with a summons from the court.

Setback Requirements—Provisions in a zoning ordinance that do not allow structures to be built within a certain distance of the property line.

Settlement—1. An agreement between the parties to a civil lawsuit, in which the plaintiff agrees to drop the suit in exchange for money or the defendant's promise to do or refrain from doing something. 2. Closing.

Settlement Statement—A document that presents a final, detailed accounting for a real estate transaction, listing each party's debits and credits and the amount each will receive or be required to pay at closing. Also called a closing statement.

Severalty Ownership—Ownership by one person alone. *Compare:* Concurrent Ownership.

Severance—1. Termination of a joint tenancy. 2. The permanent removal of a natural attachment, fixture, or appurtenance from real property, which transforms the item into personal property.

Shareholder—Individual who purchases shares in a company as an investment and has limited liability in regard to the corporation's debts. Also called stockholder.

Sheriff's Deed—*See:* Deed, Sheriff's.

Sheriff's Sale—A foreclosure sale held pursuant to a court order in a judicial foreclosure. Also called an execution sale.

Sherman Antitrust Act—The main federal antitrust law.

Special Assessment—A tax levied only against the properties that have benefited from a public improvement (such as a sewer or street light), to cover the cost of the improvement; creates a special assessment lien.

Special Exception Permit—*See:* Conditional Use Permit.

Specific Lien—*See:* Lien, Specific.

Specific Performance—A legal remedy for breach of contract in which a court orders the breaching party to actually perform the contract as agreed, rather than simply paying monetary damages.

Spot Zoning—*See:* Zoning, Spot.

Stare Decisis—The legal doctrine holding that in resolving a lawsuit, a court should try to follow precedents decided in the same jurisdiction, to make the law evenhanded and predictable.

State Action—An act of the government or a government official; only state action can violate a person's constitutional rights.

Statute—A law enacted by a state legislature or the U.S. Congress.

Statute of Frauds—A law that requires certain types of contracts to be in writing and signed by the party to be bound in order to be enforceable.

Statute of Limitations—A law requiring a particular type of lawsuit to be filed within a specified time after the event giving rise to the suit occurred.

Statutory Redemption Period—*See:* Redemption Period, Statutory.

Steering—Channeling prospective buyers or tenants to particular neighborhoods based on their race, religion, national origin, or ancestry.

Stockholder—*See:* Shareholder.

Subagent—A person that an agent has delegated authority to, so that the subagent can assist in carrying out the principal's orders; sometimes described as the agent of an agent.

Subcontractor—A contractor who, at the request of the general contractor, performs a specific job, such as plumbing or drywalling, in connection with the overall construction project.

Subdivided Lands Law—A state statute requiring consumer protection disclosures to buyers of property in subdivisions containing five or more lots.

Subdivision—A piece of land divided into two or more parcels.

Subdivision Map Act—A state law requiring that everyone who subdivides land must record a map or plan of the subdivision before selling properties.

Subdivision Plat—*See:* Plat.

Subjacent Support—*See:* Support, Subjacent.

Subject Matter Jurisdiction—*See:* Jurisdiction, Subject Matter.

Subject To—When a purchaser takes property subject to a deed of trust or mortgage, he or she is not personally liable for paying off the loan; in case of default, however, the property can still be foreclosed on. *Compare:* Assumption.

Sublease—When a tenant grants someone else the right to possession of the leased property for part of the remainder of the lease term; as opposed to an assignment, in which the tenant gives up possession for the entire remainder of the lease term.

Subordination Clause—A provision in a mortgage or deed of trust that permits a subsequent mortgage or deed of trust to have higher lien priority than the one containing the clause.

Subpoena—A document ordering a person to appear at a deposition or court proceeding to testify or to produce documentary or physical evidence.

Substantial Performance—Performance that is sufficient to discharge a party to a contract from further obligation under the contract, even though there has not been full performance.

Substantive Law—A law that establishes and defines rights and duties. *Compare:* Procedural Law.

Succession—Acquiring property through descent, by will or inheritance.

Successor in Interest—A person who has acquired property previously held by someone else; for example, a buyer or an heir.

Summons—A notice telling the defendant in a lawsuit that a complaint has been filed.

Superfund—A federal fund built up from taxes on the chemical and petroleum industries and used to pay for cleanup of toxic waste sites if the responsible parties can't be identified or are bankrupt. *See:* CERCLA.

Supplemental Assessment—In California, an additional assessment of property taxes a new owner is required to pay because of the reassessment triggered by the change in ownership.

Support, Lateral—The right to have the soil of a piece of property supported by the land adjoining it. An owner is protected by law from excavation on neighboring property that would deny this support.

Support, Subjacent—The support that the surface of land receives from the subsurface soil.

Support Rights—The right to the support of land that is provided by adjacent (lateral) or underlying (subjacent) land.

Surrender—Yielding or giving up an estate (such as a life estate or a leasehold) before it has expired.

Survey—The process of precisely measuring the boundaries and determining the area of a parcel of land.

Survivorship, Right of—A characteristic of a joint tenancy or of community property with right of survivorship; the surviving joint tenants automatically acquire a deceased joint tenant's interest in the property.

Syndicate—An association formed to operate an investment business. A syndicate is not a recognized legal entity; it can be a corporation, real estate investment trust, or partnership.

Tacking—When successive periods of use or possession by more than one person are added together to make up the period required for prescription or adverse possession.

Taking—When the government acquires private property for public use by condemnation. The term is also used in inverse condemnation lawsuits, when a government action has severely reduced the usefulness of a piece of private property.

Tax, Excise—A tax on the transfer of real property; revenue stamps or some other evidence of payment of the tax may have to be attached to a deed before it can be recorded. Also called a documentary transfer tax.

Tax, General Real Estate—An annual ad valorem tax levied on real property.

Tax, Improvement—*See:* Special Assessment.

Tax, Property—1. The general real estate tax. 2. Any ad valorem tax levied on real or personal property.

Tax Foreclosure—Foreclosure by a government agency to obtain payment of delinquent taxes.

Tax Lien—A lien against property to secure payment of taxes, such as the general real estate taxes.

Tax Sale—Sale of property after foreclosure of a tax lien.

Tenancy—Lawful possession of real property; an estate.

Tenancy, Joint—A form of concurrent ownership of property in which the co-owners have unity of time, title, interest, and possession and the right of survivorship. *Compare:* Tenancy in Common.

Tenancy, Periodic—A leasehold estate that continues for successive periods of equal length (for example, from week to week or month to month), until terminated by proper notice from either party.

Tenancy, Term—A leasehold estate for a fixed period. Also called an estate for years.

Tenancy at Sufferance—When a tenant (who entered into possession of the property lawfully) stays on after the lease ends without the landlord's permission.

Tenancy at Will—When a tenant is in possession with the owner's permission, but there is no definite lease term; as when a landlord allows a holdover tenant to remain on the premises until another tenant is found.

Tenancy in Common—A form of concurrent ownership of real property in which two or more persons each have an undivided interest in the entire property, but no right of survivorship. *Compare:* Tenancy, Joint.

Tenant—Someone in lawful possession of real property; especially, someone who has leased property from the owner.

Tenant, Dominant—A person who has easement rights on another's property; either the owner of a dominant tenement, or someone who has an easement in gross.

Tenant, Holdover—A lessee who remains in possession of the property after the lease term has expired.

Tenant, Life—Someone who has a life estate, with the right to possess the property until the death of the person whose life is the measuring life. (In many cases, the life tenant's own life is the measuring life.)

Tenant, Servient—A property owner whose property is encumbered by an easement.

Tenements—Everything of a permanent nature associated with a piece of land that is ordinarily transferred with the land. Tenements are both tangible (buildings, for example) and intangible (air rights, for example).

Tenement, Dominant—Property that receives the benefit of an easement appurtenant.

Tenement, Servient—Property burdened by an easement, so that the owner is required to allow someone else to use the property for a specified purpose.

Term—A prescribed period of time; especially, the length of time a borrower has to pay off a loan, or the duration of a lease.

Termination for Just Cause—Termination of a tenancy because of the tenant's material breach of the lease terms.

Testament—A will.

Testate—Refers to someone who has executed a will. *Compare:* Intestate.

Testator—A person who makes a will. (If it is a woman, she may be referred to as a testatrix, although that term is passing out of use.)

Third Party—1. A person seeking to deal with a principal through an agent. 2. In a transaction, someone who is not one of the principals.

Three-Day Notice to Quit—A notice that a landlord serves on a tenant who has breached the lease agreement; the first step in the eviction process.

Tier—A row of townships running east-west.

Tight Money Market—When loan funds are scarce, leading lenders to charge high interest rates and discount points.

TILA—Truth in Lending Act.

TILA-RESPA Integrated Disclosure Rule—Requires certain written disclosures for most home purchase, home equity, and refinance loans. Two main disclosure documents are the loan estimate form and the closing disclosure form.

Tie-in Arrangement—Occurs when a buyer is required to purchase one product or service in order to purchase another product or service. Also called a tying arrangement.

Time is of the Essence—A clause in a contract that means performance on the exact dates specified is an essential element of the contract; failure to perform on time is a material breach.

Timeshare—An ownership interest or license that gives the holder a right to possession of the property only for a specific, limited period each year.

Title—Lawful ownership of real property. Also, the deed or other document that is evidence of that ownership.

Title, Abstract of—A brief chronological summary of the recorded documents affecting title to a particular piece of property.

Title, After-Acquired—Title acquired by a grantor after he or she attempted to convey an interest in property that he or she did not own.

Title, Chain of—The chain of deeds (and other documents) transferring title to a piece of property from one owner to the next, as disclosed in the public record.

Title, Clear—Title that is free of encumbrances or defects; marketable title.

Title, Color of—*See:* Color of Title.

Title, Equitable—The vendee's interest in property under a real estate contract. Also called an equitable interest. *Compare:* Title, Legal.

Title, Legal—The vendor's interest in property under a real estate contract. *Compare:* Title, Equitable.

Title, Marketable—Title free and clear of objectionable liens, encumbrances, or defects, so that a reasonably prudent person with full knowledge of the facts would not hesitate to purchase the property. Also called merchantable title.

Title Company—A title insurance company.

Title Insurance—*See:* Insurance, Title.

Title Report—A report issued by a title company, disclosing the condition of the title to a specific piece of property. A preliminary title report is one issued early on in a transaction, before the actual title insurance policy is issued.

Title Search—An inspection of the public record to determine all rights and encumbrances affecting title to a piece of property.

Title Theory—A legal theory holding that a mortgage or deed of trust gives the lender legal title to the security property while the debt is being repaid. *Compare:* Lien Theory.

Tort—A breach of a duty imposed by law (as opposed to a duty voluntarily taken on in a contract) that causes harm to another person, giving the injured person the right to sue the one who breached the duty. Also called a civil wrong (in contrast to a criminal wrong, a crime).

Total Interest Percentage—The amount of interest paid over the life of the loan, expressed as a percentage of the loan amount.

Township—In the government survey system of land description, a parcel of land six miles square, containing 36 sections; the intersection of a range and a township tier.

Township Lines—Lines running east-west, spaced six miles apart, in the government survey system.

Township Tier—In the government survey system, a strip of land running east-west, six miles wide and bounded on the north and south by township lines.

Trade Fixture—*See:* Fixture, Trade.

Transferability—A condition where ownership and possession of an object can be conveyed from one person to another.

Transfer Disclosure Statement—A statement containing information about the property that a seller of residential property is required to give to the buyer.

Trespass—An unlawful physical invasion of property owned by another.

TRID—TILA-RESPA Integrated Disclosure Rule.

Trust—An arrangement in which title to property (or funds) is vested in one or more trustees, who manage the property on behalf of the trust's beneficiaries, in accordance with instructions set forth in the document establishing the trust.

Trust Account—A bank account, separate from a real estate broker's personal and general business accounts, used to segregate trust funds from the broker's own funds.

Trust Deed—*See:* Deed of Trust.

Trustee—1. A person appointed to manage a trust on behalf of the beneficiaries. 2. A neutral third party appointed in a deed of trust to handle the nonjudicial foreclosure process in case of default.

Trustee in Bankruptcy—An individual appointed by the court to handle the assets of a person in bankruptcy.

Trustee's Sale—A nonjudicial foreclosure sale under a deed of trust.

Trust Funds—Money or things of value received by an agent, not belonging to the agent but being held for the benefit of others.

Trustor—The borrower in a deed of trust. Also called the grantor.

Truth in Lending Act (TILA)—A federal law, implemented by Regulation Z, which requires disclosure of certain information to applicants for consumer loans (including residential mortgage loans). *See:* TILA-RESPA Integrated Disclosure Rule.

Unauthorized Practice of Law—Offering legal advice or otherwise practicing law without the required license.

Underwriting—In real estate lending, the process of evaluating a loan application to determine the probability that the applicant would repay the loan, and matching the risk to an appropriate rate of return. Sometimes called risk analysis.

Undivided Interest—A co-owner's interest, giving him or her the right to possession of the whole property, rather than to a particular section of it.

Undue Influence—Exerting excessive pressure on someone so as to overpower the person's free will and prevent him or her from making a rational or prudent decision; often involves abusing a relationship of trust.

Unenforceable—*See:* Contract, Unenforceable.

Uniform Commercial Code—A body of law adopted in slightly varying versions in most states (including California), which attempts to standardize commercial law dealing with such matters as negotiable instruments and sales of personal property. Its main applications to real estate law concern security interests in fixtures and bulk transfers.

Unity of Interest—In reference to concurrent ownership, when each co-owner has an equal interest (equal share of ownership) in the property. A requirement for joint tenancy.

Unity of Possession—When property is owned concurrently by two or more individuals, each co-owner is equally entitled to possession of the entire property, because their interests are undivided. This is a requirement for joint tenancy, but it is also a characteristic of all concurrent ownership.

Unity of Time—In reference to concurrent ownership, when each co-owner acquired title at the same time. A requirement for joint tenancy.

Unity of Title—In reference to concurrent ownership, when each co-owner acquired title through the same instrument (deed, will, or court order). A requirement for joint tenancy.

Unjust Enrichment—An undeserved benefit; a court generally will not allow a remedy (such as forfeiture of a real estate contract) if that remedy would result in the unjust enrichment of one of the parties.

Unlawful Detainer—A legal action to regain possession of real property; a suit filed by a landlord to evict a defaulting tenant.

Unruh Civil Rights Act—A California law prohibiting discrimination by businesses based on race, color, religion, ancestry, national origin, sex, disability, medical condition, genetic information, marital status, sexual orientation, citizenship, primary language, or immigration status; in transactions related to housing, it also prohibits businesses from discriminating based on age.

Usury—Charging an interest rate that exceeds legal limits.

VA—The U.S. Department of Veterans Affairs.

Vacation Ownership and Timeshare Act of 2004—A state law requiring that timeshare buyers receive certain property disclosures as well as a seven-day right of rescission after agreeing to purchase.

Valid—Binding and enforceable in a court of law.

Valuable Consideration—*See:* Consideration.

Valuation—*See:* Appraisal.

Value—The amount of goods or services offered in the marketplace in exchange for a given product; the present worth of future benefits.

Value, Assessed—The value placed on property by the taxing authority (the county assessor, for example) for the purposes of taxation.

Value, Market—The most probable price that a property should bring in a competitive and open market under all conditions requisite to a fair sale, the buyer and seller each acting prudently and knowledgeably, and assuming the price is not affected by undue stimulus. Also called fair market value, value in exchange, or objective value.

Variable Interest Rate—An interest rate charged on a loan that is periodically increased or decreased during the loan term.

Variance—Permission obtained from proper authorities to use property or build a structure in a way that violates the strict terms of the zoning ordinance.

Vendee—A buyer or purchaser; especially, someone buying property under a real estate contract.

Vendor—A seller; especially, someone selling property under a real estate contract.

Vested—A person who has a present, fixed right or interest in property has a vested right or interest, even though he or she may not have the right to possession until sometime in the future. For example, a remainderman's interest in the property vests when it is granted (not when the life estate ends).

Vicarious Liability—*See:* Liability, Vicarious.

Void—Having no legal force or effect.

Voidable—*See:* Contract, Voidable.

Voluntary Lien—*See:* Lien, Voluntary.

Waiver—The voluntary relinquishment or surrender of a right.

Warranty, Implied—In the sale of property, a warranty created by operation of law for the protection of the buyer, whether or not the seller intended to offer it.

Warranty Deed—*See:* Deed, Warranty.

Warranty of Authority—A doctrine that protects third parties in their dealings with agents: a person who acts in dealings with third parties as an agent, warrants that he has the authority to perform on behalf of the principal.

Warranty of Habitability—A warranty implied by law in every residential lease, that the property is fit for habitation.

Waste—The destruction, damage, or material alteration of property by someone in possession of the property who holds less than a fee estate (such as a life tenant or lessee), or by a co-tenant.

Water Rights—*See:* Riparian Rights, Appropriative Rights.

Will—A person's formal stipulation regarding how her estate will be disposed of after death. Also called a testament.

Will, Formal—A will that meets the statutory requirements for a valid will; it must be signed by two witnesses.

Will, Holographic—A will written and dated entirely in the testator's handwriting, which may be valid even if it was not witnessed.

Writ of Attachment—A court order creating an attachment lien, granted only after a hearing to determine the amount and validity of the attachment.

Writ of Execution—A court order directing a public officer (usually the sheriff) to seize and sell property to satisfy a debt.

Writ of Possession—A court order that a landlord may request after winning an unlawful detainer action, which directs the sheriff to forcibly remove the tenant and her belongings from the leased property if she refuses to leave voluntarily within five days.

Yield—The return of profit to an investor on an investment, stated as a percentage of the amount invested.

Zone—An area of land set off for a particular use or uses in a zoning law.

Zoning—Ordinances governing what land uses are permitted in certain areas (zones), separating incompatible uses, and specifying requirements for building height, setbacks, and so on.

Zoning, Spot—An illegal rezone that favors (or restricts) a particular property owner (or a small group of owners) without justification.

Zoning Amendment—*See:* Rezone.

Index